# PERSONAL
# MONEY
# MANAGEMENT:

## An Objectives and Systems Approach

**ROGER H. NELSON**
College of Business
The University of Utah

**ADDISON-WESLEY PUBLISHING COMPANY**
Reading, Massachusetts · Menlo Park, California · London · Don Mills, Ontario

# FOREWORD

Books about personal finance fall into two distinct categories, and Dr. Nelson's book is clearly distinguished as having one viewpoint, which the reader should know before he starts. One kind of book about personal finance and money management starts with the assumption that large government programs are the sole key to consumer protection. This means more regulation of consumer finance, quality control, interest rates, market operations, and the like. It notes the contributions of Ralph Nader, Betty Furness, and espouses more of such dazzling and highly publicized actions. While this is an important aspect of consumerism resources, it is not all there is. In fact, it may not be the most important.

The second approach, the one you'll find in this book in a form unique among personal finance texts is that of *individual responsibility* coupled with individual knowledge and clear personal objectives. The role of government in protection of the consumer is dealt with in Chapter Six, it's true. But that is not the main thrust of the book. This book isn't a brief for more (or less) government intervention; it's a brief, and some practical instruction, on individual responsibility and personal objectives in handling your own affairs. One might say that the most descriptive phrase for this book could be "Money Management by Objectives."

In today's world, nobody who is aware of the realities of society is proposing that government will reduce its influence. Yet, there is still much to be said for the case that individual responsibility should be increased through knowledge. While there are undoubtedly wolves in the forest lying in wait for the unwary consumer and investor, the total solution to the wolf problem and the alleviation of its evil effects can't lie solely in more commissions, bigger regulatory agencies, and denouncements of their (very real) venality. Help also rests in alert and informed individuals who can take care of themselves. If every wolf finds that Little Red Riding Hood has been trained in Karate, and can dispose of the wolves without calling for the national guard, or asking for congressional investigations, the wolf business becomes unproductive. The two hundred million consumers can't all be accompanied by Senator Hart, Ralph Nader, and Betty Furness every time they buy a car or appliance, or invest in real estate or mutual funds. Those who are capable can take care of themselves. Maybe this book should be subtitled, "Consumer Karate."

If you'd like to know how to maximize your income and minimize your expenses, all by yourself, despite snares, pitfalls, wolves, villains, bogs and swamps, this book will get you started. It is a systematic book; that is, it starts at the beginning, goes to the middle, and proceeds on to the end. This in itself makes it unique among books today. It also starts at a very fundamental point: *Define your personal objectives before you start operating your assets.*

Young business students, their professors, graduates in the professions, and average consumers will find themselves better equipped to manage their personal affairs as a result of reading this book.

*George S. Odiorne*
*Dean, College of Business*
*University of Utah*

# PREFACE

Between the first small paycheck and the last bigger one, most people make a fortune.  Tragically, though, along the way money problems usually create a lot of worry and anxiety, sometimes shatter beautiful dreams, and in some instances even cause broken homes.  This book is intended to do something about these problems.  *Personal Money Management* concentrates on the critical financial areas, areas that make the difference between economic success and failure.  It stresses a simple but very effective system for seizing control over one's financial destiny—that of setting goals and laying specific action plans for their accomplishment.  In effect, the book teaches the individual to handle his money problems systematically, just like the corporation deals with money.

It would be remiss for any book on money management today to omit the important new phenomenon of "consumerism."  While many volumes of information could be written on the subject, this text focuses on the central thrusts of "consumerism" as they affect the individual's ability to make financial decisions—buying, insuring and investing.

I have been pleased with the critiques of many professors and students on the manuscript indicating that they felt the work was "comprehensive but also fun to read."  This pleases me a great deal because it means that, at least to some degree, my philosophy that "Money management isn't dull nor necessarily complicated," has come through in the final product.

It would be pretentious indeed to imply that a work of this sort is a result solely of my own effort.  Surely such is not the case.  I've had much help from many sources.  Particularly, I am appreciative of the advice and assistance of Dean George S. Odiorne, who has written the Foreword.  It is the adaptation of Dean Odiorne's philosophy—management by objectives—which makes this book unique in its field and personal in its application.  Just as Odiorne's MBO approach has revolutionized institutional management, it is my hope that this application will have a similar positive effect in the way individuals manage their money matters.

Another sincere "thank you" goes to my dear wife, DeEtte and children, Steven, Deanne, and Mark.  These are the very special people in my life who suffered understandingly as I typed my way through Europe with them for a year and who stood by patiently and usually "silently" for several additional years while "that book" often kept us from doing all the fun "together" things that we enjoy as a family.

I am also appreciative of Ronda Brinkerhoff, my competent editorial assistant, for her help, expertise, and advice. Especially, I am indebted for her input on the food, clothing, and household buying portions of the text—areas that come naturally difficult to a man.

*Salt Lake City, Utah*                                                                        R.H.N.
*August 1972*

# CONTENTS

## PART IV
## SAFEGUARDING PERSONAL INCOME AND PROPERTY

### Chapter 12    Selecting an Appropriate Life Insurance Program

### Chapter 13    Health, Disability, and Retirement Programs

**Chapter 19    Investing in Corporate Securities: The Basics**

**Appendix to Chapter 19    Glossary of Stock Market Terms**

**Chapter 20    Investing in Corporate Securities: The Dangers and the Opportunities**

**Chapter 21    Selecting Your Porfolio of Securities**

**Chapter 22    When and How to Buy and Sell Stocks**

**Chapter 23    Management Investment Companies: "Mutual Funds"**

*This book is gratefully dedicated to four very special people—*
*My wife, DeEtte*
*My sons, Steven and Mark*
*My daughter, Deanne*

# PART I
# EARNING AND ALLOCATING MONEY

# CHAPTER 1

# CHARTING YOUR FINANCIAL OBJECTIVES

This book is about you and your money. Its goals are starkly simple, yet exceedingly important. It seeks to help you (1) make more money, (2) get more for the money you spend, and (3) keep more of the money you earn. Differing significantly from other money management texts, this volume stresses a *systems* and *objectives* approach for dealing more effectively with money. It will show you how to set meaningful financial goals without burdening you with tired theories. On the contrary, it stresses systematic action plans, not abstractions. Doing, not memorizing. Dollars, not daydreams. You will be actively working to achieve your part of the trillion-dollar American economy.

A trillion dollars is such a large amount of money that it is difficult to imagine. Yet that is the approximate sum of all the goods and services produced in the United States in one year. There is no serious argument about it, America is the goods and services leader of the world. Sharing this bounty, Americans should be, in material terms, the most satisfied people on earth. Economically no country at any time has ever had more to offer its citizens. Nonetheless, there are problems in this land of plenty. Three serious shadows—inflation, high taxes, and consumer problems—are merging their gloom to darken the finances of every American:

1. We have all had to learn something about the new math of inflation— where pluses are often minuses because of skimpier dollars.

2. Because of higher taxes, few people see extra dollars from salary increases in their take-home pay.

3. Buying decisions are more difficult. Consumers are constantly bombarded with persuasive high-pressure advertising, some of it misleading or even deceptive. We must choose from among ever-increasing numbers and varieties of products, yet most of us are ill equipped to make wise value judgments about their appropriateness, safety, or wholesomeness.

Since you will be deeply and personally affected by these broad national problems, regardless of the personal goals you set or the amount of money you earn, it is important to know at the outset what you are up against.

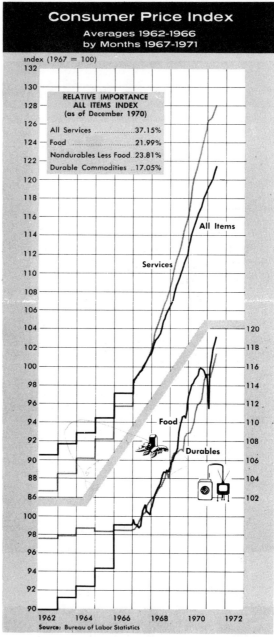

**Fig. 1–1** How prices have changed. While all prices have risen significantly over the past decade, the cost of services has shown the most spectacular increase. Durable goods such as refrigerators and other appliances have advanced the least. Reprinted by permission from *Finance Facts*, September 1971. National Consumer Finance Association.

## INFLATION

Inflation is an economic malady which decreases the buying power of your dollars. This disease of the economy is analogous to cancer in the human body. Growing uncontrolled, inflation impairs the economic health as surely as cancer impairs the physical health of its host.

While wage increases were large and cost-of-living increases small, inflation could be ignored by most people. But, in the late 1960's and early 1970's (as illustrated in Fig. 1–1) consumer prices began to show stiff annual advances. Then inflation became a household word, as skyrocketing service and grocery bills brought inflation's problems right into family budgets.

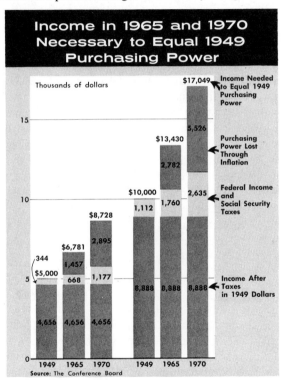

**Fig. 1–2** More and more money just to break even. Paychecks have more dollars but by the time Federal income taxes, social security taxes, and inflation are considered, the real gains are meager. Reprinted by permission from *Finance Facts*, November 1970. National Consumer Finance Association.

Figure 1–2 shows the combined effects of rising prices and higher taxes on purchasing power. To buy the same goods and services, a man who earned

$5,000 in 1949 would have needed to earn about 75% again as much in 1970. One who earned $10,000 in 1949 would have needed to earn 70% more.

On closer inspection you will see that a married couple with two children having $5,000 income in 1949 paid $344 for Federal income and social security taxes leaving $4,656 income after taxes. To have the same purchasing power in 1970, this couple would have needed income of $8,728 before taxes. Prices had increased by 54% so that $2,895 had been lost through inflation. The social security tax had increased from 1% on a maximum of $3,000 ($30) to 4.8% on a maximum of $7,800 ($374.40). Combined with the Federal income tax, the total of these two types of taxes were $1,177 in 1970.

To equal the purchasing power of $10,000 income in 1949, the married couple with two children needed $17,049 in 1970. Federal income and social security taxes took $2,635 in 1970, up from $1,112 in 1949 and $5,526 must be deducted from 1970 income to take account of inflation.

Inflation can be slowed, perhaps even halted for short periods of time. Adjustments in the Federal budget, action by the Federal Reserve Board, or other changes in national financial policy have all been used in attempts to quell spiraling costs. On August 15, 1971, President Nixon ordered a freeze on all prices and wages throughout the United States for a period of 90 days to be followed by some form of continuing voluntary or compulsory controls.

Nevertheless, economic and investment analysts seem to agree that even with some form of Federal price controls, inflation—at one rate or another—will persist. Three factors are mainly responsible for the inflationary climate: labor unions, a leveling-off in productivity advances, and government deficit spending. Other factors exert upward pressure on inflation's spiral, but the three named here stand out because of scale, pervasiveness, and strength.

**Labor unions.**  More than 17 million members strong, unions work continuously for improved benefits for their membership. Wages, pensions, insurance, longer vacations, shorter work days and shorter work weeks are some examples of the benefit improvements sought. In almost every contract negotiation between business firms and unions, some or all of these benefits are bettered. All of the benefits cost money. The firm agrees to pay higher wages, or higher insurance premiums, for example. These add to the total costs of making a product or offering a service. In turn, these higher manufacturing costs hike the wholesale and the retail prices of the products. In the rhetoric of contract negotiations and disputes, one fact is often overlooked: A firm, as well as being an employer, is an organization designed to make a profit. When it costs more to do business, the firm must charge more for its products. Ultimately, the consumer bears the brunt of the higher production costs.

**Lagging gains in productivity.**  As long as productivity (production per hour) increases faster than advances in labor costs, there is basically no reason to raise the cost of goods produced. Until recently, advancing technology, education, and automation cushioned, or at least partially compensated for, rising labor

"Remember when it meant cents instead of dollars?"

Reprinted with permission of *The Wall Street Journal* (Cartoon Features Syndicate).

costs. Now the process lags; productivity increases, while still developing, are falling behind wage increases. Here again, the cost of doing business, due to the increased cost of producing goods, is going up. And you, as a consumer, ultimately absorb the rising costs of production by paying ever rising prices.

**Government deficit spending.** The government seems to have perfected a technique by which it can be permanently and increasingly in debt. The national debt is allowed to grow, in spite of the billions of tax dollars allocated to retiring already existing indebtedness. The number and scope of government programs is ever increasing, and not surprisingly, the cost of supporting this largest service organization in the history of the world is ever increasing, too.

Some of the government's programs attempt to resolve international crises. Some are massive and zealous efforts to improve the quality of the American society. Some are simply "pet" projects of elected officials who hope to be re-elected by the beneficiaries of these projects.

When the government overextends itself in funding the bewildering array of its departments, agencies, bureaus, and other official entities, it must dig up the money somehow. When outgo exceeds income, the government "borrows" money by deficit spending. The taxpayer winds up paying interest on money borrowed to "solve" problems which no longer exist. Meanwhile, agencies offer redundant, even conflicting services. You can think of examples, or consider this one:

The Federal Communications Commission ruled that radio and television could not carry cigarette advertising after January 1, 1971. The U.S. Department of Agriculture, in an attempt to assist tobacco farmers, in 1971, masterminded a $1,500,000 grant to Iceland—earmarked for buying tobacco from the United States! At the same time, cigarette packages were required by law to state, "Warning: The Surgeon General Has Determined That Cigarette Smoking Is Dangerous to Your Health."

All government services are paid for through taxation, and as the number of services increases, the number of government employees increases, the costs go higher and higher. The increased costs must be met either by deficit spending or by raising already burdensome tax levies. Whatever else might be said of our government, one thing is absolutely certain—our government is expensive to support, and it is becoming more so.

**TAXES**

Because taxes are inextricably mixed with both inflation and lower net incomes, this discussion will combine the two effects of rising taxes.

"I wish all I had to worry about was the world -- not taxes, mortgages, rising prices, the cost of college . . ."

Reprinted with permission of *The Wall Street Journal* (Cartoon Features Syndicate).

The costs of government at all levels—national, state, county, and local— are constantly growing. Even if all these taxing agencies were run with optimum efficiency, there would still be a widening schism between increasing wants for government services and the ability of understandably reluctant taxpayers to finance those wants. The pattern runs full cycle as the various government agencies are forced to request higher tax revenues for the very expenses made costlier by former tax increases. Thus, taxes help to fuel the inflation which engenders high taxes.

Exact figures from one locality would not be representative of another because of wide variations in state and local tax laws. However, using national averages, state and local government taxes per person more than doubled between 1957 and 1969 in all but ten states, according to the most recent data compiled by Tax Foundation, Inc.

What has happened during this period tax-wise on a state by state basis is shown in Fig. 1–3. Greatest percentage rises in per person state and local taxes were Delaware (170%), Maryland (156%), New York (153%), and Nebraska (151%). Smallest percentage rises were Louisiana and Montana (86%), and Oklahoma (89%). Spending for welfare purposes by state and local governments rose 247% in the 1957–1969 period, a rate of increase greater than for any other major state-local government function, including education.

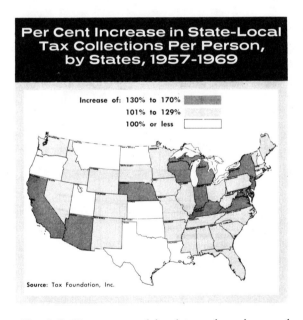

**Fig. 1–3** How state and local taxes have increased. Stiffer state and local taxes combine with the effects of Federal income taxes, social security taxes, and inflation to lower the average wage-earners purchasing power despite continuing dollar increases in his paycheck. Reprinted by permission from *Finance Facts*, April 1971. National Consumer Finance Association.

Of the $117 billion spent by state-local governments in 1969, the latest year for which figures were reported by the time of publication of your text, $47 billion went to education, $15 billion to highways and $12 billion for welfare.  Spending for education rose 234 % in the period, spending for highways, 97 %.

Combining state and local tax increases with the crunch from Federal income and social security taxes and inflation yields a grim picture indeed.  In terms of spendable purchasing power, the thing that really counts, the working American's recent wage increases are more shadow than substance.  From 1940–1965, despite rising prices and taxes, a worker's take-home pay had climbed from $25 to $43 a week in 1940 purchasing power.  However, since that time, this figure has not advanced, but has actually declined a little.

With the uncertainty as to which direction his future earning power is going to take, the wage earner is being asked to finance a veritable Pandora's box of government functions.  He is supporting the most expensive business in the world with, at times, a dubious return and prospects for even higher taxes.

Like inflation, rising taxes—at one rate or another—seem to be with us for the forseeable future.

### CONSUMER PROBLEMS

American affluence, in spite of the problems just stated, continues to be the marvel of the world.  Yet the very avalanche of products in our economy presents difficulties for the consumer.  Many products are labor-saving, durable, made to rigid specifications, and dependable.  Many are just shoddy, "quick buck" items which are not reliable, satisfactory, or even safe.  Much effort is being expended by private, government, and even commercial groups to regulate products and protect consumers.  Until such groups can regulate greed, outlaw deceptive practices, and get effective enforcement, the oldest and best advice to consumers is: *caveat emptor*—"Let the buyer beware."

But we do have to make buying decisions.  We must try to get maximum satisfaction per dollar spent.  We have to decide which of the 7–8,000 items stocked by a single large supermarket best meet our standards for comfort, safety, utility, reliability, food value, taste, and convenience—to name just a few buying criteria.  We have to choose among services, from diapers to funerals.  Of course, department stores, drug stores, automobile dealers, discount stores, furniture retailers, and a plethora of other firms also encourage spending.

Far too often, buyers simply give up and make subjective judgments which are largely a credit to the advertising industry's persuasiveness. Advertising is many things, sometimes even a public service; but it is first and foremost a service, paid for by sellers, to sell more of the sellers' goods.

Millions of products and services, millions of buying decisions, compounded by seductive advertising—is there no straightforward rational approach to buying? There is, and it is developed fully in Section III which is designed to help you get the best value (more) for the dollars you spend. Until you read that section ask yourself these four questions before buying: (1) What do I want from this purchase? (2) How does the article or service fit my needs? (3) What does the seller want? (4) Are my value requirements worth his price?

You can minimize the effect on your financial well-being of the terrible trio of inflation, rising taxes, and consumer problems. In fact, you can achieve your financial goals in spite of, and even *because* of them—following the processes described in this book. However, to make the most of the material provided here you must know *what you want to accomplish*. Thus, we move from broad economic problems to personal goals—your selection of what you want from living, with special attention to the part played by financial and career goals in your own overall life style.

## GOALS

Living without goals is like living in slavery. A slave has little choice about what he is and what he will become. A man without goals has abdicated that choice. He spends most of his life *reacting* to problems and circumstances *defensively*. He is buffeted and tossed about by changing circumstances. People who plan and set objectives to be accomplished have an entirely different kind of life. Knowing what they want to accomplish, they are on the *offense*. They create favorable conditions, do what needs doing, and reach their milestones because

Reprinted with permission of *The Wall Street Journal* (Cartoon Features Syndicate).

they know where they are going in life. This book is designed for such goal-oriented people; people who will take the time *now* to decide what they want for the *future*. It will help them set goals and then achieve them.

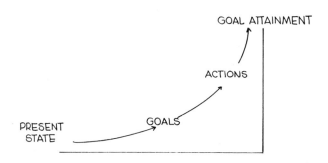

Goal achievement depends on how well you execute the following steps: First, you must define clear-cut goals and set deadlines for achievement. Second, you have to formulate a strategy which will lead to positive results. This is, basically, the development of action steps toward your goals. Third, you must expend systematic effort on these steps. To the extent you can stay on course and keep the personal commitments you have made, your goals will become reality. We do not imply that once objectives have been formulated, you should be rigid and inflexible in desperately pursuing them for the rest of your life. On the contrary, objectives often need modification. But the very fact that you start looking seriously at what you want from life—your most precious possession—will, without question, lead to greater satisfactions, and better, clearer goals as you make your way through life.

Let us briefly examine data relevant to initially making decisions on what your personal goals are going to be:

**Kind of work.** Since such a great portion of your waking hours is spent on the job, it is crucial that you be genuinely happy and satisfied with the kind of work you eventually do. As your job relates to goal setting, it is important to take a good look at yourself. Make a basic appraisal as to the kinds of activities that you not only can tolerate but toward which you can develop enthusiasm. This appraisal should involve an inventory of academic, physical as well as psychological attributes. For example, if you conclude you are a restless, energetic, and athletic type, you probably would want to stay clear of a tedious, confining desk job. Much more attention will be given career choice a little later in the chapter.

**Personal associations.** Looking at the years ahead, it is important to visualize the kind of people with whom you would most enjoy working. With what kind of friends and associates do you want to spend your time outside work? What kind of social structure do you want? Where do you want to live? What kind of environment do you want? What social and recreational events now tend to give you greatest enjoyment? Do you expect your standards to change? And if you are no longer among the *single set*, it is important that you also look at these things as a future marriage partner.

**Psychological satisfactions.** What sort of satisfactions do you anticipate will be most valuable to you—this decade and the next? Will they be quiet and personal, or noisy and social? Do you want to spend time doing things that will basically help other people? Are you more interested in tangibles rather than intangibles? Do you need to do creative things? Can you work as a team member with other people; or will you be most happy, most contented working alone?

**Other rewards.** How do you want your career remembered? What kinds of challenges do you want to meet? Do you enjoy competition, or does it threaten you? How important is the monetary reward for what you do? Do you need to be in a kind of work which will give you public visibility? In other words, do you want to be a well-known person? Or do you find satisfaction from merely knowing that you have done a commendable job?

**Kinds of goals.** Long-, intermediate-, and short-range goals are necessary. If you had only one goal, a long-range aim, you would still have implicit short-range goals of feeding, clothing, and educating yourself, and gathering the resources necessary to achieve that single larger goal. While short-range goals may be parts of a larger scheme, they may be completely separate. The kind of car you buy probably has little to do with what kind of career you pursue; but the classes you choose in college may have a great deal to do with your career and how successful you are in that career.

Temporarily, we may think of four major time considerations relative to goals. Short-term goals are those that can and should be reached within a year's time. They include providing the necessities of life, meeting and resolving day-to-day problems, and accomplishing increments of longer-term goals. An example of the latter is getting a good grade on this week's test so that you can pass this quarter's course, so that eventually you can get your bachelor's degree.

Medium range, or intermediate goals take longer. Getting your degree is one such goal. Buying your first home might be another. These goals will usually involve a 3–5 year planning period. The exact time depends on what must be accomplished: compiling the college credits you need, or accumulating the necessary money for your home, for example.

Long-range goals take longer still. Amassing wealth requires time and energy and good decisions, plus the background afforded by prior goal achievement. Retirement requires either current income from investments and savings, or using the principal itself; in either case, something must be put aside during the work years so that the retirement years are "affordable." Hence we may be talking in terms of 5–30 years, perhaps longer.

Lifetime goals are the sum of these, and something more. They result from decisions you make about what your life should be. They are quantitative *and* qualitative decisions. You can get the flavor of lifetime goals by answering such questions as: How much of what kind of experience do I want to realize during my lifetime? What will that cost in terms of thought and energy and persistence? What kinds of investments do I want to make with my life's time, with what rewards?

With this skeletal background about goals, let us begin at the beginning. The accomplishments of your life depend initially on your clear understanding of what you are setting out to do. Using a format similar to the one illustrated in Fig. 1–4, start work on a first draft of your personal goals. Be honest, accurate, and realistic (but not pessimistic). Include short-term (monthly to one year from now), intermediate (3–5 years), long-term (6–30 years), and lifetime goals. As your career plans become more certain, you will want to update carefully your life plan; but right now is a good time to start the process. The accomplishments of your life depend initially on your clear understanding of what you are setting out to do.

**Financial goals.** Do any of your goals cost money? That seems to be a naive question considering the reality of American economics at the personal level:

1. Goods and services cost money.
2. You can buy what you can afford.
3. The amount you can afford for any given purchase depends to a great extent on what you do with the money you have in relation to all the potential uses of your money.

How much do your goals cost? How are you going to pay for them? Developing a decision framework for you to pay for your goals is a major purpose of this book.

Let us precede your selection of financial goals with a brief examination of two "financial extremists." Decide which is more realistic in terms of real-world possibilities:

Abel Artist says he does not need any money to satisfy his goals. "I just

| Short-term goals monthly to one year | Steps which must be taken to accomplish this goal: | Date at which steps to be completed: |
|---|---|---|
| Goal: (Describe clearly and completely.) | 1. (list) | _____ |
| | 2. | _____ |
| | 3. | _____ |
| | 4. | _____ |
| | 5. (etc.) | _____ |
| Medium-range goals 3–5 years from today | 1. (list) | _____ |
| | 2. | _____ |
| | 3. (etc.) | _____ |
| Long-range goals 5 plus years | 1. (list) | _____ |
| | 2. (etc.) | _____ |
| Lifetime goals | 1. (list) | _____ |
| | 2. (etc.) | _____ |

**Fig. 1–4**  My personal goals.  Everyone should list his personal goals in a format most useful and meaningful to his individual situation.

want to paint . . . paint the best surrealist pictures ever. Material things mean nothing to me." Abel's ideas about materials are fine, and even workable, *unless* he wants to buy brushes and oils in order to paint, rent or buy a studio in which to paint, pay for food to ensure that posterity will see his inspirations on canvas (itself costing money). And, unless Abel wishes to limit his travels severely, he will need to buy some clothes. A. Artist represents an extreme of the goal/money relationship. He has definite goals, and claims he needs absolutely no money to achieve those goals. Still, even he must secure income and allocate income within his personal-goal framework.

Manny Millions has but one goal, entirely financial. Manny says, "I just want to make a million dollars; that's my goal, and it's my only goal." Manny

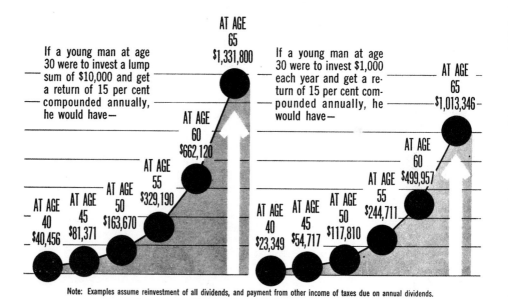

Note: Examples assume reinvestment of all dividends, and payment from other income of taxes due on annual dividends.

**Fig. 1–5** Two ways to pile up a million. While piling up a million is no easy accomplishment, it is not an impossibility. Reprinted by permission from *U.S. News & World Report*, p. 57, November 11, 1968. Copyright © 1968, U.S. News & World Report, Inc.

should look at Fig. 1–5. There, he would find two ways of reaching his goal by age 54:

1. By accumulating $10,000 in savings by age 30, investing it, and receiving a 15 percent return, compounded annually.

2. By systematically saving and investing $1,000 yearly from age 30, and achieving a 15 percent return, compounded annually.

M. Millions represents another extreme of the goal/money relationship. He has to secure income and make allocation decisions about that income. Financially, Manny's goal direction will require that he do a few more things with his money. He must invest it, insure it, and save it. Sometime in the future, he may have to borrow, or he may want to lend money.

Note the four conditions governing the success of either plan leading to the million-dollar goal: (1) saving the money to invest; (2) starting early in life, so that time, interest, dividends, and compounding can work most effectively; (3) putting money into an investment which yields the high return of 15 percent; and (4) paying income and/or capital gains taxes out of current income, along the way.

These plans are only two of many possible ways to achieve the goal of having a million dollars. Other, perhaps faster, ways will be discussed in Part V of this book. The 15 percent return could possibly be exceeded through certain kinds of investments, for example

Is it safe to predict that your financial ambitions fall somewhere between Abel Artist's and Manny Millions'? If so, where? What do you want money to do for you? How much do your personal goals cost? How are you going to pay for them? What amount of money do you want for retirement? How much down payment do you need for your dream house? Go back to Fig. 1–4, and attach price tags to personal goals, where appropriate. Jot down the financial goals, per se, which have occurred to you.

We will return to financial goals in Chapter 2, with the common-sense first step of budgeting. Now, however, we must do some work in the general area of background: we have to answer some questions about career choice and career preparation, where to get money, how money can be used, and how to use it well. You may already know some of the answers, but many Americans do not.

Despite the facts that a great deal of the average person's time is spent making economic decisions, and that these decisions are getting more numerous and more difficult—public schools have been unwilling or unable to devote much emphasis to economic education. A few groups, associations, and agencies are making praiseworthy efforts to provide information about economic matters, especially in the area of product safety, but even these efforts fall short of providing an overall background—a decision framework—for all the economic decisions that the average American wants to make. It seems fair to say that until he takes college courses in money management, or their equivalent in a comparable study discipline, the average high school graduate is poorly prepared in economic competence.

When you enrolled in this course, you indicated awareness of some of these problems and your intention to deal with them more effectively.  Good.  The time and effort you spend on this course will help you become economically successful.

## WHAT GOOD MONEY MANAGEMENT CAN DO FOR YOU

What can you do with money? There are an infinite variety of complexities involved; but, basically, there are six operations or processes: (1) earning money; (2) saving; (3) borrowing or lending money (two sides of essentially the same process); (4) insuring things (including the money earner); (5) investing, in hopes of making more; (6) spending money for goods and services.  These six processes require internal and external decisions.  For example, you might decide to spend some money, but you can not spend and then save the same dollar.  Once you have made the "external" decision to spend, how can you assure yourself of the best value from the product bought?

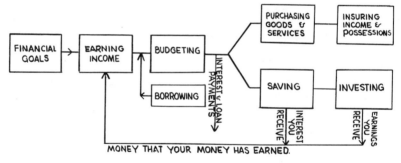

### PERSONAL MONEY MANAGEMENT SYSTEM

Now you need action plans (coordinated systems) to make sensible decisions *about* money processes, to work through the processes to your goals.  Connecting lines represent money flows and chronological and dependent relationships. (You must earn money *before* you spend it; but you insure yourself *because* you want to protect the income flow.)  These relationships will be clearer as you go on.  For now, let us define the processes, beginning with the logical question, "Where do you get the money to manage in the first place?"

## PREPARING TO EARN MONEY: CAREER CHOICE AND PREPARATION

"Them that works, eats," is as true today as when this homey statement was coined.  Wealthy or subsidized exceptions aside, most of us still have to earn our incomes, and most of us will work hard in our lifetime, but our earnings will vary greatly. This is a function within the market for labor: the more valuable the skills and abilities of labor are, the higher will be the price (wages) paid for them. Whether you earn a great deal of money or only a subsistence, depends on your own talents and training and upon your marketing those skills where they are best rewarded.

**The value of education.** You would probably not be a student if you had not drawn the conclusion that your education would result in a better job with better pay and a more prestigious way of life. That is good thinking on your part, because we live in an age when education beyond high school is almost mandatory for career success. In fact, there is hardly a safer generalization about the American economy than this: More education means more income. Look at the U.S. Bureau of Census data shown in Fig. 1–6. The figure explicitly notes that for most people in most situations, more education indeed means more income.

Besides the obvious benefits of higher income and vertical mobility that education offers, there is another, subtler benefit. We will call it adaptability. In your college experience you learn to use methods of many disciplines in handling a variety of problems and situations. Doing so, you are acquiring the ability to move with change. While it is often difficult to distinguish preparation from qualification, adaptability is one of the criteria for management. Management requires coordination of people with different qualifications, even though the manager is not specifically qualified in each of his subordinate fields.

**Where the jobs are.** Change seems to be the most prevalent characteristic of the job market. The need for educational and skill upgrading is not confined to clerical, technical, or professional fields. Changes in technology, management, and science as well as other influences have touched practically every facet of man's work. Consider two dramatic technology changes, each of recent history, each with shattering effects on what had been "good," "steady" jobs:

1. The changes in bookkeeping brought about by electronic data processing.
2. The changes in coal mining, especially in Appalachia, brought about by mechanized mining.

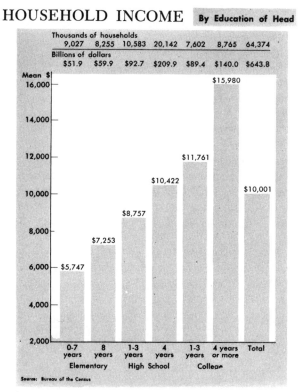

## HOUSEHOLD INCOME    By Education of Head

Fig. 1–6  What education means to your earning power.  Even though there are many personal qualities which may help account for differences in yearly and lifetime earnings of individuals, undoubtedly education has a significant impact.  Reprinted by permission from *Finance Facts*, August 1971 and December 1970.  National Consumer Finance Association.

The widespread effects of these and other technological-economic changes caused the U.S. Department of Labor to refine its forecasting.  Specifically, the department attempts to predict where occupational surpluses and shortages will occur.  To you, this means considered estimates about whether a job will be ready for you when you are ready for that job.  Take a hard look at Fig. 1–7.  Slim pickings are seen for farm workers, mathematicians, and teachers.  Government personnel are needed through 1980.  The message is: Make your career choice *realistically*.  Get the best objective viewpoints you can about a job (or alternate) which best suits your tastes and preferences.

One of the most useful guides for students entering the labor market, or for older persons considering retraining or transferring from one work category to another, is the U.S. Department of Labor's *Occupational Outlook Handbook*.*

---

* Available in the reference sections of school or public libraries or for sale by the Superintendent of Documents, U.S. Government Printing Offices, Washington D.C. 20402 (revised every two years).

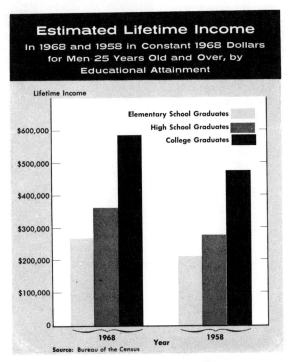

**Estimated Lifetime Income**
In 1968 and 1958 in Constant 1968 Dollars
for Men 25 Years Old and Over, by
Educational Attainment

Lifetime Income

Elementary School Graduates
High School Graduates
College Graduates

$600,000

$500,000

$400,000

$300,000

$200,000

$100,000

0

1968        Year        1958

Source: Bureau of the Census

**Figure 1–6** (*continued*)

It contains two- to three-page job descriptions of everything from barber to podiatrist, and answers such questions as: What kinds of jobs are there? What industries provide these jobs? Which fields of work are especially promising? What are the qualifications? What will the competition be like?

Here are some pertinent data from one job description in the Handbook:

**Physical Therapists.** Physical therapists help persons with muscle, nerve, joint, and bone diseases or injuries to overcome their disabilities. Following physicians' instructions, they treat patients through physical exercise, the use of mechanical apparatus, massage, and applications of heat or cold, light, water, or electricity . . .

*Where Employed.* Approximately 12,500 licensed physical therapists were employed in 1966. Nearly three-fourths of all therapists were women.

About four-fifths of all physical therapists work in general hospitals; in hospitals that specialize in the care of pediatric, orthopedic, psychiatric, or chronically ill patients; and in nursing homes.

20     Fig. 1–7   Where will the jobs be when you graduate? While overall employment will grow, there will be many industry-wide and occupational changes. You will want to take advantage of the trends, not buck them. Reprinted by permission from *Finance Facts*, October 1970 and January 1971. National Consumer Finance Association.

## Supply-Demand Imbalances in Selected Occupations
### (IF PAST STUDY AND WORK PATTERNS OF COLLEGE GRADUATES CONTINUE)

| Occupation | Projected 1980 Requirements | Percent Change 1968 to 1980 | Supply Estimated To Be |
|---|---|---|---|
| Chemists | 200,000 | 55.7 | |
| Counselors | 107,000 | 49.8 | |
| Dietitians | 42,100 | 40.3 | Significantly Below Requirements |
| Dentists | 130,000 | 31.7 | |
| Physicians | 450,000 | 53.1 | |
| Physicists | 75,000 | 63.9 | |
| Engineers | 1,500,000 | 40.2 | |
| Geologists & Geophysicists | 36,000 | 20.6 | Slightly Short of Requirements |
| Optometrists | 21,000 | 23.5 | |
| Architects | 50,000 | 47.1 | In Balance With Requirements |
| Lawyers | 335,000 | 22.7 | |
| Pharmacists | 130,000 | 7.0 | Slightly Above Requirements |
| Mathematicians | 110,000 | 60.5 | |
| Life Scientists | 238,000 | 40.8 | Significantly Above Requirements |
| Teachers, elementary and secondary | 2,340,000 | 7.8 | |

**Source:** Labor Department and National Consumer Finance Association

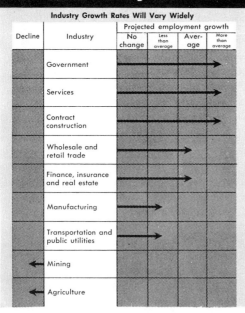

## While Total Employment Will Go Up by One-fifth by 1980 ...
### Industry Growth Rates Will Vary Widely

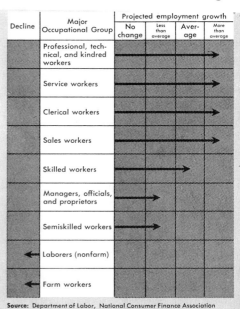

## Job Opportunities Will Increase Fastest in Occupations Requiring the Most Education and Training ...

**Source:** Department of Labor, National Consumer Finance Association

*Training.* A license is required to practice physical therapy in 48 states and the District of Columbia. To obtain a license, an applicant must have a degree or certificate from a school of physical therapy and pass a State Board examination.

*Employment Outlook.* The demand for physical therapists is expected to increase very rapidly through the 1970's as the result of increased public recognition of the importance of rehabilitation. Many new positions for physical therapists are expected to be created . . .

*Earnings and Working Conditions.* Annual salaries of inexperienced physical therapists averaged $6,500 in 1966, and those of experienced therapists ranged from $7,500 to $15,000, according to the American Physical Therapy Association.

*Where to Go for More Information.* American Physical Therapy Association, 1740 Broadway, New York, N.Y. 10019.

**Money and career choice.** "A hundred thousand dollars a year?" you say, smacking your lips. Naturally, we would all enjoy earning that kind of money, but experience has shown that the *amount* of money earned at a job is not as important to people as the *satisfaction* they get from the job itself. President John F. Kennedy inherited a million dollars on his 21st birthday, yet he went on to seek the most difficult job in the country. The key here is to choose the career which holds the most interest for you and, other considerations being equal, then seek the highest possible income in that career. An example may clarify that point: If it appears that you could teach high school psychology or be a clinical psychologist with equal competence *and* enjoyment, then you would be wise to take the latter with its higher salary. If your idea of valuable accomplishment is to provide teenagers with a basic education in personality development, then by all means become a teacher. Perhaps you could do both as a school psychologist. The point is that you will serve yourself and your employers best if you work at what is most meaningful to you. You are designing a frustrating life style, if you will constantly wish you were doing something else.

**Table 1-1**  Estimated average lifetime earnings of professional men, by level of education

| Occupation | Average | Lifetime earnings from age 18 to 64 | |
| --- | --- | --- | --- |
| | | 4 years of high school | 4 or more years of college |
| Doctors | $717,000 | $ | $721,000 |
| Dentists | 589,000 | | 594,000 |
| Lawyers | 621,000 | | 642,000 |
| Engineers: | | | |
|   Aeronautical | 395,000 | 378,000 | 418,000 |
|   Electrical | 372,000 | 327,000 | 406,000 |
|   Mechanical | 360,000 | 339,000 | 399,000 |
|   Civil | 335,000 | 285,000 | 380,000 |
|   Natural scientists: | | | |
|   Geologists | 446,000 | | 470,000 |
|   Physicists | 415,000 | | 431,000 |
|   Chemists | 327,000 | 274,000 | 351,000 |
|   Biologists | 310,000 | | 322,000 |
| Social scientists: | | | |
|   Economists | 413,000 | | 432,000 |
|   Psychologists | 335,000 | | 345,000 |
|   Statisticians | 335,000 | | 387,000 |
| Teachers: | | | |
|   Elementary School | 232,000 | | 241,000 |
|   High school | 261,000 | | 265,000 |
|   College | 324,000 | | 328,000 |
| Accountants | 313,000 | 286,000 | 362,000 |
| Clergymen | 175,000 | 156,000 | 184,000 |

"Hold it," you may be saying, "I thought this book was about how to make more money; and here it says to maybe settle for less money." Right on both counts. Remember earlier in this chapter, when we talked of your goals? There and elsewhere, especially in Chapter 2, you are encouraged to set them and proceed to achieve them. This book will help you a great deal in realizing the best use of your money, how to make money work for you. But you are reading this book within the context of your tastes, attitudes, and experience, and those determine what satisfies you, including your choice of career. Build a life full of satisfaction—not ulcers—for yourself.

**Possible job changes and your education plans.**  Other aspects of education-career relationship is education during career, and education prior to career change. The return to college by tradesmen, technical job holders, even executive and professional people, is evidence of these types of education-career activities. Not too long ago, the pattern was for a son to take up his father's trade, and continue at it throughout his life. This is no longer true. A wage earner cannot expect to remain in one occupation throughout his working life. Beginning at age 20, a man can expect to change jobs six or seven times during his 43 working years. Single women will work about 40 years; married women will work about 25–30 years. Women must also be capable of the adjustments that will be called for during their work years.

An example, which happens to be true, of education benefitting career changes is Joe:

EDUCATION:                         JOB:
B.S. in Chemistry                  Pharmaceutical Company in Oregon
    (Joe's asthmatic wife could not tolerate damp Oregon winters.)

    so............................. Laboratory assistant in Southern Idaho
                                     hospital
    (Joe found he could make more money if he were a registered technologist.)

so.......................
One year's intensive training at   Half of two-man laboratory team
accredited hospital
        (Other man left, Joe ran the lab by himself, until the job
            demands simply outweighed the job benefits.)

    so............................. Joe took a job in a retardate hospital,
                                     and became intrigued with the field of
                                     retardation

so.......................
Master's degree in biochemistry
with a special practicum in
retardation
                                   He worked his way up to lab supervisor
        (This worked out well, until the financial demands of Joe's
            growing family outweighed the position's salary.)

so.......................
Night classes in hospital          His choice of positions and salary . . . he
administration                     chose the job of Chief Administrator at
                                   a retardate hospital.

Joe's experience is not atypical. While higher pay is the main inducement in job changes, there are many other influencing factors. Perhaps you will never change jobs; perhaps you will find that switching is the key to your financial and occupational advancement. Even if you remain in a single job, to successfully absorb the training and retraining within that job, you must have a broad educational background. And, given the benefits of a broad educational background, the college graduate has the clear edge.

### COMPLETING YOUR EDUCATION: A SMART MOVE

Experience was the sole criterion for employment and career success back in the days of hereditary crafts and long apprenticeships. Now, there are three criteria: Education, career choice, and experience. Of these, experience is least important. Education, by all measures, is the most important. As we have pointed out earlier in this chapter, the rationale is that people with education can adapt to varied needs of the hiring firms. Additionally, there are many personnel administrators who believe that long experience in a single job classification may indicate that a prospective employee would have adjustment problems if faced with novel situations or challenges. Personnel officials must make hiring decisions based on what they expect of ongoing technology. The green eyeshade and sleeve garters of a bookkeeper have not been museum pieces for long.

If you are establishing your priorities of time and effort for career success, you should reconsider the Department of Labor studies shown in Fig. 1–7; then, you should review the discussion above about hiring criteria. Perhaps you will come to a conclusion which might be paraphrased, "To get a good job, and advance, professionally and financially, completing your education is priority A-1."

This is *not* to say that you should ignore opportunities to get relevant work experience. The two qualifications, in combination, are nearly unbeatable. Imagine yourself as a personnel officer for a television station. For the analogy, you interview just two candidates for your production staff:

Candidate 1:   B.A. in Telecommunications

Candidate 2:   B.A. in Telecommunications and part-time cameraman for a local station

The example is deliberately simple. Personnel departments also want to find out about work habits, ability to get along with co-workers, creativity, trustworthiness, and so on. But, if these other factors were approximately equal for both candidates, which would you choose? What does this mean to your career plans? If you can manage to, without short-changing your studies, follow Action Plan 1:

**Action Plan 1:**
**A. Stay in school**
**B. Get relevant work experience**

### BUT, COLLEGE IS EXPENSIVE

True, and becoming more so. Pressures for growth in terms of land, buildings, larger faculties, better equipment, and higher salaries for professors, administrators, and other school workers have to be matched with the colleges' ability to pay for that growth. Colleges are not immune from the effects of inflation, either.

$8,000 a year? An inkling of the rise in basic college expenses in the past five years is given in the accompanying chart (Fig. 1–8) compiled by *U. S. News & World Report*. At this pace, tuition and living costs alone will often mean $8,000 a year before the end of this decade.*

"The family that supports a son or daughter through graduate school already is laying out a relative fortune in the name of higher education. The Scientific Manpower Commission figures that a bachelor's degree at a first-rank university such as Stanford costs a student about $22,000. A doctorate from a private university will cost an additional $25,000 today. This makes up an education bill of $47,000 for a youth bright enough to be a fully trained scientist or teacher. It does not include college-overhead costs, typically not charged to students."†

### HOW WILL YOU PAY FOR COLLEGE?

Some families can afford college educations for their children. Using savings, proceeds from investments or current earnings, they purchase the college experience. Most families cannot do this, and they need to assemble a financial package which might include part-time jobs, financial aid, scholarships, loans,

---

* "Can You Afford College?", *U. S. News & World Report*, February 22, 1971, p. 25. Reprinted by permission.
† *Ibid.*

### ZOOMING PRICES ON THE CAMPUS

*Average charges for academic year at four-year colleges*

PUBLIC COLLEGES

| | FIVE YEARS AGO | THIS YEAR (est.) | NEXT YEAR (est.) |
|---|---|---|---|
| **TOTAL** | **$1,103** | **$1,417** | **$1,492** |
| Tuition and fees | $ 326 | $ 442 | $ 472 |
| Dormitory room | $ 304 | $ 416 | $ 441 |
| Board | $ 473 | $ 559 | $ 579 |

PRIVATE COLLEGES

| | | | |
|---|---|---|---|
| **TOTAL** | **$2,314** | **$3,089** | **$3,281** |
| Tuition and fees | $1,368 | $1,924 | $2,057 |
| Dormitory room | $ 418 | $ 539 | $ 575 |
| Board | $ 528 | $ 626 | $ 649 |

Averages do not include cost of clothing, books, transportation and incidentals, and are far below the annual tab for a student in an elite institution. A typical Ivy Leaguer now spends $4,000 and up a year, and out-of-State students at top State universities lay out $3,000 and up. At present increases, college by 1980 would cost $8,000 a year in many places.

### ... AND A SAMPLING
### OF TUITION BOOSTS ON THE WAY

IVY LEAGUE COLLEGES

| | Tuition for college year starting next September | Increase over present year | | Tuition for college year starting next September | Increase over present year |
|---|---|---|---|---|---|
| Brown University | $2,850 | $250 | Harvard University | $2,800 | $200 |
| Columbia College | $2,700 | $200 | University of Pennsylvania | $2,750 | $200 |
| Cornell University | $2,800 | $200 | Princeton University | $2,800 | $300 |
| Dartmouth College | $2,820 | $270 | Yale University | $2,900 | $350 |

OTHER PRIVATE COLLEGES

| | Tuition for college year starting next September | Increase over present year | | Tuition for college year starting next September | Increase over present year |
|---|---|---|---|---|---|
| Agnes Scott College | $2,000 | $100 | Franklin and Marshall | $2,550 | $150 |
| Albion College | $2,020 | $120 | George Fox College | $1,620 | $219 |
| Austin College | $3,000 | $150 | George Washington University | $2,050 | $150 |
| California Institute of Technology | $2,560 | $175 | Lehigh University | $2,450 | $150 |
| | | | New York University | $2,700 | $250 |
| Case Western Reserve University | $2,385 | $185 | Northwestern University | $2,700 | $300 |
| | | | Rice University | $2,100 | $300 |
| University of Chicago | $2,475 | $150 | Stanford University | $2,610 | $210 |
| Drake University | $1,970 | $190 | Williams College | $2,350 | $100 |
| Emory University | $2,400 | $225 | Wittenberg University | $2,286 | $165 |

PUBLIC COLLEGES

| | Tuition for college year starting next September | Increase over present year | | Tuition for college year starting next September | Increase over present year |
|---|---|---|---|---|---|
| University of California | | | State University of New York | | |
| (State residents) | $ 629 | $141 | (State residents) | $ 550 | $150 |
| (Out-of-State residents) | $1,829 | $141 | (Out-of-State residents) | $ 900 | $300 |
| University of Maryland | | | University of Oregon | | |
| (State residents) | $ 589 | $ 50 | (State residents) | $ 507 | $ 99 |
| (Out-of-State residents) | $ 939 | $150 | (Out-of-State residents) | $1,575 | $168 |

**Fig. 1–8** College costs. The cost of a college education has been rising steadily, and there is little doubt it will continue to do so. Reprinted by permission from *U.S. News & World Report*, February 22, 1971. Copyright © 1971, U.S. News & World Report, Inc.

and grants for the purpose. Some conscientious families have set aside savings for years, only to find that inflated costs of books, tuition, and living expenses have increased costs beyond their estimates.

**Federal financial aid.** The government *is* helping. The College Work-Study Program, through on-campus jobs, provides income for many students. (See Fig. 1–9.) It was authorized by the Economic Opportunity Act of 1964, a total dollar limit is established, based on relative need, and the student works for an hourly wage, a maximum of 15 hours a week while school is in session and up to 40 hours a week during vacation periods. General requirements are that the student (1) be a citizen of the United States or a foreign national in permanent residence; (2) carry a minimum of 75 percent of normal class load; and (3) present demonstration of financial need.

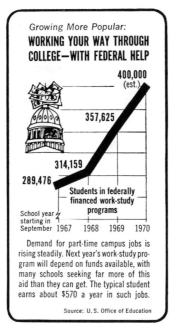

**Fig. 1–9** Work-study program. The Federal Government is providing financial assistance to college students through a variety of programs. Reprinted by permission from *U.S. News & World Report*, p. 27, February 22, 1971. Copyright © 1971, U.S. News & World Report, Inc.

Loans under two federal programs are also available. The first of these is the National Defense Student Loan Program, authorized under the National Defense Education Act of 1958. Qualifications are similar to those of Work-Study, but the academic minimum is 50 percent rather than 75 percent, of normal class load. The maximum loan is $1000 per year. Repayment is deferred while the borrower is enrolled at least half-time and during service in the military, Peace Corps, or VISTA.  Interest begins to accrue at 3 percent, nine months after the borrower ceases to carry the minimum class load. Repayment begins a year after cessation and may extend to 10 years depending on the total of the loans made.

The Federally Insured Loan Program is a second way by which students can borrow money, if they do not have access to state or non-profit loan programs. Authorized by the Higher Education Act of 1965, its academic requirements are the same as for National Defense loans.  Students may borrow up to $1 500 per year; interest accrues at the rate of 7 percent during the entire loan term, but the government pays the interest while the student is in school.  Repayment may also take up to 10 years beyond the borrower's graduation or withdrawal from school.  Detailed information on both federal loan programs is given in Chapter 6, "Consumer Borrowing."

**Other assistance.**    There are many other ways to meet the costs of college, aside from the federal programs above.  One of the best is an outright scholarship grant.  Most colleges have these gifts available, but the competition is tough, and you might not have the high academic standing to qualify.  If not, look to other loan and employment sources.  Your college personnel or placement office may be helpful in finding on- or off-campus jobs.  The local Employment Security office is a good source of part-time job information.

As for borrowing, most colleges offer, or have information about, loan services other than the two federal programs outlined here.  Contact your admissions officer or director of financial aids for information and application materials.  In some states, the Department of Education is a source of loan funds.  Inquiries should be addressed to the appropriate state agency.

One final word about paying for college: Agencies, bureaus, officials, and programs can and do assist many students.  There is a communication lag though—from the time a job becomes available to the time you hear about it through one of these intermediaries.  Paying for college is one of the primary problems in getting through college.  Your initiative, your ability to be in the right place at the right time, is itself a resource for paying your way. If you think you see an employment opportunity, do not wait until your college placement bureau lists the job—apply for it immediately.

**FEEDBACK 1**

This is the first of the action programs which follow each chapter. Their aim is understanding real-world situations; their focus is your understanding and your ability to use that understanding in achieving your goals. Feedback, like the rest of this book, and like the achievement of your level of financial success, depends on your efforts as input. You are the final judge of the output. But keep in mind that you are working on them for your own real and direct benefit. The routines are not busy work—they are exercises in the real world about the real you.

**A.** Select two or three fields which interest you. Examples (not suggestions) would be: Health professions, social sciences, communications, or laboratory sciences. Look up these areas in the *Occupational Outlook Handbook*.

- Do you see yourself as a career professional in one of them?
- Do the facts about the jobs differ from your preconceptions about them?
- Of the fields, which seems most attractive to you?
- Which jobs seem most attractive in this field? Why?

**B.** Write to sources listed in the *Occupational Outlook Handbook* for more information about any career which interests you. (Perhaps more than one— your interest is the deciding factor.) Interview at least two local firms which employ people in the field you are investigating. These people may enhance your interest or discourage it; but remember, they are making their living in a field you have only read about. They have valuable insight into the problems and the opportunities of the job. If you find your interest and ability meet a need, apply for a part-time job. Related work experience, remember?

- How do local opportunities match up with the *Handbook*'s national projections?
- What city or area is the center for work in your field? (New York is the center of national communications media, for instance.)
- Do you want to move to where the action is?
- What does the information in B. do to your interest?

**C.** Use Department of Labor publications to estimate your earnings as a college graduate in a career of your choice. Does a high school graduate qualify for this career? If yes, assume a student who graduated from high school with you has been working in this field while you have been in college:

- How does your (college graduate) starting salary compare with his starting salary? With his present salary?

- At the wage rates given, how long before you repay yourself for the money you invested in college?

- How long before you surpass the high school graduate in earning power?

**D.** If you are independently wealthy, you can skip this exercise.  If not, and especially if money is a problem: Drop into the financial aids offices of your school and fill out a Work-Study application.  And see if you need, and otherwise qualify for one of the loan programs offered.  Or both.  If worrying about money problems distracts you when you should be concentrating on your studies, your grades may be adversely affected.  The student with a part-time job often improves his grades finding that he makes better use of his time budget, as well as having fewer money budget problems.

**E.**  To clarify your present goals:

- What are the three most important reasons why you are in school?

- If you have pinpointed a career or one field interests you above all others, what are you now learning which is preparing you for your employment future?

- In light of your interest, what changes may be required in your class schedule next quarter?  Next year?  Investigate the possibility of getting a Work-Study assignment in the department related to your career preference.

## DISCUSSION QUESTIONS

1. Living in a country that produces a trillion dollars worth of goods and services in one year should be financially satisfying to its people.  Why are Americans having financial problems?

2. What happened during the late 1960's and early 1970's that gave inflation the fuel to skyrocket?

3. Has the Federal Government the right to control prices and wages as was done during the 90-day freeze in 1971?  Explain.

4. What types of government programs could be eliminated to reduce the national debt?  Should the United States do away with the national debt?

5. Should advertising be limited to reporting only facts of the product or service, eliminating all emotional appeal?

6. What goals should be most important in planning a future career?

7. Is college experience the best preparation for a job?  Where else can one become prepared for a career?

8. Why do farm workers, mathematicians, and teachers have a small job market?  What fields will be experiencing the greatest growth in jobs?

9. What is the most important outcome of a job: amount of money earned or satisfaction from the job?  Explain.

10. Is the price for going to college (tuition, books, etc.) proportionate to what you get out of it? Explain.

11. Should the Federal Government help support students in college as they are doing in their student programs? Explain.

## CASE PROBLEM

Phillip Andrews is a first-quarter senior at State University. He received good grades in high school, which gave him a scholarship in English for the first two years at college. His final year will be financed by his parents, just as was his junior year.

Phil will be graduating with a B.A. in English. He had no real reason for choosing English as his major; it was an easy subject for him in high school, so he thought he would give it a try in college. He is looking forward to getting out of school; however, he has no plans on what to do after he is out. In fact, he has even thought of dropping his last year of school to do some traveling.

Phil has not been worried about his future plans until now, when he can finally see the end of his schooling. He has no desire to teach or continue his study into graduate school. But he also feels that he is not ready to settle down into "some routine job." Phil is very confused about making future plans.

a) What should Phil have done before he went to college to avoid the confusion he is in now?

b) How could Phil have better prepared himself for a career if teaching English is not his ambition?

c) Do you believe that Phil should continue in school until graduation? After graduation?

d) What are a few short-term goals Phil should make now? What are a few long-term goals he should make?

e) Where can Phil go for possible help in making his decision?

## SUGGESTED READINGS

Ball, R. J. *Inflation and Theory of Money.* London: Allen and Unwin, 1964. 313 pp.

*Better Homes and Gardens.* "Money Management for Your Family." Des Moines: Meredith Press, 1967. 208 pp.

Blaustein, B. J., and Robert Gorman. *How to Have More Money to Spend.* New York: Julian Messner, 1962. 221 pp.

Cohen, Jerome B., Ph.D., and Arthur W. Hanson, LL.B., D.C.S. *Personal Finance Principles and Case Problems* (Third Edition). Homewood, Ill: R. D. Irwin, 1964. 865 pp.

Cohen, Martin, "What Every Young Wife Should Know About Money," *Redbook,* September 1968, reprint.

Enterline, H. G. (ed.). *Educating Youth for Economic Competence.* Somerville, N.J.: Somerset Press, 1958. 377 pp.

*Facing Facts About College Costs.* Newark: Prudential Insurance Company of America.

"How Do Those Jonses Do It?" *Changing Times.* April 1968. p. 5.

Katona, George, and others. *1967 Survey of Consumer Finances.* Ann Arbor, Mich.: Braun-Brumfield, 1968. 342 pp.

*Managing Your Money—A Family Plan.* Washington, D.C.: USDA, 1964. 12 pp.

Margolius, Sidney. *How to Make the Most of Your Money.* New York: Appleton-Century-Crofts, 1966. 241 pp.

Margolius, Sidney. *Paying for a College Education.* New York: Public Affairs Pamphlets, 1967. 29 pp.

McKay, Quinn G., and William A. Tilleman. *Money Matters in Your Marriage.* Salt Lake City: Deseret, 1971. 239 pp.

Miller, Herman P., and Richard A. Hornseth. *Present Value of Estimated Lifetime Earnings.* Washington, D.C.: Bureau of the Census, 1967. 54 pp.

Odiorne, George S. *Effectiveness—Direct Action for Your Success.* Minneapolis: DirAction Press, 1967. 273 pp.

Phillips, E. Bryant, and Sylvia Lane. *Personal Finance: Text and Case Problems* (Second Edition). New York: 1969. 536 pp.

Reader's Digest Association. *How to Live on Your Income.* Pleasantville, N.Y.: The Reader's Digest Association, 1970. 639 pp.

Smith, Carlton and Richard Putnam Pratt. *The Time-Life Book of Family Finance.* New York: Time-Life Books, 1969. 415 pp.

Wall Street Journal (ed.). "Americans and Their Pocketbooks." New York: Dow Jones & Company, 1964. 144 pp.

Weisinger, Mort. *Bonanza, U.S.A.* New York: Bantam Books, 1966. 248 pp.

Wilder, Rex. *The Macmillan Guide to Family Finance.* New York: Macmillan, 1967. 235 pp.

Yonkers Public Library. *Consumer Education Bibliography.* Washington, D.C.: U.S. Government Printing Office, no date. 170 pp.

*Your Financial Worksheet: A Guide for Women Returning to the Job World.* New York: Institute of Life Insurance, 1968.

# CHAPTER 2

# BUDGETING:
# THE WAY THROUGH THE MONEY MAZE

A small boy, sent to the bakery by his mother, returned a short time later completely empty handed: no money and no donuts—the supply had been exhausted. Questioned about the money, the child explained, "Well, it wasn't any good. I couldn't buy anything with it, so I threw it away."

We can readily assume that right then and there that youngster got his first lesson in money management. But as we think about it, his logic wasn't really so wrong. Money in and of itself is of little value. What matters is what we can do with money. And more often than we'd like to admit, most of us have—just as surely as that small boy—thrown away some of our own money through unwise decisions, about what to do with it.

After you get your money, you must decide how to use it. Good or bad advice may lead you to decisions which bring you satisfaction or despair, but you're still in charge. This is sometimes not apparent, as in the cases where expenses and time payments outrun income. You may forget that you were so excited about buying a new car or stereo outfit that the time-payment contract seemed to be just a formality which stood between you and possession. However, that decision was made, and you are now obligated to pay the bill. You made a budget decision *then*, and *now*, because of it, you must make other budget decisions.

Money, like all physical matter, simply cannot be in two places at the same time. You can't spend the *same* dollar for two *different* things.

If you have money problems, you are not alone.  People in all walks of life, at all levels of income, in every part of the country, have money problems.  If that statement seems to imply, for example, that a doctor who may earn $50,000 annually could have money problems, it does.  The scale of his problem would probably vary considerably from yours.  The rent or house payment bill which bothers him may be for $500 or even $1000: yours may be one-fifth of that.  Still, you might share with the doctor the very difficult problem of how to meet that kind of payment.  The problem—amounts aside for the moment—is matching income, of whatever size, to outgo, of whatever size.  If the point is still not clear that a great many Americans have problems managing their money, consider your classmates.  Do you believe that any of them enrolled in the course for sheer enjoyment?

If money problems are so widespread, despite variations in income, then it would seem that solutions to such problems lie not in amounts, but in approach.  Here, the relationship between life goals, financial goals, and money management should become clearer.  In Chapter 1, you were urged to make decisions on personal lifetime goals and general approaches which would lead to satisfying those goals.  In this chapter, you should set more immediate financial objectives.  Then, you should map specific dollar and cents action plans which will help you reach financial goals—immediate, intermediate, and long-term.

Before discussing planning, we must take into account a special case.  This book is addressed to the single student.  But if you are married, or when you do marry, a special dimension is added to planning; here we call it agreement.  Agreement is important to marriage, else why is so much time and energy expended in resolving disagreements?  Agreement is certainly important in *any* joint venture involving money.  Thus it seems worthwhile to digress just a bit and discuss the two-party money management team of husband and wife.

## MONEY AND MARITAL HAPPINESS

Planning is essential to the achievement of goals, and married people need planning plus agreement in the area of money management.  Without planning and/or agreement, the striving toward financial goals is plagued by problems which almost always seem to reflect upon the marriage itself.  Psychologists, sociologists and financial counselors are understandably reluctant to make such sweeping statements as: "A certain degree of proficiency in money management leads to a specific degree of happiness in marriage." Or, "This particular kind of money problem leads to that particular kind of marital difficulty."  Nevertheless, many of these same experts, whose jobs bring them into close contact with people's marital and family problems, agree that money matters represent a major cause of discord.

The degree of interrelationship between money problems and marital difficulty depends, of course, upon individual circumstances and the value a couple places on the importance of money in their marriage.  The advantages in a marriage of good economic planning and of freedom from frustrated, unrealistic goals speak for themselves. Study the fictional dialogues which follow and note especially the agreement factor in each case. What problems do you see? How might these problems be resolved? Do you have similar agreement (disagreement) problems, or do you anticipate them?

CASE 1

  He: Honey, I just found out about a terrific deal on bubble gum. We can buy 20 cases for $2 each.

  She: Wonderful! We've got more than $40 in savings, so we can buy them without borrowing.

CASE 2

  He: I spent $200 on a new set of golf clubs. I needed a heavier set, and these are beauties.

  She: But you bought a set last year, and now we can't afford a vacation this year again.

  He: Golf is recreation. I need relaxation after working so hard all week.

  She: Waste!

  He: Recreation!

CASE 3

  He: Let's save $5 more out of this paycheck.

  She: Let's spend it on a movie.

  He: When we're old, we'll be thankful that we were so thrifty during our working years.

  She: I feel old now because we never have any enjoyment from the money we earn.

CASE 4

  He: We're overdrawn on our checking account, and the department store just sent a second notice. We've got to cut out this carelessness.

  She: You're upsetting me. Now I don't feel like showing you my new outfit. I got a new purse, shoes to match, and a new blouse—I charged them so that we wouldn't have to pay for them this month. The receipts are here in my purse, I think.  Oh, and I had to charge a tank of gas because you didn't give me enough money today.

He:  Arggh!

She:  You're a mean man.

These few cases obviously do not exhaust the possibilities, but they do illustrate the necessity of having satisfactory working agreements on what you buy, how you save, how much to spend on entertainment, and so on.

### BACKGROUND

Married or single, you face routine, recurring financial decisions.  Sometimes these decisions are crucial ones.  Unless you are self-employed, even before you get your pay, taxes have already been deducted.  Out of what is left, you must decide what to buy and how much to save, realizing that even while you are saving money prices are continually going up.  Many people, perhaps yourself included, find that "there's too much *month* left over at the end of the *money*." Expenses that outrun income seem to be common to most of us; but even the ones who are "making ends meet," frequently feel that they are not really getting any place financially.

Problems.  Problems.  Problems.  By now, you are probably as tired of reading about them as you are of experiencing them.  Good.  Let's go to work on some solutions.  When we discussed general *personal* goals, we arbitrarily assumed that you had the wit and wisdom to achieve them.  In dealing with *financial* goals, however, it is well to begin with an assessment of what you have available to work with.  In other words, our discussion is not Goal—Approach, but Current Situation—Desired Situation—Approach.  Or, using a travel analogy:

**"We have to cut down on living."**

Reprinted with permission of *The Wall Street Journal* (Cartoon Features Syndicate).

1. You find out where you are now—Financial worth (current state of your budget).
2. You decide where you want to be—Financial goals.
3. You begin planning your route—Budgeting (planned, future spending).

Obviously, budget is the key word in this chapter, and you should know what budgeting means.

## WHAT IS A BUDGET?

A budget is an allocation guide for coordinating your expenses with your income. In everyday terms budgeting is organizing your finances so that you can pay bills when due; buy luxuries as well as necessities, and have some money left over to save, invest, or spend on future needs.

Budgeting is the direct, sensible approach to personal money management. The case against budgeting is that you may have to change some of the habits which are resulting in financial difficulties for you. When you analyze your spending habits and discover that they involve spending more than you want to, you will realize that the habits must be changed. By definition, habits are difficult to alter. More difficult (impossible, when you consider the paradox of borrowing your way out of debt) is the task of making ends meet when you have already spent too much money. So, the case for budgeting is the achievement of your financial goals.

## HOW DOES A BUDGET WORK?

Essentially, a budget provides a method for you and your family to get what you need and want. It is the fundamental tool used in satisfying financial goals. It is a written plan which helps the family or individual understand how to use money. Or, as someone said, "The main purpose of a budget is not to get you out of money troubles, but to keep you out of trouble in the first place."

Pertinent to this discussion of what a budget *is*—some strong words of caution about what a budget *is not*: A budget is not the bookkeeping of the cost of each and every purchase. It is not a permanent structure which involves scrimping or penny pinching forever. A budget is a tool, and tools lighten work, they do not create work.

A budget serves personal, rather than general needs. Your budget is not, and should not be, the same as your neighbor's budget. Your needs and wants are unique, and the plan to satisfy those needs and wants must itself be unique. There are as many examples of budgets as there are people who spend money. While it is interesting and useful to see how other Americans allocate their paychecks (see Fig. 2–1), each family or person should tailor a budget to fit particular goals. And every budgeter should begin with a clear knowledge of his present financial status—an inventory or personal wealth statement.

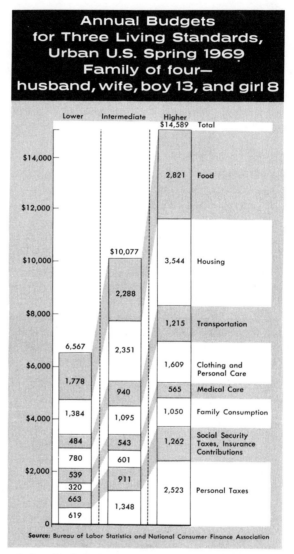

**Fig. 2–1** How much for what? Before you can make a workable budget, you need some idea of how much money you need for various expenses. Shown above are average budget allocations for a family of four at differing income levels. Your own goals, however, should determine your allocations.

## TAKING INVENTORY

For your inventory, use the form in Fig. 2–2 as a guide. Be thorough. Complete all parts of the form accurately. In Part I, list all your financial resources at this time (assets). In Part II, jot down all your financial obligations (liabilities)—the

# What's your financial health?

## I. Figure your assets:

**Estimated Amounts**

*Cash and liquid assets*
cash on hand ___ $ ___
balances in checking accounts ___
balances in savings accounts ___
U.S. Savings Bonds ___
cash value of insurance ___
savings and loan or credit union shares ___
Subtotal ___ $ ___

*Market value of securities and other investments*
corporate bonds ___
corporate stocks ___
investment company shares ___
investment club ___
notes and mortgages owned ___
Subtotal ___ $ ___

*Equity interest in personal business* ___ $ ___

*Market value of real estate*
your home ___
other property ___
Subtotal ___ $ ___

*Market value of durable goods*
home furnishings and equipment ___
clothing ___
autos ___
sporting and other equipment ___
Subtotal ___ $ ___

*Market value of special items*
furs ___
jewelry ___
art works ___
antiques ___
other ___
Subtotal ___ $ ___
**Total Assets** ___ $ ___

## II. Figure your liabilities:

**Estimated amounts**

*Current bills*
charge accounts ___ $ ___
credit card accounts ___
utilities ___
insurance premiums due ___
medical and dental bills ___
other bills due ___
Subtotal ___ $ ___

*Loan balances*
home mortgage ___
other mortgages ___
auto loans ___
insurance loans ___
personal notes ___
other debts ___
Subtotal ___ $ ___

*Taxes*
federal income tax ___
state income tax ___
real property tax ___
personal property tax ___
special assessments ___
other taxes or back taxes ___
Subtotal ___ $ ___
**Total Liabilities** ___ $ ___

**TOTAL ASSETS** ___ $ ___
**LESS TOTAL LIABILITIES** ___ $ ___
**EQUAL NET WORTH AS OF THIS DATE** ___ $ ___

Net worth by itself tells you little more than where you stand at this moment. While it's difficult to predict the future, you can anticipate certain changes in your assets and your liabilities.

In the space provided here, estimate your contingent assets and "expected liabilities." Some of these assets and liabilities will materialize in the near future, and may affect your present plans for spending and saving. Other assets and liabilities belong in the distant future, and affect present financial planning only as they increase or reduce your need to save for future goals.

## III. Estimate contingent assets:

**Estimated amounts**

pension plans ___ $ ___
profit sharing ___
expected inheritance ___
social security ___
gifts of money, property, securities or other valuables ___
bonuses ___
retirement income ___
face value of life insurance ___
other contingent assets ___
**Total contingent assets** ___ $ ___

## IV. Estimated expected liabilities:

**Estimated amounts**

repairs and maintenance on house, auto, and equipment ___ $ ___
decorating or remodeling ___
replacement of car, furnishings, or equipment ___
uninsured emergencies ___
education of children ___
purchase of major equipment and furnishings ___
other expected expenses ___
**Total expected liabilities** ___ $ ___

Weigh your contingent assets and your expected liabilities against each other—and against your net worth figure as of this date—to get a picture of your probable future financial strength.

**Fig. 2–2** What's your financial health? To be able to set and work toward the achievement of sound financial goals requires that you know just how you stand financially now. Reprinted by permission from *Better Homes and Gardens* "Family Financial Management," pp. 24, 122. October 1970. Copyright © 1970 Meredith Corporation 1970. All rights reserved.

things that pinch. Then complete the analysis by taking a look at the future—both asset and liability-wise.

Perhaps analysis will reveal that current installment payments and other obligations must be taken care of before any new plans can be executed. Or, you may find that you have no backlog of bills or obligations, and that you can proceed with some intermediate and long-range plans.

### YOUR FINANCIAL GOALS

Setting your financial goals must include consideration of what your money *must* buy; what else you *want* to buy; and, which things are *needed* now, and which can wait until next month, next year or several years from now. Similarly, a family budget involves each member in choosing these goals. In a family situation, a conference should be held, and each person's view considered.

Think about your goals carefully. Objectively determine if they are realistic. If study and discussion reveal that some of the goals are not feasible, revise or discard them. Write down the goals which remain, separating them into two categories, "Current" and "Future." Use Fig. 2–3 as a guide. Writing out your goals is important; seeing them on paper may enable you to eliminate those which are obviously daydreams. There's nothing more demoralizing than trying to achieve impossible goals, so again, be realistic.

Generally, your present goals will include the means for taking care of current living expenses—the day-to-day obligations and responsibilities. Future goals may include owning a home, taking a long vacation, or any number of long-range and expensive items. Obviously, the current goals should occupy your concentration first. They are nearer in terms of time and accessibility. Note in Fig. 2–3 that you are already applying success thinking toward your goals by breaking large, and presently unobtainable sums into small, currently available increments. The example entries show allocations per payday and per month. This is the kind of thinking ahead which pays concrete and timely dividends. By planning ahead, in an orderly and incremental fashion, you will have the money in your savings account to pay those infrequent, but large, bills

*Financial goals:*

| Goal description | Special action plans needed to achieve this goal | Cost | $ Per pay period needed to reach goal | Target date for achievement |
|---|---|---|---|---|
| *Current or near-future goals:* | | | | |
| pay car insurance | cut down dating budget | $64.50 | $8.07 | January 14, 197_ . |
| | | | | |
| | | | | |
| *Future goals:* | | | | |
| next year's college tuition | get an extra job for Sat's. | $720 | $60 | Sept. 10, 197_ . |
| | | | | |
| | | | | |

**Fig. 2–3** Planning chart for financial goals. Many of your goals, current as well as long-term, need to have action plans effected systematically if they are to be achieved. Whether you are planning for next year's tuition or for a new set of water skis, you need to know what the money requirements are, how you are going to get the money, and when you need to have it available.

like semi-annual insurance premiums. By approaching the large purchase with "prior installments," you will be able, within your schedule, to write a check for the item you want—and neatly sidestep the budget-busting time payment that you would otherwise have to consider.

## YOUR BUDGET TIME PERIOD

Most beginners at budgeting use a payday period. If they get paid weekly, they budget for a week's time; similarly, those who get paid twice monthly or every two weeks (24 and 26 times yearly), use those time periods for their budgeting period. When you become skilled at budgeting, you will probably dislike all that paperwork because a budget is a guide for action and not a report on each and every petty transaction. Veteran budgeters usually use calendar months and calendar years for their budget periods. Two very good reasons for this are (1) the billing cycles of business, landlords, and utilities, and (2) the yearly cycle of tax reporting and payment. A more subtle, but very important reason, is that long-term goals become obscured with 24 to 52 budgets per year. ($3 left over from a week's budget might look like mad money, but it is also $156 in savings, drawing interest, if less cumbersome budgeting shows it to be a more impressive $13 a month.)

As you begin to organize your finances, it might be rewarding to have immediate success with the smaller time periods. Initially, you will enjoy the feeling of being in charge (at last) of your money. With the shorter periods, your feedback will be quicker. When you are proficient and sophisticated at budgeting, you will probably evolve your own version of a monthly/yearly spending plan. So, after early success and experiments, you are encouraged to set up your budgets through the balance of this year and then on a January through December basis for the years to come. You should also keep in mind that a budget is reflection of you and not the opposite, and that you should review and revise your budget monthly so that it accurately does the kind of job you expect from it.

Whatever period best suits you today, today is the best time to begin. Start now to enjoy the benefits of control over your money.

## SETTING UP THE BUDGET

The mechanics of setting up your budget are not difficult; they merely require an orderly look at your finances. No great skill in mathematics is required, just routine arithmetic and good sense.

Specially printed household expense record books are available at most variety or stationery stores, or through a U.S. Department of Agriculture Extension Service Office. These printed budget guides are not critical. What *is* critical is the spending plan itself, and you can use an ordinary notebook, ruling columns to suit your particular needs. Use a budget worksheet for each budgeting period. Here, we'll use the calendar month and the calendar year for sample budget periods.  Use the forms like those in this chapter for analyzing specific parts of your budget.

### ITEMIZE ALL INCOME SOURCES

You must now determine the total amount of money you will have to work with. List all your anticipated income for the budgeting period as a guide, and list wages, salaries, dividends, net profits from businesses, farm or profession, rents, royalties, interest—in short, any income from any source.  Do not include raises you *might* get, or any other sort of windfall; if you don't get the raise, you might

find yourself committed to an expense you won't be able to afford.  If such items have not been deducted for you, subtract all fixed expenses such as income tax, Social Security contributions and union dues.  The amount remaining—Net income—is the total money available for you to budget.  (See Fig. 2–4.)

**Itemize your expenses.**  Use the form in Fig. 2–5 as a guide, and list the actual amount for any fixed, recurring expenses other than the taxes and deductions from gross income in your income itemizing above.  These should include such non-variables as rent or house payments, installment payments, and savings payments to yourself.  Perhaps you've never thought of savings as a fixed expense; if you had, you would now be in better financial shape, as you'll learn in Chapter 3.  Some payments, like insurance premiums, for example, are due semi-annually.  The monthly increment is one-sixth of the semi-annual amount. For obvious reasons, your expense and income period should be the same.

Estimated Money Income _____
(period)

| Item | Amount |
|---|---|
| Wage or salary of— | |
|   Husband........................... | $_____ |
|   Wife............................... | _____ |
| Net profit from business, farm, | |
|   or profession...................... | _____ |
| Interest, dividends................. | _____ |
| Other............................... | _____ |
|       Total money income...... | $_____ |

**Fig. 2–4** More than one source of income. Keeping a detailed estimate of all sources of income is an important part of budgeting. A form such as this might help.

Estimate and record the costs of household operations and maintenance expenses such as electricity, heating, and water. Receipts and cancelled checks for the corresponding period of last year are useful approximations of what those bills will be this year. You should allow for some increase in these expenses to accommodate possible higher costs. A record cold spell, for instance, could drive heating and lighting costs upward, because more people would spend more time at home.

Estimate and record amounts for other flexible expenses, including food, clothing, transportation, medical care, education, recreation, gifts and contributions, and personal allowances. You will probably have an additional expense item or two which doesn't fit neatly in the categories above. If so, be sure your expense itemizing reflects this.

When you have estimated the amounts of your expense items, compute the percentage of your income that you are allotting to each. This step may prove surprising to you, and it may cause you to think again about the *value* of (say) an automobile which *costs* you one-third of your total new income.

**MATCH UP ESTIMATED EXPENSES AND EXPECTED INCOME**

This is the first objective comparison of what you can spend with what you want to spend. Add up all the expense amounts you have listed and compare this total with your Total New Income. If the income exceeds the expenses total, you are lucky, or perhaps you have left something out. Go back over your outgoing figures; have you under-estimated some of the expense items? Were you realistic about what you will spend this month on entertainment? Did you include (one-twelfth) of such yearly expenses as automobile tax and license, property taxes, club and union dues? If there is still a surplus on the income side,

| Date | INCOME Salary | Other | Total Income | Taxes & Social Security | Savings | Insurance | Mortgage or Rent | Food | Light Telephone Fuel | Automobile | Home Furnishings and Supplies | Home maintenance | Education and Reading | Medical- Dental Supplies | Recreation Vacation | Clothing Purchases and Upkeep | Church, Charity, Gifts | Toiletries Beauty Aids | Misc. | Total Expenses |
|---|---|---|---|---|---|---|---|---|---|---|---|---|---|---|---|---|---|---|---|---|
| 1 | | | | | | | | | | | | | | | | | | | | |
| 2 | | | | | | | | | | | | | | | | | | | | |
| 3 | | | | | | | | | | | | | | | | | | | | |
| 4 | | | | | | | | | | | | | | | | | | | | |
| 5 | | | | | | | | | | | | | | | | | | | | |
| 6 | | | | | | | | | | | | | | | | | | | | |
| 7 | | | | | | | | | | | | | | | | | | | | |
| 8 | | | | | | | | | | | | | | | | | | | | |
| 9 | | | | | | | | | | | | | | | | | | | | |
| 10 | | | | | | | | | | | | | | | | | | | | |
| 11 | | | | | | | | | | | | | | | | | | | | |
| 12 | | | | | | | | | | | | | | | | | | | | |
| 26 | | | | | | | | | | | | | | | | | | | | |
| 27 | | | | | | | | | | | | | | | | | | | | |
| 28 | | | | | | | | | | | | | | | | | | | | |
| 29 | | | | | | | | | | | | | | | | | | | | |
| 30 | | | | | | | | | | | | | | | | | | | | |
| 31 | | | | | | | | | | | | | | | | | | | | |
| TOTALS | | | | | | | | | | | | | | | | | | | | |

**Fig. 2-5** Personal household income and expense record. A record of personal income and expenses is a helpful aid in planning and adjusting your budget.

after you have thoroughly accounted for your estimated outlays, you can begin to realize some of the current and near future financial goals you have set for yourself. Better yet, you can increase payments to yourself—your savings. That would be an excellent use for it, would be a step toward satisfying longer-range goals and a method of building a fund for emergencies.

If your total expenses outweigh your expected income—very often the case with many people—you will have to do some trimming and adjusting. Before you yield to the impulse to cut down on savings, you should read and under-stand Chapter 3; further, you should reconsider the earlier definition of savings as a regular and important *fixed* expense. Do not reduce the amounts allocated for medical care and recreation without carefully thinking through what these items mean to you in terms of health and general well-being. Initially, set these three categories aside for possible further consideration, and focus your attention on cutting down elsewhere. The problem then becomes one of impproving your spending habits, getting better value, and saving money on food, clothing, other household purchases, and the automobile. (Part III of your text has money saving ideas about these items.)

**Check and recheck all your budget items.** Make whatever adjustments are possible. If you still have not achieved a workable balance, you may *have* to reduce the amount allocated to savings. Do so with reluctance. In extreme cases, you may find that you are simply not able to save at all for a while. You should regard this as a strictly temporary situation, and *plan* (not hope) to remedy it at the earliest opportunity. Similarly, you may have to trim the recreation portion on a short-term basis. If your car payments are high in terms of your present budget, analyze the benefits of car ownership on a continuum with transportation at one end and ego satisfaction at the other. Perhaps you could get along with a less expensive car while you are getting your finances in better shape. Are you renting? Maybe a less luxurious apartment would better serve your current requirements.   Can you save on transportation costs by renting an apartment closer to school or work?  Is credit purchasing *too* convenient?  Do you use a credit card to purchase gasoline and automotive items? Do you have charge accounts at clothing or department stores which make it easy for you to buy more than you should in terms of your present finances? Try getting along without any credit buying for a time; pay cash for all purchases, and see if you are not more careful about the quality and quantity of your buying. This action will help you hold the line on your credit obligations while you are planning a way to meet them.  Clear up any old debts and installment payments as quickly as possible; the money formerly set aside for these items will be freed for other expenditures or for savings.  Perhaps you can pay one account off and use that "freed" money to hasten the repayment of a loan, reducing interest charged and adding a few more dollars to the amount you can allocate.  Find out how much interest you pay on your credit account purchases.  Can you really afford interest payments of 10 to 20 percent or more?  If you must borrow money during this adjustment period, be sure you know how much it costs you to "rent" the money.  Shop for credit as carefully as you do for other goods and services.  (Chapters 4 and 5 discuss consumer credit in detail.)

## MAKING A BUDGET WORK FOR YOU

No budget will work for you unless it is specifically tailored to your particular needs and desires.  Sample budgets are only guides to aid you in designing your own spending plan.  A budget which works for one individual or family will never be completely applicable to another individual or family.  Essentially, you must work and rework your spending plan until it does for you what you want it to do.  If you find that your budget is not completely effective after a month or two, do not abandon it as hopeless.  Remember you are finding your way toward effective money management and that the third edition will benefit from lessons learned in the first two.  If you need further encouragement, recall for a moment the confused state of your finances before you had a plan of any sort. Go over the plan again, making the adjustments which are necessary and desirable, and give budgeting another trial.

Your budget is not chiseled in stone; it is a reflection of your tastes, preferences, and attitudes as well as your income and outgo.  Through time, these will change and your budget should reflect the changes.  As your goals change or assume new emphasis for you, your budget must be shifted in the new directions. When you have made a spending plan which is realistic for your current situation, stick to it.  Make it serve you.  Keep records of your spending.

Use a notebook or a form like that shown in Fig. 2–5 to keep track of all your expenses and purchases for the first few budget periods.  When you compare estimates and the actual outflow of cash, you will be able to accurately adjust your estimates and your spending.  Revise estimates which are plainly unrealistic in terms of the real needs and wants they represent.  Revise spending

"It says here that women spend three fourths of the average income -- what did you do with my fourth?"

Reprinted with permission of *The Wall Street Journal* (Cartoon Features Syndicate).

if your comparison indicates you are spending too much on particular goods or services. As soon as estimate and actuality are coordinated, begin saving regularly.

Now that you have successfully adjusted what you *want* to spend with what you really *do* spend, you are ready for management—money management, that is. You can forecast your spending. Sure in the knowledge that your outgo is finally under your control, you can begin your campaign toward realizing more distant and more expensive financial goals. Going a step further, you can begin, through the overall process, to realize your personal lifetime goals.

It is unlikely that you will ever again be satisfied with spending by accident or impulse, once you have mastered the techniques and overcome the early difficulties of budgeting. The sure sense of control will be hard to give up, too. Presuming that you have experienced some of these rewards of budgeting by now, you are urged to go on to formulate your own spending plan for the balance of the year. What do you want from the remainder of this year? How can you achieve what you want in that time?

Use a detailed monthly form such as illustrated in Fig. 2–5. This form provides two columns under each budget item—one for your budget planning estimate; the other for your actual expenditures.

The summary form in Fig. 2–6 will be worthwhile in the first week of next January. With it, you can prepare the aggregate amounts of income compared with outgo. You might compute the percentage of net income that you spend on each type of expense. With the summary comparison, you can decide on policy matters about the make-up of next year's budget. You, or you and your

| INCOME | |
|---|---|
| Received From | Amount |
| Wages-Salary | |
| Gifts | |
| Rents or Royalties | |
| Interest | |
| Dividends | |
| Annuities | |
| Other (List) | |
| | |
| | |
| | |
| | |
| | |
| | |
| Total Annual Income | |

| EXPENSES | |
|---|---|
| Description | Amount |
| Social Security & Taxes | |
| Savings | |
| Insurance | |
| Mortgage or Rent | |
| Food | |
| Lights, Telephone, Fuel | |
| Automobile | |
| Home Furn. and Supplies | |
| Church, Charity, Gifts | |
| Education & Reading | |
| Medical & Dental Expense | |
| Recreation & Vacation | |
| Clothing | |
| Toiletries-Beauty Aids | |
| Miscellaneous | |
| Total Expenses | |

**Fig. 2–6** The over-all picture. A summary of income and expenses for the entire year serves as an excellent basis for a yearly budget.

family, might decide that too much is being spent on vacations, and that a portion of that money would be better used to furnish the rumpus room.

With the long-term budget and the summary comparison—to plan your spending and then see how well your plan works—you should have a clear idea of overall planning and results. As with most plans and systems, there are still some day-to-day routine matters that deserve your attention. Even the finest plans, with the best intentions, may fail if some small but important detail is not done correctly.

**HANDLING THE DETAILS**

The budgeter(s) should devise accurate and efficient methods of record-keeping and bill paying. How are these jobs going to be done, and who is going to do them? These are responsibilities which must be established early, so that the entire operation of working toward your financial objectives can proceed smoothly. If the areas are not clear, or if a poor job is being done of checkbook balancing, for example, the plan may falter or seem to be more onerous than it really is. In the balance of this chapter you will learn some of the techniques that have worked for others. Again, you should remember that your routines may vary considerably so that the final criteria must be your own.

**Cash or checks?** For visibly demonstrating to yourself how much of your money goes to which expense item, the cash system is an excellent teaching device. You are strongly urged to use checks, however, because keeping sums of money is dangerous in practice. The reasons will become clearer as we proceed.

The cash system, especially in the learning stages of money management, goes like this: You cash your paycheck. That money is the income pile. From it, you allocate expense sums to appropriate expense items. Use envelopes marked "rent," "food," "insurance," and so on. If the specific item is not payable that particular payday, you make the fractional or incremental "prior payment" to that envelope. As bills are paid, receipts or other records of a transaction should be filed.

Certainly, by this method, you *see* where the money is going; but there are serious drawbacks to the cash system, and because of these drawbacks, we discourage it. For one thing, paying bills in person takes time and travel. Utility and some other bills can be paid in this way, but seldom can *all* your bills be paid at one location. If you must send an insurance premium, for example, to another city, you may have to make two trips—one to purchase a money order or similar instrument, and another to the mailbox or post office. The cost of carfare or driving your auto to the various places to pay bills or installment accounts is another drawback. Additionally, in dealing with large sums of cash, there is the high risk of loss due to carelessness or theft. Finally, there is the temptation to borrow just a little from an "installment container" because that particular bill is not due until later on. Here is the perfect example of "robbing Peter to pay Paul," which has become a subject for humor precisely because it is so ineffective.

As you begin to think of money as a tool for goal satisfaction, rather than as a treasure to be possessed, you will probably want to keep that money in a checking account. The amount you have in the account should be sufficient for current expenses plus a small "emergency balance." Any money in excess of this total should be making more money for you—that is, drawing interest in a savings account. Most banks require their checking account depositors to maintain a minimum balance *or* to pay a small service charge. Consider the amount of money tied up, the number of checks written per month, and weigh the potential interest earnings against service charges. Determine which option is more realistic and beneficial to you, then choose the type of account best suited to your situation.

**Separate or joint accounts?** Married couples and families must choose between joint or separate bank accounts. In dividing areas of responsibility in the budget, many people decide that separate bank accounts best serve their needs. Typical is the case where husband and wife have jobs—she pays "her" bills and he pays "his." (Typically, hers are the bills for food and household operation; his include house payment or rent, car payment and/or upkeep, and expenses for the yard and house upkeep.) Other families find that a joint account works best for them, even though each member has specific responsibilities and two or more have income. There just isn't any hard-and-fast rule. Everyone in the family who helps plan the budget should do some of the spending, following through in his area of responsibility from goal conception to goal realization. The important thing is that once the family members have agreed on a plan, they should respect it and live up to their roles in it.

In most families, the husband is considered the breadwinner. Wives in these families ordinarily take care of routine household and maintenance expenses. Major purchases reflect the mutual judgment of both husband and wife (and children when they are old enough). These families generally prefer a joint checking account, but complain that balance keeping is a problem. If both have checkbooks, they find that two sets of records must each be accurate, and then accurate in sum together. If there is only one checkbook, someone is invariably tearing out a check for later use and forgetting to record the amount. (The lucky partner who finds this "extra" money in the account might then write a check which makes the account overdrawn.)

| CHECK NO. | DATE | CHECKS ISSUED TO OR DESCRIPTION OF DEPOSIT | | AMOUNT OF CHECK | √ | AMOUNT OF DEPOSIT | BALANCE FORWARD | |
|---|---|---|---|---|---|---|---|---|
| 204 | 9-4 | To | Bonus Market | 14 82 | | | Check or Dep. | |
| | | For | Food | | | | Bal. | 304 20 |
| — | 9-4 | To | Wife's Check- | 70 00 | | | Check or Dep. | 70 00 |
| | | For | book | | | | Bal. | 234 20 |
| | | To | | | | | Check or Dep. | |
| | | For | | | | | Bal. | |
| | | To | | | | | Check or Dep. | |
| | | For | | | | | Bal. | |
| | | To | | | | | Check or Dep. | |
| | | For | | | | | Bal. | |
| | | To | | | | | Check or Dep. | |
| | | For | | | | | Bal. | |

Fig. 2–7 Husband's personal check register. The figure shows a transfer of funds to the wife's checkbook. Husband and wife have a joint checking account, but budgeting is facilitated by deducting amount in the husband's register and adding the sum as a deposit to the wife's register.

One practical solution for this problem is for the husband to keep a "master record" in his checkbook. He periodically indicates disbursement of a certain amount ($70 in the example in Fig. 2–7), which would be entered in the wife's checkbook as a credit to her household operations account. Sons or daughters with checkbooks could receive such allocations for allowances and school expenses. Family members who receive allocations from the master balance would be responsible only for the amount allocated, with the restriction that they not overdraw their individual account. The wife would, for example, keep her checkbook balanced from day to day and report its balance to her husband at the end of the month. This one figure, rather than the amount of each individual check in her book, would be all the husband would need to balance his master checkbook.

## SIDE BENEFITS OF BUDGETING

Most confirmed budgeters report that the sense of accomplishment and the peace of mind resulting from successfully coordinating their income and expenses are reward enough for their efforts. What had seemed to be major sacrifices at the outset have become important contributions to improved financial position. One relevant case would be passing up the purchase of a new car (see Chapter 3) for a few years. With the car payments you don't make, you can secure other goals and save, too. After a few years you can better afford a new car, and will have achieved other goals and have savings in the bank as well. A purchase on credit will provide use, but not ownership, of a consumption good—it will result in little more than high payments that are difficult to make under your current budget.

With a workable budget, you are the boss of your own financial affairs. You are able to select and work toward your goals. Behind you is the haphazard management by accident or impulse in which your money managed you and constrained you in your choice of goals and in your ability to pay for them. You can control your spending, minimize your impulse buying, and assure yourself of getting the most value for your money when you do spend it.

Most people work hard for their money. After they earn it, their money ought to work hard for them. To be sure your money does what you want it to, use Action Plan 2:

**Action Plan 2:**  **A. Budget**
**B. Spend carefully**

## FEEDBACK 2

Here it is assumed that you have already:

● Determined your net worth.

● Made one or several budgets, and have made a workable budget.

If not, do so now. These were placed within the textual materials to provide data-at-hand for your budget program.

**A.** List your credit and loan obligation like this:

1. Account which will be paid in full in fewest months, at my present rate of payment.

2. Account which will be paid in full next, at my present rate of payment.

3. And so on.

● When account 1 is paid in full, how much faster can you pay off account

2 by applying the payment which you will not then be making on 1?

- When account 2 is paid, what will be the effect of adding payment 1 and 2 to payment 3?
- What about $1 + 2 + 3 = 4$? How fast will this repayment schedule straighten out your budget?
- What true interest rate are you paying on each of your accounts? Does paying one account more rapidly than required save you money in interest charged? What would interest paid to you mean, in dollars, if you were making one of the above payments into a savings account for a year? For two years?

**B.** If there is a New York Life Insurance Company office in your community, visit it and obtain a copy of the "New York Life Budget Book" or, write to:

New York Life Insurance Company
51 Madison Avenue
New York, New York 10010

and request a copy of this booklet. It is filled with helpful budget suggestions.

**C.** Conduct a two-part survey among (1) at least five of your single friends; and (2) at least five of your married friends.

- Do they budget? If not, do they feel that a personal spending plan would be helpful to them?
- Among the budgeters, which are most successful in reaching their objectives? Why? Least successful? Why?
- Write a report on your survey, with your conclusions, and the comments of those interviewed, if useful.

**D.** Write a brief (300–500 word) report on "How Budgeting Has Affected my Money Management." In your report, compare prior and present spending habits.

- Do you know where your money is going now?
- Do you know what your money is accomplishing now?
- Are you broke less frequently?
- Do you compare the satisfaction available from different purchases now?

**E.** If you borrowed from one of the student loan programs outlined in Chapter 1, and paid off all your current debts, how much interest—in dollars—could you save?

- With a 7% Federally Insured Loan?
- With a 3% National Defense Loan?

**F.** Although it properly belongs in Chapter 3, what would savings mean to your financial worth:

- If you had deposited just the interest you are now paying out?
- If you had saved just the depreciation, for one year on your present automobile (market worth now against one year ago)? Would you now pay cash for them, and save on credit charges?

## DISCUSSION QUESTIONS

1. How is it possible that a doctor who earns $50,000 annually can still have money problems?

2. Why is it that most people find that "there's too much month left over at the end of the money" if they don't establish a budget?

3. What is the difference between a "Goal Approach" and a "Current Situation—Desired Situation Approach?"

4. If one has set up a budget that is working for him, why might the same budget *not* work for someone else?

5. Why would it be wise for beginners at budgeting to use a payday period in their budget? Do you believe it should be for longer periods of time? Explain.

6. How can one determine what the total amount of money will be that he has to work with?

7. Why is it good to think of saving as a fixed expense?

8. Is credit purchasing too convenient? Should all purchases be made by cash to avoid overspending? Explain.

9. Should a budget determine one's tastes and preferences? Explain.

10. What is the best to use—checks or cash? Why?

11. What should a young married couple use—separate or joint checking accounts? If joint, should there be only one checkbook between them? Explain.

## CASE PROBLEMS

**1.** Charles and Ruth Carson were married last year following Ruth's graduation from State Teachers' College. They have been living on her $5,075 salary while Charles has been finishing the work for his master's degree, which he will receive in about six weeks. He has a $8,900 a year job waiting for him with a large industrial firm as soon as school is out. The work Charles will be doing is related to his college training, and although the prospects for advancement with the firm are good, he plans to work only two years and then return to college and obtain his doctorate before accepting permanent employment.

The Carsons have been renting a small furnished apartment for $110 a month. They own a six-year-old car, and have acquired a stereo and a small record collection. With Charles' job, their combined income after taxes will be $13,975, and they feel that after the scrimping and saving they have done during the past year, they are entitled to a little more freedom in spending. They would like to do more entertaining and be able to eat out more frequently than has been possible in the past; also, they would like to splurge a little more on clothing purchases.

While their one-bedroom apartment is comfortable and adequate for their present needs, they would like to have more space so that they could entertain members of their families or other out-of-town guests occasionally. Right now they are seriously considering moving into a larger furnished apartment or to a two-bedroom unfurnished unit and starting to buy furniture of their own.

The Carsons realize, however, that they must look ahead to the time when Charles will go back to school and their income will again be just about what it is now. (Ruth figures she should get annual salary increases of $125 to $170.) They feel that although their car may last another year or two, it probably will require major overhaul or replacement before Charles finishes his doctorate, and that they must keep this possibility in mind.

a) What would your advice to this young couple be?

b) Do you think they are being realistic in their thinking?

c) Do you believe it would be wise for them to buy furniture for an apartment, or should they wait until they buy their own home?

d) How much more should they budget for food, clothing, etc., than they have been doing?

e) How much should they be saving? Discuss.

2.    After almost three years of working her way through college, Janet decided to quit school and go to work full time for a year. She was tired of scrimping, especially when she saw what her working friends were able to do with the money they earned. She figured that by working full time she could have some new clothes and a few of the other things she had been doing without for so long, and that she could still save $1,000, which she felt would be enough to get her through her senior year of school.

Janet had been taking business courses and was sure that she could find a well-paying office job that would utilize her business skills. Besides, she reasoned, the experience she would gain would be invaluable later on in her teaching career.

Janet lived at home with no expenses except providing part of her own clothing and personal needs. Her parents were upset when she announced her decision to quit school, and in their effort to dissuade her, told her that if she was going to work she should pay for her own keep at home. They figured $65 a month fair payment for board and room. The best-paying job Janet has been able to find will net her $290 a month after taxes.

a) How should Janet budget her money to accomplish her goals?

## SUGGESTED READINGS

*A Discussion of Family Money: How Budgets Work and What They Do.* New York: Institute of Life Insurance, 1966.

*A Guide to Budgeting for the Family.* U.S. Department of Agriculture, Bulletin No. G-108. Washington, D.C.: Superintendent of Documents.

*A Guide to Budgeting for the Young Couple.* Washington, D.C., 1967. 16 pp.

Barlow, Robin, and James N. Morgan. *Economic Behavior of the Affluent.* Washington, D.C.: Brookings Institution, 1966. 285 pp.

Bradley, Joseph F., and Ralph H. Wherry. *Personal and Family Finance.* New York: Holt, Rinehart & Winston, 1961. 565 pp.

Burkhart, Roy A. *Money and Your Marriage.* Washington, D.C.: National Consumer Finance Association, 1963. 32 pp.

Cohen, Jerome B., and Arthur W. Hanson. *Personal Finance: Principles and Case Problems.* Homewood, Ill.: R. D. Irwin, 1964. 865 pp.

*City Worker's Family Budget for a Moderate Living Standard: Autumn 1966.* Washington, D.C.: Bureau of Labor Statistics, 1967. 40 pp.

*Consumers Expenditures and Income.* BLS Report No. 237-38. Bureau of Labor Statistics, U.S. Department of Labor. Washington, D.C.: Government Printing Office.

Coplovitz, David. *The Poor Pay More.* New York: The Free Press of Glencoe, Division of the Macmillan Company, 1963. 220 pp.

Culp, Delma K. *A System of Budget Planning and Record Keeping for Personal Finance.* Unpublished Master's Thesis, Department of Accounting, University of Utah, 1965, Salt Lake City, Utah.

*Family Budget Service.* Madison, Wis.: CUNA International, Inc.

*The Family Financial Planner.* Newark: Prudential Insurance Company of America.

*The Family Money Manager.* New York: Institute of Life Insurance.

Feldman, Frances L. *The Family in a Money World.* New York: Family Service Association of America, 1957. 188 pp.

Foote, Nelson N. *Household Decision Making.* New York: NYU Press, 1969. 349 pp.

Grass, Irma H., and Elizabeth W. Crandall. *Management for Modern Families.* New York: Appleton-Century-Crofts, 1954. 579 pp.

*Helping Families Manage Their Finances.* U.S. Department of Agriculture Bulletin No. HERR-21. Washington, D.C.: Superintendent of Documents.

*How to Plan your Spending.* Hartford, Conn.: Connecticut Mutual Life Insurance Company.

Jordan, David F., and Edward F. Willett. *Managing Personal Finances.* New York: Prentice-Hall, 1951. 381 pp.

Lasser, Jacob K., and Sylvia Porter. *Managing Your Money.* New York: Doubleday, 1963. 207 pp.

Money Management Institute, Household Finance Corp., *Money Management—Your Budget.* Chicago: Household Finance Corp., 1965. 36 pp.

National Industrial Conference Board.  *Expenditure Patterns of the American Family*. New York: 1965.  175 pp.

*New Spending Guide for Budget-Minded Families*.  New York: First National City Bank of New York.

*New York Life Budget Book*.  New York: New York Life Insurance Company, 1966.  40 pp.

Shohan, Leo B.  *Comparative Living Costs in 20 Cities*.  New York: National Industrial Conference Board, 1964.  28 pp.

"So You Think You Don't Need a Budget."  *Changing Times*.  Washington, D.C.: Vol. 19, pp 33–35.

*Where Does the Money Go?—Budget and Expense Record*.  New York: Union Dime Savings Bank.

# PART II
# SAVING AND BORROWING MONEY

CHAPTER 3

# SAVINGS: WHY? HOW?

Much emphasis was accorded savings in the previous chapter. Here, you will learn why it is considered so important. Primarily, the things people save for are: (1) retirement; (2) emergencies; (3) large purchases; (4) investment opportunities; and knowingly or unknowingly, (5) as a hedge against inflation. You may have special versions of these goals, or even additional goals. The point is that for most people, in most situations and most of the time, savings is the exit route from the difficulties and frustrations of the earn-spend-borrow-spend cycle. That cycle is not especially rewarding; and as you will learn, it is not necessary.

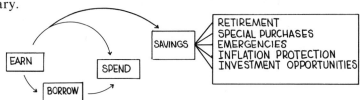

This chapter is dedicated to the promise made in Chapter 1, to show you how to make more money. You will learn about the goals of savings, the mechanics of savings, and step-by-step procedures to get your savings program off the ground. Savings, as used here, is a positive first step toward realizing your financial goals.

Let's discuss the attractions or goals of savings first, so that you understand clearly why it is necessary to have a personal savings program.

**Retirement.** If you work, even part-time, you probably have one or two savings accounts right now. Social Security contributions are deducted from your paycheck, and your account is credited with these amounts. Additionally, most unions and many companies have employee retirement plans which require employee contributions. Either program reflects legitimate and praiseworthy concern for employees. There are two drawbacks to such plans, though. The first is that the benefits are usually obtainable only at retirement. The second objection is that such plans cannot be managed by the employees to accumulate more retirement wealth through profitable investments. These types of forced, or unplanned, savings programs will not do the complete kind of job for you that your financial goals require. Something more is needed, and that something is planned savings.

**Emergencies.** Here is one of the most obvious needs met through planned savings. It is naïve to assume that no serious emergency will occur in your forseeable future. It is much more realistic to anticipate possible emergencies, and to prepare for them. What kind of emergencies? How much will they affect your financial plans? You will have to devise the answers to suit your particular life style, but you can make useful approximations by answering other questions such as these:

1. How long would you get a paycheck if an accident temporarily disabled you?
2. If you continued to get a check, would it be full or partial compensation?
3. Do you have good health and accident insurance?
4. How much do you now depend on overtime earnings?
5. How secure is your job?
6. Assuming it is stable, how steady are the hours and earnings from that job?
7. Should (do) you make special provisions for dependent relatives?

Your answers to these and similar questions will determine the amount you should earmark for emergencies. Of course, you cannot anticipate every possible emergency, but based on your knowledge and experience in living your life, you can make informed estimates. For the average person with Social Security coverage and realistic health and accident insurance, savings equivalent to one month's wages is probably adequate.

Two cautions about your emergency savings:

1. The money should be kept where it is readily available.
2. Don't succumb to the temptation of using these savings for things other than that for which they are intended. If you use your account for other purposes, or for lesser emergencies, you may find yourself short of funds to meet more serious problems.

**Special purchases.** Basically, this is *paying* by *prior installments*. If a large bill must be paid, or a large purchase is desired at a future time, you simply apportion a fractional amount (one-sixth, if six paydays fall between now and the due date) for that purchase or payment. One particular advantage of saving for special purchases is that you save the interest charged for loans or credit accounts. With savings, you should earn some interest in the interval—and have a net gain (money) plus the item purchased, or the bill paid. This systematic approach is less painful. Most of us already know it is much easier to allocate $8.34 per month than $100 out of one paycheck—but these are two ways to pay the same annual bill. If you save the smaller amount for 12 months, you accumulate the same total, with less violence to any one month's budget, as you do if you try to wrench $100 from a single month's income.

Special or seasonal sales, large appliance purchases, automobile buying, tuition, and insurance premiums are some other things which can be approached by *prior* installment through your savings program.

Christmas gift buying and after-Christmas sales are two very good uses for your savings. On any calendar, Christmas falls on December 25; that's no surprise. But how many times have you gone overboard buying presents, and wound up short of money in January? Or worse, borrowed money to tide you over? Why not take a realistic approach? Anticipate the season and save in advance for it. Besides not being in debt for Christmas purchases, you might have some money left over with which to take advantage of January sales, saving money on purchases as well. Whatever plans you make for Christmas or post-Christmas buying, *do not* put your money in a non-interest-paying Christmas Club Savings Account. We'll return to that subject later in the chapter; for now remember that savings accounts should pay interest for the use of your money. Christmas Clubs pay no interest.

**Investment opportunities.** It does take money to make money. That, to generalize, is what investment is all about. There are millions of details, but at this point we are primarily concerned with accumulating the money it takes to make profitable investments. Savings is the foundation for most people's

investment plans. Savings earn you money (interest) while amounts necessary for particular investments are being accumulated. Additionally, the interest on savings is earning you more money through compounding. Combined, these benefits make savings the logical approach to furthering your investment goals. Don't think of savings only as a deterrent to current spending, think ahead to some of your investment goals. For example:

1. Adequate savings will eventually enable you to invest in money-making opportunities which will be a welcome addition to your regular salary.

2. You might invest in real estate—land, apartment houses, commercial properties, for example.

3. You might invest in stocks and bonds.

4. You might pioneer your own business.

5. Make sure that you understand the applicable chapters of this book before you make any of those investments, to save money and make more money in each case.

6. Another reasonable investment for most people is buying a home. A large down payment (through savings) will enable you to buy a better home and have a greater choice of neighborhoods. Here, savings can be of great benefit—enlarging your potential choice range; reducing not only the total amount remaining to be paid, but also reducing the amount of your monthly payments.

Investments of whatever kind require investment funds. Accumulating those funds is perhaps the most important purpose of your savings account.

**Inflation.** Savings may help you to hold the line against the inroad made on purchasing power by inflation. Simply defined, inflation means rising prices. Simply defined, savings means increase in assets. For example:

> Over the period of a year inflation causes the price of a radio that you want to go up by five percent, from $100 to $105 in the next year. If you deposit $100 in a savings account which pays 5 percent interest compounded annually, your savings account will be worth $105 in one year. The interest credited to your account offsets the price rise. If you had no savings, you would have to make up the $5 difference from your own pocket. There are higher interest rates, and more frequent compounding schemes, but this is a simple example to make the point.

While savings is an excellent first step in diminishing the effect of inflation on the achievement of your financial goals, comparison with investment returns offered through other means will convince you that savings itself is not the most profitable use of money. In fact, in recent years the rate of inflation has actually exceeded the interest rates paid on many savings accounts. Savings is the fuel for further investment, and the main objective of this chapter is to encourage you to accumulate sufficient savings so that you can take advantage of more rewarding investment opportunities. In this respect, savings is the beginning of your investment program and investments are the way to *out-distance* inflation, not merely to keep pace with it.

One minor point remains to be cleared up here. There is some logic and some persuasion to the argument that "if inflation will eat up the purchasing power of your dollars in the future, you should buy now at today's lower prices—in effect, save in advance." Before you yield to this rationale, objectively weigh your prospects for achieving your long-range goals if you do not begin a step-by-step attack on those goals now. Put another way—if you decide to spend all your income on current consumption, what is left for next year's goals? You have to start somewhere to achieve a goal; putting off the beginning puts off the realization of goals.

## FINDING MONEY TO SAVE

If you have not already considered savings in any of the above contexts, it is strongly recommended that you do so now. They represent broad categories of intermediate and long-term goals for most people; and most people who realize these kinds of goals use a savings program. Like many of these people, you may be marking time until you have "enough" money to save. "Enough" money is a portion of your current income, whatever that income may be. Today is the time to begin to take advantage of the interaction of time, interest, and compounding. These are the main arguments in support of beginning a savings program now, if you do not already have one. But, there are "conditions" in support of procrastination, too.

Current wants and current expenses usually outrun incomes. If this is not your situation, fine. Unfortunately, it is the case for most people of all ages. Objectively, the key to starting a savings program lies in distinguishing between "gonna" and "doin'." We'll discuss the two in that order.

"When I finish college, I'm *gonna* start a savings account." The end of college expenses like tuition, books, commuting and so on will be a welcome situation. With a higher net income, and no more college expenses, there is more money to spend—and that is usually what happens to earnings in the post-college period. Former students, now in the working community, find that they can suddenly "afford" large car payments, higher rents, and other consumer luxuries they denied themselves while in school. They do remember that savings is worthwhile, but current expenses preclude opening an account, so . . .

"When I get married, I'm *gonna* start a savings plan." Good idea, but most couples combine their individual budget problems from before marriage, then add other payments to their joint budget. Furniture, drapes, perhaps a second car, a larger apartment—all seem more important than a growing balance in a savings passbook, so . . .

"When we get the down payment saved for the house we want to buy, we're *gonna* start saving for other long-range goals." Perhaps, but what about obstetrician fees, pediatrician fees, clothes, and play equipment for the children? These expenses can't be ignored. Again, the resolution might be heard, a little less convincing by now, "As soon as we get ahead of some of these bills, we're *gonna* start a vigorous savings campaign." And so goes the "gonna" approach to savings.

*Doin'* people are more direct, more realistic. They don't rely on some future change of their own attitudes or financial condition. They say instead, "We don't have a lot of money to put into a savings account, but we're *doin'* some saving." And that is precisely the key—*doin'* it. Unless and until you actually begin to save, or when you neglect your current savings program—you do injury to your whole financial future. Conversely, when you begin to save, you enhance that future and bring long-range goals closer with each deposit. As in any worthwhile endeavor, there are commitments involved; to ensure the success of your savings plan, you must make three.

### Commitment 1:  I will allocate a fixed percentage of my income to savings—now.

As a student, you may decide that five to ten percent is a good rate to begin with.  In actual dollars, that may mean only $2 or $5 or $15 is going into savings each month.  The balance in your account will grow slowly, of course, but it will grow.  More importantly, you will be developing the habit of saving regularly.  Then, when you graduate, you can shift your savings program into high gear.  With a full-time job, and the good habits you will have developed, you can direct more money and a greater percentage of income into savings.

### Commitment 2:  I will postpone buying a new car for three years after I start a full-time job.

Chapter 11 shows you many ways to save money on automobile expenses, including purchase.  Special emphasis is paid there to the possibility of saving up to 60 percent on transportation by buying a three-year-old car rather than a new one.  Being satisfied with a good used automobile for three years is worth a lot to your budget, and will save you about $40 to $75 per month—the range of difference between new and older-car payments.  Repairs and other maintenance might run higher on the older car, but you will still be ahead on a car-expense-per-month basis.  This differential can be applied to your other financial goals.  If you are lucky enough to have the use of your parents' car, perhaps you can put off any car purchase for now.

By the end of this book, you should have devised your own method of weighing today's purchases against tomorrow's goals.  The reason this commitment with respect to car purchases is so important to your goal structure is that an automobile is the second most expensive purchase in the lives of most Americans.  Because car payments are made over a shorter period of time, up to four or five years, the monthly payments for an expensive automobile may even exceed rent or house payment.  In this light, consider the advantages of owning a shiny, high-performance automobile right now: You have the use, but usually not the ownership of a rapidly depreciating consumer good.  Consider the long-term financial goals you have set for yourself to this point: home, money in the bank, travel, and so forth.  This does not mean that today's high car payment will make your goals unattainable; it does mean that those goals must be approached at a slower rate, and with less initial money to devote to them.

Suppose that you meet the girl (man) of your dreams during this time, and decide to marry!  Congratulations.  With the wife working—about 40 percent of American wives do—a couple's outlook for economic well-being and security is very good.  It is important for their plans that both husband and wife agree with the two commitments above and with one other:

**Commitment 3:   We will rent a comfortable, furnished apartment and
live there for at least three years after the husband
finishes college and takes a full-time job—before
buying a home.**

You will be better off in the long run to choose a relatively new, modern
apartment which is large enough to give you pleasure and satisfaction while you
live in it. You should not skimp on your apartment for short-run savings. Living
in an unsatisfactory apartment might prove depressing to you, and moving could
be expensive. Similarly, buying a home before your income and savings are
adequate might lead you to buy a home that doesn't suit you. So, as you hunt
for an apartment, ask yourself: "Will I be happy here for three years?"

**Commitment exceptions.** If you are *already* paying for a new car, or are buying
a new home, all is not lost. You may have to save at a lower rate for a while,
until some of your other current obligations are met. When a department store
charge account, for one example, is paid in full—allocate that payment to savings. Savings begun at any time in your life, in any amount, will help you reach
your financial goals. As you will see in the next section of this chapter, the
earlier you begin, the greater the benefits of savings.

### HOW YOUR SAVINGS ACCOUNT WORKS
So far, you have goals for saving and commitments to insure that your savings
program works. It seems logical to examine just how a savings account works.
At the outset, you should know how to protect your money in that account.

**Safety.** Be absolutely certain that your savings are adequately insured. Usually,
this means being insured by an agency of the United States Government. Those
institutions which have this insurance will advertise the fact. If an institution
does not advertise such protection for your savings, your account shouldn't be
there, unless you are otherwise satisfied with the long-term solidarity of the
institution. Some different types of savings organizations offer higher interest
to attract accounts. This is good business practice, but steer clear of *any* media
which has any uncertainty. No matter how high the rate of interest offered, if
your savings account is in a non-insured firm, you could lose the entire account
—principle, interest, and all—if embezzlement or bankruptcy takes place. The
higher interest offered is not worth the risk because eight percent of nothing is
nothing.

Agencies of the Federal Government insure accounts in qualified media such as commercial banks, savings and loan associations, and credit unions. These agencies regulate practices, reserves, and other standards of member institutions and are charged by Congress with the responsibility of guaranteeing the safety of deposits up to $20,000 at insured media. No depositor has lost a penny in an insured account. This means that your savings dollars are not lost to you, even if embezzlement or bank failure should occur. You might suffer some inconvenience, but no loss of funds.

Some uninsured savings media are backed by not much more than their directors' ability to outwit disaster, or their good intentions. A prestigious location is no guarantee of the stability of an institution, nor are its expensive and impressive brochures.

Instead of boring you by overdoing the point, let's consider this actual case:

Mr. and Mrs. Jones had retired. They had accumulated $25,000 during their work years, and they wanted to realize the greatest possible interest on their money. They planned to live on that interest plus their Social Security benefits. In their small town, a mortgage company offered the highest interest paid on savings accounts. It was not insured, but had been in the town for many years—surely, that indicated safety. Sadly, the firm went bankrupt. The Jones' account and all the other accounts were wiped out. Now, the Joneses have nothing—no savings, no interest. Social Security does not even fully cover their expenses, and they must live in semi-dependence for the rest of their lives.

The real tragedy of the Jones' story is that it was unnecessary. Although they would have received a bit less interest from a safe medium, that interest and their principal would have been intact for the entire life of their account. No great amount of research is required to assure yourself about the safety of your money—but your research will be rewarded by peace of mind, and that is why you should make safety the first order of business in your savings plans. The firms which earn money by lending it are really attempting to borrow your money for their "inventory." You should make sure that they are completely trustworthy before you lend them your money. Once you have assured yourself that several firms deserve your trust, the selection of which of these gets your savings dollars should be made by finding the one that pays you the most for the use of your money.

## TIME AND COMPOUND INTEREST

Interest itself is not difficult to understand: it is the rate, expressed as a percentage, that savings institutions are willing to pay for the use of your money. If one of them offers 5 percent, compounded annually—that firm is merely offering to pay you $5 for the use of $100 of your money for one year's time. Time is obviously important in this formula; so is the fact that the longer a medium can use your money, the more it will pay you in interest. Your money also earns more interest at institutions which compound more frequently; and higher interest earnings mean greater profits to you. You will work hard for your money, and it should work hard for you. To maximize the yield (profit) which your investment in savings earns, you should understand each element in the mechanics of saving: time, compounding, interest rates, and the result or interaction of these—yield.

**Time.** If you put $600 per year into a savings account which pays 6 percent interest, compounded annually, in 10 years, your *deposits* would total $6,000.

If your deposits were only $300 annually, and the interest and compounding period were the same, but you made those deposits over a 20-year period, your deposits would also total $6,000.

The total value, including interest earnings, of the first account would be $7,908. Interest earnings would have meant $1,908 in profits for your savings plan. That is almost $200 per year profit for the 10 years' difference.

The total value, including interest earnings, of the very same amount in deposits over a 20-year period would be $11,036. For using your money over the longer time span of 20 years, an institution pays this account more than $5,000. The difference of $3,128 ($5,036 minus $1,908) between the plans demonstrates the dollar value of an *early* beginning of the savings habit. Part of the difference is due to the effect of compounding, or of interest earning interest.

**Compounding.** Let's trace through a simple example of compounding so that you understand just what "interest earning interest" means:

> Suppose that you deposit $100 in a savings account which pays 5 percent compounded annually. Again, there are higher interest rates and more frequent compounding periods, but this is an example. The first year, your deposit earns $5, and your account total is $105. At the end of the second year, with no further deposits, your account is worth $110.25. The $5 interest of the first year has earned $.25, and your principal has earned another $5. At the end of the third year, your account is worth a total of $115.76. Prior interest paid your account is itself earning interest. This is a powerful factor in increasing your wealth. If you trace the $100 of this example through future years you will see that compounding can be said to increase the value, of your savings *at an increasing rate.*

There are wide variations among savings media in the frequency of computing and adding interest to the account (compounding). Some institutions, like our examples so far, compound only once yearly. Others compound daily, monthly, quarterly, or semi-annually. The important thing to remember is that your savings will grow faster at an institution which compounds most frequently—given the same interest rate. Table 3–1 shows how different compounding methods affect the same savings plan: $300 per year deposited January 1 each year for a 20-year period at 5 percent interest.

**Table 3–1** How compounding affects the dollar outcome of a 10-year savings program

| Annual compounding | $10,415.80 |
| Semi-annual compounding | $10,491.10 |
| Quarterly compounding | $10,529.90 |
| Monthly compounding | $10,556.30 |
| Daily compounding | $10,569.10 |

The significant differences in dollar outcome among the plans is due solely to the different frequencies of compounding. For assistance in deciphering rates as they are usually quoted in savings advertisements, Table 3–2 can be invaluable. If, for example, a figure is quoted as "annual effective rate when

**Table 3–2** Computer-prepared conversion table—showing effective annual rate of return of various interest rates with differing compounding methods

| Nominal rate | Effective annual rate when compounded: | | | | |
| | Annually | Semi-annually | Quarterly | Monthly | Daily |
| --- | --- | --- | --- | --- | --- |
| 3.5 | 3.500 | 3.531 | 3.546 | 3.557 | 3.561 |
| 3.55 | 3.550 | 3.582 | 3.598 | 3.608 | 3.613 |
| 3.6 | 3.600 | 3.632 | 3.649 | 3.660 | 3.665 |
| 3.65 | 3.650 | 3.683 | 3.700 | 3.712 | 3.717 |
| 3.7 | 3.700 | 3.734 | 3.752 | 3.763 | 3.769 |
| 3.75 | 3.750 | 3.785 | 3.803 | 3.815 | 3.821 |
| 3.8 | 3.800 | 3.836 | 3.855 | 3.867 | 3.873 |
| 3.85 | 3.850 | 3.887 | 3.906 | 3.919 | 3.925 |
| 3.9 | 3.900 | 3.938 | 3.957 | 3.971 | 3.977 |
| 3.95 | 3.950 | 3.989 | 4.009 | 4.022 | 4.028 |
| 4.0 | 4.000 | 4.040 | 4.060 | 4.074 | 4.080 |
| 4.05 | 4.050 | 4.091 | 4.112 | 4.126 | 4.132 |
| 4.1 | 4.100 | 4.142 | 4.164 | 4.178 | 4.185 |
| 4.15 | 4.150 | 4.193 | 4.215 | 4.230 | 4.237 |
| 4.2 | 4.200 | 4.244 | 4.267 | 4.282 | 4.289 |
| 4.25 | 4.250 | 4.295 | 4.318 | 4.334 | 4.341 |
| 4.3 | 4.300 | 4.346 | 4.370 | 4.386 | 4.393 |
| 4.35 | 4.350 | 4.397 | 4.422 | 4.438 | 4.445 |
| 4.4 | 4.400 | 4.448 | 4.473 | 4.490 | 4.498 |
| 4.45 | 4.450 | 4.500 | 4.525 | 4.542 | 4.550 |
| 4.5 | 4.500 | 4.551 | 4.577 | 4.594 | 4.603 |
| 4.55 | 4.550 | 4.602 | 4.628 | 4.646 | 4.655 |

**Table 3–2 (cont.)**

| Nominal rate | Effective annual rate when compounded: | | | | |
| | Annually | Semi-annually | Quarterly | Monthly | Daily |
|---|---|---|---|---|---|
| 4.6 | 4.600 | 4.653 | 4.680 | 4.698 | 4.707 |
| 4.65 | 4.650 | 4.704 | 4.732 | 4.750 | 4.759 |
| 4.7 | 4.700 | 4.755 | 4.784 | 4.803 | 4.812 |
| 4.75 | 4.750 | 4.806 | 4.835 | 4.855 | 4.864 |
| 4.8 | 4.800 | 4.858 | 4.887 | 4.907 | 4.916 |
| 4.85 | 4.850 | 4.909 | 4.939 | 4.959 | 4.969 |
| 4.9 | 4.900 | 4.960 | 4.991 | 5.012 | 5.021 |
| 4.95 | 4.950 | 5.011 | 5.043 | 5.064 | 5.074 |
| 5.0 | 5.000 | 5.063 | 5.095 | 5.116 | 5.127 |
| 5.05 | 5.050 | 5.114 | 5.146 | 5.169 | 5.179 |
| 5.1 | 5.100 | 5.165 | 5.198 | 5.221 | 5.232 |
| 5.15 | 5.150 | 5.216 | 5.250 | 5.273 | 5.285 |
| 5.2 | 5.200 | 5.268 | 5.302 | 5.326 | 5.337 |
| 5.25 | 5.250 | 5.319 | 5.354 | 5.378 | 5.390 |
| 5.3 | 5.300 | 5.370 | 5.406 | 5.430 | 5.443 |
| 5.35 | 5.350 | 5.422 | 5.458 | 5.483 | 5.495 |
| 5.4 | 5.400 | 5.473 | 5.510 | 5.536 | 5.548 |
| 5.45 | 5.450 | 5.524 | 5.562 | 5.588 | 5.600 |
| 5.5 | 5.500 | 5.576 | 5.615 | 5.641 | 5.653 |
| 5.55 | 5.550 | 5.627 | 5.667 | 5.693 | 5.706 |
| 5.6 | 5.600 | 5.678 | 5.719 | 5.746 | 5.759 |
| 5.65 | 5.650 | 5.730 | 5.771 | 5.799 | 5.812 |
| 5.7 | 5.700 | 5.781 | 5.823 | 5.851 | 5.865 |
| 5.75 | 5.750 | 5.833 | 5.875 | 5.904 | 5.918 |
| 5.8 | 5.800 | 5.884 | 5.927 | 5.957 | 5.971 |
| 5.85 | 5.850 | 5.936 | 5.980 | 6.009 | 6.024 |
| 5.9 | 5.900 | 5.987 | 6.032 | 6.062 | 6.077 |
| 5.95 | 5.950 | 6.039 | 6.084 | 6.115 | 6.130 |
| 6.0 | 6.000 | 6.090 | 6.136 | 6.168 | 6.183 |
| 6.05 | 6.050 | 6.142 | 6.189 | 6.221 | 6.236 |
| 6.1 | 6.100 | 6.193 | 6.241 | 6.274 | 6.289 |
| 6.15 | 6.150 | 6.245 | 6.293 | 6.326 | 6.342 |
| 6.2 | 6.200 | 6.296 | 6.346 | 6.379 | 6.395 |
| 6.25 | 6.250 | 6.348 | 6.398 | 6.432 | 6.448 |
| 6.3 | 6.300 | 6.399 | 6.450 | 6.485 | 6.502 |
| 6.35 | 6.350 | 6.451 | 6.503 | 6.538 | 6.555 |
| 6.4 | 6.400 | 6.502 | 6.555 | 6.591 | 6.609 |
| 6.45 | 6.450 | 6.554 | 6.608 | 6.644 | 6.662 |
| 6.5 | 6.500 | 6.606 | 6.660 | 6.697 | 6.715 |
| 6.55 | 6.550 | 6.657 | 6.713 | 6.750 | 6.769 |
| 6.6 | 6.600 | 6.709 | 6.765 | 6.803 | 6.822 |

**Table 3–2 (cont.)**

| Nominal rate | Effective annual rate when compounded: | | | | |
| | Annually | Semi-annually | Quarterly | Monthly | Daily |
|---|---|---|---|---|---|
| 6.65 | 6.650 | 6.761 | 6.818 | 6.857 | 6.875 |
| 6.7 | 6.700 | 6.812 | 6.870 | 6.910 | 6.929 |
| 6.75 | 6.750 | 6.864 | 6.923 | 6.963 | 6.982 |
| 6.8 | 6.800 | 6.916 | 6.975 | 7.016 | 7.035 |
| 6.85 | 6.850 | 6.967 | 7.028 | 7.069 | 7.089 |
| 6.9 | 6.900 | 7.019 | 7.081 | 7.122 | 7.143 |
| 6.95 | 6.950 | 7.071 | 7.133 | 7.176 | 7.196 |
| 7.0 | 7.000 | 7.123 | 7.186 | 7.229 | 7.250 |
| 7.05 | 7.050 | 7.174 | 7.239 | 7.282 | 7.304 |
| 7.1 | 7.100 | 7.226 | 7.291 | 7.336 | 7.357 |
| 7.15 | 7.150 | 7.278 | 7.344 | 7.389 | 7.411 |
| 7.2 | 7.200 | 7.330 | 7.397 | 7.442 | 7.465 |
| 7.25 | 7.250 | 7.381 | 7.450 | 7.496 | 7.518 |
| 7.3 | 7.300 | 7.433 | 7.502 | 7.549 | 7.572 |
| 7.35 | 7.350 | 7.485 | 7.555 | 7.603 | 7.626 |
| 7.4 | 7.400 | 7.537 | 7.608 | 7.656 | 7.680 |
| 7.45 | 7.450 | 7.589 | 7.661 | 7.710 | 7.734 |
| 7.5 | 7.500 | 7.641 | 7.714 | 7.763 | 7.787 |
| 7.55 | 7.550 | 7.693 | 7.767 | 7.817 | 7.841 |
| 7.6 | 7.600 | 7.744 | 7.819 | 7.870 | 7.895 |
| 7.65 | 7.650 | 7.796 | 7.872 | 7.924 | 7.949 |
| 7.7 | 7.700 | 7.848 | 7.925 | 7.978 | 8.003 |
| 7.75 | 7.750 | 7.900 | 7.978 | 8.031 | 8.057 |
| 7.8 | 7.800 | 7.952 | 8.031 | 8.085 | 8.111 |
| 7.85 | 7.850 | 8.004 | 8.041 | 8.139 | 8.165 |
| 7.9 | 7.900 | 8.056 | 8.137 | 8.192 | 8.219 |
| 7.95 | 7.950 | 8.108 | 8.190 | 8.246 | 8.274 |
| 8.0 | 8.000 | 8.160 | 8.243 | 8.300 | 8.328 |
| 8.05 | 8.050 | 8.212 | 8.296 | 8.354 | 8.382 |
| 8.1 | 8.100 | 8.264 | 8.349 | 8.408 | 8.436 |
| 8.15 | 8.150 | 8.316 | 8.403 | 8.461 | 8.490 |
| 8.2 | 8.200 | 8.368 | 8.456 | 8.515 | 8.545 |
| 8.25 | 8.250 | 8.420 | 8.509 | 8.569 | 8.598 |
| 8.3 | 8.300 | 8.472 | 8.562 | 8.623 | 8.653 |
| 8.35 | 8.350 | 8.524 | 8.615 | 8.677 | 8.707 |
| 8.4 | 8.400 | 8.576 | 8.668 | 8.731 | 8.761 |
| 8.45 | 8.450 | 8.629 | 8.722 | 8.785 | 8.816 |
| 8.5 | 8.500 | 8.681 | 8.775 | 8.839 | 8.870 |

compounded quarterly," you can find that comparable figure in the "compounded quarterly column" and then convert it to an annual nominal rate by looking at the column at the far left. Similarly, if a rate is quoted merely as an "annual rate compounded daily," you can go to the nominal rate and follow across the line to the appropriate column showing annual *effective* rate when compounded daily.

**Rate of interest.** Holding all other variables in constant, you can see the importance of selecting the medium which pays the highest rate of interest. A small difference in interest can loom very large when time and compounding begin to work on that difference. Table 3–3 illustrates the effect of various rates of interest on savings plans which are otherwise identical.

**Table 3–3** How differing rates of interest affect the dollar outcome of a 20-year savings program—$300 contributed January 1 of each year (interest compounded annually)

| Interest rate | Dollar outcome |
| --- | --- |
| 3% | $8,302.95 |
| 4% | $9,290.76 |
| 5% | $10,415.80 |
| 6% | $11,697.80 |
| 7% | $13,159.60 |
| 8% | $14,826.90 |
| 9% | $16,729.40 |
| 10% | $18,900.80 |

Now that you are familiar with the essential mathematics of savings within institutions, you will see why the emphasis in this chapter is on selecting a savings plan which will result in the highest yield. Yield, in the sense used here, is simply the profit your savings earn through the interactions of interest, compounding, and time. Higher yield for your savings should be your primary concern as you choose among insured savings media.

## OTHER GENERAL GUIDELINES

You know now what happens to your savings account once you deposit your money. You should be aware of other aspects of the relationship between you and the savings institution.

**Advertising.** The way interest is advertised is often confusing. From our discussions on yield, it will take you little time or effort to determine which institution offers the highest interest earnings—in dollars—for your savings.

Consider these four excerpts from real advertisements:

- EARN 5.41 %——when compounded quarterly for a year
- EARN 5.45 %——when compounded daily for a year
- EARN 5.30 %——current annual rate—compounded semi-annually
- EARN 5.30 %——current annual rate—compounded daily

Which of these advertisers should get your savings account? The first two institutions obscure their real rate of interest somewhat, by showing an inflated figure—an "equivalent" interest rate—after a particular interest rate has been compounded for a particular frequency. As a matter of fact, all four institutions pay exactly the same (5.30%) rate of interest, and the difference in yield is the difference caused by particular schemes of compounding.

If you will again refer to Table 3–2, you will find that:

1. Daily compounding of 5.30% yields 5.45%.
2. Quarterly compounding of 5.30% yields 5.41%.

Of the four institutions, you should choose either the 2nd or 4th. They yield identical interest earnings of 5.45%. Obviously, the third offering is the poorest, because that advertiser compounds only semiannually. Here, you should become aware of the fact that interest paid on savings may vary from year to year within an institution. There is no guarantee that a 5.30% interest rate will prevail on personal passbook accounts, for example. Interest rates may rise, and they may fall. The interest rates change directly and quickly in reaction to a Federal Reserve Board policy shift. Likewise, interest rates may vary among different media, depending on which part of the economy most directly concerns them. (Construction starts might be very important for savings and loan firms, and not as important to commercial banks, for instance.) Additionally, a particular savings firm may devise a new form of account—$5,000 minimum for one year, for example, which will offer greater yield for savings. If you are in a position to take advantage of such changes, by all means do so. Many savings firms offer "bonus" accounts which earn higher yields if savings are kept in an account for specified minimum time periods: one, two, and three-year "bonus" accounts are common.

Similar in form are the "savings certificates," "subordinated notes," and "certificates of deposit." Typically, each of these devices requires large initial deposits ($500 and up); encourages further deposits of substantial amounts ($100 and up); and offers higher-than-passbook yields for accounts remaining for periods of one year or more. It is doubtful that you will find these yields especially attractive, when weighed against the potential earning power of carefully selected investments. In every case, you should make trade-off decisions about relative earnings, relative convenience, and the kind of performance your goals require from your savings plan. If there is no better use for your money, for a year or so, you should seriously consider one of these higher yield savings plans. If you are not certain, you should not put your savings in such a plan, because not only are you giving up flexibility, but also you may sacrifice interest earnings as well if you withdraw your savings before the end of a minimum time period.

Some savers earn extra interest by taking advantage of the grace periods of different institutions. They might deposit $1,000 in bank A on the 9th of the month. Bank A compounds daily, and pays a full month's interest for funds deposited by the 10th of the month. At the end of the month, they withdraw most of the money from the account, leaving just enough to keep the account open. They deposit the money in bank B which has similar terms and conditions. On the 9th of the second month, they withdraw from bank B, again leaving a token sum and make a deposit in bank A. During the grace period at the beginning of the month, these depositors are earning interest from both banks, even though their money is physically in just one bank. There are other methods of earning slightly more in interest. Most of these methods, to be profitable, require very careful planning and execution; and unfortunately, they require large sums for principal deposits in order to earn significant dollar amounts.

**Other interest pay schemes.**    Be alert for differential interest pay schemes. Often, large print will call attention to an attractive yield possibility, and the small print will qualify that high rate.

- EARN A SIX PERCENT GUARANTEED ANNUAL INTEREST
  (On minimum balances of $10,000 and more when left on
  deposit for 35 months. Other savings accounts pay $4\frac{1}{2}$
  percent interest, compounded annually.)

These cautionary guidelines apply to all savings accounts, and deal mainly with amounts. At least two other considerations should be noted before you make that important first deposit (or withdrawal). They are functions of time—*when* you do your banking.

**Bonuses.**    Quite often, bonus amounts are added to savings accounts after 3 or 5 years. These bonuses may be $\frac{1}{4}$ or $\frac{1}{2}$ percent or perhaps more. You should remember, however, that these bonuses have considerably less effective earning power for you than do rates which are affected by the compounding process. In these instances, it is only after three or five years that the $\frac{1}{4}$ or $\frac{1}{2}$ percent is added so that it can be subsequently compounded.

**Contributions (deposits).**    Time your savings contributions so that each will earn interest for the full month or interest period in which it is deposited. Many institutions pay a full month's interest for funds deposited by the 10th of the month. Some pay interest *only* on funds which have been on deposit for the full interest period. Institutions with more liberal terms pay interest to date of withdrawal. Be sure you know when you make your regular deposit; don't lose interest earnings because you didn't watch the calendar.

**Withdrawals.**   You should know about the exact terms of withdrawal dates for your savings account. Some institutions have a grace period of a few days at the end of each month or interest period, when you can make withdrawals, yet still earn interest for the entire month.

If you must (really must) withdraw money from your savings account before the end of an interest period, it is usually possible to obtain a passbook loan for the money you need. This way, you can leave your interest-earning balance intact for the full period. Suppose you have $5,000 in savings at a bank which pays interest semi-annually. At the end of May (the fifth month of the interest period) you decide to withdraw $3,000 for an investment. It would pay you, in real dollars, to make a passbook loan, and pay one month's loan cost, rather than lose five months' interest on the $3,000.

**SETTING UP A MODEL SAVINGS PROGRAM**

Now that you know something about the mathematics and mechanics of saving, you might like to see what could happen to the finances of a male college sophomore who made the three savings commitments suggested earlier in this chapter, and kept them. He decides to complete a four-year education before going to work full time. He marries one year after graduation. His wife works for one additional year after their wedding. He had saved 10 percent of his gross earnings, and they stick to that percentage for their combined earnings. On their third anniversary, they take a look at what they've achieved, as shown in Table 3–4. Compound interest has contributed $452.02 in profits to their wealth.

Perhaps the most important single result of the young couple's savings program is that they have accumulated an investment fund early in life. Time and compound interest can now work for them, building their savings into a significant sum of money.

At this point our young couple may start thinking seriously about buying a home. Here it is appropriate to recall another reason for savings—*investments*. Left alone, with no further contributions and at the same 5 percent interest compounded semi-annually, their $3,627.82 will grow to $9,741.06 in 20 years. This may or may not be a good plan depending on what happens in regard to inflation over the same span of years. Nonetheless, if they convert the $3,627.82 to a down payment for a home now, they leave nothing in savings for economic independence in their later years, or for investments which might help them achieve a more leisurely way of life long before that. Therefore, it does make sense to keep the original savings intact for investment purposes and to continue to add to that account regularly. As Table 3–5 shows, if this young couple could continue to deposit a modest $20 per month to their original account at the same yield, it would grow to $17,913.62 in just 20 years.

Additionally at this point in time, the couple might appropriately set up a separate savings account for the purpose of accumulating a sufficient down payment for their dream home. If their desire for a home is strong, they might be

**Table 3-4** Savings and interest accumulations of suggested savings plan for college students (interest at 5 percent compounded semi-annually—10 percent of earnings allocated for savings).

| Years and earnings | Dollars saved yearly | + | Interest earned yearly | = | Total dollars |
|---|---|---|---|---|---|
| Sophomore year: | $ | | $ | | $ |
|   3 summer months | | | | | |
|   earned $265/month | | | | | |
|   9 school months | | | | | |
|   earned $78/month | 149.70 | | 5.15 | | 154.85 |
| Junior year: | | | | | |
|   3 summer months | | | | | |
|   earned $290/month | | | | | |
|   9 school months | | | | | |
|   earned $84/month | 162.60 | | 13.45 | | 330.90 |
| Senior year: | | | | | |
|   3 summer months | | | | | |
|   earned $315/month | | | | | |
|   9 school months | | | | | |
|   earned $90/month | 175.50 | | 22.83 | | 529.23 |
| First year out of school: | | | | | |
|   Full-time job | | | | | |
|   earned $460/month | 552.00 | | 41.85 | | 1,123.08 |
| Second year out of school: | | | | | |
|   Full-time job | | | | | |
|   earned $469/month | | | | | |
|   Spouse working on | | | | | |
|   full-time job | | | | | |
|   earned $315/month | 940.80 | | 82.66 | | 2,146.54 |
| Third year out of school: | | | | | |
|   Full-time job | | | | | |
|   earned $491/month | | | | | |
|   Spouse not working | 589.20 | | 124.74 | | 2,860.48 |
| Fourth year out of school: | | | | | |
|   Full-time job | | | | | |
|   earned $505/month | | | | | |
|   Spouse not working | 606.00 | | 161.34 | | 3,627.82 |

willing to make major adjustments in their budget and in their manner of living for the next five years to accommodate a sizable monthly contribution to the down payment account. Assuming they could find $60 a month (in addition to the $20 monthly for the investment account), they could rapidly accumulate ample funds for their down payment. At the 5% interest rate (compounded

**Table 3-5** Growth of hypothetical investment of $3,627.82 plus $20.00 monthly contribution at various interest rates and for various periods of time (interest compounded semi-annually).

| Years invested | Rates of interest | | | | | | | |
|---|---|---|---|---|---|---|---|---|
| | 5% | 6% | 7% | 8% | 9% | 10% | 11% | 12% |
| 5 | 6,002.38 | 6,265.43 | 6,539.83 | 6,825.64 | 7,123.95 | 7,434.43 | 7,757.82 | 8,094.87 |
| 10 | 9,041.84 | 9,810.24 | 10,647.55 | 11,559.51 | 12,552.99 | 13,634.94 | 14,813.03 | 16,095.03 |
| 15 | 12,932.92 | 14,574.33 | 16,441.82 | 18,566.77 | 20,984.38 | 23,734.79 | 26,863.85 | 30,422.19 |
| 20 | 17,913.62 | 20,976.35 | 24,615.35 | 28,939.00 | 34,078.28 | 40,186.82 | 47,448.15 | 55,964.65 |

semi-annually) they would have $4,075.23 in five years.  And if they could find a savings institution paying 6%, they would have a nifty $4,575.21 over the five years.  Now they have established two powerful approaches to their goals! They are in a position to select their home, they have substantial investment funds, and they are well underway toward many of their financial objectives.

The alternative, using their entire savings toward down payment on a home immediately, does not feature the benefits outlined above.  Home owning is expensive as well as enjoyable.  In addition to the monthly payment on the mortgage, the couple will have to pay water bills, property taxes, possibly landscaping fees, utility hookup fees, deposits on utilities.  They will probably wish to decorate.  Their furniture might look less "respectable" in its new surroundings. They will have to buy maintenance tools.  Many of the services they will have to perform or pay for are now done for them by their landlord and included in their present rental payment.  This is not to say that the expenses are not worthwhile; but the possibility exists that the new expenses will supersede their contributions to savings for other purposes.

While a home is one of the primary goals for most couples, it usually is not the only goal.  Your home should be considered in light of your other goals, and it should not make them impossible.

Do save.  Do earn the highest yield with your savings.  Do examine objectively the terms and conditions offered by various media.  Thus far, this chapter has been concerned with the "do's" of savings.  It may be unnecessary by now, but there is one important "don't" that merits your attention.

## DON'T JOIN A NON-INTEREST-BEARING
## CHRISTMAS CLUB SAVINGS ACCOUNT

Christmas Savings Clubs or similar non-interest savings accounts take in more than one-and-a-half billion dollars, earn savings institutions as much as $100 million by keeping the funds on loan, and pay absolutely no interest.  Dr. Donald A. Nicholas, a University of Wisconsin economics professor, who has served on the President's Council of Economic Advisors, has indicated that Christmas Club savings accounts cost the public about $30 million each year.  The loss is the difference of interest earnings on conventional savings or dividends ($30 million) and the amount paid club members—zero.

There are no monetary benefits accruing to a club member, so it would seem logical to avoid the clubs altogether.  But people save about $1,500,000,000 this way every year.  Why?  Members apparently like the assurance of having a certain amount of money accumulated for their Christmas shopping.  As a matter of fact, they can't do much else with the money, since it is not available to them *until* the Christmas Season.  If an emergency occurs, they cannot count on club savings to pay for it.

The value of advance installments for large purchases (or large purchase amounts, like Christmas spending) has already been pointed out to you earlier in the chapter. If you use your savings for nothing else but advance installments or for buying Christmas presents, do your saving in a regular savings account and earn some interest money while you're at it.

## STANDARDS FOR CHOOSING SAVINGS MEDIA

There are five important things you should look for in any savings institution before you decide where to deposit your savings:

1. Maximum safety (adequately insured).
2. Highest possible rate of interest.
3. Most frequent compounding of interest.
4. Quick, easy access to your money.
5. Convenience.

Finding a bank, savings and loan association, or credit union which meets all or most of these criteria may take a little time and effort, but in the long run the time and effort will be well spent.

Figure 3–1 shows the distribution of household savings among the principal financial institutions: commercial banks, mutual savings banks, and savings associations. In deciding which type would be best for your savings, rate all of them using your 5-criteria checklist. These criteria will be highlighted in discussions of specific savings institutions which follow.

**Commercial banks.** These are probably the best-known and the best-understood savings institutions. They are often called the "department stores" of banking because they offer so many different services. Most commercial banks offer several kinds of checking accounts, various types of savings accounts, security-box rentals, consumer loans, commercial loans, home loans, and trust services. Many are connected with credit card companies and offer small loans in connection with certain checking accounts. Generally the interest rate at commercial banks is lower than that paid at other savings institutions. Your decision to save at a commercial bank could be the result of a trade off: Does the convenience of many banking services under one roof offset the usually lower interest rates? Figure 3–2 is an historical summary comparison showing interest yields of selected media.

**Mutual savings banks.** This type of bank is found mostly in the Eastern United States. The word "mutual" means that these banks have no "ownership interest or group" in the usual sense, but exist and operate solely for the benefit of their depositors. "The Dime Savings Bank of Brooklyn" is a mutual savings bank, for example. Many of these institutions were founded to encourage thrift among lower income families, as the word "Dime" suggests. Today they operate much like any commercial bank. Through the years, many have grown to substantial size.

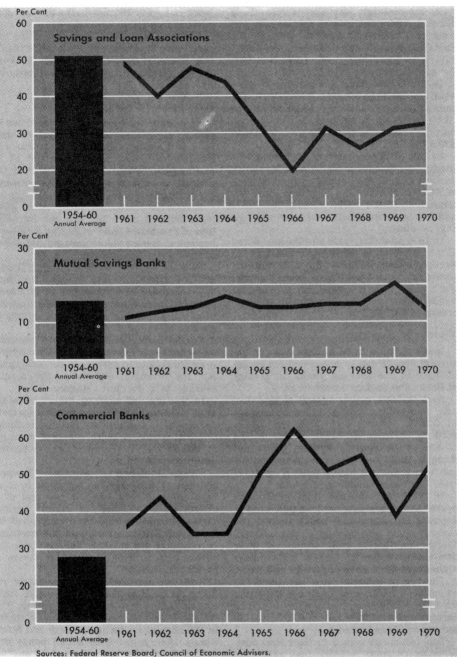

**Fig. 3–1** Household savings at major financial institutions. Most savers tend to put their money where it will earn the most interest. Historically, American families have placed the bulk of their funds in banks and savings institutions. A marked departure, however, occurred in the tight money periods of 1966 and 1969, when escalating interest rates and yields available on direct investments caused households to move directly into the market with record purchases of bonds and securities issued by the Federal Government and its agencies. Reprinted by permission from *Savings & Loan Fact Book 1971*. United States Savings and Loan League.

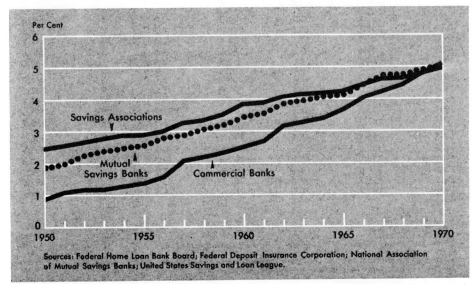

Per Cent

Savings Associations

Mutual
Savings Banks      Commercial Banks

Sources: Federal Home Loan Bank Board; Federal Deposit Insurance Corporation; National Association of Mutual Savings Banks; United States Savings and Loan League.

**Fig. 3–2** Average annual yield on savings at major financial institutions. While history is interesting, your concern is finding what interest returns are *now* being paid by the various savings institutions. Reprinted by permission from *Savings & Loan Fact Book 1971*. United States Savings and Loan League.

Deposit amounts are regulated by state legislatures. In New York State, for instance, an individual account cannot exceed $25,000; joint accounts may not exceed $50,000. On the average, mutual savings banks have paid a slightly higher return on savings than have commercial banks. Sometimes they compound interest more frequently than do commercial banks, which adds to their ·effective interest rate (yield).

**Savings and loan associations.** At the beginning of the 1970's, there were approximately 6,000 savings and loan associations throughout the United States. The assets of these associations have increased rapidly in recent years, although there are fewer associations (down from 6,320 in 1960). They have been very aggressive with advertising and promotion efforts, and typically pay from one-fourth to one-half percent more on savers' dollars than commercial banks. Individual policies differ, but money deposited in savings and loan associations is usually available on request. Many associations furnish postage-paid envelopes, encouraging the saver to make regular deposits by mail. Withdrawals are usually possible by mail also. The biggest disadvantage of saving in such institutions is that they do not offer the convenience of checking accounts. This means that if you save at a savings and loan association, you must have a checking account elsewhere.

**Credit unions.** The employees of many large and medium-size companies have chartered (state and/or federal) credit unions for their own use. If you are affiliated with such a company, you may find it convenient to deal directly with your credit union.  The interest rate paid by credit unions on savings is usually comparable to that paid by savings and loan associations.  An additional service of most credit unions is "life insurance protection" for your savings.  The usual practice is to insure the first $2,000 of an individual's savings, so that in the event of the saver's death, an additional $2,000 of life insurance would be paid to the employee's beneficiary.  Interest rates vary among credit unions, and within a single credit union, from year to year.  Often, decisions regarding the interest rate to be paid on savings during the previous 12 months are made by a credit union committee at the end of the calendar year, for the preceding 12 months. Investigate the yield and insurance features of your credit union.  Many people find payroll deduction "depositing" the most important single feature of credit union saving.  Generally, employers will cooperate by automatically deducting authorized amounts, which are credited to your credit union savings account. Accounts in qualified credit unions are being insured by the Federal Government.  (See Fig. 3–3.)

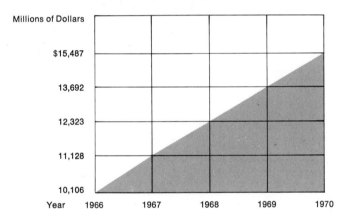

**Fig. 3–3** Savings in credit unions.  Membership in credit unions totaled about 23 million persons at the beginning of the decade.  Total savings in credit unions reached about $15.5 billion at the end of 1970.  The new Federal share insurance is apparently making credit unions even more attractive for savers.  Reprinted by permission from *Credit Union Yearbook 1971.* (Noncopyrighted.)

**Industrial loan companies.**  This type of institution frequently solicits savings by offering higher interest rates to attract your savings dollars.  Customarily, they issue "thrift certificates" for various amounts of money and at various maturity dates.  For example, you might find such a company advertising "$6\frac{1}{2}$ percent, 12-month certificates."  If you put your savings in one of these firms, you are making a commitment to leave your money with the company for at least the time specified on the certificates (12 months in the example). You should satisfy yourself about the safety of your account with such a firm. They are not insured by a Government agency.

**United States savings bonds.** Many savers have found United States Savings Bonds to be a convenient thrift medium. Employers usually offer payroll deduction service to their employees who wish to purchase bonds by this method. United States Savings Bonds are of two types: the "E" Series, and the "H" Series. The "E" bonds are pre-discounted; for example, you buy a $100 face-

value bond for $75, hold it for 5 years and 10 months, then cash it in for $100 (actually $102.92). They are available in denominations ranging from $25 to $1,000. The current rate of interest is $5\frac{1}{2}$ percent when held to maturity. The yield is 4.01 percent the first year; thereafter, the rate increases gradually; at maturity a $\frac{1}{2}$ percent bonus is added, raising the yield to $5\frac{1}{2}$ percent from issue date to maturity. The difference between the price paid for "E" bonds and the redemption value is considered to be interest. Interest is subject to Federal income tax—but not to state or local income taxes. Interest is reportable as it accrues for Federal income tax purposes, but such reporting may be deferred until the bonds are cashed, disposed of, or reach final maturity, whichever happens first. Bonds are subject to estate, inheritance, gift, and other excise taxes, whether Federal or state, but are exempt from all other taxation imposed on principal or interest by any state, United States possession, or local taxing authority.

The "H" differs mechanically, though it serves the same function, which is financing government operations. You buy a Series "H" bond at face value in denominations of $500, $1,000 and $5,000, and receive interest payments in the form of Treasury checks every six months. The yield is 4.49 percent the first year; 5.30 percent for the next four years, and 6.00 percent for the second five years, raising the rate to an average of $5\frac{1}{2}$ percent for the 10-year period. Interest must be reported for Federal income tax purposes for the year in which interest is paid.

Interest on Series "H" bonds, like Series "E" bonds, is not subject to state or local income tax.

Historically, the yield offered by either bond series has been a little less than the yield offered by savings and loan firms and credit unions. This, plus the time factor—no interest is paid for six months—makes United States Savings Bonds somewhat unattractive as a savings medium.

## UNIFORMED SERVICES SAVINGS DEPOSIT PROGRAM

If or when you serve overseas in the Armed Services, you should take advantage of the Defense Department's special savings program. It pays a high 10 percent annual interest on savings of enlisted men or officers. You can deposit monthly savings up to the total of your unalloted pay and allowances. There is one considerable disadvantage; except for emergencies you cannot withdraw your savings while overseas. The Defense Department insists that rest and recreation leaves to Paris or Tokyo do not qualify as emergencies.

Even given the inaccessibility of your savings funds, the Savings Deposit Program is still a very good one. The 10 percent return on your savings is almost as good as you could expect on good common stock investments over a long period. Also, the 10 percent return is guaranteed, which is not true for stocks.

## SHORT-TERM TREASURY BILLS AND NOTES

In addition to shopping among savings institutions for the best interest rate for your savings, you should keep track of the current interest yields on short-term United States Treasury bills and notes. Sometimes the yield is better than you can get for passbook savings or certificates of deposit. These bills and notes, too, are absolutely safe; they are backed by the ability of the government to tax. And as you know, that ability is considerable. With the notes and bills, you have an assured interest rate, so long as you do not sell before the maturity date, which is the time when the Treasury pays back the money.

Government bills and notes are also issued by the Treasury to help finance government operations. Distribution and sale are handled by the Federal Reserve System and various dealers in government securities. Once the issues have been sold originally (issued), they are actively traded—resold and repurchased—by securities dealers. You can purchase them through the investment department of your bank, through a securities dealer, or directly from the Federal Reserve. Dealer commissions are modest, ranging from $10–20 on transactions of $100,000 or less. Once you know something about these securities, buying or selling them is as easy as depositing and withdrawing your savings account money.

**Treasury bills.** Weekly, the Treasury issues bills in $10,000 and higher amounts, with 3-month and 6-month maturities. Monthly, 6-month and one-year bills are sold. The yield on Treasury bills is not difficult to determine. *The Wall Street Journal* and other financial journals publish current "Government

---
**Government, Agency and Miscellaneous Securities**

---

| U.S.Treasury Bills | | | | | |
|---|---|---|---|---|---|
| Mat | Bid | Ask Discount | Mat | Bid | Ask Discount |
| 9-11 | 7.05 | 6.15 | 12-31 | 6.99 | 6.69 |
| 9-18 | 7.20 | 6.74 | 1- 2 | 7.02 | 6.80 |
| 9-25 | 7.20 | 6.70 | 1- 8 | 7.02 | 6.80 |
| 9-30 | 6.95 | 6.30 | 1-15 | 7.03 | 6.82 |
| 10- 2 | 7.09 | 6.76 | 1-22 | 7.04 | 6.84 |
| 10- 9 | 7.10 | 6.81 | 1-29 | 7.04 | 6.88 |
| 10-16 | 7.13 | 6.84 | 1-31 | 7.02 | 6.78 |
| 10-23 | 7.15 | 6.87 | 2- 5 | 7.15 | 7.03 |
| 10-30 | 7.15 | 6.89 | 2-13 | 7.18 | 7.05 |
| 10-31 | 7.04 | 6.60 | 2-19 | 7.19 | 7.05 |
| 11- 6 | 6.99 | 6.82 | 2-26 | 7.20 | 7.10 |
| 11-13 | 6.99 | 6.83 | 2-28 | 7.11 | 6.89 |
| 11-20 | 7.00 | 6.86 | 3- 5 | 7.22 | 7.18 |
| 11-28 | 7.00 | 6.90 | 3-23 | 7.22 | 7.17 |
| 11-30 | 7.01 | 6.79 | 3-31 | 7.21 | 7.03 |
| 12- 4 | 7.00 | 6.97 | 4-30 | 7.26 | 7.15 |
| 12-11 | 7.04 | 6.84 | 5-31 | 7.33 | 7.28 |

**Fig. 3–4** How United States Treasury bills are quoted. Reprinted by permission from *The Wall Street Journal.*

Securities" quotations. Figure 3–4 shows how Treasury bills are quoted. The left-hand column gives the maturity dates—the month and day that the money will be repaid—of a particular issue of bills. The center column is the "bid" discount, and the right-hand column is the "asked" discount. Let's clarify those terms in this context by examining a particular bill in the quotations; say, the entry maturing 2–13.

(February 13)    2–13    7.18    7.05

The difference between "bid" and "asked" discounts gives the dealers their profits for handling Treasury bill transactions. When you purchase a bill, you buy at the "asked" discount. If you were to sell to a dealer before the maturity date, you would sell at the price reflecting the "bid" discount. The "7.05 asked discount" of the illustration means that you could buy a $10,000 Treasury bill at a price which would yield 7.05 percent interest on the $10,000 maturity value of the bill, that is, from today's date until the bill matures. The maturity value is usually called "par value." You should note that your actual yield would be a bit more than 7.05, since the bill is discounted, and you pay less than $10,000 for it.

**Treasury notes.** Treasury notes and Treasury bills differ in two important respects: (1) Notes have longer maturities than bills. Notes are usually for periods of three to five years, although they can be for as long as seven years or for as short as one year. (2) Semi-annual interest coupons accompany notes issued. These are clipped and deposited with your bank for an interest payment.

Treasury notes are sold in denominations of $10,000 and up. The amount of interest you can earn on notes varies. Notes are quoted at a price which excludes earned interest, often referred to as accrued interest. This earned interest is computed and added to your statement when you purchase the note. Figure 3–5 shows how Treasury notes are quoted in *The Wall Street Journal*. The left-hand column stipulates the interest rate at which the original note was written. This is *not* the interest yield you can get on the note. The selling price of Treasury notes changes as they are resold and repurchased on the money market—so they will yield the buyer interest rates consistent with the current lending practices.

### Government, Agency and Miscellaneous Securities

| U.S. Treasury Notes | | | | |
|---|---|---|---|---|
| Rate | Mat | Bid | Asked | Yld |
| 1½ | 4-70 | 97.6 | 97.22 | 6.95 |
| 5⅝ | 5-70 | 99.0a | 99.2a | 7.33 |
| 6⅜ | 5-70 | 99.13 | 99.15 | 7.36 |
| 6⅜ | 8-70 | 99.9a | 99.13a | 7.12 |
| 1½ | 10-70 | 94.18 | 95.2 | 7.10 |
| 5 | 11-70 | 97.20 | 97.24 | 7.24 |
| 5⅜ | 2-71 | 97.18 | 97.26 | 7.15 |
| 7¾ | 2-71 | 100.19 | 100.23 | 7.17 |
| 1½ | 4-71 | 91.24 | 92.8 | 7.27 |
| 5¼ | 5-71 | 97.0 | 97.8 | 7.14 |
| 8 | 5-71 | 101.5 | 101.9 | 7.11 |
| 1½ | 10-71 | 89.10 | 90.10 | 6.93 |
| 5⅜ | 11-71 | 96.15 | 96.23 | 7.12 |
| 4¾ | 2-72 | 94.22 | 94.30 | 7.16 |
| 1½ | 4-72 | 87.6 | 88.6 | 6.84 |
| 4¾ | 5-72 | 94.8 | 94.16 | 7.13 |
| 1½ | 10-72 | 84.24 | 85.24 | 6.93 |
| 1½ | 4-73 | 82.28 | 83.28 | 6.84 |
| 7¾ | 5-73 | 102.8 | 102.12 | 6.67 |
| 1½ | 10-73 | 81.6 | 82.6 | 6.72 |
| 1½ | 4-74 | 77.20 | 78.20 | 7.21 |
| 5⅝ | 8-74 | 93.24 | 94.0 | 7.12 |
| 1½ | 10-74 | 76.6 | 77.6 | 7.05 |
| 5¾ | 11-74 | 94.4 | 94.12 | 7.10 |
| 5¾ | 2-75 | 93.26 | 94.2 | 7.11 |
| 6 | 5-75 | 95.12 | 95.20 | 6.96 |
| 6¼ | 2-76 | 97.10 | 97.18 | 6.73 |
| 6½ | 5-76 | 97.14 | 97.22 | 6.94 |
| 7½ | 8-76 | 103.6 | 103.10 | 6.88 |

**Fig. 3–5** How United States Treasury notes are quoted. Reprinted by permission from *The Wall Street Journal*.

The second column (left to right) shows the maturity date of the note. The third and fourth columns indicates the "bid" and "asked" prices, respectively. The fifth, or right-hand column, shows the true interest rate you would earn on the note if you purchased it at the published "asked" price. Transactions with Treasury notes are similar to dealings with Treasury bills in that you buy at the "asked" price, and you sell at the "bid" price.

You should note that quotations printed in financial journals show what prices were on a particular trading day and not necessarily what you could buy or sell for today. Therefore, current quotes should be sought from your bank or investment broker. Further, you should note that journal quotations are based on very large transactions. Don't be surprised if your proposed buying or selling transaction cannot be made at quite so advantageous a price.

Treasury notes and treasury bills are negotiable. They should be kept, with your other securities, in a bank safety deposit box or other secure place. It is also suggested that you transact their exchange at a bank. If you should lose one of these instruments, a finder could cash them—and you would be poorer by a significant sum of money.

### SAFETY FOR YOUR SAVINGS—ONE MORE REMINDER

There are many safeguards and many supervisory agencies, state and federal, concerned with regulation and operation of financial institutions. Despite all the safeguards and regulations, four American banks were temporarily or permanently closed during 1969 as a result of financial difficulties. Unless deposits in those banks were insured, such failures could result in partial or complete loss of savers' money. In the 1930's a rash of banks and savings associations failed. These failures, and the subsequent public distrust of financial institutions, led to the formation of the Federal Reserve System and the Federal Deposit Insurance Corporation. All banks which are members of the Federal Reserve System are required to insure their deposits with the FDIC. Non-member banks may also be insured, provided they meet FDIC requirements and standards. What FDIC is to banks, the Federal Savings and Loan Insurance Corporation is to savings and loans. Qualifying savings and loan associations may insure their depositors' accounts with this organization.

Note the key words in the paragraph above. "Qualified." If an institution meets strict requirements for cash reserves, policies, and practices, it may qualify. "May." An institution which qualifies, *may* pay for and get the insurance for depositors, but it *might not*. So, however well qualified an institution may be, your savings in that institution still might not be insured. Check first. The third key word, which we've already partially defined is "federal." The FDIC; the FS&LIC; and the relative newcomer, the National Credit Union Administration, which insures qualified credit unions, are insured by the firm which has the greatest resources in the world, the taxing power of the United States Government. In terms of your savings account, of say $5,000, at an FDIC member institution, the resources backing the insurance on your account are millions to one.

### FEEDBACK 3

A. Consulting your local newspaper and available financial publications and magazines, find and clip five different advertisments of savings institutions. Neatly tape them to a sheet of paper so you can systematically analyze them.

● Which gives the highest yield?

● Is convenience (access to your account) a factor in any of the terms offered?

● Do any of the firms require that you leave your money in the account for an extended period? Which institution offers maximum safety for your money *and* highest yield? Use the computer-prepared data in Table 3–2 to assist in your analysis.

**B.** Assume (1) that you begin a savings program today; (2) that you immediately begin to work in your Chapter 1 choice of occupation after you graduate, starting at the salary you expect from your research in *Occupational Outlook*; and (3) that you save 10 percent of all earnings from today forward.

- If you save 10 percent of your current earnings until graduation, how much principal will you have in your account?
- When you begin to save 10 percent of your full-time job earnings, how does the picture change?

**C.** Using your savings program from B and 5 percent interest compounded annually, add your profits from interest paid—say for the next 10 years.

- Does your program begin to take off?
- Have you computed the effect of compounding?
- How soon will your interest earnings for a year be larger than one of your regular monthly deposits? (Not bad, getting 13 months' worth of payments to yourself for the price of 12!)
- To be even more realistic, and more profit minded, compute your account balance using the maximum insured safe yield available in your community.

**D.** Make a checklist for each of the available savings media in your area, including banks, savings and loan associations, credit unions, and industrial loan companies.

| Name | Insured safe? | Percent interest | Compounding frequency | Accessibility of funds | Convenience |
|------|------|------|------|------|------|
| Jones Bank | Yes | $5\frac{1}{2}$ | Semi-annually | Immediate | On way to school |

You should have other criteria, for your own convenience, like: Is two-way postage paid? What is the distance from home? What hours the medium is open, and so forth. If you answered *NO* to Insured safe, erase that institution from further consideration.

## DISCUSSION QUESTIONS

1. Should one buy now at today's lower prices if inflation will eat up the purchasing power of the dollar in the future? Why?
2. Should one have a fixed percentage of his income going into savings each month, no matter what his expenses may be for that month? Why?

3. Which is most important in saving money: Safety or rate of return for the money? Explain.

4. Why do savings certificates, subordinated notes, and certificates of deposit require large initial deposits of $500 and up?

5. What kind of saving device would be better than the Christmas Savings Club for those who want cash in December?

6. What advantages do the commercial banks have over the savings and loan associations? Disadvantages?

7. If the yield offered by either bond series has been a little less than the yield offered by savings and loan firms and credit unions, why have they become so popular?

8. What are some of the advantages to buying short-term Treasury bills and notes?

9. How do Treasury bills and notes differ? What are some of their similarities?

10. Can there ever be another crisis in the banking business as there was in the 1930's? Explain.

## CASE PROBLEM

Ralph Barnes is a college sophomore, and he is presently taking a personal finance course. After reading the chapter on "Savings and Savings Media" he made the following comment to a classmate:

"I don't think the author realizes how much it takes to go to college these days. I find I have to work at least 35 hours a week to keep my payments up and barely exist. In fact, my girl friend paid for the tickets to the last movie we attended. I've got $72 that goes for my Mustang payment every month. I owe over $80 at a clothing shop. And to top off the whole mess, I'm three months behind on my gas credit card. I could'nt even buy all the books I needed for my classes this semester. I know I sure can't save any money until I get out of college."

a) Discuss Ralph's financial status.

b) What do you see as his "real" problem?

c) Does he understand his own situation?

d) How would you describe his personality from what he says?

e) Is there anything he can do to improve his finances?

f) How should he proceed?

## SUGGESTED READINGS

American Savings and Loan Institute. *Savings and Loan Principles.* Chicago: American Savings and Loan Institute Press, 1965. 528 pp.

Kendall, Leon T. *The Savings and Loan Business; Its Purposes, Functions, and Economic Justification.* Englewood Cliffs, N.J.: Prentice-Hall, 1962. 173 pp.

Meyer, Martin, and Joseph M. McDaniel. *Don't Bank on It! How to Make up to 13% or More on Your Savings, All Fully Insured.* Lynbrook, N.Y.: Farnsworth, 1970. 210 pp.

Teck, Alan. *Mutual Saving Banks and Savings and Loan Associations: Aspects of Growth.* New York: Columbia University Press, 1968. 192 pp.

CHAPTER 4

## . . . AND PAY LATER
## (CHARGE ACCOUNTS, INSTALLMENT
## PURCHASES AND CREDIT CARDS)

Buying on credit has become a basic fact of life for most Americans. We enjoy its benefits daily, tending to forget—until the monthly statements rudely nudge us to reality—that besides being a wonderful convenience, credit buying is also instant debt. True, the benefits of credit buying are real, and very often the use of credit is desirable. However, the user should realize that lenders must cover substantial costs in running their business and must, of course, additionally make fair profits. Borrowers, if they are to have the convenience and utility of credit, must pay for these services. There are a few exceptions, a few important cost-free ways of using certain kinds of credit. This chapter discusses these possibilities as well as the regular credit purchases while Chapter 5 covers the subject of consumer borrowing.

Credit moves goods. Buyers who cannot afford refrigerators on a cash payment basis find that they can afford to buy them if they pay 24 or 36 "bite-size" monthly payments. Automobiles, appliances, furniture, home improvements, travel, clothes, you name it, almost everything that costs money can be purchased on installments today. Americans owe more than $127 billion in outstanding credit balances, and that does not include home or business loans. About one-fifth of that sum is owed on charge accounts and single-payment loans. The remainder is owed to financial institutions holding installment contracts. Using a rough figure of 200 million for the early 1970 American population, this means that every man, woman, and child in the country owes about $635 for credit purchases. It also means that Americans are paying more than $17 *billion* annually *in interest alone*. On a national scale, the interest accounts for more than 13 percent of the real purchase price of goods bought on credit. On the personal level, you should ask yourself every time you consider charging a purchase, "Is the convenience of not paying for this item now really worth the difference in the total cost when credit charges and interest are included?" In this chapter you will see more examples of this kind of trade-off decision making and you will learn how to avoid the added costs of credit buying.

There is genuine and appropriate national anxiety over high interest rates and other consumer finance affairs, such as unethical practices of lenders and the lack of adequate, understandable credit information. To appreciate why

"No, I haven't **forgotten you, Mr. Griggsby.**
I have your bill **right here in my file."**

Reprinted with permission of *The Wall Street Journal* (Cartoon Features Syndicate).

Congress, personal finance experts, and many others are so concerned about the use and misuse of credit, look at the case history of a young couple who recently came to the author seeking advice about their financial predicament:

The Martins (we will call them), Tom and Suzanne, were married four years ago, while both were going to college. Suzanne quit school and went to work to help Tom finish his last two years in engineering. Tom finished in the upper 25 percent of his class, and he has a responsible, well-paid position with a large structural steel firm. Suzanne still works full time.

Six months ago, they bought a new $35,000 home in a beautiful Houston, Texas, suburb. The house has seven rooms with a nice swimming pool and a sundeck adjoining their bedroom. Inside, it is furnished with everything the Martins want in the way of comfort and convenience—from plush carpet to original oil paintings. They drive a new Buick Riviera, give exciting parties, and go on exotic vacations every year. Both appreciate and buy stylish clothes. The Martins seem to "have it made." Their neighbors wonder, "How can they possibly do it?"

The Martins, sad to say, wonder the same thing. "How can we possibly do it?" The combination of unrestrained impulse buying and easily available credit have left the Martins in awkward, even frightening, financial difficulties. Letters and statements demanding immediate payment—usually in full—cram their mailbox daily. Suzanne says, "I dread answering the telephone when I come home at night; almost always it's some unpleasant person from a collection agency on the other end of the line." Finally, after months of problems and tension, they attempted to work out a budget, in the hope that it might solve their dilemma. They found that they had combined net income of $812.36; they had *fixed* monthly payments of $870.48; they had open charge accounts—immediately payable—of $1,132.00. The Martins presented the following sad details to the author for his advice:

The Martins' Finances

| Indebtedness | | Monthly payment | Monthly interest |
|---|---|---|---|
| Home mortgage: $33,000, 7½% | | | |
|   Principal and interest payment | $265.76 | | |
|   Insurance reserve | 9.05 | | |
|   Property tax reserve | 53.00 | | |
| | | $327.81 | $204.20 |
| Lease payment on Buick Riviera | | 165.00 | |
| Furniture and accessories: $3,376.00, 8% add-on interest, 36 months | | 116.28 | 22.51 |
| Carpeting: $1,807, 8% add-on interest, 60 months | | 40.66 | 10.54 |
| Draperies: $900, 8% add-on interest, 24 months | | 43.50 | 6.00 |
| Refrigerator, washer, drier: $706, 7% add-on interest, 36 months | | 23.73 | 4.12 |
| Loan from Mr. Martin's Credit Union: $1,200, 1% interest per month on unpaid balance, 24-month loan | | 62.00 | 12.00 |
| Department Store Revolving Charge Account: $300 (6-month payoff) 1½% interest per month | | 54.50 | 4.50 |
| Utilities: | | 37.00 | |
|   Total Fixed Payments | | $870.48 | |
| Landscaping Materials: $782.00, 30-day account, 1½% interest on monthly unpaid balance; all past due and payable | | $782.00 | 11.73 |
| Medical and Dental Bills: $165, 1% interest per month on unpaid balance; all due and payable | | 165.00 | 1.65 |
| Oil Company Charge Accounts: $185, 1½% per month on unpaid monthly balance; all due and payable | | 185.00 | 2.78 |
|   Total Open Accounts Immediately Payable | | $1,132.00 | |
|   Total Monthly Interest | | | $280.03 |

| | |
|---|---|
| Tony Martin's Take-Home Pay | $541.16 |
| Suzanne Martin's Take Home Pay | 271.20 |
| | $812.36 |

The Martins had realized, when they bought it, that their home, at $35,000 was probably more expensive than they could afford. But they desperately wanted it. Suzanne's parents had thought it was a good idea too, and had given them $800 to help out. Tom borrowed another $1,200 from his credit union to make the $2,000 down payment. Three home loan applications were turned down because the loan companies thought the necessary monthly payments were too steep for the Martins' income. Finally, a persistent real estate agent found a small mortgage company which was willing to lend Tom and Suzanne the money for their home, at $7\frac{1}{2}$ percent interest with only $2,000 down.

## WHY DEBT DILEMMAS?

This is a serious financial tangle for an unfortunate and unwise couple to get themselves into. Nearly 32 percent of their combined take-home income is committed to interest payments alone. The Martins limp along, juggling their payments, extending their indebtedness and their interest expense by making less than full payments on accounts. They may lose some of their possessions or property. They may even be forced into personal bankruptcy. Tom may have to get part-time work in addition to his regular job to save them from disaster. The mess they are now in could easily keep them financially strapped for the next 10 years.

The Martin case is more serious than most, but their predicament is not uncommon. How do credit difficulties, in general, come about? Perhaps the overabundance of credit cards, liberal mortgage policies, and easy terms of credit merchants give consumers a false sense of affluence. You already know some of the benefits of budgeting, but many people are not so farsighted—they do not keep accurate records of income and expense, they do not think carefully about their spending plans. Overindulgence in credit often comes about because of a lack of understanding of (1) how credit works, and (2) what credit costs. The Martins finally realized, from the ample proof offered by persistent creditors, that instant credit is nothing more than instant debt.

Certainly, there was a place for credit in the Martins' finances. Obviously, the impact should have been controlled much earlier in their situation. No one denies the value of increased buying power provided by credit. Consumer credit is a valuable financial tool, which can help provide more satisfaction and pleasure, for people who use it. In certain special situations, credit can even save money. To use credit judiciously and intelligently, the consumer must know the facts. This chapter was written to provide you with the facts you need know about credit purchasing, so that you can make the best, most sensible, use of your credit.

## TYPES OF CONSUMER CREDIT

Financing purchases which are beyond your immediate ability to pay for them, either through current income or savings, can be accomplished in either of two basic ways: (1) you can use the "sales" credit supplied by the store which sells the goods, or use a credit card; or, (2) you can arrange for a loan and borrow the funds for the purchase from a bank, credit union, or personal finance company. This chapter is concerned with the former. Chapter 5 considers consumer borrowing.

## OPEN CHARGE ACCOUNTS

One of the most common credit plans available is the "open charge" or "30-day account." Stores with these credit arrangements agree to sell merchandise or service to a customer—usually on the condition that payment be received for the purchase within 30 days after billing. Some dealers require formal application from credit customers, followed by a thorough credit investigation before opening a credit account. Other merchants, especially if they know the customer personally, will open a credit account with few or no questions asked.

The credit buyer often receives an identifying card which permits him to charge purchases at the card-issuing store. The buyer also receives a monthly statement or billing. Often, an upper limit is established, based on credit information from other accounts the buyer has used at other stores. Limits are also based on individual stores' policies, and determination of the prospective buyer's ability to pay for the credit extended.

Legally, the title to goods purchased on an open charge account generally passes to the buyer at the time of sale, rather than when the payment is made. The seller may take legal action against the buyer, for failure to pay, but the goods cannot be immediately repossessed, since they belong to the purchaser.

Careful budgeting is essential when using a 30-day account, to assure that your obligation is paid promptly and fully. When you use a 30-day account properly, you can benefit from several distinct advantages:

1. You can use the store's or seller's money, without interest or service charge, so long as your account is paid before the stipulated date.
2. You may be extended check-cashing privileges.
3. You may be given advance notice of sales, or be invited to special closed sales for charge customers only.
4. You will probably find that returns or refunds (generally, credits to your account) are easier for you than for a cash customer.
5. You can save the cost of writing many small checks and avoid the danger and inconvenience of carrying cash.

## REVOLVING CHARGE ACCOUNTS

These accounts merely modify and extend the convenience of a 30-day charge account. Many department stores have found that a large percentage of their customers are good credit risks, but are unwilling or unable to pay their 30-day accounts in full each month. For added convenience, merchants have substituted or added the revolving charge account.

Customers who use this kind of account agree to pay either (1) a specified fraction of an outstanding balance each month, say one-tenth to one-fourth, or

(2) a sliding-scale payment determined by the size of the account balance. For example, $10 for balances from $50 to $100; $15 for balances from $101 to $150; etc. Either way, interest ranging from 12 to 24 percent is charged on the unpaid portion. Here is how a revolving credit plan works for one representative family:

> The Cannons have revolving charge accounts at the Welton Department Store and at Sears, Roebuck and Company. On this month's statement from the department store, they have a balance of $210. Not desiring to pay the entire amount, they may, according to the terms of their contract, pay as little as one-sixth of the balance remaining each month. Therefore, a check of only $35 will keep their account in good standing at Welton's.
>
> The Sears statement shows an unpaid balance of $71. Being short of funds for the month, the family decides to make the smallest payment possible which, as you can see in Fig. 4–1, would be $10.

## OPTION CHARGE ACCOUNTS

These accounts are simply a combination of features of the 30-day and the revolving accounts. If a customer wishes to pay his entire balance before the stipulated deadline, no further interest is charged. If, however, he desires an extended repayment period, he may make a fractional payment and interest is charged on the balance remaining. The trend in sales credit plans is definitely toward this option system. Large oil companies, airlines, and retailers are readily adopting the more convenient features of option accounts. As the name indicates, you have discretion about repaying in full or making partial payments on your account. When you are billed for purchases against your option account, you should carefully consider the convenience of smaller payments against the cost (interest charged) for this convenience.

## INSTALLMENT CONTRACTS

The different charge plans described above are designed to help customers make relatively small purchases, using credit privileges for short periods of time. When more expensive items are purchased on credit, for longer periods of time, the merchant usually requires the customer to enter into a different type of agreement—an installment contract. Written for any length of time, from 6 months to 5 years, installment contracts are used mainly to finance purchase of "durables," such long-lasting goods as appliances, furniture, carpeting, drapes, and home-improvement projects.

Because of the amount of money involved, the seller ordinarily requires more credit information and exercises greater caution in extending the credit. Many merchants sell their installment contracts to a bank or finance company as soon as the sale has been made. To do this, they must be certain that the customer is considered creditworthy by the lending agency. After a contract has been sold, the consumer receives notice that his payments are to be made directly to the financial institution which purchased his installment contract.

## SEARS REVOLVING CHARGE SECURITY AGREEMENT

In consideration of Sears selling merchandise and services for my personal, family, or household use on my Revolving Charge Account, I agree to the following regarding all purchases made by me or on my Sears Revolving Charge Account Identification:

1. I have the privilege of a Charge Account, in which case I will pay the full amount of all purchases within 25 days from the date of each billing statement.
2. If I do not pay the full amount for all purchases within 25 days from the billing date of each statement, the following terms shall be in effect:
   (A) I will pay the deferred payment price for each purchase consisting of:
      (1) The cash price, and
      (2) A **FINANCE CHARGE** which will be the greater of a minimum charge of 50¢ (applied to Average Daily Balances of **$1.00** through **$33.00**) or an amount determined by applying a periodic rate of 1.5% per month **(ANNUAL PERCENTAGE RATE of 18%)** to the first **$500.00** of the Average Daily Balance (excluding any unpaid Finance Charge) and a periodic rate of 1% per month **(ANNUAL PERCENTAGE RATE of 12%)** on any part of the Average Daily Balance (excluding any unpaid Finance Charge) in excess of **$500.00.** The Average Daily Balance is determined by totaling the balance outstanding for each day throughout the monthly billing cycle and dividing the sum thereof by the number of days in the billing cycle. The balance outstanding for any given day is determined by adding to the previous day's ending balance (excluding any unpaid Finance Charge), any purchases or miscellaneous debits and subtracting therefrom any payments or miscellaneous credits. No **FINANCE CHARGE** will be assessed for a monthly billing period in which there is no previous balance or during which the payments and credits equal or exceed the previous balance.

(B) I will pay for merchandise and services purchased in monthly instalments which will be computed according to the following schedule:

| If the New Balance is: | | The Scheduled Monthly Payment Will Be: |
|---|---|---|
| $ .01 | 10.00 | $10.00 |
| 10.01 | 200.00 | 15.00 |
| 200.01 | 250.00 | 20.00 |
| 250.01 | 300.00 | 25.00 |
| 300.01 | 350.00 | 30.00 |

| If the New Balance is: | | The Scheduled Monthly Payment Will Be: |
|---|---|---|
| 350.01 | 400.00 | 30.00 |
| 400.01 | 450.00 | 35.00 |
| 450.01 | 500.00 | 40.00 |
| Over | $500.00 | 1/10 of New Balance |

I will pay each monthly instalment according to the schedule stated above upon the receipt of each statement. If I fail to pay any instalment in full when due, Sears may declare the entire balance due and payable and Sears may also repossess any merchandise for which Sears has not been paid in full.

(C) My monthly payment shall be applied on merchandise and services not fully paid for in the ratio that the cash price of each sale bears to the total cash price of all such sales. Ownership of the merchandise purchased on this account shall remain in Sears until I have paid the purchase price in full. I will not sell, transfer possession of, remove or encumber the property without the written consent of Sears. I have risk of loss or damage to merchandise. Upon my default, Sears may charge me reasonable attorneys' fees and court costs.

(D) Sears will send me a statement each month which will show my previous balance (last month's new balance), new balance, Average Daily Balance, scheduled payment, Finance Charge, purchases, payments and credits, the amount of my monthly instalment coming due, and a statement as to how the Average Daily Balance is determined.

(E) I have the right to pay my entire balance in full at any time without incurring a subsequent Finance Charge.

3. Sears is authorized to investigate my credit record and report to proper persons and bureaus my performance of this agreement. Upon demand, I shall return my Sears Revolving Charge Account Identification card to Sears.
4. Sears waives the right to retain or to acquire any lien arising solely by operation of law in real property used or expected to be used as my principal residence. This provision is not applicable to judgment liens.
5. The information furnished on my application is submitted to Sears for the purpose of obtaining credit, and I understand that Sears will rely upon this information in extending credit to me. I hereby certify that this information is true, correct and complete.

I understand that my Finance Charge and other credit terms will be based on my State of Residence. If I change my State of Residence, I will notify you, and you will provide me with a new agreement containing the Finance Charge and other terms applicable to my new State of Residence.

Signature_____    Date_____

Sears, Roebuck and Co. ("Sears") by _____

10898-031 (F15206) REV. 1-72  UTAH

**Fig. 4–1** Revolving charge account agreement. Before charge account privileges are extended, customers must agree in writing to the terms stipulated by the merchant. Courtesy of Sears, Roebuck and Co.

On installment purchases, a down payment, ranging from 10 to 40 percent of the selling price, is frequently required. The difference between the selling price and the amount of such a down payment, plus interest and other charges, is the amount which is financed. This contract amount is divided into a series of equal monthly payments or installments.

QUADRUPLICATE
(PURCHASER'S COPY)

CONDITIONAL SALE CONTRACT     Account No.................

The undersigned Seller hereby sells and the undersigned Purchaser hereby purchases subject to the terms and conditions hereinafter set forth, the following described property, to-wit:

| ITEM | QUANTITY | MAKE | MODEL | SERIAL NUMBER | DESCRIPTION OF EQUIPMENT | CABINET OR MOTOR NO. | SALES PRICE INC. SALES TAX IF SOLD FOR CASH |
|---|---|---|---|---|---|---|---|
| 1 | | | | | | | |
| 2 | | | | | | | |
| 3 | | | | | | | |
| 4 | | | | | | | |
| 5 | | | | | | | |
| 6 | Installation Charges | | | | | | |

| | |
|---|---|
| Total Price if sold for Cash | $ |
| Valued at | $ |
| Balance | $ |
| Cash Down Payment | $ |
| Balance | $ |
| Insurance | $ |
| Deferred Balance | $ |
| Time Price Differential | $ |
| Time Balance | $ |

LESS TRADE IN....................................

Purchaser **agrees** to pay the total time balance in................................each, ........................together with a reasonable .................equal monthly installments of $..................., commencing.........................19......., and such other sums as may become due payable on the same day of each month, commencing.........................19........, and such other sums as may become due under this contract. All payments shall be made in lawful money of the United States and shall be payable at The Continental Bank and Trust Company, Salt Lake City, Utah.

Installments remaining unpaid when due shall thereafter bear interest at the highest legal contract rate.

Purchaser acknowledges that he has been advised as to both cash price and time price of property, that he realizes the time price is greater than the cash price, and that he has elected to pay the time price.

1. Title to said property shall remain in the Purchaser until all sums due under this contract are fully paid. It is understood and agreed that this contract and the Seller's interest therein may be offered by the Seller to The Continental Bank and Trust Company for purchase, which bank shall succeed to all rights, privileges and remedies of the Seller. To induce said bank to accept such assignment the Purchaser hereby agrees and represents to such bank that such assignment shall be free of any and all defenses, set offs and counterclaims which the Purchaser may or may not have against the Seller.

2. Said chattels shall remain personal property and nothing shall prevent Seller from removing same, or so much thereof as Seller in its sole discretion may determine, from any premises to which they may be attached, upon any breach of this contract.

3. Purchaser agrees that he will not misuse, secrete, sell, encumber, remove, or otherwise dispose of or lose possession of said chattels nor permit any lien, encumbrance or charge against said chattels, and will be responsible for any loss or damage to said chattels.

4. In case of default by the Purchaser in any of his obligations under this contract; or if any levy or attachment is made or any proceeding in bankruptcy is instituted by or against the Purchaser or his property; or if any application for a receiver shall be made for Purchaser's business; or if the Seller shall at any time deem itself insecure or unsafe with respect to the amount owing hereunder; or should the property above described be in danger of misuse, confiscation or destruction, the entire balance shall, at the option of the Seller, without notice become due and payable immediately, and the Seller may proceed to collect such amount plus interest at the highest lawful contract rate; or may without notice or prior demand take possession of said property wherever found, all payments made by the Purchaser to be deemed to have been made for the use of said property and as liquidated damages for such default. The Seller resell said property so retaken, at public or private sale, and shall have the option to purchase said property at said sale. From the proceeds of any sale so made the Seller may deduct the expenses of retaking, repairing, storing and reselling said property including a reasonable attorney's fee, and apply the balance against the amount unpaid hereunder. Any surplus shall be paid to, and any deficiency shall be paid by the Purchaser, with interest at the highest legal contract rate. All rights of exemption and homestead laws are hereby waived by the Purchaser.

5. Any action to enforce payment shall not waive any of Seller's rights hereunder. Any indulgences granted Purchaser shall not constitute a waiver of any of Seller's rights. All rights and remedies hereunder are cumulative and not alternative.

6. Time is of the essence of this contract. If it becomes necessary for the delinquency of the Purchaser in making one or more payments, for the Seller to incur any expenses to restore this contract to good standing and remove such delinquency, then the Purchaser hereby agrees to pay such expenses so incurred, in addition to the principal indebtedness owing.

7. This contract constitutes the entire agreement; no waivers or modifications shall be valid unless written upon or attached hereto. There are no warranties express or implied, representations, promises, or statements in connection with the sale of the property described above except as may be set forth in manufacturer's current warranty applying, if any.

8. This contract shall apply to, inure to the benefit of, and be binding upon, the heirs, executors, administrators, successors and assigns of the respective parties, subject, however, to the above restrictions against assignments by Purchaser. Purchaser acknowledges the receipt of a true copy of this contract.

9. Purchaser further certifies that no side loan, or other extension of credit, exists, or is to be made, in connection with or to make the down payment hereinabove set forth in this Agreement.

Executed this........................day of.........................................................19..........

.........................................................  
Seller—Dealer's Name

By.........................................................  
    Sign Here

.........................................................  
Dealer's Address

.........................................................  
Purchaser

.........................................................  
Title

.........................................................  
Purchaser's Address—City and State

(ILD-168)

**Fig. 4–2** Conditional sales contract. On installment purchases, the customer is usually required to sign a conditional sales contract or a chattel mortgage.

The installment purchaser usually signs either a conditional sales contract, as shown in Fig. 4–2, or a chattel mortgage, or both. Title to the merchandise is retained by the seller or the company which owns the contract until payment is made in full. Under the terms of these contracts, the merchandise can be easily reclaimed or repossessed if the consumer fails to meet his part of the credit agreement. The customer receives copies of these agreements. Usually the customer also receives a book of coupons, or punched cards, or a payment record book to remind him of the amount and due date of his payments.

If it becomes necessary to repossess merchandise, the lender or merchant is obligated to resell the property, attempting to get a fair and reasonable price for it. In most states, any loss which the dealer sustains in reselling the goods — that is, the difference between the contract balance and the resale price — must be made up to the dealer by the original purchaser. This happens frequently, because used merchandise generally brings in only bargain prices. Sometimes, for the sake of customer good will, a merchant will write off the deficiency as a business loss, but this is the exception, not the rule.

Installment lenders quite rightfully insist that their contract terms are fulfilled by the people to whom they extend credit. To encourage regular payments of the agreed amount, installment contracts commonly assess a penalty or special charge for late payments. A grace period of a few days may or may not be allowed before such a penalty is imposed. Like each condition of any contract you sign, you should be thoroughly aware of any penalty clause and grace periods in that contract.

Fortunately for credit buyers, the majority of dealers offering installment credit plans are reputable businessmen. This majority, and the buying public, are injured by the relatively few businessmen who seek extra advantages or profits through muddy contracts, loaded with technical legal slush, in very small, hard-to-read print. Some of these undesirable terms that you should seek to avoid are:

*Add-on Clauses.* This type of clause permits the buyer to continue to purchase goods and add the cost of these additional items onto the initial contract. This practice can be very dangerous, since the add-on clause also permits the vendor to repossess *all*

**"Don't worry about that clause -- we've never
been able to understand it ourselves."**

Reprinted with permission of *The Wall Street Journal* (Cartoon Features Syndicate).

merchandise acquired under the contract. For example, if, over the years, eight items had been purchased under terms of the contract—and seven had been completely paid for—and only $1 was owed on the eighth item, all purchases could be repossessed if the buyer did not make the required payment. If you cannot avoid such a clause in a credit contract, be sure to pay off your original contract completely before making additional purchases. Then start over with a new contract.

*Wage Assignment or Garnishment Clauses.* This feature permits the seller to take, or *garnish* the wages of the buyer in case a payment is missed. Although the amount of a person's wages which can be garnished is now subject to Federal limitation under the Truth-in-Lending Law, it is still not advisable to sign a contract containing such a stipulation.

*Balloon Clauses.* In an effort to keep monthly payments at a lower and more attractive level, the balloon clause was developed. It calls for low monthly payments for most of the installments of a contract. The last or last several payments are larger than the earlier installments, often very much larger. Often, a buyer is forced to refinance the balance called for in the balloon payments—precisely what the unscrupulous lender had in mind.

*Acceleration Clauses.* This stipulation calls for the acceleration of payment if one payment is missed. Generally, all remaining monthly installments become immediately due and payable. If you are unable to pay this amount, the dealer has the legal right to repossess the merchandise.

Obviously, this short list does not exhaust the possibilities of unwanted credit terms; it does, however, point up the very real necessity of reading and understanding any contract that you sign.

## CREDIT CARDS

Pioneered by large oil companies, credit cards have multiplied in number and variety to the point that many Americans carry little if any cash. Consumers carry credit cards from airlines, travel agencies, hotel and motel chains, department stores, clubs, and financial organizations.

The greatest number of cards, and the most accepted cards, are those issued by the two giants of the credit card industry—*BankAmericard* and *Master Charge*. Bank of America owns the *BankAmericard*, and together with affiliate banks, offers services from coast to coast, as well as in England, Canada, and Japan. *Master Charge*, an organization of member banks, provides the same services on a smaller scale. American Express Money Cards have a set fee ($15 per year) but require incomes over $7,500 annually of their cardholders.

Some of the services, which have generated consumer enthusiasm for bank card credit are:

1. Participating merchants accept bank cards as if they were cash. Some cards provide interest-free, service-charge-free charges up to 30 days, much like an open charge account. Other plans impose fees and interest on the account from the day of purchase.

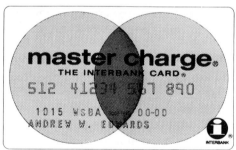

2. Cardholders may be allowed to run overdrafts on their checking accounts, being charged interest on the overdrawn amount until it is repaid.

3. Most bank cards allow automatic or semi-automatic cash loans. The cardholder can either write himself a check or go to a participating bank and ask for a cash advance.

4. Bank cardholders are usually protected by credit life insurance which repays any outstanding loan balance if a cardholder should die.

One thing appears certain: The bank credit card has become a permanent fixture in the American credit system. Doubtless, more and more consumers will become regular credit card users. It is possible that many of the different organizations offering credit card services will pool their resources and memberships to form fewer and larger, national credit card systems. The speed and extent of electronic data processing makes such mergers feasible.

Possession of a credit card, with a set amount of credit available, is not an invitation to immediately get yourself in debt to that extent. A credit card, like all your financial resources, should be used with wisdom, restraint, and judgment. In addition to purely budgetary considerations, a cardholder should safeguard his cards against loss or theft. Under recent Federal legislation, the owner of a card is now liable only for a maximum of $50 if the lost card is used fraudulently by someone else. However, you can avoid any loss by promptly notifying the credit card company. Wise credit cardholders keep a quadruplicate list of all cards in their name, indicating:

1. Account number.
2. Date issued and expiration date.
3. Name, address, and telephone number of office to be notified.

Both husband and wife should keep a copy of this list with them at all times. Another copy should be filed at home in a safe place, and still another copy should be entrusted to a close friend or relative who could provide the information should it ever be needed.

If loss through carelessness or theft should happen to your cards, immediately send telegrams to the companies involved giving all of the above information. Have Western Union send you a duplicate copy of the telegram for your records. When this is accomplished, air mail a registered follow-up letter to the companies, giving full particulars. Retain a carbon copy of the letter for your own file.

Some companies and banks offer insurance against charges made to any of your credit accounts as a result of loss or theft of credit cards. The price of this protection is low, and if you carry a lot of credit cards, such protection may be worth while.

## WHY CREDIT COSTS

State laws govern the interest and other fees which creditors may charge consumers. These laws vary considerably from state to state and the charges vary accordingly. Generally speaking, however, these are the approximate charges you can expect to pay for use of various credit schemes:

*Open, 30-day and Revolving Charge Accounts.* No credit charge if paid within 30 days; $1\frac{1}{2}\%$ per month thereafter—this is equivalent to 18 percent simple interest annually.

*Bank and other Credit Card plans.* $1\frac{1}{2}\%$ per month—18 percent simple interest—and sometimes additional fees like prediscounting cash advances.

*Installment Contracts.* $6\frac{1}{2}$ to $9\%$ add-on interest; 1 to $3\%$ interest per month; equivalent simple annual interest is 12 to 36 percent.

## HOW MUCH CREDIT CAN YOU AFFORD?

A great variety of formulas are available, each supposedly capable of accurately determining your upper credit limit. If you read four of these formulas, you would probably come up with four different limits for your credit capacity. You will be spared this exercise here, because it is of doubtful use, anyway. Some are better than others, but most of the so-called formulas are practically useless, and some are potentially dangerous.

For your credit use, you should not approach limit considerations by asking, "What is the absolute maximum I can buy, using credit?" If you are not now overextended with credit buying, perhaps a brief examination of relative costs will dissuade you from splurging in a needless and costly way. Creditors, who have their own businesses to promote, routinely recommend credit buying to "stretch" your budget. Personal finance companies and consumer finance companies even suggest installment purchase as an "excellent budgeting device." With illogical, but persuasive arguments, these firms suggest that if a person sets aside $12 per month for household improvements, this amount could quite appropriately be transferred to installment payments on a $180 television set, giving budget dollars a boost through credit. They do not mention the dollar and cents cost of such a budgeting decision, best shown by comparison:

*Consumer A* wants to buy a $180 black-and-white television set.

He puts $15 in his credit union each month for one year to save for his purchase. At year's end, he has $180.00 plus $6.02 interest, which he withdraws to make his purchase.

*Consumer B* also wants to buy a $180 black-and-white television set.

He decides that he cannot live without the set, so he buys it immediately on an 18-month installment contract, paying $12.40 monthly.

The total contract price for his set totals $223.20, or 24 percent more than the cash price.

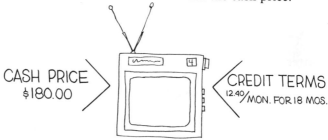

CASH PRICE
$180.00

CREDIT TERMS
12.40/MON. FOR 18 MOS.

Had Consumer B asked for a 36-month contract, as many people do, he would have paid $266.40 for his $180.00 television—*48 percent* more than the cash price.

Establishing formula limits for credit, and using credit for budgeting, are both unacceptable to any intelligent consumer who wants to achieve some degree of financial independence. If that sort of independence is one of your financial goals, it is simply impractical, unwise, and self-defeating to become ensnared by the "buy now–pay later" promotions which bombard all consumers through all communications media. Yielding to the temptation of credit purchasing means that you will have not more, but substantially less purchasing power because of the demands on your future budget made by high-cost financing charges. You have already seen the implicit trade-off: Before you buy on credit, you must determine the exact extra cost of financing the purchase. Then you must weigh this extra cost against the apparent value of immediate ownership of the item.

## A DOLLAR DELUSION

Many people who have investments and savings accounts consider themselves thrifty; yet, these same people may be paying out more in interest payments than their "thriftiness" is paying them! There is no net benefit, in fact, there is a net loss in worth, in earning 12 percent on $400 worth of stocks if the same stockholder is paying out 18 percent on a $400 department store balance. (Net loss = $24 per year.)

Consumers must be especially careful in using revolving charge plans. It is too easy to send in a minimum payment each month, then add more charges, perpetually carrying a $300 or $400 credit balance. Using credit in this way costs a lot. For example, such mismanagement means the loss of $50 to $70 every year in interest alone. Because credit buying is such a pervasive fact of consumer buying, many businesses capitalize and profit on their credit transactions—easily done, considering 18 percent potentially higher price of goods sold through credit.

## ESTABLISHING GOOD CREDIT

Credit bureaus are the information centers for the credit industry; they are located in every city of significant size throughout the country. Practically everyone who has ever made a credit purchase has a credit history on file in one or more of these bureaus, and is rated periodically on his credit performance.

Many credit bureaus are owned by community merchants; others are profit or non-profit businesses which sell credit information to subscribing firms. Most of the information in your credit file is supplied by cooperating merchants who have or expect to have an interest in your credit affairs. Many large firms use computers to make daily checks of all outstanding accounts, automatically classifying and rating their charge customers. Much of this information is passed along to credit bureaus in the marketing area. The bureaus, in turn, have interlinking arrangements with other credit checking agencies throughout the country, so that credit histories can be easily compiled on request.

Information which may affect a person's credit standing are routinely clipped from newspapers and dropped into the person's file. Samples of such information are arrests, garnishment, divorce, drunken driving convictions, and bankruptcies.

To the chagrin and bewilderment of many people, they have been summarily denied credit by a store or lending institution because of a poor credit report. More frequently than not, they have also been denied information as to "why" credit was refused. Without access to the credit files, the consumer could not hope to correct inaccurate or misleading information.

This is no longer the case. Under the Fair Credit Reporting Act,* a Credit Bureau is obligated to disclose to you the nature and substance of your credit file. An agency may make a charge for such a disclosure. Currently many credit bureaus are charging as much as $25. However, the charges will be monitored by the Federal Trade Commission (FTC), and they have indicated that they would not permit prohibitively high costs. If, within the previous 30 days, you have been denied credit or insurance, or the cost for insurance has been increased, disclosure of the files must be made to you without charge. If you find inaccuracies in the file, you have the right under the new law to submit your side of a disputed issue; and that side must be included in subsequent credit reports. Additionally, all data over seven years old must be expunged from the records. Record of Bankruptcies are deleted after 14 years. Black lists of people with poor credit ratings are against the law. Commonly, lists of people who have filed for bankruptcy have been circulated. Now such lists are illegal if sold to credit bureaus or other firms that would use the information in deciding whether to grant credit, insurance, or employment.

Superficially, it might seem that credit bureaus infringe on our privacy by keeping such detailed "personal" data. A little reflection will indicate that credit bureaus do a great deal of good for our society and our economy: First, if a person has not abused his credit, it is obviously to his advantage to have the services of an agency which can attest to his good record. Second, it would not be possible to extend credit so readily, if reliable information were not available. Third, credit agencies operate so efficiently that our credit can usually be cleared in a matter of minutes to facilitate purchasing. Fourth, the business sector can use credit ratings as indicators of trustworthiness for prospective employees. Fifth, and most important, a good credit rating is a valuable asset which can give us substantial reserve buying power when we need it most.

To build a good credit reputation, you must:

1. Make sure that your payments reach the company before the closing date for your account. Most firms use "cycle-billing" according to the alphabetical order of your last name. The date due of your payment may vary from firm to firm for this reason.

2. Be sure that your payment covers the amount due. This is no problem with

---

* This act became effective April 25, 1971.

installment payments, which are uniform amounts. You may have to do a bit of figuring with revolving accounts, where the amount might vary.

3. Notify the firm whenever you change address, or leave town for an extended period of time.

4. Accelerate the payment of your account whenever possible. Early fulfillment of credit obligations is a plus sign on your credit rating.

## WHAT TO DO WHEN PAYMENTS CAN'T BE MADE

The best of plans and the best of intentions can be disrupted by events outside the control of a credit buyer. Strikes, serious illness, investment losses, or layoffs in industry could result in an inability to meet one's credit obligations. In such cases, what can a person do to keep his credit rating?

There are no hard-and-fast rules covering all situations to apply to payment difficulties. Much depends on the seriousness of a particular problem, and whether that problem is of long- or short-term duration. Nevertheless, here are some general guides, useful in most payment crises:

1. Never let a payment become overdue without explaining to the firm involved what has happened. If the account is at a local company or store, call the credit manager and give the full details. For credit accounts with more distant companies, it is best to write a letter of explanation. Be sure to include your account number in all communications, because nearly all accounting is done by computers which require such numbers to identify accounts.

2. If possible, make at least a partial payment. Let the company know your long-term prospects, and when you anticipate being able to bring your account up to date.

3. Never ignore letters or telephone calls inquiring about your account. Most companies will be willing to extend reasonable cooperation if they have full information from you.

4. If your situation is critical, you may have to consider a consolidation loan. These loans combine the balances of several outstanding accounts into one long-term loan and one overall lower monthly payment. This step should be avoided if at all possible, since you merely push the final repayment date further into the future with consequent higher interest costs. Part of the amount financed is already interest charges; refinancing means paying interest on interest. Only the most distressing or exceptional problems should be attacked by the consolidation method.

## TRUTH-IN-LENDING LEGISLATION

The rising American interest in consumerism, with concurrent attention to consumer finance, led the 90th Congress to enact the Consumer Credit Protection Act. In essence, the law responds to two problems of consumer credit: (1) Most people do not understand the provisions of credit contracts, and (2) people do not have adequate recourse to computer oriented credit institutions. Commenting on the need for this legislation before the House of Representatives, Congressman Wright Patman of Texas said:

> "Significant segments of the population are misled by the manner in which the terms and conditions are offered and contracted for, as well as by the manner in which credit is advertised. Misleading practices engaged in by a minority of unscrupulous merchants and lenders fail to adequately disclose the credit terms offered to buyers in making purchases or in obtaining loans. This failure of adequate disclosure tends to increase the uninformed and untimely use of credit by the public, adversely affecting economic stabilization, increasing inflationary pressures, and decreasing the stability and the value of our currency."*

The bill should encourage consumers to use credit with more care and more responsibility, especially when it becomes obvious that the highest rates of interest in a century mean that credit buying is correspondingly more expensive. A law by itself will not stop the almost childish appetites of some consumers for luxuries they cannot afford, nor will it stop credit addicts from pursuing their expensive habits. The law was designed to spotlight the true costs of credit, and it succeeds—so that credit buyers can at least be forewarned about the added expenses they are contracting for.

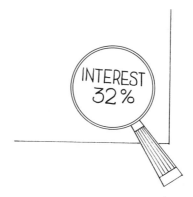

This act makes sweeping changes in most creditors' practices, requiring that written disclosure of loan facts be given before credit transactions are made. It also sets up standards to prevent misleading advertising, limits the garnishment of wages for debt payments, makes it a Federal offense to engage in loansharking, and sets up a national committee to make a comprehensive study of consumer finance activities.

---

* Congressman Patman, *Congressional Record—House*, Volume 114, Part 2, 90th Congress, January 30, 1968, p. 1426.

**Effect of the law on charge and revolving credit accounts.** Department stores, large mail-order houses, and other retailers lobbied vigorously to exclude charge and revolving credit from provisions of the Truth-in-Lending Law. But, because of the magnitude of such credit, plus its rapid growth and high cost, Congress overwhelmingly favored its inclusion. The creditor must now provide you with the following information before you open an account with him:

1. The conditions under which a finance charge may be imposed on your account, including the time period, if any, within which any credit extended may be repaid without incurring a finance charge.

2. The method of determining the balance upon which a finance charge will be imposed.

3. The method of determining the amount of the finance charge, including any minimum or fixed amount imposed as a finance charge.

4. Where one or more periodic rates may be used to compute the finance charge, each rate, the range of balances to which it is applicable, and the corresponding annual percentage rate determined by multiplying the periodic rate by the number of such periods in a year, must be given. In effect, this means that both a monthly and a yearly rate must be given. The latter rate is the most informative "True Annual Percentage Rate," which shows the cost of maintaining the terms of the credit contract for one year.

5. The conditions under which any other charges may be imposed (late fees, etc.) and the method by which they will be determined.

6. The conditions under which the creditor may retain or acquire any security interest in any property to secure the payment of any credit extended. (A Chattel Mortgage would be one example.)

Before the law was enacted, it was common practice for some creditors to print vague explanations of their credit terms, like:

> Dreamland's ABC Credit Plan is as simple as ABC. Come to Dreamland, the beautiful Department Store. Buy it, charge it—easily, swiftly.

> Pay your account before your next billing date, with no charge for credit, or take time to pay—pay one-fourth or more of your account each month, or pay your account in full at any time. If you take time to pay, Dreamland will add a small monthly charge for credit.

You can be absolutely certain that the small charge referred to here is not really so small; it was more than likely the quite large $1\frac{1}{2}$ percent per month, or 18 percent annual interest rate. Not only did creditors fail to show interest rates on their statements, but also they did not show how the charges were computed —whether the charges were based on the previous month's balance or the current month's balance. Additionally, the consumer was left in the dark about whether interest was computed before or after payments for the current month had been credited.

Present monthly or periodic statements must contain very detailed information. With every statement showing the outstanding balance on which a finance charge is imposed, the creditor must also clearly state the following:

1. The outstanding balance in the account at the beginning of the statement period.

2. The amount and date of each extension of credit during the period, and, if a purchase was involved, a brief identification (unless previously provided) of the goods or services purchased.

3. The total amount credited to the account during the period, either in payments or returned merchandise credit.

4. The amount of any finance charge added to the account during the period, itemized to show the amounts, if any, due to the application of percentage rates and the amount, if any, imposed as a minimum or fixed charge.

5. Where one or more periods may be used to compute the finance charge (for example, the usual $1\frac{1}{2}$ percent per month), each such rate, the range of balances to which it is applicable, and the corresponding annual percentage rate determined by multiplying the periodic rate by the number of such periods in a year.

6. Where the total finance charges exceed 50 cents for a monthly or longer billing cycle, or the prorated part of the total exceeds 50 cents for a billing cycle which is shorter than monthly, the total finance charges must be expressed as an annual percentage rate.

7. The balance on which the finance charge was computed and a statement of how the balance was determined. If the balance is determined without first deducting all credits during the period, that fact and the amount of such payments shall also be disclosed.

8. The outstanding balance in the account at the end of the period.

9. The date by which, or the period within which, payment must be made to avoid additional finance charges.

**How installment contracts and loans are affected.**    No longer can lenders hide the true simple interest costs of installment contracts or loans by quoting only a monthly, discount, add-on, or other deceptive or misleading rate *and* a separate list of fees and expenses.

The law says that "the amount of the finance charge in connection with any consumer credit transaction shall be determined as the sum of all charges . . . including any of the following types of charges which are applicable:"

1. "Interest, time-price differential, and any amount payable under a point, discount, or other system of additional charges.

2. "Service or carrying charge.

3. "Loan fee, finder's fee, or similar charge.

4. "Fee for an investigation of credit rating.

5. "Premium or other charge for any guarantee or insurance protecting the creditor against the buyer's default or other credit loss. (Unless the insurance is not a factor in the approval by the creditor of the extension of credit, and this fact is clearly disclosed in writing to the person applying for or obtaining credit.)"

Excepting first mortgages for home-purchase loans, the total dollar amount of the finance charge, as well as the "effective annual simple interest rate" must be provided by the creditor.

Very small loans or installment contracts are exempt from the annual simple interest rate disclosure provision if the finance charge (a) does not exceed $5, and is applicable to an amount financed not exceeding $75, or, (b) does not exceed $7.50 and is applicable to an amount financed exceeding $75. A full disclosure *is* required (total dollars, as well as interest rate) for first mortgages used for purposes other than buying a home, and for all second mortgages for any purpose.

The restrictions and regulations above may lead you to believe that all information about your credit costs will be made available to you in terms of effective annual interest. There are some exceptions, and they could be expensive. Lenders who secure their loans with real estate *may* pass certain costs on to the borrower *without* including them in the effective annual interest rate. These are:

1. Fees or premiums for title examination, title insurance, or other similar purposes.

2. Escrows (money held in trust) for future payments of taxes and insurance.

3. Fees for preparation of a deed, settlement statement, or other documents.

4. Fees for notarizing deeds and other documents.

5. Appraisal fees and credit reports.

**Restrictions on garnishment.** Congressional leaders believed that there was a strong connection between the increasing rate of personal bankruptcies (see Chapter 5) and the harsh garnishment laws in many states. A garnishment is a device to seize part or all of a worker's earnings to satisfy debt(s). The law set an upper limit on the percentage of earnings which could be attached through garnishment. Garnishment cannot now exceed 25 percent of a person's disposable weekly income (gross earnings, *less* all required tax deductions), or the amount by which a wage earner's disposable earnings exceed the equivalent of a month's pay based on the Federal minimum wage, whichever is less. The law also forbids discharging an employee because his earnings have been garnished to satisfy any one indebtedness. It had been a common practice to fire any employees whose wages were garnished—regardless of the amount or the cause of garnishment. Losing a job while already experiencing credit difficulties, tended to make those difficulties even greater.

......................................................................................... Date:.............................
NAME OF CUSTOMER

**Notice To Customer Required By Federal Law:**

**You have entered into a transaction on ............................................. which**
(DATE)

may result in a lien, mortgage, or other security interest on your home. You have a legal right under federal law to cancel this transaction, if you desire to do so, without any penalty or obligation within three business days from the above date or any later date on which all material disclosures required under the Truth in Lending Act have been given to you. If you so cancel the transaction, any lien, mortgage, or other security interest on your home arising from this transaction is automatically void. You are also entitled to receive a refund of any downpayment or other consideration if you cancel. If you decide to cancel this transaction, you may do so by notifying

**Name** ...................................................................................

**Address** ...............................................................................

.........................................................................................

**by mail or telegram sent not later than midnight of ............................. You may**
(DATE)

also use any other form of written notice identifying the transaction if it is delivered to the above address not later than that time. This notice may be used for that purpose by dating and signing below.

**I hereby cancel this transaction.**

.................................................................       .................................................................
(DATE)                                                        (CUSTOMER'S SIGNATURE)

EFFECT OF RESCISSION. When a customer exercises his right to rescind under paragraph (a) of this section, he is not liable for any finance or other charges, and any security interest becomes void upon such a rescission. Within 10 days after receipt of a notice of rescission, the creditor shall return to the customer any money or property given as earnest money, downpayment, or otherwise, and shall take any action necessary or appropriate to reflect the termination of any security interest created under the transaction. If the creditor has delivered any property to the customer, the customer may retain possession of it. Upon the performance of the creditor's obligations under this section, the customer shall tender the property to the creditor, except that if return of the property in kind would be impracticable or inequitable, the customer shall tender its reasonable value. Tender shall be made at the location of the property or at the residence of the customer, at the option of the customer. If the creditor does not take possession of the property within 10 days after tender by the customer, ownership of the property vests in the customer without obligation on his part to pay for it.

WE ACKNOWLEDGE RECEIPT OF TWO COPIES OF THIS STATEMENT

All Buyers:.......................................................... Date:.......................

.......................................................... Date:.......................

**Fig. 4–3** Rescission statement. Under provisions of the new Truth-in-Lending Law, the purchaser may cancel within three business days any credit transaction which may result in a lien, mortgage, or other security interest on the home; and the seller must return any down payment or other consideration he may have received from the purchaser.

Figure 4–3 illustrates another important feature of the Truth-in-Lending Law. Under the new code, you now have three days within which you may cancel any credit transaction which may result in a lien, mortgage, or other security interest on your home. Assume, for example, that you were approached by a salesman selling home improvements—in this instance a new roof for your house. You signed a loan agreement with him for $3,500 for the job. After he leaves, you decide to do some checking on the home improvement company. The information you get is unfavorable. All you need to do is to fill out a rescission statement which should have been supplied by the salesman at the time you signed the loan agreement. You can then mail this to the home improvement company or the bank handling the loan. If you do not have a rescission statement, you can merely notify them by mail or telegram that you are cancelling the transaction. Any downpayment made under the sale will be refunded you.

**Regulation of credit advertising.** Generally speaking, the law prohibits any credit advertising which would mislead the public. The familiar come-on, "Only $10 down and small monthly payments . . ." is no longer tolerated. If any mention is made in an advertisement of down-payments, monthly payments, finance charges, or number of payments—then all the credit data must be given. The law does not prevent very general terms like, "Credit available," which avoid detail completely.

**Extortionate credit transactions.** Extortion—the threat or use of physical force to secure payment—is one of the favorite techniques of loan sharks. The law includes stiff penalties for extortionists. This portion of the law will be discussed more fully in Chapter 5.

**Some states may exempt themselves from the law.** The Truth-in-Lending Law is enforced by the Board of Governors of the Federal Reserve Board, who delegate appropriate portions to agencies which already regulate the activities of particular kinds of creditors. States which now have or will adopt adequate truth-in-lending laws and enforcement may, at the discretion of the Board of Governors, be exempted. This means that the laws of exempt states are considered equal to, or better than, the provisions of the Federal law.

The Truth-in-Lending Law is primarily a law governing disclosure of credit terms. Naturally, this is valuable to consumers, enabling them to make informed decisions about credit buying. There are innumerable additional aspects of credit which the law does not cover, however. Especially pertinent is the lack of national standards which apply to all states. The present credit laws vary widely among the states, and to coordinate and regulate consumer credit throughout the country is the purpose of the proposed Uniform Consumer Credit Code (UCCC). As proposed, the code would unify and regulate practically all forms of consumer credit. Perhaps most importantly, it would set limits on the amount of interest or other finance charges. It would regulate credit practices of small businesses, retail installment sales, and outside sales organizations. Credit insurance, garnishment, and other provisions of existing law would be standardized.

Proponents of the UCCC hold that it offers a way out of the confusing tangle of state laws. As envisioned by its sponsors, the code would be adopted individually by states, based on the model devised by the National Conference of Commissioners on Uniform State Laws. Until it is adopted by a significant number of states, it will not have the intended force of law—currently, it is law in two states, mainly because their then-existing laws were consistent with the code before adoption.

### MONEY-SAVING TIPS ON SALES CREDIT

Remember that any number of laws will not prevent you from making bad and expensive buying decisions. Truth-in-Lending merely informs you about the cost of particular decisions; it does not regulate against willful and irresponsible buying decisions which might endanger your credit rating. How you use the information available to you is still your responsibility. Here are some guidelines to avoid credit headaches.

1. Many high-cost items are subject to impulse credit buying, when they might more appropriately be rented. Take, for instance, the homeowner who suddenly needs to drill a hole through the concrete foundation of his house. Should he spend $45 or more for a heavy-duty drill and bit for the job? Chances are, he will not use the drill again for another year or even longer. He would be much better off to rent the drill for $4 or $5.

2. Many furniture and appliance dealers offer 90 days of free credit with purchases. Some dealers offer up to one year at no additional charge. Naturally, you must compare total prices, including finance costs elsewhere, to determine if you save by buying at a particular store. Obviously, consumers pay for credit, "free" or otherwise; but large-volume dealers can minimize their bookkeeping expenses per item sold, and pass their relative savings along to customers.

3. If you must use an open- or 30-day charge account, time your purchase so that you can avoid all finance charges. On a 30-day account, you can get almost two full months of free credit by making your purchases a day or two after the "closing" date of your billing period. You will then receive a bill for your purchase about 28 days later and still have another 30 days within which to make payment without incurring any finance or service charges.

4. Learn to accept reasonable, and affordable substitutes for your consumer wants. If your finances will not permit a two-week vacation to Bermuda, take a camping trip or other budget vacation. You may have just as much fun for a lot less money. The alternative choice of charging the expensive

trip may give you monthly budget problems, instead of pleasant memories.

5. As assistance in acquiring some of your major household items, like carpeting, refrigerator, washer, dryer, etc., an occasional installment purchase may be warranted. You should make a substantial down payment, regardless of the minimum required, and limit the terms and duration of the contract. Shop around, too; compare total charges and total price including credit costs.

6. Even if you are able to pay cash for major appliances, it is a good idea to put them on a 30-day interest-free charge contract to make sure that the store or dealer will take care of any service or warranty problem that may arise when an appliance is first put in service.

7. Try to imagine how much any purchase will mean to you when you are still paying for it 6 months or 36 months from now.

## FEEDBACK 4

A. Obtain credit applications from three of your favorite department stores. On these should be plainly stated the information about credit costs required by the Truth-in-Lending Law. Compare the terms of credit offered by each.

- Is there an advantage, in true annual simple interest, to buying from one of these stores, rather than the others?

Prepare a small chart, to compare the relative merits of the credit offered by your favorite stores. Which store

- Pays postage both ways?
- Holds special sales for credit customers? (Remember that a sale is also an opportunity to spend money.)
- Bills on current, rather than past month's balance?
- Offers the most favorable billing date, with respect to your budget? Your paydays?
- Consistently offers the lowest prices for comparable goods (if all credit provisions are alike—often the case, because businesses tend to charge the maximum allowed by law in a community)?

B. Shop, without necessarily buying, for the next three "wants" on your short-term budget. For comparable goods:

- Which store offers the lowest prices?
- Which offers the lowest overall price, credit charges included, per your investigation above? (i.e., price of goods + cost of credit = total price).
- What would be the net benefit of using reserve funds—non-emergency savings—for buying the goods you want? (i.e., total price above − cost of goods = net benefit of cash purchasing = money you can spend elsewhere).

**C.** Use 20 percent, or one-fifth, as the "rule of thumb" cost of a retail charge account. This may be a little high, but adding in postage, the impulse buying of higher-priced goods, and so on makes 20 percent a useful approximation of the real cost in dollars of credit buying. List ten of your "near future" wants, their cash price, the cost of credit purchase. The first price (cash) is the cost of eventual ownership. The second is the price of immediate ownership. Compare the two; is that pair of shoes worth $4 more than the eventual ownership price?

|     | Item | Cash price | Price for immediate ownership |
| --- | --- | --- | --- |
| 1. | Shoes | $ 20 | $ 24 |
| 2. |  |  |  |
| 10. |  |  |  |

**D.** Assemble, from your records, bills and statements from the last three months. Be sure to include all statements from credit card firms, all installment statements, and charge account billings. Add the interest charges.

● What amount of interest have you paid in the last three months?

● What is your projected sum for one year? (three months × 4).

● What percentage of your income are you spending on interest?

● How many hours per week are you working just to pay interest?

● If you are buying a home, include the interest you pay on your mortgage. Recompute the answers you found in the items above.

● Does interest play too large a role in your budget? What steps can you take to lessen its impact?

**DISCUSSION QUESTIONS**

1. In what ways can the use of personal credit be advantageous? Disadvantageous?

2. What areas of business get the bulk of credit sales? Explain.

3. Why should one avoid an add-on clause? How can it be avoided?

4. Should a seller be allowed to add garnishment clauses to his credit contracts? Why?

5. Why have credit cards become the American "buyers' friend"? Are they overused? Explain.

6. What advantages do the bank cards have over cash? What advantages are there to cash over bank cards?

7. How can sellers prevent fraudulent use of credit cards? Does more action in preventing this kind of use need to be made? Explain.

8. Should buyers who use strictly cash be considered poor credit risks? Explain.
9. Should black lists of people with poor credit ratings be legal?  Why?
10. Has the Truth-in-Lending Law been too "hard" on businesses which provide credit?  Explain.

## CASE PROBLEM

States which now have or subsequently enact credit controls on a par with the Federal Truth-in-Lending Law may be exempted from it.  There is a reason to believe that many state legislatures will adopt the Uniform Consumer Credit Code proposed by the National Conference of Commissioners on Uniform State Laws.  For one thing the UCCC is even more restrictive than the Federal Law but, more importantly, states seem interested in adopting this code to bypass Federal credit controls.

a) Do you think Federal or State legislation can best regulate creditors and provide the protection consumers need?
b) Even though the UCCC may be more restrictive, do you think states would enforce such a law uniformly?
c) What effect do you suppose the Truth-in-Lending legislation or the new UCCC will have on lending activity?  Will consumers still continue to borrow and spend at record paces once they really know how much interest they are paying for credit?

## SUGGESTED READINGS

"All About Credit," *Changing Times*.  Washington, D.C.: March 1963.  16 pp.

American Industrial Bankers Association.  *An Explanation of the Consumer Credit Protection Act of 1968 and Regulation Z*.  Washington, D.C.: 1968.  30 pp.

American Institute of Banking.  *Installment Credit*.  New York: 1964.  378 pp.

Chapman, John Martin, and Robert P. Shay.  *The Consumer Finance Industry: Its Costs and Regulation*.  New York: Columbia University Press, 1967.  183 pp.

Cheyney, William J.  *Using Our Credit Intelligently*.  Washington, D.C.: National Foundation for Consumer Credit, 1963.  54 pp.

Clontz, Ralph C.  *Truth-in-Lending Manual: Forms and Procedures for Compliance with Federal Truth-in-Lending Law and Regulation Z*.  Boston: Hanover Lamont Corp., 1969. 214 pp.

*Consumer, Beware!: A Guide to Installment Buying*.  Washington, D.C.: AFL-CIO, 1966. 12 pp.

*Consumer Credit Calculator*.  Manhattan: Kansas State University, 1967.

Farnsworth, Clyde.  *No Money Down*.  New York: MacFadden-Bartell, 1963.  157 pp.

Fetterman, Elsie.  *Credit Cards: Thirty Days to Reality*.  Storrs, Conn.: University of Connecticut.  20 pp.

Giles, John LaMar. *Full Disclosure of Interest to the Consumer.* Salt Lake City: University of Utah, 1962.  55 pp.

Gregory, Brit Alan. *The Truth in Lending Bill: An Analysis of the Basic Issues: Potential Economic Impact.* Salt Lake City: University of Utah, 1965.  73 pp.

McCracken, Paul Winston, James C. T. Mao, and Cedric Fricke. *Consumer Installment Credit and Public Policy.* Ann Arbor: Bureau of Business Research, Graduate School of Business Administration, University of Michigan, 1965.  250 pp.

Moore, Geoffrey Hoyt, and Phillip A. Klein. *The Quality of Consumer Installment Credit.* New York: National Bureau of Economic Research, Columbia University Press, 1967.  260 pp.

Morr, Wallace Peter. *Consumer Credit Finance Charges: Rate Information and Quotation.* New York: National Bureau of Economic Research, distributed by Columbia University Press, 1965.  133 pp.

Thompson, Norman Samuel. *The Measurement of Consumer Credit Knowledge.* Greely: Colorado State College, 1965.  160 pp.

Walker, Courtenay, J., Larry Allen, and Brooks H. Talley. *Consumer Credit Plans: Revolving Credit, Credit Cards, Check Credit.* Frankfort, Ky.: Legislative Research Commission, 1969.  446 pp.

CHAPTER 5

# CONSUMER BORROWING: RENTING MONEY

As discussed in Chapter 4, charge and installment credit can be used to buy almost anything. When the available credit sources will not serve consumer purposes, most Americans find it easy enough to borrow cash—if they are willing to pay the going interest rate, and they are convinced their budgets can bear the burden of the added payments.

Borrowed money has a mysterious quality about it; with "extra" cash, borrowers feel wealthier. But considering the costs borrowers have incurred, they are actually poorer in dollars which they can spend without restraint. Compulsive borrowers, finding that their earlier credit obligations make a mess of their budgets, borrow *more* money to avoid the harsh reality that they are in debt, and getting deeper in debt. No one has yet devised a system to borrow his way out of debt.

**"Sorry we couldn't do business but you'll have to admit,
we had a good laugh."**

Reprinted with permission of *The Wall Street Journal* (Cartoon Features Syndicate).

The number of borrowers, the amounts borrowed, and the variety of reasons for borrowing money are all increasing. Americans borrow to consolidate and refinance existing obligations, to pay rent, for car repairs, for gifts, for automobile purchases, for home improvements, even for groceries. Some borrow so as not to upset equities in insurance, homes, and other assets. Some borrow to pay for travel and vacations. Still others borrow to pay tuition and other college expenses, or to provide themselves additional technical or professional training. All such loans—for worthy or ill-considered purposes—are generally referred to as "consumer loans." The Federal Reserve System also refers to them as "short- and intermediate-term loans." Such loans are usually small in amount, and repaid relatively quickly. "Mortgage loans" are an important source of funds for home purchases, but, since they differ in many ways from consumer loans, they are considered separately in Chapter 8, "Renting, Buying, Building."

With more than $127 billion in consumer debt outstanding, you would think that the average debtor would be knowledgeable about handling credit. After all, it is his money that is owed. Unfortunately, the average consumer's borrowing IQ has not improved nearly as fast as his indebtedness. Americans still borrow carelessly and unnecessarily, achieving a lower, not higher, standard of living. Inexperience with standard loan procedures, alternative lending sources, and lender's expectations cause widespread debtor embarrassment, resentment, and bitterness; *and* it costs them money. This chapter is designed to spare you unpleasantness in borrowing money by outlining the sources, costs, and requirements of several kinds of consumer loans.

### CREDIT CHECK: YOUR ABILITY TO REPAY CASH LOANS

Before a bank or other financial organization will lend you money, the loan officer must have considerable assurance that the money will be repaid. Not every institution has the same requirements; but, generally speaking, they will be looking for the answers to four key questions:

1. What sort of person are you, the prospective borrower? The character—trustworthiness, reliability—of the borrower comes first. The next consideration is your ability to manage your finances.

2. What are you going to do with the money? The answer to this question will determine whether or not you have a legitimate need for the money, and what type of loan will best suit your particular situation. This question is especially important for first-time borrowers; subsequent loans to the same borrower—provided he has met his prior obligations—will be based less on this "use" standard.

3. When and how do you plan to pay off the loan? The lender will want to know if your earnings, weighed against your other credit obligations, makes repayment feasible.

4. What equity (portion of the property to be purchased) and other assets do you personally own which might be pledged as security for the loan? Sometimes, if you have an excellent credit rating or previous transactions with a firm, your signature may be the only security required.

### KINDS OF LOANS

The finance industry usually classifies loans as either *secured*, meaning that some form of property or valuable (called collateral) is pledged to ensure payment, or *signature*, meaning that the lender depends solely on the character and credit rating of the borrower for repayment assurance. Loans are also classified as *installment*, to be repaid in two or more payments, and *noninstallment*, to be repaid in one lump sum. Noninstallment loans are more difficult to obtain, and lenders often insist on some form of collateral.

### COLLATERAL AND OTHER FORMS OF SECURITY

Even when a signature loan is obtainable, you might want to pledge collateral in order to get a lower-cost loan. Small loan companies and credit unions usually have fixed interest terms, which means that you can take what is offered, or leave it. Even these institutions differentiate somewhat; like the different rates offered for new cars as opposed to the rate for used cars. Banks will negotiate the terms of their loans, although they are reluctant to admit it. There may be occasions when the lender requires assurance beyond your signature and credit references that the money loaned will be repaid. The form of this assurance or collateral will vary depending on the lender's policies and the borrower's situation. The following kinds of collateral and assurances are generally acceptable to lenders:

**Real estate.**  Building lots, recreational property, buildings, homes, warehouses, apartments—almost any type of real estate makes good loan collateral.  Such property is usually pledged in the form of a mortgage.  The lending institution will want to know: (1) the property's physical condition, (2) its location, (3) its face value, in case foreclosure becomes necessary, and (4) the amount of insurance carried on the property.

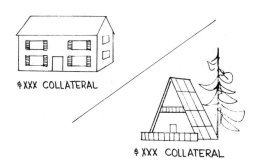

**Life insurance.**  Some forms of life insurance accumulate cash values over the years.  Lenders will usually accept this type of policy as collateral for loans not exceeding the policy's cash value.  The policy must be assigned to the lender until the loan is repaid.

**Stocks and bonds.**  If used as collateral for loans, stocks and bonds must be marketable.    As protection against market fluctuations and the possible expenses of liquidation, it is customary for banks and other lending institutions to limit loans to not more than 75 percent of the market value of high-grade stocks.  Lenders may also require the borrower to put up additional security or to pay off the loan, if the market value of the pledged stocks drops below the required margin.  On more risky, speculative stocks, loans may be limited to a much smaller percentage of the stocks' value, if the stocks are acceptable for collateral at all.

Bonds are more stable in value than even the most marketable stocks.  Stocks constitute a financial gamble, with stock buyers hoping their stocks will increase in value.  Bonds, in contrast, represent a promise of payment by Federal or municipal government, business corporation, or other entity.  Lenders may loan up to 95 percent of a bond's value.

Naturally, you will want to know more about stocks and bonds before you invest in either.  As an absolute minimum, you should be familiar with Part V of this book.

**Chattel mortgages.**  If your loan is for the purpose of buying an automobile or other piece of durable equipment, the lender may secure his money with a

# Chattel Mortgage

of ............................................................................................................mortgagor.... in consideration of

..............................................................................................................................DOLLARS

to...................................paid by...........................................................................................

of ......................................................................mortgagee...., do hereby sell and mortgage unto said

mortgagee.... all that certain personal property situated ...........................................................

in said ...............................................................................and described as follows, to wit:


This is a chattel mortgage to secure the payment of a promissory note of even date herewith, for

.....................................................................................................................DOLLARS

signed by said mortgagor.... and payable to the order of said mortgagee...................after date

at .................................................................in said ...........................................................

with ....................................................................Dollars attorney's fee for collections.

      Said property may remain in the possession of the mortgagor ... subject to the conditions herein
mentioned; but..............agree that................will not remove the same from the place where it now is.

      If default be made in the payment of said note, or if sale or removal of said property be made
or attempted, said mortgagee.... may take possession of said property wherever found, using all
necessary force for that purpose, and may proceed to foreclose. And is hereby fully authorized and
empowered to sell and dispose of the same at public auction, by advertisement, according to the
law in such case made and provided.

      Should the proceeds from such sale fail to satisfy this mortgage, costs and expenses, then the
mortgagor.... agree.... to pay the deficiency.

      For the purpose of obtaining the above loan, the mortgagor.... represent.... that.............................
the owner.... of said property, and that the same is free from all liens and incumbrances.

      Witness the hand.... of the mortgagor.... this.....................day of................................., 19.........

Witness:

..............................................................    ....................................................................................

                                                                               ....................................................................................

**Fig. 5–1**  Chattel mortgage.  A lender of money to be used for the purchase of equipment
may secure his money with a chattel mortgage.

chattel mortgage (Fig. 5–1). This gives him a *lien* (claim) on the equipment, and he assumes ownership if you default on the loan. The lender evaluates the present and future market value of the equipment, generally making loans for amounts smaller than the full purchase price—say 75 percent of new car prices, 60 percent of used car prices, or some other percentage based on current local practice. The lender will also want to know, in fact in most cases will require, that the borrower had adequate fire, theft, property damage, and public liability insurance. In determining the size of a particular loan, the lender will also compute the applicable rate of depreciation. (Most personal luxury cars depreciate faster than more popular, lower-priced models, for example.)

**Endorsers, co-makers, and guarantors.** Borrowers are sometimes asked to have other people sign a note as further promise of payment. These endorsers are contingently liable for the note they sign; that is, if the borrower fails to repay the loan, the lender expects the endorser to make the note good, and can legally insist that the endorser pay the remaining balance. Sometimes, the endorser may be asked to pledge assets or securities of his own.

You should remember, if you co-sign on a loan agreement or ask someone to co-sign with you, that both parties are equally responsible to repay the note. When repayment is due, a lender can collect directly from either the maker or the co-maker. The lender can take legal action against either. It is a responsibility that you should not take lightly, no matter what your assessment of your co-maker's character may be. A good rule of thumb is, "Don't co-sign (or co-make) a loan with anyone."

A guarantor is one who guarantees the payment of a loan by signing a guaranty commitment. This is a common practice when a person is borrowing money for a small business which is incorporated. Otherwise, under the law, a corporation is a separate entity, and an individual may not otherwise be held accountable for the business' debts, should the business (corporation) be unable to repay those debts.

## WHO THE LENDERS ARE

Since consumers have varying credit demands, various types of financial institutions have developed to meet those needs. Most of these institutions were designed originally to provide a specific type of service, like home mortgages. But diversification has blurred most of the original distinctions. Financial media now offer a variety of financial services in the competition for investor dollars.

**Commercial banks.** As their name implies, these banks were once primarily concerned with loans to business and industry. They have diversified to the point where they now offer consumer loans, especially to borrowers with high incomes. Commercial banks have outstanding more than one-third of all personal installment loans, almost three-fifths of all retail auto loans, and more than one-fourth of all loans for other consumer goods.

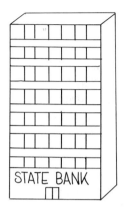

Almost every bank now has a consumer loan department making small personal loans for almost any purpose.  These loans are subject to various rates of interest, depending on the collateral and security involved.  Generally speaking, the better the risk the lower the rate of interest charged.  If a borrower has high-quality collateral (land, buildings, etc.), he probably will be able to get the lowest interest rate by dealing with a bank rather than some other institution.  This lowest secured rate varies with the interest market, but generally ranges from $6\frac{1}{2}$ to 9 percent simple annual interest.

Lowest secured rates from commercial banks compare favorably with interest rates from credit unions (generally 12 percent), which are in turn often less than rates of signature loans and loans secured by depreciable property under chattel mortgages.  Signature loans and depreciable chattel mortgage loans usually carry from 12 to 18 percent simple interest.  For comparison, loans from personal loan companies range from 18 to 36 percent simple annual interest.

The various bank card systems offer cash advances to cardholders.  Borrowing money in this way is comparable in most states to borrowing from small loans companies.  Keep an eye peeled for special transaction fees, discounts, or loan charges.  Remember, ample printed data is available describing fully the total charges on any of these plans.  Be sure you take time to find out the true interest rate you will be paying.  Do not let the ease and convenience of the bank card lead you to needless debt.

**Credit unions—a good loan source for members.**  A credit union is a cooperative association organized for the purpose of making small, low-cost loans to its members.  Funds for loans come from the complementary service offered by credit unions—savings.  Larger credit unions make more ambitious loans; some even finance homes and other real estate.  Loans are made to members for virtually any worthwhile purpose; many companies provide automatic payroll deductions to make repayment of the loans easier.  Savings are similarly deducted.  While state laws vary considerably regarding loan limits, many credit

ACME EMPLOYEES
CREDIT UNION

unions can lend as much as $750 on the member's signature alone.  Larger loans require additional security, such as shares (savings), chattel mortgages, or co-signers.

While members of some credit unions may obtain lower rates from a bank, the majority of borrowers find their credit union offers lowest rates for small loans.  Credit union rates will vary over the years in response to changes in overall economic conditions in the nation.  In the past, however, the interest rate at credit unions has not exceeded 1 percent per month (12 percent simple annual interest) and some credit unions have charged less.  Furthermore, depending on decisions by the union's board of directors, a credit union may pay an interest refund, thereby reducing the effective net rate charged for its loans.

Ordinarily, credit unions process loan applications much the same as do other financial organizations, although usually faster.  When members need funds quickly, credit unions can make emergency loans in a matter of minutes.  This ready availability of funds could be of great value to the member who needs an emergency operation, is stranded away from home without enough cash, or is caught in some other money squeeze.

Loan protection life insurance is provided without extra charge, with the premiums paid by the credit unions themselves out of operating expenses.  If a borrower dies or becomes permanently disabled, his loan is automatically cancelled.

**Industrial and small loan companies.**  Consumer finance companies, in the form of personal finance, sales finance, and industrial loan companies, operate in 49 states and Puerto Rico.  Laws in Arkansas and the District of Columbia prevent finance companies from lending cash at rates which attract responsible capital.

Two factors generally control the size of loans through consumer finance companies.  The first of these is the loan ceiling, which is determined by state legislation.  A loan ceiling is the upper limit on the size of the loan.  In California, the loan ceiling is $5,000; New York, by comparison, sets its limit at $800.  In 37 states, finance companies are permitted to make loans for more than $1,000, either under consumer finance laws or other laws which apply.  The second factor controlling the size of a loan is the relationship between the maximum authorized interest on loans and the market for loans of different amounts.

Consumer finance companies generally try to offer "full loan service"; that is, they try to serve consumers who need small loans as well as those who need larger amounts, up to the maximum permitted by law. Because the yield to the finance company for loans under $100 is considerably below the unit cost of operation, it is economically impossible for any such institution to have a large proportion of such small loans outstanding. If you are in the market to borrow $75, and the man behind the desk tells you the company has filled its quota of small loans, this interplay factor suddenly becomes very real.

Because of the variation among the states, where you live determines what you pay for a small loan, as well as the maximum amount you can borrow. In Alaska, for example, you could be charged as much as 4 percent per month (48 percent simple annual interest) on a $100 loan; but if you lived in New York, you could not be charged more than $2\frac{1}{2}$ percent per month (30 percent simple annual interest) for the same $100 loan. Usually, rates are inversely proportional to the size of the loan; that is, the more you borrow, the lower the rate charged for the loan. The appendix at the end of this chapter shows current interest charges and other information about small loans in each state.

Because the rates charged by small loan companies are so high, relative to those charged by other financial media, the question often arises as to just how much money a personal finance company makes. There are several ways to answer this question; one standard method is to figure the rate of return on the total assets. Using total assets as a base, the average net income after taxes for finance companies is about equal to, or even less than, the average net income for the 500 largest manufacturing corporations or the 50 largest merchandising firms in the country—in the range between 5.4 and 8 percent net profit.

Laws regulating maximum length of a loan contract, like other variables in loan laws, vary from state to state, and finance company policies may restrict maturities to a shorter term than allowed by law. The trend, in conjunction with higher amounts outstanding, is upward. More people are borrowing more money, from all institutions, and taking longer to repay.

Your credit should be in good enough shape that you are not likely to require the services, and pay the high interest of consumer finance companies. Of the lenders discussed so far, consumer loan companies generally charge the highest interest for their services. For that reason alone, these personal loan firms should be your least used sources of loan funds.

**Insurance companies.** Nearly all insurance policies which accumulate cash values contain a semi-automatic loan provision. If you have built up cash values in such a policy, it may be worth while to compare its interest rate with other available rates. The interest charged under most policies is similar to the rate charged by banks.

**Pawn brokers.** Cluttered with dusty cameras, jewelry, and musical instruments, pawn brokers' windows reflect the economic gloom of the people with whom these shops do business. The industry has survived because it can offer quick, confidential loans to people with bad credit. The pawn broker does not ask his customers to disclose financial information, nor does he ask for a credit report. Loans are simply secured by pawning an article of value—depositing it with the pawn broker who will safeguard the article until it is redeemed.

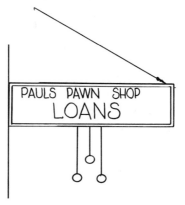

Generally, pawn shops redeem articles within a year after they are pawned. If the loan, with accumulated interest, is not paid by the end of a specified time period, the pawned item is offered for sale. In New York, pawn brokers are required to dispose of such items at public auctions. In most other states, the pawn broker sells the item any way he can, for whatever price he can obtain. New York law also requires that any excess over the amount of the loan, interest, and other charges, be returned to the person who pawned the article.

Despite the run-down appearance of the typical pawn shop, this business can yield big profits. State laws permit extremely high interest charges, currently ranging from 2 to 10 percent monthly (24 to 120 percent annually). Still more money is made when pawned articles are not redeemed since pawn shop borrowers are loaned only a fraction of the value of the article pawned. The price of unredeemed items is much nearer the real market value when those items are resold.

To get an approximate idea of what pawn brokers would lend on various items, the author went pawn shopping. In all, 10 shops in five different cities were visited over a two-week period. In each case, the author asked the pawn broker to indicate the highest amount he would lend on a Winchester pump-action 12-gauge shotgun, Model 1200—and on a Minolta SRT-101 35mm camera with fl.4 lens.  No claim is made here that this was an exhaustive survey, or that the responses are typical of other pawn shop operators across the country, but this is what the author found:

| Article to be pawned | Cost new $ | Pawn shop loan value | | | | | | | | | |
|---|---|---|---|---|---|---|---|---|---|---|---|
| | | Shop 1 | Shop 2 | Shop 3 | Shop 4 | Shop 5 | Shop 6 | Shop 7 | Shop 8 | Shop 9 | Shop 10 |
| Gun | 106 | 12 | 15 | 10 | 15 | 5 | 35 | 17 | 11 | 25 | 10 |
| Camera | 210 | 25 | 15 | 40 | 25 | 10 | 60 | 15 | 10 | 25 | 20 |

It was apparent that similar goods were priced in these shops to sell at much higher figures than those above.  With such potential margins, and the already indicated high interest charges, it must be the fervent hope of every pawn broker that few customers ever reclaim their pledged items.

**Loan sharks.**  Although it is improbable that you will ever meet, much less borrow from, one of the vicious predators known as "loan sharks,"—you should be aware of them and avoid them.  They lend money—and grief—to ill-informed, desperate people who can least afford either the usurious charges or the anxiety and physical violence often used to enforce repayment.

As noted earlier, the Federal Truth-in-Lending Law has severe penalties for such credit criminals.  The difficulty is in finding them; they shun public attention, and their "clientele" are afraid of them.  The sad fact is that loan-sharking is still a thriving business in this country, especially in the urban ghettos and slums.  A fictional story, based on factual evidence, will show you how loan-sharking works:

A minority-American, we'll call him Joe, had been out of work for 17 weeks.  For the last ten days, he'd lived in 50c-a-night flophouses.  Finally, he found work on a construction job.  Regular checks started rolling in; and with new confidence, Joe sent money to his girl in Tucson so that she could join him in Chicago.  They were married, and settled down happily in an economy apartment on Chicago's South Side.

The good life was short-lived for Joe and his bride, however.  Three months after their marriage, Joe's wife was hit by a car, breaking her back.  She would live and walk again, but required hospitalization for at least three weeks.

Joe wanted to do everything in his power to get his wife well, and he knew where he could lay his hands on some extra money.  Todd, a guy in the money business at a neighborhood tavern, had loaned Joe $10 just before Joe got his first paycheck.  Joe had repaid the loan in two days, and Todd had charged only $2 for the accommodation.  He told Joe that he'd be glad to help out any time Joe needed more cash.  Joe got the money he needed—$800—quickly and easily.  Joe's nightmare—which would last for 14 years, and cost him $14,000—was just beginning.

Sharks thrive on the poor, because the poor usually have no one else to turn to.  Misunderstanding and mismanagement often make the poor unable to borrow at institutions where better credit ratings are a requirement. The innocuous beginning in Joe's case is typical; the shark seems to be a "friend in need." Often, small loans mark the beginning of the cruel shark–victim relationship. After all, $2 seems little enough to pay for an appreciated favor, doesn't it? Perhaps, until you consider that it amounts to about 3640 percent in simple annual interest charges.

The Armed Services are not immune from loan-sharking, and the young man entering or serving in the military would be well advised to steer clear of his outfit's "money man." In some cases, the borrower must make a check, post-dated, payable to the lender, for the loan plus usurious interest. On payday, the borrower either pays the loan—buying back the check—or the check can be cashed or deposited, which gets the borrower in difficulty with his commanding officer.

Suffice to say, loan-sharking is widespread. It should be obvious that it is tremendously expensive. On small loans, this can be a temporary nuisance; on larger loans, like Joe's, the borrower may end up spending a good part of his life-time just trying to keep up with the interest payments. Little has been said here of the "repayment policy" of loan-sharks. Most simply stated, it is no policy; interest and penalty payments are whatever the shark may decide they are. The borrower who defaults has to pay the arbitrary fees, flee, or risk being beaten or killed by the shark's henchmen or "goons."

### HOW TO CHECK ON LOAN COSTS

Although the recent Truth-in-Lending legislation requires disclosure of a simple annual interest rate as well as the total dollar cost of finance charges on most loans, a sharp borrower checks the accuracy of the information he is given. To do this, you should understand several different methods of figuring loan charges. To illustrate these methods, let's assume you are making a $240 loan for one year to be repaid in equal monthly installments.

*Add-On Interest.* Interest is figured on the entire principal (amount of the loan) for the term of the loan. In this instance: $240 × 6% for one year = $14.40. The loan principal plus the interest equal the total amount which the borrower repays: $240 + $14.40 = $254.40. Payments are determined by dividing the number of install-ments into the total principal and interest: $254.40 ÷ 12 = $21.20.

*Discount Method.* Using this procedure, the interest ($14.40) is again calculated on the entire amount of the loan ($240.00). Then the interest is deducted from the loan and only the remainder is given to the borrower in cash. ($240.00 − $14.40 = $225.60 —the amount you actually get.) Installments of $20 each month repay the loan ($240 ÷ 12 = $20.)

*Monthly Interest.* Interest from 1 to 3% per month is charged on the declining loan balance—the amount still owed. If you have 1% interest on your $240 loan, at the end of the first month, the balance is still $240, so interest is 1% × $240, or $2.40 for the first month. At the end of the second month, the balance after one $20 principal payment is $220, so interest is 1% × $220, or $2.20. Interest for the entire year comes to $15.60—an average of $1.30 per month. Payments, therefore, average $21.30 per month ($20 + $1.30).

*Simple Interest.* This is the rate which should be quoted under the Truth-in-Lending Law. To compute it, divide the total loan principal by the number of installments: ($240 ÷ 12 = $20). This gives the basic monthly principal payment, without interest. Now add to the loan principal one month's basic principal payment ($240 + $20 = $260) and multiply one-half this figure by the annual interest rate: ($\frac{1}{2}$ of $260 = $130 × 6% = $7.80). If the loan is for more than one year, merely multiply this interest figure by the number of years.

When cost of credit is determined by either the add-on or discount method, the borrower can verify the equivalent simple interest rate figures which lenders must now supply. To do this, the constant ratio formula is used:

$$\text{Interest rate} = \frac{2 \times \text{number of annual payments} \times \text{\$ Cost of loan (difference between what you pay and what you receive)}}{\text{\$'s you receive} \times (\text{no. of payments} + 1)}$$

For example, using the figures given above under add-on interest:

$$\text{Rate} = \frac{(2 \times 12) \times \$14.40}{\$240 \times (12 + 1)} = 11.08\%.$$

For above figures under the discount method:

$$\text{Rate} = \frac{(2 \times 12) \times \$14.40}{\$225.60 \times (12 + 1)} = 11.68\%.$$

You can easily see that both discount and add-on methods understate the true simple interest figure. With add-on interest, you pay interest on the full loan principal, even though you do not have use of all the money for the entire loan period since you are repaying it in monthly installments. On a discounted loan, you don't receive the full amount because the interest is deducted from the loan when it is made, and again the interest is computed on the full loan, with no consideration of monthly installments.

## CONSUMER CREDIT ABROAD
The use of credit and borrowed money to raise the standard of living is held in

contempt by most of the world's governments, excepting those of the United States and Canada. Nonetheless, consumers wanting to buy more things and manufacturers wanting to increase sales have caused some softening of official attitudes toward credit. Consequently, some growth has occurred in the financing of consumer goods in West Germany, France, England, and Russia. In England, consumers may now enter into hire-purchase contracts which require a large down payment and a stipulated number of monthly installments. The title to the product belongs to the hire-purchase company until the contract has been completely fulfilled.

But cash credit is still not fully accepted as quite respectable even by the hire-purchase companies themselves. Questions are raised concerning the advisability of consumers having access to cash loans. There is also public skepticism about the right of the lender to control so stringently the purposes for which the money is used. While statistics are difficult to obtain, experts tend to agree that the personal loan industry abroad is still in its infancy.

This generally inhibited development of credit in other countries is due in part to different economic philosophies. American legislation is increasingly designed to protect consumers from credit "malpractice." Other countries seem to believe that widespread credit buying would undermine economic stability. We can see this stability philosophy in action when we realize that nearly all European countries rigidly control the down payment as well as the length of an installment or hire-purchase contract. These governments may, at any time, raise the down payment requirement on automobiles from 35 to 50 or perhaps 80 percent and shorten the maximum repayment term from 24 to six months.

### PERSONAL BANKRUPTCY

Under Federal law, an individual who runs himself hopelessly into debt may petition a court to declare him bankrupt. If the request is granted, what money or other assets he does have are distributed among his creditors, on a prorated basis. Any remaining outstanding debt cannot be recovered by creditors.

Credit grantors, lawyers, legislators, and social workers alike are demonstrating increasing concern about personal bankruptcies. Due partly to such concern, to the Truth-in-Lending Law, and to increasing sophistication about debt, bankruptcies are declining slightly in America. Still, about 180,000 are declared annually, with consequent debt cancellations totalling about $1 billion. Interestingly, there seems to be little correlation between income levels and bankruptcy rates.

While the bankruptcy law is a Federal law, it does permit different personal exemptions according to differing state regulations. These different interpretations cause confusion. Considerable work needs to be done to unify bankruptcy laws and coordinate the related state laws. Much work is going forward in these areas, but bankruptcy remains an individual problem, and credit counseling is still a prime necessity for those people who are likely prospects for bankruptcy or are problem credit users.  If you have serious credit problems, you should consider consultation with a legitimate credit counselor.  Do *not* increase your indebtedness, unless it is absolutely necessary, by debt consolidation at one of the "professional credit counselors" who are really just consumer finance companies in disguise.

## IS BORROWING WORTH THE HIGH COST?

The typical American family—man, wife, two children—has an aggregate consumer indebtedness of about $2,400.  This includes all credit purchases and loans, but excludes home mortgages.  More than $310 in interest expense is silently drained from their income yearly.  Through more careful (or no) credit spending, the family could easily divert $20 or $24 each month from "interest give-away" to money-making investments.  Over a 20-year period, such a monthly saving, invested in stocks at a 12 percent return, compounded semi-annually, would be worth nearly $19,000.

Certainly, there are legitimate reasons and occasions for borrowing money or otherwise incurring consumer debt.  The important thing is to keep this debt at a reasonable level in perspective with all your other financial objectives.  Postponing a purchase, until you can pay cash for it, does *not* mean that you will never have the item.  More conservative and intelligent use of your credit and borrowing means that you will have more, not less, in the long run.  Credit is a very sharp financial tool, but it has two cutting edges.

## FEEDBACK 5

A.  Consider that you might want to buy a new car.  Inquire at the three types of loan sources (commercial banks, credit unions, small loan companies) about the cost of borrowing the maximum amount each firm will loan for such collateral.

- How much is each type willing to loan?
- What percentage (simple annual interest) is expected by each firm?
- Including interest charges and associated loan costs, which type of loan is most expensive?  Least expensive?
- Considering the loan payments as "cost of driving," how much will it cost you to drive your dream automobile per month?  Per day?  Remember to include all the other expenses too, such as depreciation, insurance, ordinary repairs, gas and oil.  Recall that the loan payments are due whether you drive the car or not.

B.  While you are taking the above "survey," find out which of these firms will lend you money for general purposes such as vacations or consolidations.

- How much will the loan cost you in percentage of interest charged?  In dollars?

- Can you devise alternative methods of purchasing the same satisfactions?
- Can you select alternative satisfactions, for example, like a less ambitious vacation?

C.  Consider (on a *strictly hypothetical basis*) co-making or co-signing a note with the most trustworthy person you know.  Of course, he's dependable, fair, and has the best of intentions.  Suppose the note was for a monthly repayment amount of $20.  Now just imagine that your friend is laid off from his job.

- Would you give away $20 per month for absolutely no return in goods or satisfaction?
- Could you afford to?
- What adjustments would you have to make in your future budgets, for how long, to accommodate the new expense?
- What goods and satisfactions would you have to postpone, and which of your financial goals would you give up temporarily?
- Of course, special situations *do* come up, but how friendly is it to ask someone else to gamble his financial well-being?

D.  Suppose you wished to buy a $200 typewriter, and that you had $200 in a non-emergency savings account.  You are offered a one-year "easy payment" plan for purchasing the machine through a small loan company involving $1\frac{1}{2}\%$ per month interest (18 percent simple annual interest).  The payment seems manageable; only $19.67 (assuming there are no additional charges, such as insurance, discount, preparation fees, and the like).

- Could you make better use of almost $20 per month?
- Compute the true cost of the typewriter, for the duration of the one-year contract period.
- Does the typewriter seem to be as good a buy at the contract price as it was for the cash price?
- What purposes could you use the interest amount for, besides paying the costs of borrowing?

## DISCUSSION QUESTIONS

1. Have Americans' attitudes toward indebtedness changed over the last ten years?  If yes, why?  If no, explain.
2. If it can be reliably shown that borrowed money will be returned when due, should the borrower have to explain what he is going to do with the money? Why?
3. Why are noninstallment loans more difficult to obtain than installment loans?

4. Why can a borrower with high-quality collateral get the lowest interest rates by dealing with a commercial bank rather than some other institution?

5. What are the reasons for interest rates being inversely proportionate to the size of the loan from consumer finance companies?

6. Why do state laws permit pawn brokers to charge such extremely high interest rates? Is it fair to the borrower? Why?

7. Will the provisions of the Truth-in-Lending Law in fact reduce or eliminate transactions made by loan sharks? Explain.

8. What other steps, if any, need to be taken to combat the loan sharks' economic activities?

9. What is the cause for the rising number of bankruptcies over the past two prosperous decades?

10. Once a person has filed bankruptcy, should he always be regarded as a bad credit risk?

## CASE PROBLEM

John and Barbara Epping spent several days looking through travel folders planning their summer vacation. Finally they decided they would take an escorted tour into Mexico. They realized it was going to cost more than they had planned on, but figured it would be worth while to borrow what they needed. John made an application to his credit union but was told his present loan balance ($700 on small personal loans plus $3,800 on his auto loan) prevented them from making any additional loans until substantial repayments had been made.

The Eppings decided to try their bank. They filled out a loan application and were told it would have to be presented to the loan committee the following day. Two days later a letter was received which in part read:

"Our Loan Committee's unfavorable decision on your recent loan request was based upon the following credit data supplied in part by our local credit bureau:

Erratic and slow pay record at several department stores; two furniture stores; and the experience of our own mortgage loan department. Current total indebtedness approximates $8,100 in consumer credit plus your mortgage loan balance of $26,700.

Your combined monthly take-home pay of $752 does not appear sufficient to discharge your current indebtedness in a timely way."

a) How do you think the Eppings got themselves in such a financial pickle?

b) What specific steps should they take to regain a good credit rating and get on the road to financial security?

c) What part do you think creditors had in the financial jam which the Eppings now are encountering?

## SUGGESTED READINGS

Cobleigh, Ira U. *How and Where to Borrow Money.* New York: Avon Books, 1964. 160 pp.

Cole, Robert H., and Robert S. Hancock. *Consumer and Commercial Credit Management.* Homewood, Ill.: R. D. Irwin, 1964. 593 pp.

Colwell, Stephen A. *The Ways and Means of Payment.* New York: A. M. Kelley, 1965. 644 pp.

Goldsmith, Raymond W. *Financial Institutions.* New York: Random House, 1968. 207 pp.

Kedzie, Daniel P. *Consumer Credit Insurance.* Homewood, Ill.: R. D. Irwin, 1957. 212 pp.

McHugh, Helen Frances. *Differentials in Uses of Consumer Credit by Young, Urban Families.* Ames: Iowa State University, 1965. 160 pp.

National Study Service. *Family Credit Counseling, An Emerging Community Service: A Full Report of a Study of Family Credit Counseling Provided Through Non-Profit Community-Based Programs.* New York: Family Service Association of America, 1968. 127 pp.

# CONSUMER FINANCE RATE
# AND REGULATION CHART

Compiled by National Consumer Finance Association

# CONSUMER FINANCE RATE AND REGULATION CHART

*Editors warning:* National Consumer Finance Association has compiled this chart on the basis of the Consumer Finance and other loan laws referred to, and legal opinions of lawyers who are personally familiar with the laws in the different states. It was necessary to over-simplify and to generalize the statutes and legal opinions in order to present the information in this abbreviated chart form. Each NCFA member should consult his own counsel for each state statute and as to detail shown on this chart. For example, the convenience and advantage (C&A) clauses are generally similar in each state law but administrative interpretations of these clauses differ markedly among the states. In some states, insurance practices vary from company to company, depending on the opinion of different counsel and the organization of the company. Precomputation and dollar add-on laws also result in varying practices among the states and companies as to rebates and default and deferment charges. There are varying statutory and official administrative rules as to advertising, other business, security, maturities, record keeping, disclosures to customers and other matters.

| State | Maximum Rate and Loan Size (monthly rate unless otherwise stated) | Maximum Maturity | Precomp. Discount or Dollar Add-on | Default Charges | C & A Clause | Credit Insurance Life rate—per $100 per year. Disability rate—per $100 for indicated term (unless otherwise stated) | Other Laws (under which consumer finance licensees frequently operate) |
|---|---|---|---|---|---|---|---|
| Alabama | 3–2% @ $200 to $300; $1 per $5 of loans not exceeding $75; 8% a year 6 months after maturity | 25 months | Precomp. | Yes | Yes | Life, 75¢, on loans above $100 | Installment Loan Act: 6% a year add-on; no max. amount or maturity |
| Alaska | 3–2% @ $400, 1% @ $800 to $1,500; 5% on loans not exceeding $50; default fee of $3 | No max. maturity | None | Yes | Yes | NAIC. Life, premiums actually paid out. | — |
| Arizona | 3–2% @ $300, 1% @ $600 to $1,000 | 24½ months | Precomp. | Yes | No | NAIC. Life and Disability. (Proposed rates pending.) | Installment Loan Act: 8% a year add-on to $1,000, 6% on any excess to $5,000 ($10 min.) no max. maturity; 1⅓% a month on revolving loan accounts. |

| State | Rate | Maturity | Type | | | Insurance | Other |
|---|---|---|---|---|---|---|---|
| California | 2½–2% @ $200, 1½% @ $500 to $700, 1% @ $700 to $5,000; no max. above $5,000 | 24½ months to $2,000; 36½ months over $2,000 | Precomp. | Yes | No | NAIC. Life, 55¢. Disability (14 day retro): $2.42—12 months, $3.30—24 months, $4.18—36 months | General Interest Law: No limit on rate above $1,500 |
| Canada | 2–1% @ $300, ½% @ $1,000 to $1,500; 1% after maturity and after 20 or 30 months | 20 months to $500; 30 months over $500 | None | — | — | Life, 50¢ by administrative interpretation. Disability permitted by regulation. | — |
| Colorado | 3–1½% @ $300, 1% @ $500 to $1,500 | No max. maturity | Precomp. | Yes | No | NAIC. Life, 75¢. Disability (14 day retro): $2.20—12 months, $3.00—24 months, $3.80—36 months | 1913 Money Lenders Act: 2% per month on loans over $1,500; no max. amount or maturity |
| Connecticut | $17 – $11 a year per $100 @ $300 to $1,800 add-on; 12% a year after deferred maximum maturity | 24½ months to $1,000; 36½ months over $1,000 | Add-on | Yes | Yes | NAIC. Life, 50¢ | |
| Delaware | 6% a year discount; 2% service fee; 5% fine; various limitations; industrial law; loan size limited by net worth | 36 months | Discount and fee | Yes | No | — | |
| Florida | 3–2% @ $300 to $600; 10% a year 12 months after maturity | 24 months | None | — | Yes | NAIC. Life and Disability | Add-on Act: $10 a year per $100 add-on plus 20¢ per $25 limited to $2.40 per month; $600 max. size; 24 months max. maturity |

*Note:* "Precomp." means that monthly rate may be precomputed on scheduled monthly balances instead of actual balances. "Add-on" and "Discount" rates are for the contract period without regard to installment payments. Add-on is computed on and added to the original amount lent. Discount is computed on and deducted from the face amount of the note. In the Credit Insurance column, "NAIC" refers to statutes which give Insurance Commissioners some control of credit insurance premiums and which are based on a model bill of the National Association of Insurance Commissioners.

| State | Maximum Rate and Loan Size (monthly rate unless otherwise stated) | Maximum Maturity | Precomp. Discount or Dollar Add-on | Default Charges | C & A Clause | *Credit Insurance* Life rate—per $100 per year. Disability rate—per $100 for indicated term (unless otherwise stated) | Other Laws (under which consumer finance licensees frequently operate) |
|---|---|---|---|---|---|---|---|
| Georgia | 8% a year, to $2,500; discount for 18 months, add-on for longer maturities; fee of 8% of first $600 and 4% of excess | 24 months | Discount and fee | Yes | Yes | Life, $1 reducing balance, $2 level term. Disability (7 day retro.): $2.10 per annum per $5 monthly benefit | — |
| Hawaii | 3½–2½% @ $100 to $300 | 20 months | None | — | Yes | NAIC. Life, 75¢. | Industrial Loan Act: 12% a year discount for first 18 months, 9% for next 12 months, 6% for next 12 months, 3% for remaining months to 48 months; also delinquency and other charges; no max. amount |
| Idaho | 3–2% @ $300, 1% @ $500 to $1,000 | No max. maturity | Precomp. | Yes | Yes | NAIC, Life, 60¢. Disability (14 day retro.): $2.20—12 months, $3.00—24 months, $3.80—36 months | Installment Loan Act: 6% a year discount; 4% default charge ($4 max.); $3,500 max. size |
| Illinois | 3–2% @ $150, 1% @ $300 to $800 | No max. maturity | Precomp. | Yes | Yes | NAIC. Life, 65¢. Disability (14 day retro.): $2.20—12 months, $2.80—24 months, $3.35—36 months | Installment Loan Act: Annual discount rates ranging from 8½% for maturities up to 30 months down to 7.09% for 58 to 61 months. Loans over $800 to $5,000 excluding discount |
| Indiana | 3–2% @ $150, 1½% @ $300 to $1,000 | No max. maturity | None | — | No | NAIC. Life, 75¢. Disability (14 day retro.): $2.20—12 months, $3.00—24 months, $3.80—36 months | Consumer Loan Act: 8% a year add-on on loans over $1,000 to $7,500; 61 months max. maturity Industrial Loan Act: 1½% per month; precomputation with default charge; max. loan 10% of capital; no max. maturity |

| State | Rate | Maturity | | | | Insurance | Law |
|---|---|---|---|---|---|---|---|
| Iowa | 3–2% @ $250, 1½% @ $400 to $1,000 | 24½ months to $500; 36½ months over $500 | Precomp. | Yes | Yes | Life, 65¢. Disability (14 day retro.): $2.20—12 months, $2.70—24 months, $3.20—36 months Rates effective 2/15/70 | Industrial Loan Act: 9% a year discount plus fee of $1 per $50 ($40 max.); loan size limited by net worth |
| Kansas | 3–5/6% @ $300 to $2,100; 10% a year 6 months after maturity. Revolving credit permitted. | 30 months | Precomp. | Yes | No | Life and Disability | Installment Loan Law: 10% a year add-on or 1½% per month to $1,000, 8% a year or 1.2% per month on remainder ($3 min.) |
| Kentucky | 3–2% @ $150, 1% @ $600 to $800; or add-on rates $20—$15 a year per $100 @ $150, $11 @ $600 to $800 | 25 months | Add-on | Yes | Yes | Life, 75¢ (by regulation) | Industrial Loan Act: 6% a year discount plus fee of $1 per $50 or fraction thereof to $2,000; 5% discount for excess to $5,000; max. maturity 3 years, 32 days |
| Louisiana | 3½–2½% @ $150 to $300; 8% a year 1 year after maturity | No max. maturity | None | — | Yes | Life, $1 (by regulation) | Usury Law Provision: No limit over $300 as to interest included in face of loan note; no max. maturity |
| Maine | 2½–1½% @ $300 to $2,000; 25¢ min.; 8% a year after 36 months | No max. maturity (but see rate column) | None | — | Yes | NAIC. LIFE, 50¢. Disability (14 day retro.): $2.37—12 months, $2.84—24 months, $3.20—36 months | General Interest Law: 16% a year simple interest on loans over $2,000 |
| Maryland | 3–2% @ $300 to $500; 6% a year 6 months after maturity | 30½ months | None | — | Yes | Life and Disability | Industrial Finance Law: 6% a year discount plus fee of $4 or 4% up to $500, and $20 or 2% of face of any note exceeding $500; $1,500 max. face of note |

| State | Maximum Rate and Loan Size (monthly rate unless otherwise stated) | Maximum Maturity | Precomp. Discount or Dollar Add-on | Default Charges | C & A Clause | Credit Insurance Life rate—per $100 per year. Disability rate—per $100 for indicated term (unless otherwise stated) | Other Laws (under which consumer finance licensees frequently operate) |
|---|---|---|---|---|---|---|---|
| Massachusetts | 2½–2% @ $200, 1¾% @ $600 to $1,000, ¾% @ $1,000 to $3,000; 6% a year 1 year after maturity | No max. maturity | Precomp. | Yes | Not in law but by regulation | Life and Disability, each 50¢ per $100 per year | General Interest Law: No limit on rate over $3,000 except for certain home mortgage loans |
| Michigan | 2½–1¼% @ $300 to $1,000 | No max. maturity | None | — | Yes | NAIC. Life, 60¢ | — |
| Minnesota | 2¾–1½% @ $300, 1¼% @ $600 to $900 | 30½ months (by regulation) | Precomp. | Yes | Yes | NAIC. Life, 75¢ Disability (14 day retro.): $2.37—12 months, $2.84—24 months, $3.20—36 months | Industrial Loan Act: 8% a year discount plus fee of $1 per each $50 to $500 and 1% of excess, but $15 max.; loan size limited by net worth; 36 months max. maturity |
| Mississippi | Broker's service charge and lender's interest not to exceed 2% per month add-on on loans of $100 or more, graduated scale for smaller loans; no max. size | No max. maturity for $100 or more | Add-on | No | No | Loans over $99 only. Life, $1. Disability (14 day retro.): $2.20—12 months, $3.00—24 months, $3.80—36 months (by regulation) | — |
| Missouri | 2.218% to $500; 8% a year on remainder | No max. maturity | Precomp. | No | No | Life and Disability (14 day retro.) |  |
| Montana | $20—$16 a year per $100 @ $300, $12 @ $500 to $1,000 add-on; special rate for loans up to $90 | 21 months to $300; 25 months over $300 | Add-on | Yes | No | NAIC. Life over $300, 75¢ |  |
| Nebraska | 2½–2% @ $300, 1½% @ $500 to $1,000, 1% @ $1,000 to $3,000 | 36 months | Precomp. | Yes | Yes | NAIC. Life, 64¢. Disability (14 day retro.): $2.00—12 months, $2.70—24 months, $3.40—36 months | — |

| State | Rate | Maximum maturity | Type | | | Insurance | |
|---|---|---|---|---|---|---|---|
| Nevada | 9–8% a year @ $1,000 to $2,500 plus monthly fee of 1¢ per $1 to $200 and ½¢ per $1 from $200 to $400 all add-on | 24 months | Add-on | Yes | Yes | NAIC. Life, 75¢. Disability (14 day retro.): $2.20—12 months, $3.00—24 months, $3.80—36 months | — |
| New Hampshire | 2–1½% @ $600 to $1,500; 1½% on larger loans to $5,000; 6% a year 3 months after maturity | 24 months to $600; 36 mos. to $1,500; 48 mos. over $1,500 | None | — | Yes | NAIC. Life, 50¢. | — |
| New Jersey | 24–22% a year @ $500 to $1,000 | 36½ months (by regulation) | None | — | Yes | NAIC. Life, 44¢-64¢ depending on insurance volume. | — |
| New Mexico | 3–2½% @ $150, 1% @ $300 to $1,000; 10% a year 1 year after maturity and in certain other cases | No max. maturity | Precomp. | Yes | Yes | NAIC. Life, 65¢. Disability (14 day retro.): $2.35—12 months, $3.25—24 months, $4.15—36 months | Installment Loan Act: 7% a year add-on ($2 per month or $10 minimum) |
| New York | 2½–2% @ $100, 1½% @ $300 to $900, 1¼% @ $900 to $1,400.. | 24½ months to $300; 36½ months over $300 (by regulation) | Precomp. | Yes | Yes | Life and disability. Rates approved by Insurance Supt. on basis of insurance volume. | — |
| North Carolina | $18–$10 a year per $100 @ $300, $8 @ $600 to $900 add-on; 6% a year after maturity; $1 per $5 of loans not exceeding $95. Special rates on loans to $5,000 by election and for motor vehicle lenders. | 25 months to $600; 30 months over $600 | Add-on | Yes | Yes | Life, level term permitted. Disability (14 day retro.): $2.35—12 months | — |

| State | Maximum Rate and Loan Size (monthly rate unless otherwise stated) | Maximum Maturity | Precomp. Discount or Dollar Add-on | Default Charges | C & A Clause | Credit Insurance Life rate—per $100 per year. Disability rate—per $100 for indicated term (unless otherwise stated) | Other Laws (under which consumer finance licensees frequently operate) |
|---|---|---|---|---|---|---|---|
| North Dakota | 2½–2% @ $250, 1¾% @ $500 to $750, 1½% @ $750 to $1,000 | 24½ months | Precomp. but defective | Yes | No | NAIC. Life, 75¢. Disability (14 day retro.): $3.05–12 months $4.12–24 months $4.87–36 months | — |
| Ohio | $16—$9 a year per $100 @ $500, $7 @ $1,000 to $2,000 add-on; or equivalent simple interest rates | 25½ months to $1,000, 37½ months over $1,000 | Add-on | Yes | Yes | NAIC. Life, 75¢ | Second Mortgage Law: $8 per $100 a year add-on plus "reasonable" service charge up to $200 or 5% of principal |
| Oklahoma | UCCC: 30% a year to $300, 21% to $1,000, 15% to $25,000. 18% a year min. Special rates for loans to $100. Revolving credit permitted. | 25 months to $300; 37 months to $1,000; none over $1,000 | Yes | Yes | No | Life, 85¢. Disability (14 day retro.): $2.20–12 months, $3.00–24 months, $3.80–36 months (Effective 3/1/70) UCCC restrictions. | — |
| Oregon | 3–2% @ $300, 1% @ $500 to $1,500 | None | None | — | Yes | Life, 60¢ (Banking Department regulation) | Industrial Loan Co. Act: 10% a year discount plus 3% fee (min. fee $3); max. loan, 5% of net worth; max. maturity, 18 months unsecured and 24 months when secured by chattels |
| Pennsylvania | 3–2% @ $150, 1% @ $300 to $600, 6% a year after 24 months | 24 months | None | — | Yes | NAIC and Banking Department regulations. Life, 60¢ | Consumer Discount Co. Act: 7½% a year discount for 36 months, 6% for remaining period, plus max. fee of $15 ($1 for each $50); 1½% per month for default or deferment; $3,500 max. size; max. maturity 4 years and 15 days |

| | | | | | | | |
|---|---|---|---|---|---|---|---|
| Puerto Rico | 20¢–7¢ a year per $1 @ $300 to $600 add-on | No max. maturity | | Yes | Yes | No | — |
| Rhode Island | 3% to $300, 2½% for loans between $300 and $800, 2% for larger loans to $2,500 | 25 months to $1,000; 37 months over $1,000 | None | — | Yes | NAIC. Life, 50¢. Disability (14 day retro.): $2.49–12 months, $2.96–24 months, $3.51–36 months | General Interest Law: 21% a year |
| South Carolina | $20–$18 a year per $100 @ $100, $9 @ $300 to $1,000; $7 for larger loans to $7,500, add-on; plus fee of 6% up to $12 on loans to $1,000; and 5% up to $200 on larger loans; special rate for loans to $150 | 24½ months to $1,000; 36½ to $1,500; 48½ to $2,000; 60½ to $7,500 | Add-on | Yes | Yes | Life. Disability for $100 or more, 3 day retro: $1.80 per $5 monthly benefit. | — |
| South Dakota | 2½%–2% @ $300, 1½% @ $600 to $1,200, 1% @ $1,200 to $2,500; $2 min.; 8% a year 6 months after maturity | 24½ months to $1,000; 36½ months over $1,000 | Precomp. | Yes | No | NAIC. Life and Disability over $100 | — |
| Tennessee | Industrial Loan Act: 7½% a year discount plus fee of 4% or $2 to $20, 50¢ per $5 to $75, and $7.50 for larger loans, and monthly fee of $1.50 to $300 and $1 for larger loans | 36 months | Discount and fee | Yes | No | NAIC. Life, 75¢. Disability (14 day retro.): $2.39–12 months, $3.16–24 months, $3.69–36 months Subject to change after 12/31/69. | — |

| State | Maximum Rate and Loan Size (monthly rate unless otherwise stated) | Maximum Maturity | Precomp. Discount or Dollar Add-on | Default Charges | C & A Clause | *Credit Insurance* Life rate—per $100 per year. Disability rate—per $100 for indicated term (unless otherwise stated) | Other Laws (under which consumer finance licensees frequently operate) |
|---|---|---|---|---|---|---|---|
| Texas | $18–$8 a year per $100 @ $300 to $2,500 add-on; special rate for loans to $100. Revolving credit permitted. | 37 months to $1,500, 43 months over $1,500 | Add-on | Yes | No | NAIC. Over $100. Life, 75¢ plus 50¢ fee. Disability (14 day retro.): Coverage to $700: $2.25–12 months, $3.00–24 months, $3.80–36 months: Coverage over $700: $1.95–12 months, $2.60–24 months, $3.30–36 months | Consumer Credit Code, Ch. 4: $8 a year per $100 add-on; no max. amount or maturity. Revolving credit permitted |
| Utah | UCCC: 36% a year to $300, 21% to $1,000, 15% to $25,000. 18% a year min. Revolving credit permitted. | 25 months to $300; 37 months to $1,000; none over $1,000 | Yes | Yes | No | NAIC. Life, 75¢. Disability (14 day retro.): $2.20–12 months, $3.00–24 months, $3.80–36 months UCCC restrictions. | — |
| Vermont | 2½–2¼% @ $125, 1% @ $300 to $600 | No max. maturity | Precomp. | Yes | Yes | Insurance Law. Life, 44¢–70¢ depending on insurance volume. | — |
| Virginia | 2½–1½% @ $300 to $1,000; or add-on rates, $17–$12 a year per $100 @ $300; 6% a year 6 months after maturity and in certain other cases | 21 months to $600; 31 months over $600. | Add-on | Yes | Yes | Insurance Law. Life and Disability | — |

| State | Rate | Maturity | Precomp. | | | Insurance | Provisions |
|---|---|---|---|---|---|---|---|
| Washington | 3–1½% @ $300, 1% @ $500 to $1,000; $1 minimum | 25½ months | | Yes | Yes | Life, 60¢ | Industrial Loan Act: 10% a year discount plus 2% fee ($2 min. fee) and 50¢ per month; max. loan size limited by net worth; max. maturity 2 years. |
| West Virginia | 3–2% @ $200, 1½% @ $600 to $800; or add-on rates, $19–$16 a year per $100 @ $200, $12 @ $600 to $800 | 24½ months to $300; 30½ months over $300 (by regulation) | Add-on | Yes | Yes | Life, 75¢ | Industrial Loan Act: 6% a year discount plus fee of $1 per $50; loan size limited by net worth; max. maturity 2 years |
| Wisconsin | 2½–2% @ $100, 1% @ $200 to $300 | 20 months (by regulation) | None | — | Yes | No, but Life and Disability permitted under other law | Sec. 138.09: 8% a year discount on first $300, 7% on excess; 2% fee not exceeding $20; max. proceeds, $2,000; 30½ months max. maturity. Sec. 138.07: 6% a year add-on or 12% interest plus 4% fee (reduced for prepayment); no max. loan size or maturity |
| Wyoming | 3½–2½% @ $150; 1% @ $300 to $1,000; plus $1 fee on loans of $50 or less; $1 recording fee | No max. maturity | None | — | No | NAIC. Life, 60¢. Disability (14 day retro.): $2.20—12 months, $3.00—24 months, $3.80—36 months | — |

# PART III
# GETTING MORE FOR WHAT YOU SPEND

# CHAPTER 6

# CONSUMER PROTECTION SERVICES: THE GOVERNMENT'S ROLE

Despite myriad consumer problems still besetting us, Americans in the 1970's are better equipped than ever before to deal with the complexities of the marketplace. Almost daily we benefit from individual, corporate, and Congressional "consumerism" efforts aimed at (1) supplying buyers with reliable information for knowledgeable decision making, and (2) providing governmental guides and controls.

Today, we have "Truth-in-Packaging," "Truth-in-Lending," a "Buyer's Bill of Rights," "Consumer Class Action," "Truth-in-Labeling," and other products of the "Consumer Decade" which assure us that the government is watching out for us. Determining the extent and effectiveness of these Federal consumer protection services is the aim of this chapter; non-governmental efforts in the consumer's behalf are discussed in Chapter 7.

## MODERN CONSUMERISM

Aside from the scores of recently enacted consumer protection laws, probably the most significant outgrowths of the government's new concern for consumers are the Office of Consumer Affairs and the Consumer Product Information Coordinating Center. Created by Executive Order of President Richard M. Nixon in February, 1971, the OCA is charged with advising and representing the President on matters of consumer interest and with analyzing and coordinating the implementation of all Federal activities in the field of consumer protection. The CPICC was established by the General Services Administration in October, 1970, to share with the public the information and standards upon which various government agencies base their purchasing decisions. Functions of these two new agencies and of the old President's Committee on Consumer Interests, which OCA replaces, are discussed in greater detail in a subsequent section of this chapter.

**The consumer decade.** Until the dawn of the "Consumer Decade," there existed relatively few Federal laws, except for the Federal Trade Commission Act, concerned with protecting the consuming public against dangerous, impure, or falsely labeled products or against fraudulent or deceptive business practices. Spanning a 10-year period which has popularly been referred to as the "Decade of the Consumer," America's modern consumerism movement was launched in March, 1962, when President John F. Kennedy first delivered a special consumer message to Congress.

Reminding legislators that consumers were the largest economic group in the country, and that they accounted for two-thirds of all spending, President Kennedy pointed out that they were also the least organized of any economic group. Therefore, he reasoned, "the Federal Government—by nature the highest spokesman for *all* the people—has a special obligation to be alert to the consumer's needs and to advance the consumer's interest."

To fulfill this "consumer obligation" Mr. Kennedy proclaimed four basic rights for consumers:

1. *The right to safety*—to be protected against the marketing of goods which are hazardous to health or life.

2. *The right to be informed*—to be protected against fraudulent, deceitful, or grossly misleading information, advertising, labeling, or other practices, and to be given the facts needed to make an informed choice.

3. *The right to choose*—to be assured, wherever possible, access to a variety of products and services at competitive prices; and in those industries in which competition is not workable and Government regulation is substituted, to be assured of satisfactory quality and service at fair prices.

4. *The right to be heard*—to be assured that consumer interests will receive full and sympathetic consideration in the formulation of Government policy, and fair and expeditious treatment in its administrative tribunals.

President Kennedy announced to American housewives plans for appointing a consumer counsel to help formulate economic policies. This proposal met with opposition from various sources, primarily on the grounds that adding another agency would only further delay decision-making. Shortly thereafter, Mr. Kennedy invited Mrs. Persia Campbell, consumer counsel for New York State, to become "the consumer's representative" on his Council of Economic Advisors.

**Consumer advisory council instituted.** Under the direction of President Kennedy the Council of Economic Advisors in July of 1962 established the 12-member Consumer Advisory Council to "advise the Government on issues of broad economic policy of immediate concern to consumers, on governmental programs to meet consumer needs or to protect consumer interests, and on needed improvements in the flow of consumer research material to the public."*

---

* Since the Consumer Advisory Council was not created by legislative action, it was subject to dissolution on termination of President Kennedy's administration. However, when he established the President's Committee on Consumer Interests on January 3, 1964, President Lyndon B. Johnson reconstituted the Council and established it by Executive Order No. 11136. Thereby elevated to cabinet level, the Consumer Advisory Council was no longer responsible to the Council of Economic Advisors.

It was during the Kennedy administration that the Federal Hazardous Substances Labeling Act and the Kefauver-Harris Drug Amendments Act of 1962 were signed into law. (See "Significant Dates in Food and Drug Law History," on pages 167 to 169.) During the same period, the Securities and Exchange Commission was asking for tighter rules on advertising, President Kennedy was pushing for medical aid for the aging, Illinois Senator Stephen A. Douglas began his long (and up until his retirement from the Senate in 1966, unsuccessful) campaign to get enactment of a truth-in-lending measure, and Michigan Senator Phillip A. Hart was struggling to make truth-in-packaging a reality. (For a brief description of the provisions of the packaging and labeling, drugs, hazardous substances, and Medicare laws, see "Work of the 88th and 89th Congresses," on pages 156 to 157.) (See Chapter 5 for details of the truth-in-lending measure.)

**More presidential concern.**   The untimely death of President Kennedy prevented accomplishment of all his consumerism goals.   However, the challenge to champion the consumer interest was quickly accepted by his successor. Almost immediately after taking over the presidency in 1963, Lyndon B. Johnson let it be known that he held consumer problems to be a foremost concern of government. Later, declaring that in the case of consumer protection, "the President—and the Congress—speak for every citizen," and explained:

> "A hundred years ago, consumer protection was largely unnecessary.  We were a rural nation then: a nation of farms and small towns.  Even in the growing cities, neighborhoods were closely knit.
>
> "Most products were locally produced and there was a personal relationship between the seller and the buyer.  If the buyer had a complaint, he went straight to the miller, the blacksmith, the tailor, the corner grocer.  Products were less complicated. It was easy to tell the excellent from the inferior.
>
> "Today all this is changed.  A manufacturer may be thousands of miles away from his customers—and even further removed by distributors, wholesalers, and retailers. His products may be so complicated that only an expert can pass judgment on their quality.
>
> "We are able to sustain this vast and impersonal system of commerce because of the ingenuity of our technology and the honesty of our businessmen.
>
> "But this same vast network of commerce, this same complexity, also presents opportunities for the unscrupulous and the negligent.
>
> "It is the government's role to protect the consumer—and the honest businessman alike—against fraud and indifference.  Our goal must be to assure every American consumer a fair and honest exchange for his hard-earned dollar."

## PRESIDENT'S COMMITTEE ON CONSUMER INTERESTS

Subsequently, the President's Committee on Consumer Interests was established and the Office of Special Assistant for Consumer Affairs created.  Mrs. Esther Peterson, then Assistant Secretary of Labor, was named to fill the new office and to serve as PCCI chairman.  It was pointed out that, for the first time in history, the American consumer's interest—so closely identified with the public interest—was to be directly represented in the White House.  Under Presidential instruction, the voice of the consumer in Washington was to be "loud, clear, uncompromising, and effective."  Government agencies represented on the committee were the Departments of Agriculture, Justice, Interior, Commerce, Labor, and Health, Education and Welfare; also, Housing and Home Finance Administration, Federal Trade Commission, and the Council of Economic Advisors.  There was also provision for the appointment of other government officials and private citizens especially qualified to represent consumer interests.

Response to the new committee was immediate and approving.  Mail poured in from every state—more than 3,000 letters within the first week.  Said Chairman Peterson:

> ". . . people lost no time in making their voices heard.  Some (letters) were written on embossed stationery; some on dime store pads or the back of package labels.  Most had one thing in common—they were written by persons, largely housewives, who had never before corresponded with Government.  Many letters were simply expressions of approval.  Said one woman: 'It is wonderful to know that the American Housewife finally has someone in her corner rather than in her pocketbook . . .'"

**Listening post.**  Views and ideas not previously available from the general public were heard by PCCI from housewives, business and trade associations, state and local government officials, trade union officers, representatives of professional associations, leaders of consumer organizations, and representatives of women's groups and voluntary organizations.  Comments then and over the years indicate that most consumer uneasiness results from:

1. Inability to judge quality, chiefly because of rapid changes in the nature of products and the increased variety of products and services offered for sale.
2. Inability to judge "best buys" because of a lack of information and confusing marketing practices.
3. Lack of information about where a customer can seek recourse when a product or service proves unsatisfactory or when he believes he has been misled or defrauded.
4. Confusion about how prices are determined in the American free enterprise economy and why some of them rise.
5. Concern about quality deterioration.
6. Concern about the extensive use of food additives, pesticides, and the side effects of some drugs.
7. Lack of knowledge about various types of consumer credit financing and their cost to the borrower.
8. Lack of knowledge of the consumer services and information already provided by the Federal Government, and how to use these services.

9. Lack of basic education and of educational materials on how to buy, especially among persons with limited incomes.

**Other tasks.** But listening to consumer problems was not the only task of the President's Committee on Consumer Interests. Other assignments were to:

1. Develop means of keeping the public continuously informed of developments of importance in the consumer field.

2. Help the poor spend their limited funds more efficiently.

3. Examine (in cooperation with all other Federal agencies engaged in consumer educational activities) the many programs for consumer education in the schools, to stimulate the development of curricula and training materials, and to encourage larger numbers of young people to seek instruction in the fundamentals of budgeting, buying, and borrowing.

4. Work cooperatively with business in informing and educating the consumer.

5. Help existing organizations add consumer components to their programs.

6. Work with the various states and act as a clearinghouse for information in their own consumer protection programs.

7. Study unmet consumer needs and recommend appropriate Federal action to meet these needs.

**Job difficulties.** Serving as the President's Special Assistant for Consumer Affairs was no easy job for Mrs. Peterson. Nor has it been for her successors, Betty Furness, appointed by President Johnson in 1967, and Virginia H. Knauer, who took over the office in 1969 and continued in the post when the President's Committee on Consumer Interests was absorbed by the Office of Consumer Affairs upon its creation early in 1971. Over the years, numerous questions have been raised about the effectiveness of the job itself. Invested with no authority, the Special Assistants frequently have been accused of "improvising power and upsetting business." All have been plagued by small budgets and great pressures. Nevertheless, even their detractors must agree that these President-appointed "trouble shooters" have commendably performed the three tasks specifically called for by their office:

1. To serve as a direct link between the populace and the President.

2. To represent consumers at government agencies.

3. To pass along to industry and government the desires and views of consumers.

## CONGRESS AND THE CONSUMER DECADE

Paralleling the activity of the President's Committee on Consumer Interests during the period 1964 through 1970 was a tremendous upsurge of Congressional interest in consumer affairs and a flood of legislative proposals bringing Federal powers to bear in many areas of consumer protection. In addition, 1966 saw the creation of two new pieces of Congressional machinery to deal with consumer affairs: a consumer subcommittee created by the chairman of the Senate Commerce Committee, and a Special Inquiry on Consumer Representation in the Federal Government which was established within the House Committee on Government Operations.

### WORK OF THE 88th AND 89th CONGRESSES (1963–1966)

Legislative action by the 88th and 89th Congresses in the consumer's behalf includes:

*Cigarette Labeling*—passage of the Federal Cigarette Labeling and Advertising Act requiring cigarette packages to carry the statement, "Caution: Cigarette Smoking May Be Hazardous to your Health."

*Truth-in-Packaging*—passage of the Fair Packaging and Labeling Act of 1966 providing clearer and more accurate labeling of most kitchen and bathroom products.

*Child Protection*—a comprehensive measure tightening labeling requirements on potentially hazardous household items and imposing (for the first time) such requirements on other items, notably children's toys.

*Truth-in-Securities*—enactment of the Securities Act Amendments of 1964, assuring disclosure of needed information to buyers of "over-the-counter" securities.

*Housing*—enactment of the Housing Act of 1965, expanding urban renewal and public housing programs; enactment of Demonstration Cities Act to help cities meet human needs and rehabilitate physical environment.

*Automobile Safety*—passed the 1966 Traffic Safety Act (effective in 1968) requiring Federal safety standards for cars and tires.

*Highway Safety*—passed the Highway Safety Act providing funds for states establishing Federally-approved road accident reduction programs.

*Water Pollution*—in 1966, approved the Water Quality Act setting standards for purity of interstate waters, and the Clean Waters Restoration Act providing funds for sewage treatment and water purification.

*Clean Air*—in 1966, appropriated additional funds for air purification programs.

*Health Care*—passed the Health Professions Act to help increase the supply of doctors and nurses, and the Medicare Act providing adequate medical care for senior citizens.

*Dangerous Drugs*—passed Drug Abuse Control Amendment to the Food, Drug and Cosmetic Act, protecting consumers from the indiscriminate sale and use of non-narcotic dangerous drugs.

## THE 90th CONGRESS (1967–1968)

Consumer protection proposals continued to predominate in the 90th Congress, with ten major measures introduced. Popular titles and main provisions of the four of these ten measures gaining enactment in 1967 are:

*Product Safety*—establishment of a national committee to study potentially hazardous household appliances and products.

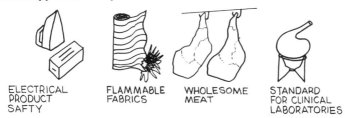

ELECTRICAL PRODUCT SAFTY     FLAMMABLE FABRICS     WHOLESOME MEAT     STANDARD FOR CLINICAL LABORATORIES

*Flammable Fabrics*—established standards of flammability for many materials used in clothing and other household articles, such as blankets and carpeting. (These Flammable Fabrics Act Amendments of 1967 increased the protection afforded consumers by the F.F. Act of 1953, which, while it protected against "explosive clothing," did not include control of many other dangerously flammable fabrics.)

*Wholesome Meat*—provides for improved standards of meat inspection, particularly on the state level, and protects against sale of "4-D" meat (that from dead, dying, diseased, or disabled animals).

*Clinical Laboratories*—Partnership for Health Amendments of 1967 provides protection against sub-standard clinical laboratories.

Detailed analysis of consumer legislation is not our purpose. However, brief comment on the meat inspection measure appears particularly appropriate, since circumstances surrounding passage of the bill bear out the whole point of the consumer section of this text—the vital importance of being informed. To a very real degree, it was the action of *one informed consumer* that finally stemmed opposition to the important wholesome meat measure. As the President's new Special Assistant, Betty Furness, observed, "Most inspection bills had been going up and down Capitol Hill for years with little hope of passage," then Ralph Nader dramatically entered the picture\* bringing with him (and spreading

---

\* Nader had been on the Washington scene the previous year, with stacks of material documenting safety defects in automobiles. His testimony before Sen. Abraham Ribicoff's auto-safety committee was the basis for the first Federal automobile safety standards, and for his best selling book, *Unsafe at Any Speed.*

across the country via the public press) documented accounts of filth, disease, and contamination in meat packing plants from Maine to California. Nader told how Iowa Representative Neal Smith had tried vainly since 1961 to secure strong amendments to the Federal Meat Inspection Act of 1906—amendments which would bring packing plants operating within state boundaries under Federal inspection. (The Federal law, passed following publication of *The Jungle*, Upton Sinclair's penetrating exposé of the deplorable conditions in Chicago plants at the turn of the century, covers only meat moved in interstate commerce.) As long ago as 1958, Nader said, Smith had noticed at livestock sales he attended that the same buyers (from plants operating only within the state) seemed to be purchasing all the diseased, sick, and maimed cattle and hogs, even outbidding other potential buyers for the obviously poor quality animals.

More of Congressman Smith's testimony:

"Some of the uninspected plants merely cut the eye out of the cancer-eyed cow, like you would cut the core out of an apple, and go ahead and use the rest of the carcass. These uninspected plants, which also process sausages and prepared products, can further reduce their cost per pound by including blood, lungs, detergents, hair, hides, antibiotics, and excessive amounts of flour and water, without having to label them in such a manner that the consumer would know what he is buying."

**Secret documents.** Nader made public other such testimony—much of it from a U.S. Department of Agriculture survey of intrastate plants which had been kept secret for four years. From a portion of the report dealing with conditions in Delaware comes this:

". . . Rodents and insects, in fact any vermin, had free access to stored meats and meat products ingredients. Hand-washing lavatories were absent or-inadequate. Dirty meats contaminated by animal hair, the contents of the animal's digestive tract, sawdust, flies, rodents, and the filthy hands, tools and clothing of food handlers, were finely ground and mixed with seasonings and preservatives. These mixtures are distributed as ground meat products, frankfurters, sausages and bolognas."

All this information is public property—testimony recorded in the Congressional hearings on the bills; still, the ill-informed or more properly, the uninformed, consumer continues to be the rule rather than the exception. But even the most ardent advocate of consumer education would not expect the ordinary, average consumer to have to plow through stacks of testimony to assure himself product safety and wholesomeness. It is reprehensible, however, that as Mr. Nader has observed, "passage of consumer-protection legislation must almost always be triggered by some horrible event that mobilizes public opinion." To illustrate, he points out that it took the deaths in 1937 of 108 persons by "elixir of sulfanilamide" to secure passage of the Food, Drug and Cosmetic Act introduced in 1933, and that the thalidomide tragedies of 1962 were needed to get passage of Senator Estes Kefauver's bill to tighten Federal control over the drug industry.

**1968, the year of the consumer.** Standing out in the Consumer Decade as a particularly noteworthy period is the year 1968. This was a year of a great deal of consumer-oriented activity not only in the Federal government, but also in the states and in industry. (State programs will be discussed in a subsequent section of this chapter; developments in nongovernmental fields comprise a part of Chapter 7, "Other Consumer Protection Services.")

In Washington, President Lyndon Johnson began the Year of the Consumer by reviewing consumer protection activities of 1967, then saying, "I think we must do more." That *more* was spelled out in his annual Consumer Message, which now had become a tradition with the President. Declaring that the "needs of the consumer change as our society changes, and legislation must keep pace," Mr. Johnson laid before the lawmakers a comprehensive eight-point program:

*Deceptive Sales Act of 1968*—To give new powers to the Federal Trade Commission, enabling it to obtain Federal Court orders to stop fraudulent and deceptive practices immediately while the case is before the Commission or the courts. (Paul Rand Dixon, FTC Chairman, testified that it was taking an average of three years, under cease and desist procedure, to receive court affirmation of Commission action.)

A main target of this bill was the "shady operator—who with false and deceptive offers of attractive home repairs or items that are more promise than product preys most of all on the poor, the elderly, and the ignorant." National Better Business Bureau estimates show that deceptive practices in the home improvement field alone cost American consumers upwards of $1 billion a year.

*Hazardous Radiation Act of 1968*—To give the Department of Health, Education and Welfare authority to conduct intensive studies of radiation hazards of television sets, and x-ray and other electronic equipment, and to require manufacturers to recall defective equipment and devices.

*Wholesome Poultry Products Act of 1968*—Following the pattern of the Wholesome Meat Act, to help the states develop their own inspection programs and train inspectors. Federal inspection requirements to prevail in states that do not, at the end of two years, have inspection at least equal to Federal standards; in the meantime, those plants which pose a health hazard will be required to "clean up or close down."

*Wholesome Fish and Fishery Products Act of 1968*—To authorize inspection programs and the prevention of health hazards and mislabeling of fish and fish products; help states develop their own programs; assure wholesomeness of imported fish products. (Prior to introduction of this measure, fish inspection was virtually non-existent.)

*Recreational Boat Safety Act of 1968*—To help states establish and improve their own boat safety programs, in an effort to cut down deaths due to boating accidents (more than 1,300 in 1967).

*Automobile Insurance*—To authorize a comprehensive study of the "overburdened and unsatisfactory" automobile insurance system (rising premiums, arbitrary coverage and policy cancellations, company bankruptcies, unfair accident compensation, slow claims processing, etc.).

*Repairs, Warranties, and Guarantees*—To authorize government cooperation with industry to (a) improve quality of service and repairs, (b) assure that warranties and guarantees say what they mean and mean what they say, (c) let consumers know how long a properly used product should last, and (d) determine whether Federal legislation is needed.

*Consumer's Lawyer*—To be appointed by the President to "act in the interest of every American consumer (to) seek better representation for consumer interests before administration agencies and courts," and be concerned with consumer matters from quality standards to frauds.

Holdover measures from the 1967 legislative session included half a dozen consumer protection proposals: Consumer Credit Protection Act (Truth-in-Lending), Interstate Land Sales Full Disclosure Act (Fraudulent Land Sales), Natural Gas Pipeline Safety Act of 1967, Fire Research and Safety Act of 1967, Mutual Funds Act, and Electric Power Reliability Act of 1967. Before the end of 1968, the Truth-in-Lending, Pipeline Safety, and Land Sale Frauds measures had been signed into law.*

**Truth-in-lending.** Considered "landmark" legislation, the Truth-in-Lending Law requires full disclosure of the true simple interest rate on all installment purchases and loans. (This bill is discussed more completely in Chapter 5, "Making Sensible Use of Installment Credit.") The pipeline safety measure gives the Federal Government authority to set safety standards for 760,000 miles of natural gas transmission and distribution lines, "creating for the first time comprehensive, complete and enforceable safety procedures regulating the pipeline transportation of flammable, toxic and corrosive gases."

Briefly, the principal provisions of the other four holdover measures are these:

*Fraudulent Lands*—The Interstate Land Sales Full Disclosure Act would require developers of land sold in interstate commerce to register with the Securities and Exchange Commission, and make full disclosure of all material facts in connection with the sale. The bill is aimed at elimination of sales (particularly by mail) of worthless land; for example, desert land or submerged lakeside or seaside lots.

*Mutual Funds*—This measure would place strong restraints on the nation's multi-billion-dollar mutual funds industry,† by limiting sales charges and selling commissions. The Securities and Exchange Commission asked for prohibition of "front-end loads" (installment plans in which up to half of the investor's first year payments are deducted for sales charges), and for a flat five percent limit on sales commissions.

*Fire Safety*—The proposed Fire Research and Safety Act of 1967 would authorize the Secretary of Commerce to conduct directly or through contracts or grants a comprehensive nationwide program of fire research and safety, and would create a National Commission on Fire Prevention and Control.

*Electrical Power Reliability*—This measure would give the Federal Power Commission more power to deal with and guard against future widespread electric power outages.

---

* Truth-in-Lending signed May 29, 1968; Pipeline Safety signed August 14, 1968.

† Estimated at $48 billion for 1967.

## UNITED STATES CONSUMER COUNSEL

Another highlight of the "Year of the Consumer" was the naming of the first United States Consumer Counsel. Following up intentions announced in his "Consumer Message," President Johnson in the Spring of 1968, created the post in the Justice Department. However, instead of the counsel being an Assistant United States Attorney General with "real legal power" and operating as head of an Office of Consumer Counsel established by legislation, as recommended by Federal Trade Commission Philip Elman and others,* the office was created by Executive Order. This meant that the Consumer Counsel Office (as well as the President's Special Assistant for Consumer Affairs, his Consumer Advisory Council, and his Committee on Consumer Interests) faced possible elimination when a new Chief Executive took office.

**Consumerism takes root.** Many observers felt that the strong emphasis placed on "consumerism" by President Lyndon B. Johnson in 1968 was, at least partially, motivated by his decision not to seek re-election. Passage of even part of the large parcel of consumer protection legislation before Congress would be an impressive victory for the retiring President. While some predicted that Lyndon B. Johnson would "go down in history as the consumer-conscious President," Mr. Johnson himself seemed quite willing to share the honor, as recorded in his 1968 State of the Union address: "This (90th) Congress— Democrats and Republicans—can earn the thanks of history. We can make this a truly new day for the American consumer, and by giving him this protection, we can live in history as the consumer-conscious Congress."

The bipartisan nature of consumerism was firmly established when President Richard M. Nixon in 1969 announced his own plans for guaranteeing the consumer rights first set forth by President Kennedy in 1962.

His Buyer's Bill of Rights was offered by President Nixon as the Administration's approach to consolidation of various House and Senate proposals introduced early in the 91st Congress, and which sought to establish or enlarge Federal participation in consumer-related areas. Among these proposals were ones which would establish, variously, a cabinet level Department of Consumer Affairs, an independent sub-cabinet consumer agency, or a statutory Office of Consumer Affairs in the Executive Office of the President—the President's own recommendation. Mr. Nixon further recommended establishment of an office of Assistant Attorney General for Consumer Protection in the Department of Justice.

Committee action on the various proposals finally resulted in an omnibus Consumer Protection Organization Act of 1970 (S 4459) which passed the

---

* In 1966 Congressman Benjamin Rosenthal of New York had introduced a bill to create a Department of Consumers, and in 1967, Senator Philip A. Hart of Michigan introduced a measure to establish a National Consumer Service Foundation. Bills introduced in 1961 and again in 1963 by Senator Estes Kefauver to establish a Department of Consumers had also failed.

Senate in the closing weeks of the 91st Congress, but which died with adjournment in the absence of final action in the House.

**Buyer's bill of rights.** Disappointed over its lack of complete success in the 91st Congress, President Nixon at the beginning of the new 92nd session resubmitted his 11-point proposal designed to provide a Buyer's Bill of Rights by:

1. Creating by Executive Order a new Office of Consumer Affairs in the Executive Office of the President which will be responsible for analyzing and coordinating all Federal activities in the field of consumer protection.

2. Recognizing the need for effective representation of consumer interests in the regulatory process and making recommendations to accomplish this after full public discussion of the findings of the Advisory Council on Executive Organization.

3. Establishing within the Department of Health, Education and Welfare, a product safety program. The Secretary of Health, Education and Welfare would have authority to fix minimum safety standards for products and to ban from the marketplace those products that fail to meet those standards.

4. Proposing a Consumer Fraud Prevention Act which would make unlawful a broad but clearly-defined range of practices which are unfair and deceptive to consumers and would be enforced by the Department of Justice and the Federal Trade Commission. This act, where appropriate, would also enable consumers either as individuals or as a class to go into court to recover damages for violations of the act.

5. Proposing amendments to the Federal Trade Commission Act which will increase the effectiveness of the Federal Trade Commission.

6. Calling upon interested private citizens to undertake a thorough study of the adequacy of existing procedures for the resolution of disputes arising out of consumer transactions.

7. Proposing a Fair Warranty Disclosure Act which will provide for clearer warranties, and prohibit the use of deceptive warranties.

8. Proposing a Consumer Products Test Methods Act to provide incentives for increasing the amount of accurate and relevant information provided consumers about complex consumer products.

9. Resubmitting the Drug Identification Act which would require identification coding of all drug tablets and capsules.

10. Encouraging the establishment of a National Business Council to assist the business community in meeting its responsibilities to the consumer.

11. Proposing other reforms, including exploration of a Consumer Fraud Clearinghouse in the Federal Trade Commission, increased emphasis on consumer education, and new programs in the field of food and drug safety.

## OFFICE OF CONSUMER AFFAIRS

Superseding the old President's Committee on Consumer Interests, the Office of Consumer Affairs was created by Presidential Executive Order* early in 1971. Appointed first director of the new agency was Mrs. Virginia Knauer, former chief of PCCI, and who retained the title of Special Assistant to the President for Consumer Affairs.

Specific duties of the Office of Consumer Affairs include:

1. Encouraging and assisting in the development and implementation of consumer programs; coordinating and reviewing policies and programs; seeking the resolution of conflicts; advising and making recommendations to Federal agencies with respect to policy matters, the effectiveness of their programs and operations, and the elimination of duplications with respect to consumer interests in Federal policies and programs.

2. Assuring that the interests of consumers are presented and considered in a timely manner by the appropriate levels of the Federal Government in the formulation of policies and in the operation of programs that affect consumer interests.

3. Conducting investigations, conferences, and surveys concerning the needs, interests, and problems of consumers, and avoiding duplication of activities of other Federal agencies.

4. Submitting recommendations to the President on how Federal programs and activities affecting consumers can be improved.

5. Taking action on consumer complaints by referring complaints and other information to the Federal agency charged with enforcing the particular law, rule, or order being violated.

6. Performing the duties formerly assigned to its predecessor, the President's Committee on Consumer Interests.

7. Coordinating and disseminating information of interest to consumers in language that is readily understandable by laymen.

8. Assisting in consumer education programs.

9. Cooperating with state and local governments and with private enterprise in promoting and protecting consumer interests.

One of the main duties of the Special Assistant for Consumer Affairs is the establishment and distribution to every school district in the nation of guidelines for consumer education at the elementary and high school levels. Likewise, suggested guidelines for adult and continuing education have been established as steps toward developing informed consumers in all socio-economic groups.

In its efforts to keep the public informed about what the Federal departments

---

* No. 11583, February 24, 1971, as amended May 26, 1971.

and agencies are doing for the consuming public, OCA publishes a monthly newsletter, "Consumer News." Aim of the newsletter is to bring readers, in one publication, a brief account of the latest government programs to benefit the consumer and to keep the public up to date on plans for the future. Subscription cost is $1 per year, and the publication may be ordered from the Superintendent of Documents, Washington, D.C. 20402. Address of the Office of Consumer Affairs itself is New Executive Office Building, Washington, D.C. 20506.

## CONSUMER PRODUCT INFORMATION COORDINATING CENTER

Directed by Executive Order of the President,* the General Services Administration in 1970 set up the Consumer Product Information Coordinating Center to develop and distribute information based on government's purchasing know-how.

In establishing the new Center, President Richard M. Nixon pointed out that numerous agencies of the Federal government purchase from private industry a wide variety of consumer products for government use. He noted that the making of such purchases requires the development of extensive documents, reports, and other information for evaluating the products purchased, and that the government has an opportunity to help the consuming public by sharing with it the knowledge accumulated in the process of purchasing items for government use with tax dollars.

In cooperation with the Office of Consumer Affairs, the Consumer Product Information Coordinating Center publishes a "Consumer Product Information Index," listing various selected Federal publications of consumer interest. The index may be obtained from the Superintendent of Documents, Washington, D.C. 20402, or through the General Services Administration, Washington, D.C. 20405.

## OTHER CONSUMER PROTECTION ACTION IN THE 1970's

Both inside and outside the halls of Congress, a number of other important consumer protection measures gained approval in the years immediately following the now-famous Consumer Decade. Among them were:

1. Creation by the Justice Department of a new Consumer Affairs Section in its Antitrust Division.
2. Passage of the Consumer Class Action Act, allowing one or more persons acting on behalf of a larger group (class) of consumers, to bring civil actions in Federal courts in cases of fraud or deceptive practices. (A classic early case was a suit against Montgomery Ward on behalf of thousands of customers who involuntarily became policyholders of Ward's credit life insurance.)

---

* No. 11566, October 26, 1970.

3. Congressional action extending the life of the National Commission on Product Safety.

4. Senate passage of the Fair Credit Reporting Act (S823) requiring credit bureaus to disclose to consumers information in their credit files, delete inaccuracies, reinvestigate disputed items, permit consumers to file explanatory statements, destroy old files, and limit circulation.

5. Passage by the House of the Federal Credit Union Act to set up an independent Federal agency to supervise federally chartered credit unions.

6. Amendment of the Child Nutrition Act, making foods more readily available to needy children.

7. Food and Drug Administration proposal requiring all eyeglass lenses to be impact resistant or shatterproof.

8. Consumer product fact sheets prepared by U.S. Army Natick Laboratories to translate Federal Government purchasing specifications into plain English for the general public.

9. National Business Council for Consumer Affairs established in the Department of Commerce, as a vehicle through which government can work with business leaders to establish programs for fostering a marketplace which is fair both to those who sell and those who buy, and to encourage everyone who does business to do a better job of establishing competitive prices for high quality goods and services.

10. Establishment of the National Institute for Consumer Justice, to study adequacy of procedures for resolving disputes arising out of consumer transactions, including small-claims courts and arbitration.  Particular focus to be given to increasing incentives for voluntary settlements and to recommending more effective ways of assisting consumers in obtaining rapid satisfaction of claims. The Institute forwards recommendations to the President and to Congress.

11. Establishment by the Food and Drug Administration's Bureau of Product Safety an electronic system of reporting product-related injuries and enabling the Bureau to take prompt investigative and remedial action.

12. Warranty and guaranty legislation which enables consumers to choose reliable long-lasting products by requiring free repair or replacement of any malfunctioning product if that product malfunctions within the warranty period.

## THE ACTION LAG

It is difficult to understand why it should take six or eight years to effect such seriously needed consumer protection measures as the Truth-in-Packaging and Truth-in-Lending Laws.  But a look behind the scenes may help clarify the mystery—a handful of dedicated congressmen, uncertain as to the amount of backing they can count on from an often apathetic public, versus anti-legislation lobbying groups.    Representative Wright Patman, chairman of the House Banking and Currency Committee, expressed the feelings of himself and his colleagues on the subject during the late 1960's:

> "While (the consumerism movement is) gaining growing recognition, I feel that there are some tremendous gaps—some great weaknesses—in consumer action.    I must honestly say that I am gravely disappointed that there is so little mail, so little meaningful action, from consumers and consumer organizations on legislative issues.    This is particularly disappointing when your well-heeled opponents are beseiging the Congressional mail boxes and filling the halls with lobbyists."

Or, as another observed, ". . . never before . . . have so many been swindled so often in so many different ways out of so much . . . with so few protesting voices."*

**Unaware consumers.**    Obviously, the blame cannot all be laid at the doorsteps of the sellers.    The simple truth is that a seller cannot sell if a buyer will not buy. Resolution of consumer problems begs at least as much for informed consumers as for increased regulation, and there probably is some validity to the argument that the public does not even know what consumer services their government is providing.    Actually, almost every government agency either directly or indirectly performs some sort of consumer service, as we shall see.    Unfortunately, the fact that so much of government has so many "fingers in the stew" has not resulted in a tastier stew.    On the contrary, results have often been an overlapping of services, poorly defined responsibility, and the general confusion which is a recognized product of the proverbial "government red tape."    We offer no cure for the red tape, and no comment except to reiterate its inevitability—it is the price we pay for living in a democracy.

## GENESIS OF FEDERAL CONSUMER PROTECTION AGENCIES

Before considering a current listing of governmental consumer services, let us review the early beginnings of the Federal consumer protection movement in this country, including taking a detailed look at several of the most important consumer protection agencies.

**First Federal consumer protection laws**    In 1872, the 42nd Congress enacted legislation prohibiting fraudulent use of the United States mails.    Today, Postal Inspection Service authorities spend some $2 million a year to protect the public against mail fraud.    In one recent year, they received a record high of 130,000 complaints, action on which resulted in more than 1,500 arrests, 633 convictions, and discontinuance of more than 5,000 fraudulent promotions.

The first pieces of really dramatic Federal consumer protection legislation

---

* Curt Gentry, *The Vulnerable Americans.*    Garden City, N.Y.: Doubleday and Company, Inc., 1966, p. 11.

were the Meat Inspection and Pure Food and Drug Acts in 1906. In 1848, Congress had passed the Edwards Law prohibiting the importation of adulterated drugs, and more than 100 food and drug measures had been introduced in Congress between 1879 and 1906, but then, as now, it took a good deal of "muckraking" to stir up public alarm and bring legislative action. For example, disclosures of filthy, fraudulent, or dangerous products—foods dosed with chemical preservatives, candy colored with poisonous dyes, narcotic soothing syrups for babies, and the tragic consequences which followed when people believed in the cure-all promises of some "patent" medicines.

## THE FOOD AND DRUG ADMINISTRATION

Enforcement of the 1906 Food and Drugs Act was begun by the Bureau of Chemistry of the U.S. Department of Agriculture, which also administered the Filled Milk Act of 1923. In 1927, two new consumer protection measures, the Caustic Poison Act and Import Milk Act, were passed and a separate law-enforcement agency known as the Food, Drug and Insecticide Administration was formed; it became the Food and Drug Administration in 1931. Events in the period 1900 to 1930, and particularly during the "roaring twenties," resulted in complete revision of the 1906 law, and in 1938 it emerged as the Food, Drug and Cosmetic Act.

Cosmetic sales volumes had grown from $5 million at the turn of the century to $336 million in 1938.* Safety controls among manufacturers were virtually non-existent; reports of consumer injuries mounted. According to FDA Publication No. 26:

"Some of the products were very bad, indeed. Thallium—an ingredient now considered too dangerous for ordinary use even in rat poison—was used in a dipilatory, and it caused hair to fall from the head. High-mercury-content ointments were sold as skin-bleach creams. Chemicals capable of causing blindness were used in eyebrow dyes."

In addition to its control over cosmetics, the mission of the Food and Drug Administration is to "insure that foods are safe, pure, and wholesome, and made under sanitary conditions; drugs and therapeutic devices are safe and effective for their intended uses; and that all of these products (including cosmetics) are honestly and informatively labeled and packaged."

With its broad scope, the FDA functions today as a potent protector of American health and well-being. Significant dates in food and drug law history from 1938 to the present are summarized in the accompanying illustration.

## SIGNIFICANT DATES IN FOOD AND DRUG LAW HISTORY

1938  The Copeland Bill was passed by Congress. It was known as the Federal

---

* Today, cosmetics sales approach $4 billion annually.

Food, Drug and Cosmetic Act of 1938 (52 Stat. 1040) and contained these new provisions, among others:

Extended coverage to cosmetics and devices.

Required predistribution clearance of safety on new drugs.

Prohibited addition of poisonous or deleterious substances to foods, except where required or unavoidable.

Provided for tolerances for unavoidable or required poisonous substances.

Authorized standards of identity, quality, and fill of container for foods.

Authorized factory inspections.

Added the remedy of court injunction to previous remedies of seizure and prosecution.

1940 July 1—FDA transferred from the Department of Agriculture to the Federal Security Agency.

1945 July 6—Federal act amended to require certification of the safety and efficacy of penicillin. Later amendments extended this requirement to other antibiotics.

1948 June 24—Miller Amendment affirmed United States jurisdiction over products adulterated or misbranded after interstate shipment.

1951 October 26—Durham-Humphrey Amendment specifically required that drugs which cannot be safely used without medical supervision bear the prescription legend on the label and be dispensed only upon prescription.

1953 April 11—Federal Security Agency became U.S. Department of Health, Education and Welfare.

1954 July 22—Miller Pesticides Amendment, streamlines procedures for the setting of safety limits for pesticidal residues on raw agricultural commodities and greatly strengthened consumer protection.

1957 FDA reorganized by establishment of five bureaus, with scientific functions grouped into Bureau of Biological and Physical Sciences, and Bureau of Medicine. Administrative and enforcement functions were assigned to Bureau of Program Planning and Appraisal, Bureau of Field Administration, and Bureau of Enforcement.

1958 September—Food Additives Amendment enacted, prohibiting use of new food additives until promoter establishes safety and FDA issues regulations specifying condition of use.

December—Division of Public Information established to promote industry compliance and consumer protection through information and education program.

1960    July 12—Color Additive Amendments enacted to allow FDA to set safe limits on the amounts of colors which may be used in foods, drugs, and cosmetics and to require manufacturers to retest previously listed certifiable colors.

Federal Hazardous Substances Labeling Act passed to require prominent warning labeling on hazardous household chemicals.

1962    October 10—Kefauver-Harris Drug Amendments passed to assure a greater degree of safety, effectiveness, and reliability in prescription drugs and to strengthen new drug clearance procedures.

1965    Drug Abuse Control Amendments passed to stop indiscriminate sale and use of non-narcotic dangerous drugs.

**Other FDA services.**   Modern scientific methods required to enforce the Food, Drug and Cosmetic Act (at a cost of approximately 20 cents per person per year), mean that FDA scientists must know the normal composition of products to be tested and devise methods to detect those that are substandard.  They study the toxicity of ingredients used in the manufacture and production of foods, drugs, and cosmetics, paying particular attention to potential danger of long usage. Testing and evaluating the potency and effectiveness of vitamins and medicines is part of their job; so is the investigation of adequacy of controls over processing, preserving, packaging, and storage methods.   Specialists in bacteriology, chemistry and biochemistry, microanalysis, pharmacology, entomology, human and veterinary medicine, and many other sciences make up the FDA investigation staff.  In addition, approximately 1,000 specially trained inspectors visit factories, warehouses, and stores to collect samples for laboratory analysis in the Administration's 18 regional offices throughout the country.*

## CONSUMER AND MARKETING SERVICE

Another important consumer protection agency of the Department of Agriculture is the Consumer and Marketing Service.  Some of its activities, along with those of various other USDA agencies, are discussed in the chapters dealing with the purchasing of food and clothing.  Its major functions for consumers are:

1. Assuring that meat, poultry, and their products in *interstate* commerce are wholesome, fully and truthfully labeled, and free of disease.

---

* Detailed information on FDA consumer protection services, including material on standards, enforcement of the FDA Act, career opportunities with FDA, etc., may be obtained from any FDA Regional Office or by writing Food and Drug Administration, Department of Health, Education and Welfare, Washington, D.C. 20204.  Ask for "Packet A; Consumer Protection—Foods," or for "Packet B; Consumer Protection—Drugs and Cosmetics."   FDA Regional Offices are located in Atlanta, Baltimore, Boston, Buffalo, Chicago, Cincinnati, Dallas, Denver, Detroit, Kansas City, Los Angeles, Minneapolis, New Orleans, New York, Philadelphia, St. Louis, San Francisco, and Seattle.

2. Providing a system of grading food products to indicate quality, size, shape, etc.

3. Safeguarding competition and fairness in the marketing of farm products.

4. Providing money to help buy milk and other foods for school children for breakfasts and lunches, and donating food for needy adults and school children. Supplying food stamps to increase food buying power of low-income families.

5. Alerting consumers to foods currently abundant and likely to be good buys.

Activities of the Consumer and Marketing Service are carried out through cooperation with farm, industry, and research groups in establishing grade standards, acquiring and donating food for distribution to the needy (families, institutions, and schools), providing cash assistance for school lunch programs, providing matching funds to the states to initiate their own marketing programs, and issuing marketing orders which help stabilize the marketing of farm and dairy products.

Federal inspectors in the CMS prevent the sale in interstate commerce of meat and poultry products that do not meet Federal standards. They provide for grading of foods on a voluntary basis, with costs paid by producers and distributors. Also, they are authorized to issue orders banning deceptive or fraudulent practices in the labeling, marketing, and distributing of perishable fruits and vegetables, and banning unfair, deceptive, discriminatory, and monopolistic practices in the marketing of livestock, poultry, and meats.

Consumers make direct use of CMS when they buy foods bearing the Federal inspection mark, or when they rely on grade designations to determine relative quality of grade-labeled products. They can alert themselves to current good buys in the food market by following reports on plentiful foods issued weekly by USDA through local papers and other news media.*

## FEDERAL EXTENSION SERVICE

This agency of the Department of Agriculture operates as a part of a three-way partnership with state and county governments sharing in the financing, planning, and administration of out-of-school programs for youths and adults in agriculture, home economics, and related subjects. The partnership is known as the Cooperative Extension Service.

Major function of the Federal Extension Service is to extend to families and individuals practical consumer information, mostly evolving out of research done by the nation's land-grant universities and private industry.

Extension agents are usually located at the courthouse, post office, or other

* Details of CMS programs can be obtained by directing inquiries to Consumer and Marketing Service, U.S. Department of Agriculture, Washington, D.C. 20250, or to the local CMS office at the address listed in your local telephone directory.

government building in the county seat. Consumers may telephone, write, or visit for information or publications, many of which are available without charge. State Extension Service offices are located at land-grant universities.

## FEDERAL TRADE COMMISSION

The Government's chief protector of the consumer interest is the Federal Trade Commission, and in this capacity the Commission works to maintain free competitive enterprise as the keystone of the American economic system. The FTC was organized as an independent administrative agency in 1915, pursuant to the Federal Trade Commission Act of 1914, considered the single most important piece of consumer protection legislation ever enacted. Duties of the Commission are many and varied under the statutes, but underlying them all is one basic responsibility of preventing the free enterprise system from being stifled or fettered by monopoly or corrupted by unfair or deceptive practices.

Principal functions of the Commission are:

1. To promote free and fair competition in interstate commerce through prevention of price-fixing agreements, boycotts, combinations in restraint of trade, and other unfair methods of competition.

2. To safeguard the consuming public by preventing the dissemination of false or deceptive advertisements of food, drugs, cosmetics, and therapeutic devices, and other unfair or deceptive practices.

3. To prevent discriminations in price, exclusive-dealing and tying arrangements, and corporate mergers when such practices or arrangements may substantially lessen competition or tend toward monopoly; interlocking directorates under certain circumstances; the payment or receipt of illegal brokerage, and discrimination among competing customers in the furnishing of or payment for advertising or promotional services or facilities.

4. To enforce truthful labeling of textiles and fur products.

5. To prevent the interstate marketing of dangerously flammable wearing apparel or fabrics intended or sold for use in wearing apparel.

6. To regulate packaging and labeling of most consumer commodities so as to prevent consumer deception and facilitate value comparisons.

7. To supervise the registration and operation of associations of American exporters engaged solely in export trade.

8. To petition for cancellation of the registration of trade-marks which were illegally registered or used for purposes contrary to the intent of the Trade-Mark Act of 1946.

9. To gather and make available to the Congress, the President, and the public, factual data concerning economic and business conditions.

In regulating trade and commerce between the various states and within the District of Columbia, the FTC allows the accused party to agree to a consent judgment and stop the unlawful practice without admitting any violation of law. Failure to comply with this provision leaves the accused liable to being charged in a formal complaint and ordered to a hearing. An examiner who hears the case makes an initial decision, which may be appealed to the full Commission; the Commission's decision may, in turn, be appealed to the courts. Violation of an FTC order carries a maximum fine of $5,000 for each violation each day.

The FTC has no authority to act for you to recover your money if you are the victim of a deceitful or unfair practice. It can, however, investigate the case and take steps to halt illegal practices.

Anyone may file a complaint with the Federal Trade Commission by writing to one of its regional offices (located in major cities) or the FTC Headquarters, Washington, D.C. 20580. The complaint should be accompanied by as much supporting evidence as possible. Identity of the complainant is not disclosed by the FTC.

As a side-light, it is interesting to note that the Federal Trade Commission operates its consumer protection program on approximately $14 million a year —considerably less than the annual advertising budgets of many of the firms whose advertising it polices.

## OFFICE OF ECONOMIC OPPORTUNITY

A new agency within the Executive Office of the President is the Office of Economic Opportunity (popularly called the Anti-Poverty Agency) created in 1964 to "help low-income people break out of poverty and help others to avoid falling into it." Much of its activity is consumer-oriented. For example, it:

1. Helps low-income consumers learn how to get the most for their money in the purchase of goods and services.
2. Helps low-income consumers to solve consumer problems requiring legal assistance.
3. Improves living conditions and home management skills of low-income persons.
4. Provides low-income consumers with access to existing low-cost credit and savings institutions.
5. Helps low-income consumers create their own economic institutions designed to help them solve their own community consumer problems.

Programs are developed by local Community Action Agencies. Such a program might include, for instance, buying clubs, credit facilities, comparison shopping tours, consumer discussion groups, financial counseling, budgeting and debt reduction clinics, legal assistance, home management instruction, etc.

Information on OEO services may be obtained by contacting a local community action agency, state technical assistance agency, the regional office of OEO, or its national office at 1200–19th Street, N.W., Washington, D.C. 20506.

## OTHER FEDERAL AGENCIES

Space limitations prevent detailed reports concerning the activities of all those Federal offices and agencies listed by the President's Committee on Consumer Interests as being involved in "advancing and protecting the interest of the American consumer." However, if the programs of these agencies are to produce their full intended benefits, consumers must be at least acquainted with them. The following brief summaries provide you with basic information on current consumer programs. Where the agency is a subdivision of a government department, name of the parent department is shown in parentheses. Unless otherwise indicated, all of the agencies are headquartered in Washington, D.C., and all maintain information services from which additional details of their programs and specific instructions for obtaining service may be obtained, usually free of charge. Many of the agencies maintain regional offices from which help may be secured. To find a regional office of a particular agency, consult the listing in your local telephone directory under "United States Government." To contact the headquarters office, address your request to the agency by name, Washington, D.C. and use the zip code number shown in parentheses following the name as listed below:

*Administration on Aging* (20201)—strengthens and assists state and local agencies concerned with problems of aging, including consumer problems.

*Agricultural Research Service* (Agriculture, 20250)—protects food and fiber supplies from diseases and pests; regulates marketing of pesticides; breeds better crops, livestock, and ornamentals; finds new consumer uses for agricultural products; devises balanced diets; disseminates nutrition information, including calorie and vitamin content of food.

*Bureau of Family Services* (Health, Education and Welfare)—provides for financial assistance, through state agencies, for needy families with dependent children; provides for financial support, through state agencies, to needy blind, aged, disabled, mentally ill or tubercular people; provides for free medical care, through state agencies, for needy individuals and families not covered by Medicare and other services; provides for advice and counseling on a wide variety of personal and family matters as home management, child care, marital discord, homemaking and budgeting.

*Bureau of Federal Credit Unions* (HEW, 20201)—grants Federal credit union charters to qualified groups; regulates the operations of Federally chartered credit unions throughout the country to ensure sound operation.

*Bureau of Labor Statistics* (Labor, 20210)—provides technical information on cost of living, family expenditures and standards of living, through the monthly Consumer Price Index.

*Bureau of Public Roads* (Commerce, 20230)—improves highway systems in cooperation with the states; surveys and constructs roads on public lands (such as parks, forests, and defense installations); stimulates improvement of auxiliary facilities such as freeway lighting, snow and ice removal, and electronic guidance systems; develops and promotes programs for highway safety.

*Children's Bureau* (HEW, 20201)—helps states extend and improve their maternal and child health, crippled children's and child welfare services; provides comprehensive health care for preschool and school children, particularly in areas with concentration of low-income families; provides medical care to women who during the maternity period are unlikely to receive necessary health care because of low incomes or for other reasons (including health care for mothers and infants following childbirth); issues guides and publications for parents, teenagers, and professional personnel; conducts research in child health and welfare problems.

*Civil Aeronautics Board* (20482)—encourages development of an air transportation system that fits the needs of commerce, national defense, postal service, and the general public; promotes efficient service at reasonable charges; provides for enough competition to assure sound growth of air service to meet the public need; assists in development of international air service.

*Department of Defense* (20315)—protects military personnel as consumers of commercial products and services by prescribing certain minimum standards, thereby affecting some consumer services to the public because of the large number of business firms involved; provides free burial to military veterans and their immediate family; sets standards for procurement of supplies that may affect standards of quality available to the public because of the large quantities purchased; arranges for civil defense; provides a wide variety of civil functions for the public benefit through the U.S. Army Corps of Engineers.

*Environmental Sciences Services Administration* (Commerce, Rockville, Md., 20852)—forecasts the weather and warns of floods, hurricanes, tornadoes and blizzards; provides nautical and aeronautical charts, many of which are useful in recreational pursuits. Provides local up-to-the-minute weather information through local news media or by telephone. (See "Weather Bureau" under United States Government listings in local telephone directories.)

*Federal Aviation Agency* (20553)—promotes air transport safety and ensures efficient operation of air transportation; promotes development of supersonic transport; establishes safety standards for air operations; conducts research into all phases of aviation safety.

*Federal Communications Commission* (20554)—assures that adequate facilities are available at reasonable rates to meet the needs of the public and for interstate and foreign communication service; regulates the number and type of radio and television stations and community antenna television (CATV) services; sees that holders of licenses operate in the public interest; promotes more effective use of radio and television for public purposes such as marine and aviation safety, police and fire, business radio (taxicabs, etc.), the new non-broadcast television service for in-school instruction, and the citizens ("ham") radio service; promotes communication satellite to meet public needs at reasonable rates.

*Federal Deposit Insurance Corporation* (20429)—insures deposits in banks which are eligible for Federal deposit insurance. The insurance covers deposits of every kind, whether public or private, including regular commercial deposits, time deposits, savings, and trust funds awaiting investment. Maximum protection to a depositor in an insured bank is $15,000.

*Federal Housing Administration* (Housing and Urban Development, 20410)— by insuring home loans, brings home ownership within the reach of people who otherwise might not be able to afford it; provides means of repairing and improving houses on borrowed funds; assures house purchasers of quality construction; stabilizes interest rates and improves availability of mortgage money in the housing market.

*Federal Power Commission* (20426)—regulates rates charged at the wholesale level by electricity and gas producers in interstate commerce; regulates construction of interstate pipelines and hydro-electric projects; insures adequate supplies for the present and anticipated needs of the public; stimulates development of public recreational facilities at hydro-electric projects; promotes interconnection and coordination of electric systems to assure adequate supplies with the greatest possible economy and utilization and conservation of natural resources.

*General Services Administration* (20405)—in purchasing supplies for the Federal Government, GSA sets product standards which often influence the quality of goods available to consumers on the open market.

*Government Printing Office* (20402)—furnishes government publications free or at minimum cost. About 25,000 titles are currently available, and free lists of titles under 47 subject headings are available on request. A price list of government consumer publications (Price List 86) including order blanks is available at 10 cents a copy. Address requests for price list or lists of titles (specify subject) to Superintendent of Documents, U.S. Printing Office, Washington, D.C. 20402.

*Department of the Interior* (20240)—seeks to assure adequate supplies of water for public use; provides certain park and recreation areas and facilities for public use; supervises facilities and services operated within the National Parks for concessionaires under contract; markets electric power within certain regions of the country where Federal hydroelectric power dams have been constructed; provides protection for purchasers of Indian and Eskimo arts and crafts.

*Interstate Commerce Commission* (20423)—seeks to ensure reasonable transportation charges, adequate and efficient service, and public safety. (The safety functions of ICC were transferred to the Department of Transportation on April 1, 1967.)

*Department of Justice* (20530)—enforces Federal laws for consumer protection through cases referred to it by other government agencies, such as FDA, FTC, Post Office, and SEC.

*National Bureau of Standards* (Commerce, 20234)—develops criteria with which to measure the quality and performance of materials, many of which are used in consumer goods; sets standards for certain consumer goods and industrial materials used in making products of various types; promotes development of uniform laws governing weights and measures.

*National Traffic Safety Agency and National Highway Agency* (Transportation, 20590)—ensures that all new cars manufactured after January 1, 1968 will conform to Federal motor vehicle safety regulations; make roads and highways safer for drivers and pedestrians; set national standards of tests and regulations for drivers.

*Office of Education* (HEW, 20202)—stimulates the development of new courses, new programs, facilities, and buildings for educational purposes; encourages the development of special programs, which may include consumer education, in the Nation's schools; identifies educational problems of national concern and recommends solution.

*Office of Metropolitan Development* (HUD, 20410)—fosters the planning and construction of public works projects to provide water, sewer, transit, street, school, and park services and beautification in metropolitan areas.

*Office of Renewal and Housing Assistance* (HUD, 20410)—makes more low-rent housing units available for low-income persons, especially the elderly and handicapped; helps tenants in public housing projects to improve their spending habits through consumer education; works with manufacturers to improve household appliances and other products used in public housing projects; seeks to improve environmental standards of neighborhoods, including better services and facilities for consumers; helps home owners in urban renewal areas to improve their homes and ease the hardship of moving.

*U.S. Postal Service* (20260)—provides mail service; provides insurance for valuables sent through the mails; sells international money orders; protects people from dangerous articles, contraband, fraudulent promotion material, and pornography transmitted by mail; sells U.S. Savings Bonds.

*Public Health Service* (HEW, 20201)—stimulates development of medical and dental facilities and public health services; develops programs to prevent accidental injuries and to control communicable and chronic diseases; helps maintain a healthful environment by stimulating action against air pollution and other environmental health hazards; conducts and supports health and health-related research; aids the development of programs and facilities to train health workers; fights mental illness through research and support for community facilities construction and mental health programs; provides assistance to states and communities in combatting epidemics and natural disasters; guards against the introduction of communicable diseases into the United States; provides medical services to merchant seamen, American Indians, Alaskan natives, and others eligible to receive direct government medical services.

*Rural Development and Conservation* (Agriculture, 20250)—includes the Rural Community Development Service, Farmers Home Administration, Forest Service, Rural Electrification Administration and Soil Conservation Service. RCDS helps rural people obtain better access to Federal programs, which are not now fully used in rural areas. FHA provides credit and management assistance to farmers for ownership and operation of family-size farms; provides credit to both farm and non-farm rural residents to build and improve homes (including some rental housing); provides loans and grants to build rural community water and waste disposal systems; makes loans for soil conservation, watershed and forestry development, and rural community recreation centers; provides loans administered for OEO. The Forest Service promotes conservation and best use of the Nation's forest land resources. SCS offers technical assistance to landowners in stabilizing and improving soil, water, plant and wildlife resources on private lands; helps rural landowners establish income-producing recreation areas.

*Securities and Exchange Commission* (20549)—protects the public in the purchase and sale of stocks and bonds and in the operation of investment companies.

*Social Security Administration* (HEW)—information and service available from any of more than 700 offices listed in local telephone directories, or write to Social Security Administration, 6401 Security Blvd., Baltimore, Md. 21235—provides an insurance program to furnish income to persons and their families in old age and in the event of disability or death; provides a health insurance program to help pay health care expenses for persons 65 years of age or older; studies problems of poverty and insecurity to see how social insurance can alleviate them.

*Department of the Treasury* (20226)—among its many bureaus and offices, those most closely affecting consumers include the Internal Revenue Service, Secret Service, Customs Service, Savings Bonds Division, Bureau of Narcotics, and Comptroller of the Tax Division—is charged with preventing consumer deception in the labeling and advertising of alcoholic beverages, preventing the re-use of liquor bottles, and regulating other products containing alcohol. The Secret Service guards against counterfeiting of currency, the forging of government checks, and protects the President and Vice President. The Savings Bonds Division promotes the sale of government bonds. The Customs Service renders services to the traveling public and the commercial community. The

Bureau of Narcotics controls the import and manufacture of narcotics. The Comptroller of the Currency protects the depositors in 4,800 national banks throughout the country.

*Veterans Administration* (20420)—for veterans only, furnishes hospitalization and other medical care; for veterans, their dependents, and their survivors (depending upon their eligibility), provides various kinds of financial benefits and other assistance.

## CONSUMER PROTECTION IN THE STATES

Even the most enthusiastic proponents of Federal consumer protection programs agree the job is not Washington's alone. Nor should it be. The voice of the consumer needs to be heard and heeded at home as well as in Washington. State—and to only a slightly lesser degree, county and municipal—governments share the responsibility. Some are accepting the challenge. In other instances, however, meaningful action is slow in developing.

Actually, many aspects of consumer protection *must* be carried out at the state level if at all, and there are some others that can be dealt with more effectively locally than under Federal programs. For example, the Federal Government possesses no jurisdiction over products which move in *intrastate* commerce—almost 50 percent of the nation's total food, drug, and cosmetic production. The other 50 percent moved across state boundaries is *interstate* commerce and is, of course, subject to Federal regulation.

State and local licensing and business regulation departments can screen out many unscrupulous operations. Much consumer fraud can be controlled by effective use of police power. "Hot line" telephone alert systems to inform local officials of fraudulent operations have proved effective both within and between states. The value of publicity is cited by some, including a North Dakota Assistant Attorney General who says: "One of our best weapons has been immediate press releases warning the citizens of the state with regard to fraudulent practices which have been reported to this office." Another potential weapon employed thus far by only a handful of the states is the "Little FTC Law," which outlaws *any* deceptive practice and eliminates the need for piecemeal legislation to control specific objectionable practices as they arise.

As might be expected under democratic law, where each state develops its own course of action, no two have identical consumer protection programs. In fact, appraisals by officials of the various states themselves of their respective programs run the gamut from "excellent" to "poor."* For example:

> "We are very fortunate in getting our legislature to pass good consumer protection legislation."

* Responses of Attorneys or Assistant Attorneys General to the author's survey to determine the current status of consumer protection in each state. Only four states failed to reply; one which did, summarily dismissing the request, wrote: ". . . has no consumer protection law; . . . (and) we do not have the time or the personnel to answer this type of inquiry."

"We believe (ours) is the most comprehensive package of consumer protection legislation of any state."

"It is our belief that ours is the leading state in the area of consumer protection."

"Our present laws leave much to be desired."

"Proposed legislation to protect the consumer was defeated."

"Generally, (the law) does not appear to have been actively enforced."

It is not our purpose here to evaluate the relative merits of various consumer protection proposals or programs, but rather to point out *what is being done* in various states. Nevertheless, it seems appropriate to consider one recommendation of Washington Senator Warren G. Magnuson: *

> "The ease with which states could assume the legal authority to fight wholesale fraud, if state legislators were so inclined, is phenomenal. The Federal Trade Commission, which is capable of stopping nearly every type of scheme imaginable, operates under a statute singular in its simplicity and brevity. The heart of the statute (Section 45, Title 15 of the U.S. Code) is but nineteen words. It reads: "Unfair methods of competition in commerce, and unfair or deceptive acts or practices in commerce are hereby declared unlawful."
>
> The mark of effectiveness that distinguishes this law from many of the states' criminal statutes is that it is a civil statute aimed solely at stopping deceptive activities without the need to prove the wrongdoer guilty of a crime . . . the FTC can simply order him to "cease and desist" from his "unfair, false or misleading" business practice. If he does not do so, he is subject to civil penalties of up to $5,000 per day for each violation.
>
> Proof of intent to deceive is not necessary. . . . It is sufficient that the claims are false and are likely to mislead prospective purchasers."

**Surveys of state programs.** It is conceivable that, acting on Senator Magnuson's recommendation, states which do not yet have consumer protection laws could come up with programs superior to many of those which already exist. But let us turn now from speculation to reality. In response to the previously mentioned survey, as well as one conducted by the Office of Consumer Affairs in 1971, it was determined that:

1. Legislators of 43 states have enacted *some* consumer protection measures.

2. In 18 of the states there have been established specific agencies (Department of Consumer Protection, Office of Consumer Services, etc.) to handle programs and services.

3. In 36 states the consumer protection service operates as a division of the Attorney General's office.

4. The Bureau of Consumer Frauds and Protection of one state (New York) was established as early as 1957; in 1959, a Department of Consumer

* Warren G. Magnuson and Jean Carper, *The Dark Side of the Marketplace: The Plight of the American Consumer*. Englewood Cliffs, N.J.: Prentice-Hall, Inc., 1968, p. 64.

Protection was set up in Connecticut, and an Office of Consumer Counsel was established in California; the special consumer protection agencies of three states (Arizona, Florida, and Massachusetts) were organized as recently as 1967.

5. Consumer protection measures are pending before the legislatures of eight states.

6. A majority of the responses stressed the importance of consumer education. "The best protection against fraud and deception is an alert and wary consumer," was a typical comment.

**Local programs.** Local consumer counsels (and/or councils) have been organized in recent years in a number of municipalities, including New York City; Los Altos and Palo Alto, California; Miami, Florida; and Nassau County, New York. In addition, there are a number of private consumer organizations operating nationally and within the various states, some of which are discussed in Chapter 7, "Other Consumer Protection Services." The same chapter includes a look at the international consumer movement.

### EDUCATION AS AN AID TO THE CONSUMER
Growing complexities of the marketplace make the need for consumer education urgent. Just as an individual needs work skills to get and hold a job, he needs buying skills if he is to get the most for the money he earns. There is little question that education is the potentially most valuable of all government aids to the consumer.

Recognizing this, the President's Committee on Consumer Interests has sought to stimulate action by appropriate groups, from parents to school administrators, and to urge Federal agencies and others to provide materials for use in teaching. Accomplishments of the PCCI in this regard include cooperating with the United States Office of Education to publish the helpful booklet, "Sources of Federal Assistance for Consumer Education," establishing an information committee to further consumer education programs for both youths and adults, and publicizing sections of those laws authorizing Federal assistance. The Committee has also been a co-sponsor (with the National Committee for Education in Family Finance) of a number of "Consumer Education and Financial Planning" workshops. Working with the Office of Economic Opportunity, the PCCI encouraged establishment of consumer education components in Community Action Programs and other anti-poverty projects throughout the country.

**State participation.**  As interest in consumer education has increased, and as educators as well as producers of consumer goods have begun to recognize the buying potential of American youth (disposable income of over $25 billion a year) several states have instituted consumer economics courses in their public schools.  One of the most comprehensive is that developed at Lincoln High School in Yonkers, New York.  The program consists of a one-year elective course in consumer problems plus a series of assemblies in which experts in business and government deal with frauds.  Additionally, consumer education is integrated into the entire curriculum from seventh grade on up.

Similar programs are being instituted elsewhere in New York State, and in New Jersey, Idaho, and Washington.  One elementary school (Meadow Moor) in Salt Lake City, Utah, has instituted a unique program to teach consumer credit principles at the fourth grade level.  And schools in New York City, Chicago, Baltimore, Norfolk, Oklahoma City, Minneapolis, and Hartford offer separate courses in the field or include consumer education as part of other courses.  On the junior high school level, the women's program of New York State Commerce Department has gained nationwide attention staging its teen-age consumer assemblies throughout the state.  Most of these programs are traceable to the impact of government interest and concern.

**Work of other groups.**  It is impossible to determine the full extent of government influence on the development of consumer education programs throughout the nation.  To give government all the credit, however, would be unjust.  From the business community—working to improve information to the consumer—have come such important committees as the Textile Advisory Council and the Industry Advisory Committee on Footwear Information.  Labor organizations, women's clubs, and church groups have made important contributions.  The efforts of these private groups are discussed in Chapter 7.  But who gets the credit is not nearly so important as the fact that the action is taking place.

## FEEDBACK 6

**A.**  On your next grocery shopping trip, take special notice of meat grades. These are regulated by the Department of Agriculture, and each grade specifies certain qualities about the meat which you buy.  Through the local office of the Department of Agriculture, or by interviewing your butcher, find out what is meant by "Prime," "Choice," "Good," "Commercial."

- Given your taste and pocketbook, which grade meets your standards for food you want to buy?
- Which requires special, at-home preparation to be palatable?
- Based on your acquaintance with other markets in your area, what is the best combination of grade, price, and palatability for meat sold in your shopping area?
- Which meat counter trims closest? The meat you eat is what you pay for, and fat and bone you throw away actually raise the relative price of the meat.

**B.** Read the label on several brands of aspirin, including the high-priced, well-advertised brands.
- Is there a difference in content?
- Is there a difference in price?
- By dividing the quantity by the price, which brand and size is the best buy *per tablet*?

**C.** Through a Food and Drug Administration office, or a Consumer and Marketing office (USDA) obtain definitions for these contents of food you buy daily or weekly:
- Sodium nitrate, sodium nitrite, benzoate of soda, monosodium glutamate, stabilizers, tripe, meat by-products, BHT, Lecithin, "Fortified," heavy syrup.
- Which of these are nutritional?
- Discuss in class the probable or defined reasons for these additives.

**D** Find out which brands of bread your classmates buy. Avoiding duplication, have five brands of white bread brought to class.
- Compare weight and price of each.
- Compare ingredients of each.
- Compare size of loaf and weight.
- On equivalent brands (interchangeable), is there one which is a better buy?

**E.** In a pharmacy, or the drug section of a supermarket, examine the labels of non-prescription drugs and cosmetics. Pay special attention to warnings, weight, potency, U.S.P. rating and tablet count.
- Without a prescription, can you buy drugs with "habit forming" potential?
- Find three different examples of specific cautions, like: "Do not swallow." "Not to be taken internally." "Do not use near eyes." "Avoid contact with skin." "Use in a well-ventilated room."

**DISCUSSION QUESTIONS**

1. Why was there such a rise in awareness of consumer problems during the "Consumer Decade"?

2. Is it the Government's duty to protect consumers? Explain.

3. What is your opinion of the Cigarette Labeling Act? Is it doing the job that it was set up to do? Explain.

4. Why did Congress have trouble passing most inspection bills in the past? What caused the change in recent years?

5. Do most consumers know what services their government is providing in consumer affairs? Explain.

6. How does the Federal Trade Commission help the individual consumer?

7. What are some of the consumer protection measures that are operating in your state?

8. Is consumer protection so widely needed that it should be a duty of the Federal Government instead of the state or local levels?

9. What is the best way to go about educating the public about getting the most from money that they earn?

10. When should consumer education begin for a person? Why?

**CASE PROBLEM**

One evening, Mr. Jackson and his neighbor were having a heated discussion about politics and the government. It started out as a general discussion but later turned to the role of the Federal Government in the lives of private citizens. Mr. Smith stressed the point that the laws made by Congress were representative of the people and should not be thought of as some unreasonable standards interfering with the public's private lives—what Government does should be regarded as something done in the best interests of its people.

"But take a look at what Congress has gone and done now!" the neighbor responded. "I can't even buy a pack of cigarettes without the government telling me that they're bad for me. I'm the one that is putting out the money, not them —nobody should have to tell me what's good to buy and what's not!"

a) How do you think Smith explained the Federal Cigarette Labeling and Advertising Act to his neighbor?

b) What other measures made by Government do you believe Smith spoke about to support his views?

c) How would Smith view the work of Ralph Nader? How would the neighbor view it?

**SUGGESTED READINGS**

Bishop, James, and Henry W. Hubbard. *Let the Seller Beware*. Washington: National Press, 1969. 195 pp.

Clason, George Samuel. *The Book of Cures for Lean Purses.* Denver: Institute of Financial Education, 1937.

Directory of Government Agencies. *Safeguarding Consumers and Environment.* Alexandria, Va.: Serina Press, 1968.

Dunkman, William Edward. *Money, Credit and Banking.* New York: Random House, 1970. 470 pp.

Gentry, Curt. *The Vulnerable American.* Garden City, N.Y.: Doubleday, 1966. 333 pp.

Joyce, George. *The Black Consumer.* New York: Random House, 1971. 369 pp.

Magnuson, Warren Grant, and Jean Carper. *The Dark Side of the Marketplace; The Plight of the American Consumer.* Englewood Cliffs, N.J.: Prentice-Hall, 1968. 240 pp.

Margolius, Sidney. *Buyer, Be Wary!* New York: Public Affairs Pamphlets, 1967. 28 pp.

Margolius, Sidney. *How to Buy More for Your Money.* New York: Doubleday, 1947. 128 pp.

McNeal, James U. (ed.). *Dimensions of Consumer Behavior* (second edition). New York: Appleton-Century-Crofts, 1969. 446 pp.

Mowbray, A. Q. *The Thumb on the Scale; Or the Supermarket Shell Game.* Philadelphia: Lippincott, 1967. 178 pp.

Sanford, David. *Hot War on the Consumer.* New York: Pitman, 1969. 280 pp.

Schoenfeld, David, and Arthur A. Natella. *The Consumer and His Dollars.* Dobbs Ferry, N.Y.: Oceana Publications, 1970. 365 pp.

*Service: USDA's Report to Consumers.* Washington, D.C.: USDA, 1968. 4 pp.

Troelstrup, Arch W. *The Consumer in American Society.* New York: McGraw-Hill, 1970. 668 pp.

CHAPTER 7

# OTHER CONSUMER PROTECTION SERVICES

Certainly, government's recent involvement in furthering consumer interest, as detailed in the preceding chapter, is commendable. But it would be naïve indeed for consumers to rely solely on the protective arm of government to shield them against unfair marketing practices or to always guide them to prudent purchasing.

In the first place, all too often there are wide gaps between passage of laws and their enforcement. In the second place, government is not the only—nor necessarily the best—source of consumer protection services and information. Business and industry deserve much credit; so do countless individuals and organizations, as will be discussed shortly.

Unquestionably, personal experience is the best teacher and, therefore, your most valuable source of consumer protection. Once you *get stung*, you protect yourself against the same or similar offenses in the future. However, this kind of personal experience can be a devastatingly expensive learning process. As the old saying so aptly expresses it, "Experience keeps a dear school, but the fool will learn in no other."

Making experienced fools of ourselves to gain consumer know-how is not necessary. From the experience of others much information and many services are accessible to the consumer who avails himself of them. As a matter of paradoxical fact, if consumers made greater use of *private* sources of information and services, there would be much less need for governmental consumer protection programs.

This does not mean that *no* government action is called for. Government can do some jobs more effectively than can any individual or group. But it is to the consumer's benefit to recognize that (1) government is not and should not be doing the whole job, (2) help is available from other sources, and (3) consumers will benefit in direct proportion to their discovery and use of consumer protection aids from various sources.

The purpose of this chapter is to identify not all of these aids, but at least a useful variety. The discussion provides information about the various kinds of services offered and indicates possible sources of detailed consumer protection information. In this chapter you will be learning what to look for and where and how to find it.  You will be getting help in becoming a wise, informed consumer, equipped to make educated choices rather than irrational guesses.

## DEFINITION OF TERMS

It may be well to determine what distinction, if any, should be drawn between the terms *information* and *services* as they are employed in this chapter.  Taken out of context, they do have separate and distinct definitions.  But within the present frame of reference, *consumer protection information* must be considered a *consumer protection service*, and vice versa.  To the consumer, information and service are equally important.  Therefore, either or both of these terms will be used interchangeably throughout the chapter.

## SOURCES OF INFORMATION AND SERVICES

It has already been pointed out that the primary sources of consumer protection information and services are our own personal experience, plus the experiences and advice of family, friends, and neighbors reporting to us in informal conversation; producers of goods telling their stories in the labels attached to their products; the sellers of those products through their advertisements, and individuals and organizations communicating their knowledge to us through technical reports.

**What to look for and where to find it.**  Consumer information dispensed by personal acquaintances is often invaluable, and there is little need for advice about how to obtain assistance from these sources.  One can hardly escape it!  Let us, therefore, turn our attention to the efforts of the producers and sellers of goods and to the somewhat more objective evaluations of those engaged in product testing and research.  But before we proceed, it is important to bear in mind one significant observation: Consumer protection information or service, from whatever source, is reliable only to the degree that its dispensers are truthful and just in their evaluations and judgments.

## HOW PRODUCERS AID CONSUMERS

A hundred or even 50 years ago, when families raised most of their own food and made much of their own clothing, they had little cause for concern about quality.  They *knew the product* and what to expect of it.  Even later, when individuals and families began relying on each other to supply their needs and wants, their concern about quality and value for their money was minimal, because they *knew the producer*; he was their friend or neighbor.  Their chief concern was the development of good personal relationships; hence, the persons who served one another did so efficiently and truthfully.

But over the years, technology and progress have brought us wonderful new products in great abundance and variety.  There are upwards of 10,000 different items in some large grocery stores.  And along with this superabundance have come myriad consumer problems, not the least of which is determining which buy will provide the most and/or the best for the money. Except in rare instances, producers and their consumers are no longer neighbors, or even members of the same communities. Personal contact between them seldom exists, yet unless the producer tells a convincing story of the merits of his wares to the prospective buyer, he has no market for those goods. So, the producer has devised labels to speak for him.

## VALUE OF LABELS TO CONSUMERS

Labels carry a twofold message: (1) information the producer *wants* to tell the consumer—which may also, but does not necessarily, include (2) information the government *requires* the producer to tell the consumer. In other words, the government demands that labels disclose certain information whether or not the producer desires to do so. In considering these two types of information, we shall discover the real value of labels.

Some of the legal aspects of labeling were discussed among government aids to the consumer in Chapter 6. However, government regulation is an integral part of consumer goods labeling and one which makes labels the effective private aid to the consumer that they are. Indeed, by faithfully complying with government regulations regarding labeling, producers provide invaluable service to consumers. For these reasons, the ensuing discussion is included in this, rather than the preceding, chapter.

**Labels and the law.** We have already seen that labels contain information demanded by law for consumer protection. They must contain none of the exaggerations or deceptions which have made it difficult, if not impossible, for the consumer of a few decades ago to know what he was getting when he made a purchase. Labels must state clearly and exactly the product's contents or composition, and must do so in a manner which does not mislead the buyer. They must be easy to read (without the aid of a magnifying glass) and to understand under ordinary conditions of purchase and use. Labels which do this can help the buyer obtain value for his money and guard his health.

The label must include the name and address of the producer or distributor, identity (name, and usually a picture) of the product, and the quantity of contents in terms of weight, measure, or count. Generally, the label also includes the product brand name and the manufacturer's trade mark (a word, letter or other symbol which identifies the manufacturer and which may be, but is not necessarily, evidence of product quality). Sometimes, labels also include directions for use and claims for performance.  Hazardous and inflammable substances must bear warning legends on the labels.

Provisions of the Fair Packaging and Labeling Act of 1966 put an end to such deceptive labeling as *king size*, *giant size*, or *large household size*.  Now, the label must state exactly the net quantity in ounces or pounds and fractions thereof—certainly a boon to the housewife trying to make value/price comparisons between different weight *king size* packages of laundry detergent, for example.  Or, another example, the label on a bottle of cooking oil which formerly read *one pint, eight ounces* must now state the contents as *24 ounces* or *1½ pints*.

NET WT. 1ᴸᴮ.6ᴼᶻ. (22 oz.)

## LABELING OF PROCESSED FOODS

Fortunately for the consumer, who generally spends a major portion of his income on groceries, labels on processed foods must state several facts in addition to those listed above.  Except in the case of *standardized* food, which will be discussed later, the labels on any food product containing two or more ingredients must list each one by its common name, *in order of its predominance in the product*.  For example, by reading the label a consumer could get a fair idea of the proportion of meat to vegetables in a can of beef stew (which she might well decide should have been labeled vegetable-beef stew) on which the ingredients are listed as follows: potatoes, water, carrots, beef, food starch, salt, flavoring, cereal, caramel coloring, and monosodium glutamate.  Or, consider the list of ingredients for a 4½-ounce bottle of strained baby food labeled "Vegetables and Bacon": water, carrots, tomatoes, bacon, food starch, modified defatted soy flour, onions, dehydrated potatoes, salt, celery, smoked yeast.

Imitations must be prominently labeled.  For example, unless it is pure vanilla extract, it must be labeled "imitation vanilla flavoring," and so on.  In stating net contents, if the food is liquid it must be labeled in terms of liquid measure; if it is solid or a mixture of solid and liquid it must be labeled in terms of weight.  Container size must not be misleading.  Even though the correct quantity of contents is listed on the label, the product must fill the package.

For some fruits and vegetables, the label must state variety (for example, yellow cling peaches), style of pack (whole, sliced, etc.) and the packing medium (sugar syrup, water, etc.).  Artificial coloring or flavoring and/or chemical preservatives must be listed, and labels on food that does not meet certain established standards must state that fact.

**"Standardized" foods.**  Special standards which have been set by the Food and Drug Administration for many foods include Standards of (1) Identity, (2) Quality, (3) Fill of Container, and (4) Standards for Enriched Products.

Food standards are designed to promote honesty and fair dealing by preventing the production and sale of goods that cheat the consumer or compete unfairly with the products of honest manufacturers. Federal law provides for the establishment of such definitions and standards for foods "whenever the Secretary of Health, Education and Welfare decides that such action is in the best interest of the public."

**Standards of identity.** This type of standard, also called a *"Definition and Standard of Identity,"* defines any given food product, that is, what the consumer can expect when selecting food by its common or usual name. The standard sets the minimum amounts of the "valuable ingredients" in a food product, and may even set a limit on a secondary ingredient such as water. In other words, a Definition and Standard of Identity (DSI) tells what ingredients are in the food, and may specify the proportions. It requires that for certain foods certain basic ingredients must be used, and designates the only other ingredients which may be used at the packer's option.

Because the ingredients of a food product for which a DSI has been established are named in the standards, they need not be listed on the label. However, optional ingredients must be named when the interests of the consumer require it. An example is canned mushrooms, on which the label states, "salt added." In this case, mushrooms are the "valuable" or standard ingredient and salt is optional.

To cite another illustration, the DSI for cheddar cheese protects the consumer against paying cheese prices for excess water, by requiring that the product contain at least 40 percent milk fat and not more than 39 percent moisture.

**Standards of quality.** These are *minimum* standards only, which establish specifications for such quality factors as color, tenderness, and freedom from defects. Standards of Quality do not grade foods, i.e., "fancy," "select," "A," etc., but provide for special labeling of any product not up to usual consumer expectation. In other words, they set a minimum quality below which foods must not fall without being labeled with such appropriate legends as these:

| | |
|---|---|
| **BELOW STANDARD IN QUALITY**<br>GOOD FOOD—NOT HIGH GRADE | **BELOW STANDARD IN QUALITY**<br>NOT WELL-PEELED, UNEVENLY TRIMMED |

**BELOW STANDARD IN QUALITY**
EXCESSIVE DISCOLORED PEAS

"Below Standard in Quality. Good Food—Not High Grade," or "Below Standard in Quality. Not Well-Peeled, Unevenly Trimmed." When these legends are used, they must appear in bold letters and be of a size proportionate to the size of the package.

**Standards of fill of container.** These are standards which specify how full a container must be to avoid charges of consumer deception of *slack fill*, which is the practice of selling air, water, or space in a container which could have held more of the product. Standards of Fill of Container are especially important in the packaging of products such as cereal and crackers, for example, which settle after filling.

> THIS PACKAGE IS SOLD BY WEIGHT, NOT VOLUME. SOME SETTLING OF CONTENTS MAY HAVE OCCURRED DURING SHIPMENT AND HANDLING.

**Standards for enriched food products.** These standards provide that *enriched* food actually has been improved by the addition of significant amounts of vitamins or other nutrients, and that the enriching ingredient is not merely a minute amount added just for advertising purposes. If a label claims vitamin content, the food must indeed contain the amount of the vitamin stated, and these foods (or foods for special dietary use) must state the percentage of the minimum daily requirements of those vitamins supplied by a stated portion (or a reasonable daily amount) of that food.

**Other helpful food labels.** Food grading standards established by the United States Department of Agriculture are discussed in Chapter 6 and in the Foods section of Chapter 9. Grade labeling based on these standards provides consumers with valuable buying guides for meats, fish, dairy and poultry products, and fresh fruits and vegetables.

### LABELING OF DRUGS AND DEVICES

As with food labels, those on drugs and health devices are strictly regulated by the Food and Drug Administration, and producers and distributors can best aid consumers by adhering to these regulations. For drugs that can be sold

> **DIRECTIONS FOR USE IN RELIEF OF OCCASIONAL CONSTIPATION**
> When Needed, Take One Tablet at Bedtime

> **WARNING**
> Do not use when abdominal pain, nausea, or vomiting are present. Frequent or prolonged use of this preparation may result in dependence on laxatives.

```
┌─────────────────────────────────────────┐
│                                           │
│              WARNING                      │
│                                           │
│   If pain persists for more than 10 days  │
│   or redness is present, or in conditions │
│   affecting children under 12 years of age,│
│   consult a physician immediately.        │
│                                           │
└─────────────────────────────────────────┘
```

without a prescription, the label must:

1. Give adequate directions for use.

2. Give appropriate warnings against misuse.

3. List active ingredients.

4. Declare the quantitative percentage of certain specified ingredients (for example, alcohol).

5. Give the established ("generic" or "nonproprietary") name of the drug or of each of the ingredients.

6. Tell name and address of manufacturer or distributor.

7. State plainly the quantity of the contents in units of weight or measure, or by numerical count. (Metric measures are permissible.)

The *U.S. Pharmacopeia* and *The National Formulary* list the officially set standards for some drugs. These standards are recognized under Federal law, but drugs purporting to be "official" must have the same composition and meet all the other requirements set for them in these official books. Such drugs may carry the legend "U.S.P." on their labels. If a drug differs from the official standards in strength, quality, or purity, this must be clearly stated on the label.

If a drug purports to be an official drug, it must have the same composition and must meet all of the other requirements set for it in the official text. For example:

| BLATT'S | MUST MEET SAME | HOSTETTER'S |
|---------|----------------|-------------|
| Iodine Tincture, U.S.P. | STANDARDS AS | Iodine Tincture, U.S.P. |

If the drug differs from the official drug in strength, quality or purity, the difference must be clearly stated on the label.

```
┌──────────────────────────────────────────┐
│            MILK OF MAGNESIA                │
│  Differs from the U.S.P. product, Magnesia Magma.  Con-  │
│  tains only 5% magnesium hydroxide.   U.S.P. preparation │
│  must contain 7 to 8% magnesium hydroxide.             │
└──────────────────────────────────────────┘
```

The labels of all drugs, whether official or not, must list active ingredients and must quantitatively declare certain ingredients, whether active or not.

```
┌──────────────────────────────────┐
│        CAMPHOR SPIRIT, N.F.       │
│      Active Ingredients—Camphor,  │
│             Alcohol 90%           │
└──────────────────────────────────┘
```

**Prescription drugs.**   Drugs which may be harmful if used without a physician's supervision can be sold only on prescription.  Manufacturers or distributors of such products must label them with the warning: "Caution: Federal Law prohibits dispensing without prescription."  The package must also contain complete directions and information about possible side effects.

Many drugs may be harmful if used without a physician's supervision. These can be sold only on a prescription.  For the guidance of the physician the package must contain complete directions and warnings, and information about any side effects.  Your physician is your safeguard in the use of prescription drugs.

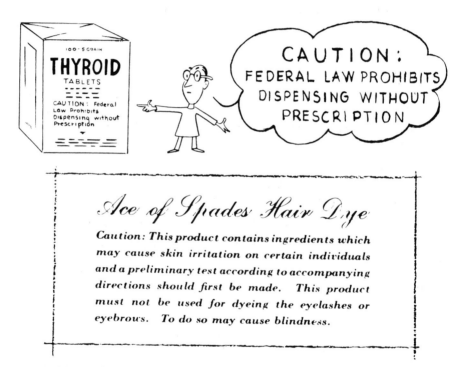

**Health and medical devices.**   Like other consumer goods any health or medical devices offered for sale are labeled with information helpful to the buyer.  Such labels must give the name and address of manufacturer, and electrical devices must carry warnings that they may cause severe burns or other injury if misused. It is a violation of Federal law to label any such devices with misleading claims for the treatment or cure of disease or illness.  Thousands of gadgets have been removed from the market because of their false claims of cures ranging from arthritis to zymosis.

Since 1938, the Food and Drug Administration has had responsibility for control over all devices used in diagnosis and treatment of disease.  While there are legitimate machines, such as x-ray units and other equipment used by licensed physicians in their offices or in clinics and hospitals, there are no devices or machines recognized by the FDA for the cure of disease by the patient in his own home.  A few devices, such as heating pads and infrared lamps, are recognized as beneficial—but only for providing *temporary relief*, not for effecting cures.  Still, thousands of useless contrivances are foisted upon the ailing public year after year.  And because of the gullibility of consumers and the *modus operandi* of promoters of worthless or dangerous products, efforts of the FDA to control this type of medical quackery are seriously thwarted.  Consumers who feel that they are being victimized can help protect themselves by writing to FDA officials* and giving the name of the device, its manufacturer, and where they bought it or received treatment with it.

## LABELING OF OTHER CONSUMER GOODS

Much of the helpful information buyers can find on the labels of other consumer goods is pointed out in the discussion of those goods, i.e., clothing and textiles, furniture, and other household products, in Chapter 10.  However, two important facts for consumers to remember about labels on any products are these:

1. Whether the label information is that furnished voluntarily by the producer or manufacturer or that required by law, it is the buyer's guide to quality and value.
2. The label information is put there for the consumer's benefit, but it will not protect or serve him if he does not read it.

## WHAT ADVERTISING DOES TO AND FOR THE CONSUMER

Whether the seller of consumer goods is the producer or manufacturer dealing directly with the buyer, or a middleman distributor or retailer, advertising is one of his best tools.  He makes use of newspapers, radio, television, letters and circulars, store windows, billboards, utility poles, the containers in which his products are packed, the trains and trucks in which deliveries are made, and the word of satisfied customers to extoll the virtues of his wares.

Advertising makes the consumer buy or want to buy.  That is its main function.  But it also can, and often does, confuse the prospective buyer, as he is bombarded on all sides with its messages.  Typical response to the statement, "Advertising helps the consumer," is one of disbelief.  When we hear, "It pays to advertise," we all agree that, "It pays the *seller* to advertise."  But what of the buyer?  How does advertising help him?

First of all, it tells him a great deal (though rarely everything he needs to know) about what is available on the market, and it tells him where he can find products or services and usually at what prices.  It aids him in value comparisons.

---

* Food and Drug Administration, U.S. Department of Health, Education and Welfare, Washington, D.C.  20204.

Most importantly, truthful advertising—from which the discerning consumer can distill the necessary facts and discard unneeded frills—guides him to wiser buying choices by providing information on which to base purchasing decisions. The importance of truthful advertising will be discussed in greater detail shortly. But first, let us look at one other significant function of advertising.

The services thus far enumerated represent the direct benefits derived by the consumer from the advertising copy itself. But an indirect and often overlooked function that may actually be more important than any other is advertising's financial support of the mass media of communications—newspapers, magazines, radio, and television. Traditionally, newspaper and magazine subscriptions have barely covered circulation expenses. It is advertising that really pays the bill (an estimated $20 billion advertising bill in 1971) for most of the educational material and entertainment provided by these and the broadcast media.

ENTERTAINMENT
&
EDUCATION

**Discerning the truth in advertising.** Separating fact from attention-getting fiction in advertising is not always easy. Usually, he who does the best job of it has cultivated at least a degree of skepticism for the glib pronouncements and persuasive arguments of the advertiser. Hostility is not necessary; what is required is the realization that to sell is the advertiser's main objective, to inform only a secondary aim, and that overly zealous advertising copywriters do in fact exist. Most of us will agree that advertising men seem to spend much of their time concocting half-truths, and that, we rarely will find the whole truth in any advertisement.

Such criticisms have been leveled at the "ad-men" for decades, but striking back, they call attention to a long history and wide range of self-regulations and are of the opinion that there are few sectors of American business which are subjected to so many types of federal, state, and local legislation. Claims by the advertising men that more government regulation is neither desirable nor necessary seems to be substantiated in part at least by reports of the Federal Trade Commission, which under the Wheeler-Lea Amendment of 1938, has power to prohibit and police false advertising. The Commission's Bureau of Deceptive Practices regularly receives and reviews a steady flow of advertising disseminated by all advertising media. In 1966, the review resulted in 1,210 formal investigations, out of which only 109 formal complaints were issued.

**Other policing agencies.** Besides the Federal Trade Commission and the Food and Drug Administration, whose activities have already been discussed, several other federal agencies exercise restraints over various aspects of advertising. Among them are the Department of Agriculture, U.S. Postal Service, Securities and Exchange Commission, Federal Communications Commission, and the Alcohol and Tobacco Division of the Internal Revenue Service. Additionally, numerous state and local regulations prevail. The most notable example of these is the "Printer's Ink Model Statute,"* which makes it a misdemeanor to represent to the public (by means of virtually any medium) advertising containing "any assertion, representation, or statement of facts which is untrue, deceptive, or misleading."

**Printer's Ink Model Statute**
**(1945 Revision)**

Any person, firm, corporation or association, or agent or employee thereof, who, with intent to sell, purchase or in any wise dispose of, or to contract with reference to merchandise, real estate, service, employment, or anything offered by such person, firm, corporation or association, or agent or employee thereof, directly or indirectly, to the public for sale, purchase, distribution, or the hire of personal services, or with intent to increase the consumption of or to contract with reference to any merchandise, real estate, securities, service, or employment, or to induce the public in any manner to enter into any obligation relating thereto, or to acquire title thereto, or an interest therein, or to make any loans, makes, publishes, disseminates, circulates, or places before the public, in this state, in a newspaper, magazine or other publication, or in the form of a book, notice, circular, pamphlet, letter, handbill, poster, bill, sign, placard, card, label, or over any radio station, or in any other way similar or dissimilar to the foregoing, an advertisement, announcement, or statement of any sort regarding merchandise, securities, services, employment, or anything so offered for use, purchase or sale, or the interest terms or conditions upon which such loan will be made to the public, which advertisement contains any assertion, representation or statement of fact which is untrue, deceptive, or misleading, shall be guilty of a misdemeanor.

Sponsored by *Printer's Ink*, trade journal of the advertising industry, the statute or a modified version of it has now been adopted by all but six states— New Mexico, Arkansas, Mississippi, Georgia, Alaska, and Delaware. Sponsors did not push for a federal law because they felt it was possible to obtain action more readily in state courts than in the federal courts.

The Printer's Ink Model Statute grew out of an early campaign by the advertising industry for self-regulation of advertising media and legislation "to protect the public from false advertising." Heading the campaign was the Associated Advertising Clubs of the World which adopted as its slogan, *Truth-in-Advertising*, and developed for its own guidance a set of standards known as the *Ten Commandments of Advertising*.

---

* Drawn up in 1911 as suggested legislation for the various states, the Model Statute was revised in 1945. In addition to other items, the changes included adding radio—but not television—to the list of media involved. Reprinted by permission.

Today, the association has a new name, Advertising Federation of America, but its announced goals remain essentially as originally set forth, which were: "To explain advertising to the public; to raise continually higher the standards of truth and good taste in advertising; to help make advertising more effective for business and more useful to the public; to help protect advertising against harmful restrictions and possible taxation; to encourage improvement in education for men and women in or preparing for advertising."

Another outgrowth of the 1911 Truth-in-Advertising movement was the development by the AACW of several vigilance committees which later evolved into the National Better Business Bureau, potent force in the industry's self-regulation program. Its purposes, as defined by BBB publications, is to protect business, investors, and consumers against unfair and fraudulent practices, including fraudulent advertising and repeated misrepresentations. Over the years, BBB's *Do's and Don'ts of Advertising Copy* has been a standard reference in the industry. Other activities of Better Business Bureaus in the consumer's behalf will be discussed in a subsequent section of this chapter.

**Self-regulation of advertising industry.** According to the United States Department of Commerce, self-regulation in advertising takes one of four forms:

1. *Individual Advertisers* adopting and enforcing their own specific codes of advertising standards and ethics.

2. *Individual Industries*, or a group of companies in the same field (e.g., footwear, furniture, etc.) working together to formulate and enforce a standard code of ethics and practices for its members.

3. *Advertising Trade Associations, Clubs, Bureaus, and Related Organizations* regulating the activities of many industries and many media. (For example, the American Association of Advertising Agencies.)

4. *Advertising Media*, publishers and broadcasters acting both independently and through their own media associations.

**Cost of advertising.** We have seen that advertising is a multi-billion-dollar-per-year industry. And those billions eventually come out of the consumers' pockets. Statistics of the Internal Revenue Service show that in a typical recent year, of every $100 spent on consumer goods of all types, $1.10 went to pay advertising costs. But, does advertising *really cost* the consumer? If advertising results in increased sales volume, which, in turn, results in lower per-unit manufacturing and marketing costs, the savings can be passed on to the buyers in the form of lower prices. This, say advertisers, is what happens in many instances, and when it happens often enough advertising begins to pay, not cost, the consumer. It is something to consider.

## TECHNICAL SERVICES THAT AID CONSUMERS

Thus far, we have discussed the roles of labeling and advertising as consumer information and protection services. We should not overlook the instances in which consumer aids, perhaps developed during product testing for example, are incorporated into manufacturers' products and accrue to the consumer automatically. In addition, there is available to the consumer a reservoir of technical information resulting from research and from the testing and rating of consumer goods.

**Research, testing, and rating.** Sometimes, the technical information derived from product analysis comes from the producers or manufacturers themselves, a by-product of their efforts at product upgrading. In some instances, such information is developed by professional and trade associations or by other independent organizations engaged in product testing and rating. These groups have developed such devices as seals, certifications, ratings, and grade standards to assist consumers in making educated purchasing choices.

There are a great many different groups involved in the testing and rating of consumer goods, and it is necessary to limit our discussion to a representative few. But before we proceed, there is a need for this word of caution: As in the case of tangible consumer goods, the results of information produced by testing organizations are valid only in proportion to their integrity and to the reliability of their methods. However, with reputations at stake, and with everything to lose by supplying false or misleading information, reliability can be assumed in most cases.

**Consumer services of manufacturers and merchants.** Quality control of their product is the policy of many manufacturers who believe it is the basis of customer satisfaction and business success. For example, spokesmen for Revlon, a large cosmetic firm, are quoted in a Department of Commerce report as saying: "Any statement we make must bear scientific verification. We have 122 people in our laboratories, including doctors and scientists at the Ph.D. level. Final precaution becomes the responsibility of an officer of the company and our Legal Department."

In the earliest days of the J. C. Penney Company Stores, Jim (James Cash) Penney himself instituted product testing in his fledgling dry goods firm which opened its doors to the public in Kemmerer, Wyoming, in 1907. Quality control through product testing is a practice which today extends to practically all merchandise sold in the huge nationwide Penney chain. The firm's Research and Testing Laboratory was officially established in New York City in 1930, mainly to test fabrics used in Penney clothing for color fastness, weight, wearing qualities, composition, resistance to fire, susceptibility to water, warmth, and to find methods for mothproofing woolens. Unofficially, however, the work began nearly 65 years ago, while J. C. Penney was still an employee of the old Golden Rule Stores.

"A washbasin, a cake of soap, and a pitcher of water were the tools; and a room in a small hotel in New York was J. C. Penney's first testing laboratory . . .

Penney, sleeves rolled up, busy scrubbing samples . . ." writes his biographer.*

Safeway and A & P Food stores are other national chains with programs for testing and grading many of their products. Among the well-known department stores with similar services are Macy's of New York, Chicago's Marshall Field, and Gimbels and Lit Brothers of Philadelphia. Macy's established a bureau of standards in 1927, to study, from the consumer's point of view, the adaptability, performance, durability, and care of merchandise sold in their store. They also adopted the policy of labeling their goods with instructions and information derived from their laboratory studies.

**Seals and certifications.** Seals or *laboratory insignia* are found on labels or sometimes, as in the case of appliances, on the name plate, of many consumer goods. How important are they? How much faith may be placed in them? Officials of Consumers' Research, Inc., say:

> The presence or absence of a particular seal may sometimes mean the difference between a product which will give years of satisfactory service and one that will have to be discarded after a short time or may cause injury or even death to the user, while it lasts.†

Figure 7–1 shows representative seals, with a brief explanation of each.

Publishers of some popular magazines require that products be tested and meet certain standards before advertising for them is accepted. Some companies maintain their own testing laboratories; others employ independent agencies to conduct the examinations. Many consumers are influenced by such seals as those illustrated; however, the mere fact that the seal appears on a product is not out-and-out guarantee of quality. Seals never imply any more protection than is specifically stated, and each should be carefully read so that the consumer knows exactly what is claimed or promised. Undoubtedly, the seals are at least as valuable to publishers eager to protect themselves as to consumers.

**Protective services of business and professional groups.** Trade associations working to assure quality and performance provide consumer assistance with respect to certain specific classes of goods. The following are examples selected at random:

*American Gas Association*—Organized in New York City in 1918 by manufacturers of gas appliances, equipment, and supplies to provide information on all phases of these goods. It develops operating and performance standards, conducts research, and publishes a newsletter and approved appliance lists.

*American Home Economics Association*—Founded in 1909; headquartered in Washington, D.C. Its objectives are fostering of wholesome family life and improvement of homes through education, welfare, and consumer protection, and it supports legislation aimed at protecting consumer interests. It sponsors publication of consumer guides; works for standards of quality and identity,

* Norman Beasley, *Main Street Merchant.* McGraw-Hill Book Co., New York, p. 170.
† Reprinted by permission from *Consumer Bulletin,* July 1963, by Consumers' Research Inc.

*We satisfy ourselves that products and services advertised in GOOD HOUSE-KEEPING are good ones and that the advertising claims made for them in our magazine are truthful.* If any guaranteed product or service advertised in GOOD HOUSEKEEPING proves to be defective, it will upon request and verification be replaced, or the money the consumer paid for it will be refunded. Insurance, realty, automobile, public transportation, travel facilities, and institutional advertisements are not guaranteed.

*The following points should be noted as practical applications of the Guaranty in certain areas:* Advertising claims of taste, odor, beauty, etc., are subjective, and accurate measurements are often impractical. Unless such claims are patently in error, we permit them to be made in our pages, even though we may not share the advertiser's opinion. Some products must be installed, used and serviced as the manufacturer directs to give satisfactory performance. We cannot be responsible for faulty installation or service by dealers or independent contractors.

The "seals of approval" of *Parents'* and *Good Housekeeping* magazines mean products bearing them have been tested and have met certain specific requirements, including the requirement that the product must perform as claimed in the advertisement for it in that particular publication.

AMERICAN GAS ASSOCIATION
Seal indicates that gas appliances and equipment on which it appears meet AGS standards of operation and performance.

UNDERWRITERS'
LABORATORIES, INC.
Found on electrical, gas, or chemical products, the seal indicates the product has been tested and meets safety and performance standards.

UNITED STATES TESTING
COMPANY, INC.
Seal awarded to products tested which meet its specifications regarding materials, construction, use and performance.

**Fig. 7–1** Testing seals. The appearance of these and similar seals on products indicates that the product has been tested and meets specifications of materials, construction, performance, and safety. Reprinted by permission from *Consumer Bulletin*, July 1963, Consumers' Research, Inc.

informative labeling and advertising, and laws prohibiting sale of harmful goods and services.

*American Medical Association*—Chicago-based organization representing the nation's physicians. Works through special councils and committees to sponsor testing of medical products to improve their safety and performance; publishes *Today's Health.*

*American Standards Association*—Organization of industrial firms, trade associations, technical societies, consumer organizations, and government agencies founded in 1918 to serve as a clearinghouse for nationally coordinated voluntary safety, engineering, and industrial standards.

*Architectural Aluminum Manufacturers' Association*—Does testing of aluminum products for quality of materials, construction and strength of component sections, resistance to air and water infiltration, etc., labeling those which meet its specifications, "Quality Certified by AAMA."

*Underwriters' Laboratories*—Organized by groups of insurance companies to promote product safety guarantees, thus minimizing claims of policyholders. While U.L. encourages product quality, the seal means only that the product is safe. (Consumers are cautioned to be sure the U.L. seal appears on all components of an electrical appliance or device; for example, not just the cord or plug.) In November, 1967, U.L. set up a consumer advisory council to help channel results of safety research to the public and publicize consumer experiences.

*United States Testing Company*—Conducts confidential testing and research for industry and government; awards its "Seal of Quality" to products meeting its materials, construction, use, and performance specifications.

*Water Conditioning Research Council*—Sponsors studies at a large midwestern university on the quantitative savings of soaps, detergent, clothing, utensils, plumbing, etc., made possible by changing from hard to soft water; publishes materials for schools on water conditioning and project ideas.

## CONSUMER-SPONSORED TESTING AND RATING
Consumers Union of U.S., Inc. and Consumers' Research, Inc., are well known as the country's major consumer-supported testing and rating organizations. Each publishes a monthly magazine reporting its findings. Although the names of both these organizations and their publications are similar, there is no official connection; indeed, their methods of operation and final results are quite dissimilar.

**Consumers Union of U.S., Inc.*** This non-profit organization was established in 1936 to provide consumers with information and counsel on consumer goods and services, to give information on all matters relating to the expenditure of

---

* Address: 256 Washington Street, Mount Vernon, New York 10550.

## 258   *COLOR TV SETS*

that distance and, if yours is a console with legs, block off the underside so that a child or pet cannot sit with his legs underneath the set. (CONSUMER REPORTS, SEPTEMBER 1968).

Though 1969 models are now available, some 1968 sets will probably still be found in the stores, and our Ratings of these models follow.

*CU plans a new project on table model color TV sets for 1969.*

**RATINGS.** *Consumer Reports, January 1968. Listed in order of estimated overall quality, based on laboratory tests, engineering evaluations of performance in strong- and medium-signal areas, and judgments of convenience, with picture quality the primary criterion. Picture-quality judgments cover both color and monochrome performance. Judgment on fringe-area performance is given in each Rating. Dimensions are in order of height, width and overall depth to the nearest ¼ in. All are console models and were judged good in VHF interference rejection and automatic gain control (AGC); all provide individual channel preadjustment and automatic degaussing; and all have a picture area of 295 sq. in. and a tone control. Except as noted, all have two color controls (intensity and hue), a relatively effective ACC circuit, channel selector light for both VHF and UHF, and a switch or control for adjusting sharpness of picture.*

### ACCEPTABLE

✔ **SYLVANIA CF210M** (Sylvania Electric Prod., Inc., NYC), $579.95. 30x36x23½ in. Overall picture quality, good. Fringe reception: VHF, good; UHF, good. Has AFC. According to the manufacturer, the following models have essentially the same chassis: CF210W-1, CF211K, CF212WS-1, CF213BT, CF214C, CF215P, CF216H, CF217M, CF220W, CF221K, CF223BT, CF225BT and CF225C.

✔ **RCA VICTOR GJ733** (RCA Sales Corp., Indianapolis), $699.95. 28½x40x22¾ in. Overall picture quality, good. Fringe reception: VHF, good; UHF, good. Has AFC. UHF tuning judged easiest of any all-channel TV set tested to date. According to the manufacturer, the following models have essentially the same chassis: GJ737, GJ741, GJ745, GJ749, GJ753, GJ795, GJ797, GJ799 and GJ801.

✔ **GENERAL ELECTRIC M904DWD** (General Electric Co., Syracuse, N.Y.), $549.95. 31½x 36¾x23¼ in. Overall picture quality, good. Fringe reception: VHF, fair-to-good; UHF, good. No AFC, but meter made manual fine tuning relatively convenient (CU's sample required adjustment before meter indication correlated with best tuning). Provision for reducing warm-up time. Input for coaxial antenna cable. Lacks ACC circuit, not a serious omission. According to the manufacturer, the following models have essentially the same chassis: M900DBN, M901DWD, M902DWD, M903DMP, M905DMP, M910DWD, M912DMP, M914-DPN, M980DWD, M981DCD, M984DPN, M920DWD and M922DMP.

✔ **PHILCO R6511WA** (Philco-Ford Corp., Philadelphia), $579.95. 29½x33x23 in. Overall picture quality, good. Fringe reception: VHF, good; UHF, good. No AFC, but "eye" made manual fine tuning relatively convenient (one of two samples required adjustment before eye operated properly). No external control for adjusting sharpness of picture, a minor deficiency. Did not match the standard monitor colors as well as most other sets tested. According to the manufacturer, the following models have essentially the same chassis: 6508WA, 6513EA, 6528WA, 6534CH, 6530MA, 6532PC, 6536PC, 6560WA, 6562CH, 6580-XLCH, 6582XSP and 6590PC.

✔ **ZENITH Y4518** (Zenith Radio Corp., Chicago), $589.95. 30x33¼x22½ in. Overall picture quality, good. Fringe reception: VHF, good; UHF, good. Has AFC. According to the manufacturer, the following models have essentially the same chassis: Y4519W, Y4520M, W4523R, Y4523H, Y4526, Y4528H, Y4532, Y4533W, Y4537M, Y4539R, Y4539H, Y4541, Y4543, Y4545 and Y4547.

**MAGNAVOX 1T740S** (The Magnavox Co., Fort Wayne, Ind.), $625. 29¼x35½x22¾ in. Overall picture quality, fair-to-good; some lack of crispness and detail in picture. Fringe reception: VHF, good; UHF, good. Has AFC. Provision for reducing warm-up time. Two-

**Fig. 7–2** A typical page from "The Buying Guide Issue" of *Consumer Reports.* This handy booklet includes ratings for over 2,000 items by brand and model. Reprinted by permission from *Consumer Reports.* Copyright by Consumers Union of U.S., Inc., a nonprofit organization.

family income, and to initiate and cooperate with individual and group efforts seeking to create and maintain decent living standards.

Consumers Union derives its income solely from the sale of its publications, *Consumer Reports*, issued monthly, and an annual "Buying Guide Issue" (see Fig. 7–2), both included in the $6-a-year subscription. Consumers Union accepts no advertising or product samples, and it is not beholden to any commercial interest. Expenses of occasional public-service research projects may be met, in part, by nonrestrictive, noncommercial grants.

Products tested are bought on the open market by CU's shoppers. Ratings are based on laboratory tests (see Fig. 7–3), controlled use tests, and/or expert judgments of the purchased samples. Consumers Union ratings offer comparative buying information to assist consumers in getting their money's worth. CU pledges that any opinions entering into its product ratings shall be as free of bias as it is possible to make them.

Consumers Union advises that consumers having trouble with a product,

**Fig. 7–3** Consumers Union engineers at work. Reproduction of "color bars" on TV sets under test is compared with that on the wall-mounted monitor at Consumers Union. *Consumer Reports* publishes the findings of such tests, providing reliable ratings on thousands of products. Courtesy of Consumers Union of U.S., Inc., a non-profit organization.

during or after the warranty period, write to the manufacturer and send carbon copies to Consumers Union, the Federal Trade Commission (Washington, D.C. 20580), and their local Better Business Bureau.

**Consumers' Research, Inc.**\* This non-profit organization was established in 1929 in White Plains, New York. Consumers' Research is not supported by manufacturers, dealers, or the government, and accepts no advertising. Products are rated by make or brand name on the basis of scientific tests or expert examination by Consumers' Research. Consumers' Research, Inc., publishes a monthly *Consumer Bulletin* plus *Consumer Bulletin Annual* which provides a summary of previous product ratings. Monthly issues report on brand name products as well as on the latest recordings and motion pictures, and contain consumer news. The yearly subscription rate is $5 for 12 issues, with *Annual*, $7; *Annual* alone, $2.60. (Braille edition of monthly issues of *Consumer Bulletin* are available from Volunteers Service for the Blind, 332 South 13th Street, Philadelphia, Pa. 19106.)

**Consumer's Digest.**† One other consumer protection service best described as "quasi-consumer-supported," is *Consumer's Digest*. A recent addition to the field, it appeared in the early 1960's. The bi-monthly magazine is supplemented by an annual *Consumers' Price Buying Directory*. While it claims no affiliation with any manufacturer and support by means of membership subscription, *Consumer's Digest* does accept advertising.

According to its officers, "*Consumer's Digest* is a dedicated organization whose primary interest is to serve you, the consumer—to give you accurate and valuable price buying information which will help you save hundreds of dollars."

Membership, at $7 per year, includes the 256-page *Price Buying Directory*, which lists thousands of the most popular nationally advertised brand names products complete with model number, description, manufacturer's list price (when available), and the lowest possible discount purchase price.

### OTHER CONSUMER SERVICE PUBLICATIONS

**Changing Times** ("The Kiplinger Service for Families"). This publication is issued monthly by The Kiplinger Washington Editors, Inc.†† Articles are geared to money-saving themes and advice on investments and income management. Typical titles include: "Advice for the Family Treasurer," "Sure, You Can Cut Your Milk Bill," "Don't Get Careless About Using Credit." A special feature in each issue is "The Months Ahead," preview of consumer-oriented legislation, price indexes on consumer goods, and other consumer news.

---

\* Address: Washington, New Jersey 07882.

† Address: 6319 North Lincoln Ave, Chicago, Ill. 60645.

†† Address: Editor's Park, Maryland 20782.

Available by subscription only, *Changing Times* contains no advertising.* Subscriptions are $6 for one year, $10 for two, including the annual *Family Success Book—99 New Ideas on Your Money, Job and Living.*

**Women's Magazines.**  Today, virtually all of the popular women's magazines and many other general audience periodicals include as regular features special consumer service sections or articles giving factual information to assist readers in making intelligent buying choices.  No attempt is made to list them all, but representative are the "Money Management" section of *Better Homes and Gardens*, "The Better Way" and "Institute Reports" of *Good Housekeeping*, and similar articles in *McCalls, Redbook, Ladies' Home Journal, Woman's Day*, and *Family Circle.*

**General Interest and Men's Magazines.**  *Pageant* often carries reports to consumers, and condensations.  Full-length consumer service articles frequently appear in *Reader's Digest.  Popular Mechanics, Popular Science*, and similar male-oriented periodicals include test and performance reports on automobiles, boats, construction materials, toys, tools, etc.

**BBB Publications.**  Some services of the National and local Better Business Bureaus have already been discussed.  Another is the distribution of "Facts You Should Know About . . ." booklets covering such subjects as health care, used car purchases, credit, home building or buying, investments, insurance, and many others.  Write or call your local BBB for these publications, most of them are free.

**Books.**  A number of recently published books which are valuable references and sources of consumer protection information are listed in the bibliography accompanying each chapter in the consumer section of this text.

## CONSUMER FEDERATION ASSISTS BUYERS

One of the most powerful efforts in behalf of the nation's buyers is the young but vigorous Consumer Federation of America.†  Described as the "unifying force in the growing consumer movement," CFA works to promote the rights of all consumers, in harmony with the general welfare.  There are no individual members in CFA, only groups.  Any consumer organization—city, county, regional, state, or national—which supports the programs and objectives of CFA may join by submitting an application to its national offices, Suite 406, 1012 14th Street, N.W. Washington, D.C. 20005.

Designed to provide consumer groups a powerful voice in public affairs, the Federation sharply criticizes many existing business and pricing practices and

---

* *Changing Times* and other "subscription only" publications are available in public and university libraries.

† Founded in 1967 with 56 charter members, it now includes upwards of 200 groups in almost every state and the District of Columbia.

urges members to take grassroots action against them. Main objectives of the Federation are to:

1. Coordinate lobbying activities in Congress.
2. Disseminate information to state groups.
3. Assist in setting up local groups.
4. Perform legal and research functions.
5. Sponsor the *Consumer Assembly*, an annual consumer forum in the nation's capital, which brings together members of consumer groups from across the nation to focus attention on consumer issues.
6. Publish "Consumer Action," the Federation's official newsletter.

## GETTING YOUR MONEYSWORTH

One of the more flamboyant entrants on the recent consumerism scene is "Moneysworth," a fortnightly newsletter. Published by Avant-Garde Media, Inc., 110 W. 40th Street, New York City 10019, it is available at 50 cents an issue or $10 per year. Articles in the first issue (October, 1970) of "Moneysworth" appeared under such provocative headings as "How to Buy a New Car for $125 Above Dealer's Cost," "Getting a Low-Cost Legal Abortion," "Value Judgment: Best Buys in 35-mm Cameras." Each issue features a "Dollars and Sense" section of brief notes on money saving on a variety of purchases.

## BUSINESS AND THE CONSUMER

Business—and indirectly, but importantly, individual consumers—will benefit from a new service of Commerce Clearinghouse, Inc. In mid-1971, CCH began publication of "Consumerism—New Developments for Business." This weekly newsletter is designed to alert business as to how consumer demands from public and government sources affect their business interests and decisions in production, advertising, sales, and related areas. The service has grown out of the realization that manufacturers are facing more direct demands by the consumer, and that government and public pressure is being directed toward the manufacturer and drawing him more and more into the consumer-protection spotlight in the marketing and ultimate use of his products.

While the "Consumerism" newsletter is primarily available to businesses, it is also provided to libraries and thereby to individual interested consumers.

### WORLD-WIDE CONSUMER PROTECTION SERVICES

Programs to improve the lot of consumers are by no means limited to the United States. The past decade has seen the birth and development in many parts of the world of consumer services which closely parallel the independent, cooperative, and governmental efforts at work here. Officials of the International Organization of Consumer Unions (organized in Amsterdam in 1960) report that the number of national consumer protection organizations throughout the world expanded from only 16 in 1960 to 80 in 1968.

In Europe, the work began in the late 1950's when a group of consumers in England organized and began testing products and publishing results. Britain's National Federation of Consumer Groups, founded in 1963, attracted world-wide attention several years later when it began posting on public bulletin boards comparative lists of local food stores.

A National Consumer League organized in Jamaica in 1965 goes directly to manufacturers with complaints about pricing, packaging, etc. In remote Malaysia, a Consumer's Association was set up in 1965, to improve shopping conditions there. A main problem in that country is that there are three (Malay, United States, and Chinese) systems of weights and measures, and shoppers who did not understand all three often felt they were being cheated.

These are only a few examples. Other similar organizations with like problems are now operating in New Zealand, Australia, Japan, Ireland, Scandinavia, Switzerland, France, Belgium, Italy, India, Canada, Denmark, Israel, and Holland. Some 34 nations sent delegates to the fifth Biennial Conference of the International Organizations of Consumers Unions in Bronxville, N.Y., in June of 1968.

### FEEDBACK 7

**A.** Write or visit the non-Federal consumer protection agencies in your town and state. Ask them: "What consumer safety and satisfaction protection services are provided by your agency? What remedies can your agency provide for abuses of consumer confidence?"

Your inquiries should be addressed to at least the following agencies and whichever new ones are available as a result of growing public and official concern with consumer protection:

- The Better Business Bureau. Determine who sponsors the Bureau in your area. What are the responses of the Bureau to consumer complaints? What are the services of the Bureau to the consumer?
- Chamber of Commerce. Who are the members of the Chamber?
- State agencies.

**B.** From your experience, which stores in your area take pains to ensure that their customers are satisfied with the merchandise and service the stores offer? Which stores back up their claims to make the customer "King"? Are small stores or large stores in your community most dependent on good will? Why? Consider the recourse that you, as a dissatisfied customer, have if you buy a deficient product from the three sellers below:

- If a door-to-door salesman sells you a defective vacuum cleaner, can he be held accountable for repairs? Is there a local agency which will back up the guarantee or warranty? Do you have to write the national headquarters for a response to your problem?

- If a chain store sold you a vacuum as in item 1, how would it respond to your complaint? Does this store have its own repair facility? Can the store make repairs or adjustments to your satisfaction, or must they "pass the buck" to higher headquarters?

- If a locally owned store sold you that vacuum, is it prepared and equipped to solve your repair and service problems? Is it a complete facility in that respect, or merely a sales agency for the vacuum?

- Of the three sellers considered above, which has the most to lose from your dissatisfaction?

C. Read and compare the advertising copy for several brands of a similar product. What is the purpose of the advertisement? What is the approach of the advertisement?

- What satisfaction do you seek from the product advertised? Clean clothes, dependable transportation, cold storage for your food?

- What satisfactions do the advertisements imply? Decor improvement, ego satisfaction, success with the opposite sex, eye-appealing menus.

- How do the two approaches differ—yours and the advertiser's? How are the approaches related? Do you see more satisfaction implied than the particular product can offer, in and of itself?

## DISCUSSION QUESTIONS

1. What types of consumer problems should the Federal Government become involved with? Explain. What types should non-government groups become involved with? Explain.

2. How have technological changes and progress brought about consumer problems?

3. Why must a label include the name and address of the producer or distributor?

4. How much attention does the average consumer pay to labels on products?

5. Does advertising make people buy something that they actually do not want? Explain.

6. What are the advantages to advertising? Disadvantages? Does it cost the consumer too much?

7. Is there a need for more Government regulation of advertising? What types of controls? On what types of advertising?

8. Would producers follow fair-trade practices if there were no controls over them? Why?

9. How much reliance should be placed on seals or laboratory insignias? Do some mean more than others? Which ones?

10. What benefits can come from a world-wide protection service? Is it needed? Why?

## CASE PROBLEM

Richard is majoring in art at his university. His instructor assigned the students in the class to design the packaging and advertising layout for an imaginary snack product made of corn. Richard designed a package that was unusually large. He thought in order to sell the product it should stand out from the rest on the markets' shelves and appear to have much more product stored inside than it really did. Also, the only identification he put on the package was the name of the product, so it wouldn't look "cluttered" with other printing. Besides, he thought if the ingredients of the contents were printed on the package, it would be easy for competitors to copy its make-up for themselves.

For the advertising layout, Richard planned to stress how the product was the best snack anyone could buy for his money. He figured, in order to sell the product, advertising better make the product appear worth buying.

a) Are Richard's ideas good ones? Explain. What mistakes has he made in the package design? In his advertising scheme?

b) Are the restrictions that would be put on Richard's ideas reasonable? Explain. Who would enforce them?

c) Explain other consumer protections that Richard must be aware of if he is planning an advertising career.

## SUGGESTED READINGS

Blackwell, Roger D., and others. *Cases in Consumer Behavior*. New York: Holt, Rinehart and Winston, 1969. 431 pp.

Chase, Stuart, and Frederick John Schlink. *Your Money's Worth: A Study in the Waste of the Consumer's Dollar*. New York: Macmillan, 1927. 285 pp.

Dowd, Merle E. *How to Live Better and Spend 20% Less*. West Nyack, N.Y.: Parker, 1966. 237 pp.

*How to Stretch Your Money*. New York: Public Affairs Pamphlets, 1968. 28 pp.

Preston, Lee E. (ed.). *Social Issues in Marketing*. Glenview, Illinois: Scott, Foresman, 1968. 313 pp.

Ryan, Kerry Jean. *Stop, Consider, Before you Buy.* Yonkers, N.Y.: Yonkers Public Library, 1968. 8 pp.

Troelstrup, Archie William. *Consumer Problems and Personal Finance.* New York: McGraw-Hill, 1965. 611 pp.

Trump, Fred. *Buyer Beware!* New York: Abingdon Press, 1965. 207 pp.

Wharton, Don. "Five Common Frauds, and How to Avoid Them," Pleasantville, N.Y.: The Reader's Digest Association, December 1967. 4 pp.

Wilhelms, Fred T., and others. *Consumer Economics* (Third Edition). New York: Gregg Division, McGraw-Hill, 1966. 495 pp.

Wilson, W. Harmon, and Elvin S. Eyster. *Consumer Economic Problems* (Seventh Edition). Cincinnati: South-Western Publishing Company, 1966. 650 pp.

CHAPTER 8

# RENTING, BUYING, BUILDING

Personal finance experts often debate the pros and cons of renting versus buying. Their usual conclusion is that economically a person is better off renting. However, this appears to be an oversimplification of the problem. For most persons, there is—psychologically as well as economically—a time to rent and a time to buy or build.

For single persons or newly married couples, a compact rental unit can prove very satisfactory. But as a family grows, apartments or even duplexes become confining. Additional bedrooms are needed. So is more space to entertain friends and associates. It is at this point that families should consider buying or building.

Later in life, as children leave home—to go to college, marry, or enter military service—homeowners often decide to sell and again rent a nice apartment. Such a move may not only save money, but also provide more leisure hours.

## RENTING AND LEASING

Unless you were born under a very lucky star, apartment hunting has its inevitables: disgust, disappointment, despair. Hopefully, though, the foot- and mind-tiring search will turn up a suitable "cliff dwelling" at a reasonable rental. If you're an "old pro" at this game, then certainly you need no advice. Instead, this section is addressed to persons who haven't had the bewilderment of looking for an apartment. Once the decision to move has been made, start the search as soon as possible. Usually, the Sunday paper's classified section is the place to begin. In many cities, an early Sunday edition is on sale Saturday evening. If you're clever enough to get one of these advance copies, red pencil likely prospects in the rental ads and get on your way.  It's a distinct advantage to have a few hours headstart on other apartment seekers.   Here are some general suggestions:

1.  Don't waste time sight-seeing.  Limit your search to the type of rental unit you want—apartment, duplex, house—and to those you can afford.

2.  You might find just the right place the first time you go out looking.  But there is more likelihood it will take many days of shopping and comparing. Don't rush.  Allow yourself enough time to really know what is available.

3.  Limit your search to five or six units in any one day.  If you see many more than that, they all become a blur.  In disgust, you might grab just anything and be sorry later.

4.  Be certain to get complete cost information as you check each unit.  Find out what utilities are included in the rental.  (Watch out for units that are electrically heated.  Often you end up paying the electric bill, which can amount to a sizable sum.)  Is a lease required?  Is there a cleaning, garage, or parking fee?

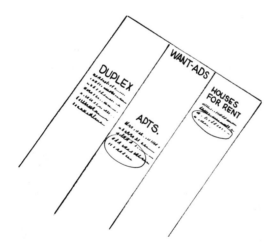

Now, down to the nitty-gritty of the hunt: the many things that make for comfortable, pleasant living.  Even though you may not consider the rental unit as permanent living quarters, take enough time to go over the "Checklist for Apartments" on the following page.  It will help you make an objective comparison and take some of the guesswork out of the search.  If you're looking for a duplex or a home to rent instead of an apartment, use the "Checklist for Houses" on pages 225 to 227.

# CHECKLIST FOR APARTMENTS

## *Building and Grounds*

____ attractive, well-constructed building

____ good maintenance and upkeep

____ clean, well-lighted and uncluttered halls, entrances, stairs

____ reliable building management and supervision

____ attractive landscaping with adequate outdoor space for tenants

____ locked entrances, protected from outsiders

____ clean, attractive lobby

## *Services and Facilities*

____ laundry equipment

____ parking space (indoor or outdoor)

____ receiving room for packages

____ convenient trash collection and disposal

____ adequate fire escapes

____ storage lockers

____ locked mail boxes

____ elevators

____ engineer on call for emergency repairs

____ extras—window washing, decorating, maid service, shops, doorman

## *Living Space in the Apartment*

____ adequate size

____ convenient floor plan

____ suitable wall spaces and room sizes for your furniture

____ adequate daylight

____ pleasant views

____ soundproof.  Listen for talking, plumbing, footsteps, equipment from other apartments or hallways.

____ attractive decorating and fixtures

____ good ventilation

____ easy cleaning and maintenance

____ attractive, easy-to-clean floors or carpets

____ furnished appliances in good condition

____ clean, effective heating

____ individual heat controls

____ up-to-date wiring

_____ agreeable size, type and placement of windows

_____ windows with screens and storms, blinds or shades

_____ conveniently placed electric outlets

_____ well-fitted doors, casings, cabinets and built-ins

_____ extras—air conditioning, carpeting, dishwasher, disposal, fireplace, balcony

_Source: Money Management, Your Housing Dollar_, copyright by Household Finance Corporation. Reprinted by permission.

## BUYING OR BUILDING

Usually, the largest single purchase of your lifetime is a home. Mistakes in buying and building are costly and not easily undone. If you happen to purchase a color TV or wrist watch that turns out to be a lemon, you may find it disagreeable and annoying. But if the house you buy is unsatisfactory, it is quite another matter. With the TV or watch you might have had to pay for it on a 6-month or even 12-month installment contract; with the home you generally will be paying it off for the next 20 or 25 years. And, of course, you pay a much

**"Try to picture it after you've poured $20,000 into it."**

Reprinted with permission of _The Wall Street Journal_ (Cartoon Features Syndicate).

higher price—a price commensurate with its importance, size and long life, as well as the happiness it will afford you and your family. Because buying a home is so important, it should be given the utmost thought and study.

There is no wizard way to assure you will make all the right decisions. However, you will find in the next few pages answers to some of the most perplexing questions frequently asked by prospective homeowners:

1. What are the advantages I can expect as a homeowner?
2. How much can I safely spend for a house?
3. What should I look for in choosing a neighborhood?
4. What are the advantages and disadvantages of buying an existing home or building a new home?
5. What should I look for in the construction of a home?
6. How do I go about getting the best financing for a home?

It is no exaggeration to expect that study and implementation of the suggestions given here can save you several thousand dollars in buying or purchasing an average home.

## ADVANTAGES OF OWNING A HOME

While your own personal goals will tend to dictate the kind of house and neighborhood you choose—or for that matter whether you even want to buy a home —most people will find the chief advantages of living in a home are:

*1. You will live in a better community.* In general, owner-occupied homes are symbolic of the better residential neighborhoods. The density of population is smaller than in apartment building sections. There is less street traffic, congestion, dirt, and noise. Because of the financial stake home-owning families have in their homes, individual homes are usually better maintained than rental property. Home owners typically take more of an interest than do renters in such community affairs as the building and maintenance of good schools, playgrounds, parks and streets, adequate police and fire protection, and other public services.

*2. You will live in better housing.* Homes generally offer more space, more rooms, better design, and the use of bigger and better appliances and other equipment than do apartments. Anyone with a growing family knows the importance of that extra space, that third or fourth bedroom, that recreation room in the basement, or that backyard equipped with swings or sand boxes for the youngsters. Another all-important aspect of home ownership is privacy— freedom from noise, prying eyes, or "big ears," and complaints of janitors and landlords or other apartment dwellers.

*3. You will enjoy congeniality of neighbors.* Most home-owning neighborhoods are comprised of people of similar social, economic, and educational backgrounds. The similarity of interests usually means a minimum of friction, and a maximum of opportunity for developing lasting and enjoyable friendships, not only for parents, but for their children as well.

*4. You may have a much greater sense of personal contentment.* In knowing that you own a house and the plot of ground on which it stands, you will feel more secure, and perhaps better able to meet the uncertainties of a rapidly changing world. In addition, you will enjoy an intangible feeling of stability that only comes with having "roots"—belonging to a community of congenial neighbors, participating in community activities, knowing your children are growing up in a wholesome environment. Among other things you will enjoy many hours puttering in your garden or your workshop, or just chatting over the back fence. And in fixing up your house the way you and your family want it, you enjoy a certain feeling of independence, creativity, and personal satisfaction usually not available to renters.

Aside from the more general considerations, there are some real financial advantages associated with home ownership. These must be weighed in light of your overall financial situation.

*5. You will be able to deduct mortgage interest and home taxes.* Even though a sizable portion of your monthly payment for a home goes to pay interest charges, all that interest plus real estate taxes are deductible from your Federal and State income taxes. This can mean substantial tax savings. These deductions, which are usually sizable in the early years of your mortgage, usually put you in a lower effective tax bracket. Besides interest and tax deductions, you might be able to take other deductions (depreciation, maintenance and utilities) on part of your home if you have some legitimate use of the space for your job or profession. For example, a salesman might have to use half of his garage or basement for storage plus one room for an office. A portion of one's rent might, of course, be similarly deducted for a renter.

*6. You benefit from forced savings with an inflation hedge.* A portion of each monthly payment on a mortgage is credited against the loan principal. Over the years, your investment (often referred to as *equity*) in the property increases. Should you decide to sell the home, you usually can recover this equity. Because of this country's inflationary patterns, you may additionally profit from the increased value of the home. Construction costs seem continually to be on the increase. For the past several years, construction has been rising 7 percent each year. It can be expected, therefore, that a home costing $20,000 to build today may cost $21,500 a year from now. Interestingly, too, that profit you may make is not taxable if you turn around and buy another home. The tax chapter later in this book will give you the details on how you can avoid tax on the sale of a home.

Budget-wise, buying a home gives you a distinct financial advantage in being able to make long-range plans for fixed expenses. Taxes and maintenance costs for homes will likely keep pace with inflation, but the mortgage payment will remain "fixed." (Unless you choose a flexible interest loan which is discussed later.) Younger persons' paychecks should continue to benefit directly from changes in the cost of living as well as professional advances. Therefore, if inflation continues, your mortgage payment should be easier and easier to meet five or ten years from now than it is today.

7. *You usually have an improved credit rating.* Other things being equal, people who own or are buying their own homes are given preferential credit treatment. Homeowners are considered more stable. They have firmer roots in the community. They also have equity in their property.

8. *You will find that comparable living space of a home costs less than an apartment.* Although people usually rent an apartment for less money than they would pay for a home, they do not get the same amount of living space. The author has made a number of detailed comparisons of total annual costs per square foot of living space on a variety of homes and apartments. On this basis, homes prove to be more economical for virtually every class of dwelling whether they be economy, moderately priced, or luxury units.

These then, are among the major advantages of owning your own home. Of course, there are some disadvantages and headaches, too, and before you buy a house, you should become acquainted with them.

### DISADVANTAGES OF HOME OWNERSHIP

Many a homeowner complains that there are seemingly unending extra money demands associated with a home. To keep a place in good repair requires paint, patching plaster, water gaskets, plumbing repairs, furnace filters, and a thousand and one other things that the apartment dweller seldom thinks about. Not only do you have to pay for these things, but you will find that you will be required to give a certain amount of time to maintenance, such as cutting the grass, trimming shrubs, painting and decorating, and other minor tasks. How agreeable or disagreeable these tasks are depends solely on your temperament and your life goals. Many people do not find these tasks burdensome, but rather enjoyable, and a refreshing change of pace from normal employment. As for maintenance cost, you will need to set aside a small portion each month to meet these needs, the amount dependent on the age and construction of your house and how well you keep it up.

As time goes on, you will probably have some extra expense for remodeling, or adding on a new bedroom, or putting a recreation room in the basement, or adding new equipment. To some extent, of course, this extra expense will be offset by increased family happiness due to the increased livability of your home.

You must also realize that besides your principal and interest payments, and maintenance co, ts, you will be required to pay real estate taxes, hazard insurance and your own ut.'ity bills. However, when you are renting, part of your rent pays for these thin, s; and, in addition, you pay for an additional amount as a profit for your landlord. Usually, however, you can count on home ownership being more of a monthly drain on your budget than renting, even though you get more space for your "ownership" dollar and build up equity in the property.

For many people, the advantages and benefits of home ownership outweigh the additional costs and responsibility. And, over the long run, you will probably find that on the day you own your home free and clear or have a substantial equity in it, that the cost usually has been less than renting. Dependent on your life style and goals, you and your family will most likely have had a much happier life living in a home of your own than if you had rented.

## HOW MUCH SHOULD YOU SPEND ON HOUSING?

A classic rule of thumb is that a family can safely spend about one week's salary each month for rent or mortgage payments—including property insurance and taxes. Another is that you can purchase a home costing roughly $2\frac{1}{2}$ times your annual income. Each family, however, is unique. Some families want to be out-of-doors and away from home much of the time. They enjoy fishing, boating, water-skiing, or other sports. Still other families find greater pleasures in home-centered activities such as back-yard barbecuing, practicing on musical instruments, or caring for flowers and shrubs. Because they are so different, it is important that each family spends an amount of money on the home which will complement rather than detract from their overall living patterns and pleasures.

Young couples, regardless of their lifestyle, will be wise to spend somewhat less than a week's pay each month for housing during the early years of their marriage. Economizing on rentals for the first few years of married life can bolster their savings considerably. And in the long run, such economy-minded couples will end up being able to afford a nicer home and having more money for investments and other pleasures.

## SELECTING A NEIGHBORHOOD

No mistake can be quite so tragic as the "right" house in the "wrong" neighborhood. Even if the home is appropriate otherwise for you and your family, a house won't prove to be a good buy if it is unsuitably located. There are psychological, comfort, economic, convenience, and zoning factors that should be investigated thoroughly before a site is chosen.

If you are a long-time resident of a city, you will already know the preferred areas. However, when moving to a new community, don't be too surprised if it takes you up to six months to get all the information you need. Never rush into buying a home. Rent a comfortable apartment for a while. Give yourself and your family time to get acquainted with the city. Only then can you really be sure of finding the right neighborhood.

**Psychological and comfort factors.** Look for a neighborhood which exhibits the topographical features which appeal to you. Are you attracted by a hillside site which has an imposing view of the city, or the privacy of a wooded area? The location also has a great deal to do with comfort factors. For example, smog or other weather problems are sometimes more severe in one part of a city than another. Drainage is definitely a factor that you should investigate. There are many parts in nearly every community where it is impossible to have basements, below-ground storage, or living facilities because of high water problems.

Most couples find that they and their children are happier if they choose a neighborhood where other families have comparable backgrounds—especially age, education, and income level. Having something in common with neighbors makes it easier to strike up a conversation, make sincere friendships, and develop lasting ties.

The upkeep and general appearance of homes and landscaping can tell you much about a neighborhood. If you want to maintain a neat, well-kept home, then you certainly want it located in a neighborhood where other people take proper care of their property. One of the dangers of buying a new home in a recently built subdivision is that you can never be sure how the homes are going to be maintained. Homes and yards may look perfectly fine initially with their new paint and recently planted lawns, but both the homes and yards may look quite different in five or ten years.

**Economic factors.** The total cost of your new home—whether you build or buy—will be significantly influenced by the location you choose. In most urban areas, you'll find a wide range of prices. It is wise to remember that the initial cost of the land or the home is not the final cost. Even though money can be saved initially by moving to the suburbs, the daily expense of commuting to work and social functions may offset any savings. Here are other cost items that should be looked into:

1. *Taxes*—Most cities levy property taxes on real estate. Talk to homeowners in the neighborhood and find out what they pay for property taxes. Since taxes are usually levied by districts, taxes may vary from one side of the street to another. If you can't find out about taxes from the property owners, call the city or county assessor's office for the information.

2. *Utility Costs: Water, Sewer, Gas, and Electricity Fees*—It is not uncommon to find several different water, gas, or electric companies serving different parts of a large metropolitan area. Although it seems ridiculous, the author knows of many instances where the utility costs are three and four times as great in one suburb as in an adjoining one. Since these are ongoing costs, it's well to make a few comparisons.

In addition to these specific economic considerations, you must be very concerned with projecting the resale value of the prospective property. Get the opinions of local real-estate men, bankers, or other businessmen.

**Zoning regulations.** Check these carefully. Nearly all cities have zoning commissions. In effect, such a commission classifies all the land within the city and determines what type of structures may be built and what, if any, business may be conducted. Without good zoning restrictions, orderly development of a city would be nearly impossible. A typical zoning classification system might read something like this:

1. *Residential A1*—Single residences only; duplexes, all other multiple-dwelling units, and all businesses are prohibited.
2. *Residential A2*—Single residences or duplexes; all other multiple-dwelling units and all businesses are prohibited.
3. *Residential A3*—Single residences, duplexes, and multiple-housing units; all businesses are prohibited.

**Deed restrictions.** Beyond zoning, land-developers or subdividers often write in restrictive covenants on the deeds to the property in an attempt to protect the quality of a neighborhood. These restrictions may cover a wide variety of things relating to how a home may be designed and constructed, such as: how many stories; architectural style; how many garages; whether or not you may build any detached structures on the lot aside from the house; minimum square footage in home; whether or not you can build a duplex or other rental property; types of trees that may be planted; height or style of walls and fences.

**Convenience factors.** Although the nearness to the husband's and/or wife's place of employment is vitally important, there are many other convenience factors that must be weighed. Some of the key questions you might ask about prospective neighborhoods are:

1. Is the location close to good-quality schools for your children?
2. Are there sidewalks for the safety and protection of yourself and family?
3. Does the area have access to convenient exits and entrances to freeways and other major highways?
4. Are there nearby shopping centers, theaters, restaurants?

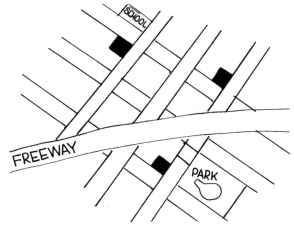

## TYPES OF CONSTRUCTION

Regardless of whether you prefer a bungalow, ranch, Cape Cod, split-level, or other style of home, you should be aware of the different types of construction used for homes. Maintenance costs, as well as heating and air conditioning expenses, can be greatly influenced by the way a house is built. These are the most widely used types of construction:

1. *Frame*—Construction consists basically of wood framing with exterior walls faced with either wood or aluminum siding. Wall cavity must be filled with excellent insulating material because of thinness of wall. Exterior walls generally require heavy upkeep expenses, especially if surfaced with wood siding.

2. *Brick*—Exterior walls are built from brick, usually a large size brick. Interior walls consist of plaster or sheetrock applied directly to the inside surface of the brick. This construction has a good appearance, but poor insulating qualities. Cold and heat are conducted directly to interior walls.

3. *Block*—Large concrete blocks are generally used. The blocks are hollow which provides somewhat better insulation than does the brick construction outlined above. The exterior surface of concrete block is not particularly attractive.

4. *Brick-Block*—Outer walls are made from brick, backed by large cement blocks. Better, more stable construction than either brick or block alone. Somewhat better insulation value. However, both brick and block tend to conduct heat and cold to interior space.

5. *Brick Veneer*—This is undoubtedly the most desirable type of construction. It is also the most expensive. The home is first framed from wood. Then, outer brick walls are layed. Insulation is installed in the inner wood-framed walls. Interior walls are sheetrocked or plastered.

Nearly all builders now use large sheetrock panels to form inner walls. Sheets are glued or nailed in place; the joints taped and plastered. This is an excellent interior wall material and usually results in better, smoother surface than does plastering. Added insulation value can be attained by using sheetrock backed with aluminum foil. It's wise to insulate a home heavily. A few extra dollars spent on insulation during construction will be saved many times over in the life of a home, especially in locations that have extremely hot and cold temperatures.

Another way to save on heating and air conditioning costs is to limit the number and size of windows. Where it is advantageous to have large picture windows, it would be well to consider using double pane insulating glass. This product is expensive, however, and may not be practical for use throughout the home.

**BUYER'S CHOICES**

Today's prospective home buyer is offered many interesting properties—old and new homes, condominiums and co-ops, as well as row houses. Frequently, the purchase of an existing home is more economical than building. Naturally, there are many things about each kind of property which should be taken into account. Let's turn our attention to the most important of these considerations:

**Older homes.** Exploding, sprawling suburbia disenchants many people. In search for a better way to live, these Americans choose to move back into the city, buy, and renovate an older home. They may be able to avoid many hours of commuting to work each week. If they choose they can leave the car in their garage and ride a bus, trolley, or subway. Moving into a well-established neighborhood with stately trees and abundant shrubbery also must be considered on the plus-side of buying an older home.

Besides the advantages of location, there are other important extras usually included in the purchase price of an older home—carpeting, drapes, and finished basement living area. Landscaping is also complete; air conditioning may be included. Naturally, the price of an older home is influenced by many factors—prestige of the neighborhood, architecture of the home, and how well the home has been maintained. Nonetheless, the extras discussed here are not usually reflected fully in the selling price of the older home.

Many prospective home buyers also find the architectural style of older construction appealing. To these persons, the warmth and charm of the older motif is more important than the efficiency and functionality of a new home. Basic construction of some older homes is superior to new construction. For instance, older homes may have such features as massive foundations, thick rock walls, very spacious rooms, excellent hardwood floors, paneling, molding, and doors.

On the negative side of the ledger, the older home may need painting and redecorating, new heating or cooling equipment, new plumbing and plumbing fixtures, and/or roof repairs. The home could still possibly be a good buy, but only if purchased at a low enough price that you could also afford the remodeling and refurnishing work.

**New homes.** There is something special about being able to move into a brand new home. Everything is fresh and bright. You have the latest built-in appliances, fixtures, and hardware. New building materials create a home that is easy to keep clean and one which requires little maintenance. Floor plans of a new home are generally very functional and make economical use of space. Garage and carport areas tend to be more generous than those of older homes. A new home is also more apt to be adequately wired for today's many electrical gadgets and appliances than is the older home.

Construction quality and equipment of new homes vary a good deal. It is important, therefore, that you know something about the builder and that you go over the home very carefully in accordance with the checklist on page 225. Find out what warranties or guarantees come with the home and its contents. These are especially important on roofing, cement walks and driveways, plumbing, heating, cooling equipment, electrical wiring, and built-in appliances. You must be assured, too, that the builder will be in business long enough to back up the warranties.

With any new home, you most likely will have to add to the sale price the costs of landscaping, carpets, and drapes. When these are tallied, you can make comparisons with existing older homes to see which is the best overall deal.

**Condominiums and cooperatives.** Having their beginning in the larger cities of our country, both cooperatives and condominiums, especially the latter, are enjoying increasing popularity. Either may be detached, semidetached, rowhouse or multi-family structures designed to compete with single homes. The apartments are usually larger and better equipped than the standard rental apartment. Mortgage interest and taxes paid on the units are fully tax deductible.

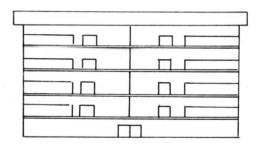

They differ considerably, however, in many important ways. Consider the following:

*The Purchaser of a Condominium:*

1. Actually buys a particular apartment unit, receiving full legal title to his property.

2. Receives joint ownership of parking lot, swimming pool, and other common areas and facilities of the development.

3. May have to agree to a perpetual management contract with the developer of the unit for

*The Purchaser of a Cooperative:*

1. Buys membership stock in a corporation which owns the apartment building. As part of his share purchase he also leases the apartment unit he wishes to occupy.

2. May gain the privilege of using common facilities of building or may be required to additionally subscribe for privileges.

3. Gains a vote according to the by-laws of the cooperative for electing a board of directors.

maintenance and other services; or more usually is given a vote in the election of a management group which supervises such activities.

Usually each member has one vote.

4. Assumes financial responsibility only for maintenance charges imposed by the management group and for the mortgage on his particular unit.

4. Assumes broader financial responsibility for maintenance charges, his contract payments and additionally any added amounts that may arise from the failure of other cooperative members to meet their obligations.

5. Is usually able to sell his unit freely to other persons, but may have to agree to some restrictions on sale.

5. Must usually obtain approval of cooperative before selling or leasing the unit.

The advantages offered by both types of housing are chiefly these: (1) Since multiple units can be built less expensively than single homes, you usually get much more value for your housing dollar. (2) Heating and air conditioning costs are usually considerably less than for comparable single dwellings. (3) Gardening, maintenance and garbage disposal services are economically shared, as are common facilities such as tennis courts, putting greens, and swimming pools.

Either type of unit can prove to be a good investment. Even though a cooperative member does not have legal title to his particular unit, equity accrual can be anticipated upon resale, as in the case of a condominium or private home, if the cooperative is successfully operated. Overall, there is somewhat less financial risk in buying a condominium since you obligate yourself only to your particular living unit (plus a maintenance agreement) rather than to your share of the entire project as for a cooperative. Nonetheless, you should shop around a good deal even for condominiums to make sure you get the best value for what you spend. Be sure to read the management contract *carefully* which goes along with the purchase. In some instances, a developer will sell the condominium at a bargain price, but require you to sign a perpetual management contract which requires you to pay inflated monthly maintenance and upkeep payments.

**Mobile homes.** A casual drive through the countryside in almost any part of the nation will disclose a new fixture on the landscape: the immobile mobile home. These "stretch" versions of the camper and trailer dot every state from New York to California. Thousands of special mobile home parks (some attractive—some dismal) have risen to accommodate this new pre-engineered, factory-built substitute for the traditionally built one-family home. The reasons for the spectacular growth in the mobile homes are many and varied, but probably the most compelling is the inability of the tradition-bound housing industry to supply enough homes at prices people can afford.

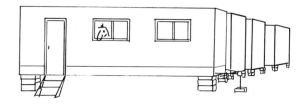

Many manufacturers are scrambling to cash in on the popularity of the mobile home. Consequently, the buyer has many choices. Although often convenient and well planned, the mobile home is much smaller than the customary home. Even more important than a consideration of space, however, is the style of living provided by mobile park communities. While many persons may be perfectly satisfied with such an environment, don't buy a mobile home without seeing firsthand "where" it will be rooted. Even the best mobile parks are crowded and offer little privacy. This can be especially undesirable where children are involved. Many concerned people are seriously asking what will happen to the millions of mobile homes which are resting and rusting on concrete blocks across America. Many fear they may become the shanties and slums of the future.

Even if you are merely considering a mobile home for a short-term living space, you must evaluate carefully overall costs—including resale value. While ordinary homes usually increase in value in inflationary times, mobile homes may instead show substantial depreciation. Mobile park fees are often very steep. In hot or cold climates, air conditioning and heating a mobile home can be troublesome and costly.

On the more positive side, the purchase of mobile homes is now possible under the GI loan program. This was authorized for the first time by the Veterans Housing Act of 1970. Also, in that same year, the Department of Housing and Urban Development began insuring 12-year mobile home loans.

**Row houses.** First used in Europe, the row house is now a common sight in many of our larger American cities. With handsome, crisp, innovative architectural treatment, there is today revived interest in this type of housing. Because they share common walls, foundations, roofs, and parking areas, row houses economize both land and construction costs.

Small private patios or garden courts are often an integral part of each unit; however, the owner of a row house does not usually have to worry about yard maintenance. If there is a common landscaped park area, or perhaps a swimming pool, maintenance is provided for a small monthly fee by the project's developer.

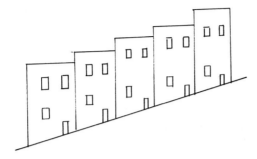

The "Checklist for Houses" set out below is an easy way to inventory the good and bad points of each house you consider.

## CHECKLIST FOR HOUSES

### Outside House and Yard

_____ attractive, well-designed house

_____ suited to natural surroundings

_____ compatible with houses in the area

_____ good drainage of rain and moisture

_____ dry firm soil around the house

_____ mature, healthy trees—placed to give shade in summer

_____ convenient, well-kept driveway, walks, patio, porch

_____ suitable use of building materials

_____ lot of the right size and shape for house and garage

_____ enclosed yard for children

_____ parking convenience—garage, carport or street

_____ distance between houses for privacy

_____ sheltered entry—well lighted and large enough for several to enter the house together

_____ attractive landscaping and yard

_____ convenient service entrance

### Outside Construction

_____ durable siding materials—in good condition

_____ solid brick and masonry—free of cracks

_____ non-corrosive gutters and downspouts, connected to storm sewer or splash block to carry water away from house

_____ copper or aluminum flashing used over doors, windows, and joints on the roof

____ solid foundation walls—six inches above ground level— eight inches thick

____ screens and storm windows

____ weather-stripped windows and doors

## *Inside Construction*

____ well-done carpentry work with properly fitted joints and moldings

____ properly fitted and easy-to-work doors and drawers in built-in cabinets

____ sound, smooth walls with invisible nails and taping on dry walls; without hollows or large cracks in plaster walls

____ dry basement floor with hard smooth surface

____ properly fitted, easy-to-operate windows

____ adequate basement drain

____ level wood floors with smooth finish and no high edges, wide gaps or squeaks

____ dry, well-ventilated attic

____ well-fitted tile floors—no cracked or damaged tiles—no visible adhesive

____ sturdy stairways with railings, adequate head room—not too steep

____ good possibilities for improvements, remodeling, expanding

____ leakproof roof—in good condition

____ adequate insulation for warmth and soundproofing

## *Living Space*

____ convenient floor plan and paths from room to room

____ suitable wall space and room size for your furnishings

____ convenient entry with foyer and closet

____ outdoor space convenient to indoor space

____ work areas (kitchen, laundry, workshop) with adequate drawers, cabinets, lighting, work space, electric power

____ windows located to provide enough air, light and ventilation

____ private areas (bedrooms and bathrooms) located far enough from other parts of the house for privacy and quiet

____ agreeable type, size and placement of windows

___ social areas (living and dining rooms, play space, yard) convenient, comfortable, large enough for family and guests

___ rooms conveniently related to each other—entry to living room, dining room to kitchen, bedrooms to baths

___ adequate storage—closets, cabinets, shelves—in attic, basement, garage

___ usable attic and/or basement space

___ possibilities for enlarging the house if and as necessary

___ attractive decorating and fixtures

___ extras—fireplace, air conditioning, porches, new kitchens and baths, built-in equipment, decorating you like

*Source: Money Management, Your Housing Dollar*, copyright by Household Finance Corporation. Reprinted by permission.

## BUILDING A CUSTOM-DESIGNED HOME

Sometimes a family cannot find an existing home that fits its needs or desires. And, even though it probably will cost more money, they finally decide that for them it is best to have a home custom-designed and built. In addition to the extra money, the family will probably find building more time-consuming and fraught with decisions. Also, there will be a few uncertainties sprinkled in for added flavor. In the long run, though, building may certainly be more satisfying.

**Getting house plans.** The planning phase is very important if you are to be assured that your new home will be pleasing and functional. If you can afford to do so, employ the services of a well-qualified architect. Ordinarily, architects' fees for residences run from 10 to 15 percent of the contract price. Therefore, if you are planning on building a $25,000 home, architects' fees could run from $2,500 to $3,750. This may sound like a great deal of money, but an architect's services can be a very sound investment. He is a professional and may very well save you the cost of his fees in economies effected in design and construction of the home. For example, he knows how to get the very best possible utilization of space and the most economical and satisfactory choice of construction methods and materials. Depending on the fee, the architect may actually supervise and inspect construction for you. If you decide to employ an architect, however, be sure that you talk to several before making the final selection. Most architects have particular styles in which they specialize. Make sure your tastes and the architect's run along the same lines. Talk with former clients of the architect—get their frank opinions.

Unfortunately, not all persons have enough money to employ an architect. Most usually, the architectural fees must be paid in cash. By the time you pay for a lot and accumulate a down payment, you may find it simply impossible to get hold of that extra money for such fees. If you can't, there are several alternatives:

1. In many cities you will find reputable "house planning firms." (See Fig. 8–1.) These firms employ skilled draftsmen, often people with considerable architectural training. They will plan a home for you for a fee only a fraction of that required by a licensed architect (usually $250–$500). The capabilities of such firms differ greatly one from another; if you decide to proceed along these lines, make some very thorough checks. Talk to some of their recent customers to find out about the quality and thoroughness of the planners' work.

2. Purchase standard stock plans from house planning firms or home magazines. At any magazine stand, you can also find house plan books. Detailed construction plans are available from any of these sources at quite nominal cost. Usually the plans include a set of material specifications. Here are the names and addresses of some of the companies which sell complete sets of plans.

   Companies that sell house plans:

   Hiawatha Estes
   P.O. Box 404-P
   Northridge, California 91324

   L. M. Bruinier and Assoc.
   1304 S.W. Bertha Blvd., Dept. E
   Portland, Oregon 97219

   Home Planners, Inc.
   16310 Grand River Avenue
   Detroit, Michigan 48227

   Home Building Plan Service
   Studio 12C, 2454 N.E. Sandy Blvd.
   Portland, Oregon 97232

   Garlinghouse
   Dept. NHG 58
   Box 299
   Topeka, Kansas 66601

   House Plan Headquarters, Inc.
   48 West 48th Street
   New York, New York 10036

   The only difficulty with stock plans is that they have to be adapted to your own lot. This may complicate things for the contractors who will bid on your home. If you use stock plans, make certain of just how the contractor proposes to modify the plans to fit the house on your lot. You also should have a statement from the builder to the effect that the plans are satisfactory and that the necessary adaptations will be made at no additional cost to you outside the terms of the contract.

3. Builders often have sets of plans from which you may choose. They may even furnish these at no charge to you and will give you firm bids on each of several models. Such plans may be entirely satisfactory; however, you will not have the opportunity of comparing bids from several contractors if you

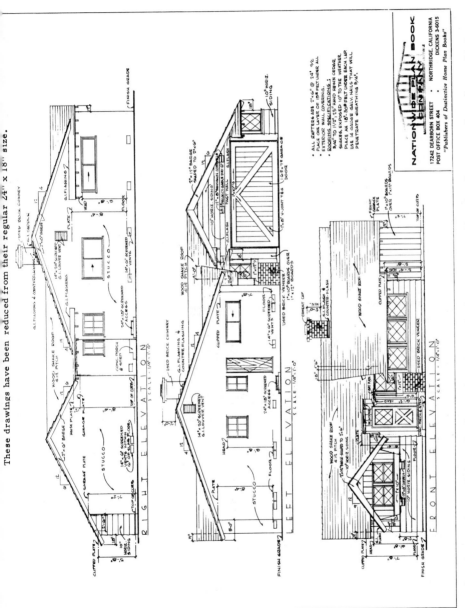

**Fig. 8–1** House plans. High-quality house plans can be obtained at reasonable prices from a number of reputable home-planning companies and magazines. This particular plan is available from the Nationwide Plan Book Company, 18323 Parthenia Street, Northridge, California.

# GENERAL SPECIFICATIONS

For a Residence and..................................................................................Contract No..............................................

Contractor.................................................................................................................................................

Owner.......................................................................................................................................................

We hereby certify that we have seen the property, read the following General Conditions and Specifications and agree to same.

Owner's Signature....................................................................Contractor, D.B.A..........................................

Owner's Signature....................................................................Contractor's Signature..................................

Owner's Address......................................................................Contractor's Address....................................

Owner's Phone.........................................................................Contractor's Phone......................................

The General Conditions and Specifications, the Addenda, if any, and drawings shall be known as the Contract Documents and are part of the contract. The Contract Documents are complementary and what is called for by one document shall be as binding as if called for by all.

Whenever required by the context or facts the singular shall include the plural and vice versa, and the masculine shall include the feminine and neuter.

The word "Contract," when used includes the Contract Documents.
The word "Job," when used, includes the entire improvements as called for by the contract.
The word "Work," includes any or all things done upon or furnished to, or to be done upon or furnished to, the job.
The word "Contractor," refers to the person who is obliged to construct the job called for in the contract.
The word "Owner," refers to the person for whom and upon whose premises the job is to be constructed.

When Owner and Contractor are identical, the Owner shall do and perform all things and comply with all conditions called for hereunder on the part of the Contractor.

The word "Company," refers to................................................................................................................

Words and expressions used in the contract providing for the exercise of a discretion or determination of an uncertain amount or thing, such as "approved," "satisfactory," "estimated," shall mean that such discretion or determination is vested solely in the Company and that on such matters its determination exercised in good faith shall be final.

**SUPERVISION**—The Company shall exercise general supervision to insure the performance of the contract by the Contractor. It, through its representatives, shall have access to any and all parts of the building at all times to inspect work done, and it may inspect, sample and test any materials furnished or ordered to be used in the structure. All work and materials are subject to the approval of the Company.

**CONTRACTOR RESPONSIBLE TO COMPANY**—The Contractor shall be responsible and answer directly to the Company for his acts and omissions and for the acts and omissions of his sub-contractors, and of all persons directly or indirectly employed or retained by him in connection with the job.

**DRAWINGS AND SPECIFICATIONS**—The general conditions and specifications, addenda, if any, and drawings are intended to co-operate so that any work exhibited in either of them whether exhibited in the order or not is to be executed according to the true intent and meaning hereof, the same as if set forth in all. Provided, however, that should any law, ordinance or regulation of the State or of any County or Municipality prescribe additional requirements or should any of the work so called for be in violation of the requirements of any such law, ordinance or regulation, then the requirements of such laws, ordinances or regulations shall prevail and shall be complied with by the Contractor as a part of the work called for and no extra compensation shall be allowed therefor.

**LABOR AND MATERIALS**—The Contractor shall furnish all labor and material necessary to do all that may be termed ordinary or customary or essential to the completed job, notwithstanding any omissions from the drawings or Contract Documents, and should anything be omitted therefrom which is necessary to a clear understanding of the job, or should any error exist therein, or in work done by other contractors affecting work included in the contract, it shall be the duty of the Contractor to notify the Company.

**QUALITY, MATERIALS AND WORKMANSHIP**—All materials furnished for and used in the job and workmanship on the job shall be the best of the kind and grade specified, and where the grade is not specified, shall be first class. The job shall be completed as a first class, high grade job throughout.

**PERMITS AND REGULATIONS**—The Contractor shall obtain and pay for all permits and licenses and shall give all notices, pay all fees and comply in every respect with the laws, ordinances, rules and regulations bearing on the job.

**IMPROPER WORK**—The Contractor shall remove all improper work upon being directed to do so by the Company. If the Contractor should refuse or neglect to remove such improper work, the Company may remove the same or cause it to be removed by another and the Contractor shall not only suffer a deduction for the expense occasioned thereby, but shall also be responsible for all damage suffered which may be deducted from the contract price. Any cost caused by defective or ill-timed work shall be borne by the Contractor.

**ARBITRATION**—If no "Company" is being utilized in the performance of this contract, any controversy between the Owner and the Contractor which may arise from this contract shall be settled by arbitration. Each shall choose an arbitrator and these two shall choose a third. The decision of any two of these shall be binding upon both the Owner and the Contractor. The Owner and the Contractor shall equally share the expense of this arbitration.

**CHANGES IN THE CONTRACT**—Without invalidating the contract, the Owner may make alterations or additions to the original contract. The Contractor shall make no changes until written authorization has been received from the Owner. The contract price will be adjusted according to the changes and this information will be included in the written authorization and signed by both the Owner and Contractor.

**Fig. 8–2** Building specifications. Like house plans, building specifications can be obtained from a number of sources and generally accompany a set of house plans. Courtesy of Nationwide Plan Book Company.

use this procedure. You may also find that you cannot modify the plans to meet your own needs.

**The specifications.** A very important document required for bidding which accompanies the plans is the "List of Specifications." (See Fig. 8–2.) This is an extremely detailed list indicating the type and grade of lumber, roofing, insulation, concrete mixtures, etc. Essentially, it must indicate the grade, quality, model number, etc. of everything used in constructing or equipping the home. This exacting document provides your best assurance of getting just the fixtures and appliances and construction quality which you desire and are paying for. Don't get discouraged with all the detail. Take time to get a complete list of all the information needed.

It is customary to include broad dollar allowances for certain types of things. Usually there is an allowance for "hardware"—all the doorknobs, hinges, locks, door and drawer pulls, etc. Also, it is customary to include an allowance for all the electrical and plumbing fixtures. This procedure is all right, but make sure that the allowance is going to be sufficient. Instead of taking someone else's word for it, do some spot checking and estimating to be sure. Find out what you want. Specify exactly.

If the contractor helps you prepare the specifications, he may purposely eliminate some very vital and significant items. Similarly, he may "up" your total costs by special clauses or restrictions in the formal building contract. Notable among these are:

1. Sewer and water trenching, pipes, meters, and hookup from the house to street connections.
2. Underground electrical and telephone cable hookup fees.
3. Sidewalk and curbing charges or assessments.
4. Earth removal and rough grading of lot to facilitate proper drainage and prepare for landscaping.
5. Rain gutters and downspouts.

**Sub-contracting or general contractor?** If you have had previous experience in the building trade, you might consider acting as the general contractor yourself. In doing so, you would advertise for bids from many different experts for each individual phase of the building job. For example, you could get a bid from carpenters to do all the wood framing and finish carpentry work. Other sub-contractors would lay brick or siding; others would do the roofing, electrical, plumbing, heating, etc.

If you have the time to supervise the construction yourself and you know what you're doing, you might be able to save money sub-contracting the work. However, if you don't know the business, stay far away from this approach. Certainly for the average person, finding a general contractor who can give you one overall firm bid on the entire house is preferable.

**Selecting a contractor.**  Once house plans and specifications are complete, you are faced with one of the final and important choices—choosing the builder to do the job for you.

The majority of general contractors build individual homes as well as subdivision homes on contract.  Therefore, you will find it worth your time to visit open houses of many local subdivisions.  Look carefully at construction details and finished work.  Make a list of the contractors whose work impresses you.  Then call the contractors and ask if they would be interested in bidding on your home.  The bidding process often takes considerable time and follow-through.  Be sure to ask each contractor to submit a written proposal to you.  Don't be too surprised if you lose a few sets of plans in the bidding process.  Often contractors will take a set of plans to bid on a home, and you'll never hear from them again.  The building business is notorious for its "booms and busts."  If the past is any indication of the future, the majority of building contractors who may wish to bid on your home today will not be in business five years from now.  Therefore, you will probably be better off and have fewer risks if you narrow your selection to reputable contractors—men who have been in the trade and proven themselves for some time.

If you can find six to ten good prospects, that should be sufficient.  However, if all the bids appear too high, you might want to continue the bidding process.  In getting bids from 12 contractors on the author's home, there was a difference of $11,000 from the high to the lowest bid.

Once you have all your bids complete, re-examine recent work to make sure the quality of the workmanship is still of a standard that will satisfy you.  Check credit ratings.  This is very important.  For one reason or another, it may be that you will decide not to accept the very lowest bidder.  Or you might choose to do some negotiating with one of the contractors.  Talk it over, see what you would have to change to reduce the contract price to a level you can afford.

**Some hazards in building.**  Among the numerous hazards in building are:

1. Never knowing for certain the quality of the finished product.
2. Costs exceeding contract because of changes you decide to make while building is in progress.
3. Builder going bankrupt before construction is complete, or failing to pay for labor and materials used in constructing your home—leaving the owner liable for the charges.

Even though you may have investigated and been satisfied with buildings constructed by your contractor, builders sometimes do spotty work.  Unfortunately, your home may not be finished quite to your expectations.  Even though nearly every community has a building inspector, the thoroughness of inspections varies a great deal.  Unless the finished work is grossly poor, the inspector will, in all probability, approve what the contractor has done.  Your only recourse is to convince the builder that the work should be done over again, or to withhold signing the completion papers with the lending institution until the work has been completed to your satisfaction.

One of the most disconcerting things about building is that as the work progresses, you inevitably see things that you'd like changed. Most building contracts have a "change clause" stating that any changes will be made at cost plus 10 or 15 percent. However, it is easy for builders to "pad" the actual cost of these changes. Unless you have an exceptionally honest contractor, you'll find the changes costly. Nonetheless, if changes are required, be sure you have a written agreement between you and the contractor on "each" and "every" change. Then there won't be misgivings or disagreements when it comes settlement time. Be sure to keep a running list of change costs so that you'll be able to meet your obligations to the contractor when the house is completed.

Undoubtedly, the most dangerous aspect of building a home comes from the possibility that the contractor may go bankrupt or that he might fail to pay for labor and materials used for your home. Although laws vary somewhat from one state to another, most states have "lien statutes" that can be invoked by laborers or suppliers against your property if the contractor fails to meet his obligations on the home. For example:

> The Elkinds had lived in an apartment for ten years saving money to build. They had saved $8,500. Subsequently, they purchased a nice building lot, had plans drawn, and gave a contract to a local builder to construct the home. When the home was about 80 percent complete, the builder left his wife, and took out bankruptcy. He had already drawn about 75 percent of the money for the house from the bank. The bank had made the contractor submit "lien waivers" from each of his suppliers before they had paid him the money. (A lien waiver is a form which in effect says that the supplier or laborer has been paid and that he waives the right to impose a lien on the property.) However, the bank subsequently found that the contractor had fraudulently had the waivers signed by friends and not the real subcontractors or laborers. Consequently, liens were placed on the owners for over $11,000 for the work already completed. The contractor (deeply in debt and near bankruptcy) was finally jailed for forgery, but there was no way to recover the tragic economic loss suffered by the Elkinds.

How can you protect yourself against liens? The best protection is to require the contractor to furnish a "performance bond." The bonding company will investigate the contractor's credit rating and financial ability. If he satisfies their requirement, the company will issue a bond guaranteeing that the contractor will do his job as stipulated in the contract. Bonding is quite expensive—usually running 5 percent of the total job cost. If the contractor is required to furnish it, undoubtedly he will pass the cost along to you. This, however, is the only positive way you can avoid the possibility of lien difficulty in building.

## SOURCES OF HOME MORTGAGE LOANS

The principal sources of home mortgages are:

1. Commercial banks.
2. Savings and home-loan institutions.
3. Mortgage and investment companies.
4. Insurance companies.
5. Private lenders.

Probably the most convenient and complete local listing is provided in the "Yellow Pages" of your telephone directory. Look under "Mortgages."

Don't feel out of place in visiting any of these sources. Mortgage companies make their profits by making loans. They advertise because they want you to come and see them. Before a loan is actually granted, a formal application must be submitted; then a thorough credit check is made, and the request is considered by a loan committee. However, in just a brief conversation with the loan officer, you can find out your prospects for getting a loan and the terms under which it could be written. The subsequent topics dealing with (1) types of loans, (2) special mortgage features, and (3) costs of home loans will summarize the main points you will want to compare.

## TYPES OF HOME LOANS

**FHA loans.** Promoting widespread home ownership was the principal goal of the Federal Housing Administration established by Congress in 1934. FHA loans are actually made by a bank, building and loan association, mortgage company, insurance company, or other FHA-approved lender. The loan is merely "insured" by the FHA. It is not a government loan. The FHA does not lend money or build homes.

Since the FHA mortgage insurance protects the lender against any possible loss on the loan, the lender can allow borrowers very liberal terms. Low down-payment, long-term home loans have become standard, permitting many families that could not otherwise afford to do so to become home owners. For the mortgage insurance, the buyer pays a yearly premium equal to $\frac{1}{2}$ of one percent of the average loan balance outstanding during the year. Monthly payments include an amount for taxes, insurance, mortgage insurance, interest, and principal payments.

The FHA determines what the maximum interest shall be. However, if this interest rate is lower than the prevailing rate for conventional loans, lenders become disinterested in participating in the insured-loan program. If they should make FHA loans at such times, they would want to charge a discount — an extra fee — to compensate for the difference. Discounts may not be charged buyers of existing homes. However, if a person is going to build a home for himself or for resale, the FHA also permits the lender to charge the borrower a discount. If you are building, therefore, it is wise to investigate the discount fully before deciding on the most economical loan.

Since FHA interest rates change, it would be well for you to check with your local FHA office for the now-current rate. In addition to the interest, you pay an additional $\frac{1}{2}$ of one percent for the insurance feature.

**VA loans.** There are two important aspects of the Veterans Administration GI loan program: (1) The government enters into an agreement with the lender to guarantee a significant portion of a qualified applicant's loan. (2) If the ex-GI cannot find anyone willing to make a loan, the veteran can make application to the VA for a direct government loan.

Since the risk of the lender is reduced, there is more likelihood that the applicant can secure favorable loan terms—low downpayment, reasonable interest, and long-term repayment. Maximum interest rates are established by the Veterans Administration. They vary from time to time to keep pace with the availability and cost of money in the conventional loan market. The VA loans are always $\frac{1}{2}$ of one percent below total FHA rates, since there is no insurance charge made on the VA loans. Post-Korean veterans, however, pay an initial one-time fee of $\frac{1}{2}$ of one percent of the total amount of the loan. This fee, which may be included in the loan, is remitted to the VA by the lender. For example, if the loan amount is $16,000, the fee would be $80. No commission or brokerage fees may be charged to a veteran for securing a GI loan. However, the lender may charge reasonable closing costs usually paid by a borrower.

**Conventional loans.** Any loan which is not insured by FHA or the VA is referred to in financial circles as a "conventional loan." Quite often, the borrower of a conventional loan must meet higher credit standards. These may include (1) a larger downpayment, (2) greater job stability, and (3) well-established bank credit. Conventional loans may not be written for as long a term as an insured mortgage. They may contain more restrictive clauses on advance payments and early loan payoffs. Nonetheless, every home buyer should determine what conventional loan terms are available to him. Since individual lenders may vary greatly, you may find more liberal terms offered under a conventional loan than is the case under insured loans. Persons having excellent credit and sizable downpayments, may find a conventional loan at a lower-than-average interest rate.

**Which loan is best?** Among other things, you should also know the differences in time required for processing the various types of loans. This can be particularly important where you have already sold your present house, or where your lease is expiring. You will generally find that you can get a conventional loan much more quickly than the other two—in as short a period as two weeks—compared with six weeks to two months and more for the other two, and that it involves much less paper work and red tape.

And remember, while under the two government loans, you might get by with a smaller downpayment, and smaller monthly payments by virtue of the longer term in which you have to repay the loan, these easier terms over the long pull will cost you a lot more money. For the bigger the loan you take out, and the longer you take to repay it, the more money you will pay out in interest cost.

The additional interest cost can add thousands of dollars on to the overall cost of your home, as well as greatly postponing the day when you will own your own home free and clear.

## SPECIAL FEATURES OF HOME MORTGAGES

It is standard for all mortgages to require a monthly reserve payment for property insurance and taxes in addition to the mortgage payment. This is certainly desirable from a budgetary as well as a convenience standpoint. Aside from this, though, there are other features that differ considerably from one lender to another, and usually lending offices will give you a frank and accurate explanation about these stipulations. However, you must take the responsibility of actually reading the mortgage before signing the papers. These are the principal points you will want to clarify:

*Prepayment clauses and/or penalties.* The ideal loan from the borrower's standpoint would have no restrictions on early payoff. Then should a person be able to accelerate repayment, he could freely do so. A loan without any such restrictions, however, is rare. Therefore, you should attempt to find a mortgage written with the most liberal prepayment terms.

*Open-ended clauses.* After paying off a portion of your mortgage, there may be many legitimate needs for extra money to finance home projects—remodeling, adding extra living area, making major repairs. If the mortgage has an "open-end" feature, you may re-borrow the difference between what you still owe and the original amount of the mortgage. Since home mortgages are based on simple interest, the open-end feature may be your most economical source of home-improvement money. The open-end mortgage is highly desirable; but you should be aware that each mortgage may have different stipulations. Additional funds borrowed may be at the same or at a different rate than that specified in the original mortgage. Sometimes, you end up paying a higher rate on the entire mortgage.

*Loan-Modification Agreement.* This is an excellent feature which permits adjusting the terms of the original loan in accordance with a serious change in your financial situation. This does much for your "peace of mind" because in the event of a drop of income through change of job, loss of overtime payments or serious illness, you know you can adjust your monthly payments accordingly.

*A Package Provision.* This, like the last provision, may be quite desirable for the buyer, particularly if you are moving into a newly built home. It is a feature which enables you to finance certain major appliances and other necessary items (such as landscaping, carpeting, drapes) as part of the original loan at the original interest rate.

## COSTS OF HOME LOANS

Mortgage interest rates for permanent home mortgages are determined by a variety of complex economic factors of which construction activity and demand for home mortgages are only a part. National monetary policy and fiscal policy and the demand for funds by governments and individuals all play a part. Fluctuations in mortgage interest rates can be substantial, depending upon how these numerous factors converge at any one time. Moreover, differing local conditions and sluggish responses to demand and supply pressures in local areas make for differences in prevailing rates in various localities and regions at any one time.

Financing charges are levied by the lender in two ways. First, they are imposed as the stated interest charges on the unpaid balance of the mortgage loan. In this form they are borne directly by the home owner in the monthly payments; second, they take the form of *Points* charged (as a one-time fee) against the mortgage amount (one point equalling 1 percent of the principal) at the time the loan is made.

Charges for points arise primarily in connection with FHA-insured mortgages. They are a device by which the lender can achieve a market yield on his loan despite the imposition by FHA of a ceiling on stated interest rates. In recent years points have also been used in connection with conventional mortgages to increase yields where State usury laws impose ceilings below going market rates. Under FHA regulations the buyer of a house cannot be required to pay more than 1 point; the seller must pay the rest. In fact, however, the seller of new housing considers his payment for points as a cost and thus passes it along to the buyer by padding the selling price.

The combination of the stated interest rate and points is the effective yield to the lender and, in one form or another, it is you the buyer who bears these costs. Despite occasional short-term declines in home mortgage interest rates, the postwar trend has been almost steadily upward. In the early 1950's, yields on conventional mortgages commonly were about $5\frac{1}{4}$ to $5\frac{1}{2}$ percent. For the last few years, they have more normally been about $7\frac{1}{4}$ percent, and still more recently, they have been over 8 percent.

As noted, points paid for by the seller are, like other development costs, all included in selling price. Points charged to the buyer, like the down payment, require *immediate* payment at the time of closing. The mortgage interest rate is paid each month on the unpaid balance of the mortgage loan. Monthly debt service payments (which include interest and amortization of principal) will vary with the interest rate, principal amount, and term of the mortgage. They will vary proportionally with the principal amount, other things being equal. Thus a 10 percent increase in the mortgage principal will produce a 10 percent increase in monthly payments.

The proportion of monthly payment attributable to the interest charge steadily decreases as time goes on, since the principal amount outstanding, on which the interest charge is levied, is being reduced. Thus, for example, assuming a $10,000 mortgage at 6 percent for 20 years, monthly payments will be $71.65. At the end of one year, only $267.08 will have been applied against the principal amount and $592.72, or 68.9 percent, of the year's payments will have gone toward interest. Not until well into the eighth year (month 102) do payments toward the principal exceed interest charges. The total amount paid over the life of the mortgage will vary with the amount of the mortgage principal, the rate of interest, and the term.

Because of the long-term commitments which lenders must make on mortgage loans, there is growing sentiment favoring a variable or flexible interest mortgage loan. While new in this country, the flexible interest loan has long been used successfully in Europe. Essentially, it is a special contractual arrangement whereby the lender can adjust interest upward or downward in response to general changes in the money market. The homeowner generally may respond to changes in interest charges in one of two different ways: (1) by paying a larger or smaller monthly payment, or (2) by continuing to pay the current monthly payment and lengthening or shortening the payoff time for the mortgage.

The desirability of such a mortgage depends completely on the future general trends in interest rates. If rates are relatively low at the time you are shopping for a mortgage—with some expectation that interest may go higher— obviously the flexible plan is not the one to choose. But if interest rates are very high with a likelihood that they may soften—go lower—you could benefit from this arrangement. Figure 8–3 illustrates how this might work.

## IF YOU BUY A HOME WITH A "VARIABLE RATE" MORTGAGE—

Under a new-type mortgage, the interest rate is adjusted up or down at specified intervals as the cost of money generally rises or falls. Over the life of the loan, rates might both rise and fall.

Suppose interest costs climb steadily on a 30-year, $25,000 mortgage. Here's how monthly payments might run if rates were adjustable every five years:

| | IF RATE IS— | MONTHLY PAYMENT WOULD BE— |
|---|---|---|
| FIRST FIVE YEARS | 8.0% | $183 |
| 6-10 years | 8.5% | $191 |
| 11-15 years | 9.0% | $198 |
| 16-20 years | 9.5% | $204 |
| 21-25 years | 10.0% | $209 |
| 26-30 years | 10.5% | $211 |

Suppose interest rates fall steadily:

| | IF RATE IS— | MONTHLY PAYMENT WOULD BE— |
|---|---|---|
| FIRST FIVE YEARS | 8.0% | $183 |
| 6-10 years | 7.5% | $176 |
| 11-15 years | 7.0% | $169 |
| 16-20 years | 6.5% | $164 |
| 21-25 years | 6.0% | $160 |
| 26-30 years | 5.5% | $158 |

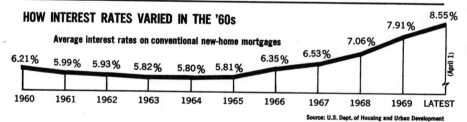

### HOW INTEREST RATES VARIED IN THE '60s

Average interest rates on conventional new-home mortgages

6.21%    5.99%    5.93%    5.82%    5.80%    5.81%    6.35%    6.53%    7.06%    7.91%    8.55%

1960    1961    1962    1963    1964    1965    1966    1967    1968    1969    LATEST (April 1)

Source: U.S. Dept. of Housing and Urban Development

**Fig. 8–3** Variable rate mortgage chart. A variable rate mortgage allows for adjustable interest rates in response to changes in the money market. Reprinted by permission from *U.S. News & World Report*, April 27, 1970. Copyright© 1970, U.S. News & World Report, Inc.

Knowing something about the general mechanics of how mortgages work, let us now look at the specifics of how you can cut home-financing costs:

*1. Find the lowest interest rate.*  Usually you will find that the largest single cost in buying a home is not the lot nor even the house itself, rather it is the interest which must be paid on the mortgage.  Consequently, finding the most economical mortgage rate is as important as finding the right home.

Too often, a home buyer eagerly takes the first loan offer.  He needn't.  He can shop for mortgage terms just as he can shop for the best buy when purchasing a fishing pole or a camera.  Regardless of where you live, considerable differences in interest rates and loan closing costs exist among lenders.  So before you make a mortgage commitment, shop and compare.  Especially in times of more abundant mortgage money and competitive rates, such shopping can save a great deal of money.  Table 8–1 which follows shows you the tremendous impact which the interest rate has on mortgage costs.

**Table 8–1** Comparison of total interest charges and monthly payments for each $1,000 borrowed on a twenty-year mortgage.

| Rate of interest (percent) | Total amount repaid | Total interest over life of mortgage | Monthly payment |
|---|---|---|---|
| $5\frac{1}{2}$ | $1,651.20 | $ 651.20 | $6.88 |
| 6 | 1,718.40 | 718.40 | 7.16 |
| $6\frac{1}{2}$ | 1,790.40 | 790.40 | 7.46 |
| 7 | 1,860.00 | 860.00 | 7.75 |
| $7\frac{1}{2}$ | 1,934.40 | 934.40 | 8.06 |
| 8 | 2,008.80 | 1,008.80 | 8.37 |
| $8\frac{1}{2}$ | 2,083.20 | 1,083.20 | 8.68 |
| 9 | 2,160.00 | 1,160.00 | 9.00 |
| $9\frac{1}{2}$ | 2,239.20 | 1,239.20 | 9.33 |
| 10 | 2,318.40 | 1,318.40 | 9.66 |

Aside from shopping for the best "going" interest rate, you should look down the road a year or two as to (1) what trends seem to be emerging in interest rates and (2) what inflation is doing to home prices.  If inflation were halted and there seemed to be good indication that interest rates were falling, you would logically decide that it would save you money to postpone your home purchase.  However, if construction costs continue to increase at their current pace—about 7 percent a year—interest rates would have to decline by more than 0.8 percent on a 25-year loan to benefit from a year's wait.

*2. Keep repayment period reasonable.*  Another influential factor in reducing your mortgage costs is the length of time you take to repay.  If you repay a $15,000, $5\frac{3}{4}$ percent mortgage in 25 years, at $94.50 per month, your total repayment is $28,350.  If you pay the same $15,000 mortgage in 35 years, at $5\frac{3}{4}$ percent, your total repayment will be $34,902.  However, very long mortgages often require a higher rate and in any case, a higher total repayment.

The chief reason why a family might want a long mortgage is to reduce monthly payments. However mortgages longer than 25 or 30 years really do not reduce monthly payments enough to justify the higher total interest. On a $15,000 mortgage at 5¾ percent, your monthly payment for a 25-year term would be $94.50; for 30, $87.60; for 35, $83.10.

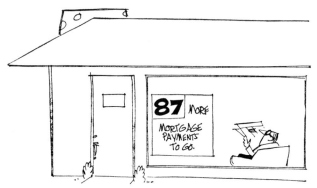

Reprinted with permission of *The Wall Street Journal* (Cartoon Features Syndicate).

*3. Make a sizable down payment.* The third influence on your total cost is the amount of down payment. This may be a double-barreled one. For example, a lender may require 7¾ percent or 8 percent if you pay only 10 percent down, but 7½ percent if you can put down 25 percent, and as little as 7 percent if you put down one-third or more (depending on the general rate level in your area).

**REFINANCING CAN SAVE MONEY**
As has already been pointed out, interest rates are now at or near their 20-year peak. Interest costs may go higher, or they could decline. If and when you become a new homeowner, keep track of prevailing interest rates on home mortgages. Should rates go down, it could pay you to "refinance your home." This simply means that you would go shopping for another mortgage to replace the one you already have. For example, in five years you may find that rates are ¾ of one percent lower than your existing mortgage. By getting a new loan and paying off the old one, you may be able to lower your monthly payments, or better still, cut one or two years off the life of the mortgage and keep payments at the same rate.

Mortgages are usually written with a "prepayment or early-payoff penalty." Such a penalty clause states that should you pay off your loan within a certain period (usually three or five years), you must pay a stipulated penalty. Penalties may be fixed dollar sums; more usually, they are stated as a percentage of the outstanding principal. If your mortgage has such a clause, and most mortgages do, it may be best to wait until the penalty period has elapsed before refinancing. At least any penalty must be considered as an offsetting cost against any savings you would make from a lower interest rate on a new loan. Other offsetting expenses are those fees and closing costs associated with getting the new mortgage.

If interest rates do decline, you will very likely find that getting a new loan is easier than getting your initial loan. You will have built up some equity in the home, established a better credit rating from prompt payment on your first loan, and in all probability will be earning a higher salary.

## MOVE-IN STRAINS ON THE BUDGET

Unless you've gone through the move from apartment living to a home, it's safe to say that you're in for a bit of a shock. To avoid a complete nervous breakdown to yourself and your budget, it's well to be prepared for the economics of the move. Admittedly, some of the items here can be postponed, but all eventually must be taken care of. Here are the major things you should plan for:

1. Direct moving expenses for furniture and household belongings to your new home.
2. Expenses for drapes, carpeting, additional furniture, new appliances such as washer, drier, and refrigerator.
3. Costs for landscaping, sprinkling system, yard maintenance equipment and tools, fertilizer, insecticides, etc.
4. Utility expenditures are likely to increase for heat, lighting, and telephone service.
5. Commuting distances often are greater, requiring additional expenditures for your automobile. Often there is a need for a second car.

Setting aside money for the move can help make the move a pleasant one and avoid the distress of suddenly finding yourself way out on a limb financially.

## FEEDBACK 8

A. Develop your criteria for home buying by analyzing your requirements, desires and means. Within 50 miles of where you now live:

- What neighborhood is best for you? A growing family?
- What location is best for your employment plans?

- What kind of construction materials should go into your home, especially considering local climates?

- Are the homes in certain neighborhoods higher priced than their construction warrants?

- Which is a better buy in your town; new or established homes?

**B.** Begin a "want" list of features, conveniences, floor plans, decor ideas— in short, a list of what you want in your home. When you have, with the agreement of your family, completed your list and "designed" your future home:

- Should (or could) you find these features in an older house?

- Does an existing subdivision have the kind of home you want?

- Should you build a home to incorporate the unique features you want?

- How does the information in B match up with your data from A? (For example, if the home of your dreams is 50 miles from your job, you will have to find an exceptional home and exceptional satisfaction to pay the costs in time and money of commuting 500 miles in a five-day work week.)

**C.** Anticipate hidden move-in expenses by estimating what it will cost you to move from where you now live to, and *into* your new home.

- Can you rent or borrow a truck for the job? Will you really save over professional moving costs, or do you have more profitable work to do?

- What additions are immediately required in your new home? You should carefully consider items listed on page 241 and painting, air conditioning, carpet cleaning, and other renovations which are most easily accomplished before you move all your furniture and belongings to your new home.

- Will you have to plant a lawn and shrubs immediately? Do you want a sprinkling system put in before you move in? What additional garden tools will you need?

- Do you want to do any extensive remodeling before you move? It might be more efficient to take care of new cabinets, built-ins and remodeling the basement before you live in your new home. This way, the sawdust, lumber trimmings and paint spills can be cleaned up before they become a nuisance.

### DISCUSSION QUESTIONS

1. Should rent be the determining factor for apartment hunting? Explain. If not, what is the most important factor?

2. Why is building a home better than buying one that is already built? Why is it better to buy one already built?

3. If one decides to build his home, how does he go about finding a reputable general contractor? Where should he look for the construction plans?

4. What are the factors that have caused suburbs to expand so quickly?

5. Why do building specifications call for such a detailed list of items? Is it necessary to have such detail? Explain.

6. What is best source of home mortgages? Why?

7. What are the differences between the two government home building loans?

8. Why would a borrower want no restrictions on early payoff on his loan? Why are loans without such restrictions so hard to find?

9. How do national monetary policy and fiscal policy play a part on mortgage interest rates?

10. What are the advantages to flexible-interest mortgage loans? Disadvantages?

## CASE PROBLEM

The Finlays, Chuck and Margaret, are both 28 years old. They were married shortly after graduation from college five years ago. They are currently renting a small but attractive apartment, paying $171 monthly plus utilities. They have no children but want to start their family soon. They are tired of apartment living and are considering the purchase of an attractive new home.

Study the details concerning the home and the young couple's financial standing. Discuss the advisability of the purchase; other alternatives they should consider:

*The Prospective Home:* Located in a new, restricted, suburban housing development, the home has just been completed. It has 2,410 square feet of living space—spacious rooms—including three bathrooms, kitchen, living room, dining room, family room, and four bedrooms. The lot is also large—frontage of 135 feet and a depth of 170 feet. The lot is not landscaped. The builder will sell for $42,000. Financing is available on a 20-year, $7\frac{1}{2}$ percent loan with a 10 percent downpayment. Monthly payments total $380.67—$304.67 for principal and interest; $62.00 for property taxes; $14.00 for insurance.

*The Finlays' Finances:* Chuck is permanently employed in the accounting department of a large local bank. His take-home pay amounts to $591 monthly; for the past two years he has worked evenings and on Saturdays for a small accounting company, earning an extra take-home amount of $176 monthly. Margaret works as a secretary for the district manager of a large dairy firm; she has worked in this capacity for 6 years. Her take-home pay amounts to $328 monthly. They own two cars—an economy auto 6 years old which is paid for; a year-old medium-sized car on which a loan balance of about $2,900 is outstanding with two years' monthly payments of $120.82 remaining; they have no other indebtedness. They have $6,780 (current market value) in common stocks and a savings account of $2,950.

a) Discuss the advisability of the purchase.

b) What other alternatives should they consider?

## SUGGESTED READINGS

Abrams, Charles. *Home Ownership for the Poor: A Program for Philadelphia.* New York: Praeger, 1970. 225 pp.

*An FHA "Quick Guide" to Buying a House.* Washington, D.C.: 1966. 12 pp.

Clurman, David, and Edna L. Hebard. *Condominiums and Cooperatives.* New York: Wiley-Interscience, 1970. 395 pp.

Coons, Alvin E., and Bert T. Glaze. *Housing Market Analysis and the Growth of Non-Farm Home Ownership.* Columbus: Ohio State University, 1963. 174 pp.

*Estimating Ability to Pay for a Home.* Washington, D.C.: Federal Housing Administration, 1962. 8 pp.

Herzog, John P., and James S. Earley. *Home Mortgage Delinquency and Foreclosure.* New York: Columbia University Press, 1970. 170 pp.

Margolius, Sidney. *How to Finance Your Home.* New York: Public Affairs Pamphlets, 1964. 20 pp.

Marshall, Robert A. *Before You Buy a House.* Washington, D.C.: Kiplinger Washington Editors, Inc., 1964. 96 pp.

Watkins, Arthur M. *How Much House Can You Afford?* New York: New York Life Insurance Co., 1963. 30 pp.

Watkins, Arthur M. *How to Avoid the Ten Biggest Home-Buying Traps.* New York: Meredith Press, 1968. 138 pp.

CHAPTER 9

# SAVING MONEY ON FOOD AND CLOTHING

Single young men or women maintaining their own apartments or young couples without children usually have few financial obligations, and rarely feel compelled to analyze their buying habits. Within a few years, however, as these same young people assume the responsibilities of parenthood and family money management, wise spending becomes increasingly important. Obviously, money saved on any consumer purchases can mean extra money for other needs or wants. In this chapter you will learn ways of saving money on food and clothing purchases. First, however, let us look at one important consideration which applies not only to the buying of these two basic necessities, but also to the other household purchases discussed in the following chapter. That is "Where to Buy."

## DETERMINING WHERE TO BUY
Prestige is wonderfully important in our lives, but it can be an expensive luxury that the budget-minded consumer can ill afford. Getting full value for each dollar spent means spending it for *only* the product plus a reasonable amount of merchandising, not the frills of a fancy name, exclusive location, fancy packaging, delivery service, charge accounts, or "atmosphere." Comparison shoppers soon learn that it is often possible to buy identical merchandise in several different stores at widely different prices. They know, too, that some retailers have arrangements with manufacturers to use the store's own label on its wholesale purchases from those particular suppliers. Except for price, this merchandise usually is identical to that sold by other retailers under the manufacturer's brand name. So-called prestige stores often mark up their "private-brand" merchandise, while many department stores and discount houses may sell their private-label goods at substantially lower prices.

Plush surroundings and "super" service particularly in clothing and furniture stores cost money, and to enjoy them customers pay higher retail prices. If you cannot, or do not want to pay for the extras, find out where you can purchase the goods without the frills. But do not think that discount stores or those big, sprawling warehouse-type self-service markets that sell everything from abridged dictionaries to zithers are necessarily the answer to more consumer purchasing power. Careful observation of their operating methods will reveal that most of them follow a well-defined pattern of austere surroundings combined with a minimum of customer service. This kind of merchandising— lack of merchandising may be more nearly correct—*usually* does add up to lower prices for the customer. Often, however, such practices benefit retailers more than customers. A perceptive look at the tactics of this interesting new breed of merchandisers is detailed in the informative volume, *The Great Discount Delusion.**

**Membership discount stores.** About midway through the 1900's there dawned on this country a unique selling gimmick, the membership discount department store. For a fee, usually $2 to $5, "selected" individuals are initiated to membership in an "exclusive purchasing program" which, they are informed, will save them dimes and dollars on every purchase at "their" store. Membership cards must be displayed to a doorkeeper to gain entrance to the store whose physical surroundings and merchandising policies usually parallel those of conventional discount stores discussed previously. Membership is not nearly so selective as prospective members may be led to believe—after all, these are captive customers, and "the more the merrier," so to speak. It is the old idea of making something more desirable by making it just a little difficult to obtain, and the philosophy pays off handsomely for membership discount marts.

Usually, prices in the membership stores are a little lower than in regular department stores. But unless purchases are large, it may take considerable time to recoup the membership fee. Brand name merchandise is usually scarce, and in appliance departments it is common to find that many items are the previous year's models. Many clothing items are "seconds" or "irregulars."

**Mail-order and catalog stores.** Although few food items are sold in mail-order and catalog stores, these are important merchandising tools for many retailers of clothing, furniture, and other household goods. Prior to World War II, outfitting the home and family by mail was an accepted way of life for millions of rural Americans. After the war, when automobiles and gasoline were again available, farmers and small-city dwellers began to discard the "look book" and drive to the cities to shop. But by the mid-1960's, with traffic choking highways and city parking space scarce or unavailable, many people apparently decided city shopping was not worth the effort, with the result that many old, established

---

* Walter Henry Nelson, *The Great Discount Delusion.* New York: David McKay Company, Inc., 1965.

mail-order houses are enjoying a comeback and hundreds of new ones—particularly those that feature gifts and household specialty items—have appeared in recent years.

Parts of most mail-order catalogs are shown in color, and modern printing methods result in remarkably accurate reproductions.  Catalog descriptions usually give pertinent product specifications and instructions on care and upkeep.  Prices for mail-order merchandise may be a little lower than those charged by local retailers, but apparent savings are likely to be wiped out by mailing or shipping costs.  On the other hand, the savings of time, gasoline, and nerves may offset disadvantages.

Comparison shopping by mail is difficult, but not impossible.  While the mail-order customer cannot be sure of what he is getting until he has it, most mail-order businesses do allow returns and exchanges, so our advice is to "try it and see."  Before ordering for the first time from a mail-order house, check with the Better Business Bureau to see if there are numerous complaints against the company.  When doing business by mail rather than in person, it is especially important to deal with reputable firms.  After the order is placed, allow several weeks for delivery.  If the order is paid by check, many firms wait until the check clears the bank before sending the merchandise.  When the merchandise is received, it should be inspected for damage in shipping and for accuracy in filling the order.  If the merchandise must be returned for some reason, sending it by certified mail gives you proof that the company did receive the goods, and that your account should be credited.  Most complaints against mail-order houses arise from "no record of receipt" of returned goods.

Shop around by mail.  Find out what quality of merchandise is handled by the various firms.  Only after examination and comparison will you be able to judge value and quality and decide whether or not mail-order shopping is for you.

## STRETCHING YOUR FOOD DOLLARS

It is not only extravagant, but also foolish to spend more money than necessary for food when the best buys are those which most adequately supply the family's nutritional needs and satisfy their tastes at the lowest cost.  This does not mean that people should not eat well, nor is it any attempt to abolish the social pleasantry of good food shared with friends and associates.  In fact, personal and family budgets should include provisions for entertaining at home and dining out—in harmony with desires and financial means.  But, it does mean that the average American family, which spends nearly one-fourth its income for food, can eat well and still save money on every trip to the grocery store.

Although the emphasis may appear to be on food *for the family*, the principles set forth below are sound ones which can be applied with equal effectiveness by single persons or couples without children.

Reprinted with permission of *The Wall Street Journal* (Cartoon Features Syndicate).

## BALANCING NEEDS, TASTES, AND MONEY

Food's basic functions are to satisfy hunger and to provide nutrients for body building and health maintenance.  While expensive cuts of meat and exotic fruits and vegetables usually do an excellent job of satisfying hunger—and the ego, as well—they are not necessarily superior when it comes to providing nourishment.  Likewise, the cheapest buy is not necessarily the *best* buy.  Family approval is important.  Food that is not eaten is hardly a bargain.  Taking these factors into account, the wise food buyer studies the family's food requirements and tastes and learns the nutritional value of various foods so that all three can

be matched against each other and against the money available for food buying. To assist with the important task of planning menus to meet food requirements, the *Daily Food Guide* (Fig. 9–1) is typical of the excellent tools available from the United States Department of Agriculture.*

## A Daily Food Guide

### MEAT GROUP

**Foods Included**

Beef; veal; lamb; pork; various meats, such as liver, heart, kidney.

Poultry and eggs.
Fish and shellfish.
As alternates—dry beans, dry peas, lentils, nuts, peanuts, peanut butter.

**Amounts Recommended**

Choose 2 or more servings every day.
Count as a serving: 2 to 3 ounces of lean cooked meat, poultry, fish—all without bone; 2 eggs; 1 cup cooked dry beans, dry peas, or lentils; 4 tablespoons peanut butter.

### VEGETABLE-FRUIT GROUP

**Foods Included**

All vegetables and fruits. This guide emphasizes those that are valuable as sources of vitamin C and vitamin A.

paragus tips; raw cabbage; collards; garden cress; kale; kohlrabi; mustard greens; potatoes and sweetpotatoes cooked in the jacket; spinach; tomatoes or tomato juice; turnip greens.

*Sources of Vitamin C*

Good sources.—Grapefruit or grapefruit juice; orange or orange juice; cantaloup; guava; mango; papaya; raw strawberries; broccoli; brussels sprouts; green pepper; sweet red pepper.
Fair sources.—Honeydew melon; lemon; tangerine or tangerine juice; watermelon; as-

*Sources of Vitamin A*

Dark-green and deep-yellow vegetables and a few fruits, namely: Apricots, broccoli, cantaloup, carrots, chard, collards, cress, kale, mango, persimmon, pumpkin, spinach, sweetpotatoes, turnip greens and other dark-green leaves, winter squash.

**Amounts Recommended**

Choose 4 or more servings every day, including:
1 serving of a good source of vitamin C or 2 servings of a fair source.
1 serving, at least every other day, of a good source of vitamin A. If the food chosen for vitamin C is also a good source of vitamin A, the additional serving of a vitamin A food may be omitted.
The remaining 1 to 3 or more servings may be of any vegetable or fruit, including those that are valuable for vitamin C and for vitamin A.
Count as 1 serving: ½ cup of vegetable or fruit; or a portion as ordinarily served, such as 1 medium apple, banana, orange, or potato, half a medium grapefruit or cantaloup, or the juice of 1 lemon.

### MILK GROUP

**Foods Included**

Milk—fluid whole, evaporated, skim, dry, buttermilk.

Cheese—cottage; cream; Cheddar-type, natural or process.
Ice cream.

**Amounts Recommended**

Some milk every day for everyone.
Recommended amounts are given below in terms of 8-ounce cups of whole fluid milk:

| | | | |
|---|---|---|---|
| Children under 9 | 2 to 3 | Adults | 2 or more |
| Children 9 to 12 | 3 or more | Pregnant women | 3 or more |
| Teen-agers | 4 or more | Nursing mothers | 4 or more |

Part or all of the milk may be fluid skim milk, buttermilk, evaporated milk, or dry milk.
Cheese and ice cream may replace part of the milk. The amount of either it will take to replace a given amount of milk is figured on the basis of calcium content. Common portions of cheese and of ice cream and their milk equivalents in calcium are:

| | |
|---|---|
| 1-inch cube Cheddar-type cheese | = ½ cup milk |
| ½ cup cottage cheese | = ⅓ cup milk |
| 2 tablespoons cream cheese | = 1 tablespoon milk |
| ½ cup ice cream | = ¼ cup milk |

### BREAD-CEREAL GROUP

**Foods Included**

All breads and cereals that are whole grain, enriched, or restored; check labels to be sure. Specifically, this group includes: Breads; cooked cereals; ready-to-eat cereals; cornmeal;

crackers; flour; grits; macaroni and spaghetti; noodles; rice; rolled oats; and quick breads and other baked goods if made with whole-grain or enriched flour. Bulgur and parboiled rice and wheat also may be included in this group.

**Amounts Recommended**

Choose 4 servings or more daily. Or, if no cereals are chosen, have an extra serving of breads or baked goods, which will make at least 5 servings from this group daily.
Count as 1 serving: 1 slice of bread; 1 ounce ready-to-eat cereal; ½ to ¾ cup cooked cereal, cornmeal, grits, macaroni, noodles, rice, or spaghetti.

### OTHER FOODS

To round out meals and meet energy needs, almost everyone will use some foods not specified in the four food groups. Such foods include: unenriched, refined breads, cereals, flours; sugars; butter, margarine, other fats. These often are ingredients in a recipe or added to other foods during preparation or at the table. Try to include some vegetable oil among the fats used.

**Fig. 9–1** Daily food guide of the United States Department of Agriculture.

Basic to wise grocery shopping is knowing nutrition. Learn from investment of a little time and perhaps a few dollars for a good cookbook, the essentials of human nutrition and the foods which provide these needed nutrients.

**Planning—an essential step.** A cardinal rule for economy in food buying is to "plan your purchases." Plan your menus around featured items from the weekly grocery ads. Although many items listed on the ads (especially in smaller print) are everyday prices, the featured items are usually real bargains.

---

* For information on ordering USDA bulletins, see Appendix 9–A.

Put these items down first and plan accompanying courses to complement them.

A few more minutes at the table after the actual menu planning will save time and countless steps in the store: You probably have a favorite supermarket where you do most of your shopping. Arrange your list to match the store aisles so you need to go up and down each aisle only once. Start at one end of the store and work your way across—for instance, list all canned fruits and vegetables, staple items (sugars, flours, spices), cereals, non-grocery items, convenience package meals, fresh produce, dairy products, meat products, frozen foods and bakery items. Pick up frozen food and bakery items last so that they will not melt or get crushed during the rest of the shopping trip.

After planning your purchases, "purchase your plan." This will help you resist impulse buying. Be flexible enough, however, to substitute unadvertised specials for other items you had listed, and to compare variety, quality, and price at the store.

Planning ahead for at least a week, and longer if possible, allows you to take advantage of bargains that may be spotted *now*, even though these particular items may not be actually needed until some later time. Having cupboards adequately stocked with the "staples" will cut down on emergency trips to the grocery store—times when shoppers are most tempted to make impulse purchases of non-essential or luxury items. Restraint should be exercised, however, to avoid overstocking of infrequently used or highly perishable items.

**Non-grocery items.** Do your food buying plans and your grocery budget include non-grocery items? If not, perhaps they need revision. Cleaning supplies, toiletries and drug products, children's toys, and household gadgets probably account for a larger share of grocery store purchases than most shoppers imagine. To see if this is true in your own case, ask the cashier to check out only groceries on one tape and everything else in your shopping cart on another.

## MAKING YOUR OWN BUYING GUIDE

When you grocery shop, do you *know* whether the advertised "specials" and the "sale" prices represent legitimate savings, and are not just gimmicks? Be sure, by making your own buying guide. First, list the food items and other grocery store products you regularly purchase, indicating brand names, sizes, and other identifying information. Then, using this list, do comparison shopping at several stores, indicating on your list the cost in each particular store for each specific item. Now, by averaging the costs at the various stores, you can arrive at a "base" against which to check future purchases and advertised specials for each item. Be sure to update your personal shopping guide about every six to 12 months, or whenever there is an announced increase or decline in food prices or in the national cost of living.

## LEARNING THE TACTICS OF FOOD MERCHANTS

To get the most for food dollars, shoppers need to know something about marketing tactics, or the "tricks of the trade." Not that grocers are an unscrupulous lot "out to get you"; most of them are honest merchants working to gain your good will. But they want you to spend *your* money in *their* store so they study, do research, conduct surveys, and train employees in good salesmanship, all to induce the customer to spend more money with them. Customers should be just as diligent about saving at the supermarket.

Merchants have learned that only one out of three shoppers prepares even a partial shopping list, and that "impulse" buying accounts for nearly 50 percent of all purchases. Putting this information to work for them, grocers have come up with these and similar means of keeping customers looking *and* buying:

Offering free coffee and samples of store items.

Arranging shelves in rows running the full length of the store, making it necessary for you to pass by hundreds of different items as you travel the aisles.

Displaying related-use items adjacent to each other. For example, shortcake from the bakery department displayed with strawberries in the produce section.

Providing a "kiddie corral" where children can look at comic books or ride coin-operated animals while mother shops.

Piping pleasant music throughout the store via an intercom system.

Air conditioning the store.

Installing lunch counters where shoppers can stand up for a quick cup of coffee or sit down for a leisurely snack.

Urging shoppers to buy more units through multiple unit pricing. For example, marking an item "3 for 87 cents," suggesting that this is a better price than 29 cents per each individual unit.

Displaying toys and games at the ends of aisles and elsewhere (on low shelves, especially) to catch the eyes of children accompanying parents on shopping trips.

Displaying chewing gum, candy, prepared breakfast foods, cookies and peanut butter on low shelves and within sure reach of small children.

Attracting attention with extender display racks, dangling signs, and blinking lights.

Advertising immediate and trouble-free check cashing service—which may turn out to be neither.

Selling pre-packaged meats (to keep butcher shop costs down by allowing the butcher to cut and wrap during slack periods of the day). While there is generally nothing wrong with this sort of operation, it should be remembered that you see only the best side of pre-packaged meat. Also, it is fairly common practice that when ground meat has been in the display case longer than one day, the butcher opens the package, spreads a thin layer of newly ground meat around the darker, older meat, then rewraps and reprices the package.

Offering trading stamps (the cost of which is borne by the customer) but sometimes failing to give them unless the customer asks, and frequently shorting buyers on the number of stamps given.

Providing carry-out service from the store to your automobile.

Making it unnecessary for customers to shop elsewhere by stocking a large variety of non-food items including dry goods, hardware, housewares, cleaning supplies, books and magazines, tobacco, small appliances and kitchen gadgets, toiletries, lotions, and gardening equipment and supplies.

### SHOPPING THE GROCERY ADS

Traditionally, homemakers do their family food buying on the weekend, and nation-wide it is customary for grocers to advertise weekly specials for Thursday, Friday, and Saturday. Object of the specials, of course, is to attract customers who will also purchase non-special items. Even so, it may be possible to trim 10 percent from the average grocery bill just by shopping for the specials. One study of some 200 grocery items shows that prices were 7 to 10 percent higher on Tuesday than on Friday.

### SELECTING YOUR SHOPPING TIME

As important as the right time of the week for grocery shopping are the right time of day and the right amount of time for the job. Shop before noon, if possible, when shelves have been restocked and produce has been sorted and trimmed. Also, this is the time of day grocers have more time to give customers individual attention. Allocate sufficient time so that the trip to the store is not hurried.  When you are under pressure, you are unable to give proper attention to studying labels, computing prices per serving, and making necessary comparisons in quality and price.  Avoid grocery shopping when you are hungry—when everything in the market looks good and the temptation of impulse buying, particularly at the fresh produce and bakery counters filled with delicious but perishable items, may be too great to withstand.

### WATCHING FOR SEASONAL OR ANNUAL "SPECIALS"

Learn what products are featured at special prices at certain times during the year by certain grocers, and time your purchases of these particular items accordingly, especially of items that can be stored for later use.  In the fall, most grocers feature case-lot sales of canned fruits and vegetables.  While such sales are timed to the current year's harvest, the products may or may not be new crop.  Frequently, they are left-overs being pushed to make room for new supplies coming from the processors.  While there is little noticeable deterioration in canned goods over a period of one or two years, it is unwise to store them for longer periods.

With case-lot merchandise, too, it is important to be sure that the advertised price actually is a bargain.  Divide the case price by the number of units, and check unit price against your buying guide.  Also, be careful about purchasing case lots of off-brand merchandise until you have checked for family approval.  Buy one can and try it first to know what you are getting.

### MAKING USE OF GOVERNMENT AIDS

A valuable aid to the consumer is the United States Department of Agriculture's localized food marketing news service, in which home economists, nutritionists, and marketing specialists prepare information on best food buys, menu planning, food preparation and storage, and related subjects.  This information is distributed locally through radio and television programs, through newspaper columns, through "newsletters," and through lectures and demonstrations before club or school groups.  Typical is *Consumer Alert*—"News, Clues, Do's," illustrated in Fig. 9–2.  To find out if such information is available in your

# CONSUMER ALERT

NEWS CLUES DO'S

MONEY SENSE
FOOD TRENDS

**COOPERATIVE EXTENSION SERVICE, UTAH STATE UNIVERSITY**

VOL. II NO. VII                                                                July

FRUIT BUYING KNOW-HOW. Questions to us ask what kind to use, when available, where, and how to preserve. The fruits of this part of our state come mostly from three counties: Box Elder, Davis, Utah. Some apples are grown in Salt Lake County, and the roadside stands located mostly in the south and east parts of the city usually have a good supply of Utah fruits available. Peaches also grow in Weber County, the north Ogden area and into Roy. Most of the good pears come from Utah County.

This fruit belt stretches from Bountiful, north, along Highways 89-91 through Davis County, then picks up just before you get to Willard in Box Elder County and on through Brigham City. In those areas you will find many good growers with roadside stands to serve you. (They also grow a good supply of seasonal vegetables.)

In Davis County, Bountiful, on to Farmington, north Farmington and the mountain road (Route 89) that goes over to Weber Canyon, are the tree fruit areas. In Utah County, Orem bench, Mapleton, the west mountain area, and Payson are the places to look.

## CHERRIES

Royal Ann--available about the last week in June. There aren't many and their season is short. These are the big, white ones used for making maraschino cherries.

Bing--look for them the first week in July. Deep red beauties, wonderful for eating out-of-hand, and good for canning or jam making.

Lamberts--available a few days later than the Bings. Larger than Bings but used for the same purposes. It isn't easy to tell them apart and both are scrumptious.

Sour or Pie Cherries--ripe by July 15. Ideal for pie making and canning or freezing for pies.

## APRICOTS

Chinese--are usually the first to arrive, about July 10. Small, with sweet pits, these are wonderful for canning; they hold their shape and do not become stringy.

Moor Park--the common variety, are ripe by July 15. They are also used for canning but do become soft and stringy, so are better for juice, puree, or jam.

## PEACHES

There are many varieties, the earliest ones for canning ripen about August 1, and one variety or another is available into October

Red Haven--ripe about August 7 and is the first good freestone peach for canning.

Golden Jubilee--ripe about August 14. A delicious peach for eating fresh; yellow color, high quality, tender. Doesn't ship well.

Johnson Elberta--)
Lemon Elberta-- )August 28--September 11
Early Elberta-- )
Late Elberta--September 15

Lemon, Johnson, and Early Elbertas are the most popular for canning.

Hale--September 15, is also a good canner. The flesh is coarser than in the Elbertas, but the flavor is delicious and the red color of the stone cavity adds beauty.

## EARLY APPLES

Red Astrachan--July 15; short season and doesn't last well. Has delicious tangy flavor and crisp texture for eating. Makes marvelous applesauce, pies, jelly.

Yellow Transparent--July 21. Greenish-yellow; medium size; tart flavor; similar to Red Astrachan and has same uses.

**Fig. 9–2** *Consumer Alert News* is one of many nationally distributed publications containing suggestions for food buying, planning, preparation, storage, and related items.

community, contact your county USDA Extension Service office or the USDA Extension Service of your local university.*

A list of current USDA publications concerned specifically with food buying, preparation, care and preservation, along with instructions for ordering the bulletins, appears at the end of this chapter as Appendix 9-A.

## UTILIZING CONSUMER SERVICES OF NEWS MEDIA

Many women's magazines, as well as daily and weekly newspapers throughout the country, feature valuable articles on food purchasing and preparation. While some of the suggestions could be devastating to the average household budget, especially if one attempts to follow too precisely the details of some exotic menus or recipes, these articles can serve as useful guides. In addition, reports on food products often appear in the specialized "consumer service" publications discussed in Chapter 7.

## "CULTIVATING" YOUR GROCERYMAN

If you shop in a small store, get to know the grocer and the butcher personally. They can be your food budget's best friends. And even in the large, more impersonal supermarkets, employees are usually happy to give you information and assistance, if you just ask. They are there to serve you. The produce manager knows how fresh particular products are, and how to tell if melons, pineapples, avocados and such are ripe.

Meat purchases account for a large share of the average food dollar, so the importance of careful shopping at the butcher counter is readily apparent. Let your butcher help you. Even though the trend in recent years has been to install pre-packaged meat service in many stores, most still have meatcutters on duty during store hours. They are glad to honor requests for special cuts. The customer who knows what he wants, and who speaks the butcher's language (knows the names of various cuts, etc.), soon gets special attention at the meat counter.

Be sure that you know how many servings per pound you get from various kinds of meat, then compute the price per serving to figure your best buy. For

---

* Each year, the USDA publishes new information and updates old publications on hundreds of subjects in seven major categories: (1) soil, water, domestic animals, fruits, vegetables, flowers, trees and shrubs, (2) foods, their preparation, care, preservation, and how to buy them, including USDA grades, (3) nutrition, (4) planning kitchens or houses, (5) making or mending clothes, repairing carpets, purchasing clothing, (6) laundering, removing stains, and (7) controlling insects.

You can get a bulletin covering a subject, or a personal reply to specific questions, simply by writing a post card to U.S. Department of Agriculture, Washington, D.C. 20250. Many of these pamphlets and bulletins as well as information tailored to a particular locality are available from State USDA offices or from local county agricultural agents or home demonstration agents listed in the telephone directory under "United States Government."

example figuring on a 3-oz. serving of lean, cooked meat, round steak at $1.29 per pound will actually cost less per serving than pork chops at $1.09. Table 9–1, showing comparative prices per pound and per serving of typical meat, fish, and poultry items is a useful guide.

Table 9–1  Per pound and per serving prices—meat, fish, poultry

|  | Price per pound | Price per 3–4 oz. serving |
| --- | --- | --- |
| Beef, ground | $ .79 | $ .20 |
| Beef liver, frozen | .65 | .16 |
| Chicken, fryer | .45 | .21 |
| Chuck roast, bone in | .82 | .38 |
| Haddock, fillet | .89 | .22 |
| Ham, whole | .72 | .34 |
| Lamb chops | 1.89 | .78 |
| Lamb, leg of | 1.09 | .56 |
| Pork chops | 1.09 | .56 |
| Pork, roast, bone in | .79 | .38 |
| Steak, round, bone out | 1.31 | .44 |
| Steak, sirloin | 1.49 | .54 |
| Turkey, roaster | .49 | .22 |

## RELYING ON USDA GRADING

United States Department of Agriculture grades for goods are a dependable, nationally uniform guide to quality and a means of making valid comparisons of quality and price. Food bearing the USDA grade shield is clean and wholesome and has been examined by a Government inspector who has certified that it measures up to a definite standard of quality.

Under the Wholesome Meat Act of 1967 and the Wholesome Poultry Products Act of 1968, consumers are assured that all USDA inspected poultry and red meat are "safe, wholesome, unadulterated and truthfully labeled."

Inspection is not required on fruits and vegetables and many other foods; however, they may be inspected and marked with the USDA stamp. It is beef, lamb, butter, poultry, and eggs that are most likely to carry the inspector's label, usually with the designation, "U. S. Grade A, or AA, or B" for poultry and eggs; "U.S. Prime, Choice, Good, Standard, Commercial, or Utility," for meats. (Two other grades, "Canner" and "Cutter," rarely reach the retail market.)

These USDA standards are widely used by processors and packers for their own quality control programs. Use of the grading services is on a voluntary basis unless state or local law or an industry program requires it. They are not provided at government expense, but on a fee-for-service basis. However, federal law has for many years required government inspection for wholesomeness of meat and poultry destined for interstate or foreign trade, and this service is paid for by the government.

The official grade mark for eggs is in the form of a shield. It always carries the grade name, the letters "USDA," and the words "Federal-State Graded," "Graded Under Federal-State Supervision," or a similar term. The grade mark may be on a gummed label which seals the carton, or it may be printed on the carton.

*United States Department of Agriculture*

Inspection and grade marks for poultry

*United States Department of Agriculture*

*Federal grade and inspection stamps on products of fisheries*

Department of Agriculture specialists have developed grade standards for more than 300 farm products. A valuable shopping guide summary of the kinds of products graded, the various grade names, and an explanation of what the grades mean appears as Appendix 9–B.

## BUYING IN QUANTITY

Families having storage space and/or a freezer may be able to make substantial savings by purchasing grocery items, especially staples and other frequently used products, in quantity when they are "on special." Unless storage is adequate, however, waste due to spoilage may more than offset any savings on the original purchases. Stored foods should be used and replaced on a rotating basis. Table 9–2 shows maximum storage periods of home frozen foods for best eating quality. To freeze successfully, choose foods of original high quality and be sure they are well packaged and held continuously at zero or below in the freezer or the freezer compartment of the refrigerator, not in the ice-cube compartment. Various kinds of food which are best stored under refrigeration and the approximate lengths of time they may be stored without losing appreciable amounts of nutrients, color, flavor and texture are shown in Fig. 9–3.

**Table 9–2**  Maximum storage periods for home-frozen foods

| Kind of food | Time can be stored (months) |
|---|---|
| Meat: | |
| Beef roasts and steaks | 12 |
| Ground beef | 3 |
| Lamb roasts and chops | 12 |
| Patties | 4 |
| Pork (fresh) roasts and chops | 8 |
| Sausage | 2 |
| Pork (smoked or cured) | 2 |
| Veal roasts and steaks | 8 |
| Chops and cutlets | 6 |
| Cooked meat dinners, meat pies, swiss steak | 3 |
| Poultry: | |
| Whole chicken or turkey | 12 |
| Cut-up chicken | 9 |
| Cut-up turkey | 6 |
| Goose or duck (whole) | 6 |
| Cooked chicken or turkey: | |
| Sliced meat and gravy | 6 |
| Pies | 12 |
| Fried chicken | 4 |
| Ice cream and sherbet | 1 |
| Fruits: | |
| Cherries, peaches, raspberries, strawberries | 12 |
| Fruit juice concentrates | 12 |
| Vegetables: | |
| Asparagus, beans, peas, cauliflower, corn, spinach | 8 |
| Bakery goods: | |
| Bread and rolls | 3 |
| Angel and chiffon cakes | 2 |
| Chocolate layer cake | 4 |
| Fruit cake | 12 |
| Doughnuts | 3 |
| Unbaked pies (fruit) | 8 |
| Cream pies | 1 |

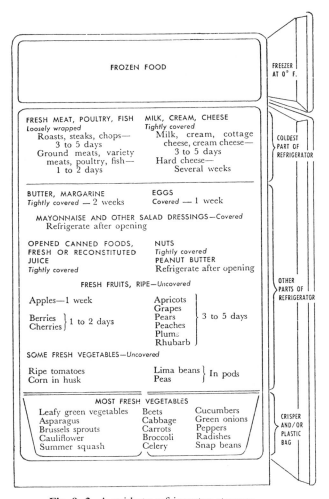

**Fig. 9-3** A guide to refrigerator storage.

## CANNING FOODS FOR STORAGE

Home canned foods, purchased at low cost in season or produced at home, can give good food value and variety to family meals. However, home canning requires considerable know-how. Expert guidance in this area of home management can be obtained from USDA home demonstration agents, nutritionists, and home economists working out of state or county offices. A telephone call or written inquiry will bring personalized replies as well as offers of helpful publications, usually free. Selected USDA publications dealing with home canning and freezing are shown as double-starred (**) items in Appendix 9-A.

## LEARNING FROM THE EXPERIENCE OF OTHERS

Probably the best grocery shoppers of all are the heads of large families—people who *must* get full value for every food dollar.  Some of their methods for saving at the grocery store, in addition to the suggestions already presented, are listed below.  As you study them, analyze your own buying habits.  Which of these ideas can be profitable for you?  What others can you add to the list?

Carry with you those money-off coupons you get through the mail or in newspapers and magazines, and redeem them as you purchase the products they advertise.  Be sure you use coupons before their expiration date if they have one.  Coupons *can* save you money, if you use the items they advertise.  For example, one recent issue of a magazine at a newsstand price of 35 cents contained 65 cents worth of money-off coupons.

Select from grocery shelves only cans and packages on which the price is clearly marked; checkers can forget.

Check prices in superdrug stores on cleaning and kitchen supplies, paper goods, and the food items they carry against prices for the same items in grocery stores.  There is sometimes as much as 25 percent difference.

If you wear dark glasses, remove them in the produce department to see the true color of fruits and vegetables.

Investigate "thrift stores" which may be operated by a large wholesale bakery in your area.  Their day-old products, sold at reduced prices, may be as fresh as if you purchased the same brand in the grocery store.

Learn can sizes and what they mean in terms of number of servings.  This is especially important when you are "shopping the ads."

Shop the "bargain basements" of food stores for canned goods with damaged labels or for "banquet size" canned goods which offer worthwhile cost-per-serving savings for families which use foods in these quantities.

Find out whether or not convenience foods such as packaged mixes, frozen dinners, etc., are comparable in price to the same foods in their usual state. Studies have shown, for instance, that you can almost always save money by purchasing frozen concentrated orange juice rather than squeezing the oranges yourself. Also, studies by home economists have shown that most expensive of the pre-prepared foods are brown-and-serve rolls and other bakery products.

Investigate cooperative programs for group purchasing. Programs vary greatly, so it is important to study the possibilities of a plan or plans and then to decide if it suits your purposes.

Consider forming neighborhood or family groups to purchase in bulk or extra large sizes of such items as detergents, powdered milk, etc. Packaging costs money; perhaps you can save by doing your own.

Learn what to look for when shopping for food. For instance, in buying oranges for juice, appearance is of little importance, but weight is.

Try "store name" brands to see how they compare in quality and family acceptance with higher priced brands.

## GETTING VALUE FOR YOUR CLOTHING DOLLARS

It just may be, as the old adage goes, that "clothes make the man" (or woman). But it is also true that clothes can literally break the person who cannot resist

"Where would the economy be if people didn't buy things they can't afford!"

Reprinted with permission of *The Wall Street Journal* (Cartoon Features Syndicate).

them, who is a slave to high fashion, or who will not exert the effort to identify and shop for value and quality in clothing. For many people—and particularly for young men and women—the real test of effective personal money management is working out a realistic clothing budget and learning to live within it.

### IDENTIFYING QUALITY IN CLOTHING

Usually the first, and sometimes the only, consideration given to the purchase of clothing is whether or not the garment looks attractive with respect to current trends in style, color, and fit. Purchases made under these circumstances often turn out to be poor choices, with inferior quality in both materials and workmanship showing up after the items have been worn a few times. This is both unfortunate and unnecessary. When one knows what to look for, real quality can be determined before purchases are made.

An especially helpful rule is, "stick with brand names." Do a little investigating—reading a company's advertising is one way—to determine a firm's claims to quality and workmanship. Learn what manufacturers' policies are with respect to quality control. One example is illustrated in Fig. 9–4.

**Fig. 9–4** Quality control. Many manufacturers maintain testing laboratories to check products at each step in the manufacturing process, from raw material to finished item. Courtesy of Jantzen, Inc., Portland, Oregon.

**Purchasing "real" style.** Fads, high fashion, and real or imagined needs for particular, specific items of clothing "right now" can devastate a clothing budget.

Extremes in clothing and accessories that are "in" today are likely to be completely out of style three months from now. Clothing of this sort is just too expensive for the wardrobe of the average budget-minded person.

*Adjustments*

"We can't give you a refund because we've already spent the money."

Reprinted with permission of *The Wall Street Journal* (Cartoon Features Syndicate).

This is no indictment against high style. People can dress economically and still dress well. In fact, being stylishly dressed does not necessarily mean appearing in the latest or most flamboyant fashions. Rather, it means carefully selecting clothes of good quality, of basic but becoming design, of proper fit, and in materials and colors most complimentary to one's own personality—all at the most economical, though not necessarily the cheapest, price—and leaving "haute couture" and fads to those who can, or think they can, afford them.

Does the garment look "right," or does it appear skimpy or cheap? Is the fit "easy," with no binding, pulling, or sagging? Are garment parts cut on the grain of the material so that clothing hangs correctly and is not so apt to pull out of shape? Is the style so extreme as to elicit surprised stares instead of admiring glances? Is it overdone with fussy trimmings, or is it elegant in its simplicity? These are questions truly well-dressed persons ask themselves as they consider clothing purchases.

**Examining construction details.** Careful buyers are quick to notice that if clothing material is figured or checked the patterns match at important joinings. They check for spots, snags, or other evidence of damage. They inspect closures to see that buttons, snaps, or hooks and eyes are accurately placed and securely sewn. They notice whether buttonholes run with the grain of the material; for strength and durability, they should. Also, buttonholes should fit easily over buttons, should be evenly and firmly stitched or bound, and reinforced at each end. Look for reinforcement, too, at other strain points such as pockets, seams, and closures. Examine the sleeves. Are they sewn in smoothly and correctly, with underarm seams of sleeves (except on men's coats) matching exactly the side seam of the garment? How about the collar? Is it properly attached, not longer on one side than the other, and does it lie smoothly without buckling?

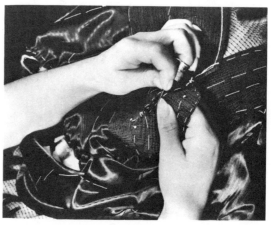

**Fig. 9–5** Hand-tailored quality. Tailoring unites 145 pieces into a fine suit, the manufacture of which may require as many as 200 different stitching, shaping, steaming, pressing and inspecting operations. Invisible felling or stitching of the collar gorge (shown above) identifies a well-tailored collar as well as a finely tailored suit. (Courtesy of Hart Schaffner & Marx, Chicago.)

After examining the outside of the garment, look on the inside. Inspect seams, hems, facing, and stitching. It is the "inside story" that tells the difference between cheap and quality clothing. As shown in Fig. 9–5, the tailoring of a fine suit requires up to 200 different operations. While many of these steps are not discernible, you can detect many aspects of quality by carefully inspecting seams, hems, facing, and stitching. Be sure seams are even in width all the way, and that they are at least one-half inch deep. If not, they could fray out with wear or during cleaning. Seams of good-quality garments are double stitched, overcast, tape bound, or finished in some other appropriate manner, and pressed flat. Machine stitching is close and even, and facings are firmly attached and lie flat. Seams are flat, even in width, and pucker-free. Pocket openings should be smooth and neat.

# CLOTHING FABRICS

Few of man's attempts at improving on nature have been more remarkable than his successes with fibers and fabrics. During the past decade, particularly, fabulous new synthetics have poured from the chemists' laboratories in almost overwhelming quantity and variety. At the same time, nature's age-old standbys,

## Natural Fibers

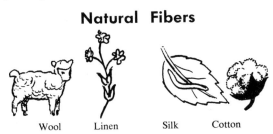

Wool    Linen    Silk    Cotton

cotton, wool, linen, silk, mohair, cashmere, and furs and pelts have been modified, improved, and imitated. Natural fibers as well as synthesized ones have been given new properties of appearance, wear, and cleanability. Some have been given stretch, others have been made water and stain repellent, flame retardant, heat and soil resistant, bacteriostatic, shrink-proof, and dye-fast. In some instances, the natural fibers and the fabrics made from them have been almost completely replaced by synthetics with equal or superior properties. Sweaters that look and feel like wool, but which are vastly easier to clean and which cost half as much, are just one example.

| Trademark | Generic Name | Trademark | Generic Name |
|---|---|---|---|
| "Acele" | acetate | "Chromeflex" | metallic |
| "Acrilan" | acrylic | "Chromspun" | acetate |
| "ANIM/8" | anidex | "Coloray" | rayon |
| "Antron" | nylon | "Coneprest" | durable-press |
| "Arnel" | triacetate | "Creslan" | acrylic |
| "Avisco" | acetate | "Cumuloft" | nylon |
| "Avisco" | rayon | "Cupioni" | rayon |
| "Avisco Vinyon HH" | vinyon | "Dacron" | polyester |
| "Avlin" | polyester | "Dan-Press" | durable-press |
| "Avril" | rayon | "DLP" | olefin |
| "Avron" | rayon | "Durastran" | metallic |
| "Belfast" | wash-and-wear | "Dynel" | modacrylic |
| "Bemberg" | rayon | "Enkalon" | nylon |
| "Beta Glass" | glass | "Estron" | acetate |
| "Cantrece" | nylon | "Fiberglas" | glass |
| "Caprolan" | nylon | "Fibro" | rayon |
| "Celanese" | acetate | "Fortisan" | rayon |
| "Celanese" | rayon | "Fortrel" | polyester |
| "Celaperm" | acetate | "45" | vinyon |
| "Celara" | acetate | "Glospan" | spandex |
| | | "Herculon" | olefin |

| Trademark | Generic Name | Trademark | Generic Name |
|---|---|---|---|
| "Jetspun" | rayon | "Sanforized Plus" | wash-and-wear |
| "Kodel" | polyester | "Saran 25S" | saran |
| "Koratron" | durable-press | "Spandelle" | spandex |
| "Lactron" | rubber | "Strawn" | rayon |
| "Lamé" | metallic | "Suprenka" | rayon |
| "Lastex" | rubber | "Tebilized" | wash-and-wear |
| "Lus-Trus" | saran | "Trevira" | polyester |
| "Lurex" | metallic | "Unel" | spandex |
| "Lycra" | spandex | "Vectra" | olefin |
| "Nupron" | rayon | "Velon" | saran |
| "Nylmet" | metallic | "Verel" | modacrylic |
| "Nyloft" | nylon | "Vincel 64" | rayon |
| "Orlon" | acrylic | "Vitron" | glass |
| "Penn Prest" | durable-press | "Vycron" | polyester |
| "PPG" | glass | "Wrinkl-Shed" | wash-and-wear |
| "Qiana" | nylon | "Zantrel" | rayon |
| "Rayflex" | rayon | "Zefran" | acrylic |

**Synthetics and blends.** Man-made fibers account for almost half of the total textile fibers used in the United States today. Some are totally new; others are modifications, treatments, or combinations (blends) of synthetics with other synthetics or of synthetics with natural vegetable or animal fibers. Table 9–3 shows the major man-made fibers, their makers and trade names, and the primary uses of each. Some of the more common blends of fibers and their use by garment manufacturers are shown in Table 9–4, while Table 9–5 provides useful information concerning the common natural vegetable fibers, their properties, and major uses.

**Difficult choices.** Each new addition to the already large variety of clothing fabrics available on the market increases the problems of identifying advantages of one over another. How will that one wear? Can this be laundered? Will it stretch out of size? Does "wash and wear" mean *no* ironing? The Federal Trade Commission has, since 1960, required that fabric labels bear the generic (common) name of all fibers present in amounts of 5 percent and above, and that the mill list the content of each fiber as a percentage by weight in order of predominance. Unfortunately, most clothing labels usually give far less information about the fabrics than is desirable, and you may have to look for it from other sources. Salespeople may be able to help. Reading recently published books or magazine articles dealing specifically with fabrics, and studying and examining clothing materials firsthand will be useful. Go to a fabric shop or to the yardage department of a large store. Study the labels on bolts of materials. Manufacturers who are proud of their product are happy to have their name identified with it, so look for the maker's name on the bolt label or along the tightly woven edge (selvage) of yardage. For detailed information on any

**Table 9–3** Major manmade fibers

| Generic name | Manufacturer's trade name | Manufacturer | Fiber type | Major end uses |
|---|---|---|---|---|
| Acetate | Celanese<br>Estron*<br>Avisco*<br>Acele* | Celanese Fibers Co.<br>Eastman Chemical Products, Inc.<br>American Viscose Div. (FMC).<br>E. I. du Pont de Nemours & Co. | Secondary cellulose acetate, filament and staple | Lingerie, dress goods, drapery, sports and casual wear. Fiberfil. |
| Triacetate | Arnel* | Celanese Fibers Co. | Cellulose triacetate, filament and staple. | Tricot lingerie and outerwear dress goods, sports and casual wear. |
| Acrylic | Orlon*<br>Acrilan*<br>Creslan* | E. I. du Pont de Nemours & Co.<br>Chemstrand Co.<br>American Cyanamid Co. | Polyacrylonitrile (primarily staple) | Sweaters, knit goods, men's and women's slacks, carpets, blankets. |
| Nylon 66 | Du Pont*<br>Chemstrand*<br>Celanese<br>Beaunit | E. I. du Pont de Nemours & Co.<br>Chemstrand Co.<br>Celanese Fibers Co.<br>Beaunit Fibers. | Polyamide (primarily continuous filament) | Hosiery and socks, lingerie, dress goods, blouses, upholstery, carpets, knit sports goods, uniforms and work clothing, and industrial yarns. |
| Nylon 6 | Caprolan*<br>Enka*<br>Beaunit<br>Firestone* | Allied Chemical Corp.<br>American Enka Corp.<br>Beaunit Fibers.<br>Firestone Synthetic Fibers Co. | Same as for Nylon 66 | Same as for Nylon 66. |
| Polyester | Dacron*<br>Fortrel*<br>Kodel*<br>Vycron* | E. I. du Pont de Nemours & Co.<br>Fiber Industries, Inc.<br>Eastman Chemical Products, Inc.<br>Beaunit Fibers. | Polyester (primarily staple), filament for special applications | Blends with cotton for shirting, sports clothing, dress goods, slacks. Blends with wool for suitings. Knit goods for shirting and sports wear. Fiberfil. |
| Rayon | Avril*<br>Zantrel*<br>Cuprammonium | American Viscose Div. (FMC).<br>American Enka Corp.<br>Beaunit Fibers. | Regenerated cellulose filament and staple | Men's and women's slacks and suitings. Women's wear. Linings and drapery. Blankets, carpets, industrial yarns. |

**Table 9–3** Major manmade fibers (*continued*)

| Generic name | Manufacturer's trade name | Manufacturer | Fiber type | Major end uses |
|---|---|---|---|---|
| | Fibro* | Courtaulds North America, Inc. | | |
| Glass | Fiberglas* | Owens-Corning Fiberglas Corp. | Silicon dioxide (sand) plus fluxes to lower melting point | Nonflammable drapes, curtains, bedspreads, industrial fabrics. |
| | Beta Fiberglas | Owens-Corning Fiberglas Corp. | | |
| | PPG* | Pittsburgh Plate Glass Co. | | |
| | Garon* | Johns-Manville Fiber Glass, Inc. | | |
| | Vitron* | Johns-Manville Fiber Glass, Inc. | | |

* Registered trademark.

*Source:* U.S. Department of Agriculture.

**Table 9–4** A few of the important blends and their applications

| End use | Fiber blends | Fabric construction | Important properties |
| --- | --- | --- | --- |
| Dress shirts | 65/35 polyester/cotton | Batiste<br>Broadcloth<br>Oxford | Ease of care, fast drying, wrinkle resistant, durability. |
| Blouse | 65/35 polyester/cotton | Broadcloth<br>Crepe<br>Combinations<br>Taffetas<br>Failles | Ease of care, lightweight, appearance retention, fast drying, durability. |
| Dress goods<br>Printed and plain<br>Dyed | 65/35 polyester/cotton<br>50/50 polyester/cotton<br>50/50 polyester/rayon<br>50/50 triacetate/cotton | Broadcloth<br>Challis<br>Checks<br>Crepes<br>Twills<br>Linens | Washability, ease of care, color styling, shape retention. |
| Sportswear<br>Shirting<br>Circular knit goods<br>Slacks | 65/35 polyester/cotton<br>50/50 polyester/cotton<br>55/45 acrylic/wool<br>50/50 acrylic/rayon | Sharkskin<br>Serge<br>Twills<br>Linens<br>Poplins<br>Sateens<br>Oxfords<br>Flannels | Ease of care, durability, appearance retention, color styling, pleatability. |
| Slacks<br>Casual<br>Dress | 65/35 polyester/cotton<br>50/50 polyester/cotton<br>55/45 polyester/wool | Gabardine<br>Twills<br>Tropicals | Appearance retention, washable or dry-cleanable (wool), ease of care. |

**Table 9–4** A few of the important blends and their applications (*continued*)

| End use | Fiber blends | Fabric construction | Important properties |
| --- | --- | --- | --- |
| | 55/45 acrylic/wool<br>70/30 polyester/acrylic<br>50/50 triacetate/rayon<br>50/50 acetate/rayon | Denims<br>Sharkskin | |
| Lightweight | 55/45 polyester/wool<br>50/50 acrylic/wool | Gabardine<br>Tropical worsted<br>Twills<br>Flannels<br>Serge | Durability, shape retention, ease of care. |

*Source:* U.S. Department of Agriculture.

**Table 9-5** Important natural fibers and their properties and end uses

| Fiber | Fiber characteristics | Important end-use properties | Major end uses |
|---|---|---|---|
| Cotton | Very short lengths—$\frac{7}{8}''$ to 1.5″. Strong, low elongation. High moisture absorbing. | Excellent washability and comfort. Can be made "ease-of-care" by chemical finishing but loses strength and abrasion resistance. Slow drying. | Sheets and pillowcases, toweling, dress goods, work clothing, shirting. Blended with polyester fibers. |
| Wool | Short length, 1″ to 8″. Coarsest of the natural fibers. High moisture absorbency. Low strength. | High moisture absorbency. Comfort at high relative humidity. Fabric can be felted and fulled. Excellent wrinkle performance and crush resistance dry. Drycleanable. Careful washing and ironing. | Suitings, coating, blankets, carpets, sweaters and knit goods. Women's suiting, slacks, dress goods. Blended with polyester or acrylic fibers. |
| Silk | Long filamentous fibers 300–1,000 yards. Very fine, strong, and elastic. | Semilustrous and crisp feel. High strength makes possible sheer fabrics. Careful washing and ironing, drycleaning preferred. | Dresses, scarfs, hosiery, blouses. Combined with acetate, nylon, etc. |
| Linen | 6–18 inches. Very coarse, strong, stiff fiber. | Silky luster, very strong and durable, poor wrinkling properties. | Tablecloths. Satin damask, dress goods, lace (blended with polyester fibers). |

*Source:* U.S. Department of Agriculture.

particular clothing material, write to the home economics or education department of fabric manufacturers; most are happy to answer questions regarding their products.

It is well to remember in considering clothing fabrics that something new is not necessarily something better—what it really is, is something "different." Find out that difference, and whether the difference is really important with respect to your own needs. Remember, too, that if it is very new it may carry a higher price tag than some other similar but more familiar product. Before you pay the added cost, be certain that it is justified.

## OTHER IMPORTANT ASPECTS OF CLOTHING SELECTION

After inspecting workmanship and material and determining suitability with respect to style and fit, what other factors ought to be considered before purchasing clothing? For one thing, it is important to read the labels carefully and completely. Although they may not, as mentioned earlier, contain *all* you would like to know, labels on better-quality clothing often give information about workmanship, special finishes which may have been applied to the fabric (wash and wear, crease-resistancy, etc.). There may also be instructions on caring for the garment, indicating whether it must be dry cleaned, or if special laundering procedures should be followed. For instance, a label may indicate that the material has been "Sanforized," which means that the residual shrinkage will not exceed 1 percent. "Sanforsetting" is a process applied to rayon fabrics and limits their residual shrinkage to 2 percent. Terms such as "non-shrink" are not guarantees of limited shrinkage, and are not to be confused with "Sanforized" and "Sanforsetting." For example, a "non-shrink" without any qualifying limits may actually mean that the fabric will not shrink *more than*, say, 6 or 8 percent. And 8 percent shrinkage in a dress or pair of trousers could mean a difference of two whole sizes.

Something else worth considering is whether or not an otherwise suitable garment that does not fit exactly as it should can be successfully altered, and whether or not the store will guarantee alterations to your satisfaction. Also, is the cost of necessary alterations included in the purchase price, or will it be extra?

Finally, careful consideration should be given to whether or not the garment in question is precisely what you want and need. Does it come up to all your expectations of quality and price? Could you do better to purchase it somewhere else, to have it made, or to make it yourself? (Many women who sew for themselves or their families get a lot of good ideas and valuable sewing and tailoring information just by "shopping around.") But, whatever you do, be careful not to let a salesperson "fast talk" you into purchasing against your better judgment. If you have considered the purchase in light of all the foregoing factors, your own judgment is worth while, so rely on it. You are developing powers of discrimination that will pay off in extra value for your money. You are on your way to becoming a discerning shopper.

## SHOPPING BY MAIL

Many mail-order stores retain fashion experts and designers to assure that the clothing styles are smart and up-to-date. Catalog descriptions usually contain information about fabric content and properties, as well as cleaning instructions. Actual measurements should be carefully checked against size charts of each particular firm, since there may be noticeable size variations from one company to another; however, strict compliance with measuring instructions will usually avert any major fitting problems. The general considerations regarding mail-order buying, which were discussed earlier, apply also to clothing.

## SAVING MONEY ON SHOES

Too often, good fit, comfort, and style are not combined in the same pair of shoes. Consequently, many people are constantly purchasing more and more shoes to replace little-worn ones that sit in the closet because they are out of style or do not fit. Results to clothing budgets are obvious—bad enough in the case of relatively inexpensive shoes; downright serious when it is expensive footwear. Solution to the problem, however, is just as obvious—more attention to good fit and less concern with high fashion.

Another costly practice of many persons is buying high-priced dress shoes but inexpensive work or school shoes when, in most cases, it is the latter that get the most wear. Often, it is possible to save as much as 50 to 70 percent on high fashion footwear by delaying purchases until the middle or end of a season. Store owners are anxious to move style merchandise rapidly, and shoes that have not sold in the first few weeks of a new season often go on sale at half price or less.

Since dress shoes are usually worn less frequently than work shoes, there is not the same necessity for quality and durability—generally prime factors in price determination. There may not even be the same necessity for comfort, and if these dress shoes are going to get infrequent and "easy" wear anyway, it follows that lower-priced shoes will give more value per dollar than more expensive ones.

Getting the greatest possible value for shoe dollars also requires recognition of quality, a task considerably easier in the days before synthetics and today's impressive array of new textures and colors. However, Fig. 9–6 presents some useful guidelines for judging quality in footwear.

## SUMMARY OF MONEY-SAVING SUGGESTIONS

Whether you are a single person concerned only with your personal wardrobe, or a parent faced with the challenging job of clothing a family, the ideas listed below can help you stretch your clothing dollars to cover some of the desired extras as well as the necessary basics.

*Quality* in footwear depends largely on the way they are made and the materials used. New construction methods and shoe materials make it possible to buy well-made shoes at different price levels.

**To judge the quality of footwear inspect:**

- *construction details.* Look for a smooth lining, free of wrinkles; smooth seam edges; even stitching with no loose threads. When buying footwear for bad weather, find out whether it is waterproof and warm enough for your purpose.

- *shoe uppers.* A variety of materials are used for shoe uppers. Look for the color, texture, durability, flexibility and care features you want.

    *Leather* comes in different colors, textures and types. It conforms to the foot and is porous and flexible.

    *Poromeric*—a man-made, breathable shoe material—comes in a variety of colors, textures and types. This light weight, colorfast material offers complete shape retention and requires only minimum care. Because material does not stretch, proper fit is especially important.

    *Fabric* comes in different colors and textures. It is flexible, comfortable, porous and conforms to shape of the foot. Fabrics give comfort but may not be as durable as other shoe materials. Find out how fabric can be cleaned.

    *Plastic* comes in a variety of colors, textures and finishes. Generally, plastic is not as flexible as leather or fabric and it is not porous. Fabric backing adds to durability and comfort.

    *Straw* comes in different colors and may be closely or loosely woven. It is generally comfortable but not durable.

- *shoe linings.* Both comfort and durability depend in part on shoe linings. They should be smooth and wrinkle free, porous, absorbent, treated to resist rotting and fungus growth.

- *inner soles.* Comfort also depends on the inner sole. It is normally cushioned at the ball of foot and may include reinforcement over arch of shoe. Many inner soles are ventilated and treated to resist moisture and fungus. They may have extra padding for comfort.

**Fig. 9–6** Judging shoe quality. Reprinted by permission from *Money: Management: Your Clothing Dollar.* Money Management Institute of Household Finance Corporation.

1. Keeping in your purse or wallet an up-to-date record of shoe, hosiery, and clothing sizes for each member of the family makes it possible for you to know if the one-of-a-kind or other special bargain items you run onto unexpectedly will fit. This is important because sale items usually cannot be returned or exchanged. But remember that it is no bargain at any price if it is not needed.

2. Read the labels and learn the fabric content and its properties and characteristics for all clothing you buy. Find out about wearability and cleanability, as well as any special care that may be required.

3. Mark clothing hangtags ("John's blue dacron shirt," "Helen's green plaid skirt," etc.) and file them near the laundry center for quick reference regarding any special washing instructions.

4. Resist the urge to splurge on fads or latest styles and to buy too much children's clothing—children's growth is rapid and clothes are usually outgrown before they are outworn.

5. Watch for end-of-season bargains in clothing or shoes that can be saved for the following year.

6. Keep your weight and shape under control. Clothing bargains frequently are the reward of persons who can wear, without expensive alterations, standard sizes in ready-mades.

7. If you have need for water- or soil-repellent clothing, investigate the do-it-yourself products now available. It may be that you can buy regular clothing and treat it for considerably less than the cost of pre-treated garments.

8. Give your clothing proper care, including cleaning and mending, and teach all members of the family to do the same.

9. Plan a basic wardrobe of good-quality clothing and give it variety and interest by the addition of low-cost accessories.

10. Shop a number of clothing and department stores in your area to acquaint yourself with the quality of merchandise and prices charged. Find out if these stores sell different quality merchandise in different sections of the store, and if they have self-service or bargain-basement sections where you might make additional savings on particular items. Remember, however, that most stores with bargain basements stock those sections with poorer quality or "bargain" merchandise, and that they seldom move higher quality goods from another part of the store to the basement. Instead, they conduct sales and feature specials in each respective department, so that you might actually find better bargains at a sale of "better quality" merchandise on the second floor, for instance, than in the bargain basement itself.

11. Find out the merchandising practices of various stores. Do they have a quick turnover policy which might mean, for instance, that they take a markdown on merchandise not sold within a specified time (30 days in many stores)? Do they feature seasonal sales on certain types of merchandise or in a particular section of the store? Do they remove the label and sell at half price or less certain "name" or "prestige" brand clothing which is unsold at the end of a planned promotion? (Some retailers have arrangements with manufacturers to do this.) Is it store policy to include in its "sales" merchandise from regular stock, or is it the policy to bring in for a special sale inferior quality merchandise which actually is no bargain even at the advertised bargain prices? Can sale merchandise be returned or exchanged if size or color is not correct?

12. Curb impulse buying of something you need in a hurry or because it lifts your spirits.

**FEEDBACK 9**

**A.** Brush up on your mental arithmetic, or take a small notebook and pencil with you on your next trip to the grocery store. Calculate, as nearly as you can, the real cost of the food you eat.

- On the four or more different sizes of canned tomato juice, for only one example, what is the cost per ounce of each size? Considering only this factor for the present, what size is your best buy? As examples of factors, you may have to weigh your family's acceptance of quality, flavor, appearance, and so on.

- If the largest size is the best buy, on a strict cost-per-ounce basis, are there still other costs involved? Say a 50-pound bag of onions was priced at 5 cents per pound, but your family does not use that quantity of onions in six months. Are storage and spoilage hidden costs of some food items for your family?

- Next time you clear (or watch someone else clear) the dinner dishes, check to see if your family customarily throws away portions of certain menu items. Recall if you can, any pattern to this process. If a third of a can of corn is thrown away every time it appears on the menu, could you save money by purchasing smaller amounts of corn? Or would a survey of family members discover that no one really liked corn that much anyway and that all prefer green beans?

**B.** Make a hard-nosed shopping list next time you go grocery shopping. Resolve to depart from that list as little as possible. As you shop, take note of your inclinations to purchase other items.

- How well is your grocer doing his job of tempting you with impulse items like candy at the check-out stand, end displays of items you do not need, hanging displays near the items on your list—like nonfood items.

- Take note of the traffic design on your favorite store. Where is the bread counter? The meat counter? The dairy case? The produce racks? These are staple items; food which almost everyone is looking for when grocery shopping. What items do you have to pass to get to the staples? Why?

**C.** Make a small survey of marketing techniques used in clothing stores. Take special notice of:

- Related items. (Example: with shirts, do you find neckties, cuff links, pocket organizers, tie-tacks and even sport coats?)

- Sketch the floor plan of your usual clothing store. How are the various sections placed in relation to one another? Why do you suppose the store is laid out this way?
- If the store carries three price levels of a particular kind of clothing, which level does the sales clerk show you first?
- Does your store feature high style, competitive prices or special service, or another market advantage?
- Do you often take advantage of your credit arrangements at this store— even buy more than you came for because you can "charge it"?

## DISCUSSION QUESTIONS

1. What are the reasons behind the growth of the sprawling warehouse-type self-service markets? How does their merchandising differ from more "exclusive" stores?
2. Why should a food list be made before going grocery shopping? How closely should one follow it?
3. What are the advantages to limiting food buying at one particular market? Disadvantages?
4. Food merchants are known for their "tricks of the trade." How can one get around them?
5. Should the USDA be required to inspect fruits and vegetables? Explain. How can one be sure that they are fresh?
6. How susceptible is the American public to changes in fashion fads?
7. Why have synthetics and blends in clothes become so popular? Are they superior to natural fibers? Why?
8. Is the buying public more concerned with the fabric make-up and quality of wearing apparel or the style and way it will look while wearing it? Why?
9. How can one be sure of quality if the shopping is done by mail?
10. Why will people pay more money for dress shoes that they wear only occasionally than they will pay for shoes that they wear every day?

## CASE PROBLEM

Chris Ann was raised by her grandparents since she was 8 years old. She lived with them in an apartment house located in a big city until she was 22, when she married her long-time boyfriend, Alan, and moved to a smaller city in the state.

Alan and Chris Ann have been on a tight budget to make ends meet since they were married. They divided up the household duties so each had some duties to manage. Chris Ann was in charge of food buying, and it was this area they were having trouble budgeting correctly. The purchase amount always exceeded the budget.  Alan could not understand this problem, because he knew that the two of them did not eat that much food.  He decided to make a check and found that Chris Ann was doing all the food purchasing by phone to a near-by corner market that delivered the food to her door.  She would call up the market when she needed food or other items and give them her order.  She explained to Alan that her grandmother had always done it that way and found it saved time to let others do the shopping for her.

a) Is Chris Ann wise to do her shopping by phone?  Explain.

b) What can Chris Ann do to cut down the food expense?  Where can she find good food at the lowest prices?

c) What advantages will Chris Ann find by planning the meals for a week at a time?

# 9-A   USDA BULLETINS ON FOOD BUYING, PREPARATION, CARE AND PRESERVATION

**FOOD SHOPPING**

Cheese Buying Guide for Consumers.  Uses, flavor, texture, and care of cheese; characteristics of various natural cheese; what to look for when buying.  1961. (MB-17) 10c.

Family Fare: Food Management and Recipes.  Also includes tips on buying. 1960.  (G-1) 35c.

Family Food Budgeting . . . For Good Meals and Good Nutrition.  1964. (G-94) 10c.

Fresh Fancy or Grade AA Eggs.  Describes and illustrates.  1963.  (MB-26) 5c.

How to Buy Eggs by USDA Grades and Weight Classes.  Tips on buying, storing, using.  1958.  (L-442) 5c.

How to Buy Poultry by USDA Grades.  Explains grades, classes, uses.  1963. (MB-1) 5c.

Know the Eggs You Buy.  Illustrates and describes how to know quality.  1956. (PA-70) 10c.

Know the Poultry You Buy.  A guide to buying quality poultry.  1963.  (PA-170) 10c.

Know Your Butter Grades.  Tips on buying, storing.  1960.  (MB-12) 5c.

Shopper's Guide to U.S. Grades for Food.  Meaning of grades, suggested uses. 1962.  (G-58) 10c.

Tips on Selecting Fruits and Vegetables.  1961.  (MB-13) 20c.

USDA Poultry Inspection: A Consumer's Safeguard.  Meaning of inspection, how it is done.  1959.  (PA-299) 5c.

U.S. Grades for Beef.  Facts on grades, cuts, suggested cooking methods, amounts to buy.  1960.  (MB-15) 10c.

## PREPARATION AND CARE OF FOODS

Apples in Appealing Ways. Varieties, uses, recipes. 1959. (L-312) 10c.

** Cold Facts About Home Food Protection. 1964 (6) p. il. Catalog No. FS 2.50:121. Tells about pathogenic (disease-producing) bacteria and how we can prevent growth by refrigerating food. 5c.

Conserving the Nutritive Values in Foods. Effects of storage, cooking. Tips on best procedures. 1963. (G-90) 10c.

Dry Beans, Peas, Lentils . . . Modern Cookery. Kinds, how to cook, recipes. 1957. (L-326) 15c.

* Family Fare: Food Management and Recipes. Good basic cookbook. 1960. (G-1) 35c.

* Family Food Budgeting . . . For Good Meals and Good Nutrition. 1964. (G-94) 10c.

* Family Meals at Low Cost. Includes recipes using donated foods—dried eggs, lard, rice, rolled oats, wheat, etc. 1962. (PA-472) 10c.

* Food for Families With School Children. Meal planning, shopping, menus. 1962. (G-13) 15c.

* Food for the Family With Young Children. Food planning, reducing food bill. 1963. (G-5) 10c.

* Food for Fitness. A daily food guide. Basic information. 1963. (L-424) 5c.

* Food Guide for Older Folks. Meal planning, cooking tips. 1963. (G-17) 10c.

* Food for the Young Couple. Menus, meal planning, food buying. 1962. (G-85) 10c.

** Freezing Combination Main Dishes. Directions for stews, meat loaves, casseroles, etc. 1954. (G-40) 10c.

** Freezing Combination Main Dishes. Rev. 1965. 20 p. il. Catalog No. A 1.77:40/2 10c.

** Freezing Meat and Fish in the Home. Yields of meat from carcass. Cutting directions. Cleaning, dressing, filleting fish. Directions for wrapping, freezing, storage. 1963. (G-93) 20c.

** Green Vegetables for Good Eating. Buying, storing, cooking. 1954. (G-41) 10c.

** Home Canning of Fruits and Vegetables. Procedures; steam-pressure canner and water-bath methods. 1957. (G-8) 20c.

** Home Canning of Fruits and Vegetables. Rev. 1965. 32 p. il. Catalog No. A1.77:8/3. 15c.

---

* These bulletins also provide nutrition guides.
** These bulletins provide home canning and storage guides.

** Home Canning of Meat. Directions for meats and some meat-and-vegetable mixtures; proper canning equipment; timetable for hot pack and raw pack methods. 1963. (G-6) 10c.

** Home Canning of Meat, Reminders for Success.  Rev. 1963.  16 p. il. Catalog No. A1.77:6/3. 10c.

** Home Care of Purchased Frozen Foods.  Table of storage periods; tips on purchasing; care of freezer. 1960. (G-69) 5c.

** Home Freezing of Fruits and Vegetables. Directions; what to freeze, type of containers to use. 1957. (G-10) 20c.

** Home Freezing of Fruits and Vegetables. Rev. 1965. 48 p. il. Catalog No. A1.77:10/3. 20c.

** Home Freezing of Poultry.  How to do it; also recipes and directions for freezing cooked-poultry dishes. 1960. (G-70) 15c.

** How to Make Jellies, Jams, and Preserves at Home.  Directions; reasons for unsatisfactory results. 1957. (G-56) 15c.

** Making Pickles and Relishes at Home. 1964. 30 p. il. Catalog No. A1.77:30. 5c.

Meat for Thrifty Meals.  Selecting and cooking cheaper cuts of beef, pork, lamb, and veal.  Using leftovers, canned meat. 1953. (G-27) 20c.

** Potatoes in Popular Ways.  Buying, storing, cooking recipes. 1957. (G-55) 15c.

Peanut and Peanut Butter Recipes. 1954. (G-36) 10c.

** Pressure Canners, Use and Care. 1953. 6 p. il.  Catalog No. A1.77:30.  5c.

Recipes for Quantity Service.  Directions for quantities for 25, 50, or 100 portions. 1958. (HERR-5) FOR SALE ONLY.  $2.50.

** Storing Perishable Foods in the Home.  Directions for different kinds of foods; refrigerator temperatures. 1961. (G-78) 10c.

Sweetpotato Recipes.  Storing, cooking, recipes. 1946. (L-293) 10c.

Tomatoes on Your Table.  Ripening, cooking, recipes, marmalade, preserves. 1961. (L-278) 10c.

Turkey on the Table the Year Round.  Buying, preparing, cooking, recipes, leftovers. 1961. (G-45) 15c.

** What To Do When Your Home Freezer Stops.  Steps to keep food from spoiling. Rev. 1957. (L-321) 5c.

**HOW TO ORDER BULLETINS**

USDA will send free up to 10 different publications in response to any one request.

In requesting bulletins from USDA, please order by number, not name of publication.  For example, to obtain the publication "Removing Stains from Fabrics," order it by its G number (G-62) rather than by its title.  This speeds up service to you.  Group the L numbers, G numbers, etc., and list them numerically within these groups.  For instance: G-1, G-10, G-30; L-307, L-424.

Send request (post card means faster service) to Office of Information, U.S. Department of Agriculture, Washington, D.C. 20250.

If USDA's free supply of a particular bulletin becomes exhausted because of demand, you will be referred for that publication to the Superintendent of Documents, U.S. Government Printing Office.  Bulletins listed here as FOR SALE ONLY must be obtained from that source.

You also can buy any of the other bulletins listed, unless they are marked FROM USDA ONLY or another source is given.  Prices are listed for your convenience.  USDA *does not sell bulletins*.  All *purchases* must be made from the Superintendent of Documents.

If you buy 100 or more copies of *one* publication, you are entitled to a 25 percent discount.

To make purchases from the Superintendent of Documents, give the full title of the publication along with the number, and send with check or money order (no stamps) to: Superintendent of Documents, Government Printing Office, Washington, D.C. 20402.

# 9-B SUMMARY OF
# USDA GRADING STANDARDS

Six kinds of meat are graded: Beef, veal, calf, lamb, yearling mutton, and mutton.

The Grade names, U.S. Prime, U.S. Choice, and U.S. Good, can apply to all, except that mutton is not eligible for the Prime grade. There are lower grades for each of these meats, also, which differ slightly in terminology but are not likely to be seen in retail stores.

The next three lower grades for beef, U.S. Standard, U.S. Commercial, and U.S. Utility, may appear on occasion on retail counters. A store usually carries only one grade—the one it has found pleases most of its customers.

U.S. Prime, the top grade of beef, is produced from young and well-fed beef-type cattle. Meat of this grade is liberally marbled. Roasts and steaks are tender, juicy, and flavorful. Most of the supply of Prime beef is sold to restaurants and hotels.

U.S. Choice is the grade preferred by most consumers and is widely available at retail. It is of high quality and usually has less fat than Prime beef. Roasts and steaks from the loin, rib, and top round in this grade are tender and juicy. Other cuts, such as those from the bottom round or chuck, which are more suitable for pot roasting or braising, are juicy and have a well-developed flavor.

U.S. Good grade beef is lean but of fairly good quality. Although cuts of this grade lack the juiciness and flavor associated with a higher degree of fatness, their relative tenderness and high proportion of lean to fat please many thrifty shoppers.

U.S. Standard grade beef has very little fat and a mild flavor. It lacks juiciness but is relatively tender, since it comes from young animals.

U.S. Commercial beef comes from older cattle and therefore lacks tenderness. Long, slow cooking with moist heat is required for most cuts to develop the rich, full flavor of mature beef.

Veal is produced from animals that are 3 months or less in age; calf from animals between 3 months and 8 months old. The higher grades of veal, U.S. Prime and Choice, are more thickly fleshed than the lower grades and have a higher proportion of meat to bone.

Also, they have more fat and therefore are more juicy and flavorful. No grade of veal, however, has enough fat intermingled with the lean to make cooking with dry heat practical. Moist heat is needed to insure juiciness and development of flavor. Calf is intermediate between veal and beef in its texture, flavor, and tenderness.

Meat produced from sheep is divided into three classes, according to its age when slaughtered—lamb, yearling mutton, and mutton.

Most of the sheep produced in this country are marketed as lamb. Because lamb is produced from young animals, most of the cuts of the higher grades are tender enough to be cooked by dry heat—roasting, broiling, and pan broiling.

Yearling mutton comes from animals between 1 and 2 years old. It is produced in limited quantities, but is preferred by some people because it is more flavorful than lamb. Chops and legs of the higher grades are tender enough to be cooked by dry heat.

Mutton, which comes from mature animals, lacks natural tenderness and should be braised or pot roasted.

Six kinds of poultry are graded: turkey, chicken, duck, goose, guinea, squab.

The grade names are U.S. Grade A, U.S. Grade B, and U.S. Grade C.

Poultry grades are based on the conformation, or fleshing, of the bird—the proportion of meat to bone; the finish—the amount of fat in and under the skin, which tends to keep the meat moist and tender while cooking; and the absence or degree of defects such as cuts, tears, and bruises.

The "class" of the bird, which will appear on the label, is a guide to tenderness and to the appropriate cooking method. "Class" is indicated by the words "young," "mature," or "old," and by such terms as "broiler," "roaster," "stewing hen."

Much of the poultry produced is graded and is identified at retail with the USDA grade shield.

Usually only U.S. Grade A is identified. Lower grades are seldom, if ever, labeled as such.

Eggs are graded for size and for quality. There is no relation between size and quality.

The grade names for quality are Fresh Fancy Quality or U.S. Grade AA, U.S. Grade A, and U.S. Grade B.

For size, the names are U.S. Jumbo, Extra Large, Large, Medium, Small, and Peewee.

The two higher grades of quality have a large proportion of thick white, which stands up well around a firm, high yolk. They are delicate in flavor. Grade B eggs have a thinner white, which spreads over a wide area when broken. The yolk is rather flat and may break easily.

The term "Fresh Fancy Quality" is used only on eggs that have been produced under a special quality-control program designed to insure freshness as well as high quality.

Official egg sizes are based on weight per dozen, not size of the individual egg, although variation of sizes of individual eggs within a dozen is limited by the standards.  Minimum weight of a dozen Large eggs is 24 ounces; Medium, 21 ounces; Small, 18 ounces, and so on.  There is a 3-ounce difference between each weight class.

Of the dairy products, butter, Cheddar and Swiss cheese, and nonfat dry milk are graded.

A quality-control program and "Quality Approved" rating is available for process cheese, cottage cheese, sour cream, and buttermilk.

Grade names: U.S. Grade AA, U.S. Grade A, and U.S. Grade B for both butter and Cheddar cheese.  They are the same for Swiss cheese, except there is no U.S. Grade AA.  (There is also a Grade C for Cheddar and C and D grades for Swiss cheese.)

Grades for nonfat dry milk are U.S. Extra Grade and U.S. Standard Grade.

The higher grades of butter have a pleasing and desirable sweet flavor and are made only from cream that has such flavor.  Grade B butter is generally made from selected sour cream and therefore lacks the fresh flavor of the top grades.

The top grades of cheese indicate desirable and consistent flavor, body, and texture, as appropriate for the type of cheese, which in Cheddar includes sharp, mellow, and mild.  Labeling of cheese with the U.S. grade shield is not widespread, though much of it is graded at wholesale.

The U.S. grade shield on a package of nonfat dry milk is assurance of dependable quality and compliance with sanitary requirements.  It is also assurance, in the case of "instant" nonfat dry milk, that the milk powder will in fact dissolve instantly.

Most fresh fruit and vegetables are packed and sold on the wholesale market on the basis of U.S. grades.  There are standards for 72 different kinds. Thirteen "consumer standards" have been developed for use at the retail level but are seldom used.

The typical range of grades used at wholesale for fresh fruit and vegetables includes U.S. Fancy, U.S. No. 1, U.S. No. 2.  There are sometimes grades above and below that range.  For instance, grades for apples are U.S. Extra Fancy, U.S. Fancy, U.S. No. 1, and U.S. Utility.  The "consumer grades" are, generally, U.S. Grades A, B, and C.

Grades for fresh fruit and vegetables are determined on the basis of the product's color, size, shape, degree of maturity, and freedom from defects. Defects may be those caused by dirt, freezing, disease, insects, or mechanical injury.

Grades have been developed for a great variety of processed fruits and vegetables, canned, dried, and frozen, and a number of related products, such as peanut butter, jams, jellies, pickles, olives, honey, and orange juice crystals.

The usual grade names are U.S. Grade A or U.S. Fancy; U.S. Grade B or U.S. Choice or U.S. Extra Standard; U.S. Grade C or U.S. Standard.  There are few exceptions to this pattern.

U.S. Grade A (or Fancy) indicates an excellent quality in processed fruit and vegetables, uniformity in size and color, virtual freedom from defects, and the proper degree of maturity or tenderness. This grade is suited for special uses, as in desserts or salads, where appearance and texture are important.

U.S. Grade B is a good quality, just as nutritious as the top grade, but the product may be less uniform in size and color and less tender and free from blemishes. Most processed fruit and vegetables are of this grade. It is quite satisfactory for most uses.

U.S. Grade C indicates fairly good quality. The product is just as wholesome and may be as nutritious as the higher grades.

Only a limited amount of processed fruits and vegetables and related products are marked with the U.S. grade shield, which means that a Government grader has examined the product and certified that it is the quality stated.

Hundreds of processors, however, employ the grade standards in packing and selling processed fruit and vegetables. They may use the grade name, without the "U.S." in front of it, on their labels, even though the product has not been examined by a Government grader, as long as the quality actually is as good as indicated by the grade name.

If the quality does not measure up to the grade claimed, the processor is liable to prosecution under laws on mislabeling.

Milled (white) and brown rice, dry edible beans, peas, and lentils are graded.

The grades are: For milled (white) rice, U.S. Grades 1, 2, 3, 4, 5, and 6; for brown rice, U.S. Grades 1, 2, 3, 4, and 5; for beans and peas, U.S. Grades 1, 2, and 3; for lentils, U.S. Grades 1 and 2.

For dry beans there are also special handpicked grades that are adapted to use at retail. They include U.S. No. 1 Choice Handpicked, U.S. No. 1 Handpicked, U.S. No. 2 Handpicked, and U.S. No. 3 Handpicked.

The grades for rice are based on such factors as the absence or degree of defective kernels (broken kernels or those damaged by heat, water, or insects); mixed varieties (which may affect cooking qualities); and objectionable foreign material. General appearance and color also are considered.

Grades for beans, peas, and lentils are based on factors such as color and absence or presence of defects, foreign material, and beans, peas, or lentils of different classes.

Grades for all of these products are widely used in the trade but seldom appear on retail packages. Some packages of rice are marked with the grade name.

## SUGGESTED READINGS

*A Consumer's Guide to USDA Services.* Washington, D.C.: USDA, 1966. 49 pp.

*Be a Good Shopper.* Washington, D.C.: USDA, 1965. 8 pp.

Biesdorf, Heinz B., and Mary Ellen Burris. *Be a Better Shopper: Buying in Supermarkets.* Ithaca: Cornell University, 1968. 42 pp.

Burack, Richard. *The Handbook of Prescription Drugs: Official Names, Prices and Sources for Doctor and Patient.* New York: Pantheon Books, 1967. 181 pp.

Cross, Jennifer. *The Supermarket Trap: The Consumer and the Food Industry.* Bloomington: Indiana University Press, 1970. 258 pp.

*Family Expenditures for Clothing.* New York: National Industrial Conference Board, 1955. 40 pp.

*Family Food Budgeting.* U.S. Department of Agriculture, Home and Garden Bulletin No. 94. Washington, D.C.: U.S. Government Printing Office, 1964. 16 pp.

*Food for Families with School Children.* Washington, D.C.: USDA, 1963. 24 pp.

Garrett, Pauline G., and Edward J. Metzen. *You are a Consumer of Clothing.* Boston: Ginn and Company, 1967. 177 pp.

*How to Buy Beef Roasts.* Washington, D.C.: USDA, 1966. 15 pp.

Money Management Institute, Household Finance Corporation. *Money Management — Your Shopping Dollar.* Chicago: Household Finance Corporation, 1965. 36 pp.

*Vegetables in Family Meals: A Guide for Consumers.* Washington, D.C., 1968. 32 pp.

Wright, Carlton E. *Food Buying; Marketing Information for Consumers.* New York: Macmillan, 1962. 410 pp.

# CHAPTER 10

# SAVING MONEY ON HOME FURNISHINGS
# AND OTHER HOUSEHOLD PURCHASES

All those items used to transform an empty house or apartment into a liveable home, whether it be simple or elegant, may be grouped into the broad category, "home furnishings." Included besides furniture and appliances are floor coverings, draperies, bedding and other linens, dishes and silverware, cookware, and accessories including pictures, lamps, and miscellaneous art objects.

But actual household operation requires many items other than home furnishings. Consider for a moment all the cleaning and laundry supplies, the toiletries and health needs, that most of us think of as basic necessities; add to them the phonograph records, stereophonic tapes, toys, games, and other recreational equipment that are desirable, if not necessary. Over the period of a lifetime or perhaps even over the period of only a year or so these myriad personal possessions represent the outlay of thousands of dollars. It seems hardly necessary, therefore, to point out that saving a dollar here or a dime there on the purchase of home furnishings and other household items can add up to an impressive total. Such savings *are* possible, as will be shown in this chapter.

## HOME FURNISHINGS

Many people find that except for the purchase of a home itself, the money spent on home furnishings represents their largest financial outlay. In fact, the total cost of completely outfitting a three-bedroom house with good-quality yet moderately priced furnishings will be very close to one-half the cost of the house alone. And this does not take into consideration any expensive art objects, only those pieces of furniture and the appliances, draperies and so forth that most people consider essential to comfortable living. In other words, the family that buys a $20,000 home will—after living in the house long enough to acquire all the essentials—probably have spent about $10,000 to furnish it.

Bear in mind that these are costs for *initially* furnishing a home. Redecorating and replacement of a part of all furnishings would, of course, affect the total expenditure proportionately. For example, *complete refurnishing* an entire home even once could make the total lifetime cost for furnishings run as much as or more than the original cost of the house itself. Consider too, the probable expenditures by persons who rent unfurnished houses or apartments and who, by choice or necessity, purchase new furnishings with each move.

**"Do you have enough money to go window shopping with me today?"**

Reprinted with permission of *The Wall Street Journal* (Cartoon Features Syndicate).

These facts seem startling, since relatively few people start "from scratch" to furnish a home. As a matter of fact, few persons actually *completely furnish* one room *at one time*. But even when household furnishings are acquired over a period of years, the total cost—whether it be $10,000 or only half that—represents a large expenditure, and it should be money wisely spent. The purchase of a $25 lamp should be given as careful consideration as the buying of a $1,000 carpet, if one is going to get the best possible value for his money.

## FURNITURE

Fortunate, indeed, are young persons or newlyweds who can start housekeeping with a furniture "nest egg"—a few good pieces of furniture already bought and paid for. Those who do not would do well to borrow, accept as gifts from their family, or purchase a few second-hand items to "tide them over" until they can make the careful, unhurried selections that will assure them getting the right thing at the right price.

If there is one area of consumer buying in which the average person needs a reminder to "go slow," it is in the purchase of furniture. Here, even a small investment in time and study can mean a big saving in money. Make your first rule in furniture purchasing: "Study and plan before you shop; *shop* before you buy."

Here are other good rules you would do well to follow:

1. Consistently read one or more of the good "home" magazines. If possible, take a course in interior decorating so that you can learn the basic elements of good design and color coordination. Many stores offer free interior decoration services. However, make sure you don't sacrifice your tastes to theirs.

2. Study your furniture needs and wants in light of your own personality, the layout of your house or apartment, and what your budget will sensibly allow. You will then be assured of getting what you really want and can afford.

3. Shop the "ads." You can learn much about a store's merchandising policy and learn how its prices compare generally with those of other stores in the same area.

4. Choose a reliable store or stores with which to do business. Check their status with the local Better Business Bureau. Talk with friends and acquaintances about their experiences with particular dealers.

5. Go in and look around. Salesmen may try to pressure you into quick decisions or offer on-the-spot discounts to get you to buy "right now." But take your time. If they can discount a piece of furniture today, they can discount it tomorrow or next week. And furniture dealers expect you to look around, no matter how fast talking they may be.

6. Watch for legitimate furniture sales. See how much a store cuts its prices. Be sure that the sale merchandise consists of regular stock items, and that it is not a special carload of "cheap" furniture shipped in just for the sale.

7. Try bargaining. If a certain store routinely has annual or semi-annual sales at, say 20 percent or 30 percent discount, you may be able to get that same

discount at *any time of year*.  Bear in mind the fact that no store can stay in business if it sells at prices that do not yield a *profit*, and if it can sell at "30 percent off" in June, it can probably sell at 30 percent off in May, February, or any other particular time.

8.  Remember that furniture stores are like service stations—one on every corner—and when you are investing hundreds or thousands of dollars, you can afford to drive a few miles, if necessary, to protect that investment by getting the best possible buy.

9.  Find out if the item you buy carries any guarantee or warranty and just what is covered.  If the guarantee requires you to send a registration card to the factory or dealer, be sure to fill it out and mail immediately.  Many guarantees are not enforceable unless this "proof of purchase date" registration is filed with the manufacturer or dealer within a specified time.

10.  Choose established, reliable brands.  Look for the manufacturer's name on the underside, back, or inside the drawer of a piece of furniture.  A maker who is proud of his product will stand behind it.  Also, he will likely have on hand replacement drawer pulls or other parts with which you may have trouble.

**Fig. 10–1**  Learn to identify quality materials and workmanship.  While wood is the most widely used furniture material, metal and plastic are also appropriate for many items.  Courtesy of American of Martinsville.

11.  Learn to identify quality materials and workmanship.  (See Fig. 10–1.) While wood is the most widely used furniture material, metal and plastic are

also appropriate for many items.  In wooden furniture, look for:

a) Hardwoods—maple, birch, oak, mahogany, gum, and the fruitwoods (walnut, pecan, cherry, and hickory) are the commonly used ones.  Pine is generally considered too soft for quality furniture.  Furniture may be made from "solid" or "veneered" wood.  Solid wood is planks of lumber, edge-glued together.  Veneered wood is three to seven layers of cabinet-grade plywood laminated together.  Beautiful selected veneers over solid hardwood frames make excellent furniture material.

b) Woods with straight grain.  This is especially important for furniture legs, arms, and other weight-bearing parts, since cross grain or slope of grain weaken the wood.  Tabletops, drawer fronts, and similar parts are also best made of straight grain to minimize the chance of warpings due to humidity changes.

c) Absence of irregularities in construction or finish.  Examine the piece at a low angle (about 15 to 30 degrees) under a fairly strong light, looking for flaws you might ordinarily overlook.

d) Clean lines.  Be sure that edges and corners are smoothly finished, and that there are no protruding parts.

e) Instructions for care.  If the finish requires special attention, be sure you understand.

f) Firmness and steadiness.  Make certain that the item rests squarely and firmly on all legs.  If there are coasters, rollers, drawers, or other moving parts, see that they move freely without sticking or binding.

g) Joints that are sturdy and tight fitting.  Look for double dowel or mortise and tenon joinings on the outer frame and dovetail joints on drawers. Notched and screwed corner blocks of wood or metal give added strength to parts subjected to heavy strain.

h) Glue and screws—not nails.  See that all glue joints are tightly closed and that screws are tight.

i) On dropleaf tables, check the hinges.  A piano-type hinge the length of the joint or at least three 3-inch hinges are required to support all but the smallest dropleaf.

12. The above checkpoints should also be applied in evaluating the framework and exposed wood parts of upholstered furniture.  In addition, look for:

a) Closely interlaced seatbase of steel, rubber, plastics, or jute.

b) Coil springs made of tempered steel (flat springs may be used in "slim line" furniture where bulkiness is undesirable).  Springs should be anchored to frame and webbing and securely mounted to prevent shifting.

c) Durable filler material on padding or cushions.  (Federal law requires manufacturers to affix labels which identify filling in upholstered furniture.)

d) Firmly woven, durable upholstery fabrics.  Find out what you can expect of the fabric and what special care it may require.  Decide if you need any of the special finishes which may be applied to upholstery fabrics (for example, to provide resistance to mildew, fading, shrinkage, wear, etc.) and determine whether or not they are worth the extra amount they cost.

13. Visit a furniture repair shop.  Observe the defects that are being repaired; notice the parts that have held up under use.  Then, remember what you have seen when you go furniture shopping.

14. When buying sofas or chairs, sit on them; lie on the beds.  Find out *before you buy* if they are comfortable and provide the support you desire.

15. Just because the bedroom furniture is not often seen by visitors, do not assume that it need not be just as comfortable and durable as that of any other room.  Beds, especially, need to be carefully selected.  You spend a fourth to a third of your lifetime sleeping.  Your job efficiency, your disposition, and even your health depend a great deal on the quality of the rest you get, so do yourself a favor by buying the best bed you can afford.  The best bed will cost more than a poor one, but price alone is no indication of real quality.  Here are some other important things to look for:

a) Correct size.  Choose a bed that is six inches to a foot longer than the sleeper.  Oversize beds (queen and king size) have become extremely popular, but costs are still much higher than for standard-sized sleep sets.  (The degree of firmness and support you choose are largely matters of personal preference.)

b) Matched spring and mattress sets.  Pieces designed to be used together will give better service than mismatched springs and mattresses.

c) Construction.  Bedsprings are of three types, "box," "metal coil," and "flat."  Mattresses are available in "innerspring" and plastic or rubber "foam" types.

Box springs consist of wire coils which are mounted on a wood frame, padded, and covered with fabrics.  Metal coil springs are similar, except that they are not padded and not usually covered.  Flat springs are made of metal strips or links attached to a frame.  Flat springs are less expensive than coil types, but they are also less comfortable and less serviceable.

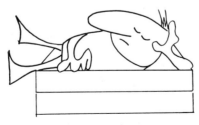

Both spring and foam type mattresses come in various grades.  Those of best quality will have strong borders (usually a rolled edge), sturdy handles and firmly woven covers. Spring type mattresses should have at least four metal or plastic vents on each side for air circulation.

d) Coils. Number of coils is the primary indicator of quality in both coil type mattresses and springs. Look for a minimum of 500 coils in the mattress and 500 matched coils in the springs for a standard double-bed size sleep set. Generally, the more coils, the greater the comfort. "Independent action" springs are preferred by many people since such springs adjust themselves to the weight load on the mattress to prevent sagging.

e) Foam. If you are buying a foam mattress (best used over good quality boxsprings), be sure you get the latest market information regarding the various foam fillers. Latex rubber may be a little more expensive than newer synthetic materials, but it is also time tested and has proved itself. Urethane and other synthetics show good promise, and like synthetic clothing fabrics, are constantly undergoing change and improvement. However, get the latest word before you buy.

f) Water beds. A new innovation of the early 1970's is the water bed, a vinyl mattress filled with water which can be heated or cooled as desired. Manufacturers of water beds advertise their great comfort and even claim some therapeutic value for these innovative beds. However, they require special installation, and may be difficult if not impossible to move either within a room or from house to house.

g) Covering. Good-quality mattress covering is important, but more important is what is inside. Fancy ticking may be only a cover up for poor-grade material or workmanship inside. Look for a sturdy, firmly woven fabric and for well built borders and edging.

---

Under Penalty Of Law This Tag Is Not To
Be Removed Except By The Consumer

## ALL NEW MATERIAL CONSISTING OF

## POLYESTER FIBER

---

### REG. NO. CAL-155

| # 5029 | CERTIFICATION IS MADE BY THE MANUFACTURER THAT THE MATERIALS IN THIS ARTICLE ARE DESCRIBED IN ACCORDANCE WITH LAW. |
|---|---|

---

SOLD BY
**SEARS ROEBUCK & CO.**
CHICAGO, ILL.

Date of Delivery.............................................
**Finished Size 20"x 26"**

---

**FEDERAL REQUIREMENT**    RN-24270
**COVER: 100% COTTON**

16. Check the impulse to buy bedroom suites if you really don't need them. Modern home construction is including many built-ins including cupboards and drawers in bedrooms. Ample closet space may eliminate the need for expensive dressers and chests. If a bed is all you need, buy it separately; or match it to those extra items you actually do need, instead of several unnecessary pieces just because they come as a set. Plenty of stores carry open stock bedroom furniture and cater to the discriminating shopper who knows what he wants and goes after it. Also, it is likely that you can get a much better price (seasonal sale or close-out) on a single piece than on a suite.

## RUGS AND CARPETS

The salesman will tell you why the carpet you buy is a good one. He'll tell you if it's worth the money, and how it ought to wear. But since carpeting is probably the most expensive home furnishing item you ever buy for your house, for your own peace of mind, double check not only the salesman but also the store. Be sure you are dealing with a reputable firm and honest, knowledgeable people. If you are not sure, check with the local Better Business Bureau.

But even before you start to look for a place to buy, you ought to learn a few basics about rugs and carpets—things that will let the salesman see he is dealing with someone he need not try to fool just in case he might be tempted to do so. For example you should know that:

1. Handmade rugs, products of a centuries-old profession, are still produced today in some parts of the world. Even in the United States, where the power carpet loom was invented in 1839, Indians of the Southwest are famous for beautiful handwoven rugs and blankets.

2. The early Wilton, Axminster, and velvet rug looms were developed in England to reproduce handmade rugs, and excellent broadloom machine reproductions are possible with today's modern methods. In addition, modern manufacturers produce chenille and tufted rugs.

3. "Broadloom" means carpeting in widths of 6, 12, 15 and 18 feet. (Originally, looms produced 27-inch strips which were sewn together to make roomsize rugs.)

4. "Wilton" is the name applied to rugs woven on a jacquard loom which raises the correct color yarn to the surface to make the pattern. Since all but

the pattern yarn are left buried beneath the surface, such rugs have greater depth and strength than some other types.

5. "Axminster" rugs, named for the English town where they were created, are made by attaching the pile yarn to the backing one tuft at a time.

6. "Velvet" weave is the simplest machine rug process. A layer of pile yarn loops is attached to a layer of jute backing, then the loops are cut to form the smooth velvety finish. Uncut pile results in "looped pile" carpeting.

7. "Chenille" rugs are made in a two-step weaving process. Fuzzy yarns are woven, then cut into strips, and used for the pile, which is interwoven with the backing material (usually jute or heavy cotton).

8. "Tufted" rugs are the result of a high-speed method of sewing face yarns through a woven jute or canvas backing with wide, multineedle machines. To finish the carpet, it is passed over a roller which coats the back with latex and locks the tufts in place.

9. Wool, once the universal choice of material for rug making, is now sharing the spotlight with a host of serviceable synthetics.

10. Carpet wools are coarse and strong (some handmade wool rugs several hundred years old are still in use today). But if carpet wools are adulterated by apparel weight wools—as is legal and frequently done—durability of the rugs woven from them diminishes accordingly, and it is extremely difficult to know how much apparel wool has been used in a particular rug or carpet.

11. Cotton rugs, while not as durable (and not as colorfast because of their need for frequent cleaning) as wool ones, may give sufficient service in bedrooms or other minimum traffic areas. They have a tendency to soil very rapidly.

12. Synthetics used for rug making fall into five generic classifications: acrylic, modacrylic, nylon, polypropylene, and rayon. As with synthetic clothing fabrics, each manufacturer has his own brand name within these five genera. For example, Acrilan by Chemstrand; Creslan by American Cyanamid; Orlon by E. I. du Pont de Nemours, and Zefran by Dow Chemical, are all acrylics.

Giant strides have been and are constantly being made in improving the old and developing new synthetic carpet materials. Resistance to soil and stain, to wear, mildew, moths and carpet beetles and to fire, easier cleaning, brighter colors, greater resilience are all properties manufacturers are building into their rug materials. The changes and improvements come so rapidly that any listing of standards today would probably be obsolete in a few months or a few years. For latest information, check current development and marketing news from the U.S. Department of Agriculture and the periodical reports of testing organizations.

13. In carpets made of synthetics or wool, the fibers of the pile alone do not determine quality of the finished product. The backing on the carpet and pad-

ding or cushion used beneath it are of major importance. If the backing gives way, the face yarns will be damaged. Jute, a vegetable fiber imported largely from India, and the most widely used backing fiber, comes in a variety of different grades. So do cotton, Kraftcord cellulose fiber yarn, and the various synthetic backings developed in recent years. The padding gives resilience and softness to a carpet, and extends its life—up to 100 percent, according to some manufacturers. Until recent years, felted hair or a jute and hair combination were the most frequently used carpet cushioning materials. Newer ones are made of hair fiber and rubber combinations, 100 percent sponge rubber, or urethane foam. Again, each comes in different grades, and comparisons need to be made on the basis of up-to-date information and test reports. Usually padding grades are specified by weight in ounces.

**Other suggestions for saving money on carpeting.** Type and grade of carpeting should be considered in light of the use to which it will be put—higher quality for heavy traffic areas, and so forth. Room-size rugs which can be moved about to distribute wear may be more economical than wall-to-wall carpeting and are sensible for apartment dwellers. Likewise, depending on color and pattern, some wall-to-wall carpet can be turned and relaid, perhaps stretching its usefulness several years. Also, the good part of a carpet that has begun to show wear in certain areas can perhaps be moved to a smaller room for added service.

Shop around. Never buy rugs or carpets on an impulse. Firmly resist pressures to rush you into buying something you do not need or want. Take your time to examine carpet samples and deals of several sellers. Fortify yourself with as much information as you possibly can. If possible wait until a seasonal close-out or stock liquidation comes along. Armed with knowledge, you can tell whether or not the goods offered at "fantastic savings" really are bargains.

Good care is essential to maximum carpet life and therefore to saving money on carpet purchases. Top surface dirt should be vacuumed out several times a week (or daily if subjected to hard use). Postpone having the carpet cleaned for as long as possible. Cleaning often takes much of the "body" and "life" out of the carpet. And, when you must have it cleaned, have it done by a reputable, professional cleaner. Moisture in the air affects carpets and for best results a relative humidity ranging from 40 to 50 percent should be maintained. Stiletto heels can cut carpet pile backing. Spilled water should be quickly wiped up before it soaks through to the backing. Most stains on carpeting *can* be removed by a professional, particularly if he is called in *first* and not after you have tried and failed, or have made it worse by using some cleaning agent not suited to the job.

## DRAPERIES AND LINENS

In the selection of draperies and household linens, we are again dealing with fibers and fabrics. The same considerations, therefore, that apply to clothing and carpeting with respect to wearability, cleanability, and suitability for the

job they are to do should be applied. Wise choices here can mean not only dollar savings on the original purchase and on upkeep, but can also eliminate the need for costly, too-early replacement.

**Draperies.**  Labor charges for professional drapery making run high.  Even so, the greater satisfaction usually provided by custom-made drapes designed and created in accordance with your own specific needs and desires may justify their extra cost.  Besides, there *are* ways to save money even on custom-made draperies.  During a short two- or three-week period each year, many stores feature free labor with drapery material purchases.  Still others offer free lining material with the purchase of drapery yardage.  Finding out if stores in your area hold such annual promotions and then delaying your drapery purchases long enough to take advantage of these special sales can save you money.

If custom-made draperies appear out of your financial reach, or if suitable ready-mades cannot be found, you might consider doing the work yourself. Most drapery making is not complicated, and step-by-step instruction booklets can be obtained free of charge or at nominal cost from fabric stores or sewing centers.  Watch these stores, too, for drapery fabric sales or promotions, and buy when you can get the most for your money.  Plan ahead, so that you are not faced with making expensive short-notice decisions.

**Linens.**  Annual and semi-annual "white goods" sales are now well-established events throughout the country.  These sales, usually held during May or January, offer many genuine bargains in bath, bed, and table linens.  However, for the best bargains and greatest satisfaction, be sure that you are buying brand-name items from the store's regular stock, not off-brand goods stocked especially for these seasonal promotions.

Often "seconds," or merchandise with flaws of some sort, are offered at white sales.  In many instances, the imperfection is slight and will not be notice-able nor affect the usefulness of the item.  Seconds may actually be very good buys, but be sure to inspect the items first and know exactly what you are getting.

Look-ahead shoppers often find white sales excellent sources of wedding and shower gifts at money-saving prices, and many a clever young bride has converted a pair of colored bed sheets into inexpensive curtains that have served well until she could afford permanent or custom-made draperies.

## EQUIPMENT, APPLIANCES, AND PRODUCTS

Good household equipment and appliances are expensive—too expensive to be bought and not used or to be replaced in a year or so because performance falls short of expectations.

**"Here's where your trouble is -- your 90-day guarantee has run out."**

Reprinted with permission of *The Wall Street Journal* (Cartoon Features Syndicate).

Individual and family needs and circumstances, which are the bases for planning equipment purchases, vary considerably. Also, attention must be given to future as well as present conditions. In evaluating needs before buying equipment for the home, therefore, the wise consumer asks:

Is the item under consideration really necessary? Will it make homemaking easier? Is it needed right now, or would waiting until some later date be more sensible? Is the deluxe model the best buy, or would a "stripped down" version serve just as adequately? How much will it cost to operate? Is home wiring in good condition and adequate to handle the proposed new equipment? Will improvements in the wiring or plumbing systems be necessary to handle future equipment additions? Will the proposed equipment take up space needed or preferred for something else? Are the special features of a particular model worth the extra money they cost, or do they merely add eye appeal or only minor convenience?

Even with all these questions resolved, the thrifty consumer will not be ready to begin the actual shopping process. First, he will want to do some reading, especially in periodicals such as *Consumer Reports, Consumer Digest,* and *Changing Times,* and the special annual issues of these magazines which take the form of consumer buying guides.

Many women's magazines, notably *Better Homes and Gardens* and *Good Housekeeping*, include excellent reports to consumers in practically every issue. In some of the reports to readers, products are identified by name, manufacturer, and manufacturer's "list" price, giving the consumer an excellent basis for comparison shopping.

Armed with this type of information, the consumer is probably as well informed as—or perhaps even better than—the average equipment or appliance salesman. Combining this knowledge of product with a thorough understanding of his own or his family's needs, he has the tools for critically evaluating, rather than merely relying on, claims of manufacturers and dealers. In other words, he is able to make intelligent decisions for himself. And this, after all, is the most effective way of getting his money's worth on any purchase.

## SHOPPING FOR EQUIPMENT

When and where to buy are especially important factors in saving on equipment and appliance purchases. If at all possible, needs should be anticipated weeks or months in advance in order to take advantage of seasonal sales or other promotions. Close-out or inventory reduction sales planned by dealers to provide space for new models can be excellent sources of bargains. Frequently, year-to-year model changes are changes that affect cabinet design more than the real working parts of the equipment, and it is often possible to make a real saving if one is willing to settle for a little less than the very latest style.

Discount stores frequently advertise their washing machines, vacuum cleaners, freezers, and other household equipment at prices lower than those of other furniture or equipment dealers. This merchandise may provide good buys for the consumer. However, a close check of model numbers and designs is likely to reveal that part, if not all, of the items are previous years' models. While the prices asked might be considerably lower than those of current year's merchandise, they may well be out of line for last year's models. Again, the important thing is knowing what you are getting and determining whether the price is right for that particular merchandise. Discount stores are more likely than other dealers to carry "off" brands, for which parts and service may be difficult to obtain. Before purchasing an unknown or little-known product, the consumer ought to find out all he possibly can about it.

Another word of caution about dealing with discount stores is appropriate. Such establishments have a high mortality rate. Many go out of business within a few months or years after opening, leaving customers without recourse when and if mechanical problems arise. The implications here are so obvious that it seems almost unnecessary to call attention to one other principle of wise buymanship: the importance of doing business with a well-established firm which stands behind its merchandise and which, in turn, has the backing of reliable manufacturers.

It is not unreasonable to expect of the dealer from whom equipment is purchased that he will: (1) provide proper and efficient installation; (2) give estimates beforehand regarding costs for installation and servicing; (3) provide service and replacement of parts at a fair price; (4) give prompt and efficient service; and (5) demonstrate use of equipment.

Similarly, the purchaser should be able to expect of an equipment manufacturer that he: (1) provide specification and parts sheets with each unit; (2) provide detailed information about construction, finish, special features and performance of the equipment; (3) give detailed instructions regarding use and care of the product; and (4) provide a written warranty of the manufacturer's responsibility in case of failure of equipment to perform properly within a certain time limit.

With respect to any warranty, however, the purchaser should read it carefully and be certain he understands all its conditions. No warranty gives blanket coverage for *all* problems which may arise, nor does it offer protection for an unlimited period of time. There are responsibilities of the purchaser as well as of the manufacturer, and the consumer needs to be fully aware of the terms of the warranty in each specific instance.

## EQUIPMENT FOR NEW HOMES

In tract homes and other houses offered for sale by the builder (as distinguished from custom homes built to the specifications of the buyer), the choice of equipment is usually that of the contractor. Since he is in business to make money, he wants to get the best possible price on the equipment he buys. For this reason, he may order "standard" rather than "deluxe" models, white rather than colored finishes, small- or average-sized units, and second- rather than first-quality products. Many contractors are willing, however, for the home buyer to specify makes and models of equipment, with the understanding, of course, that any major price differences will be borne by the purchaser. Persons fortunate enough to buy a home at a time prior to or during construction so that they have this choice have a distinct advantage over those who must get along with someone else's selections. While the new choices may mean extra money for the buyer, they will probably be well worth the expenditure from the standpoint of convenience and personal satisfaction, since the selection will have been made according to the buyer's estimate of needs rather than on price alone.

## KITCHENWARE

As any homemaker knows, the average kitchen all too soon becomes a clutter of little-used pots and pans, dishes, plasticware, chinaware, silver and stainless steel flatware, crystal, and an endless variety of tools and kitchen gadgets. And kitchenware that is not used because it is not really needed or because it fails to perform as expected is costly, indeed. Besides the money wasted on their purchase in the first place, these unused dishes and cookware may not even be worth the space they occupy and might as well be discarded.

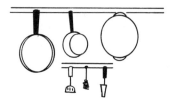

How many of these worthless items can you find in *your own* kitchen? Probably quite a stack if you are living at home or if you are a newlywed with the usual array of wedding gifts.  On the other hand, if you are a bachelor or a bachelor girl doing light housekeeping in your own apartment, you are likely operating with one or two cooking pots, a fry pan, half a dozen plates and bowls, and three or four place settings of silverware—and you probably have all the kitchenware you actually need.  This is not to say you may not *want* more, nor that you should not necessarily have more.  But it does serve to illustrate the point that most kitchen cupboards are overstocked with unnecessary and useless items.  Taken by themselves, these pieces may be relatively inexpensive, but a large collection adds up to a lot of money that might better have been saved or spent for something else.

The most important rule, therefore, when it comes to saving money on dishes and cookware is this: Buy cautiously.  Be certain of your needs, then carefully select only the items that specifically meet those needs.  Other suggestions are:

1.  Resist the temptation and pressure to buy "complete sets," unless you are certain this is the wisest choice.  Such sets usually include a number of rarely-used items.
2.  When buying dishes and chinaware, especially, be certain it is "open stock" merchandise so that broken pieces may be replaced.
3.  Shop around for the best price, remembering that merchandise identical to much of that sold in department, hardware, or gift stores may also be purchased in variety and discount stores at considerably lower cost.
4.  Keep purchases to a minimum.  Keep in mind that friends and relatives very frequently choose cookware and dishes as wedding and shower gifts.
5.  Avoid buying from door-to-door or "special appointment" salesmen, whose merchandise is practically always (a) available only in sets, and (b) priced considerably higher than items of comparable quality in a store.  Another thing to remember is that while the door-to-door salesman makes a real selling point of the fact that his particular brand of merchandise cannot be purchased anywhere else, this factor alone does not make it superior to any other brand.  Such salesmen often use high-pressure techniques to sign young women up for large purchases on long-term, high-interest contracts.

## CLEANING AND LAUNDRY SUPPLIES

Nowadays, choosing the right cleaning or laundry products—the ones that will give most satisfactory results at the lowest cost—is a complicated job. Soaps, synthetic detergents and other cleaners come in liquid, cake, powder, premeasured packet, aerosol spray, and tablet forms, with or without pigments and with or without bleach. They have high suds, low suds, or no suds.

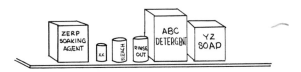

With literally hundreds of products available and new ones appearing almost daily, the consumer's choice is practically endless. Advertisements on television and radio, in newspapers and magazines, and on billboards, plus the recommendations of neighbors and friends, all loudly proclaiming the merits and magic of the various formulations, frequently confuse rather than clarify. Whom and what shall the consumer believe? How shall he choose?

Actually, selection can be simplified considerably by classifying the various products according to their general characteristics and intended purposes. When this is done, it is relatively easy for the consumer to make choices between various products within a particular classification on the basis of cost and personal preference.

**Laundry agents.** Soaps and synthetic detergents (or "syndets," as they are frequently called) clean by (1) wetting the fabric and the soil; (2) emulsifying soil (surrounding insoluble oily substances with a detergent film, thereby separating it from the fabric); (3) dispersing or breaking up the soil into smaller, more easily removed particles; and (4) holding the soil in suspension to be flushed away in the wash water.

Soap is made of animal fat and caustic soda (lye), and is most effective when used in a slightly alkaline solution. Synthetic detergents are made by chemical conversion of petroleum derivatives or animal and vegetable fats and oils into complex products suited for a variety of cleaning jobs. Because soap decomposes in acid solutions, and because heavy soil may produce acidity in wash water, manufacturers of some soaps and syndets add alkalinity to their products to improve cleaning power. These "built" agents are identified as "heavy-duty" or "all-purpose" cleaners, in contrast to the "light-duty" or "unbuilt" products intended for lightly soiled fabrics and items of delicate construction such as hosiery and lingerie, and for fabrics containing silk or wool.

Whitening and brightening powers of both the built and unbuilt laundry products are enhanced by the addition of colorless fluorescent dyes. These "optical whiteners" increase light reflection, thereby improving the appearance of laundered articles. Effectiveness of these whiteners varies with different fabrics and with different laundering and drying processes. Color of the soap or detergent itself has no effect on its cleaning power. Pigments are added primarily to make a more attractive looking product.

Properly used, either soap or detergent does a good job. Soap does have the disadvantage of forming insoluble curds which may combine with particles of

**Fig. 10–2** Waste and danger. Excess suds not only waste soap, but can also run over onto this washer's unshielded motor. Consumers are advised to use low-sudsing detergent and be sure to ground the case. Reprinted by permission from *Consumer Reports*. Copyright by Consumers Union of U.S., Inc., a nonprofit organization.

soil and settle into the fabric rather than being carried away in the laundering process. Soap curd is not dissolved in water, and is not washed out in subsequent launderings. In addition, no soap is available for the cleaning job in a washerload of clothes until all the calcium or magnesium salts in hard water are precipitated or separated out of the water by the soap. Soap does produce good results, however, when used with naturally soft or chemically softened water. Synthetic detergents work well in moderately or even fairly hard water. Extremely hard water may call for the use of more detergent or detergent plus a softener.

In determining the amount of laundry agent to use, the rule for soap is simple: enough to maintain a good suds throughout the washing cycle. A drop in the suds level indicates that the soap has picked up all the soil it can hold, and that more soap is needed to complete the removal of soil and prevent its redeposition in the fabric being washed. Syndets vary as to the amount of suds produced, so suds level cannot be used to determine how much of the product is needed. Best guide is the manufacturer's directions on the container, taking into consideration, of course, the degree of soiling, washload size, and softness or hardness of the water.

Using the *right* amount of soap or detergent is important. Too little results in incomplete cleaning and the danger is redeposited soil, which is harder to remove than the original dirt. On the other hand, too much of the product may complicate rinsing operations or cause suds overflow and consequent mechanical difficulties with the washing machine, as illustrated in Fig. 10–2. These, and some of the water-pollution and other ecological problems relating to soap and detergent residues, have been minimized in recent years, however, with the development of low- and extra-low sudsing detergents, as well as products which are phosphate free and/or biodegradable (made of material which rots away, leaving no residue harmful to plants or animals).

By way of summary, the following points can serve as useful guides in the selection of laundry products:

1. Heavy soil calls for "heavy-duty" or "all-purpose" cleaner.
2. Delicate fabrics and lightly soiled articles are best washed in "unbuilt" laundry products.
3. Labels indicate whether soap or detergents are for special or all-purpose use.
4. White or colorfast fabrics including cottons, linens and man-made synthetics can be laundered safely with either soap or detergents.
5. Fabrics that are not colorfast are best washed with unbuilt soap or syndets.
6. It may be necessary to choose between maximum cleanliness with a heavy-duty product that could damage the fabric or safeguarding the fabric by using an unbuilt soap or syndet with less cleaning power.

**Household cleaners.** As with soaps and detergents, the array of household cleansers and cleaners on the market today is indeed impressive. And again, choice of the right product for each cleaning job is a baffling one. Shoppers who pay strict attention to the advertising may feel compelled to purchase a special agent for each particular cleaning problem. On the other hand, there can also be found strong support for the "all-purpose" products said to be equal to most, if not all, cleaning jobs throughout the house.

Actually, the most realistic money-saving solution is a middle-road course, keeping selection to as few different products as possible, but being sure—by paying careful attention to the manufacturers' directions and suggested uses— that what you are getting will do the job you want done.

It is important to remember that many cleaning agents contain chemicals or other ingredients whose harsh action may damage certain surfaces or finishes. For example, the abrasive in even the gentlest scouring cleansers can, with prolonged use, roughen the porcelain finish of a sink or bathtub. This allows staining that perhaps cannot be removed except with high-powered cleanser which could, in turn, damage the finish even more. However, some cleansers contain bleaches which make stain removal easier and thus cut down abrasive wear. But another example of hidden danger is in the case of an oven cleaner which may do an excellent job of removing burned-on grease from the porcelainized oven interior, but which may damage chrome or enamel finishes or may literally eat holes in linoleum if accidentally allowed to come in contact with these surfaces.

Abrasive cleansers should not be used on Formica or laminated plastic counter tops, nor on teflon-coated or other plated metal cookware. Also, the finish of freezers, refrigerators, ranges, washing machines, and dryers might be damaged by the abrasive action. For safety, carefully follow the appliance manufacturer's directions for cleaning household equipment.

Painted surfaces may be damaged by abrasive type cleaners and by some liquid or paste-type preparations. Here again, strict compliance with the manufacturer's directions is called for. After all, there is no saving if paint damage caused by a strong cleaner has to be repaired with an expensive paint job.

**Cleaners in spray containers.** In recent years, along with the flood of new products, have come numerous packaging innovations—packages designed primarily to provide greater convenience for the consumer. Especially important is the spray type dispenser. And while convenience and ease of use have been achieved with push-button cans, bottles, and plastic containers, this new convenience has added significantly to product cost. In few, if any, instances does the spray dispenser improve the quality of the product itself, and the careful shopper must ask himself if the extra convenience is worth the extra cost. Even those who say "yes," may begin to doubt it when the push button fails to function and it is impossible to get the contents out of a can—a not infrequent occurrence with aerosol dispensers!

**Where to buy.** Purchasing laundry and cleaning supplies along with meat and potatoes on your regular trips to the grocery store may be the convenient way to buy these items, but it is probably not the most economical. In fact, sales of non-food items in food stores are commonly considered the money makers, particularly for the small independent grocers operating on a narrow profit margin.

But discount, variety, and super-drugstores can—and usually do—sell non-food items at lower prices, and while the quality of some merchandise (clothing, for example) in this type outlet may not be equal to that of other retail stores, there is no difference in certain other items, including cleaning and laundry supplies. Brand name soap, paste wax, or liquid cleanser are the same wherever they are sold. Cost becomes the only real consideration in deciding where to shop to save money—unless, perhaps, it is necessary to go far out of one's way to shop at the super-drugstore or discount store.

Another money-saving practice, particularly for the consumer who can anticipate needs over a relatively long time period and is in a position to purchase in quantity, is to buy at janitorial supply houses or from industrial suppliers. Small sizes are seldom available from these sources, and often the products are sold in concentrations that may be diluted with several parts of water to bring them down to commercial or non-institutional strength. Such concentrations mean savings in packaging, transportation, and warehousing costs that may be passed on to the consumer.

Before making "bulk" purchases of cleaning and laundry supplies (or any other merchandise, for that matter), the consumer should be sure he is getting the right product for the job he wants it to do, and that it will not cause any allergic reaction or other health problems.

## TOILETRIES AND HEALTH NEEDS

As is the case with cleaning and laundry products, many health needs and toiletries can be purchased more economically from discount and super-drugstores than from department stores and "conventional" drugstores. And, again, if these are brand name products, it is only sensible to buy where the price is lowest. On the other hand, the discount and super-drugstores, particularly if they are members of chains, will probably feature their "own store brand" in many of the items carried.

Usually, but not always, the price of such "store brand" merchandise is lower than that of so-called "name brand" items. However, it must be remembered that price is not the only consideration in getting value for money spent.

Quality and performance must also be proved. This means that a certain amount of product testing by the consumer may be desirable, but it hardly seems necessary to point out the extravagance of constantly trying out new products without first using up supplies already on hand.

With such items as toothpaste, mouthwash, creams and lotions, shampoos, and other grooming aids, the usual "sales pitch" is that it is possible to make considerable savings by purchasing the "large economy size." But the real bargain hunter will not rely on someone else's say so; he will compare weights as well as prices to be certain that he really is getting more for his money when he buys the larger size package. He will remember, too, that even a small package of any product that is not used after it is purchased is no bargain at any price.

As with the purchase of food and other consumer goods, one of the surest ways of saving money on toiletries and health needs is to plan ahead and anticipate requirements in advance of the time they are actually needed. Such practice will not only allow for taking advantage of store "specials," but will also eliminate many of those costly, unplanned trips to the store.

## TOYS AND RECREATION EQUIPMENT

A shortened work week and increased automation at home as well as in industry has made the pursuit of leisure-time activities an almost full-time job for many Americans. Grown-ups as well as children have more time for play than ever before, and they are spending more money than ever for play equipment, musical supplies and equipment, and other items for leisure time enjoyment.

To begin with, watch for seasonal sales. Buy at the end of the season for the coming year. Leftover Christmas toys and games often may be purchased on December 26 for half price or less. Many of these items make excellent birthday gifts or may be saved for the following Christmas. (Incidentally, Christmas cards are another item that may be purchased at tremendous savings *after* Christmas and stored for a year.)

When shopping for toys and games, look for durability; many are shoddy and the quality is far out of line with respect to price. Keep in mind that, as a rule, one well-built toy is more economical in the long run than are half a dozen cheap or poorly made ones.

Toy-making is big business, and except for a relatively small number of "old standbys," toys come and go with amazing rapidity. Wait for the current craze to die down a bit before rushing to purchase the latest new toys, games, or other recreation equipment. Experience has shown that the price of a "hot" new item is apt to drop 25 to 50 percent within a few weeks or months of its introduction. Where you buy toys and games is important. Invariably, those items sold in grocery stores are higher priced than the same items sold in variety or discount stores.

Delaying purchase of phonograph records or stereophonic tapes until the tide of popularity has begun to subside can often mean big dollar savings. Likewise, savings are possible by purchase of these items in discount or variety stores or supermarkets instead of in exclusive music shops.

## SUMMARY OF MONEY-SAVING SUGGESTIONS

Except for the relatively few to whom "money is no object," those who have studied the preceding pages of this chapter should be impressed with the necessity for carefully planning their purchases of home furnishings and other household items. Numerous helpful ideas for stretching the consumer's dollar as he deals with vendors of furniture, appliances, carpets, draperies and linens, dishes and cookware, toiletries and health needs, cleaning and laundry supplies, and miscellaneous items have been detailed. In concise outline form below are summarized a number of these tested money-saving suggestions:

1. Make your Number One Rule with respect to purchasing household furnishings: "Study and plan before you shop; shop before you buy."

2. Start early (before marriage and while you are still living at home, if possible) to accumulate a "nest egg" of good furniture pieces.

3. Consider getting along with a few borrowed or second-hand furniture items as the "firsts" in your new home or apartment, until you can make careful, unhurried selections that will assure you of getting the right pieces at the right prices.

4. Buy from trusted salesmen in reputable stores. If you are not certain, check their rating with the local Better Business Bureau.

5. Watch for "legitimate" furniture sales, and "bargain" with the dealers.

6. Learn to identify quality materials and workmanship. Find out the special properties and characteristics of various furniture, rug and drapery materials, and the care required by each.

7. Shop the periodic "white sales" for household linens.

8. Find out all you can about appliance performance tests and ratings before you buy. Find out if there are guarantees and what *you* must do to ensure protection under the guarantee or warranty.

9. Beware of buying from discount houses until you know exactly what they carry and how reliably they back the products they sell.

10. Choose the furniture, appliances, laundry supplies, linens, etc. that you buy on the basis of how well they will do the specific job for which they are intended.

11. Buy "brand name" items where you can get the best possible price. On other items, be sure you are purchasing from a reputable dealer.

**FEEDBACK 10**

**A.** At your choice of furniture stores, compare construction of a couch retailing at about $100 with couches costing $200 and $300.

- Which has the best frame construction? The most durable fabric or covering material? The best detail?
- Recalling the furniture you have seen in use, which of the three couches do you think will last longest?
- Which couch has the most up-to-the-minute styling? Which style do you estimate you will like the appearance of for the longest time?

**B.** Based on your experience or your evaluation of various advertising messages, make a preliminary choice of a major appliance (washer, dryer, refrigerator, or air conditioner, for example).

- At the library, look up your choice in the most recent issue of *Consumer Reports* magazine. How does your choice compare with the other brands rated there?
- Compare warranties and guarantees for various brands of appliances. Remember that only what is guaranteed in writing is, in fact, guaranteed.
- Which appliance rates highest for durability? A single service call on an inferior appliance can wipe out the seeming difference in price between it and a more expensive brand.

**C.** When you've determined your selection of the best appliance, seek out the best dealer in your area.

- Which of the dealers offering your selection has his own service department?
- Which dealer offers the lowest installment cost?
- Remember that house brands are often manufactured by firms whose appliances are competing with those house brands. For equivalent value, is there a price differential between the house brands and brand name appliance?

**D.** Prepare a shopping list of toiletry and home cleaning products. Rule columns for comparing prices at a large department store, a grocery store, a super-drugstore.

- Are the brands you prefer available in each store?
- If so, which store features the best prices for each item?
- Which store has the best total cost for the items on your shopping list?

**DISCUSSION QUESTIONS**

1. How can one decide what kind of furniture he wants to furnish his home? Should style and appearance take precedence over quality and durability? Explain.

2. What type of carpeting would be best suited for a living room? Hallway? Kitchen? Bedroom? Explain.

3. How can one be certain that he is getting the best in furniture? In carpeting?

4. What types of equipment and appliances are essential to the maintenance of a house? Why?

5. If appliances are previous years' models, should they be purchased? Why? Should they be purchased if the newer models are considerably more expensive? Explain.

6. Why are people reluctant to move into homes that are already furnished with equipment and appliances?

7. Why have door-to-door salesmen been successful in their selling? To whom is their merchandising aimed? Explain.

8. Are all laundry soaps primarily alike? Explain. What is the difference between soaps and detergents?

9. Why is "store brand" merchandise usually lower priced than "name brand" items? Are there any major differences between the two? Explain. Why are "name brands" usually more popular?

10. Why is after-Christmas shopping more economical? Why does the price of a "hot" new item usually drop 25 to 50 percent within a few weeks or months of its introduction?

## CASE PROBLEM

Steve and Martha lived in student housing while Steve finished his schooling at the University. They found their apartment to be very small; but it was completely furnished (major kitchen appliances, living room and bedroom furniture, lamps, etc.), and they were happy they could use their money for things other than furnishings.

Steve got a job offer immediately after graduation, which transferred them to the East Coast. They were surprised to find that furnished apartments were extremely expensive there—in fact, much too expensive for the money Steve would be making. They had no home furnishings but realized an unfurnished apartment was all they could afford for now.

a) What could Steve and Martha have done while in school to prevent their present situation?

b) Should they look for an apartment that is at least furnished with a refrigerator and stove? Why?

c) What suggestions would you make to Steve and Martha concerning furniture buying? Where should they go to look for good buys? What about carpets and drapes?

d) Should they consider buying a clothes washer and dryer? Why?

e) How should they plan their purchases if they expect to buy a house in a few years?

## SUGGESTED READINGS

Austin, Ruth Erma, and Jeannette O. Parvis. *Furnishing Your Home.* Boston: Houghton Mifflin, 1961. 282 pp.

Bennett, H. *More For Your Money.* New York: Chemical Publishing Co., 1970. 220 pp.

Calvert, David P., and Marilyn O. Moody. "Help Yourself." Wichita, Kansas: Office of the County Attorney, Consumer Protection Division, 1971. 32 pp.

Margolius, Sidney. *The Responsible Consumer.* New York: Public Affairs, 1970. 20 pp.

Mather, Lays L., Ed. *Economics of Consumer Protection.* Danville, Illinois: The Interstate Printers and Publishers, 1971. 148 pp.

Stern, Louis L. "Consumer Protection via Self Regulation." *Journal of Marketing.* Chicago. Vol. 35, July 1971. pp. 47–53.

"Washing Machines: Selection and Use." Washington, D.C.: USDA, 1964. 22 pp.

"When You Buy Furniture." Knoxville: University of Tennessee, 1962. 5 pp.

# CHAPTER 11

# SAVING MONEY ON AN AUTOMOBILE

Most people spend too much money on automobiles. Cars are necessary for transportation and enjoyable hours of recreation, but newness and glamour usually cost more than they are worth. Your automobile may be more of a strain on your monthly budget than it need be. Do not allow your car payments to rob you of money that otherwise could go toward savings, special goals, and even for other more rewarding kinds of recreation. Instead, learn how to make substantial savings by wise buying and financing of either a used or a new car.

## WHEN TO TRADE—WHAT KIND OF CAR?

Almost everybody has his own ideas as to how long he should keep an automobile before trading for a newer model. The answer, of course, largely depends on the individual and the use which he makes of his car. A salesman who drives 100,000 or more miles annually may find it necessary to trade every year. Another person may not drive that far in ten years. To some people, a car is a hobby and a major part of their recreation. For some it is a status symbol that seems more important than home, clothing, or anything else. To others, the automobile is merely a necessity, a means of getting to and from work. A frank evaluation of your own goals, needs, and personality should set the framework for your decision of *when* to buy and *what* to buy.

## UNDERSTANDING DEPRECIATION

When you decide to purchase a car, you must be concerned with the cost: how much it will cost when you buy it; how much it will be worth when you sell it; how much impact inflation will have on your subsequent replacement purchase.

Depreciation in its simplest form is merely the difference between the purchase and the selling price. However, a broader and more meaningful definition of depreciation would also take into consideration the inflated price of the replacement vehicle at the time the old car is sold. Therefore, true or realized depreciation (or ownership cost) of an auto is best shown by looking at the cash difference required at the time a trade is made.

Table 11–1 shows how a new car depreciates when it becomes a used car. In 1971, a new Ford Torino cost $3,372. If you had previously bought a new Ford Torino in 1968, its value would have dropped to approximately $1,250 by 1971. You would have had to make up about $2,122 to trade the 1968 for the 1971. The difference would have been your realized depreciation.

Compare the yearly average depreciation figures on each car in Table 11–1. As you can readily see, the value of a new car drops tragically the first year, nearly 40 percent. You will also note from the chart that the yearly average rate of depreciation becomes smaller for each of the years shown. Consider the VW as an example. The first year's depreciation would be about $624. For two years, the average yearly depreciation drops to $425; and for three years it averages only $383. This is a typical pattern for most cars—large or small.

Depreciation is not the only cost in owning a car. Different cars average different miles per gallon of gasoline; have different insurance, finance, and upkeep costs. Table 11–2 provides an eye-opening roundup of estimated annual costs of owning and operating several different kinds of cars. Actual costs, of course, will vary from one vicinity to another depending on actual insurance rates, financing arrangements, etc. Different drivers will get considerably different performance from the same vehicle—gas mileage, maintenance, and tire expenses. Yet, despite all the possible variations, a realistic picture of automobile ownership and operation costs can be seen. At the low end is the VW, the Bug, at about $1,300; at the prestigious other extreme, the luxury-class Lincoln shows an annual cost of about $3,300. The final choice of a car, however, depends on much more than a consideration of cost. Safety, comfort, styling, and handling characteristics must all be properly weighed.

## CARS FOR COLLEGE STUDENTS

Owning and operating any car, new or used, can cost a great deal of money. For some college students, owning a car may be such a drain on their finances that they are forced to leave school and assume a full-time job. Whether a student really needs a car depends to a great extent on where he lives and where he goes to school. Some cities have excellent public commuter transportation; others have virtually none. A sense of values as well as practical considerations are involved. If owning and caring for a car interferes with your education, the temporary fun of the car may not be worth long-term, discouraging setbacks in working toward your more important life's goals. Put first things first. Your college education

**Table 11-1** Comparisons of yearly automobile depreciation costs for selected American and foreign cars based on estimates of one-, two-, and three-year old trade-in values for similar makes and models*

| | 1971 new-car prices, options as indicated, $90 delivery charge, $265 of extras, 6% discount, and 4% sales tax | Three-year old trade (1968) | | Two-year old trade (1969) | | One-year old trade (1970) |
|---|---|---|---|---|---|---|
| | | Estimated cash difference required | Yearly depreciation | Estimated cash difference required | Yearly depreciation | Cash difference and yearly depreciation |
| Ford Torino, V-8, 4DS, AT, PS | $3,372 | $2,122 | $707 | $1,847 | $923 | $1,272 |
| Chevrolet Biscayne, V-8, 4DS, AT, PS | $3,677 | $2,652 | $884 | $2,227 | $1,114 | $1,752 |
| Plymouth Fury I, V-8, 4DS, AT, PS | $3,526 | $2,451 | $817 | $1,976 | $988 | $1,526 |
| Mercury Monterey, V-8, 4DS, AT, PS | $4,021 | $2,821 | $940 | $2,421 | $1,210 | $1,821 |
| Pontiac Catalina 252, V-8, 4DS, AT, PS | $3,971 | $2,696 | $899 | $2,271 | $1,135 | $1,721 |
| Chevrolet Nova-6, 4DS, AT | $2,860 | $1,860 | $620 | $1,360 | $680 | $1,085 |
| Maverick 6 cyl., 4DS, AT (Falcon) | $2,711 | $1,661 | $554 | $1,411 | $706 | $1,086 |
| Valiant 6 cyl., 4DS, AT | $2,871 | $1,846 | $615 | $1,546 | $773 | $1,196 |
| Cadillac DeVille, 4DS, AT, PB, PS, Air, 6-way Seat | $7,332 | $4,307 | $1,436 | $3,257 | $1,629 | $2,282 |
| Lincoln Continental, 4DS, AT, PB, PS, Air, 6-way Seat | $7,410 | $4,760 | $1,586 | $3,835 | $1,918 | $2,810 |
| Volkswagen, 2DS, AT | $2,224 | $1,149 | $383 | $849 | $425 | $624 |
| Renault, 4DS, AT | $2,256 | $1,431 | $477 | $1,181 | $591 | $906 |

* Based on low-book or wholesale values for used cars and factory advertised delivered prices for 1971 cars as listed in *NADA Official Used Car Guide*, Pacific Southwest Edition, December 1970.

4DS = 4-door sedan     AT = Automatic Transmission     PB = Power Brakes
2DS = 2-door sedan     PS = Power Steering     Air = Air Conditioned

**Table 11–2** Estimated total annual costs of owning and operating selected automobiles

| Make | Gas[a] | Maintenance, tires, and oil[b] | Depreciation[c] | Finance charges[d] | License, registration fees[e] | Insurance[f] (19 to 21 years old) | Average yearly total |
|---|---|---|---|---|---|---|---|
| Chevrolet Biscayne, 4DS, AT, PS | $370 | $139 | $884 | $162 | $39 | $569 | $2,163 |
| Lincoln, 4DS, AT, PS, PB, Air | $444 | $149 | $1,586 | $326 | $39 | $752 | $3,296 |
| Pontiac Catalina 4DS, AT, PS | $404 | $139 | $899 | $175 | $39 | $569 | $2,225 |
| Volkswagen 2DS, AT | $158 | $110 | $383 | $98 | $39 | $521 | $1,309 |

[a] Based on author's estimates and owners' reports: assumes 80% city driving; 20% open-road driving; Chevrolet 12 MPG, Lincoln 10 MPG, Pontiac 11 MPG, and VW 25 MPG. Calculations are for premium gasoline @ 0.37/gallon for all vehicles except for VW figures which are for regular gasoline @ 0.33/gallon.

[b] Calculations based on author's estimates: Chevrolet and Pontiac at 1.16¢/mile; Lincoln at 1.24¢/mile; VW at 0.92¢/mile.

[c] Based on figures listed in *NADA Official Used Car Guide*, Pacific Southwest Edition, December 1970. Shows average of approximate trade-in difference for 3-year-old trade on similar model. from Table 11–1.

[d] Based on 80% loan of 1971 prices as listed in Table 11–1; average yearly cost of 36-month installment contract at 10 percent interest.

[e] Estimate, does not include property taxes.

[f] Insurance costs include comprehensive, $100 deductible collision, $100/$300/$25,000 property damage and liability coverage; owner operators in the 19–21 age category. Costs will vary according to area and driver classification.

is almost certain to increase your earning power and should help pay for many new cars in your working lifetime.

Few students (and many other people as well) can afford to buy and operate a *new* car. If you must have an auto and have to pay for it yourself, be satisfied for the time being with a used one.

### SAVINGS ON A USED CAR

Because of the very steep depreciation suffered in the first few years of owning a new car, considerable savings are possible by carefully selecting and buying a used auto. To get some idea of the savings possible, let us again refer to Table 11–1. You will recall that this chart shows the effect of both depreciation and inflation by indicating cash differences required in trading old autos for new models. Had you purchased a Chevrolet Biscayne in 1968, traded it for a new model in 1971, you would have had to pay a cash difference of $2,652. The inflated new-car price and depreciation resulted in a yearly ownership cost of about $884. However, had you purchased the same model four years old (at about $1,200) and subsequently traded it after three years (then worth about $375), your annual ownership cost would have sunk to only about $228. The total three-year ownership-cost saving of the used rather than the new car would have run about $1,967. Net or actual savings would naturally be less, however, because of higher upkeep costs. But you would still be far ahead financially.

You can easily see, therefore, why a good used car is a sensible choice for the student or the "young married." For that matter, anyone who uses a car only moderately can economize by buying one that is four or five years old. Or perhaps you can well afford a new car for the main family auto and also want the added convenience of a second car for the family—a good used car can be just the thing for the second car.

**"Irma, you're just supposed to kick the tires!"**

Reprinted with permission of *The Wall Street Journal* (Cartoon Features Syndicate).

**How to Select a Used Car.**  As soon as you begin looking at used car lots or answering ads in the daily paper, you find that it is not an easy task to determine the mechanical condition of the prospective car.  The following pointers will help.

1. *Mileage.*  Mileage is a good (but not infallible) criterion on which to base wear—that is, if the true mileage can be determined.  As a practical matter, however, buyers are seldom able to discern whether or not the mileage on the car is "actual."  The mileage indicator on most automobiles can be very easily reset, although some states now have laws against this procedure.  Usually, all one needs to do to make the change is to visit a speedometer shop and instruct the personnel to adjust the dials.  Nonetheless, there are a few checks one can make to catch a fraudulent seller.

First, always look at the oil change stickers on the side of the door.  Sometimes sellers will forget to remove stickers that show the true mileage.

Second, look over any items in the glove compartment.  You may uncover inspection tickets, tire or parts guarantees which would also show the correct mileage of the auto.

Third, look at the condition of the carpeting on the driver's side of the car, and the rubber covers on the brake, clutch, and accelerator pedals.  If heavily worn, these may be clues to the real mileage on the vehicle.

2. *Usage.*  Perhaps as reliable as mileage as an indication of the car's condition is an investigation of the owner's occupation and his driving habits.  You would certainly want to know, for example, if the owner were a rancher who had to drive his automobile hundreds of miles every day over rough unimproved roads.  Under those circumstances, the wear and tear on the vehicle could be substantial.  Likewise, you would want to know whether or not the car were ever used for freeway or out-of-city driving.  Contrary to what some people think, an automobile which has been driven very little, such as the auto owned by the proverbial "little old lady," may not be as good a buy as a vehicle which has been used for freeway and long-distance driving.  Engines of vehicles which have also been used only in start-and-stop city traffic tend to build up damaging sludge.  Also, autos that stand unused for long periods can develop serious oil

and fluid leaks. Autos have hundreds of seals around and between connecting parts, and daily use keeps these seals lubricated and prevents shrinkage.

   3. *Leaks.* It is always a good idea to inspect an automobile for oil and fluid leaks. There are a number of places which are particularly prone to leakage: transmission, rear axle, differential, power steering, brakes, and, of course, the radiator and cooling system. After test driving the car, park it on a clean patch of cement. Let it sit for a few minutes; then inspect for leaks.

   If it is not possible to locate the source of an oil leak, it may be that you can identify the origin by examining the type of oil on the pavement. If the oil is of a very light consistency, usually having a somewhat orange-red tint, it is probably from the transmission or power steering. If the fluid is very light in consistency, with a rather strong odor, and usually clear in color or slightly brown, the fluid is probably leaking from the braking system. On the other hand, if the oil leakage on the pavement is very dark in color and sticky, it is almost certain that this is regular motor oil leaking from the crank case or differential of the car. Water leaks can usually be detected by examining the radiator for rusted spots.

   While one would not eliminate the purchase of a vehicle just because of an oil or fluid leak, the defect ought to be considered when agreeing on a purchase price. For example, if the transmission is leaking on a medium-sized vehicle, one can expect a charge of $50 to $60 for replacement of the seal. Power steering leaks ordinarily run $30 to $35 for replacement.

   4. *Brakes.* Another important safety check of a prospective automobile is the braking system. The brakes can be repaired easily, but you ought to know what you are getting into in the way of repair costs. There are two general malfunctions which occur in the braking system. The first relates to the brake drums and shoes. Braking on most American cars is accomplished by applying pressure

to the brake shoes, creating enough friction on the round brake drum to cause the wheels to stop turning. Consequently, the friction causes the shoes to wear out in approximately 20,000 to 30,000 miles. Replacement costs typically run from $15 to $45 depending on the type of automobile.

Normal wear on the braking system eventually results in deterioration and leakage from the pistons which operate the brake shoes. It is a very good idea to get down on your hands and knees and take a look at the inner sides of the wheels and tires to check for any stains or fluid. Any fluid dripping over the tire is almost a sure indication that a complete brake overhaul job is required. This involves replacement of the pistons (commonly referred to by mechanics as brake "kits").

You should always make a brake pedal test of the vehicle. If the brake pedal sinks slowly to the floor as one depresses it firmly, the master cylinder is leaking. This condition requires immediate attention for safe operation. A complete brake overhaul can run as much as $80. On the other hand, if the pedal goes very near to the floor immediately as it is depressed but does not sink further, this is an indication that the brakes need adjustment or additional brake fluid. This is a relatively inexpensive proposition costing perhaps as little as $2.

5. *Test-Driving.* In test-driving the vehicle, make special note of its steering performance. Does the vehicle maintain its stability on the road at moderate speed? Is there a noticeable vibration coming through the steering column? If the car seems to pull to one side or the other or there is a noticeable vibration, the front end may be out of alignment. This can be expensive and result in drastic tire wear, which by the way, is usually *not* covered by the used-car dealer's warranty. Therefore, alignment should be one of the factors ascertained before purchasing the vehicle. Frequently, the dealer can be talked into correcting it. Vibration may also be caused by out-of-balance tires. Balancing is only a minor item and relatively inexpensive. There is always the possibility, too, that there are more serious problems in the steering linkage system. If in doubt, let a mechanic make a diagnosis for you.

Is the body in poor condition? Does it have squeaks and rattles? These are perhaps some of your best clues that the car has been badly misused.

The transmission can be checked by test driving the car and listening to its operation. If there is jerky shifting from one gear to another, or continual or erratic noise, one would suspect serious transmission difficulties. Rebuilding or overhauling the transmission can run anywhere from $175 to $450, depending on the car.

6. *Engine Performance.* What about checking the performance of the engine in a used car? Several factors here will give a "fair" determination of the engine's condition. If you are seriously thinking about buying the car, take it to a good service station and ask the attendant or mechanic to make a simple pressure test on each of the cylinders. The mechanic should have a chart which indicates what the correct operating pressure of each cylinder should be. If the

test indicates adequate pressure, you can be fairly sure that the engine is in reasonably good operating condition.  If the automobile engine is badly worn, however, the piston rings will allow excessive amounts of oil to enter the burning chamber; and, consequently, the automobile will burn large amounts of oil.  As this condition progresses, replacement of the piston rings is necessitated.  This is a costly proposition and indicates that a general motor overhaul is necessary. Such an overhaul can run from $90 to $300.

There is one other test that should be made.  Take a drive down a rather long hill and let the engine idle as you make the descent, braking to a stop at the bottom.  Then, start out rapidly, yet safely, looking behind the automobile to note any excessive amounts of exhaust coming from the car.  Black smoke being emitted from the exhaust (noticeable in the air as you drive away), indicates that the automobile is poorly tuned and is not operating properly and is burning too much fuel.  However, heavy gray smoke is a sign that the engine is consuming too much oil and needs an overhaul.

As a final engine check, lift the hood of the car while the engine is running and carefully listen for any unusual engine noises.  Normally, any car's power plant will make some metallic clicking sounds.  However, if these are erratic or too pronounced, you probably can expect that the auto's engine is in need of repair.

7. *Body*.  A final check of the automobile body ought to be made for evidence of major re-painting.  If the automobile has been involved in a severe accident, major body work can sometimes be detected by examining the car surface in direct sunlight.  Usually, there are subtle differences, if not pronounced ones, between the re-finished and original surfaces.  Doors may also reveal wreckage—poor fit, looseness, rattles, etc.  If you suspect that the automobile has been involved in a major accident, the owner should be quizzed carefully regarding this point.  If such is the case, it may spell nothing but continuous service difficulties for any make of car.

8. *Tires*.  A last check should be made of the tires of the vehicle to determine if they are wearing evenly.  Sometimes, it is impossible to keep the wheels aligned properly after a major accident, and peculiar tire wear would be a symptom of such a problem.

9. *Auto Diagnostic Clinics.* Most metropolitan areas now have electronic auto clinics with sophisticated computer-like testing equipment for diagnosing the mechanical condition of the automobiles. Typically, the clinics take a car through a battery of 100 to 150 individual checks and tests to spot malfunctions in any operating portion of the car's anatomy. The original specifications established by the manufacturer are the standards against which the car's ignition, carburetion, steering, transmission, etc. are compared. These testing centers vary in test equipment and personnel, but generally are quite reliable. Typical clinic activity is illustrated in Fig. 11–1. Such centers usually do not offer repair services themselves, but merely perform diagnostic tests. Under these circumstances, the owner or prospective purchaser of the car is assured that the evaluation he receives is objective because the lab has no vested interest in the repair work.

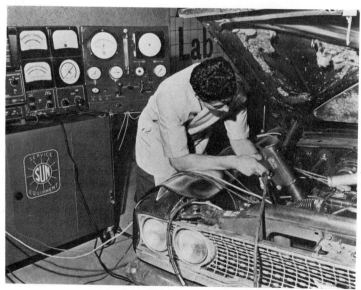

**Fig. 11–1** Auto diagnostic laboratory. Most large metropolitan areas now have labs with highly sophisticated test equipment capable of diagnosing the mechanical condition of autos. Such testing is highly recommended before purchasing a used car. Courtesy of Auto Lab, Inc.

The results of the tests, which usually take about an hour, are discussed in detail with the customer. The diagnostic center's personnel will usually prepare an accurate cost estimate of the needed repairs. Diagnostic fees range from $10 to $20. It certainly seems sensible to use such a test facility for checking out any automobile that you are seriously considering buying. Even if you end up testing three or four cars before you find the one that is in good condition, you will usually save a good deal more in the long run than you spend on auto lab fees. If the test reveals some major difficulty, you may be able to get the used car dealer to repair it; or if the seller is an individual, perhaps the selling price can be adjusted to take care of the repairs.

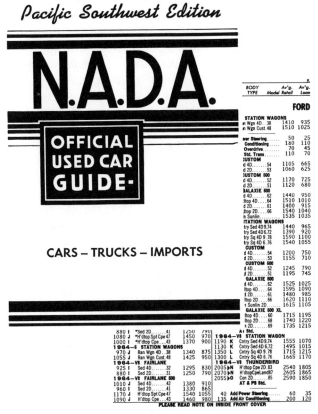

**Fig. 11–2**  The NADA "Used Car Guide" is an authoritative source of current information regarding used car prices. Average wholesale (low-book), average retail (high-book), and average loan values are clearly identified.  Courtesy of National Automobile Dealers Association.  The "Used Car Guide" is available by subscription from the association at 2000 K Street, N.W., Washington, D.C. 20006.

10. *Used Car Prices.*  Before you make any final deals on a used car, you should check its value in the "Official Used Car Guide" published by the National Automobile Dealers Association. The monthly guide's data are based upon reports of actual transactions by dealers and wholesale auctions throughout the various geographical areas of the country, and is available through the auto loan department of any bank or credit union. The automobiles are listed alphabetically and then chronologically in the guide. You will note from Fig. 11–2 that the first column of each page lists the average wholesale price in dollars.

At the right of the body description is the average retail price followed by the average value of the loans granted on that particular model.

If you buy a used car from another individual, rather than a dealer, you should not pay full retail price. The private seller cannot offer any guarantee or warranty (other than that which may still be in effect from the auto manufacturer—which, incidentally, must be transferred through a local dealer) as might a dealer. A fair price depends ultimately on the auto's condition and upon the general used car market at the time of your purchase.

### PURCHASING A NEW CAR

The purchase of a new automobile is a major financial undertaking. As such, it deserves very special and detailed attention in order to get the very best possible deal. A 10 percent saving, or for that matter a 4 to 5 percent saving, is significant. It is wise to take a tip in tactics from the fleet-buyer—the purchaser who buys a large number of vehicles each year for his company—to see how he proceeds in buying an automobile. In every case, you will find that the fleet-buyer requires a dealer to submit a written bid for automobiles. While most dealers refuse to follow this procedure with an individual because of the dealer's fear that he may reveal prices to the competition, an individual can certainly go from dealer to dealer and get a fixed, definite cash price quote from each of the dealerships. New car dealers commonly sell their autos at 5 to 15 percent below factory listed prices.

"Oh gosh, yes! -- We sell them faster
than we can call them back!"

Reprinted with permission of *The Wall Street Journal* (Cartoon Features Syndicate).

Before getting their quotations, decide upon a definite make and model of automobile and list all the extras that are to be included—such optional features are power steering, power brakes, power windows and seats, whitewall tires, premium tires, disc braking system, custom trim, radio, heater, etc.  Only after a bid has been received from several agencies is one in a position to make reasonable and objective comparisons.  If one is going to trade in a car, follow the same procedure by getting a fixed quote from each dealer of the "cash difference" required to complete the purchase of a new vehicle.  But be very certain to talk about the same model of automobile with comparable equipment; otherwise, price comparisons are meaningless.

**A word about sticker prices.**   Comparison shopping is a time-honored technique, but you have to know what you're comparing.  One of the meaningful bases for comparison is the manufacturer's suggested retail value, called the "sticker price."

New cars come to the dealer with sticker prices, but the fact is, they are seldom sold for that amount.  As a buyer, you want to consider how much you can get discounted from the sticker.  As a seller, the dealer wants to consider how much he can add on to the wholesale cost he has paid—a cost which averages around 20 percent less than the sticker price.

This 20 percent amounts to $500 to $1,000, depending on the car you choose.  As you can see, there is a lot of leeway for price negotiation, and the result is that most new cars sell for something between wholesale and full-sticker value.  Factors in the negotiation could include trade-in value of your old car, payment arrangements, etc.

**Wholesale prices.**   Fortunately, actual dealer costs on new autos and optional equipment can now be easily obtained (see Fig. 11–3).  Most newsstands carry these publications which give reliable comprehensive listings of wholesale costs as well as regional delivery charges:

*American Car Prices Magazine*, 7 Editions Yearly
*Edmund's New Car Prices*, 5 Editions Yearly

Knowing the dealer's costs puts you in a much better bargaining position.  You will be less likely to expect unrealistic discounts and less likely to accept fattened bids from glib salesmen.

**Which model?**   It is a very good idea not to take the first production of new cars of a new year's model.  Inevitably, there are dozens of minor changes which the factory makes in the first month or so of production to iron out the bugs.  By waiting for only 30 to 60 days, you will be fairly well assured that most of these engineering and production imperfections will have been corrected.

Although dealers may spend a good deal of money advertising spectacular prices and savings on the previous year's close-outs, seldom would they make good new-car bargains.  Recall if you will the new math of depreciation which we covered earlier in this chapter:  Even should the new-car dealer sell the close-out model to you at his cost (about 20 percent under sticker price), that last year's

# PONTIAC

| 1971 PONTIAC | FED. TAX INCL. | DEALERS COST* | WINDOW STICKER RETAIL* |
|---|---|---|---|
| out 582 . . . . . . . . . . . . . . . . . . . . . . | 25.00 | | 31.60 |
| —Models with 582 . . . . . . . . . . . . . . . . | 8.33 | | 10.53 |
| 714- Rally gauge cluster, clock & tachometer—All models except 22887 . . . . . . . . . . . . . . | 74.99 | | 94.79 |
| 718- Rally gauge cluster & clock—All models except 22887 . . . . . . . . . . . . . . . . . | 37.49 | | 47.39 |
| 722- Electric clock—All models except 22887 . | 12.50 | | 15.80 |
| 731- Custom trim group (Includes fitted trunk mat, rear quarter ash trays, body color door handle inserts, deluxe front bucket seats, roof panel insulation & custom door & quarter interior trim)— All models except 22487 . . . . . . . . . . . . | 61.99 | | 78.99 |
| 734- Bumper guards, rear . . . . . . . . . . . . | 12.50 | | 15.80 |
| TGR- WSW fiberglass F78x15 tires—22387,22487 | 34.16 | | 43.18 |
| THR- WSW fiberglass E78x14 tires—22387,22487 | 20.83 | | 26.33 |
| TMF- BSW fiberglass F70x14 tires—22487 only | 28.33 | | 35.81 |
| —22387 only . . . . . . . . . . . . . . . . . | 28.33 | | 35.81 |
| TML- White letter fiberglass F70x14 tires—22687 | 30.83 | | 38.97 |
| —22387 or 22487 only . . . . . . . . . . . . . | 59.16 | | 74.78 |
| TNL- White letter fiberglass F60x15 tires—22687 | 57.49 | | 72.67 |

## 1971 PONTIAC LEMANS

| | FED. TAX INCL. | DEALERS COST* | WINDOW STICKER RETAIL* |
|---|---|---|---|
| **T-37 Models** | | | |
| 23327- Coupe . . . . . . . . . . . | 153.00 | 2224.17 | 2740.0 |
| 23337- Hardtop Coupe . . . . . . . | 156.00 | 2273.34 | 2800.00 |
| 23369- 4 Door Sedan . . . . . . . | 155.00 | 2262.62 | 2787.00 |
| **LeMans Models** | | | |
| 23527- Coupe . . . . . . . . . . . | 160.00 | 2323.51 | 2861.00 |
| 23536- 2 Seat Wagon . . . . . . . | 185.00 | 2704.91 | 3326.00 |
| 23537- Hardtop Coupe . . . . . . . | 163.00 | 2372.68 | 2921.00 |
| 23539- 4 Door Hardtop . . . . . | 170.00 | 2476.88 | 3048.00 |
| 23546- 3 Seat Wagon . . . . . . . | 191.00 | 2792.58 | 3439.00 |
| 23569- 4 Door Sedan . . . . . . . | 162.00 | 2361.96 | 2908.00 |
| **LeMans Sport Models** | | | |
| 23737- Hardtop Coupe . . . . . . . | 172.00 | 2518.58 | 3099.00 |
| 23739- 4 Door Hardtop . . . . . | 179.00 | 2625.20 | 3229.00 |
| 23767- Convertible . . . . . . . . | 185.00 | 2710.58 | 3333.00 |
| **GTO Models** | | | |
| 24237- Hardtop Coupe . . . . . . . | 189.00 | 2776.14 | 3413.00 |
| 24267- Convertible . . . . . . . . | 201.00 | 2964.72 | 3643.00 |

these are approximate freight rates
**FREIGHT MUST BE ADDED TO COST AND RETAIL COLUMNS**

| | | | |
|---|---|---|---|
| Calif, Oregon, Wash | 200.00 | Arizona, Utah, Nevada | 200.00 |
| Denver, Colorado | 160.00 | Miami, Florida | 158.00 |
| Atlanta, Georgia | 120.00 | Chicago, Illinois | 56.00 |
| New Orleans, La | 136.00 | Boston, Mass | 96.00 |
| St. Louis, Missouri | 88.00 | New York, New Jersey | 96.00 |
| Pittsburgh, Pa | 66.00 | Charleston, S.C. | 130.00 |
| Dallas, Texas | 146.00 | Houston, Texas | 148.00 |
| Norfolk, Virginia | 102.00 | Washington D.C. | 94.00 |

**Fig. 11–3** Shown above is a portion of a page from *American Car Prices*. Consulting such a guide lets you know your dealer's exact cost on a new auto so you can be in a better bargaining position with him when shopping for a new car. Courtesy of *American Car Prices* Magazine, 2777 Foothill Blvd., La Crescenta, California 91214.

model (even though still new from the standpoint of use) immediately loses almost 40 percent of its sticker value through depreciation when you drive it away from the dealer.

In general, there are only two situations in which it would make sense to buy a year-end model: (1) when the true discount is greater than the first year's depreciation, or (2) if you knew that you would keep the car for several years and the true discount was greater than the *yearly average depreciation* for that period of time.

**New-car warranties.**   A new-car warranty is a manufacturer's promise to stand behind the quality of the automobile.   In the early 1960's the big auto producers began making long-term vows against manufacturing defects.   Originally, warranties were extended from 90 days or 4,000 miles to 12 months or 12,000 (whichever came first).   Later, in attempts to out-do each other, manufacturers pushed the coverage to two years or 24,000 miles.   Additionally, the drive-trains and a few other specified parts were warranted for five years or 50,000 miles.

Millions of car buyers found, however, that the warranties were better on paper than in practice.   Instead of being a protection to the buyer, many a disillusioned customer found that the warranty was carefully written to protect the manufacturer and his dealer.   Because of the numerous complaints, and some prodding publicly from Ralph Nader, the Federal Trade Commission conducted an in-depth report on Detroit.   The report substantiates what many disgusted auto buyers knew all along:

1. There are serious quality-control problems in the automobile industry.
2. Dealers often lack the equipment, personnel, or know-how to correct manufacturing defects.
3. Manufacturers, through tight-fisted reimbursement policies for warranty work, encourage dealers to give car owners the run around.

The "FTC Staff Report on Automobile Warranties" concludes that the long-term warranties are of unquestioned value and that "scrapping the warranty or reducing its terms are not acceptable options for a sound public policy, which must seek to assure a high degree of safety and convenience in the daily operation of automobiles and must have as a prime objective the reduction of the shocking annual toll in lives, injuries, and property damage resulting from motor vehicle accidents."

Despite all the public attention and the customer wrath, the car buyer today probably has less protection "warranty-wise" than he had in the previous decade. Instead of extending time and mileage coverage, most of Detroit has cut the warranty terms to one year and 12,000 miles.   Unexpired warranty coverage is available to used-car buyers only upon payment of $25 or $50 transfer fee.   A further bit of discouragement for the new-car buyer comes from test results published by the nonprofit Insurance Institute for Highway Safety.   The Institute crash-tested four 1971 model sedans and four 1970 models—Chevrolet Impala, Ford Galaxie, Plymouth Fury and American Ambassador. In single-car, five-mile-per-hour front-end collisions into barriers, the average repair cost for the four sedans was $332 for the 1971 models; only $216 for the 1970 models. Despite the high repair bills, auto manufacturers apparently are not making any all-out effort to make cars less fragile.

## SAFETY INFORMATION NOW AVAILABLE

The Federal Government's Transportation Department has amended Federal Motor Vehicle Safety Regulations on Consumer Information to make it easier for consumers to obtain safety information about new cars. When shopping for a new car, you will be able to obtain and take home the consumer information about new autos that usually has been available only in dealer showrooms. This data will explain a new car's stopping distance, acceleration and passing ability, as well as tire reserve loads. If you don't want to go to a showroom to pick up the information, you may request your dealer to send it to you.

## HOW DO YOU RATE AUTO REPAIR SERVICE?

You buy a new car from the dealer who gives the best deal. When the car needs service or repair, you take it to the dealer's service department. After the work is done and you pay the bill, you learn something about the reliability of the dealer's service. Maybe excellent, maybe good, maybe bad. Maybe you've been had.

Virginia Knauer, Special Assistant to the President for Consumer Affairs, agrees with consumers that auto repair should not be by chance. "Too many consumers have paid for unnecessary repairs, and too many consumers have had repairs made with unsatisfactory results," she said. "Consumers should know the reliability of a dealer before—not after—repairs are made."

She has asked the major auto makers and the National Automobile Dealers Association to back a plan for a public rating system of auto service quality provided by dealers. She said an effective public rating system could increase competition in service and provide rewards for superior service. American Motors Corp., Ford Motor Corp. and NADA have indicated approval of the rating concept; General Motors Corp. and Chrysler Corp. have suggested other methods to improve auto service.

But until such data are available, you'll have to depend on your own survey. Friends, neighbors, relatives, and business associates can often give you valuable information on how your local auto dealers rate on service.

## SELLING YOUR PRESENT CAR

Take a serious look at the feasibility of selling your own used car to another individual rather than trading it in. The new car dealer may quote you an inflated trade-in price for your present car to be deducted from an equally inflated full retail or factory list price of the new car. Or the dealer may simply quote you a "cash difference" deal. Whichever way it may be, the fact remains that the dealer must make his overhead plus a profit in handling both the new and used car. Salesmen's commissions, rent, electricity, heat, air conditioning, advertising, and other costs all run high. For this reason, the dealer will seldom be able to offer you top dollar value for your trade-in.

If you compare the cash price at which new vehicles are sold as opposed to cash-difference prices in transactions involving trades, you will nearly always find that the actual trade-in value of your car allowed by the new-car dealer would be little or no more than the average wholesale or low NADA "book" price. For this reason, you sometimes may be able to realize 5 to 10 percent more on your used car by selling it yourself and then making a separate deal on the new car.

Generally speaking, if your present used car is in excellent condition, requiring little or no repair or fix up, you will be better off at least making a try at selling it yourself. On the other hand, should it be necessary to effect costly repairs such as engine or transmission overhauls or major body work, you could find it advantageous to trade. In the latter case the dealer has a distinct advantage over the individual, since he is able to have the repairs made for 30 to 50 percent less than the consumer would be charged.

Local economic conditions may also affect your decision. If car sales are very slow in your area, you may be wise to trade in the car to the dealer. Also, if you are not inclined to be patient and are unable or unwilling to spend a number of hours in concerted effort trying to sell the vehicle, then it is probably not a good idea to attempt selling it yourself. It frequently takes 30 to 90 days to sell an automobile; and, of course, there is no guarantee that you will be able to sell it at all. Advertisements in the daily newspaper may be necessary, and these can run into a sizeable amount of money, depending on the area.

If you should decide to sell your own car, here are a few tips that will help maximize its selling price:

1. Concentrate on those things that show up in appearance rather than on mechanical factors. For example, if the car has scratches or dents in the body, cracked windows, torn upholstery, dirty or worn-out carpeting, these are items that you would want to correct.

2. Set up a budget for the refurnishing of the car so you will be sure that you are going to come out financially ahead for all your efforts. Normally speaking, one would not want to spend more than $35 to $75.

3. Make sure that the car is kept spotlessly clean and freshly waxed. This one thing more than any other will affect the sale.

4. Advertise on weekends. Most of the calls or inquiries will be made on Saturday, Sunday, and Monday. Therefore, in most areas it would be virtually a waste of money to have ads running throughout the week.

5. It is not a good idea to include the asking price of the vehicle in an ad. Buyers always shop around with the hope of getting an exceptionally fine deal price-wise and tend not to call or check out ads unless the price is extremely low. However, if you can interest them into coming and seeing the vehicle without revealing the price, there is a good chance the buyer may pay what you are asking if the car is in very good shape.

### ADVANTAGES AND DISADVANTAGES OF LEASING AN AUTO

In the last few years there has been a noticeable increase in the number of auto leasing plans offered both to business and to the general public. In fact, they have become so numerous that it is impossible to pick up a newspaper without seeing advertisements pushing the supposed advantages of leasing versus buying the automobile. If one takes the bare prices which are quoted in these advertisements as representing the total costs of the plans, the lease arrangements look very attractive. In actual experience, however, leasing does not offer the dramatic savings that are sometimes claimed by the leasing companies.

There are usually many costs over and above the basic monthly rate. For example, in nearly every instance the person leasing the automobile is required to pay local property taxes and license fees, as well as collision and liability insurance on the vehicle. Additional charges are customarily made for tire wear or tire replacement. When the lease contract is read carefully, one may also find very rigid stipulations on the total mileage which may be driven over the lease period without paying additional charges. For example, permission may be granted to drive 10 or 12 thousand miles per year at the basic contract rate with a graduated scale of additional charges for excess mileage due at the end of the contract period. A cash deposit of $100 to $300 is often required.

*If you do lease . . .* Before signing any lease agreement, make certain what type of lease it is and the term or length of the lease period. It is, perhaps, most common for leasing companies to advertise rates for two- or three-year leases. The rate for a three-year lease would be somewhat lower than for a two-year period because of savings in depreciation. If you require a new car every year, naturally, the lease rate would be considerably higher. In any case, one ought to be absolutely certain of the term of the lease.

The type of lease is perhaps of greatest importance in determining whether or not a lease arrangement is really economic or even satisfactory. For example, many companies now offer "open-ended" leases. This lease typically offers a low monthly rate. In fact, the rate may not be totally representative of the overall cost of the lease for the total lease period. The reason is this: the lease is worded such that the person leasing the car (called the lessee) agrees to pay a fixed monthly sum which is calculated on the assumption that the vehicle will be worth a certain amount at the end of the lease period. It is not uncommon to have the leasing company purposely overstate the anticipated value of the auto at the end of the lease period. The effect of such an over-statement is that the monthly payments may appear more competitive than those of other companies. But at the end of the lease period it may be necessary for the lessee to pay a lump sum to make up the difference between the actual value and the amount which was approximated or perhaps purposely overstated in the original lease agreement. In many instances individuals have had to pay out from $300 to $700 at the end of a two-year lease period because of the open-ended feature of the lease.

The only way to be absolutely certain of a fixed dollar monthly cost of a lease is to make sure that it is a "closed-end" lease, with no strings attached at the end of the lease period.

A general statement cannot be made regarding the advisability of leasing. Leasing contracts are not that well standardized; rates vary tremendously from one company to another, and from one area to another. Potentially, leasing may offer a reasonably good way of budgeting for transportation since depreciation is automatically being paid for with each lease payment. The large leasing company also has a distinct advantage in buying the automobile, since it buys in large quantities at low fleet prices. However, the buying advantage may be, and usually is, offset by the additional administrative overhead which the leasing company assumes in running the business, and by the profit to which he is entitled — both of which must be included in leasing fees. Before deciding whether or not leasing is advisable for you, estimate total automobile expenditures which you have experienced through past purchases and sales of vehicles and compare this with the total costs of a closed-end lease program for a term equivalent to your normal trade-in time. Essentially, it is a matter of comparing the monthly depreciation and interest costs of ownership with the monthly lease rate. Since insurance expense, licensing fees, and property tax assessments are paid by you whether you buy or lease, they can be excluded from the analysis.

## FINANCING THE PURCHASE OF AN AUTOMOBILE

Chapters 5 and 6 discussed credit and loans in a general way. There are, however, a few things concerning automobile loans that deserve particular emphasis here. To begin with, arrangements for a loan should be made well in advance of the actual purchase. This will allow for shopping around and comparing the total costs of the auto loan. Otherwise, one may get high-pressured into letting the auto dealer handle the financial arrangements. It is not at all uncommon to find interest charges varying from 10 to 18 percent on new-car loans. Another significant advantage in arranging for the auto loan in advance of its purchase is that you will tend to set more logical budget limits on how much you wish or can afford to spend for the automobile purchase.

Here are a few additional points that may save dollars:

1. Don't trade for a new car or newer model until the equity in your present car plus what cash you can invest in the car to be purchased equal at least one-third of the total purchase price. This substantial downpayment will

materially reduce the amount of interest cost on the loan and will result in lower monthly payments or faster payoff.

2. Since the auto loan is usually substantial, determine whether or not "credit life insurance" is available or included in the loan. In the event that you should be accidentally killed or should die before the loan is repaid, such indebtedness could leave your family with a serious financial obligation. Usually credit unions offer this insurance at no extra charge. Other lenders may make such insurance available at nominal rates. But be sure you compare total costs! Insurance charges on the loan shouldn't be more than about $\frac{1}{2}$ of 1 percent over and above the prevailing interest rate.

3. Make sure that the quoted monthly payments will completely pay off the loan in the specified contract period. Some contracts have "balloon" payoffs, that is larger final payments.

4. Some auto dealers arrange with lending institutions to include an extra $300 to $500 cash over and above the amount needed to finance the purchase of an auto. The dealer then turns around and gives this extra amount to the purchaser to use as he pleases. They do this, of course, as a sales gimmick. Similarly, dealers often advertise that you can buy now and have your first payment delayed for as much as three months. The end result of any such inducements is just added interest charges and more strain on the monthly budget.

**FEEDBACK 11**

**A.** What can an automobile do for you?

● Provide transportation, of course, but what kind? How often? How far?

● Support your ego, a little perhaps. But at what cost? Can you make your present or proposed car payment and still afford your education? Rent? Food? Other obligations? Other free-time activities?

● If you want to "trade up," and especially if you want to buy a new car—make a priority list of your goals (again).

Right now, the most important financial goal I have is
the second most important financial goal is
the next most important financial goal is

and so on until you have fixed a new car in its proper perspective for your overall situation.

**B.** Using a NADA Official Used Car Guide, compute the cost of just having (not necessarily driving) the car of your dreams. Remember to include depreciation, options, insurance, state and local taxes, finance charges, and any storage or garage fees. Observe that your total reflects the cost of keeping your dream car *parked*. Any wear and tear, gas and oil, tires and other maintenance costs are to be *added*—if you should want to drive the car.

**C.**  When you intend to buy your next automobile, visit one of the diagnostic clinics in your community, *before* you begin looking.  Ask for an explanation of the findings:

- Estimate the costs involved if the front tires are excessively worn in terms of new tires, realignment, balancing, steering linkage.
- Proceed through the diagnostic check-list, noting discrepancies to look for before you buy a car.
- Using the possibilities found in the second item and the procedure in the first item, compile your own checklist and approximate costs of repairs for discrepancies for the particular car you have in mind.

**D.**  If you plan to sell your present car, devise an estimate of the price you should ask for it.

- Find out what dealers will offer in trade deals for the kind of car you want next.
- While at the dealers', compare the prices of cars like yours on his used car lot.
- Shop the want ads for information about the asking price for cars similarly equipped, the same age, the same features as yours.
- Evaluate the information from the above.  Add to the price, if your special maintenance is a feature; add to the price if your car's body work is in better shape; add for performance options, if your area has a demand for such features.  Subtract the value of any defects, especially if they cost more to fix than would be offset by the gain in apparent value.  This can be an inducement to buy for a man who is handy with tools, or who has a discount arrangement for parts.
- Compare the data from the four items presented in *D* above, and set your price.  You are now ready to discuss prices with potential buyers.  In your mind, you should also set a "floor" price, below which you will not be satisfied.  One possibility for the "floor" price is a figure slightly above the best trade-in offer you get.

## DISCUSSION QUESTIONS

1. What do people look for in buying a new car?  What is the most important consideration?  What causes a person to decide he needs a new car?
2. Why do new cars depreciate so quickly after their first year?
3. What are the advantages of buying a used car?  Disadvantages?
4. What are the ways of determining whether a used car has been involved in a major accident?
5. How does one go about bargaining for a fair price on a new car?  Should people be expected to pay the sticker price?  Why?

6. Are cars being put together as well as they were in the past? Explain.

7. Are the safety devices now being put into cars by the manufacturer wanted by the public? Explain. Who pays the cost for increased safety standards?

8. Why have most warranty coverages been reduced?

9. If one decides to sell his car, what is the best way to go about it? How can he be sure that he is asking a realistic price?

10. What are the differences between open-end and closed-end leases? Which is best for the buyer? Explain.

## CASE PROBLEM

Richard L. Cushman is a freshman at a junior college. He is currently taking 8 credit hours of course work and working 32 hours a week. His parents are paying for all his college expenses, and he is living at home. His take-home earnings are $39.04 each week. The Cushman family has two cars—a new Mercury, which Mr. Cushman drives to work and which is off limits to Richard and a 1961 Plymouth that is driven mostly by Richard and occasionally by Mrs. Cushman. Richard has $85 in savings and has decided to buy a new Ford Mustang. He believes he has ample earnings to support it. He can get the car for only $300 down, and the dealer has indicated that he can get a 48-month loan at $7\frac{1}{2}$ percent discount interest. Richard plans to borrow the balance of his downpayment from his father, that is if he can convince Mr. Cushman that the purchase is a good idea.

a) Based on the data supplied in this chapter, can Richard afford to own the car he proposes buying?

b) Do you think Richard has considered all the costs involved in owning and operating the car?

c) What do you think about the financial arrangements for buying the car? About how much interest will he end up paying?

d) What would be your recommendations to Richard if you were to have the opportunity to be his financial counselor?

## SUGGESTED READINGS

"Auto Buying Guide." *Consumer Reports*, April, 1968. pp. 172–219.

Crowther, Sam, and Irwin Winehouse. *Highway Robbery: True Story of How American Motorists Are Swindled out of More Than $7 Billion Every Year.* New York: Stein and Day, 1966. 189 pp.

Jackson, Charles R. *How to Buy a Used Car.* Philadelphia: Chilton, 1967. 90 pp.

Moolman, Val. *Get the Most for Your Money When You Buy a Car (Used or New).* New York: Simon & Schuster, 1967. 144 pp.

Rosevear, Robert Edwin. *An Analysis of Automobile Leasing.* Salt Lake City: Unpublished Master's Thesis, University of Utah, 1969. 87 pp.

CHAPTER 12

# SELECTING AN APPROPRIATE
# LIFE INSURANCE PROGRAM

College students, like most other people, shy away from talking or even thinking about life insurance protection since it inevitably causes them to consider death and its implications. It's certainly not surprising that healthy, robust young people in the prime of their lives would seriously question *why* they should bother with life insurance. Nonetheless, each of us has to deal with death as one of the certainties of life. And while we all hope to live to a ripe old age, we cannot afford to gamble with the financial security of those we love. In the event of premature death, insurance is for most people the only way they can create an immediate estate of sufficient size to clear up bills, pay off a home mortgage, and provide continuing income for their dependants. (See Fig. 12–1.)

**CLEARANCE FUND**

Creditors come first.
Your family gets
what is left.

**MORTGAGE OR HOME FUND**

So they will inherit a home where
proper values can be taught.

**DEPENDENCY PERIOD INCOME**

The greatest gift a father
can give his children
is their mother's time.

**LIFE INCOME FOR YOUR WIFE**

Give her the dignity of financial independence.

**Fig. 12–1** Illustrated above are four important reasons for buying life insurance. Courtesy of Beneficial Life Insurance Company.

There is such a bewildering array of life insurance programs offered to the public today that it is difficult to know what type(s) of protection one should have. More than 1,800 companies have eager-beaver salesmen trying to convince the public that their life insurance programs are the best. Due to lack of understanding about life insurance, most people make one of two financial mistakes: (1) they postpone buying life insurance until it is actually needed—and then, of course, it is too late; or (2) they are talked into subscribing for an insurance program which is ill-suited to their particular needs. This chapter should help you avoid falling into either group. It explains the kinds and costs of life insurance, shows what protection you get from Social Security, and provides you with computer-prepared tables which will help determine how much coverage you need.

## HOW LIFE INSURANCE WORKS

Life insurance is a system whereby a person shares with other people certain risks specified by the *policy* (an agreement, between the person and the insuring company). By relatively small contributions (called premiums) from many policyholders, large amounts of money can be paid to those few who actually sustain a loss.

**Life expectancy.** Fundamental to insurance mathematics is a comprehensive understanding of life expectancy patterns of the people being insured. Consequently, life insurance statisticians, known in the business as *actuaries*, make intensive studies of the life expectancy of the general population and various segments of the population. Actuaries classify individuals not only by age, but by sex, occupation, race, family health history, and so forth. They then tabulate the data for these groups. One such tabulation is shown in Table 12–1.

Although man's maximum span of life remains at about 100 years, more people today are surviving to older ages than did their parents or grandparents. Because more people live to older ages, the average lifetime has increased. However, the prolongation of life has not affected the span of life. Moreover, this century's advances in medicine, public health and safety have added years to people's lives, but the benefits have not been distributed equally among all Americans. By far the largest increases in life expectancy have been among the newborn, as a result of sharp reductions in mortality among infants and small children. Increases at all ages have been smaller for men than for women.

Taking a closer look at Table 12–1, you can identify clearly the changes in life expectancy in comparisons for groups of the same age, sex or race. The overall average in the United States has increased strikingly since 1900, with most of the gains taking place during the *first* half of the century. The overall data are also summarized graphically for you in Fig. 12–2. From 1900 to 1968, the life expectancy of a newborn American boy increased by 20.4 years while a newborn girl's increased by 25.7 years. While the difference between life expectancy of

**Table 12–1**  Expectation of life at birth in the United States

| | White | | | Nonwhite (Years) | | | All races | | |
|---|---|---|---|---|---|---|---|---|---|
| Year | Male | Female | Both sexes | Male | Female | Both sexes | Male | Female | Both sexes |
| 1900 | 46.6 | 48.7 | 47.6 | 32.5 | 33.5 | 33.0 | 46.3 | 48.3 | 47.3 |
| 1910 | 48.6 | 52.0 | 50.3 | 33.8 | 37.5 | 35.6 | 48.4 | 51.8 | 50.0 |
| 1920 | 54.4 | 55.6 | 54.9 | 45.5 | 45.2 | 45.3 | 53.6 | 54.6 | 54.1 |
| 1930 | 59.7 | 63.5 | 61.4 | 47.3 | 49.2 | 48.1 | 58.1 | 61.6 | 59.7 |
| 1940 | 62.1 | 66.6 | 64.2 | 51.5 | 54.9 | 53.1 | 60.8 | 65.2 | 62.9 |
| 1950 | 66.5 | 72.2 | 69.1 | 59.1 | 62.9 | 60.8 | 65.6 | 71.1 | 68.2 |
| 1951 | 66.5 | 72.4 | 69.2 | 59.1 | 63.3 | 61.0 | 65.6 | 71.3 | 68.4 |
| 1952 | 66.6 | 72.7 | 69.4 | 59.1 | 63.7 | 61.1 | 65.7 | 71.6 | 68.6 |
| 1953 | 66.8 | 72.9 | 69.6 | 59.7 | 64.4 | 61.7 | 65.9 | 71.9 | 68.8 |
| 1954 | 67.4 | 73.6 | 70.3 | 61.0 | 65.8 | 63.1 | 66.7 | 72.7 | 69.6 |
| 1955 | 67.3 | 73.6 | 70.2 | 61.2 | 65.9 | 63.2 | 66.6 | 72.7 | 69.5 |
| 1956 | 67.3 | 73.7 | 70.2 | 61.1 | 65.9 | 63.2 | 66.6 | 72.8 | 69.6 |
| 1957 | 67.1 | 73.5 | 70.0 | 60.3 | 65.2 | 62.7 | 66.3 | 72.5 | 69.3 |
| 1958 | 66.2 | 73.7 | 70.3 | 60.6 | 65.5 | 63.0 | 66.4 | 72.7 | 69.4 |
| 1959 | 67.6 | 74.2 | 70.7 | 61.4 | 66.5 | 63.8 | 66.8 | 73.2 | 69.9 |
| 1960 | 67.4 | 74.1 | 70.6 | 61.1 | 66.3 | 63.6 | 66.6 | 73.1 | 69.7 |
| 1961 | 67.8 | 74.5 | 71.0 | 61.9 | 67.0 | 64.4 | 67.0 | 73.6 | 70.2 |
| 1962 | 67.6 | 74.4 | 70.9 | 61.5 | 66.8 | 64.1 | 66.8 | 73.4 | 70.0 |
| 1963 | 67.5 | 74.4 | 70.8 | 60.9 | 66.5 | 63.6 | 66.6 | 73.4 | 69.9 |
| 1964 | 67.7 | 74.6 | 71.0 | 61.1 | 67.2 | 64.1 | 66.9 | 73.7 | 70.2 |
| 1965 | 67.6 | 74.7 | 71.0 | 61.1 | 67.4 | 64.1 | 66.8 | 73.7 | 70.2 |
| 1966 | 67.6 | 74.7 | 71.0 | 60.7 | 67.4 | 64.0 | 66.7 | 73.8 | 70.1 |
| 1967 | 67.8 | 75.1 | 71.3 | 61.1 | 68.2 | 64.6 | 67.0 | 74.2 | 70.5 |
| 1968 | 67.6 | 74.9 | 71.1 | 60.3 | 67.6 | 63.9 | 66.7 | 74.0 | 70.2 |

*Source:* National Center for Health Statistics, U.S. Department of Health, Education and Welfare. *Life Insurance Fact Book*, New York: Institute of Life Insurance, 1970, p. 97.

men and that of women has increased, the difference in expectancy between white and nonwhite Americans has been greatly reduced in this century.

**Paying for the risk.** Life expectancy of the prospective policyholder obviously must determine the cost of the insurance. Fortunately for Americans, the longer life expectancy in turn has contributed to keeping down the cost of life insurance, reflecting the lengthened average time during which the policyholders are expected to be paying period installments or *premiums*.

The younger one is when purchasing a life insurance policy, the smaller will be the premium. The reason is obvious: the younger you are, the greater is your life expectancy and the longer is the period during which you are likely to be able to pay premiums. Conversely, if you buy the same amount of insurance

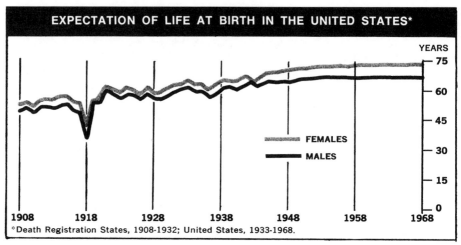

**Fig. 12–2**  Life expectations.  The life insurance industry keeps close tab on birth and death statistics.  Such data enable life insurance underwriters to establish fair and reasonable rates for the policies.  Reprinted by permission from *Life Insurance Fact Book*.

late in life, the premiums will be higher.  Since life expectancy by then is shorter, you have less time to pay premiums.

The premium payments help pay administrative costs and create profits for the insurance company as well as providing a reserve to pay the surviving family (the *beneficiaries*) at the time of a policyholder's death.  The premium paid is somewhat less than the amount needed to cover these items, however, since most of the premium goes into a reserve fund which is in turn reinvested by the insurance company.  Profits from the investments help build up the reserve fund which is eventually used to pay policy benefits.

### TYPES OF LIFE INSURANCE POLICIES

Although companies offer policies under several commercial headings to improve sales, there are basically only five types of life policies: (1) straight or whole life insurance, (2) term insurance, (3) limited payment life insurance, (4) endowment insurance, and (5) accidental death insurance.  Sometimes plans combine two or more of the basic types of insurance.

**Whole life insurance.**  Most life insurance salesmen will advise you to purchase a *whole* or *straight* life insurance policy.  Sometimes this type of protection is also referred to as *permanent* or *ordinary* insurance.  Basically, this coverage offers two financial services for the buyer:

1. It provides the amount of financial protection established as the amount of the policy, perhaps $5,000, $10,000 or $20,000.  In the event of an individual's death, the full amount of the policy is paid to whomever the

policyholder indicates as his or her beneficiary. This life protection is an efficient way for anyone to establish an immediate estate of considerable worth to take care of loved ones should death preclude his doing so himself.

2. Whole or straight life insurance provides an added benefit—that of a forced savings program. Part of the premium paid on a whole life policy goes for actual insurance protection. The other portion of the premium could be looked upon as a savings account, since it ultimately builds up cash value. The cash value which accumulates on the policy is added security for the policyholder since he may, if he chooses, surrender his policy for stipulated cash values at prescribed intervals of time.

Since whole-life insurance policies build up cash values, such policies usually provide "nonforfeiture options" in the event the policyholder runs into financial difficulties and finds he is unable to make further premium payments. Two choices are usually offered the policyholder: (1) Extended-term protection can be selected which keeps the policy in effect for a fixed period of time. How long extended-term protection is available depends entirely on how long the policy had been in effect, as shown in Table 12–2. (2) Reduced paid-up insurance to continue for life can be selected. The amount of insurance available is determined by provisions of the policy, in addition to the length of time it has been in effect. Typical amounts of paid-up insurance are given in Table 12–3. If the financial reverses of the policyholder are temporary, it is best to borrow on the cash values of the policy to pay the current premiums to continue the policy in full force with no changes in length or amount of coverage.

Many families look to *loans* on whole life policies as sources of cash to meet an emergency, to seize an investment opportunity, or as we have just explained above, to pay the premium, if necessary, to keep protection in force. Life insurance companies can make policy loans quickly and without complication. The interest rate, guaranteed in the policy, is often lower than could be obtained elsewhere; and the loan can be repaid at the borrower's convenience.

**Table 12–2** Approximate time for which life insurance will be continued at face amount for policies issued at age 18

| Type of policy | End of 10th yr. | 15th yr. | 20th yr. |
|---|---|---|---|
| Term | 0 | 0 | 0 |
| Straight Life | 22 yr. 235 days | 25 yr. 305 days | 26 yr. 101 days |
| 20-Payment Life | 36 yr. 51 days | 40 yr. 325 days | Paid Up |
| 20-Year Endowment | $527* | $781* | Matured |

\* Full protection to maturity plus this cash for each $1,000 of face amount.

*Source: Policies for Protection.* New York: Educational Division, Institute of Life Insurance with the cooperation of Health Insurance Institute, 1963, p. 19.

**Table 12–3** Approximate amount of paid-up insurance for each $1,000 face amount for policies issued at age 18

| Type of policy | End of 10th yr. | 15th yr. | 20th yr. |
|---|---|---|---|
| Term | 0 | 0 | 0 |
| Straight Life | $230 | $361 | $462 |
| 20-Payment Life | $515 | $767 | $1,000 |
| 20-Year Endowment | $536* | $783* | Matured |

* Terminates at maturity when this amount is paid in cash.
*Source: Policies for Protection.* New York: Educational Division, Institute of Life Insurance with the cooperation of Health Insurance Institute, 1963, p. 20.

Whole life insurance policies are written so that the buyer pays what is called a *level premium*. This means that the premium remains the same from year to year. Although rates vary from one insurance company to another, a whole life policy usually costs about $16 per $1,000 of protection annually if taken out at age 20; at age 30, the yearly cost is approximately $20. At these rates, $50,000 of life insurance at age 30 costs $1,000 or more a year.

You can readily see that *high cost* is one serious disadvantage of whole life protection. There is another serious weakness: the interest rate on the *savings part of the premium* is often *lower* than interest rates paid by banks, savings and loan associations, or the gains realized from common stocks and other kinds of investments. Most insurance salesmen attempt to pass off this weakness by saying that "even though the rate is somewhat low, whole or ordinary life insurance gives the individual a forced savings plan—an advantage because the policyholder probably wouldn't save if he weren't obligated to do so." This seems to be a weak argument. If the person buying insurance is not the type who would discipline himself to set aside a small additional amount in savings, then it is quite unlikely that he would maintain the payments on a life insurance program.

In an effort to make whole life coverage more attractive to young people, many life insurance companies are offering innovative new packages. The new approach allows you to buy a large whole life policy and *borrow* yearly against the cash value of the policy to help pay the premiums. Normally, after the first couple of years, the amount you can borrow to help pay premiums brings the net cost of the insurance down to approximately the same cost as for term insurance (life insurance written as pure protection with no cash build-up portion). New administrative procedures make this kind of arrangement easy and automatic. Furthermore, if you keep your life insurance program in force for a long period of time, you will probably have lower net cost for the insurance protection over the years—even as compared with term insurance.

Another sensible approach for young persons in buying insurance is to combine a small amount of whole life with a large lump of term insurance. The cash values accumulating on the whole life policy would be available to pay premiums for both policies if economic difficulties should keep you from being able to pay out of your normal earnings. The principal features of term insurance are discussed next.

**Term life insurance.**  The main reason a breadwinner buys life insurance is to give dependants continuing economic support in case he dies prematurely. Life insurance fringe benefits such as accumulated savings or investments are usually handled most sensibly by separate plans. Term insurance is *pure* life insurance protection without fringe benefits—it builds no cash values. It is sold for specified periods of time, such as units of five or ten years.

Two very good points about term protection are (1) You can buy the amount you need for only as long as you think you will need it; and (2) its cost is very low. There are certain times in your life when you need more insurance than at other times. For example, when you marry, have children and assume a mortgage on a home, you have need for substantial life insurance coverage. However, as your children near the completion of their education and begin to earn their own way, and as you make final payments on your mortgage, your financial responsibilities are much lighter. Term insurance is adjustable to your needs and makes a lot of sense for young marrieds.

Some term policies are written on a *decreasing* or *reducing coverage* basis. As an example, a policy may offer $10,000 of protection for the first 10 years; $8,500 worth of protection for the second 10 years, $6,250 for the third 10 years, and so on. Decreasing term policies normally have a level premium. This type of policy is usually very economical. At least one major company offers a 20-year $30,000 decreasing term policy for a person 30 years old for only $10 per month.

Many term policies have options for additional family protection. Several large insurers offer $10,000 term policies with decreasing term insurance on the wife, ranging from $2,500 protection down to $800 protection over 30 years. Children are protected for a level amount of $500 each. This type of protection is called a *family rider* and costs only about $2 per month over and above the regular premiums on $10,000 term policies. Children born after purchase of the policy with such a rider are usually automatically insured. Coverage and rates vary, however, from company to company.

A characteristic of most term insurance is that the premium increases at the end of each term. For example, a 20-year-old would pay approximately $7 annually for each $1,000 of ten-year term insurance. At age 30 the term rate would *increase* to approximately $8 annually per $1,000. By age 40 the rate would be increased to about $12. The insurance company must charge increasingly higher rates because they are taking an increasingly higher risk. Figure 12-3 shows the difference in premiums for whole or straight life insurance, and ten-year term insurance. The straight life premium is higher in the beginning

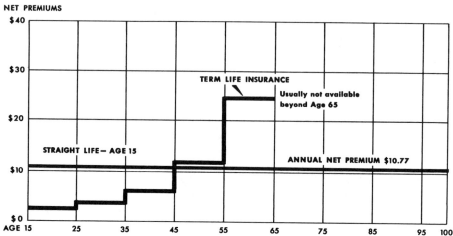

NET PREMIUMS

**Fig. 12–3** A comparison of net annual premiums for two kinds of life policies—ten-year term and straight life. Since term insurance provides "pure" protection, its premium increases every ten years. The straight life premium is higher in the beginning (because it is part protection, part investment) but continues at the same level throughout the life of the policy. Reprinted by permission from *The Mathematics of Life Insurance*, 1961. Institute of Life Insurance.

because it is part protection, part investment, but continues at the same level throughout the life of the policy. Since term insurance provides pure protection, its premium increases, along with the risk, every ten years.

Insurance salesmen make a much smaller commission on term policies than on other policies; consequently, some salesmen may not recommend term insurance. However, insurance professionals are paying increasingly closer attention to the real needs of the client. Reputable insurance agents describe term insurance and all the options available. Good companies nearly always offer term insurance which is guaranteed *renewable*. This means the insurance company will not drop your insurance after any term. A policy with such a feature can usually be continued to age 65 by paying successively higher premiums for each term period. Another feature which is usually available on term policies is that of *convertibility*. A policy with a convertibility option allows the owner to convert his term policy to whole or straight life insurance or other family plans at specified periods of time. Many people mistakenly assume that term insurance is inappropriate for their needs since it will cover them for only a short period of time. If you buy term protection, find a company which provides *convertible and renewable* policies.

The major disadvantage of term insurance is that there is no cash value to fall back on in the event the insured is unable to pay the premiums. Usually all life policies (term or whole) are cancelled after a 31-day grace period if the premium is not paid. A regular savings or investment program or a combination of whole and term insurance would help you avoid letting a policy lapse.

What type of job you have makes a difference in what type of insurance you should have. For example, a salesman expects that his earnings may fluctuate more widely than the income of pharmacists, dentists, or teachers. Anyone who has or anticipates a somewhat erratic income would be wise to have a greater amount of whole life insurance with its cash value build-up to help assure that premiums can be met. The man with a very steady income would probably be wise to lean heavily on term insurance.

**Group life insurance.** Many unions as well as professional associations have influenced insurance companies to offer inexpensive group life insurance which can be provided by employers as a fringe benefit for the worker. With few exceptions, *group life* is term insurance. However, these policies usually have *conversion privileges.* In other words, if you leave the company it is possible to continue the coverage by converting to a *straight life policy* within a specified period of time. Group contracts normally offer considerable savings. Such plans usually accept all employees even though some of the people may otherwise be uninsurable because of some existing health condition if they were considered on an individual application for insurance. It is certainly advisable for one to participate in group plans when they are available.

**Credit life insurance.** Another kind of term insurance is "credit life," a policy which is usually issued to a borrower, and covers many kinds of indebtedness. Installment purchases of furniture, automobiles, major appliances, loans from banks or from other financial institutions and even mortgages, are often covered through special arrangements with insurance companies. In addition to life insurance provisions, credit life policies usually provide for payment of monthly installments should the insured become totally disabled and unable to work during the contract period. Sometimes the installment contract automatically includes credit insurance. If not, check the cost of the protection and weigh its need carefully. Remember that for most installment contracts, you are paying off part of the obligation monthly. Over the entire term of the contract, you will receive average protection for only about half the original or face

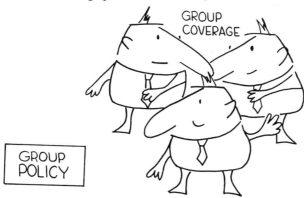

GROUP COVERAGE

GROUP POLICY

amount of the contract. Looked at in these terms, credit life can be quite expensive when compared with regular term insurance.

**Limited payment life insurance.** The limited payment policy differs little from the whole or straight life policy except that the premiums are a little higher, and the individual pays fewer of them. Many companies put emphasis on policies which will be paid up at age 65 so that the individual will not have to pay premiums from his retirement income.

**Endowment insurance.** As was previously indicated, part of a whole life policy's premium goes toward insurance, part toward savings. This is also true for limited payment life insurance. For an endowment policy, a much greater portion of the premium is earmarked for cash-value buildup. Figure 12–4

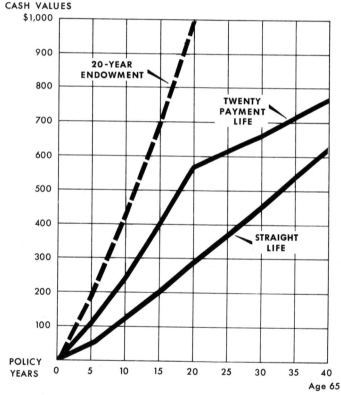

**Fig. 12–4** Cash value accumulations for 20-year endowment, 20-payment life, and straight life insurance policies. Chart shows the approximate cash values per $1,000 of insurance for each of the three different kinds of policies purchased at age 25. Reprinted by permission from *The Mathematics of Life Insurance*, 1961. Institute of Life Insurance.

gives you an interesting comparison of cash-value accumulations for endowment, limited payment and straight life policies.

There are many types of endowment programs, but all are alike in that they have definite savings or value-goals for stipulated payment periods. Endowment premiums are much higher than for other policies; but, as you have seen, cash values build rapidly, too. The face value of the policy is payable in cash or in other settlement options to the policyholder at the end of the endowment term if the policyholder is living; or payable at any time to the policy beneficiary upon the death of the insured before maturity of the policy.

**Accident insurance.** Because of the increased risk of death in motor vehicle mishaps and other accidents, it is wise to enroll for low-cost accidental-death policies which are available to supplement your basic insurance program. For as little as $3 to $5 per month, it may be possible to purchase a group policy providing $50,000 worth of accident life protection. Family accident insurance covering one's spouse and children can also be added for a small additional premium. When you buy an accident policy, make certain that it has *broad* accidental death coverage, for some accident policies are written to cover only *specified* accidents.

## PACKAGED PLANS: INSURANCE + STOCKS

Over the past couple of decades, the insurance industry has continually lost ground in attracting the public's savings. Whereas the industry was getting about 25 percent of the savings during the early fifties, its share is now less than 10 percent, according to data published by the Securities and Exchange Commission. Much of the decline in the popularity of cash-value insurance is attributable to the villain: inflation. People have diverted their dollars into stocks or other investments as an inflation hedge.

Near the close of the decade of the sixties, insurance companies began moving pell-mell into the mutual fund business. As will be explained more fully in a later chapter, mutual funds invest the buyer's dollars in stocks. Because of the very poor showing of the stock market over those same years, however, many of the insurance firms which had made plans to move into mutual funds became discouraged and shelved the idea—at least temporarily. Nonetheless, there are thousands of insurance salesmen now licensed to sell mutual-fund shares and many hundreds of different packaged plans available which provide both insurance and fund investment. While many of these plans may have merit, it is important to be able to identify clearly how much you are paying for insurance and how much is going into funds.

## SPECIAL POLICY OPTIONS

There are two very important options you should select with your life insurance policy, regardless of the type of policy you decide to purchase.

First is the *premium waiver for disability*. Under such an option, the company agrees to waive all future premiums on the policy should the policyholder become disabled and unable to work. It is common to have a three-to-six-month waiting period after a person becomes disabled before the waiver option takes effect.

The second important option is *double indemnity*. This option doubles the face value of the insurance policy if the insured dies accidentally. Because of the high incidence of accidental deaths in this country, as previously discussed, this option is a valuable one. Both double indemnity and premium waiver options add little cost to the basic premium.

### KINDS OF INSURANCE COMPANIES

There are two kinds of regular life insurance companies: mutual and stock. Both types are known as "legal reserve companies" since they must set aside a prescribed portion of premiums received to provide a reserve for future benefit payments under the insurance contracts which they write.

**Mutual companies.** These organizations are, generally speaking, the older and larger insurers. They are formed as associations of policyholders and work much like cooperatives. When a person purchases an insurance contract (policy) from a mutual company, he becomes a *part owner* with voting rights in the company. He usually pays larger premiums than are necessary to meet reserve requirements and cover administrative expenses. Excess funds collected through premiums are refunded annually, semiannually, or quarterly to the policyholders in the form of *dividends*. Such policies written by mutual companies are known as *participating policies*. There are a few mutual companies that offer non-participating policies, but this is the exception rather than the rule.

**Stock companies.** These insurers organize as regular corporations. Investors purchase the shares of stock offered by the company and receive voting rights to determine who will run the corporation and who has rights to profits which may be distributed by the corporation as dividends. The policyholder of a stock company is a client rather than an owner and has no voting rights. Premiums are established to cover the risk (provide the necessary reserve) and give a fair operating profit.

In actual practice, the protection provided by policies of either mutual or stock companies is usually identical. Theoretically, the ultimate costs of mutual policies should be somewhat lower because of the absence of a profit factor. Such a general assertion in favor of the mutual company, however, can be misleading. What is important to the prospective policyholder is a detailed comparison of *net costs* and *coverages* of competing plans. Since the operating record of mutual companies is quite constant, previous dividend payment records will approximate quite accurately what can actually be expected in the future. Therefore, when comparing mutual and stock company plans, projected dividends should be deducted from premium costs to equate the premiums.

## HOW POLICY BENEFITS ARE PAID

To the policyholder and to his beneficiary, the provisions for paying benefits are one of the most important parts of a life insurance policy. Benefits, after all, are what give meaning to life insurance. Policy benefits do not have to be death benefits. Endowment insurance, as already discussed, becomes payable to the policyholder himself, if he is living, upon a certain date named in the policy. In the event an insured dies, the beneficiary receives payment. Also, loans may be made against the cash values of endowment, limited payment, and whole life policies; this, too, is a policy benefit. The various choices then for receiving policy benefits are: at maturity (as in the case of endowments), at death, or upon the withdrawal of the cash value.

In practically every life insurance policy, the benefits may be paid in one of four general ways. The first of these is to pay the policy proceeds in a single lump sum. The other three methods of paying policy benefits are called *settlement options*.

1. The benefit can be received in a single cash payment. The beneficiary could then deposit the sum in the most advantageous savings institution and subsequently make withdrawals monthly as needed. Or part or all of the funds could be invested.

2. The policy proceeds can be left with the company to earn interest.* Interest payments would then be paid every year for as long as the money remains with the company. Such interest payments are considered taxable income. The principal could be withdrawn at a time the beneficiary may choose, or he/she can instruct the company to make it payable to some other person.

The interest payments paid by insurance companies are typically somewhat less than the rates offered by insured savings and loan institutions. Beneficiaries should always investigate and compare the current rates payable by the insurance company and local insured savings institutions and then put their money where it will earn the biggest return.

3. The life insurance company can be instructed to pay the proceeds to the beneficiary in installments as a regular monthly income. The amount of income received each month will be determined by *how long* it is to continue and how much each payment is to be. As will be explained more fully in Chapter 17, the prorated amount of the principal of the insurance withdrawn yearly is con-

---

* Most policies are based on a guaranteed rate of $2\frac{1}{2}$ percent interest, compounded annually. Some are written at lower and some at higher guaranteed rates. Companies announce each year the interest rate which they will pay on settlement options. Currently, most companies are paying $3\frac{1}{2}$ percent.

sidered non-taxable income. Also up to $1,000 interest yearly may be excluded from Federal tax where the principal is left with the insurer.

4. The insurance company will also pay the beneficiary a lifetime income. The size of the monthly payment depends on the beneficiary's age, the interest rate, and sex. The older a person is, the larger will be the monthly payment because fewer years of life remain. If the beneficiary is a man, the payments will be somewhat larger each month than for a woman, because women live longer than men. Therefore, the income for women must be figured to last a few years longer.

Companies often guarantee ten years of lifetime income—usually specified in life insurance language as "ten years certain." If the beneficiary dies during that ten years, the remaining payments are made to a subsequent beneficiary until the end of the tenth year. If death does not occur, the payments continue for as long as the person lives.

In summary, most life insurance policies provide four settlement options: (1) cash; (2) interest payments; (3) installment payments; and (4) life income. These various methods of paying benefits make it possible for life insurance to meet a variety of family needs.

## THE INCONTESTABLE CLAUSE

After a life insurance policy has been in force for a stipulated period of time (usually two years), the insurer must continue the policy in force as long as premiums are paid. Even if the policy has been obtained through misstatements or even fraud concerning one's health, occupation, or other data, the policy must be continued and benefits must be paid to the beneficiary in the event of the insured's death. Any disability income benefits under a rider to a life policy are usually *excluded* from the incontestable clause.

## WHO CAN BUY INSURANCE?

Most Americans who apply for life insurance are able to get it. Life companies are accepting about 97 percent of the applications for ordinary life insurance (whole or straight) submitted in the United States. The 3 percent of life applications that are not acceptable are related to serious health impairments and other factors such as extremely hazardous jobs. These data are further detailed in Fig. 12–5.

Such a high rate of acceptance indicates how successful life insurance companies have been over the years in solving the problems presented by two conflicting underwriting objectives. On the one hand, companies want to provide the benefit of insurance protection to the greatest possible number of people. On the other hand, in fairness to all policyholders, companies must take into account individual differences among applicants in health condition, occupation, habits, and family health background, so that the premiums charged will

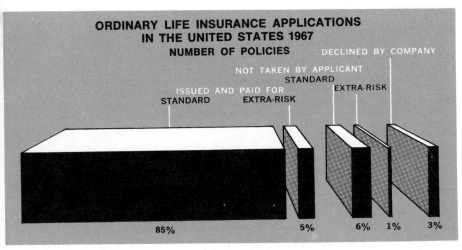

**Fig. 12–5** Disposition of life insurance applications in the United States, 1967, by number of policies. Notice that only 3 percent of all life insurance applications were declined by the insurance companies. Reprinted by permission from *Life Insurance Fact Book*, 1968. Institute of Life Insurance.

be adequate for the risks involved. Figure 12–6 shows a typical life insurance application. From this information and that supplied by physicians, if a medical examination is required, the insurer determines an applicant's eligibility.

Several developments have contributed to the high rate of applicants' acceptance. Extra-risk policies at higher premiums have made insurance available to many who could not otherwise have obtained it. And advances in medicine, job safety, and public health have made it possible to issue policies to many persons who would formerly have been considered uninsurable because of their health or occupation.

A survey of ordinary life insurance applicants and of extra-risk insurance reveals that 5 percent of all the ordinary policies purchased, and 6 percent of all ordinary policies in force at the end of the year, were extra-risk. A sample of these extra-risk policies showed the following reasons for extra ratings: heart disease, 30 percent; weight problems, 20 percent; other physical impairments, 24 percent; hazardous occupations, 18 percent; other reasons, 8 percent.

More life insurance is becoming available. For instance, some companies now insure diabetics who can show that their disease is under control. Airline pilots, who formerly had to pay higher premiums for insurance if they could get it at all, now can usually obtain policies at standard rates.

Life companies are constantly investigating the effects of various health and occupational hazards on life expectancy and mortality. Such studies help make life insurance widely available at equitable costs. They also provide medical information and help to educate the public in matters affecting health and lifespan.

TEACHERS INSURANCE
AND ANNUITY ASSOCIATION
OF AMERICA

**APPLICATION FOR INSURANCE**

PLEASE BE SURE TO ANSWER
EVERY QUESTION. GO BY
QUESTION NUMBERS

730 Third Avenue, New York, N. Y. 10017

(Please Print Name)    First Name    Middle Name or Initial    Last Name

1. Full
   Name

2. Male ☐
   Female ☐

3. Addresses: State both and place a cross (X) in ☐ for address to which mail shall be sent.

| | Number | Street | City or Town | State | Zip Code |
|---|---|---|---|---|---|
| A. Residence ☐ | | | | | |
| B. Business ☐ | | | | | |

4. Nonprofit Employer: college, university, private school, or other educational or scientific institution by which you are currently employed.

Institution    Title    Department    Date Employed

5. What are your exact duties?
   (If other than office and classroom, give full details.)

6. Where    State or Country
   born

7. When    Month    Day    Year
   born

8. Married ☐
   Single ☐
   Widowed ☐
   Divorced ☐
   Separated ☐

9. How do you wish to pay premiums?
   Annually ☐
   Semi-annually ☐
   Quarterly ☐
   Monthly ☐

10. Do you wish premiums deducted from your salary? *Available only for monthly premiums and only if your employer agrees.*
    Yes ☐    No ☐

11. Do you wish to elect the Automatic Premium Loan option?    Yes ☐
    *Not available on Term or Home Protection insurance.*    No ☐
    (Automatic loan to you from the cash value, if sufficient, to pay a premium you have not paid by end of grace period. No additional charge for this option.)

14. State ALL of the life, health and accident insurance carried by you. (If none, so state.)

12. **Insurance Being Applied For.**
    *State exact title of policy or policies.*

| | Face Amount | Name of Company | Amount | Plan | Year Issued |
|---|---|---|---|---|---|
| | | | | | |
| | | | | | |
| | | | | | |
| | | | | | |

13. To whom shall the proceeds be payable in case of your death? Give first name, middle initial and last name: Mary A. Smith (not Mrs. John Smith). For your children, you may simply use the term "My Children" and leave the Date of Birth and Relationship columns blank. This term will provide equal treatment among your children—present and future—born of any and all marriages and any children legally adopted at any time.

Date of Birth Mo. Day Yr.

Relationship to you? (If none, state whether friend, creditor or other.)

**Primary Beneficiary(ies) (Class I):**

Contingent Beneficiary(ies) (Class II), if any:

The right to change beneficiaries is reserved to me.

Note: If no Primary Beneficiary (Class I) is living at time of insured's death, the proceeds are payable to the Contingent Beneficiary(ies) (Class II). If a Class includes more than one person, the proceeds are divided equally among the living beneficiaries of the Class.

Details Here. **Use reverse side if necessary.**

NOTE: Answer questions numbered 15 to 22 "yes" or "no" and as to any answered "yes" **give full details in space provided below.**

15. Will this insurance replace any existing insurance?

16. Have you, within the past two years, engaged in any work other than as stated in Nos. 4 and 5 above?

17. Do you plan to engage in any work other than as stated in Nos. 4 and 5 above?

18. Are you now connected (or plan definitely to become connected) with any military or auxiliary service?

19. Have you any definite plan (or understanding with your employer) to travel or reside outside the U. S. and Canada?

20. Have you taken aerial flights other than as a fare-paying passenger on regularly scheduled airlines during the past two years (or plan to do so)?

21. Have you ever piloted an aircraft (or plan to do so)?

22. Have you ever applied for life or disability insurance which was declined, postponed, or modified in any way?

If less than age 56 nearest birthday and insurable for the total permanent disability waiver of premium benefit, I understand that the policy applied for will include such benefit. The answers to the above questions are true and complete. These answers and those I make on the statements to physician form at the time of my medical examination are my application.

I hereby tender $_____, the amount of the first premium on the policy applied for, which shall be returned to me if the Association does not grant the insurance.

Dated at_____this_____day of_____19_____

_____
Signature of Applicant

18.26-6-66    **Kindly review your application and see that all questions have been answered. Go by question numbers.**    BS-67

**Fig. 12–6** Typical application for life insurance.

## SOCIAL SECURITY SURVIVORS' BENEFITS

Before you can make a meaningful evaluation of just how much life insurance you should purchase, you must consider the survivor's benefits which might be available to your dependant or dependants under the Social Security system of the Federal Government. The insurance you receive under Social Security is much the same as life insurance, except that the coverage is broader. During your working years, you and your employer pay Social Security contributions which go into special funds; when your earnings stop or are reduced because you retire, die, or become disabled, monthly cash benefits are paid from the funds to replace part of the earnings the family has lost. Self-employed persons may also contribute to the program for full coverage.

Today, nine out of ten working people in the United States are building protection for themselves and their families under the Social Security program. Almost every kind of employment and self-employment is now covered by Social Security. Some occupations, however, are covered only if certain conditions are met. Workers in these occupations have special conditions: farmers or ranchers, family employees, ministers and members of religious orders, household workers, employees who receive tips, employees of nonprofit organizations, employees of state and local governments, farm employees, Federal employees, military service, railroad employees, American citizens working abroad, foreign agricultural workers, and foreign exchange visitors.

The original Social Security Act was enacted by Congress in 1935 during this country's greatest depression. Prior to that time, public assistance (both state and federal) to individual citizens was based solely on poverty or need. With the Social Security Act, this country embarked upon what is actually a compulsory insurance program. Although some people may disagree philosophically about compulsory programs, the Social Security system undoubtedly has done a great deal of good. It not only has assured a basic subsistence for each family insured, but has given this protection without requiring the indignity of having to plead poverty to get help.

If you are employed, your contribution to the Social Security program is automatically deducted from your wages each payday. In effect, this wage deduction is the premium on your Social Security insurance. Your employer sends it, with an equal amount as his own share of the contribution, to the District Director of Internal Revenue. Contribution rates under the present law are given in Table 12-4.

You must have a Social Security number if your work is covered by the Social Security law or if you receive certain kinds of taxable income. Your Social Security number is also your tax number. It should be shown to your employer when you start to work. Upon request, show it to anyone who pays you dividends, interest, or other income that must be reported.

You can get a Social Security card (Fig. 12-7) at any Social Security District Office. The number shown on your card will be used to keep a record of your earnings and of any benefits to which you and your dependants become entitled.

**Fig. 12–7**  Specimen Social Security card.

You need only one Social Security number during your lifetime. Notify your nearest Social Security office if you ever get more than one number. If you change your name, or if you lose your Social Security card, go to a Social Security office to get a card showing your new name or to obtain a duplicate of the card you lost.

**Checking your Social Security account.** Each employer is required by law to give you receipts for the Social Security contributions he deducted from your pay. He must do this at the end of each year and also when you stop working for him. These receipts, such as Form W-2, will help you check on your Social Security account. They show the wages paid you and the amount deducted from your pay. For most kinds of work, your wages paid in forms other than

**Table 12–4**  Social Security contribution rates*

| Years | Employer, employee, each percent of covered earnings | | | Self-employed percent of covered earnings | | |
|---|---|---|---|---|---|---|
| | For retirement, survivors, and disability insurance | For hospital insurance | Total | For retirement, survivors, and disability insurance | For hospital insurance | Total |
| 1968 | 3.8 | 0.6 | 4.4 | 5.8 | 0.6 | 6.4 |
| 1969–70 | 4.2 | 0.6 | 4.8 | 6.3 | 0.6 | 6.9 |
| 1971–72 | 4.6 | 0.6 | 5.2 | 6.9 | 0.6 | 7.5 |
| 1973–75 | 5.0 | 0.65 | 5.65 | 7.0 | 0.65 | 7.65 |
| 1976–79 | 5.0 | 0.7 | 5.7 | 7.0 | 0.7 | 7.7 |
| 1980–86 | 5.0 | 0.8 | 5.8 | 7.0 | 0.8 | 7.8 |
| 1987 and after | 5.0 | 0.9 | 5.9 | 7.0 | 0.9 | 7.9 |

* The contribution rates apply to earnings up to $9,000 a year.

cash—for instance the value of meals, or living quarters—must be included. For domestic work in a private household or for farm work, however, only cash wages count. You should also keep a record of the amount of self-employment income you have reported.

It's a good idea to check your account from time to time to make sure your earnings have been correctly reported. This is especially important if you have frequently changed jobs. Simply ask your Social Security Office for a postcard form to use in requesting a copy of your record. Complete, sign, and mail it. Information about your earnings cannot be released without a signed request from you. What should you do if there is a discrepancy? The easiest and speediest way to get your account set in order is to make photo copies of all the W-2 forms for the years in question and submit these copies to your nearest Social Security Office with a tabulation of the total withholdings. If you keep good personal accounting records, the W-2 forms should be stapled to each year's Federal tax return.

**Social Security death benefit.**   Social Security embodies a number of insurance programs. (See Table 12–5.) The principal benefit relevant to life insurance is the *death benefit* which is payable to the widow, children, or dependent parent following a worker's death. For survivors to receive such death benefits, however, the worker must first qualify as *fully* or *currently insured* under Social Security.

If a person stops working under Social Security before he becomes insured, credits for the earnings reported for him will remain on his Social Security record. He can add to them if he later returns to covered work. No benefits based on his earnings can be paid to him or his family, however, until he has credit for enough earnings to become insured.

**Currently insured.**   Even if a worker is not fully insured, certain kinds of benefits may be paid to his survivors if he is *currently insured* when he dies. He is cur-

**Table 12–5**   Types of survivors' benefits payable under Social Security

| Monthly payments to your | If at death you are |
|---|---|
| *Widow 60 or over | Fully insured |
| Widow (regardless of age) if caring for your child who is under 18 or disabled and is entitled to benefits | Either fully or currently insured |
| Dependent child | Either fully or currently insured |
| Dependent widower 62 or over and disabled dependent widower 50–61 | Fully insured |
| Dependent parent at 62 | Fully insured |
| Lump-sum death payment | Either fully or currently insured |

* Under certain conditions, payments can also be made to your surviving divorced wife.

rently insured if he has credit for at least $1\frac{1}{2}$ years of work within 3 years before his death.

**Fully insured.**   No one can be fully insured with credit for less than $1\frac{1}{2}$ years of work and a person who has credit for 10 years of work can be sure that he will be fully insured for life.   Having credit for sufficient work, however, means only that certain *kinds* of benefits may be payable—it does not determine the amount. Most non-farm employees get credit for $\frac{1}{4}$ year of work (called a "quarter of coverage") if they are paid $50 or more in a 3-month calendar quarter.   Also, a person may receive a full year of credit if his self-employment net income is $400 or more in the year.   A person who has covered farm wages receives $\frac{1}{4}$ year of credit for each $100 in wages he has (up to $400) in a year.   In addition, any employee who earns the maximum wages creditable for Social Security for a year ($9,000 in 1972 and later) receives a full year of credit, even if he works only part of the year.

Table 12–6 shows how much credit for work under Social Security a worker needs to be fully insured.

**Table 12–6**   For workers born after 1929

| If the worker dies when his age is | He will be fully insured with credit for this much work |
|---|---|
| 28 or younger | $1\frac{1}{2}$ years |
| 30 | 2 |
| 32 | $2\frac{1}{2}$ |
| 34 | 3 |
| 36 | $3\frac{1}{2}$ |
| 38 | 4 |
| 40 and so on | $4\frac{1}{2}$ |

*NOTE*: A person is fully insured if he has credit for $\frac{1}{4}$ year of work for each year after 1950 up to the year he reaches retirement age, becomes disabled, or dies.   In counting the years after 1950, a person born in 1930 or later would omit years before he was 22.

The amount of the benefit will depend upon the average yearly earnings of the deceased and the number of dependants.   (See Table 12–7.)   The maximum

**Table 12-7**  Examples of monthly cash payments

| Average yearly earnings after 1950* | $923 or less | $1,800 | $3,000 | $4,200 | $5,400 | $6,600 | $7,800 |
|---|---|---|---|---|---|---|---|
| Widow at 60 | 61.10 | 80.10 | 104.20 | 127.20 | 149.40 | 171.90 | 197.30 |
| Widow or widower at 62 | 70.40 | 97.40 | 120.20 | 146.70 | 172.30 | 198.30 | 227.60 |
| Disabled widow at 50 | 42.80 | 56.10 | 72.90 | 89.00 | 104.50 | 120.30 | 138.00 |
| Widowed mother and one child | 105.60 | 167.90 | 218.40 | 266.60 | 313.20 | 360.60 | 413.80 |
| Widowed mother and two children | 105.60 | 167.90 | 222.70 | 308.90 | 389.90 | 435.20 | 482.70 |
| One surviving child | 70.40 | 84.00 | 109.20 | 133.30 | 156.00 | 180.30 | 206.90 |
| Maximum family payment | 105.60 | 167.90 | 222.70 | 308.90 | 389.90 | 435.20 | 482.70 |

* Generally, average earnings are figured over the period from 1951 until the worker reaches retirement age, becomes disabled, or dies.  Up to five years of low earnings or no earnings can be excluded.  The maximum earnings creditable for Social Security are $3,600 for 1951–1954, $4,200 for 1955–1958, $4,800 for 1959–1965, and $6,600 for 1966–1967.  The maximum creditable for 1968–1971 is $7,800, and beginning in 1972, $9,000; but average earnings usually cannot reach these amounts until later.  Because of this, the benefits shown in the last column on the right generally will not be payable until later.  When a person is entitled to more than one benefit, the amount actually payable is limited to the larger of the benefits.

payable under Social Security is paid to a wife with two or more dependent children. Although there is no possible way you can determine exactly what the benefits will be under Social Security in the future, there doubtless will be legislative modifications to increase benefits somewhat if the cost of living continues to rise. The original 1935 Act has been amended frequently. The overall result of these changes has been to increase benefits, broaden the protection, and extend the system to cover more workers.

**Applying for Social Security benefits.**  When a person who has worked under the Social Security law dies, some member of his family should immediately get in touch with the nearest Social Security office. A long delay in filing an application can cause loss of some benefits, since back payments can be made for no more than 12 months. An application for a lump-sum death payment must ordinarily be made within two years after the worker's death. A woman applying for a widow's benefit should take her marriage certificate to the local Social Security Office; if children are eligible, take along their birth certificates, too. Also provide the Social Security people with the insured's W-2, Wage and Tax Statement, for the previous year. Proof that the applicant was being supported by the insured person is required before benefits can be paid to a parent after the death of a working son or daughter, or to a husband or widower whose wife has died. The people in your Social Security Office will explain how the fact of support can be best shown.

If you have occasion to apply for survivor's benefits, your Social Security Office can explain how any earnings you may have in that year or later years will affect your payments and will tell you when and how to report your later earnings to the Social Security Administration. The explanation that follows is intended to give you a general idea of the conditions under which benefits are paid to beneficiaries who are still working. For taxable years ending after 1967, the following rules apply:

1. A person earning $1,680 or less in a year gets all the benefits.
2. For a person earning more than $1,680 in a year while under 72, the general rule is that $1 in benefits to you (and your family) will be withheld for each $2 earned from $1,680 to $2,880. In addition, $1 in benefits will be withheld for each $1 of earnings over $2,880.

Regardless of total earnings in a year, benefits are payable for any month in which the insured neither earns wages of more than $140 nor performs substantial services in self-employment. Benefits are also payable for all months in which the insured is 72 or older, regardless of the amount of earnings in months after reaching 72.

It is very important to note that the earnings of a person who is receiving benefits as a dependant or as a survivor affects *only his own* benefits and will not stop the payments to other members of his family. For example, a widow under 62 with two children may, depending on the husband's income record, receive a maximum benefit of $483 for herself and the two children. If she subsequently decided to take a full-time job and received a salary of $500 per month, she would no longer be eligible for continued payment under the system. However, her two dependent children would continue to receive payments amounting to about $414. To qualify for benefits, dependants must fall in one or more of these categories:

1. Unmarried children 18 years of age or between 18 and 22 if they are full-time students.
2. Unmarried children 18 years and over who were severely disabled before they reached 18 and who continue to be disabled.
3. A wife or widow, regardless of her age, if she cares for a child under 18 or disabled and the child is getting benefits based on the worker's Social Security account.
4. A wife 62 or widow 60 or older, even if there are no children entitled to payments.
5. A widow 50 or older (or dependent widower 50 or older) who becomes disabled not later than 7 years after the death of the worker, or in the case of a widow, not later than 7 years after the end of her entitlement to benefits as a widow with a child in her care.
6. A dependent husband or widower 62 or over.
7. Dependent parents 62 or over after a worker dies.

In addition to monthly benefits, a lump-sum payment may be made after the worker's death.

Under the law in effect before February 1968, there were circumstances in which benefits could be paid to children of a woman worker *only* if she had worked $1\frac{1}{2}$ out of the last 3 years before she retired, became disabled, or died, or if she had actually provided most of the child's support. This provision, which prevented payment of benefits in some cases, has been removed. Now children are considered dependants of both their mothers and their fathers, and they may become eligible for benefits when *either* parent becomes entitled to retirement or disability benefits or dies.

Payments may also be made under certain conditions to a divorced wife at 62 or a surviving divorced wife at 60 (or a disabled surviving divorced wife 50 or older). To qualify for benefits, a divorced wife must have been married to the worker for 20 years and also meet certain support requirements. Benefits also can be paid a dependent surviving divorced wife at any age if she is caring for her deceased former husband's child under 18 or disabled who is entitled to benefits. For more information about the provision, get in touch with your Social Security Office.

Monthly payments to the wife or dependent husband of a person entitled to retirement or disability payments generally cannot be made until the marriage has been in effect at least 1 year unless the couple are parents of a child. Payments can be made to the widow, stepchild, or dependent widower of a deceased worker if the marriage lasted 9 months or longer; or in the case of death in line of duty in the uniformed services, and in the case of accidental death if the marriage lasted for 3 months.

Life insurance proceeds in no way affect a survivor's eligibility for Social Security payments.

## WHO NEEDS INSURANCE AND HOW MUCH?

There are a few people who perhaps actually need no life insurance protection. An unmarried person with no dependent relatives or friends who has sufficient savings or investments to pay for funeral costs certainly has no urgent or real need for life insurance protection. However, most people become involved with a home and a family, and with other people who are financially dependent on them. Therefore, sooner or later, most people need a life insurance program.

Since life insurance costs a younger person less, the time to start a basic life insurance program most cheaply is probably while you are still in college. However, even though you may pay a low premium, you may also be paying for insurance that you actually *don't need* until later. Although there is always some risk that your health may deteriorate and make you uninsurable later, it is probably advisable to postpone the purchase of life insurance until you marry and assume family responsibilities.

What about life coverage for dependants? Since the main purpose of life insurance is to replace the financial resources of the breadwinner in case of unexpected death, there are sound arguments *against* spending large amounts of money on life insurance for dependants, particularly children. Money spent unnecessarily on life insurance could better go into good investments. The first and foremost consideration is to protect the family unit against the hardships which would arise from the death of either parent. If the husband dies, the wife and children must depend upon Social Security benefits plus life insurance for their economic survival. Even though the wife may be able to find work, it may be quite undesirable for her to have to work with the responsibilities of a young family. On the other hand, if the wife dies, sufficient life insurance funds should be available to help assure proper child care and household help.

Before you can decide on the kind and amount of protection you need, consider the following relevant factors:

1. Your yearly income basically determines how much you can afford to pay for insurance and sets the basic standard of living to which your family members have become accustomed. Your earnings also determine the amount which your family will receive under Social Security.

2. The number and ages of your children also influence the amount of Social Security benefits and the number of years which they are payable, and Social Security in turn influences the amount of ordinary life insurance you need.

3. Your net worth or ownership (often referred to as equity) in your home, investments, and other property must be skillfully evaluated in determining how much money will be available to your heirs.

4. On the other side of the ledger, you must also be aware of all the liabilities or indebtedness which you now owe—mortgages, loans, notes, installment credit, etc.

5. If you participate in a retirement plan (sometimes called an annuity), cash benefits may be available to your family in the event of your death. This could lessen the amount of life insurance necessary.

6. Your spouse's ability to earn a living for herself is also an important factor in the assessment.

7. As was mentioned earlier in the book, continuing inflation is to be expected. Therefore, it makes sense to enroll for somewhat more insurance than you actually think will be required now to offset increasing prices.

Now let us take a look at how you can make a determination of how much insurance you need. You should begin by attempting to convert the foregoing considerations into dollar terms. You need to specifically answer these questions:

1. How much money does the family need on a monthly basis to sustain its living pattern and goals?

2. What would Social Security Survivor's Benefits be?

3. What, if any, assets (money, business income, property, and so forth) would be available? Remember, even though you may have equity in a home or business, you may not want the family to have to sell the property or increase the mortgage.

4. Could, or should, the wife assume employment? When? How much could

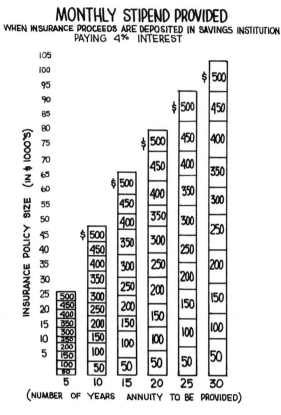

**Fig. 12–8** Computer-prepared data showing how much monthly supplementary money is needed over and above Social Security benefits.

she earn? Similarly, what economic contributions could older children make to the family's and their own needs?

Once you have determined approximately how much monthly supplementary money over and above Social Security will be required, the computer-prepared data in Fig. 12–8 will give you a speedy determination of about how much insurance you need. This figure shows how much money would have to be deposited in a savings institution paying 4 percent interest to provide specified monthly payments for various lengths of time. More precise data and data for other rates of interest are given in the computer-prepared tables of Appendix 12-A.

Now that you have tentatively determined *how much coverage* you need, you must decide on the kind of insurance to buy. You may have already discovered that you cannot afford all the protection you need if you have to pay a whole-life premium on the full amount.  Your best alternatives are probably these:

1. Purchase a small amount of whole-life and a large amount of term insurance.

    or

2. Purchase a whole-life plan which allows you to borrow automatically on the cash-value buildup.  This may cost you more than term for the first couple of years, but may save you money if you want to keep your policy in force for a long period of time.

Don't be disheartened if you still can't afford all the protection you feel you need.  If you are interested in investments and are willing to learn the in's and out's of investing, you might be better off keeping insurance coverage to a minimally acceptable level and diverting more money now or later into investments.

## WHICH COMPANY? WHICH AGENT?

Insurance salesmen may be affiliated exclusively and directly with a particular insurance company—selling only the insurance of that company.  Other salesmen may work for or be an independent insurance broker.  In the latter case, the salesman may handle insurance from a number of different insurers.  There is some advantage to talking with a broker since he may be able to better handle your total insurance needs (including property, liability, and health insurance)

by choosing the best policy in each category from among the various insurance companies he represents.

One of the best ways to begin finding a good insurance salesman is by asking your parents, friends, neighbors, and others for recommendations. It is important to ask them such questions as, "Have you discussed insurance with this agent? Did you like the way he worked with you? Was he professional in his approach? Why?"

You may also want to know something about an agent's membership in professional groups. Agents who belong to local Life Underwriters Associations are often among the more experienced agents in their communities. Those who are Chartered Life Underwriters have also passed a series of college-level examinations on insurance and related subjects. These agents are entitled to use the letters "C.L.U." after their names.

Because insurance programs are structured differently by different companies and because they also set rates independently, you should talk to more than one agent. If you find yourself confused by unfamiliar terms, things not discussed already in this chapter, turn to Appendix 12-B. This handy reference section gives an easy-to-find alphabetic reference to standard insurance terminology.

Rates for basic kinds of coverage can be quickly checked over the telephone, saving you hours of time otherwise spent in listening to "canned" salesmen's pitches in your home. Once you've narrowed down the field, you can invite one or two agents in for personal interviews and make a final selection.

## FEEDBACK 12

A. Review Table 12–2. From it, and your understanding of the chapter, select the type of life insurance which best suits your particular goals, your age, and your income. Answer to your satisfaction:

● How long do you want protection?

● If you should die, how many insurance dollars would your survivors require immediately, for one year, for five years? Compute the monthly income payments necessary for them to meet the obligations which you think worth while.

● What is the value of life insurance, which makes it a must for careful financial planners, even if those planners are actively pursuing growing investment goals?

B. Make an insurance check on yourself.

● Are you insured with a group life policy? In what amount?

● Do your financial obligations (installment payments, loans, etc.) have "credit life" provisions? Are you paying too much for this protection?

● What would your death-by-accident mean to your beneficiaries?

- What would disability mean to your continued payment of insurance premiums?

C. With your local Social Security Office, or using the tables in this chapter, compute benefits for survivors of:

- Yourself.
- Your wife or husband.
- Your parent (or either parent, if both have accrued Social Security credits).

## DISCUSSION QUESTIONS

1. Why do so many people postpone their buying of life insurance until it is actually needed? When is the best time of one's life to buy it?
2. What are the advantages to whole life insurance? Why is it unattractive to young people?
3. What are the advantages to term insurance? Disadvantages?
4. Why are accident insurance premiums so low?
5. What are the differences between stock and mutual companies? What are their similarities?
6. In what ways may policy benefits be paid? Who would benefit most from each way?
7. In what ways is the insurance coverage broader under Social Security than under life insurance?
8. What conditions brought about the enactment of the Social Security Act?
9. Who actually needs insurance? Why?
10. How can one inform himself as to the best company from which to buy?

## CASE PROBLEM

Harold Capella is 29; his wife, Ann, 28. They have two boys 6 and 4. Harold has been a machinist for a large aircraft manufacturer for eight years. He recently was made production foreman and given a hefty pay increase (from $9,500 to $14,200 annually). A dear aunt passed away a year ago, leaving a substantial bequest for the boys' education. Harold now has a $15,000 term policy with a family rider providing $1,000 on each child, and $3,000 coverage for Ann. In discussing their favorable turn of events, the Capellas feel they need to be putting substantially more money into savings.

a) Should they continue their present life insurance program? Add more term protection?

b) Do you think it would be advisable to add a large straight life policy to their protection—funneling money into this form of forced savings?

c) What other alternatives should they consider?

d) How would their planning differ should Harold temporarily have lost his job, subsequently taking a position paying less money?

## SUGGESTED READINGS

American College of Life Underwriters. *C.L.U. Teachers Manual.* Philadelphia: 1953.

Cah, William. *A Matter of Life and Death.* New York: Random House, 1970. 309 pp.

*Consumers Union Report on Life Insurance, The.* Mt. Vernon, N.Y.: Consumers Union, 1967. 218 pp.

Eilers, Robert, and Robert M. Crowe. *Group Insurance Handbook.* Homewood, Ill.: R. D. Irwin, 1965. 972 pp.

Fraine, Harold George. *Valuation of Securities Holdings of Life Insurance Companies.* Homewood, Illinois: R. D. Irwin, 1962.

Gollin, James. *Pay Now, Die Later: What's Wrong with Life Insurance; A Report on Our Biggest and Most Wasteful Industry.* New York: Random House, 1966. 267 pp.

Gregg, Davis Weinert. *Group Life Insurance; An Analysis of Concepts, Contracts, Costs, and Company Practices,* 3rd ed. Homewood, Illinois: Published for S. S. Huebner Foundation for Insurance Education, University of Pennsylvania by R. D. Irwin, 1962.

Harper, Floyd S., and Lewis C. Workman. *Fundamental Mathematics of Life Insurance.* Homewood, Illinois: R. D. Irwin, 1970. 394 pp.

*How to Get the Most Life Insurance Protection at the Lowest Cost.* Larchmont, N.Y.: J. K. Lasser Tax Institute, 1968. 210 pp.

Huebner, Soloman S., and Kenneth Black. *Life Insurance.* New York: Appleton-Century-Crofts, 1969. 875 pp.

Life Insurance Association of America. *Life Insurance Companies as Financial Institutes.* (A monograph prepared for the Commission on Money and Credit.) Englewood Cliffs, N.J.: Prentice-Hall, 1962.

Lovelace, Griffin M. *Life and Life Insurance.* Hartford, Conn.: Life Insurance Agency Management Association, 1961.

McCahan, David. *The Beneficiary in Life Insurance.* Rev. ed. Edited by Dan M. McGill. Homewood, Illinois: Published for the S. S. Huebner Foundation for Insurance Education, University of Pennsylvania by R. D. Irwin, 1956.

Mehr, Robert Irwin. *Life Insurance, Theory and Practice.* Austin, Tex.: Business Publications, 1970. 956 pp.

Nash, Chester C. *Getting the Most for Your Family's Life Insurance Dollar.* New York: Association Press, 1966. 26 pp.

Oates, James Franklin. *Business and Social Change; Life Insurance Looks to the Future.* New York: McGraw-Hill, 1968. 99 pp.

Pendleton, Oswald William. *How to Find Out About Insurance: A Guide to Sources of Information.* New York: Pergamon Press, 1967. 196 pp.

Pfeffer, Irving. *Insurance and Economic Society.* Homewood, Illinois: Published for S. S. Huebner Foundation for Insurance Education, University of Pennsylvania by R. D. Irwin, 1956.

Redeker, Harry S., and Charles K. Reid, II. *Life Insurance Settlement Options.* Boston: Little, Brown, 1957.

Russell, George Hugh, and Kenneth Black, Jr. *Human Behavior and Life Insurance.* Englewood Cliffs, N.J.: Prentice-Hall, 1963. 267 pp.

Willett, Allan Herbert. *The Economic Theory of Risk and Insurance.* Philadelphia: University of Pennsylvania Press, 1951.

## 12-A COMPUTER-PREPARED TABLE SHOWING AMOUNT OF INSURANCE PROCEEDS NEEDED TO PROVIDE VARIOUS AMOUNTS OF MONTHLY BENEFITS AT DIFFERING INTEREST RATES

| Monthly payment | Years | Policy size needed when invested at | | |
|---|---|---|---|---|
| | | 4% | | 6% |
| 50 | I | 587.15 | 586.45 | 580.90 |
| 50 | 5 | 2714.95 | 2649.50 | 2586.25 |
| 50 | 10 | 4938.50 | 4714.05 | 4503.65 |
| 50 | 15 | 6759.60 | 6322.75 | 5925.15 |
| 50 | 20 | 8251.05 | 7576.25 | 6979.00 |
| 50 | 25 | 9472.60 | 8553.00 | 7760.30 |
| 50 | 30 | 10473.10 | 9314.05 | 8339.55 |
| 100 | I | 1174.30 | 1172.90 | 1161.80 |
| 100 | 5 | 5429.90 | 5299.00 | 5172.50 |
| 100 | 10 | 9877.00 | 9428.10 | 9007.30 |
| 100 | 15 | 13519.20 | 12645.50 | 11850.30 |
| 100 | 20 | 16502.10 | 15152.50 | 13958.00 |
| 100 | 25 | 18945.20 | 17106.00 | 15520.60 |
| 100 | 30 | 20946.10 | 18628.10 | 16679.10 |
| 150 | I | 1761.45 | 1759.35 | 1742.70 |
| 150 | 5 | 8144.85 | 7948.50 | 7758.75 |
| 150 | 10 | 14815.50 | 14142.20 | 13511.00 |
| 150 | 15 | 20278.80 | 18968.30 | 17775.40 |
| 150 | 20 | 24753.20 | 22728.80 | 20937.00 |
| 150 | 25 | 28417.80 | 25659.00 | 23280.90 |
| 150 | 30 | 31419.20 | 27942.20 | 25018.70 |
| 200 | I | 2348.60 | 2345.80 | 2323.60 |
| 200 | 5 | 10859.80 | 10598.00 | 10345.00 |
| 200 | 10 | 19754.00 | 18856.20 | 18014.60 |
| 200 | 15 | 27038.40 | 25291.00 | 23700.60 |
| 200 | 20 | 33004.20 | 30305.00 | 27916.00 |
| 200 | 25 | 37890.40 | 34212.00 | 31041.20 |
| 200 | 30 | 41892.20 | 37256.20 | 33358.20 |
| 250 | I | 2935.75 | 2932.25 | 2904.50 |
| 250 | 5 | 13574.80 | 13247.50 | 12931.30 |
| 250 | 10 | 24692.50 | 23570.30 | 22518.30 |
| 250 | 15 | 33798.00 | 31613.80 | 29625.80 |
| 250 | 20 | 41255.30 | 37881.30 | 34895.00 |
| 250 | 25 | 47363.00 | 42765.00 | 38801.50 |
| 250 | 30 | 52365.30 | 46570.20 | 41697.80 |

| Monthly payment | Years | Policy size needed when invested at | | |
|---|---|---|---|---|
| | | | 5% | 6% |
| 300 | 1 | 3522.90 | 3518.70 | 3485.40 |
| 300 | 5 | 16289.70 | 15897.00 | 15517.50 |
| 300 | 10 | 29631.00 | 28284.30 | 27021.90 |
| 300 | 15 | 40557.60 | 37936.50 | 35550.90 |
| 300 | 20 | 49506.30 | 45457.50 | 41874.00 |
| 300 | 25 | 56835.60 | 51318.00 | 46561.80 |
| 300 | 30 | 62838.30 | 55884.30 | 50037.30 |
| 350 | 1 | 4110.05 | 4105.15 | 4066.30 |
| 350 | 5 | 19004.70 | 18546.50 | 18103.80 |
| 350 | 10 | 34569.50 | 32998.40 | 31525.60 |
| 350 | 15 | 47317.20 | 44259.30 | 41476.10 |
| 350 | 20 | 57757.40 | 53033.80 | 48853.00 |
| 350 | 25 | 66308.20 | 59871.00 | 54322.10 |
| 350 | 30 | 73311.40 | 65198.40 | 58376.90 |
| 400 | 1 | 4697.20 | 4691.60 | 4647.20 |
| 400 | 5 | 21719.60 | 21196.00 | 20690.00 |
| 400 | 10 | 39508.00 | 37712.40 | 36029.20 |
| 400 | 15 | 54076.80 | 50582.00 | 47401.20 |
| 400 | 20 | 66008.40 | 60610.00 | 55832.00 |
| 400 | 25 | 75780.80 | 68424.00 | 62082.40 |
| 400 | 30 | 83784.40 | 74512.40 | 66716.40 |
| 450 | 1 | 5284.35 | 5278.05 | 5228.10 |
| 450 | 5 | 24434.60 | 23845.50 | 23276.30 |
| 450 | 10 | 44446.50 | 42426.50 | 40532.90 |
| 450 | 15 | 60836.40 | 56904.80 | 53326.40 |
| 450 | 20 | 74259.50 | 68186.30 | 62811.00 |
| 450 | 25 | 85253.40 | 76977.00 | 69842.70 |
| 450 | 30 | 94257.50 | 83826.50 | 75056.00 |
| 500 | 1 | 5871.50 | 5864.50 | 5809.00 |
| 500 | 5 | 27149.50 | 26495.00 | 25862.50 |
| 500 | 10 | 49385.00 | 47140.50 | 45036.50 |
| 500 | 15 | 67596.00 | 63227.50 | 59251.50 |
| 500 | 20 | 82510.50 | 75762.50 | 69790.00 |
| 500 | 25 | 94726.00 | 85530.00 | 77603.00 |
| 500 | 30 | 104731.00 | 93140.50 | 83395.50 |
| 550 | 1 | 6458.65 | 6450.95 | 6389.90 |
| 550 | 5 | 29864.50 | 29144.50 | 28448.80 |
| 550 | 10 | 54323.50 | 51854.60 | 49540.20 |
| 550 | 15 | 74355.60 | 69550.30 | 65176.70 |
| 550 | 20 | 90761.50 | 83338.80 | 76769.00 |
| 550 | 25 | 104199.00 | 94083.00 | 85363.30 |
| 550 | 30 | 115204.00 | 102455.00 | 91735.00 |

| Monthly payment | Years | Policy size needed when invested at | | |
| --- | --- | --- | --- | --- |
| | | 4% | 5% | 6% |
| 600 | 1 | 7045.80 | 7037.40 | 6970.80 |
| 600 | 5 | 32579.40 | 31794.00 | 31035.00 |
| 600 | 10 | 59262.00 | 56568.60 | 54043.80 |
| 600 | 15 | 81115.20 | 75873.00 | 71101.80 |
| 600 | 20 | 99012.60 | 90915.00 | 83748.00 |
| 600 | 25 | 113671.00 | 102636.00 | 93123.60 |
| 600 | 30 | 125677.00 | 111769.00 | 100075.00 |
| 650 | 1 | 7632.95 | 7623.85 | 7551.70 |
| 650 | 5 | 35294.40 | 34443.50 | 33621.30 |
| 650 | 10 | 64200.50 | 61282.70 | 58547.50 |
| 650 | 15 | 87874.80 | 82195.80 | 77027.00 |
| 650 | 20 | 107264.00 | 98491.30 | 90727.00 |
| 650 | 25 | 123144.00 | 111189.00 | 100884.00 |
| 650 | 30 | 136150.00 | 121083.00 | 108414.00 |
| 700 | 1 | 8220.10 | 8210.30 | 8132.60 |
| 700 | 5 | 38009.30 | 37093.00 | 36207.50 |
| 700 | 10 | 69139.00 | 65996.70 | 63051.10 |
| 700 | 15 | 94634.40 | 88518.50 | 82952.10 |
| 700 | 20 | 115515.00 | 106068.00 | 97706.00 |
| 700 | 25 | 132616.00 | 119742.00 | 108644.00 |
| 700 | 30 | 146623.00 | 130397.00 | 116754.00 |
| 750 | 1 | 8807.25 | 8796.75 | 8713.50 |
| 750 | 5 | 40724.30 | 39742.50 | 38793.80 |
| 750 | 10 | 74077.50 | 70710.80 | 67554.80 |
| 750 | 15 | 101394.00 | 94841.30 | 88877.30 |
| 750 | 20 | 123766.00 | 113644.00 | 104685.00 |
| 750 | 25 | 142089.00 | 128295.00 | 116405.00 |
| 750 | 30 | 157096.00 | 139711.00 | 125093.00 |
| 800 | 1 | 9394.40 | 9383.20 | 9294.40 |
| 800 | 5 | 43439.20 | 42392.00 | 41380.00 |
| 800 | 10 | 79016.00 | 75424.80 | 72058.40 |
| 800 | 15 | 108154.00 | 101164.00 | 94802.40 |
| 800 | 20 | 132017.00 | 121220.00 | 111664.00 |
| 800 | 25 | 151562.00 | 136848.00 | 124165.00 |
| 800 | 30 | 167569.00 | 149025.00 | 133433.00 |
| 850 | 1 | 9981.55 | 9969.65 | 9875.30 |
| 850 | 5 | 46154.20 | 45041.50 | 43966.30 |
| 850 | 10 | 83954.50 | 80138.90 | 76562.10 |
| 850 | 15 | 114913.00 | 107487.00 | 100728.00 |
| 850 | 20 | 140268.00 | 128796.00 | 118643.00 |
| 850 | 25 | 161034.00 | 145401.00 | 131925.00 |
| 850 | 30 | 178042.00 | 158339.00 | 141772.00 |

| Monthly payment | Years | Policy size needed when invested at | | |
|---|---|---|---|---|
| | | 4% | 5% | 6% |
| 900 | 1 | 10568.70 | 10556.10 | 10456.20 |
| 900 | 5 | 48869.10 | 47691.00 | 46552.50 |
| 900 | 10 | 88893.00 | 84852.90 | 81065.70 |
| 900 | 15 | 121673.00 | 113810.00 | 106653.00 |
| 900 | 20 | 148519.00 | 136373.00 | 125622.00 |
| 900 | 25 | 170507.00 | 153954.00 | 139685.00 |
| 900 | 30 | 188515.00 | 167653.00 | 150112.00 |
| 950 | 1 | 11155.90 | 11142.60 | 11037.10 |
| 950 | 5 | 51584.10 | 50340.50 | 49138.80 |
| 950 | 10 | 93831.50 | 89566.90 | 85569.30 |
| 950 | 15 | 128432.00 | 120132.00 | 112578.00 |
| 950 | 20 | 156770.00 | 143949.00 | 132601.00 |
| 950 | 25 | 179979.00 | 162507.00 | 147446.00 |
| 950 | 30 | 198988.00 | 176967.00 | 158451.00 |
| 1000 | 1 | 11743.00 | 11729.00 | 11618.00 |
| 1000 | 5 | 54299.00 | 52990.00 | 51725.00 |
| 1000 | 10 | 98770.00 | 94281.00 | 90073.00 |
| 1000 | 15 | 135192.00 | 126455.00 | 118503.00 |
| 1000 | 20 | 165021.00 | 151525.00 | 139580.00 |
| 1000 | 25 | 189452.00 | 171060.00 | 155206.00 |
| 1000 | 30 | 209461.00 | 186281.00 | 166791.00 |
| 1050 | 1 | 12330.20 | 12315.50 | 12198.90 |
| 1050 | 5 | 57014.00 | 55639.50 | 54311.30 |
| 1050 | 10 | 103709.00 | 98995.10 | 94576.70 |
| 1050 | 15 | 141952.00 | 132778.00 | 124428.00 |
| 1050 | 20 | 173272.00 | 159101.00 | 146559.00 |
| 1050 | 25 | 198925.00 | 179613.00 | 162966.00 |
| 1050 | 30 | 219934.00 | 195595.00 | 175131.00 |
| 1100 | 1 | 12917.30 | 12901.90 | 12779.80 |
| 1100 | 5 | 59728.90 | 58289.00 | 56897.50 |
| 1100 | 10 | 108647.00 | 103709.00 | 99080.30 |
| 1100 | 15 | 148711.00 | 139101.00 | 130353.00 |
| 1100 | 20 | 181523.00 | 166678.00 | 153538.00 |
| 1100 | 25 | 208397.00 | 188166.00 | 170727.00 |
| 1100 | 30 | 230407.00 | 204909.00 | 183470.00 |
| 1150 | 1 | 13504.50 | 13488.40 | 13360.70 |
| 1150 | 5 | 62443.90 | 60938.50 | 59483.80 |
| 1150 | 10 | 113586.00 | 108423.00 | 103584.00 |
| 1150 | 15 | 155471.00 | 145423.00 | 136278.00 |
| 1150 | 20 | 189774.00 | 174254.00 | 160517.00 |
| 1150 | 25 | 217870.00 | 196719.00 | 178487.00 |
| 1150 | 30 | 240880.00 | 214223.00 | 191810.00 |

| Monthly payment | Years | Policy size needed when invested at | | |
|---|---|---|---|---|
| | | 4% | 5% | 6% |
| 1200 | 1 | 14091.60 | 14074.80 | 13941.60 |
| 1200 | 5 | 65158.80 | 63588.00 | 62070.00 |
| 1200 | 10 | 118524.00 | 113137.00 | 108088.00 |
| 1200 | 15 | 162230.00 | 151746.00 | 142204.00 |
| 1200 | 20 | 198025.00 | 181830.00 | 167496.00 |
| 1200 | 25 | 227342.00 | 205272.00 | 186247.00 |
| 1200 | 30 | 251353.00 | 223537.00 | 200149.00 |
| 1250 | 1 | 14678.80 | 14661.30 | 14522.50 |
| 1250 | 5 | 67873.80 | 66237.50 | 64656.30 |
| 1250 | 10 | 123463.00 | 117851.00 | 112591.00 |
| 1250 | 15 | 168990.00 | 158069.00 | 148129.00 |
| 1250 | 20 | 206276.00 | 189406.00 | 174475.00 |
| 1250 | 25 | 236815.00 | 213825.00 | 194008.00 |
| 1250 | 30 | 261826.00 | 232851.00 | 208489.00 |
| 1300 | 1 | 15265.90 | 15247.70 | 15103.40 |
| 1300 | 5 | 70588.70 | 68887.00 | 67242.50 |
| 1300 | 10 | 128401.00 | 122565.00 | 117095.00 |
| 1300 | 15 | 175750.00 | 164392.00 | 154054.00 |
| 1300 | 20 | 214527.00 | 196983.00 | 181454.00 |
| 1300 | 25 | 246288.00 | 222378.00 | 201768.00 |
| 1300 | 30 | 272299.00 | 242165.00 | 216828.00 |
| 1350 | 1 | 15853.10 | 15834.20 | 15684.30 |
| 1350 | 5 | 73303.70 | 71536.50 | 69828.80 |
| 1350 | 10 | 133340.00 | 127279.00 | 121599.00 |
| 1350 | 15 | 182509.00 | 170714.00 | 159979.00 |
| 1350 | 20 | 222778.00 | 204559.00 | 188433.00 |
| 1350 | 25 | 255760.00 | 230931.00 | 209528.00 |
| 1350 | 30 | 282772.00 | 251479.00 | 225168.00 |
| 1400 | 1 | 16440.20 | 16420.60 | 16265.20 |
| 1400 | 5 | 76018.60 | 74186.00 | 72415.00 |
| 1400 | 10 | 138278.00 | 131993.00 | 126102.00 |
| 1400 | 15 | 189269.00 | 177037.00 | 165904.00 |
| 1400 | 20 | 231029.00 | 212135.00 | 195412.00 |
| 1400 | 25 | 265233.00 | 239484.00 | 217288.00 |
| 1400 | 30 | 293245.00 | 260793.00 | 233507.00 |
| 1450 | 1 | 17027.40 | 17007.10 | 16846.10 |
| 1450 | 5 | 78733.60 | 76835.50 | 75001.30 |
| 1450 | 10 | 143217.00 | 136707.00 | 130606.00 |
| 1450 | 15 | 196028.00 | 183360.00 | 171829.00 |
| 1450 | 20 | 239280.00 | 219711.00 | 202391.00 |
| 1450 | 25 | 274705.00 | 248037.00 | 225049.00 |
| 1450 | 30 | 303718.00 | 270107.00 | 241847.00 |

| Monthly payment | Years | Policy size needed when invested at | | |
|---|---|---|---|---|
| | | 4% | 5% | 6% |
| 1500 | 1 | 17614.50 | 17593.50 | 17427.00 |
| 1500 | 5 | 81448.50 | 79485.00 | 77587.50 |
| 1500 | 10 | 148155.00 | 141422.00 | 135110.00 |
| 1500 | 15 | 202788.00 | 189683.00 | 177755.00 |
| 1500 | 20 | 247532.00 | 227288.00 | 209370.00 |
| 1500 | 25 | 284178.00 | 256590.00 | 232089.00 |
| 1500 | 30 | 314192.00 | 279422.00 | 250187.00 |

# 12-B GLOSSARY OF LIFE INSURANCE TERMS

**Accidental Death Benefit.** A provision added to an insurance policy for payment of an additional benefit in case of death by accidental means. It is often referred to as "Double Indemnity."

**Actuary.** A person professionally trained in the technical aspects of insurance and related fields, particularly in the mathematics of insurance such as the calculation of premiums, reserves, and other values.

**Agent.** A sales and service representative of an insurance company. Life insurance agents may also be called life underwriters.

**Annuitant.** The person during whose life an annuity is payable, usually the person to receive the annuity.

**Annuity.** A contract that provides an income for a specified period of time, such as a number of years or for life.

**Annuity Certain.** A contract that provides an income for a specified number of years, regardless of life or death.

**Application.** A statement of information made by a person applying for life insurance. It is used by the insurance company to determine the acceptability of the risk and the basis of the policy contract.

**Assignment.** The legal transfer of one person's interest in an insurance policy to another person.

**Automatic Premium Loan.** A provision in a life insurance policy authorizing the company to pay automatically by means of a policy loan any premium not paid by the end of the grace period.

**Beneficiary.** The person named in the policy to receive the insurance proceeds at the death of the insured.

**Broker.** A sales and service representative who handles insurance for his clients, generally selling insurance for various kinds and for several companies.

**Business Life Insurance.** Life insurance purchased by a business enterprise on the life of a member of the firm. It is often bought by partnerships to protect the surviving partners against loss caused by the death of a partner, or by a corporation to reimburse it for loss caused by the death of a key employee.

**Cash Surrender Value.** The amount available in cash upon voluntary termination of a policy before it becomes payable by death or maturity.

**Claim.** Notification to an insurance company that payment of an amount is due under the terms of a policy.

**Convertible Term Insurance.** Term insurance which can be exchanged, at the option of the policyholder and without evidence of insurability, for another plan of insurance.

**Credit Life Insurance.** Term life insurance issued through a lender or lending agency to cover payment of a loan, installment purchase, or other obligation in case of death.

**Declination.** The rejection by a life insurance company of an application for life insurance, usually for reasons of the health or occupation of the applicant.

**Deferred Annuity.** An annuity providing for the income payments to begin at some future date, such as in a specified number of years or at a specified age.

**Deferred Group Annuity.** A type of group annuity providing for the purchase each year of a paid-up deferred annuity for each member of the group, the total amount received by the member at retirement being the sum of these deferred annuities.

**Deposit Administration Group Annuity.** A type of group annuity providing for the accumulation of contributions in an undivided fund out of which annuities are purchased as the individual members of the group retire.

**Disability Benefit.** A provision added to a life insurance policy for waiver of premium, and sometimes payment of monthly income, if the insured becomes totally and permanently disabled.

**Dividend Addition.** An amount of paid-up insurance purchased with a policy dividend and added to the face amount of the policy.

**Double Indemnity.** An accidental death benefit providing for additional payment of an amount equal to the face of the policy in case of death by accidental means.

**Endowment Insurance.** Insurance payable to the insured if he is living on the maturity date stated in the policy, or to a beneficiary if the insured dies prior to that date.

**Expectation of life (Life Expectancy).** The average number of years of life remaining for persons of a given age according to a particular mortality table.

**Extended Term Insurance.** A form of insurance available as a nonforfeiture option. It provides the original amount of insurance for a limited period of time.

**Face Amount.** The amount stated on the face of the policy that will be paid in case of death or at the maturity of the contract. It does not include dividend additions, or additional amounts payable under accidental death or other special provisions.

**Family Income Policy.** A life insurance policy, combining whole life and decreasing term insurance, under which the beneficiary receives income payments to the end of a specified period if the insured dies prior to the end of the period, and the face amount of the policy either at the end of the period or at the death of the insured.

**Family Policy.** A life insurance policy providing insurance on all or several family members in one contract, generally whole life insurance on the husband and smaller amounts of term insurance on the wife and children, including those born after the policy is issued.

**Fraternal Life Insurance.** Life insurance provided by fraternal orders of societies to their members.

**Grace Period.** A period (usually 31 days) following the premium due date, during which an overdue premium may be paid without penalty. The policy remains in force throughout this period.

**Group Annuity.** A pension plan providing annuities at retirement to a group of persons under a single master contract, with the individual members of the group holding certificates stating their coverage. It is usually issued to an employer for the benefit of employees. The two basic types are deferred and deposit administration group annuities.

**Group Life Insurance.** Life insurance issued, usually without medical examination, on a group of persons under a single master policy. It is usually issued to an employer for the benefit of employees. The individual members of the group hold certificates stating their coverage.

**Individual Policy Pension Trust.** A type of pension plan, frequently used for small groups, administered by trustees who are authorized to purchase individual level premium policies or annuity contracts for each member of the plan. The policies usually provide both life insurance and retirement benefits.

**Industrial Life Insurance.** Life insurance issued in small amounts, usually not over $500, with premiums payable on a weekly or monthly basis. The premiums are generally collected at the home by an agent of the company.

**Insurability.** Acceptability to the company of an applicant for insurance.

**Insurance Examiner.** The representative of a state insurance department assigned to participate in the official audit and examination of the affairs of an insurance company.

**Insured.** The person on whose life an insurance policy is issued.

**Lapsed Policy.** A policy terminated for nonpayment of premiums. The term is sometimes limited to a termination occurring before the policy has a cash or other surrender value.

**Legal Reserve Life Insurance Company.** A life insurance company operating under state insurance laws specifying the minimum basis for the reserves the company must maintain on its policies.

**Level Premium Insurance.** Insurance for which the cost is distributed evenly over the period during which premiums are paid. The premium remains the same from year to year, and is more than the actual cost of protection in the earlier years of the policy and less than the actual cost in the later years. The excess paid in the early years builds up the reserve.

**Life Annuity.** A contract that provides an income for life.

**Life Insurance in Force.** The sum of the face amounts, plus dividend additions, of life insurance policies outstanding at a given time. Additional amounts payable under accidental death or other special provisions are not included.

**Limited Payment Life Insurance.** Whole life insurance on which premiums are payable for a specified number of years or until death if death occurs before the end of the specified period.

**Mortality Table.** A statistical table showing the death rate at each age, usually expressed as so many per thousand.

**Mutual Life Insurance Company.** A life insurance company without stockholders whose management is directed by a board elected by the policyholders. Mutual companies, in general, issue participating insurance.

**Nonforfeiture Option.**  One of the choices available to the policyholder if he discontinues the required premium payments.  The policy value, if any, may be taken in cash, as extended term insurance or as reduced paid-up insurance.

**Nonparticipating Insurance.**  Insurance on which the premium is calculated to cover as closely as possible the anticipated cost of the insurance protection and on which no dividends are payable.

**Ordinary Life Insurance.**  Life insurance usually issued in amounts of $1,000 or more with premiums payable on an annual, semiannual, quarterly, or monthly basis.  The term is also used to mean straight life insurance.

**Paid-Up Insurance.**  Insurance on which all required premiums have been paid.  The term is frequently used to mean the reduced paid-up insurance available as a nonforfeiture option.

**Participating Insurance.**  Insurance on which the policyholder is entitled to receive policy dividends reflecting the difference between the premium charged and actual experience.  The premium is calculated to provide some margin over the anticipated cost of the insurance protection.

**Permanent Life Insurance.**  A phrase used to cover any form of life insurance except term; generally insurance, such as whole life or endowment, that accrues cash value.

**Policy.**  The printed document stating the terms of the insurance contract that is issued to the policyholder by the company.

**Policy Dividend.**  A refund of part of the premium on a participating life insurance policy reflecting the difference between the premium charged and actual experience.

**Policy Loan.**  A loan made by an insurance company to a policyholder on the security of the cash value of his policy.

**Policy Reserves.**  The amounts that an insurance company allocates specifically for the fulfillment of its policy obligations.  Reserves are so calculated that, together with future premiums and interest earnings, they will enable the company to pay all future claims.

**Preauthorized Check Plan.**  A plan by which a policyholder arranges with his bank and insurance company to have his premium payments drawn, usually monthly from his checking account.

**Premium.**  The payment, or one of the periodical payments, a policyholder agrees to make for an insurance policy.

**Premium Loan.**  A policy loan made for the purpose of paying premiums.

**Rated Policy.**  An insurance policy issued at higher than standard premium rate to cover the extra-risk involved in certain cases where the insured has impaired health or a hazardous occupation.

**Reduced Paid-Up Insurance.**  A form of insurance available as a nonforfeiture option.  It provides for continuation of the original insurance plan, but for a reduced amount.

**Renewable Term Insurance.**  Term insurance which can be renewed at the end of the term, at the option of the policyholder and without evidence of insurability, for a limited number of successive terms.  The rates increase at each renewal as the age of the insured increases.

**Revival.**  The reinstatement of a lapsed policy by the company upon receipt of evidence of insurability and payment of past due premiums with interest.

**Settlement Option.** One of the ways, other than immediate payment in a lump sum, in which the policyholder or beneficiary may choose to have the policy proceeds paid.

**Stock Life Insurance Company.** A life insurance company owned by stockholders who elect a board to direct the company's management. Stock companies, in general, issue non-participating insurance, but may also issue participating insurance.

**Straight Life Insurance.** Whole life insurance on which premiums are payable for life.

**Supplementary Contract.** An agreement between a life insurance company and a policyholder or beneficiary by which the company retains the cash sum payable under an insurance policy and makes payments in accordance with the settlement option chosen.

**Term Insurance.** Insurance payable to a beneficiary at the death of the insured provided death occurs within a specified period, such as five or ten years, or before a specified age.

**Underwriting.** The process by which an insurance company determines whether or not and on what basis it will accept an application for insurance.

**Waiver of Premium.** A provision that under certain conditions an insurance policy will be kept in full force by the company without further payment of premiums. It is used most often in the event of total and permanent disability.

**Whole Life Insurance.** Insurance payable to a beneficiary at the death of the insured whenever that occurs. Premiums may be payable for a specified number of years (limited payment life) or for life (straight life).

CHAPTER 13

# HEALTH, DISABILITY,
# AND RETIREMENT PROGRAMS

After studying about life insurance in Chapter 12, you realize that there can be *living* values associated with that kind of insurance. Nonetheless, there's a great deal of truth to the old adage that, "You have to die before you get anything back on life insurance." There are several other kinds of insurance and financial programs you should consider as you work out your total financial goals and action plans. Fortunately, these programs don't make the same demands for *payoff* as does life insurance. To the contrary they are intended to provide *living* financial assistance to you as well as your family.

These programs are designed to give your finances a boost when illness or disability strikes and when you retire from your job or profession. Consideration is given to Social Security protection and to private nongovernmental plans.

## HEALTH, DISABILITY INSURANCE, AND MEDICARE

Today's highly specialized and complex world of health insurance is seen in best perspective by examining the introduction and evolution of health insurance as it changed in response to each new social and economic demand which arose over the past century.

In the United States today the great majority of health care is financed through the broad, competitive network of private health insurance. The broad scope and continued growth of health insurance coverage stems from century-old origins. In response to the public's demand for coverage against the frequent rail and steamboat accidents of the mid-nineteenth century, the nation's earliest accident insurance company was organized in 1850. By 1864, coverages were available for accidents of virtually every description. By the turn of the century, 47 American companies issued accident insurance.

The first company organized specifically to write health insurance was founded in 1847. Health insurance began to show substantial growth toward the end of the century with the entry of accident companies into the field. At about the same time, life insurance companies began to enter both the accident and health fields.

In its embryonic stage, the primary emphasis of the health insurance policy

was directed toward *replacement* of income rather than hospital or surgical benefits. The early insurance company policy insured the policyholder against the loss of earned income due to a limited number of diseases, including typhus, typhoid, scarlet fever, smallpox, diphtheria, diabetes, and a few others. This policy contained a provision for a seven-day waiting period to take place before the start of benefit payments. The policy's indemnity was limited to 26 consecutive weeks. Although subsequent policies were to liberalize the number of diseases covered, eliminate medical examinations, and include surgical fee schedules, this emphasis on the income aspects of the insurance continued until 1929.

### MODERN HEALTH INSURANCE

In that year, a powerful socio-economic upheaval—the start of the Depression —ushered in the beginning of modern health insurance. As the Depression deepened, the public became increasingly aware of the rising costs of medical care. Hospitals were faced with empty beds and declining revenues.

At this time, a group of school teachers banded together to form an arrangement with Baylor Hospital in Dallas, Texas, to provide themselves with hospital care on a *prepayment* basis. This was the origin of the Blue Cross service concept for the provision of hospital care, and it had a profound effect on the traditional writers of insurance, the insurance companies, by foreshadowing the development of the reimbursement policy for hospital and surgical care.

A further major change occurred during World War II. The freezing of industrial wages made the fringe benefit a significant element of collective bargaining. Group health insurance became a large part of the fringe benefit package.

In the postwar period, three powerful stimuli interacted to provide modern health insurance with its strongest impetus. The first of these was a decision of the United States Supreme Court which held that fringe benefits, including health insurance, was a legitimate part of the bargaining process wherein labor negotiated its contracts with management. The second was the sharply escalating costs for care which prompted the public to find a way to protect itself against the expense. The third force was the continuing improvement of health insurance itself, through the introduction and the broadening of coverages.

The emergence of the nation from a depression economy to the beginnings of an affluent society also brought the introduction of the broadest form of health insurance devised to date: major medical expense insurance. From its start as an executive coverage, major medical insurance grew rapidly in response to the family's need for protection against serious and prolonged illness in an age characterized by swiftly rising hospital, surgical, and medical costs.

With the country's economy in full and rapid expansion following World War II, the newest major development in health insurance, long-term disability income coverage, led the health insurance business to a re-emphasis on the income replacement concept of insurance during times of disability and other financial emergencies.

Concerned with the rapidly increasing costs of medical care, Congress in 1965 passed historic amendments to the Social Security Act which created Medicare. This new form of governmental hospital insurance and supplementary medical insurance was a bold step toward providing better care for America's aged.

**Term of income benefits increasing.** The length of time for which disability income benefits are payable has been increasing steadily in recent years. Many long-term coverages now provide that when a disability results from an accident, benefits continue for the duration of the disability for as long as the policyholder lives. For short-term disabilities caused by accident or sickness, benefit payments are generally limited to 13 to 26 weeks up to one or two years.

Loss-of-income benefit patterns may approximate two-thirds of an individual's normal weekly net earnings up to a maximum dollar allowance. Policies may also provide benefits for total or partial disability, medical expenses, accidental loss of life, dismemberment, and loss of sight.

A clearly discernible trend today is the considerable interest in insurance protection against long-term disability, especially on a group basis. Group long-term disability policies have evolved from group key man and insured salary continuance programs. Some of these group policies provide maximum monthly benefits as high as $1,000 or more until age 65 in the event of illness, or benefits for life where a disability was caused by accident.

**Coverages growing broader.** The general trend of health insurance has been not only to provide protection against a wider spectrum of health care services, but also toward coverages which were broadened to reflect changes in the economic environment. Since the end of World War II, benefits for hospitalization, spurred by the exceptionally sharp cost increases, have rapidly become more comprehensive. These benefit amounts have risen from the $5 or $10 per day level to $30 or higher. Concurrently, the number of covered hospitalized days per illness has increased sharply from 31 to 70 days, to today's common periods of 120 to 365 days. Paralleling this pattern, benefits for ancillary or special hospital services have increased from $100 to $200, to $300, to $500, and higher. Coverages for surgical care have also shown comparable increases.

Prior to Medicare, individual hospital, surgical, and major medical policies guaranteed renewable for lifetime were widely available, reflecting the progress which had been achieved over the years in the broadening of individual coverages. Most individual and family major medical policies terminate at age 65, the eligibility age for Medicare. However, lifetime coverage on a guaranteed renewable basis is still available in some companies.

Among the newer coverages, one which is stimulating wide interest is health insurance for dental care. Considered little more than an idle dream a decade ago, dental care coverage is generally available today through group insurance programs offered by insurance companies. The two main deterrents which retarded pioneering efforts in dental insurance were the feasibility of insuring dental care and the question regarding the demand for the coverage. Pilot programs operated by dental service corporations and insurance companies proved that dental insurance is workable on a group basis. These programs demonstrated that the risk in insuring care is not the incidence of dental need, which is almost universal; the unknown factor is the matter of overutilization. Accumulation of utilization data is answering that question.

**Nursing home coverage.** A relatively new form of coverage in a rapidly evolving field is for skilled nursing care in a nursing or convalescent home. An increasing amount of protection against the costs of this care, which can be of considerable importance in long-term illness, has been made available by insurance companies in very recent years. Since most nursing home patients are over 65, and since Medicare covers extended care facilities, nursing homes have taken on a new aspect in recent years. Many insurance companies now offer this kind of protection for persons of all ages through basic hospital-surgical or under major medical coverage. In general, such coverage is designed for convalescent care (rather than custodial care) following a period of hospitalization. The duration of coverage ranges from 30 days to two years. The most common duration in new group plans is 60 days.

The problem with the development of nursing home coverages has been the lack of qualified nursing homes. Major steps toward eliminating the problem have been taken with the entrance of the Joint Commission on Accreditation of Hospitals into the picture and with the establishment of the nursing home standards under Medicare.

Nevertheless, insurance companies are making coverage available. Several companies have indicated their intention of matching or improving on the Medicare benefits for nursing home care for their policyholders under 65 years old.

The fact that the rubber and automotive industries have included nursing home benefits in their contracts, which are underwritten by both insurance companies and Blue Cross, indicates that such coverage is generally available now to employers who are willing to provide such benefits.

**Coverage for mental illness.** Another significant trend in health insurance is increasing insurance company coverage for the treatment of mental illness. In years past, mental illness was often deemed the responsibility of government, similar to tuberculosis and the epidemic diseases. However, advances in treatment, theory, and techniques have gradually brought psychiatry out of the institution to the point where it is now considered an integral part of the community's health resources.

Today, insurance company group coverages for mental and emotional disorders, under supplementary and comprehensive major medical plans, is widespread. A sample study of new group health insurance policies issued in 1968 shows that four out of five persons covered (excluding those covered by short-term or long-term disability only) had some form of major medical coverage. Ninety-seven percent of those covered by either supplementary or comprehensive major medical plans were covered for nervous and mental disorders as hospital in-patients. Seven out of eight were also covered for out-of-hospital treatment for mental illness.

Early experience indicated some disproportionately large claim costs under major medical policies for ambulatory psychiatric care for personality adjustments. As a result, some insurers found it necessary to increase the coinsurance factor for these ambulatory services from 20% to 50%. Other companies have limited the number of reimbursable out-patient visits to a fixed number— in some cases 50 visits a year—and have imposed a further limit on the maximum covered expense per visit, such as $20 or $25.

Most insurance written on an individual basis provides further limitations on mental illness coverage, such as a requirement of hospital confinement, and some eliminate this form of coverage entirely.

Major medical insurance written on small groups of 25 or fewer sometimes limits the maximum mental illness benefit to a smaller amount than for other illnesses. In such cases, the usual mental illness limitation has been $1,000. Another form of restriction on this form of coverage for the small group has been to limit benefits for mental illness to the care rendered while the insured is an in-patient in a hospital. In some cases, both forms of restrictions are used.

**Alcoholism.** In keeping with modern medical thinking, alcoholism is considered a sickness under most health insurance contracts written by private insurance companies, although it is still found listed as an exclusion in a diminishing number of policies in the area of individual and family coverage. Further, while health insurance in its general forms may be issued to applicants with alcoholic histories, there is no specially designed alcoholics policy.

The extent of treatment of alcoholism, as covered by a health insurance contract, can vary with the definition of "hospital" in the policy. Some policies define "hospital" in the widest sense, to include sanitarium or special hospital; others limit reimbursement for treatment to the facilities of the acute short-term general hospital. Whether or not physicians' services, nursing, psycho- or physio-therapy are included will again depend on the coverage extent of the particular policy. When alcoholism is diagnosed or treated as an alcoholic psychosis, reimbursement will be determined by the "nervous and mental" provision of the policy. Such provisions in major medical expense policies or comprehensive policies may or may not provide benefits for in-hospital or in-and-out-of-hospital treatment. Under disability income policies, alcoholism is a compensatable sickness, if it renders the insured totally disabled under the policy and is not listed as an exclusion in the policy.

**Out-of-hospital drugs.** As total health care coordinated by the physician becomes increasingly recognized as a single service, insurance coverage for prescription drugs may be expanded correspondingly beyond what is currently available under major medical plans.

A primary factor prompting insurance entry into the field has been the unusually rapid development of the number of drugs now available to the public. The Health Insurance Institute reports that of the some 1,500 drugs currently available, fewer than 600 were manufactured in the early 1950's.

Most of the plans written by insurance companies or service plans which offer prescription coverage on an out-of-hospital basis make use of (1) a 75% or 80% coinsurance factor, (2) a deductible of the calendar year type, and (3) restrictions to the so-called legend drugs, those which by law require a written prescription. Among the common exclusions are surgical gases, oxygen, and therapeutic lamps.

**Business income insurance.** Another new coverage is the extension of health insurance into the area of business income insurance, as well as a disability income policy, to cover professional office overhead expenses. These special policies are now being made generally available on an individual basis to doctors, architects, and other professionals, as well as on a group basis through their societies and organizations.

Covered items include rent, mortgage interest payments, office payroll, utilities, building maintenance, professional car, depreciation of furniture and equipment, professional dues and other regular outlays. Generally excluded are mortgage principal payments, salaries of other employed professionals, and the cost of equipment and pharmaceutical supplies.

The latest development in business income insurance is its application to the purchase of stock options in closed corporations and the buy-sell contracts of partnerships.

Noncancellable overhead policies to age 65 are now relatively common. Most policies call for a two-week or 30-day waiting period. Some policies will pay up to 80% of overhead expenses. Others pay a stated maximum, usually $1,000 a month. Coverage is generally limited to 12 to 24 months.

The response of health insurance coverages to the changing needs of the American public, to the point where these coverages have become an ingrained part of the society's economic and social fabric, can be expected to adjust and adapt as required by the public's need. Already, health insurance explorations have begun in such areas as vision insurance, group travel insurance, and special risk insurance. As insurers gain more experience and knowledge in these and other fields, even more diverse forms of coverage may be expected to evolve.

## MEDICAL CARE COSTS

The cost of health care like everything else seems to be increasing continually. As you can see from glancing at Table 13–1, total medical care costs had advanced 55 percent at the close of the previous decade compared with the base years 1957–1959. Physicians' fees and hospital room rates continue to take giant

**Table 13–1** Consumer price indexes for medical care items in the United States (1957–1959 = 100.0)

| Year | All medical care items | Physicians' fees | Dentists' fees | Optometric examination and eyeglasses | Hospital room rates | Prescriptions and drugs |
|------|------|------|------|------|------|------|
| 1935 | 49.4 | 53.9 | 52.0 | 69.0 | 23.8 | 69.2 |
| 1940 | 50.3 | 54.5 | 53.5 | 70.8 | 25.4 | 69.3 |
| 1945 | 57.5 | 63.3 | 63.3 | 77.8 | 32.5 | 73.2 |
| 1950 | 73.4 | 76.0 | 81.5 | 89.5 | 57.8 | 86.6 |
| 1955 | 88.6 | 90.0 | 93.1 | 93.8 | 83.0 | 92.7 |
| 1960 | 108.1 | 106.0 | 104.7 | 103.7 | 112.7 | 102.3 |
| 1961 | 111.3 | 108.7 | 105.2 | 107.0 | 121.3 | 101.1 |
| 1962 | 114.2 | 111.9 | 108.0 | 108.6 | 129.8 | 99.6 |
| 1963 | 117.0 | 114.4 | 111.1 | 109.3 | 138.0 | 98.7 |
| 1964 | 119.4 | 117.3 | 114.0 | 110.7 | 144.9 | 98.4 |
| 1965 | 122.3 | 121.5 | 117.6 | 113.0 | 153.3 | 98.1 |
| 1966 | 127.7 | 128.5 | 121.4 | 116.1 | 168.0 | 98.4 |
| 1967 | 136.7 | 137.6 | 127.5 | 121.8 | 200.1 | 97.9 |
| 1968 | 145.0 | 145.3 | 134.5 | 125.7 | 226.6 | 98.1 |
| 1969 | 155.0 | 155.4 | 143.9 | 131.1 | 256.0 | 99.2 |

*Source*: United States Department of Labor.

**Table 13–2**  Consumer price index in the United States (1957–1959 = 100.0)

| Year | All items | Food | Apparel | Housing | Trans-portation | Medical care | Personal care | Reading and recreation | Other goods and services |
|---|---|---|---|---|---|---|---|---|---|
| 1935 | 47.8 | 42.1 | 47.2 | 56.3 | 49.4 | 49.4 | 42.6 | 50.2 | 52.7 |
| 1940 | 48.8 | 40.5 | 49.6 | 59.9 | 49.5 | 50.3 | 46.4 | 55.4 | 57.1 |
| 1945 | 62.7 | 58.4 | 71.2 | 67.5 | 55.4 | 57.5 | 63.6 | 75.0 | 67.3 |
| 1950 | 83.8 | 85.8 | 91.5 | 83.2 | 79.0 | 73.4 | 78.9 | 89.3 | 82.6 |
| 1955 | 93.3 | 94.0 | 95.9 | 94.1 | 89.7 | 88.6 | 90.0 | 92.1 | 94.3 |
| 1960 | 103.1 | 101.4 | 102.2 | 103.1 | 103.8 | 108.1 | 104.1 | 104.9 | 103.8 |
| 1961 | 104.2 | 102.6 | 103.0 | 103.9 | 105.0 | 111.3 | 104.6 | 107.2 | 104.6 |
| 1962 | 105.4 | 103.6 | 103.6 | 104.8 | 107.2 | 114.2 | 106.5 | 109.6 | 105.3 |
| 1963 | 106.7 | 105.1 | 104.8 | 106.0 | 107.8 | 117.0 | 107.9 | 111.5 | 107.1 |
| 1964 | 108.1 | 106.4 | 105.7 | 107.2 | 109.3 | 119.4 | 109.2 | 114.1 | 108.8 |
| 1965 | 109.9 | 108.8 | 106.8 | 108.5 | 111.1 | 122.3 | 109.9 | 115.2 | 111.4 |
| 1966 | 113.1 | 114.2 | 109.6 | 111.1 | 112.7 | 127.7 | 112.2 | 117.1 | 114.9 |
| 1967 | 116.3 | 115.2 | 114.0 | 114.3 | 115.9 | 136.7 | 115.5 | 120.1 | 118.2 |
| 1968 | 121.2 | 119.3 | 120.1 | 119.1 | 119.6 | 145.0 | 120.3 | 125.7 | 123.6 |
| 1969 | 127.7 | 125.5 | 127.1 | 126.7 | 124.2 | 155.0 | 126.2 | 130.5 | 129.0 |

*Source*: United States Department of Labor.

leaps each year. When all medical services are considered together, these costs showed a greater increase over the previous decade and also during the early years of the Seventies than any other kind of personal expense. (See Table 13–2.)

Why the rapid increase? A rising economy and a variety of other factors have influenced the cost of hospital care: (1) the improved quality of hospital services; (2) more intensive care of patients; (3) the use of new and expensive drugs that were not available just a few years ago; (4) the increase in hospital personnel and wages; and (5) the public's increased utilization of hospital facilities made possible by more numerous health insurance programs.

### FREQUENCY OF MEDICAL AND DENTAL CARE

According to the latest National Health Survey conducted by the Federal Government, the average American makes 4.5 visits to a doctor and 1.6 visits to a dentist each year. The average person from a family with an income of less than $4,000 per year did not make a single dental visit during the year. Persons who averaged two or more dental appointments per year were from families with annual incomes of $10,000 or more. This compares with 4.8 visits to physicians per year for the same income group. Figure 13–1 illustrates how the typical American spends his medical-care dollars.

Each year, about one out of every seven Americans can expect to be admitted to a hospital for medical or surgical treatment or diagnostic services. This

## DISTRIBUTION OF PERSONAL CONSUMPTION EXPENDITURES FOR MEDICAL CARE 1969
### In the United States

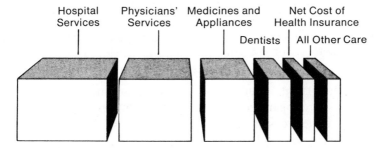

**Fig. 13–1** Personal expenditures for medical care. Americans spent a total of $42 billion in private expenditures for health care in 1969. This represented 7 percent of the public's expenditures on all personal needs, and a 12 percent increase over the previous year. As more recent figures become available, it is anticipated that similar increases will be shown. According to the American Hospital Association, the average expense to treat a patient in a community hospital was $69.93 per day in 1969. Reprinted by permission from *1970 Source Book of Health Insurance Data.* Health Insurance Institute.

amounts to some 72,500 persons entering hospitals each day of the year. Because of the likelihood of a family needing doctor and hospital services, health insurance, particularly group health insurance, has become very popular. Most people feel that the relatively small monthly contribution for a health insurance policy is preferable to the possibility of having to pay large amounts at uncertain times for hospital and surgical costs. Money spent for health insurance premiums is considered by the Federal government as a "medical expense," and is, therefore, partially tax-deductible, regardless of whether or not illness occurs during the taxable year.

## TYPES OF HEALTH INSURING ORGANIZATIONS

About 1,800 voluntary (non-government) insurance organizations currently make health insurance protection available to the American public. Such voluntary insurers include: insurance companies, Blue Cross-Blue Shield organizations, medical society-approved plans, and a variety of independent health insurance plans; for example, industrial, community, private group clinics, and college health programs. Additional health protection is afforded older citizens under the Federal government's Social Security Medicare Program. Each of these principal insurers is discussed in the following pages.

**Insurance companies.** Originally, most insurance companies were chartered exclusively to provide life insurance coverage. As we have already noted, after World War II many of these companies saw the need for mass coverage under group and individual health policies. The results of their sales efforts have been dramatic. By 1950, more than 50 percent of the population of the United States was covered. Now about 85 percent of the people have such protection. (See Fig. 13–2.)

Today, there are more than a thousand insurance companies issuing health insurance policies. Some of these companies sell life, health, and disability insurance; others specialize exclusively in health and/or disability protection.

**Blue Cross-Blue Shield organizations.** These organizations operate on a non-profit basis and are organized in cooperation with the doctors and hospitals in various geographic areas of the country. Blue Cross plans provide protection against *hospital* costs, while Blue Shield pays for *surgical* and other items of medical care. Today, there are 75 Blue Cross-Blue Shield plans operating across the United States. The plans are frequently sold under group contracts to companies, or they may be subscribed to on an individual or family basis. Usually these plans provide coverage for actual *services* of both hospital and doctor rather than allowing a *fixed* amount of money for specified items.

**Independent health insurance plans.** Many private companies provide independent health services for their employees. Mining enterprises and large industrial organizations sometimes hire their own doctors and some maintain their own clinics and hospitals. Such health services may be made available

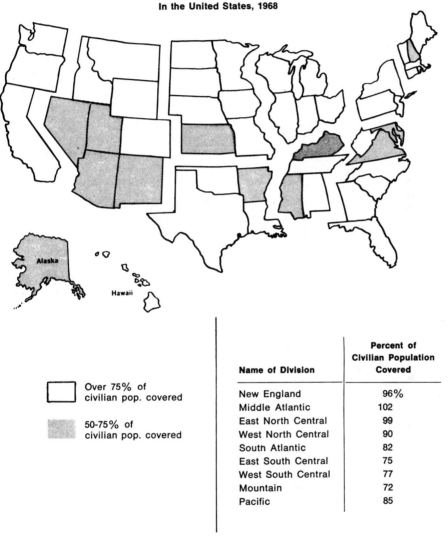

**PERCENTAGE OF THE CIVILIAN POPULATION UNDER AGE 65
WITH SOME FORM OF HEALTH INSURANCE PROTECTION
BY STATE AND BY GEOGRAPHIC DIVISION**

**In the United States, 1968**

|  | Over 75% of civilian pop. covered |
|---|---|
|  | 50-75% of civilian pop. covered |

| Name of Division | Percent of Civilian Population Covered |
|---|---|
| New England | 96% |
| Middle Atlantic | 102 |
| East North Central | 99 |
| West North Central | 90 |
| South Atlantic | 82 |
| East South Central | 75 |
| West South Central | 77 |
| Mountain | 72 |
| Pacific | 85 |

Note: In general, individual insurance coverage is tabulated on the basis of a
person's residence, whereas group coverage is tabulated on the basis of
a person's place of employment. For this reason, coverage may exceed
100% of the population in a particular state or division.

**Fig. 13–2** Percentage of United States population with some form of health insurance
protection. Reprinted by permission from *1969 Source Book of Health Insurance Data.*
Health Insurance Institute.

only to employees, while others include the employees' families. Communities, in conjunction with local medical societies, often establish non-profit medical and hospital plans. In all, there are nearly 600 independent-type health insurance plans now in operation throughout the country.

**Federal Government Social Security—Medicare.** One of the weakest areas of health care in the United States has been the protection of those past retirement age. Nearly four out of every five dollars of health insurance benefits now come from group insurance, and group coverage generally ends when an employee retires. On the average, elder citizens have substantially less income; consequently, they frequently do not receive adequate medical care during the years they need it most. For these reasons Congress enacted the present Medicare Law which augments other Social Security programs.

Under Medicare, nearly all Americans 65 and over are eligible for two kinds of health insurance protection: hospital insurance, and, for those who choose to take it, medical insurance.*

All persons 65 or over who are entitled to Social Security or railroad retirement benefits are automatically eligible for hospital insurance. Even if a person is not entitled to regular Social Security benefits, he may qualify for Medicare. Nearly everyone who reached 65 *before* 1968 is eligible for hospital insurance. Those who reached 65 in 1968 and later who are not eligible for cash benefits, will need to have worked under employment covered by Social Security to qualify for hospital insurance benefits. The amount of work credit needed depends upon the year of their 65th birthday. Eventually the amount of work required for hospital insurance will be the same as for Social Security cash benefits. A health insurance card is issued to those persons who have established their eligibility.

**Hospital insurance under Medicare.** Your hospital insurance will pay the cost of covered services for the following care:

> Up to 90 days of in-patient care in any participating hospital in each benefit period.†
> For the first 60 days, it pays for all covered services except for the first $60. For the 61st through the 90th day, it pays for all covered services except for $15 a day. (For care in a psychiatric hospital, there is a lifetime limit of 190 hospital benefit days.)
>
> A lifetime reserve of 60 additional hospital days. You can use these extra days if you ever need more than 90 days of hospital care in any benefit period. Each lifetime

---

* Some Federal employees and some former Federal employees who are not eligible for Social Security benefits are not eligible for hospital insurance. They may, however, enroll in the medical insurance program.

† A "benefit period" begins the first time you enter a hospital after your hospital insurance starts. It ends after you have not been an in-patient for 60 days in a row in any hospital or in any facility that mainly provides skilled nursing care.

reserve day you use permanently reduces the total number of reserve days you have left. For each of these additional days, hospital insurance pays for all covered services except for $30 a day.

Up to 100 days of care in each benefit period in a participating extended care facility, a specially qualified facility which is staffed and equipped to furnish skilled nursing care and many related health services. Hospital insurance pays for all covered services for the first 20 days and all but $7.50 a day for up to 80 more days, *but only if*:

You are admitted because you need additional care for a condition treated while you were in a hospital;

You need continuing skilled nursing care, not just help with such things as bathing, eating, dressing, walking, and taking medicine at the right time;

You are admitted within 14 days after your discharge from a hospital where you were an in-patient for at-least three days in a row;

You are in an extended care facility which is approved for Medicare payments.

Up to 100 home health visits by nurses, physical therapists, speech therapists, or other health workers, *but only if*:

Your condition is such that you need skilled nursing care on an intermittent basis or physical or speech therapy;

The services are ordered by a doctor and are furnished by a home health agency which takes part in Medicare;

A plan for your care is established by a doctor within 14 days of your discharge from the hospital or extended care facility;

Your care is for further treatment of a condition for which you were treated in the hospital or extended care facility;

The visits are made within 12 months after a qualifying stay of at least three consecutive days in a hospital or after your discharge from an extended care facility.

If you sign up for medical insurance, you will also be eligible for the other home health visits described later.

**Medical insurance under Medicare.** Generally, your medical insurance will pay 80 percent of the reasonable charges for the following services after the first $50 in each calendar year.

Physicians' and surgeons' services, no matter where you receive the services—in the doctor's office, in a clinic, in a hospital, or at home. (You do not have to meet the $50 deductible before your medical insurance will pay physician charges for X-ray or clinical laboratory services when you are a bed patient in a hospital. The full reasonable charge will be paid, instead of 80 percent.)

Home health services ordered by your doctor even if you have not been in a hospital—up to 100 visits during a calendar year.

A number of other medical and health services, such as diagnostic tests, surgical dressings and splints, and rental or purchase of durable medical equipment.

Out-patient physical therapy services—whether or not you are homebound—furnished under supervision of participating hospitals, extended care facilities, home health agencies and approved clinics, rehabilitation agencies, or public health agencies.

All out-patient services of participating hospitals, including diagnostic tests or treatment.

Certain services by podiatrists (but not routine foot care or treatment of flat feet or partial dislocations of the feet).

**Enrolling for medical insurance.** The medical insurance part of Medicare is voluntary and no one is covered automatically. You will receive this protection only if you enroll within a specified period. You will have protection at the earliest possible time if you enroll during the 3-month period just before the month you reach 65. You may also enroll the month you reach 65 and during the 3 following months, but your protection will not start until 1 to 3 months after you enroll.

If you do not enroll during your first enrollment period, you will have another opportunity during the first 3 months of each year, provided this period begins within 3 years after you had your first chance to enroll. However, if you wait to enroll, you may have to pay a higher premium for the same protection; and your coverage will not begin until 3 to 6 months after you enroll.

Medical insurance is financed with monthly premiums paid by people 65 and over who have enrolled for this insurance. The Government matches these premiums dollar for dollar. The basic medical insurance premium is $5.60 per month and will remain at that rate at least through June 1972. Once you enroll for medical insurance, you do not have to do anything to keep your protection. It continues from year to year without any action. If you wish to drop your medical insurance, you may give notice to do so at any time. Your medical insurance protection will stop at the end of the calendar quarter following the quarter you give notice.

## CHOOSING THE RIGHT POLICY

Generally speaking, buying health insurance is usually less complicated than buying life insurance coverage. There is no question of planning benefits to make them available when the beneficiary will need them. Most health insurance benefits are paid when the hospital and medical bills come in—and that is when they are needed.

Planning health insurance is further simplified for most people because much of their coverage, sometimes all of it, is group insurance, planned by employers or their benefit committees. Because costs of administering large groups are relatively low, group insurance is less expensive than individual health insurance. Also, companies often pay part or all of the cost for their employees.

But if a person is not enrolled in a group plan, how can he choose the kind of coverage that will serve best? Because policy provisions and premiums vary widely, it is important for individuals or families to consider how a particular policy will provide for their needs before making any decision. Here are some of the questions that need to be answered in finding the right policy for a given individual or family situation.

Does the policy cover expenses that the family may have trouble paying without insurance? Are the benefits of the kind and of a size likely to fit their needs? Do the policy benefits fall in the range of hospital and medical expenses in the community? How long will benefits be paid? Table 13–3 will assist you in judging the adequacy of the hospital and surgical benefits of policies you may be considering.

**Table 13–3** Average expense per patient day, average length of stay and average expense per patient stay in community hospitals in the United States

| Year | Average expense per patient day | | | Average length of stay (days) | Average expense per patient stay |
| | Total | Payroll | Other | | |
| --- | --- | --- | --- | --- | --- |
| 1946 | $9.39 | $4.98 | $4.41 | 9.1 | $85.45 |
| 1950 | 15.62 | 8.86 | 6.76 | 8.1 | 127.26 |
| 1955 | 23.12 | 14.26 | 8.86 | 7.8 | 179.77 |
| 1960 | 32.23 | 20.08 | 12.15 | 7.6 | 244.53 |
| 1961 | 34.98 | 21.54 | 13.44 | 7.6 | 267.37 |
| 1962 | 36.83 | 22.79 | 14.04 | 7.6 | 279.91 |
| 1963 | 38.91 | 24.01 | 14.90 | 7.7 | 299.61 |
| 1964 | 41.58 | 25.26 | 16.32 | 7.7 | 320.17 |
| 1965 | 44.48 | 27.44 | 17.04 | 7.8 | 346.94 |
| 1966 | 48.15 | 29.41 | 18.74 | 7.9 | 380.39 |
| 1967 | 54.08 | 32.44 | 21.64 | 8.3 | 448.86 |
| 1968 | 61.38 | 36.61 | 24.77 | 8.4 | 515.59 |

*Source: 1969 Source Book of Health Insurance.* New York: Health Insurance Institute.

When these questions are answered, it is time to look at how "renewal provisions" affect premiums. The less expensive policy is usually the kind that can be renewed each year, subject to review by the insuring organization. This type of health policy, however, is quite hazardous for the policyholder, since there is every likelihood of the policy being cancelled by the company at the end of the premium year if the insured has become seriously ill. So, generally speaking, it is wise to avoid these low-cost policies. A policy that is guaranteed renewable (or renewable up to a certain age limit) costs somewhat more, but does provide continued protection. With this type of policy, the company must renew the policy (up to the age limit—frequently 50) if the premiums are paid. However, although the insuring company may not adjust premiums for just one individual, it may change the premiums for the policy if premiums are adjusted for an entire classification of policyholders.

Most expensive, because it offers the strongest guarantee, is the policy that is both guaranteed renewable and noncancellable. This kind of protection can be continued as long as the agreed-upon premiums are paid. In addition to the renewable feature described above, the policy can be continued in force until a certain age—usually 50—at a stipulated or guaranteed premium rate.

**Insurability.**  One of the chief advantages of group plans is that all employees regardless of their present health are insurable if they are working full time at the time the contract is made. Even if the employee suffers a recurrence of a previously existing physical condition, the insuring company will pay regular benefits. However, if a person is self-employed, retired, or working for a company that does not have group health insurance, he must apply directly to an insurance company for individual or family health insurance. He will be required to complete a health statement very similar to that required for life insurance. Similar statements must be made for all members of the family who would be covered under the policy for which he is applying.

## WHAT EACH TYPE OF HEALTH INSURANCE DOES

As has already been pointed out, there are five basic types of health insurance. Each type is available both under "group" and "individual" policies. A brief description of the basic coverages and exclusions under these various plans follows.

**Hospital expense insurance.**  In general, these policies are intended to pay all or part of hospital bills for room, board, nursing care, and other regular charges associated with hospital confinement. An additional payment, again sometimes limited to a maximum stated in the policy, is allowed for such items as use of an operating room, anesthesia, administration of blood and plasma, drugs, X-ray, and so on. More people have this kind of health insurance than any other.

Few policies pay all hospital costs on a blanket basis. Therefore, it is very important to read the entire policy carefully. Never sign up for a hospital policy (or other health plan) until you have taken time to read the contract provisions. Sometimes health insurance salesmen will make inaccurate representations concerning a policy and not offer the prospective buyer a chance to read the actual contract before enrolling. Ask for a copy of the policy provisions so you can take time to read, study and compare. Look particularly at the "exclusions and restrictions" in the policy. Typically, the following limitations will be found in reputable health policies:

1. The insurer will not pay for hospitalization connected with an illness or condition existing prior to subscribing to the health policy. (Group policies, however, usually cover all conditions under a blanket policy agreement, whether or not the condition existed before the present plan took effect.)

2. Policies normally limit payment to a fixed daily sum for the hospital room, board, and general nursing care or stipulate that the company will only pay for such services for a room having three or more beds. Policies also frequently limit coverage to a maximum of 60 or 90 days.

3. Confinement to sanitariums or rest homes is not covered.

4. Hospital admissions primarily for diagnostic studies are frequently excluded.

5. Radiation therapy including X-ray therapy, radium therapy, and radio-isotope therapy are generally not covered or covered in a very limited way.

6. Generally, policies specify a maximum amount payable for obstetrical care. The figure is typically $100, or $150 for Caesarean section. Also policies normally exclude such care unless the pregnancy occurs after the date of enrollment.

7. The cost of blood or plasma is not ordinarily covered.

8. Ambulance services are usually not included.

9. Coverage under certain contracts may well be limited to "member" or participating hospitals. People who travel frequently may want to take particular care in making certain they get a policy that gives coverage in any regular hospital regardless of location.

Special mention should be made concerning health policies that are written to provide a fixed monthly sum to cover all hospital and surgical costs. Many of these plans advertise that they will pay $500 a month for hospitalized illnesses. This may sound attractive, but actually such a policy may pay only for a small part of actual hospitalization and surgical charges at today's prices. The average stay in a hospital, as you will see from again referring to Table 13–3, is about eight days with charges running in excess of $500. This figure is for hospital costs only and does not include doctor's fees. For the average hospital stay, the policy of this type would pay only $133 toward the total bill. It must be realized too that many health conditions cost much more than the average. With the fixed monthly benefit policy, the amount paid would be prorated on the days hospitalized regardless of actual costs. Occasionally, too, such policies specify that they pay if the hospital confinement results from an accident. Even though the premium for this policy appears low, it probably is no bargain because of the very limited coverage.

**Surgical expense insurance.** This pays all or part of the surgeon's fee for an operation. Most policies list a variety of operations and the maximum fee allowed for each. The higher the maximum fees allowed in the policy, the higher the premium. This kind of insurance is often bought in combination with hospital expense insurance. Generally excluded are:

1. Physician's services for extraction of teeth or other dental processes.

2. Plastic surgery performed for cosmetic purposes.

3. Hospital expense or nursing services. (This is provided under hospital expense policies.)

4. Office calls to a physician or surgeon.

5. Surgical fees resulting from a condition existing prior to the issuance of the policy, unless it is a group policy.

It is not uncommon to see hospital and surgical protection written together in one health policy.

**General medical expense insurance.**  This pays all or part of a physician's bill, other than surgical fees.  The coverage may include visits to the doctor's office and the doctor's calls on the patient at home or in the hospital.  Medical expense policies also list maximum benefits for specific medical services and maximum total payments.  This type of insurance is usually bought in combination with hospital and surgical insurance.  The three together are often called "basic health coverage."  Generally speaking, unless a person is under a group plan, the added cost of this general coverage may not warrant its purchase.  Most people can afford to pay for drugs and for office calls to a physician, whereas they would find it difficult to handle the much higher costs associated with hospitalization and surgery.

**Major medical expense insurance.**  This type of policy protects against the large expenses of serious injury or a long illness.  It is the newest type of health insurance, the fastest-growing and probably the most significant type of health coverage.

Major medical insurance can add greatly to the protection offered by basic coverage under hospital, surgical or general medical expense policies.  Hospital, surgical, and medical policies list maximum benefits, and serious illness can easily exceed these maximums.  At that point, major medical insurance takes over and pays a high percentage of additional costs.  The maximum benefits payable under major medical insurance are high—$5,000, $10,000, sometimes $20,000.

This kind of insurance helps pay many kinds of expenses both in and out of the hospital when they are for treatment prescribed by a doctor.  These may include doctor bills, nursing care, and almost all other costs of a major illness or accident.  Because it offers such a wide range of benefits and provides such high maximums, major medical insurance contains two features to keep the cost reasonable:

1. A "deductible" provision calls for the policyholder to pay a basic amount before the policy benefits begin.  For example, the policy might require the policyholder to pay the first $100.  When major medical insurance covers groups or individuals who also have a basic hospital and surgical plan, the "deductible" is sometimes set so it is the same as the maximum paid under the basic plan.  One particular kind of major medical insurance has a very low "deductible," often $50 or $100, and is offered without any basic plan.  This kind of all-inclusive health insurance is called "comprehensive major medical."

2. Nearly all major medical policies have a "co-insurance" provision which calls for the policyholder to share the expenses above the deductible amount. Commonly, the insurer will pay 75 or 80 percent of expenses above the deductible amount. The policyholder pays the rest.

If a person cannot afford complete health insurance coverage, it would be well for him to buy major medical only to protect against the eventuality of a serious, lingering illness which could without "major medical" benefits be financially disastrous.

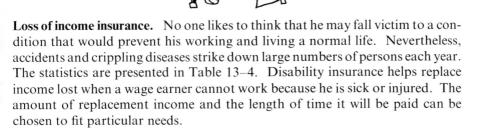

**Loss of income insurance.**   No one likes to think that he may fall victim to a condition that would prevent his working and living a normal life.   Nevertheless, accidents and crippling diseases strike down large numbers of persons each year. The statistics are presented in Table 13–4.   Disability insurance helps replace income lost when a wage earner cannot work because he is sick or injured.   The amount of replacement income and the length of time it will be paid can be chosen to fit particular needs.

**Table 13–4**  Disability days by family income and type of disability in the United States, 1968

| Type of disability | All incomes | Under $3,000 | $3,000–$4,999 | $5,000–$6,999 | $7,000–$9,999 | $10,000 and over |
|---|---|---|---|---|---|---|
| | | | Family income | | | |
| **Restricted activity** | | | | | | |
| Days (in millions) | 2.996 | 701 | 437 | 502 | 534 | 649 |
| Days per person per year | 15.3 | 29.8 | 17.8 | 13.7 | 12.6 | 11.3 |
| **Bed disability** | | | | | | |
| Days (in millions) | 1,233 | 270 | 179 | 213 | 227 | 274 |
| Days per person per year | 6.3 | 11.5 | 7.3 | 5.8 | 5.4 | 4.8 |
| **Work-loss days** | | | | | | |
| Days (in millions) | 413 | 41 | 56 | 80 | 93 | 119 |
| Days per person per year | 5.4 | 7.0 | 6.9 | 5.6 | 5.4 | 4.6 |

*Note*: The data refer to disability because of acute and/or chronic conditions.  The category "All incomes" includes unknown income.  The category "Work-loss days" represents currently employed persons.

*Source*: *1970 Source Book of Health Insurance.*  New York: Health Insurance Institute.

Some policies pay benefits from the first day out of work, but most provide for a wait of a week, a month, two months, or perhaps six months. The purpose of this wait, or "elimination period," is to offer a policy to fit each family's financial condition. The choice depends partly on how long the wage earner's employer will pay him while he is not able to work. Another consideration is the family's savings. By planning to meet expenses of a short illness out of savings and using insurance to protect against longer disability, a family can buy protection at much lower cost.

Some policies pay benefits for only a few months or a year, while others pay for many years or even for life. Many people choose a shorter term policy paying benefits for perhaps two years. The purpose is to provide for "readjustment" income while the family is planning what it will do should the wage earner's disability continue. This shorter term policy is less expensive, but it may not always be the right choice. Most people would more sensibly choose a policy with a longer "elimination period" that would continue to pay benefits to age 65. Insurance companies scrutinize applicants very carefully before issuing disability insurance. Nearly always they insist on a physical examination. Savings can generally be made by adding a "disability rider" to the life insurance policy.

**Social Security disability coverage.**   Benefits can be drawn for disability by those covered under the Social Security system. For most people, the Social Security disability provision provides a substantial cushion of income protection. Private disability income insurance can be used to supplement this protection for greater security. Here is how the Social Security disability plan works:

If you become disabled before 65, you and certain members of your family may be eligible for benefits. Do not wait too long after you are disabled to apply for benefits; if you wait more than a year, you may lose benefits. Payments may begin with the 7th month of disability. If you are found eligible for disability insurance benefits, you will remain eligible as long as you are disabled. When you reach 65, your benefit will be changed to retirement payments at the same rate.

Who is considered disabled? A person is considered disabled only if he has a severe physical or mental condition which (1) prevents him from working, and (2) is expected to last (or has lasted) for at least 12 months or is expected to result in death.

A person with a severe medical condition could be eligible even if he manages to do a little work.

How much work credit is required for a disabled worker? If you become disabled before you are 24, you need credit for $1\frac{1}{2}$ years of work in the 3 years before you become disabled. If you become disabled between 24 and 31, you need Social Security credits for half the time after you are 21 and before you become disabled. To get disability benefits if you become disabled at 31 or later, you must be fully insured and have credit for 5 years of work in the 10 years just before you become disabled.

The amount of your monthly disability payment is generally the same as the retirement benefit you would get if you were 65. This is outlined in Table 13–5 on p. 401. Figure your average earnings as if you reached 65 (62 for a woman) at the time you become disabled. If you are a disabled widow, surviving divorced wife, or dependent widower, the amount of your benefit is figured from what your spouse would have received.

Everyone who applies for Social Security disability benefits is referred for possible services to his State rehabilitation agency. These services help many people to return to productive employment. Social Security often helps pay the cost of services provided to applicants by rehabilitation agencies. For more information about the disability benefits for blind people and disabled widows, disabled surviving divorced wives, and disabled dependent widowers, get in touch with your Social Security office.

## WHEN SOMEBODY ELSE IS LIABLE FOR YOUR HOSPITALIZATION

Nearly all health policies have a "subrogation clause." This, in effect, means that should the policyholder be caused injury by another party which results in hospitalization and perhaps surgery, the insurance company can sue the other party for damages. If, however, a lawsuit is instituted by the policyholder and damages subsequently awarded, the policyholder must reimburse the insurance company for any payments made relative to his hospitalization from the accident.

## RETIREMENT PROGRAMS

"What's with this retirement stuff? As yet, I haven't even decided for sure on a profession." These sentiments may very well parallel your own thoughts as you begin study of programs to provide income for your retirement years. Difficult as it may be for college-age people to take time out of their busy lives to consider retirement, it nevertheless is one of the essential steps in rounding out your financial goals. Unhappily, most people reach retirement *before* they start to worry about how they're going to keep afloat financially during later life. Many, if not the majority, of these same people had the mistaken idea that Social Security payments would take care of their needs.

The rude fact is that nearly 25 percent of retired persons today are living in or on the edge of poverty. The dreams they had of leisure time and travel quickly evaporate with the hard reality of their meager retirement incomes.

If you work, you are already making contributions to your own retirement program through Social Security or perhaps some other government administered program. However, eventually, you may want to make other arrangements for supplementing this basic coverage. The concluding portion of this chapter outlines the present provisions of the Social Security system and other government retirement plans and provides quick reference to private retirement income programs called annuities.

## SOCIAL SECURITY RETIREMENT BENEFITS

As you are already aware from discussion in this and the previous chapter, Social Security is a broad compulsory Federal insurance system. Once you've worked long enough under Social Security to qualify, you can count on a continuing cash income for yourself and your family if you become disabled; and your survivors would receive monthly cash benefits if you should die. Another important provision pertinent to our present discussion is the *retirement program* which builds up while you work.

Even though you cannot count on Social Security for all your retirement needs, it is a good program and the protection you earn stays with you when you change jobs; when you move from city to city; when you move to another state; when you change occupations; or when you change employment from one company to another.

**How much you receive.** The average earnings of workers in the United States today are such that most people can expect to receive *maximum* or near maximum payments under Social Security when they retire. For example, a husband and wife would get $413.70 each month (based on current payment schedules) after retirement if the husband's yearly earnings had averaged at least $7,800. It's important to note that these benefits will be paid regardless of retirement income received from other sources. Table 13-5 gives a detailed breakdown of the current benefit schedule.

**Keeping up with changes in Social Security.** In order to get the full idea of the value of Social Security to you and your family, you will find it helpful to keep abreast of the changes made in the Social Security law. Since the program began in 1935, it has been changed and improved many times. Both contributions and benefits have increased over the years. The Social Security deduction of only 1.5 percent of earnings back in the fifties has jumped to 5.2 percent; the salary base on which contributions are made has gone from $4,200 to the present $9,000. Furthermore, a special government fact-finding committee has recommended that the base be pushed up to $12,000 by 1974 with a deduction of 6 percent.

No one can predict just what kind of changes in the overall Social Security system—or the retirement provision in particular—might be made in the future. However, there is every likelihood that both benefits and contributions will continue their upward pattern, particularly if inflation continues to plague the economics of the nation.

By keeping up with changes made in the Social Security law, you will be able to see fully the role that the protection you are earning plays in your financial goals and plans of the future. Good planning requires that responsible members

**Table 13-5** Examples of monthly retirement payments under Social Security

| Average yearly earnings after 1950* | $923 or less | $1,800 | $3,000 | $4,200 | $5,400 | $6,600 | $7,800 |
|---|---|---|---|---|---|---|---|
| Retired worker—65 or older | 70.40 | 111.90 | 145.60 | 177.70 | 208.80 | 240.30 | 275.80 |
| Disabled worker—under 65 | 35.20 | 56.00 | 72.80 | 88.90 | 104.40 | 120.20 | 137.90 |
| Wife 65 or older | 56.40 | 89.60 | 116.50 | 142.20 | 167.10 | 192.30 | 220.70 |
| Retired worker at 62 | 26.40 | 42.00 | 54.60 | 66.70 | 78.30 | 90.20 | 103.50 |
| Wife at 62, no child | 61.10 | 80.10 | 104.20 | 127.20 | 149.40 | 171.90 | 197.30 |
| Widow at 60 | 70.40 | 92.40 | 120.20 | 146.70 | 172.30 | 198.30 | 227.60 |
| Widow or widower at 62 | 35.20 | 56.00 | 77.10 | 131.20 | 181.10 | 194.90 | 206.90 |
| Wife under 65 and one child | 35.20 | 56.00 | 72.80 | 88.90 | 104.40 | 120.20 | 137.90 |
| One child of retired or disabled worker | 35.20 | 56.00 | 72.80 | 88.90 | 104.40 | 120.20 | 137.90 |

*Source: 1969 Source Book of Health Insurance.* New York: Health Insurance Institute.

* Generally, average earnings are figured over the period from 1951 until the worker reaches retirement age, becomes disabled, or dies. Up to 5 years of low earnings or no earnings can be excluded. The maximum earnings creditable for Social Security are $3,600 for 1951–1954; $4,200 for 1955–1958; $4,800 for 1959–1965; and $6,600 for 1966–1967. The maximum creditable for 1968–1971 is $7,800, and beginning in 1972, $9,000; but average earnings usually cannot reach these amounts until later. Because of this, the benefits shown in the last column on the right generally will not be payable until later. When a person is entitled to more than one benefit, the amount payable is limited to the larger of the benefits.

of the family understand in advance when benefits would be payable and have some idea of what the amount of the benefits would be.

## OTHER GOVERNMENT-ADMINISTERED PENSION PLANS

In addition to Social Security, the Federal Government administers special retirement programs for federal civilian employees as well as the Railroad Retirement System. State and local governmental units also offer a variety of special retirement programs for their employees.

**Federal civilian employee plans.** There are more than a dozen retirement systems for employees of different branches of the Federal Government, but the major programs for federal civilian employees (other than the District of Columbia) are: the United States Civil Service Retirement System; the Tennessee Valley Authority Retirement System; the Foreign Service Retirement System; and the Retirement System of the Federal Reserve Banks, which includes the Bank Plan and the Board of Governors' Plan. By far the largest is the United States Civil Service Retirement System, with over 2.7 million active workers on its roll at the end of the sixties. The other plans are considerably smaller.

**State and local government employee plans.** These cover teachers and other employees in education, as well as policemen, firemen, and other employees of states, counties, and cities. State and local retirement plans paid over $2.6 billion in benefits in 1969 to 1,167,000 retired workers and other recipients. The assets of such plans at the end of 1969 were about $51 billion. Total contributions amounted to $6.5 billion.

An amendment to the Social Security Act in 1950 permitted elective OASDI coverage for state and local government employees not under the provisions of any retirement system; a further amendment in 1954 made OASDI coverage possible under certain conditions for state and local employees who were members of existing retirement systems. As a result of these changes, some two-thirds of all state and local employees are now covered by the OASDI program; of these, about 70 percent are covered by both OASDI and their own pension plans, and 30 percent by OASDI alone.

**Railroad Retirement System.** The Railroad Retirement System, established by the Railroad Retirement Act of 1935, is unique in that it is the only social insurance system administered by the Federal Government which covers a single private industry The Act was amended in 1937, as a result of the joint efforts of railroad management and labor, to create a unified retirement system for the industry. Railroad workers are not covered by OASDI but the benefit structure provides payments at least equal to comparable coverage under OASDI.

## ANNUITIES: INDIVIDUAL AND GROUP RETIREMENT PLANS

Where can you find those extra dollars to supplement the basic Social Security retirement system? You have several choices and may well end up using a combination of programs: (1) Your future employer may provide a good retirement program as part of the fringe benefits of your job. Even if your employer doesn't *give* you such a program, the company may subsidize part of the cost or at least afford you the opportunity to contribute to such a plan. (2) Alternatively, you can purchase a supplementary program individually through a life insurance agent. Incidentally, the values of life insurance policies may also be used to set up such a program. Or (3) you can rely wholly or partly on your own investment program.

Pension contracts are usually spoken of as "annuities"—whether they be individual or group plans. There are today over 9 million such contracts in force. Group annuities issued under insured pension plans remain the largest and fastest-growing segment of the annuity field. The number of group annuity certificates outstanding with United States life insurance companies is now more than 7 million.

**Fixed and variable annuities.**  Most annuities are intended to provide guaranteed retirement income in a predetermined amount, usually for life. The long-standing disadvantage of the fixed annuity has been the fact that insurance companies have invested premiums in bonds and mortgages which provide "safe" but often "small" yields. One relatively new retirement plan is the variable annuity, all or part of which may be based on common stock investments, or on a cost of living index. Part or all of the funds normally placed in common stocks or other investments are maintained in a separate investment account. Considerably more investment latitude is permitted in separate accounts than in life insurance investments generally. With one type of variable annuity, income payments are fixed and guaranteed once they begin, although their initial size depends upon the value of the fund. With another type of variable annuity, the income payments themselves vary with the current value of the investments on which the annuity is based. Many variable annuity plans provide for a combination of fixed and variable incomes under one contract.

There are several sources of annuity plans. They are available on a group basis, most often as insured pension plans set up by employers; or they can be purchased individually through a life insurance agent. The cash surrender value of life insurance policies may also be used to set up an annuity.

**Tax-sheltered annuities.**  Two general groups of persons can take advantage of tax-sheltered annuities: (1) employees of charitable and educational institutions, and (2) self-employed persons.

**Plans for employees of charitable and educational institutions.**  Certain tax-exempt organizations and public educational institutions are permitted by the Internal Revenue Code to purchase and to pay for premiums, within certain limits, on annuities for their employees under what is commonly known as a tax-sheltered annuity. Such premiums are not subsequently includible in the current gross income of the employee for Federal income tax purposes. These are the organizations which qualify:

1. Educational organizations operated by a state, a political subdivision of a state, or an instrumentality thereof.
2. Any corporation, community chest, fund or foundation organized and operated exclusively for religious, charitable, scientific, or educational purposes, or for the prevention of cruelty to children or animals.

Under this arrangement, the tax is postponed, not forgiven. The amount of retirement income generated by such tax-sheltered funds will be taxed when received. If a person anticipates having a lower income during his retirement years, as many persons do, he will benefit from such a tax-sheltered arrangement, provided our tax laws remain structured on a progressive basis. (With a lower retirement income, as compared with his present earnings, he would pay a lower percentage rate of Federal tax.)

**Plans for the self-employed.**   Under the "Keogh Law," self-employed persons or groups may now establish a pension plan for themselves. The annuity must be funded through a trust or a custodial account or through the direct purchase of non-transferable annuity policies from an insurance company.

Beyond the possible net tax savings over the years, there is another significant advantage: The dollars which are sheltered now from taxes have an opportunity to earn compound interest over the years in other investments, ultimately providing more income.

### SUMMARY TIPS FOR RETIREMENT PLANNING

1. If your employer provides a group retirement plan to which he and you both contribute, you will likely find it to your advantage to enroll.
2. Take advantage of the tax shelter provision in the Federal Internal Revenue Code if you work for an educational or charitable institution; or of the "Keogh Law" if you are self-employed.
3. Because fixed annuity contracts have a low yield, you will do better to put more money into your own investment program and little or none into an individual fixed annuity—unless you qualify for a tax-sheltered plan.
4. If you do want the security of an individual annuity, or if you have the choice at work between a fixed and a variable plan, enroll for the variable one which should give you some inflation protection.

### FEEDBACK 13

**A.**   As well as you can remember, estimate what your personal medical expense amounted to last year.

● How many times did you visit a physician? What was his fee for each visit?

Estimate the cost of medical care items if any were prescribed for you.  If you were treated in a hospital, how many days were you there?  What was the cost per day?

- Check with the administrative office of a local hospital and obtain the current costs for a physician's care, hospital room, and medical care items.  Is there an increase in costs for any care that you may have received last year?  Which costs increased most rapidly?  Least rapidly?

- Determine if you are able to meet these costs without any assistance from an insurance program.

**B.**  Make a health insurance check on yourself.

- Are you covered with any type of health or disability insurance?  By what organization is it sponsored?  What is the extent of its coverage; and do you feel that you are paying too much for that coverage?

- Are you a member of any organization that offers group insurance?  What would be the cost of obtaining such protection?

- Do you belong to any organization that offers independent health services to its members?  Who is eligible for those services?

**C.**  Retirement time may be in the distant future, but now is the time to plan your financing of those years.

- Refer to Table 13–5 and imagine yourself in one of the classifications of a retired person.  Do you feel that you could live as you would like on the corresponding payment?  If not, how much more income would you need?

- Consider the many possibilities of supplementing the Social Security retirement system.  Investigate different employers' retirement programs.  Check with a life insurance agent on retirement programs that are offered through his company.  Establish an investment program of your own that you feel will get you through those retirement years.

## DISCUSSION QUESTIONS

1. Why do you suppose early health insurance programs were directed toward replacement of income rather than hospital or surgical benefits?

2. Do you agree with the Supreme Court's decision that health insurance benefits have a place during wage discussions between labor and management?  Why?

3. What would be some of the major problems in insuring dental care?

4. Do you believe that psychiatric care should be covered by insurance?  Why?

5. Should policies be issued which specifically cover alcoholism?  Why?

6. Are the present costs of medical services equivalent to the services and care that one receives?  Explain.

7. Of insurance companies, Blue Cross-Blue Shield organizations, and independent health insurance plans, which do you believe offers the best protection at the lowest cost? Explain.

8. What are the differences between hospital insurance and medical insurance under Medicare? What are the similarities?

9. Do you believe that it was necessary for the Federal Government to establish a health care program such as Medicare for the aged? Explain.

10. Do Social Security retirement benefits provide adequate income to those who qualify? Explain.

11. What is the difference between fixed and variable annuities?

## CASE PROBLEM

Shauna Handlemeyer is 21 years old and is helping support her husband Jack, 22, who is going to college. She is working for a medium-sized company that offers an excellent health care program to its employees for $15 a month. It covers all medicine, semi-private room, and physician fees incurred while in the hospital for both her and Jack. It also includes maternity and other additional benefits. Shauna is making $350 a month and feels that it would be difficult to part with $15 each month especially when they are now on a tight budget. Besides, Shauna believes that there is no worry for them of serious illness since they are both young and healthy.

At Jack's college, health insurance for both of them is available for $22.50 covering three months. This insurance includes payment for only half the coverage available through Shauna's employer, yet it has a more appealing cost to them.

a) Do Shauna and Jack need any health insurance since they are young and healthy?

b) What are the advantages and disadvantages to being covered under Shauna's employer's program? Under Jack's college's program?

c) What are other health programs available to Shauna and Jack outside their work and school? What are the advantages and disadvantages of each?

## SUGGESTED READINGS

Brinker, Paul A. *Economic Insecurity and Social Security*. New York: Appleton-Century-Crofts, 1968. 566 pp.

Carroll, John Joseph. *Alternative Methods of Financing Old-Age, Survivors, and Disability Insurance*. Ann Arbor: Institute of Public Administration, University of Michigan, 1960. 187 pp.

Cohen, Jerome B. *Decade of Decision*. New York: Institute of Life Insurance with the cooperation of Health Insurance Institute, 1966. 56 pp.

Dickerson, Oliver Donald. *Health Insurance.* Homewood, Ill.: R. D. Irwin, 1968. 773 pp.

Duarte, Alfonso. *Long-Term Disability: A Report to Management.* New York: American Management Association, 1968. 23 pp.

Gregg, Davis Weinert. *Life and Health Insurance Handbook.* Homewood, Ill.: R. D. Irwin, 1964. 1,348 pp.

Griffin, Frank L., and Charles L. Trowbridge. *Status of Funding Under Private Pension Plans.* Homewood, Ill.: R. D. Irwin, 1969. 106 pp.

*Guide to Your Disability Income Insurance, Guide to Medical Expense Insurance,* and *Your Health Insurance Check Up.* New York: Health Insurance Institute.

Hepner, Harry Walker. *Retirement—A Time to Live Anew: A Practical Guide to Managing Your Retirement.* New York: McGraw-Hill, 1969. 298 pp.

Hoyt, Edwin Palmer. *Your Health Insurance: A Story of Failure.* New York: John Day, 1970. 158 pp.

Katona, George. *Private Pensions and Individual Saving.* Ann Arbor, Michigan: Cushing-Malloy, 1965. 114 pp.

McCahan, David. *Accident and Sickness Insurance.* Homewood, Illinois: Published for the S. S. Heubner Foundation for Insurance Education, University of Pennsylvania by R. D. Irwin, 1954–1956.

McGill, Dan Mays. *Fundamentals of Private Pensions.* Homewood, Illinois: R. D. Irwin, 1964. 421 pp.

*Medicare and Social Security Explained.* Chicago: Commerce Clearing House, 1965.

Melone, Joseph J., and Everett T. Allen, Jr. *Pension Planning: Pensions, Profit Sharing and Other Deferred Compensation Plans.* Homewood, Ill.: R. D. Irwin, 1966. 404 pp.

*Modern Health Insurance.* New York: Health Insurance Institute, 1969. 60 pp.

Oakes, Mansur Bradford. *Bedside Money.* Indianapolis: Taylor, 1942.

*Our Family's Health Insurance: Do We Know the Answers?* New York: Institute of Life Insurance, 1966.

Pickrell, Jesse Fredrick. *Group Disability Insurance.* Homewood, Ill.: R. D. Irwin, 1958. 255 pp.

*Policies for Protection.* New York: Health Insurance Institute, 1963. 35 pp.

*Primer of Accident and Health Insurance,* a handbook for agents. Chicago: Health Insurance Association of America, 1956.

Somers, Herman Miles, and Ann Ramsay Somers. *Medicare and the Hospitals: Issues and Prospects.* Washington: Brookings Institution, 1967. 303 pp.

*Source Book of Health Insurance Data.* Annual. New York: Health Insurance Institute.

Tax Foundation. *Issues in Figure Financing of Social Security.* New York, 1967. 52 pp.

Werbel, Bernard G. *Health Insurance Primer.* Greenlawn, N.Y.: Werbel, 1963.

# CHAPTER 14

# ESTATE PLANNING

Don't be thrown for a loop by the word *estate*. Its meaning is not limited to fancy homes set on rolling hills with servants, greyhounds, thoroughbred horses, and miles of bridle paths. Practically speaking, everyone has an estate—your estate being simply the sum total of your assets. While in college, your estate may be relatively insignificant. But with the aid of the action money plans already undertaken and those you'll effect later, your estate will grow in size and include investments as well as home and automobile. Estate planning is the process of analyzing your assets, whether they be many or few, and making the necessary legal arrangements to make sure they are passed on to your heirs with the least possible trouble and loss.

Make no mistake, this chapter is not a do-it-yourself law course. You will not learn how to save the $50 to $75 it may cost to have an attorney draw up a will. Quite the opposite is the case, for this chapter shows you *why* estate planning is such a vital element of your overall financial scheme; and *why* you must get competent legal advice to effect this plan.

Besides furthering your own estate planning, you might also find these data important to you financially in another way. Someday, you may be a beneficiary of an estate which your parents or other relatives or friends have amassed. Because you've had the benefit of college training, you may very well be called on to give counsel to such persons, however embarrassing it may be, concerning their estate matters.

Having spent much of a lifetime working and saving to accumulate what they have, parents and others are naturally concerned that their beneficiaries

get the estate, intact, with as little being drained away in taxes and attorney fees as possible. To you as a potential beneficiary, the matter is of great practical concern too. If matters aren't handled properly, inheritance taxes can eat up a sizable chunk of the assets before they ever get to you—particularly if the estate is large. The nice part is that the material presented in this chapter—knowledge of probate procedures, joint property ownership, inheritance taxes, trusts and so forth—will assist you in assessing the adequacy of your parents' as well as your own estate planning.

## WHAT HAPPENS WHEN THERE IS NO WILL?

Regardless of how you would have divided your estate, and regardless of whom you would have included or excluded, if you die intestate (without a will), state law takes over. A court will distribute the assets in a predetermined manner without sentiment. While the law is not intended to be harsh or unfair, these court decisions can make things difficult for survivors. Consider the following actual case involving a young couple:

> Mr. and Mrs. G were in their late 20's. They had two young children and had recently acquired a home and a mortgage. Other assets included $12,500 in common stocks which had been given the husband by his parents, and $1,700 in a savings account in the husband's name. This energetic, successful couple had their plans cut short when the husband was struck down as a pedestrian by a hit-and-run driver. He died several days after the accident, and left no will.

Excepting for the home, which was owned under a joint survivorship deed (to be discussed later), the estate was divided two-thirds to the children, one-third to the wife. Had the accident occurred in a community property state, the assets might have been divided differently. Just how the division would be made would depend on the particular state law in question.

Because the wife was faced with the responsibility of raising her young family, perhaps the husband would have preferred to have the entire estate go directly to her. But without a will, this is not possible; the wife is hamstrung by her husband's lack of foresight. Of course, leaving one's estate to be handled by law is not exactly like leaving it to chance; there is a system, and it is meticulously adhered to—to the advantage or disadvantage of your heirs. It is evident that even if you aren't super-rich, you can make things easier for survivors if you do make a will.

## WHAT YOU SHOULD KNOW ABOUT WILLS

As we have seen, inheritance laws (sometimes called laws of descent) determine *who* inherits your property if you die intestate (without a will). Therefore, anyone who cares what happens to his property should make a will—young and old alike.

Even if you don't care what happens to each specific item—whether Uncle Charlie's ivory chess set goes to Aunt Ethel or to Cousin Dave—you do care about the people surviving you who will depend on your assets, just as they have depended on you. This means that when you start assuming family responsibilities, buy a home or other property, or amass savings, you should sit down with a lawyer and decide how those dependants will be taken care of if something happens to you. It makes no sense to put off estate planning until you're older, or until you're seriously ill.

**What can be included in a will?**  Almost anything may be included in a will so long as it is not illegal. However, here are some of the more common provisions:

1. You may specify to whom and in what proportion your estate shall be divided, so long as you do not disinherit your wife.
2. You can name the person you wish to carry out the provisions which you establish in your will—an "executor" if you choose a man; an "executrix" if you choose a woman.

**"He names each of you in his will, but I hesitate to
say what he calls you."**
Reprinted with permission of *The Wall Street Journal* (Cartoon Features Syndicate).

3. You can direct that your estate, or part of your estate, be paid to a special trust for reasons discussed in detail later in this chapter.
4. You can outline special provisions for handling investments or business properties.
5. You can name a guardian for your children in the event your spouse does not survive you. This is discussed in greater detail later in the chapter.
6. You can specify the manner and place of burial.

**Who should prepare your will?**   Most states recognize the legality of holographic wills—those which are handwritten, dated and signed by the testator.   When persons are victims of accidents and under certain other circumstances, some states will allow oral wills.

However, neither holographic nor oral wills can be counted on to do what you intend them to do.  It may be a blow to your ego, but the fact is that you, by yourself, are not the best-qualified individual to make your will.  You need help, but not of the wrong sort.  A Notary Public is not the one to prepare your will, unless he also has a law degree.  Nor is it a good idea to use form wills supplied in stationery stores or in paperback books.

The right sort of help is a lawyer.  A will is a very personal document, drafted to meet the special provisions of the state in which the property is to be probated; and it must be designed to reflect the individual needs of the testator (the person making the will).  This is one case where you need the services of an expert—an attorney—and nothing else will do.  If you have never dealt with an attorney before, you'll need to do some talking with friends, business associates, and

| HOME *illegible* <br> LOT  *illegible* <br> AUTO *illegible* | WIFE *illegible* <br> *illegible* <br> TOM *illegible* <br><br> SALLY *illegible* <br> *illegible* | RETIREMENT <br> INCOME *illegible* <br> *illegible* <br> SCHOOL <br> EXPENSES <br> *illegible* <br> *illegible* |

relatives to help you make a selection. Attorneys—like surgeons—differ in skill and ability. Sometimes they specialize in a particular form of legal practice. In this instance one would want to deal with a person specializing in estate planning. The choice is yours to make, but it should be made thoughtfully and carefully, just as you would choose an insurance agent.

Before you actually sit down for a planning session with the attorney you select, you should do a little homework. To save time and to help the attorney draft a will that's tailor-made for your situation, you should:

1. Take inventory and make an evaluation of all your property and how it is held.
2. List all the people you want that property to benefit.
3. Consider the objectives you want to accomplish for those people by means of that property.

Then pay a visit to your lawyer. Share your information with him, and together you will complete the final step—setting up suitable machinery to achieve those objectives.

**Legal terms commonly used in wills.**  So that you may fully understand the provisions of your will, it is a good idea to become acquainted with some of the special legal terms your attorney is likely to use in preparing the will:

*Administrator*:   A person appointed by the probate court to settle the estate of a person who died without a will. The term Administratrix is used when a woman is given such an appointment.

*Beneficiary*:   The individual (beneficiaries/individuals) named to receive property or other benefits of the will.

*Bequeath*:   The giving of personal property to persons named in the will.

*Codicil*:   A change or addition to a will—signed by the testator, witnessed, and notarized.

*Decedent*:   The deceased person.

*Devise*:   The giving of real property such as a home, land, store, etc.

*Devisee*:   A person who is designated in the will to receive real property.

*Executor:*    The individual named in the will to settle the estate—pay your final bills, sell your property, and divide your estate among your heirs in the manner you prescribe.  Such a person, if a woman, is called an "executrix."

*Legatee:*    The person who is designated to receive personal property in a will.

*Testator:*    The person leaving the will.  If a woman, "testatrix."

*"If it will make you feel any better, I don't understand half of this gobbledygook myself."*

Reprinted with permission of *The Wall Street Journal* (Cartoon Features Syndicate).

**Your will should be kept current.**    Drawing up a will is not a one-time event.  In fact, the American Bar Association recommends that wills should be reviewed at least every three years or whenever your estate and your circumstances change.  Particularly, a review should be made when:

1. A child is born to your family.
2. You adopt a child.
3. You go into business for yourself or buy new and different kinds of property.
4. Your estate enlarges substantially, causing new inheritance tax problems.
5. You have a substantial increase in earnings.
6. You change your marital status through marriage or divorce.

If your review indicates that your will should be modified, you can either (1) make the change by means of a codicil, an addition to the will which should be signed and witnessed just like the will itself originally was, or (2) rewrite the entire document.

**Where to keep your will.**    A will is of little legal consequence if it can't be located when it is needed.  Therefore, you must make certain it is amply safeguarded and that the proper people know where it is kept.  Ask your attorney if he will keep a signed copy in his files. Another copy can be kept in a safe deposit box in a bank with any other important papers—deeds, contracts, bonds, and so forth. The executor of your will should also be given a signed copy of the document and know the location of the other copies.

## SOME IMPORTANT CONSIDERATIONS

Chances are you will be quite surprised if you make a list of all the property (real and personal) that you own. If you are planning to make a will, this information will be necessary—so consider each of these items carefully:

Real Property

1. House.
2. Investment property (lots, apartment building, etc.).
3. Business property (office building, etc.).

Personal Property

1. Automobile(s), boat.
2. Household furnishings, tools, jewelry, sports equipment, and other personal items.
3. Employee benefits (retirement and pension funds; group life insurance).
4. Credit union accounts and other savings.
5. Notes (secured and unsecured).
6. Stocks and bonds.
7. Life insurance (including credit union life savings and loan protection insurance).

This is a partial list. Some of these items, such as life insurance and jointly held property, may not be controlled by your will, but it is important to consider them. To determine your net estate, add up the total estimated value of your real and personal property, then deduct the estimated costs of your last

illness and burial; the fees for the administration of your estate; and your outstanding debts.

With this information available, you can probably answer most of the
questions asked by the lawyer who assists you in writing your will.

**Appointing a guardian for your children.**    Parents consider their children far more
precious than their home, automobile, or any investment. Wills usually make
adequate provision for transfer of assets to children, but it is amazing how many
attorneys and parents fail to consider that the continued happiness and welfare
of young children are greatly dependent on *who* would care for them and love
them should their parents die.

Admittedly, it is unpleasant to consider the tragic possibility of both parents
being taken, but in this day of frantic freeway driving and frequent air travel,
disasters do happen. If no guardian is named in the respective wills of the
deceased husband and wife, the court is obliged to make an appointment. However, such an appointment may not coincide with your preferences and may not
be the best choice for your children. Any intelligent couple will certainly prefer
to have the right of determining guardianship themselves. So when your
attorney drafts your will, tell him who you have chosen to be named guardian.

Since the matter of guardianship intimately involves the person(s) you
name, you should discuss the responsibilities and get the consent of the prospective guardian(s) prior to drawing up the will. Neighbors or intimate friends,
couples that have mutual respect and admiration for each other, often jointly
agree to be named in respective wills of one another in the guardianship capacity.
Many people prefer to name a brother, sister, grandparent, or other close
relative.

How recently have you read a newspaper write-up of something like this?

Mr. and Mrs. M were in their early 30's; they had no children. One night as they were
returning home from a long trip, they hit a truck head-on. Their estate consisted of a
large equity in a valuable home, a savings account, and two excellent subdivision
building lots. The husband died within an hour of the accident; but the wife lived for
several weeks before succumbing to her injuries. They left no will.

In the eyes of the law, the wife, Mrs. M, inherited the estate upon the death of the husband. Subsequently, upon her death, even if it had been only minutes later, the wife's relatives inherited the entire estate, with nothing going to the husband's family.

The ironic thing is that in many states the same type of inequity could have resulted even if both Mr. and Mrs. *had* left wills, *unless* the wills contained a *common disaster clause*. Such an inclusion, sometimes called simultaneous death clause, explains how property will be disposed of if husband and wife die at the same time, or near the same time as the result of some accidental occurrence. These clauses may be worded to suit the particular testator, but the device's net effect is to keep the actual chain of inheritance in line with the testator's intent.

## WHAT YOU SHOULD KNOW ABOUT TRUSTS

Simultaneous death clauses are better than nothing as an attempt to protect against unwanted results following a common disaster involving both the testator and the beneficiary. However, courts have ruled such clauses inapplicable in situations where the beneficiary outlived the testator by a day or even an hour.* Such rulings do not seem in accordance with common sense, and are rare, but they do point to a potential weakness of the simultaneous death clause—that it may be ineffective.

To avoid this potential pitfall and to achieve the same results which a common disaster clause is designed to obtain, a *trust* may be used. A trust is a legal device for transferring your assets to some person, bank or company to manage for you or for your heirs. Your attorney creates the trust so that your assets will be managed just as you direct and so that they will benefit whomever you select. In the case of Mr. and Mrs. M, his will would have created a trust fund to give Mrs. M a life income, with a large gift to go to Mr. M's family after the death of Mrs. M.

The strategy behind a trust is to place the responsibility for managing the bequeathed wealth on the shoulders of a qualified individual or representative of an institution (this managing party is called the trustee). The trustee makes the money work to the advantage of the beneficiaries without saddling them with the management responsibility—a responsibility for which they may be unsuited or unqualified in terms of skill and know-how.

---

* White v. Taylor, Texas, 1956; American Safe and Trust Deposit Co. v. Eckhardt, Illinois, 1928.

To create a trust, you go to your lawyer and say, "I have so-and-so many dollars and property to put in a trust and I want them ultimately to serve such-and-such purposes. Can you draw up a trust document to accomplish this?" He can and will. By means of this document, money and other assets are committed to the trustee, who invests and manages the trust. The initial amount is called the *corpus* (body) or the *principal*; the money returned on the investments is the *income*.

**Kinds of trusts.**   There are two basic types of trusts: (1) testamentary, that which is created through your will and which becomes effective after your death; and (2) living or *inter vivos*, that which is effected while you are living. An example of a testamentary trust would be the trust Mr. M could have made under his will. Under the terms of this imaginary trust, the life income for Mrs. M would be the income from the investments made with the principal. The gift to the members of Mr. M's family upon Mrs. M's death would be the principal itself, called a gift of corpus. In trust language, Mrs. M would be designated as a "life-tenant" since her income from the trust is only during his lifetime. The members of Mr. M's family, as beneficiaries who receive the principal after the life-tenant (there may be more than one) has died, would be called "remainder-men."

The testamentary trust is created, generally speaking, to relieve the beneficiaries of the responsibility of managing the corpus. The motive of the person creating the trust (called the "settlor") may be to *spare* the beneficiaries that responsibility (if they are very busy with other things and don't want to be bothered); or the settlor's intent may be to *prevent* the beneficiaries from taking that responsibility (if they are incompetent, whether or not they want to be bothered). Whatever your reasons, if all you want is the assurance that the legal title to your property (held by the trustee) and the equitable title (held by the beneficiary) will not rest with the same individual, a testamentary trust will see to that.

A living or inter vivos trust, on the other hand, serves myriad purposes. There are two sorts of living trusts, revocable and irrevocable, and these two options serve to make the living trust a versatile tool. If you are the settlor of a revocable trust, you retain control over your assets. You have the power to revoke. This power is not confined to ending the trust; "to revoke" in this context includes any alteration you wish to make, from very minor details all the way to negating the whole agreement. With an irrevocable trust, on the other hand, you have no say about either the corpus or the income. But irrevocable trusts have another advantage revocable ones don't have—possible tax savings.

The theory which determines the taxability or non-taxability of trusts is simple: As long as the settlor remains in control of his assets, those assets will be included in his estate. Therefore, a revocable trust is subject to estate tax, paid after the settlor's death. An irrevocable trust, on the other hand, is not subject to estate tax, since the settlor divests himself of control over both corpus and income, as well as any *power* to revoke.  Irrevocable trusts, however, are taxable as gifts; the gift tax will be discussed later.

If the estate planner elects to use a living trust, his choice of which form to use—revocable or irrevocable—should be a closely reasoned decision.  The settlor should avoid having his vision fogged by possible tax savings; he must remember that irrevocable trust means just what it says—you can't get your property back.  An irrevocable trust should never, never be created if there is a chance you will need the money tied up in it.  You don't want to make a decision you might regret; the fact that somebody else will avoid estate tax after you die is poor comfort if you are 75 and destitute because you put all your money in an irrevocable trust.  It isn't inherently evil as an estate planning tool; you just need to think twice before you use it.

**Special trusts.**    There are certain living trusts, not to be dealt with here, which may be useful in special cases.  Short-term trusts, partial income retained trusts, life insurance trusts, and trusts for charity and real estate all may be useful to the estate planner.  Your attorney can help you with these special trusts.  A common objection to trusts is that they are impersonal.  In theory, this may be so; but in fact, the chances are that you and your heirs will deal with a single trust officer at a bank, and that you'll find him an understanding adviser.  At the same time, no matter how sympathetic he is, his personal involvement is tempered by professionalism, and his objective, unemotional handling of your money can be an advantage in carrying out your directions.

Generally speaking, trusts are perhaps most useful for large estates with varied assets and investments.  If your estate is small, you can probably rely on a will, your insurance, and perhaps a joint-ownership deed (discussed later) for your home to take care of your estate-planning needs.  However, you might find the living trust beneficial even for small estates in avoiding probate expenses.

### WHAT IS PROBATE?

Every state has a special court organized to oversee the administration of estates. Usually this is called the probate court.

After one's death, the executor or executrix presents the will to the probate court.  The court determines the will's validity and monitors the executor's actions to make sure they are in accord with the intent of the will.  The court will post a legal notice indicating that the will is being probated.  Creditors and other interested persons may then file any claims they may have against the estate.  The validity of these claims will be determined by the court.

If the executor you name is unable to fulfill his duties because of sickness or other reasons, the court will appoint another qualified person to act for you.  In some instances you may specify in your will that you desire the court to appoint an appropriate person as executor of the will.  However, it is better to name someone whom you know is qualified in business matters.

If you die without leaving a will, the probate court is charged with the responsibility of seeing that your estate is properly divided among your relatives. The court will appoint an administrator who will attend to duties similar to those of an executor, except that the estate will be divided according to the inheritance laws applicable in your particular state. State statutes designate who has priority to act as administrator—usually according to relationship. If the person who is first entitled does not carry out his or her responsibility within the statutory time, another interested party may do it.

**Costs and delays of probate.** Many informed persons argue that our present probate laws are ridiculous. They complain that probate is too complicated, usually requiring the services of an attorney. If nearly always results in long delays, sometimes causing financial inconvenience or hardship to heirs. But the biggest complaint usually concerns probate's cost. First of all, the executor receives a fee set by statute according to the size of the estate. For example, on a $5,000 estate, the commission would be $210; on $10,000, the fee is $360; for $100,000 it is $1,910. The fee decreases percentagewise as the estate increases in size. The attorney's fee is usually larger. It is usually determined by the court. Often there are minimum fees of $250 or more regardless of estate's size. Additionally, there are court expenses, appraisers' fees, etc. to be paid.

**Table 14–1** Table for determining probable probate and administration expenses

| Gross estate less debts, etc. | | Probate and administration expenses | |
|---|---|---|---|
| From (1) | To (2) | Amount on (1) (3) | Rate on excess (4) |
| 0 | $50,000 | 0 | 8.6% |
| $50,000 | 100,000 | $4,300 | 7.8 |
| 100,000 | 200,000 | 8,200 | 7.2 |
| 200,000 | 300,000 | 15,400 | 6.8 |
| 300,000 | 400,000 | 22,200 | 6.5 |
| 400,000 | 500,000 | 28,700 | 6.3 |
| 500,000 | 600,000 | 35,000 | 6.0 |
| 600,000 | 700,000 | 41,000 | 5.9 |
| 700,000 | 800,000 | 46,900 | 5.8 |
| 800,000 | 900,000 | 52,700 | 5.7 |
| 900,000 | 1,000,000 | 58,400 | 5.6 |
| 1,000,000 | 1,500,000 | 64,000 | 5.6 |

*Source:* Beneficial Life Insurance Company.

All these costs raise the shrinkage (loss) tally. Table 14–1 shows the estimated costs of estate administration which includes the cost of lawyers, executors, appraisers, and probate court. Estate taxes, however, are not included.

## AVOIDING PROBATE

If you consider all the complaints waged against the probate court system, you probably will be quick to surmise that avoiding probate is desirable. Believe it or not, this can be done!

If property passes to beneficiaries through a will or if a person dies intestate, the estate must be probated. However, under certain circumstances it may be possible to avoid the necessity of probate with its inherent delays and costs. There are two ways probate can be avoided:

1. In some cases, joint-ownership deeds eliminate the necessity of probate.
2. Setting up the inter vivos (living) trust may also keep the estate out of probate.

Let us consider both of these:

**Joint ownership of property.**  It is commonplace for a couple to have joint checking and savings accounts. They may also hold joint ownership in their home, stock investments, land and other property. Such joint holdings may or may not be desirable—depending on your circumstances and on the state in which you reside. Get the advice of your attorney; find out how these jointly held properties are treated under your state's laws.

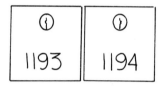

In some states, joint checking and savings accounts are immediately blocked upon the death of one of the co-owners. Similarly, the bank may not allow access to a safe-deposit box. The assets in the accounts may be blocked until the court has probated the estate; access to the safe deposit box may not be given until a member of the probate court and/or state inheritance tax officials are present. If these conditions exist in your state, it might be well to rent two separate safe-deposit boxes—for HIS and HERS safekeeping—placing the husband's will, insurance papers and other valuables in HER box and the wife's will and other valuables in HIS box.

Some states have very liberal survivorship laws for joint property, posing other problems. Here is one illustration:

> An elderly lady had accumulated a large estate. She had two sons who both lived out-of-state. — Not desiring to leave her home, the lady requested the help of a sister who lived near by. — Unable to do anything for herself, the lady opened up a joint checking account for herself and the sister so that the sister could take care of household expenses, doctor and hospital bills, etc. She put $25,000 in the account. What verbal agreement concerning the account was actually made may never be known, but upon the death of the lady, the sister quickly withdrew the remaining money—some $19,000.

There was no will that could be found.  Subsequently, the surviving sons hired an attorney to reclaim the money, but they were unsuccessful.  The sister insisted that the money was intended for her, and the court upheld her right to the money.

Most estate planners recommend that the home be held in joint ownership. The deed should read something like this:

> Theodore D. and Sandra S. Graham as joint tenants with full rights of survivorship and not as tenants in common.

Or this:

> Theodore D. and Sandra S. Graham as joint tenants, or the survivor of them.

Then upon the death of one of the owners, the home reverts automatically to the survivor and does not usually have to be probated.  If all one's assets consist of real property, it may be possible to avoid probate by jointly holding all such property.  However, this is not a method that should be used indiscriminately. There are instances when it may not be wise to hold a home in joint ownership. Here is one example:

> Harold and Patsy Menning had two children.  Mr. Menning died, leaving his wife a valuable home.  Later she was remarried to a divorcee with two children of his own. Patsy had a joint-tenancy deed made on the home for herself and her second husband. When she died—intestate—the home became the second husband's property.  When he too died intestate, the Menning home went to *his* children by the previous marriage.

In addition to showing that joint ownership isn't always the best thing, this example certainly points out the importance of making a will.  Without one, the letter of the law must be followed, in this case costing the Menning children their share in the estate.

Besides making a will, and besides keeping the home out of joint ownership in the first place, there is another way this inequity could have been avoided: adoption.  Adoption is not exactly an estate-planning tool, but here is at least one case in which it would have gained a fair result.

Another disadvantage to joint ownership of property, especially for large estates, is that in the eyes of the Internal Revenue Service, the total value of such property is included in the gross estate of either husband or wife, regardless of who might die first.  Half of the value may be deducted only if the survivor is able to prove that he or she actually contributed to acquisition cost of the property. This may be difficult to do—especially for a wife.

**Inter vivos or living trust.**  One of the most vocal of modern crusaders for probate reform is Norman F. Dacey.  You may have seen or read his popular book, *How to Avoid Probate*, in which he charges that, "In most areas of this country, the probate procedure is a scandal, a form of tribute levied by the legal profession upon the estates of its victims, both living and dead."\* He enthusiastically

---

\* Taken from *How to Avoid Probate* by Norman F. Dacey.  Copyright 1965 by the National Estate Planning Council.  Used by permission of Crown Publishers, Inc.

recommends use of a self-declared revocable trust (see Fig. 14–1), which he calls a "financial bridge from one generation to another."* In effect you say, "I hereby declare that I hold this property in trust for the benefit of so-and-so, I appoint John Smith as successor trustee and I direct that at my death the successor trustee shall dispose of the property as follows, etc."*

The advantage of using the living trust is that it can eliminate the need for probating your estate—which in turn can insulate your estate from the eroding effects of high probate expenses. Using the trust to achieve this aim is not, however, something you should try by yourself. If you seek to avoid probate by using the revocable trust, that trust must be a carefully drafted agreement between you (the property owner) and the trustee. As always, the person to advise you in creating the trust is your attorney.

But if the revocable trust is such a handy tool, why isn't it used more often? One reason is this: Oddly, the living trust in estate planning was not brought into sharp focus until the last decade, when a rash of articles appeared expressing lawyers', bankers' and laymen's views about how and when it should be used.

Despite recent publicity about the living trust, many attorneys remain unknowledgeable about the concept's uses and advantages. Unfortunately, too, there are probably some attorneys who are only too well aware of how the trust can help their client's beneficiaries avoid probate fees. Not all the blame lies with the legal profession, however, for many attorneys attempt unsuccessfully to get their clients to use the living trust. For some strange reason, there is considerable reluctance on the part of many persons to depart from the time-honored concept of a will—even when the living trust has been carefully explained to them. Sometimes clients have the belief (incorrect) that a trust is only for the use of the wealthy.

There is one technical factor, however, which should be mentioned which does limit the effectiveness and use of the living trust: to completely sidestep probate *all* of your assets must be inventoried and included in the trust. Even so, it may save you money and may work very well for you in your particular state. It is certainly something you should discuss with your attorney.

### DECREASING THE COSTS OF PROBATE

It may not be feasible for you to plan for your estate to completely by-pass probate. If this is the case, there are still ways to decrease the costs involved in probating your estate. These are:

1. Irrevocable trusts.
2. Gifts.
3. Keeping insurance proceeds out of probate.

---

* Taken from *How to Avoid Probate* by Norman F. Dacey. Copyright 1965 by the National Estate Planning Council. Used by permission of Crown Publishers, Inc.

𝔇eclaration of 𝔗rust     DT-1

WHEREAS, I, _____John J. Smith_____ of the

~~City~~/Town of _____Jonesville_____, County of ____Fairfax____, State of ____Connecticut____

am the owner of certain real property located at (and known as) ____525 Main Street____

in the said ~~City~~/Town of ____Jonesville____, State of ____Connecticut____

which property is described more fully in the Deed conveying it from ____Henry B. Green____

to____John J. Smith____, as "that certain piece or parcel of land with buildings thereon

standing, located in said____Jonesville____, being

the rear portions of Lots #34 and 35, on Map of Building Lots of George Spooner,said map being dated May 3, 1952, and filed for record in the office of the Town Clerk, Jonesville, Connecticut, in Book 5, Page 16, of said Maps. Said parcel of land is more particularly described as:

Beginning at a point on the south line of Lot #34, on said map, 73.5 feet East of the East line of Park Avenue --- running thence North along land of James E. Beach, 100 feet to a point on the North line of Lot #35 on said map, 70.44 feet East of the East line of Cornwall Street, thence East along land of the said James E. Beach (being Lot #51 on said map) 55 feet --- thence South along land of Thomas Cook (being Lot #56 on said map) 100 feet to the aforesaid North line of Bartram Street --- thence West to the point of beginning.

NOW, THEREFORE, KNOW ALL MEN BY THESE PRESENTS, that I do hereby acknowledge and declare that I hold and will hold said real property and all right, title and interest in and to said property and all furniture, fixtures and real and personal property situated therein, IN TRUST

    1. For the use and benefit of

(Name)____Mary A. Smith (my niece)____

(Address)____750 Porter Street____    Jonesville    Connecticut

     Number      Street      City      State

Upon my death, unless the beneficiary shall predecease me or unless we both shall die as a result of a common accident or disaster, my Successor Trustee is hereby directed forthwith to transfer said property and all right, title and interest in and to said property unto the beneficiary absolutely and thereby terminate this trust; provided, however, that if the beneficiary hereunder shall then be a minor, the Successor Trustee shall hold the trust assets in continuing trust until such beneficiary attains the age of twenty-one years. During such period of continuing trust the Successor Trustee, in his absolute discretion, may retain the specific trust property herein described if he believes it in the best interest of the beneficiary so to do, or he may sell or otherwise dispose of such specific trust

re... ....ation, and in ...... ...vent, I reserve ....
designate such new beneficiary, this trust shall terminate upon my c.... and the ...... ....operty shall revert to ....

    5. In the event of my death or legal incapacity, I hereby nominate and appoint as Successor Trustee hereunder whosoever shall at that time be beneficiary hereunder, unless such beneficiary be a minor or legally incapacitated in which event I hereby nominate and appoint

(Name)____Henry P. Adams____

(Address)____125____    Barnum Street    Jonesville    Connecticut

     Number      Street      City      State

to be Successor Trustee.

    6. This Declaration of Trust shall extend to and be binding upon the heirs, executors, administrators and assigns of the undersigned and upon the Successors to the Trustee.

    7. The Trustee and his successors shall serve without bond.

    8. This Declaration of Trust shall be construed and enforced in accordance with the laws of the State of Connecticut

**Fig. 14–1**
Typical trust document. Courtesy of Crown Publishers, Inc.

4. Selling property.

5. Having one attorney handle all probating procedures.

Each of these will be taken up in turn.

**Irrevocable trusts.**   You already know that the irrevocable living trust is not subject to estate taxation.  It is obvious, then, that if a portion of your estate is tied up in irrevocable trust, that portion will by-pass probate, decreasing court costs.  Keep in mind, however, the care with which this device should be used—it can leave you high and dry, as we said earlier.

**Gifts.**   If you were to give away *all* your money and property obviously there would be no probate proceedings after your death, since you would have left no estate to be probated.  However, no one knows just how long he will live, and certainly most parents wouldn't want to give away their home, money and property and then have to depend on their children to give them a living—just to avoid probate.

However, by giving part of a substantial estate away, it is possible to significantly reduce probate costs and inheritance taxes since the value of the gross estate is lowered.  This does make sense.

**Keep insurance proceeds free of probate.**   A warning should be included about life insurance proceeds.  It is possible to name your estate as beneficiary of your life insurance policy.  Attorneys may recommend this to their own advantage, since the allowable legal fee for probating an estate is based on the assets probated.  However, this is generally not a good idea, for it simply raises probate costs and ties up insurance money for as long as two years or until probate is completed.  While insurance proceeds are considered as part of the decedent's gross assets for tax purposes, they do not have to go through probate if the beneficiary is directly named as such in the policy.

**Selling property.**   Clearly, if you sell part of your estate, then the part which you sell is no longer included in your estate; therefore, that part is not subject to probate.  You can see the advantage, then, in selling liquid assets to the person you want to benefit, so that he already owns the property when you die, and does not have to receive it via probate at added cost.

**One attorney.**   This method of decreasing probate costs doesn't always apply, but is good for the beneficiary to remember when the deceased has property in two or more states in one geographical region.

Costly complications can arise when persons own property in more than one state.  Such property usually will have to be probated in the state in which it is located.  Often, the lawyer handling the probating of your estate in the state where you live will hire another lawyer to function at the court where the out-of-state property is located.

If the states are near each other, it might be cheaper to pay the home-state attorney's travel expenses to the other state's probate proceedings, *if* the other court will permit him to participate as though he were a member of the bar in that state too.

## WAYS TO SAVE ON ESTATE TAXES

Federal estate taxes (paid on the deceased's estate) range from 30 percent on the taxable portion of small estates to 39 percent on estates exceeding $1,000,000. You can see the full range in the tax table given in Step 5, Fig. 14–2. For larger estates with taxable income exceeding $10,000,000 the rates reach 77 percent. It is well to remember that in figuring your gross estate, the Internal Revenue Service requires that insurance proceeds be included.

To begin with, all estates have a $60,000 automatic exemption. Only if the total estate exceeds this amount are there Federal taxes to pay. However, if you know what you are doing, you can avoid paying any estate tax on small or moderate-sized estates which exceed the exemption. Furthermore, you can reduce significantly the amount of tax on larger estates. Here is how to effect these savings:

1. *Qualify your estate for the marital exclusion.* If you leave your estate outright to your wife under the terms of a valid will, one-half of your adjusted gross estate (after debts, final bills, and administration expenses) may be excluded in addition to the $60,000 exemption. This is another important reason for making a will. However, if the wife owns as much or more property than the husband, this type of arrangement actually may be to the expense of her estate. Ultimately this could be costly to the surviving children.

2. *Utilize gift exclusions.* If your parents have a very large estate, you as beneficiary can avoid much if not all Federal estate taxes if your parents take advantage of the tax-free gifts permitted under present laws. Later, as your own estate grows, you may want to benefit your children in a similar way.

Each person is allowed an annual $3,000 exemption for gifts he may choose to make. If husband and wife jointly make a gift, they may give up to $6,000 tax-free in any one year. In addition to the yearly exemption, each person is given a lifetime gift exemption of $30,000. Thus, a husband and wife, should they choose, could give as much as $66,000 tax free in one year. Thereafter, they would be restricted to $6,000 per year. And remember, this gift is completely free of tax—both to the person receiving the gift and to the one giving the gift.

There is only one thing to watch out for: gifts given in the three years immediately prior to one's death may be subject to inclusion in the gross estate if they are considered gifts in contemplation of death.

Irrevocable living trusts qualify as gifts and so qualify for benefits under the gift tax exclusion. Of course, it is very difficult to be certain that one will not need property conveyed to an irrevocable living trust, and this is a factor to be weighed carefully. A revocable living trust does not, however, qualify for the gift-tax exclusion as it is considered an incomplete gift.

# THE ESTATE OF:

## STEP ONE

### ESTATE INVENTORY*

| | |
|---|---|
| Real Estate | $ |
| Personal Property | $ |
| Stocks, Bonds, Securities | $ |
| Notes and Accounts Receivable | $ |
| Life Insurance | $ |
| Business Interests | $ |
| Cash | $ |
| Other Assets | $ |
| Total Gross Estate | $ |

*Include both separate and community property in community property state.

## STEP TWO

### DEDUCTIONS

| | |
|---|---|
| Debts | $ |
| Funeral Expenses | $ |
| Administration Expenses | $ |
| Total Deductions | $ |

## STEP THREE

### ADJUSTED GROSS ESTATE

| | |
|---|---|
| Total Gross Estate | $ |
| (Less) Total Deductions | $ |
| Adjusted Gross Estate | $ |

## STEP FOUR

### ESTIMATE OF TAXABLE ESTATE

| | |
|---|---|
| Adjusted Gross Estate | $ |
| Marital and/or Community Deduction** | $ |
| Specific Exemption | $ |
| Total Personal Exemption | $ |
| Net Taxable Estate † | $ |

** Consult your attorney for the legal and technical analysis of marital and community deduction.

† A credit against Federal Estate Tax is allowed for State Inheritance Taxes.

## STEP FIVE

### APPROXIMATE TAX

| Net Estate | Basic Tax | Rate on Excess in First Column | Excess Tax | Total Tax |
|---|---|---|---|---|
| $1,000,000 | $325,700 | 39% | | |
| 750,000 | 233,200 | 37 | | |
| 500,000 | 145,700 | 35 | | |
| 250,000 | 65,700 | 32 | | |
| 100,000 | 20,700 | 30 | | |
| 60,000 | 9,000 | 28 | | |
| 50,000 | 7,000 | 25 | | |
| 40,000 | 4,800 | 22 | | |
| 30,000 | 3,000 | 18 | | |
| 20,000 | 1,600 | 14 | | |
| 10,000 | 500 | 11 | | |
| 5,000 | 150 | 7 | | |
| | | 3 | | |

## STEP SIX

| | |
|---|---|
| Transfer Charges (Use step 2—Total) | $ |
| Federal Estate Tax (Use step 5—Total) | $ |
| Total Cash to Transfer Estate | $ |
| Liquid Cash or Assets Available | $ |
| Shortage or Excess | $ |

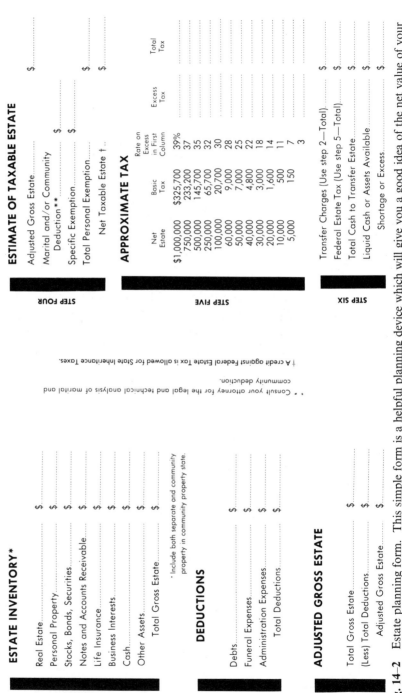

Fig. 14–2  Estate planning form.  This simple form is a helpful planning device which will give you a good idea of the net value of your estate after probate expenses and inheritance taxes.  Because they vary so greatly, state taxes are excluded from the form.  However, they may reduce your net estate.  Courtesy of Beneficial Life Insurance Company.

**FEEDBACK 14**

**A.** Although you may have only personal property to consider passing on to heirs, consider and plan for some of the transactions and events of the next five or ten years with the idea in mind of getting *which* property to *which* person with the least difficulty and expense.

- What objectives will your estate planning have when you marry? Have your first child? Additional children?

- How will you plan your home buying, in order that your home goes to the person you select?

- When your business or career takes a successful and profitable turn, what should you do to insure that these benefits are received substantially intact by your survivors?

- As a potential heir, how can you advise and assist your parents or older relatives so that your inheritance or your brothers' and sisters' is unencumbered?

**B.** Recheck your intangible assets (here, your non-property assets) and satisfy yourself that they name the correct beneficiary. This is an especially valuable step if your family situation has changed recently through marriage, divorce, births, or deaths. At a minimum, you should make sure that the following name the person of your choice:

- Life insurance. This is an obvious, but sometimes overlooked item.

- If your home is under joint survivorship deed, provisions should be made in your will for passing the home to others in the event of common disaster. (This is a consideration with many other properties, but particularly appropriate for a home because for most people a home is the most valuable property they acquire.)

- You should also check joint or surviving ownership, or the beneficiary clauses of your savings account, your stocks and bonds (including U.S. Savings Bonds), and your employee benefit package including retirement, pensions, and bonuses. Make sure that any creditor life insurance still benefits your choice of beneficiaries.

**C.** Write or visit the Legal Aid Society near your home (or write the Attorney General of your state) and obtain data about the inheritance laws in your state. You should inquire about:

- Any peculiarities in the state probate laws.

- Survivorship regulations.

- Common disaster, or simultaneous death regulations.

- Special provisions of trust regulations.

- Applicable tax information.

## DISCUSSION QUESTIONS

1. Why is it that many people die without any will?
2. What should be included in a will?
3. Why should not holographic nor oral wills be counted on to do what they were intended to do?
4. Why is it important to review the will at least every three years?
5. Why should the will be kept safeguarded?
6. What considerations should be given in choosing guardians for children?
7. In what ways can a trust be better than a common disaster clause? When are trusts most useful?
8. What are the problems with the present probate laws?
9. Why do most estate planners recommend that homes be held in joint ownership?
10. How can one save on estate taxes?

## CASE PROBLEM

Three couples from different age brackets and with differing financial standing are described below. Study the data on each couple and discuss the particular estate planning problems which each couple faces. In what ways are their estate problems similar and dissimilar?

*Couple A*:  Ted and Julia Mackintosh are newlyweds in their early twenties and have just completed college. Both work. They have a $5,000 savings account, owe $2,100 on an automobile, and are buying their home. They currently have an equity in their house of $1,600 and owe a mortgage balance of $26,000. They have mortgage insurance which would pay off the mortgage on their home in the event Ted should die. They have no children now, but plan on having a family sometime in the future.

*Couple B*:  Reid and Elva Burton are in their late 30's. Elva is a full-time housewife. They have a $3,300 savings account, stock investments worth approximately $19,000, own two cars, have an equity in their home of $14,700, and owe a mortgage balance of $22,000. Additionally, they own several pieces of investment real estate worth approximately $11,000. The Burtons have three children ages 8, 11, and 14.

*Couple C*:  Herbert and Maud Jensen are in their late 60's. Both have worked, but are now retired. They own their own home worth $72,000, a beach home worth $32,000, real estate acreage worth $405,000, and common stocks worth $782,000. They also own three cars, have a savings account of $31,000, and have no debts. They have three married children.

## SUGGESTED READINGS

Bowe, William Joseph. *Tax Savings Through Estate Planning*. Nashville, Tenn.: Vanderbilt University Press, 1963. 102 pp.

Brosterman, Robert. *The Complete Estate Planning Guide for Business and Professional Men and Women and Their Advisers.* New York: McGraw-Hill, 1964. 327 pp.

Casner, Andrew James. *Estate Planning.* Boston: Little, Brown, 1961.

Dacey, Norman. *How to Avoid Probate.* New York: Crown Publishers, 1965. 341 pp.

Domgaard, John Neil. *Estate Planning: Tax Considerations.* Salt Lake City: University of Utah, 1963. 74 pp.

Hull, Addis E. *Stock Purchase Agreements in Estate Planning with Forms.* Englewood Cliffs, N.J.: Prentice-Hall, 1969. 201 pp.

J. K. Lasser Tax Institute, and Ralph Wallace. *J. K. Lasser's How to Save Estate and Gift Taxes.* Garden City, N.Y.: Doubleday, 1969. 266 pp.

Wormser, René Albert. *Personal Estate Planning in a Changing World.* New York: Simon and Schuster, 1952. 271 pp.

CHAPTER 15

# AVOIDING PROPERTY
# AND LIABILITY LOSSES

Justifiably, Americans show intense personal pride in their beautiful homes and automobiles. Next to family and friends, the home and automobile probably number among our most valued possessions and usually represent the costliest things purchased in a lifetime. According to Commerce Department figures, the average home purchased today costs about $24,000. However, if you complete college, build a successful career and stick to your financial goals, you will probably spend much more than that on a home. On top of the original purchase price, you will add mortgage interest, home improvements, household furnishings, appliances, and a potpourri of personal belongings. Then consider the money invested in an automobile. While tastes and prices are diverse, you may have $2,000 to $6,000 or even more in your family auto; and if you have two or more cars the investment jumps even higher.

It becomes crystal clear that major damage or loss of the home, its contents, or the automobile would seriously disrupt your budget, hindering the attainment of your financial goals. This chapter completes the book's insurance discussions by surveying the major perils faced by property owners and showing how to buy insurance at most reasonable costs. We begin by looking at auto insurance, since it usually represents a person's most sizable outlay for property and liability coverage.

## INSURANCE FOR AUTOMOBILES

The bright, shiny automobile—impressively big or stylishly small—has won its place as an American status symbol. From a practical standpoint, too, it has become a necessity, a way of life. Yet the very popularity of the automobile has created seemingly unreal ecological problems. At the beginning of the seventies there were about 109 million vehicles on the nation's roads. Not only do these vehicles pump alarming levels of vile pollution into the air, but they take a great accident toll.

Sharing the crowded highways with these millions of vehicles means that your automobile has much greater likelihood of being damaged or destroyed or inflicting damage than does anything else you may own or use. In 1970 alone, there were 22,116,254 motor vehicle accidents and 4,983,328 related injuries according to the Insurance Information Institute. These accidents resulted in a whopping economic loss of $16.2 billion. The perils of driving are further under-scored by looking at the number of tragic deaths inflicted by motor accidents. Figures for 1970 supplied by the National Safety Council showed that 55,300 people died in that one year.

There is a slim ray of hope shining through this grim picture. Federal safety standards for automobiles *are* having a positive effect. Such things as better passenger packaging, collapsible steering columns, ballooning windshields, seat belts, shoulder belts, impact absorption materials, and more have according to many insurance experts started to turn the grim tide. They point out that the number of injuries was down about 26,000 and deaths 1,100 fewer for the first year of the decade compared with only a year earlier even though there were more vehicles on our roads and 91,000 more accidents.

**"It's my own plan for making automobiles safe!"**

Reprinted with permission of *The Wall Street Journal* (Cartoon Features Syndicate).

Economic losses from auto accidents dropped an estimated 3.5 percent to approximately $16 billion. This was the *first* downward trend in losses in the 25 years that good records have been kept. Hopefully stringent legislation, diligent enforcement, and greater commitment to safety engineering by the automobile manufacturers will dramatically reverse the monstrous toll of injuries and deaths. However, the Institute of Life Insurance which keeps statistical data on automobile accidents cautions that improvements in the traffic toll have occurred briefly in the past only to be cancelled by a reversal in trend. It also points out that while a continuing and significant downward trend in economic loss ultimately would lead to a reduction in auto insurance rates, such a reduction would take some time to develop because of the many months —even years—it takes for accident experience to be reflected in rate-making statistics. It noted that the total number of accidents is still rising and the costs of auto repairs and medical and legal services—which are paid by auto insurance—are skyrocketing.

## FINANCIAL RESPONSIBILITY LAWS AFFECT ALL DRIVERS

Regardless of your automobile's safety features and no matter how careful a driver you may be, you cannot predict when you may be involved, innocently or otherwise, in a traffic mishap. Your car may be sideswiped tomorrow by an intoxicated driver unable to control himself or his vehicle. Late for an appointment, a worried student or businessman may run a red light. Brake failure could send your car careening into a crowd of people. Macabre as these are to think about, just a casual analysis of the statistics already cited seem to justify the conclusion that *no one* should be without some form of automobile insurance. Even though you might handle the financial loss incurred by damage or even total destruction to your own vehicle, you cannot afford the threat of a financially crippling judgment resulting from injury to other people or their property.

Because of the widespread risk associated with driving, every state has a *financial responsibility law* on its books. If you are involved in an accident, your state's financial responsibility law may require that you furnish proof of financial responsibility (usually done in the form of automobile liability insurance) up to certain minimum dollar limits. Table 15–1 lists the minimal limits required for each state. If you drive in any neighboring countries, Canada and Mexico, it's well to know that they too have similar laws. Although Mexico has no financial responsibility law as such, it does require an auto liability insurance policy *written* with a *Mexican* company. Three states, Massachusetts, New York, and North Carolina, have laws requiring their registered car owners to have liability insurance.

## NATIONAL CONCERN ABOUT AUTO INSURANCE

If you are a college-age driver, you know only too well how auto insurance rates have jumped. You may also have had the unpleasant experience of hassling with a miserly insurance adjuster to get a claim settled; or worse, you may have been one of the unfortunate drivers who found they could not collect on their insurance because the insurer had become insolvent. Auto insurance problems are many and severe. So much so that they have captured the attention of many industry leaders and public officials who moved during the early part of the

**Table 15–1**  Automobile Financial Responsibility Laws in the United States and Canada

| UNITED STATES State | Liability* limits | State | Liability* limits |
|---|---|---|---|
| Alabama | 10/20/5 | Rhode Island | 10/20/5 |
| Alaska | 15/30/5 | South Carolina | 10/20/5 |
| Arizona | 10/20/5 | South Dakota | 15/30/10 |
| Arkansas | 10/20/5 | Tennessee | 10/20/5 |
| California | 15/30/5 | Texas | 10/20/5 |
| Colorado | 15/30/5 | Utah | 10/20/5 |
| Connecticut | 20/20/5 | Vermont | 10/20/5 |
| Delaware | 10/20/5 | Virginia | 20/30/5 |
| District of Columbia | 10/20/5 | Washington | 15/30/5 |
| Florida | 10/20/5 | West Virginia | 10/20/5 |
| Georgia | 10/20/5 | Wisconsin | 15/30/5 |
| Hawaii | 10/20/5 | Wyoming | 10/20/5 |
| Idaho | 10/20/5 | | |
| Illinois | 10/20/5 | CANADA | |
| Indiana | 10/20/5 | Alberta | $35,000 inclusive† |
| Iowa | 10/20/5 | | |
| Kansas | 10/20/5 | British Columbia | $50,000 inclusive |
| Kentucky | 10/20/5 | | |
| Louisiana | 5/10/1 | Manitoba | $35,000 inclusive |
| Maine | 20/40/10 | | |
| Maryland | 15/30/5 | New Brunswick | $35,000 inclusive |
| Massachusetts | 5/10 | | |
| Michigan | 10/20/5 | Newfoundland | $35,000 inclusive |
| Minnesota | 10/20/5 | | |
| Mississippi | 5/10/5 | Nova Scotia | $35,000 inclusive |
| Montana | 10/20/5 | | |
| Nebraska | 10/20/5 | Ontario | $50,000 inclusive |
| Nevada | 15/30/5 | | |
| New Hampshire | 15/30/5 | Prince Edward Island | $35,000 inclusive |
| New Jersey | 10/20/5 | | |
| New Mexico | 10/20/5 | Quebec | $35,000 inclusive |
| New York | 10/20/5 | | |
| North Carolina | 10/20/5 | Saskatchewan | $35,000 inclusive |
| North Dakota | 10/20/5 | | |
| Ohio | 12.5/25/7 | Northwest Territories | $35,000 inclusive |
| Oklahoma | 5/10/5 | | |
| Oregon | 10/20/5 | Yukon | $50,000 inclusive |
| Pennsylvania | 10/20/5 | | |

* The first two figures refer to bodily injury liability limits and the third figure to property damage liability. For example, 10/20/5 means coverage up to $20,000 for all persons injured in an accident, subject to a limit of $10,000 for one individual; and $5,000 coverage for property damage.

† The "inclusive" limit means there is $35,000 of liability insurance available to settle either bodily injury or property damage claims—or both—up to that amount.

decade to get better, cheaper protection for the consumer. While some disagreement exists as to what changes are called for, there is a general consensus that changes must be made, and soon.

**Poorly designed autos.** Insurance leaders continue to stress those aspects of automobile design and construction which in their judgment endanger human life and increase the number and size of automobile insurance claims. For example, mention was made in the book's chapter on purchasing autos about the frailty of present-day cars. A series of crash tests conducted by the Insurance Institute for Highway Safety in 1970 were briefly discussed. These tests involved cars driven into barriers at speeds of 5, 10, and 15 miles an hour. (Five miles an hour is considered walking speed; 10 miles an hour, jogging speed.) Estimated dollar damage ranged from a low of $65 in the 5-mile-an-hour, rear-end crash of a small imported car, to a high of $1,050 in the head-on crash of an American sports car at 15 miles an hour. (See Table 15–2.)

**Table 15–2**  Insurance Institute for Highway Safety 1970 Crash Test Results

|  | 5 MPH Front | 5 MPH Rear | 10 MPH Front | 10 MPH Front/ Rear | 10 MPH Front/ Side | 10 MPH Front/ Pole | 15 MPH Front |
|---|---|---|---|---|---|---|---|
| **SEDANS** | | | | | | | |
| Chevrolet Impala | $196.20 | $247.30 | $491.40 | $421.30 | $481.80 | | $ 740.40 |
| Ford Galaxie | $185.80 | $325.25 | $459.05 | $513.45 | $478.35 | NOT TESTED | $ 703.10 |
| Plymouth Fury | $171.30 | $202.05 | $600.05 | $483.60 | $515.75 | | $ 652.30 |
| AMC Ambassador | $309.25 | $100.05 | $615.75 | $813.80 | $521.55 | | $ 819.50 |
| Averages | $215.64 | $218.66 | $541.56 | $558.04 | $499.36 | | $ 728.83 |
| **PONY CARS** | | | | | | | |
| Ford Mustang | $160.30 | $147.05 | $400.70 | $615.65 | $402.35 | | $ 661.35 |
| Plymouth Barracuda | $176.60 | $197.10 | $332.90 | $379.75 | $409.70 | NOT TESTED | $ 876.05 |
| AMC Javelin | $262.67 | $132.40 | $618.85 | $550.59 | $502.05 | | $ 686.65 |
| Chevrolet Camaro | $130.10 | $174.00 | $599.35 | $465.60 | $437.90 | | $1,052.60 |
| Averages | $182.42 | $162.64 | $487.95 | $502.90 | $438.00 | | $ 819.16 |
| **SMALL CARS** | | | | | | | |
| Volkswagen | $120.25 | $ 64.45 | $322.35 | $228.20 | $381.55 | $335.75 | $ 518.70 |
| Toyota | $133.70 | $ 69.30 | $410.94 | $305.57 | $316.34 | $370.03 | $ 486.86 |
| Maverick | $153.10 | $204.75 | $427.35 | $449.80 | $423.30 | $400.55 | $ 590.55 |
| Hornet | $204.50 | $193.85 | $508.40 | $590.20 | $591.75 | $474.60 | $ 636.75 |
| Averages | $152.89 | $133.09 | $417.26 | $393.44 | $428.24 | $395.23 | $ 558.22 |

*Source*: Insurance Information Institute, *Insurance Facts 1970*.

One suggestion which has emerged from these and other tests is a new bumper, designed to replace the current "cosmetic model" in the interests of automotive safety and reduced damage under impact. Experts say such bumpers could save as much as $1 billion a year in car insurance premiums.

**Poorly designed insurance.** Under traditional forms of auto insurance, your insurance company tries to establish who was at fault before settling personal injury or certain property damage claims. For example, if you were hit by another car, the accident was the fault of the other driver, both vehicles were damaged, and there were persons injured in both cars as well, your insurance company would sue or press out-of-court settlement with the *other driver* or *his insurer*. As a consequence, the courts have become almost hopelessly tangled with the backlog of lawsuits involving liability claims.

A new kind of auto insurance, a no-fault system, seems to be emerging as a favored solution to the motorist's dilemma. Six states now have no-fault plans in operation and more than half the states are looking favorably at similar systems. Although a Federal bill is being sought which would provide a standardized no-fault plan nationwide, there is more likelihood that the no-fault system will be adopted state by state.

The new plan is based largely on the first-party principle; that is, persons who suffer losses are compensated by their own insurance company. Recently, two powerful insurance trade associations, the American Mutual Insurance Alliance and the National Association of Independent insurers, which in the past have strongly supported the present third-party form of auto accident compensation, offered new plans, each of which espouses a program containing elements of both the present lawsuit system and the no-fault concept. The American Insurance Association, on the other hand, favors a complete no-fault program.

The following pages tell more about the no-fault concept as well as other kinds of policies being written by automobile insurers and show how each protects you. No-fault insurance generally covers only bodily injury, although it *may* extend to property damage. Three of the other coverages pertain specifically to bodily injury: Bodily Injury Liability, Medical Payments, and Protection Against Uninsured Motorists. The other major plans relate to *property damage*, and these are: Property Damage Liability, Comprehensive Physical Damage, and Collision Insurance.

## NO-FAULT INSURANCE

Though there are many variations in the no-fault approach, generally these are the provisions under which the new system works:

1. Each driver is required to carry a new form of liability insurance which protects himself, his passengers and pedestrians against *bodily injury*.

2. In the event of an accident in which he, a passenger, or a pedestrian is injured, the driver's insurance company immediately pays the damages directly. Presently, there are long delays since the driver's insurance company attempts to *first* determine who was at fault *before* any payments are made.

3. While most no-fault systems encompass bodily injury only, some states have adopted plans extending payments to auto and property damage.

4. Most plans have stipulated limits on damage payments such as $10,000 for medical payments, loss of earnings and the like.

5. Those injured in an accident are usually prohibited from suing the other driver until payments have been made by the insurer up to the limits provided by the policy.

The hopes for the new system are that there will be speedier settlement of claims and reduction in administrative overhead and legal costs resulting in a general reduction in auto insurance premiums.

## BODILY INJURY LIABILITY INSURANCE

Under this coverage, your insurance company agrees to pay all sums which you may become legally obligated to pay as *damages* because of injury to pedestrians, persons riding in other vehicles, or passengers (other than family) in your own car. You, members of your immediate family and others who have permission to drive your car are covered.

Bodily injury coverage is usually stipulated as 10/20, 20/50, or other combinations. The first number refers to the maximum amount of liability in thousands of dollars assumed by the insurance company for injury in *any one* accident to *any one* person. The second figure indicates the dollar protection applicable to the total liability coverage for *all* persons affected in any one accident. There are a few companies that write a flat liability coverage for any one accident or occurrence which includes both bodily injury and property damage.

It is very significant that under liability insurance—both bodily injury and property damage—your insurance company will defend you in any suit alleging bodily injury or property damage and seeking damages which are payable under the terms of the policy, even if any or all of the allegations of the suit are groundless, false, or fraudulent. The insurance company's financial interest in any court action brought against one of its policy-holders assures competent legal assistance in preparing a defense, which could otherwise prove expensive to the driver should he not have liability insurance.

## PROPERTY DAMAGE LIABILITY INSURANCE

Vehicles and property of any sort *other than the insured's* are included in this coverage. The policy covers damage to other persons' property caused by your car so long as the auto was driven by you, members of your family, or by other persons driving the auto with your permission. Or, if you are driving someone else's vehicle by permission, you are extended liability protection as would be members of your immediate family. This insurance even covers damages caused by the insured's car should its brakes fail when parked and it subsequently collides with something.

Naturally, the insurance company limits its liability to that amount stated in the policy. As explained in the discussion on bodily injury liability insurance, the first two numbers in the liability quotation refer to the thousands of dollars of coverage for bodily injury. A third and final number in the quotation (for example: 10/20/5) makes reference to the amount of coverage for property damage—in this instance, $5,000.

No driver can afford to be without bodily injury and property damage liability insurance. Keep in mind the following incident in determining how much coverage you require:

Mrs. Stevens stepped into her car one morning and headed for the shopping center. She drove on a cross-town freeway for about two miles. She then took her usual freeway exit which was near the shopping center. She entered the exit at a somewhat faster than usual speed and hit her brakes to slow down as she made a turn around the rather steep ramp leading from the freeway. Her brake pedal went completely to the floor without taking hold. She frantically steered the car and fortunately kept on the ramp, but then went careening out of control and crashed into the front of a large discount center opposite the ramp. Miraculously, no one was injured, but the property damage amounted to $31,000. The family carried 100/300/25 liability insurance—a more than ample coverage, they thought. Actually, the Stevenses ended up having to borrow $6,000 to settle the court award to the store, since their policy limit was only $25,000.

Premiums differ greatly from one area to another on liability coverage. Insurance companies keep records of losses in particular geographic areas and establish appropriate premium rates to cover anticipated claims and provide normal operating costs and profits. Rates are approved by the various state agencies or commissions established to control and regulate insurance companies. While premiums differ, double or triple the amount of liability coverage can usually be obtained for relatively small additional premiums.

### MEDICAL EXPENSE INSURANCE

This protection applies to the insured, members of his family, or other occupants of his car should injury occur. Coverage is also extended to injuries sustained by the insured received as a pedestrian. The insurance company agrees to pay all reasonable medical expenses incurred within one year from the date of the accident, including those for necessary medical, surgical, x-ray, and dental services, prosthetic devices, ambulance, hospital care, professional nursing, and even funeral services. As with bodily injury and property damage liability, you can get a lot more if you pay a little more.

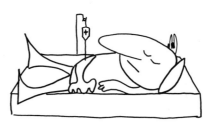

How much medical-expense coverage you need depends mainly on your driving habits. If you have frequent occasion to transport friends, family or perhaps neighbor's children, you should purchase higher amounts of medical insurance.

### PROTECTION AGAINST UNINSURED MOTORISTS

This type of protection is devised so that the insurance company will pay all the sums which the policyholder shall be legally entitled to recover as *damages* from the owner or operator of an uninsured automobile because of *bodily injury* inflicted on him (the insured). It must, of course, be established that the owner or driver of the uninsured auto was legally liable and that collection from him is impossible because of his lack of insurance or financial resources. This insurance also pays for injuries sustained in a hit-and-run accident. Every state, except Maryland and North Dakota, now requires that insurers offer this coverage with every auto liability policy. In most states, this coverage also extends to losses caused by anyone whose insurance company is or becomes insolvent.

The amount of protection afforded under this coverage is specified in a manner identical to the bodily injury liability provision, 10/20 or 25/100, etc. The first number refers to injury to any one person in any one accident; the second to total liability to any number of persons in any one accident. In addition to you, the policyholder, immediate members of your family and occupants of your car are insured. People commonly make the mistake of believing that this coverage will pay for damage to their automobiles by an uninsured motorist. It does not. *It covers only bodily injury.*

## COMPREHENSIVE INSURANCE COVERAGE

This aspect of auto insurance protects the vehicle against *all* physical damages except those caused by collision. It covers a large number of possible perils: fire, theft, larceny, explosion, earthquake, windstorm, hail, water, flood, malicious mischief or vandalism, riot or civil commotion, falling objects, and glass breakage.

## COLLISION COVERAGE

Like comprehensive insurance, collision protection covers the policyholder's car. It protects you from financial loss sustained in repairing or replacing your automobile, should it be involved in an accident with another car or motor vehicle or if you should wreck the car yourself. It does not, as some people think, cover liability for damage to *another person's vehicle.* If you are hit by another vehicle, and the accident is the sole responsibility of the other party, it may be possible through a court judgment to force payment for repairs. However, if you have collision insurance, your insurance company will authorize and pay for *immediate* repairs, and then take the responsibility of collecting from the offending party. It's a different story, as we have already seen, if there are personal injury claims involved in such an accident. Unless you are protected under a no-fault scheme, you would have to sue or force settlement with the guilty party.

Rates for collision protection are expensive. Like other coverages, premiums vary according to local loss rates and also the type and age of vehicle insured. If your automobile is being purchased on an installment basis, the lender usually requires you to have collision insurance. The lender will probably also try very hard to sell the insurance so he can make the commission on the policy.  However, you do not necessarily have to purchase the insurance from the auto dealer or finance company.  If you have had previous insurance dealings with a reputable company and agent, it is wise to ask him to come to the dealer's office so that he can provide the needed coverage.

All drivers need bodily injury and property damage liability coverage.  However, there are many instances where collision and comprehensive coverage is not essential.  For example, the value of a five or six year old car is likely to be approximately $400 for middle-priced cars.  It may not be feasible to pay the $60 to $125 yearly required to keep comprehensive and collision protection in force.  Usually all collision insurance is sold on a "$50 or $100 deductible" basis which means that you would collect only $300 to $350 if the vehicle were totally destroyed.  The premium in relation to the available coverage is prohibitively high.  Another point to consider is that any financial loss sustained as a result of a collision can be deducted from the taxable earnings on the next Federal tax return.  This results in a sizable tax saving which reduces the net effect of your loss.

Figure 15–1 graphically summarizes the basic coverages of auto insurance which have been discussed in this chapter.

| TYPE OF COVERAGE | WHERE COVERAGE APPLIES | | | | |
| --- | --- | --- | --- | --- | --- |
| | persons | | property | | |
| | The Insured Including Family | Persons Other Than Insured | The Insured's Car | Cars Other Than Insured's | Property Other Than Cars |
| 1. Bodily Injury Liability | | ● | | | |
| 2. Property Damage Liability | | | | ● | ● |
| 3. Medical Payments | ● | ● | | | |
| 4. Comprehensive Physical Damage | | | ● | | |
| 5. Collision | | | ● | | |
| 6. Uninsured Motorist Protection | ● | ● | | | |

Fig. 15–1   A summary chart of the six basic coverages of auto insurance policies. Reprinted by permission from *A Family Guide to Property and Liability Insurance*. Insurance Information Institute.

## CHOOSING AN AUTO INSURANCE COMPANY

Legislators and officials of reputable automobile insurance companies have expressed considerable concern in the last several years over the rising number of auto insurance company failures. Most of these failures have arisen from the ranks of relatively new companies which make a habit of insuring "poor risk" drivers—those who have a record of traffic citations and accidents. Inadequate premiums and sub-standard financial reserves have resulted in many drivers being unable to collect. Especially serious are the large number of liability judgments which have been defaulted by the defunct auto insurance companies. Legislative proposals in Congress range from establishing a Federal agency similar to the Federal Deposit Insurance Corporation to setting up a plan that would backstop programs initiated at the state level. About half the states now have laws providing for assessment of solvent insurance companies to satisfy claims against companies which are declared insolvent. Undoubtedly, additional legislative action to set higher standards and controls on automobile insurers will result. In the meantime, you must rely on the reputation of the company with which you deal.

As with property insurers, comparison of rates is important, but should be secondary to comparison of reputation for fair dealing, fast settlement of claims and financial ability. Some companies are known for their inefficiency and slowness of settlement. Others insist that repairs be made by their own shops or by body repair contractors. Five competitive bids may be required by some insurers; only two or three by others. Find out some of these things before you buy the insurance. Ask the agent for two or three names of persons in the community who can comment on their recent experience with claim settlement.

## AUTO INSURANCE COSTS

As with all types of insurance, auto insurance premiums relate directly to expenditures which the insurer must make to cover the claims arising from the policyholders. The number of accidents and the cost of repairs ultimately determine the rates you pay. Table 15–3 shows that repair costs have risen dramatically in recent years reflecting the inflationary trend of the economy, more expensive design (such as wrap-around windshields and bumpers), and more complicated mechanical equipment.

The number and severity of traffic accidents vary a great deal from one locality to another. Large metropolitan centers typically have the largest ratio of accidents; and, correspondingly, insurance companies must charge higher rates. Geographically, each state is divided into rating territories. A rating territory may be a large city, part of a large city, a suburban or a rural area. The overall loss statistics from each rating territory determine the basic insurance rates.

However, there are other items that influence what you must pay for auto insurance. The major factor is driver classification, which is based on the insured's age, sex, marital status, driving record, and use of the automobile—pleasure, business, etc. Other factors are the year, make and model of the car or cars, the amount of protection, the deductible provision which one chooses, and the number of cars to be insured. A more detailed discussion on how rates are determined is contained in the Appendix to this chapter.

**Table 15–3**  Auto repair costs

| Year of model | Change in cost of parts* as of December 31, 1969 |
| --- | --- |
| 1963 | plus 26% |
| 1964 | plus 26% |
| 1965 | plus 21% |
| 1966 | plus 20% |
| 1967 | plus 20% |
| 1968 | plus  7% |
| 1969 | plus  6% |

* Includes lower control arm, front bumper, rear bumper, radiator grille, radiator core, front fender, hood, front door shell and trunk lid. The study showed that hourly labor costs as of December 31, 1969, depending on locality, ranged from as low as $4.50 to as high as $13. The most commonly quoted hourly labor charge was $7.

*Source*: Insurance Information Institute.

**Your driving record.**  Safe driver plans are in effect in most states. Under a safe driver plan, if you and everyone in your household who drives your car have had a *clean driving record*, you qualify for a discount on your automobile premiums. The discount is 10, 15 or 20 percent, depending upon the state where you live.

A *clean driving record* means that you have not been involved in any accident where you were at fault nor have you been convicted of a serious traffic law violation for the past three years. It is estimated that more than 75 percent of all motorists qualify for the safe driver discount.

A driver *without* a clean record pays more than the basic premium. How much more he pays depends upon how bad his record is. So the way one drives affects what he pays for his insurance.

**Farmer discount.**  Persons engaged in farming or ranching may qualify for a 25 to 30 percent discount on the insurance premiums for their private passenger cars, station wagons, or jeep-type automobiles. Farmers' trucks with a load capacity of 1,500 pounds or less are regarded as private passenger cars.

To qualify for the farm discount, a farm *automobile* must be one that is garaged on a farm or ranch and *is not used* in any occupation other than farming, ranching, or used in driving to and from an occupation other than farming.

**Driver education discount.**   More than 12,000 high schools and colleges through-out the country offer driver education courses which are designed to teach young men and women to drive safely, to avoid accidents, and to save lives.   Standards for these courses are set by the National Conference on Driver Education of the National Education Association.   They include classroom instruction and experience behind the wheel.

Youthful operators who have successfully completed a driver education course meeting national standards, may be eligible for a discount on automobile insurance premiums.   In some states this discount is applicable when every male driver under age 25 in your household has completed a recognized course, and applies to liability, collision, and medical payments premiums.   In other states the discount may be obtained if every driver—both male and female—under age 21 has successfully completed such a course.   In these states, the discount applies to all coverages.   Young drivers who own a car also are eligible for this discount.

**Two or more cars discount.**   In some states, owners of two or more private pas-senger cars are eligible for a discount on the liability, collision, and medical payments premiums on each car provided the cars are insured under the same policy, are not all used for business purposes and are not driven by a male under age 25.   Where one of the cars is used for business, the discount applies only to the pleasure car.

The new classification plan now in use in many states contains a more liberal application of the two or more cars discount.   Under this plan, the discount is extended to include all multi-car families provided the cars are under one owner-ship.

**Good student discount.**   In most states, your classroom performance can have an important effect on your insurance premiums.   When comparing insurance plans, be sure to ask about this discount.   Find out what the qualifications are. Get the necessary forms to verify your scholastic standing.

### HOW AUTO INSURANCE RATES ARE DETERMINED
Since significant statistical differences exist in the accident rates and average insurance claims of different types of vehicles and drivers, auto insurance com-panies adjust basic rates so that each person will pay a more equitable rate.   The following material explains how rates are set.

**Driver classification.**   The highest rates are paid by unmarried young males who own or are the principal operators of automobiles.   This is because they have a higher accident rate and more costly accidents.   In some states all single youthful male operators under age 25 are bracketed in one group for rate-making pur-poses.   In most states, however, a distinction is now being made among youthful drivers under a revised rating system developed on behalf of a large segment of the automobile insurance business.

Under this revised rating system, which applies to all coverages, the cost continues to be highest for young unmarried males, but is scaled downward year by year from age 17 through 29. Unmarried young female drivers also pay more than the base rate, with their costs subject to a downward scaling from age 17 through 20. However, a premium credit is allowed if the youthful driver of the family car is a resident student at a school or college more than 100 road miles from his home. Women drivers age 30 through 64, if they are the only operators resident in their household, have been placed in a new low-premium class. Relative costs of automobile insurance by driver classification under the revised rating system are shown in Fig. 15–2.

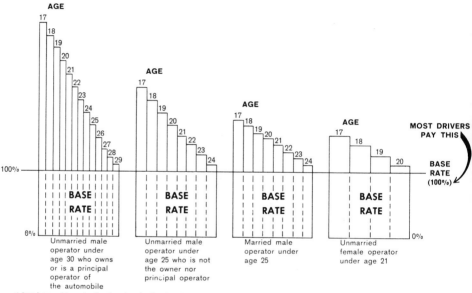

Fig. 15–2 Cost of automobile insurance by driver classification. Reprinted by permission from *A Family Guide to Property and Liability Insurance*. Insurance Information Institute.

## INSURANCE FOR HOMES

Natural as well as man-made perils—such as fire, windstorms, accidents, crime, and riots—pose possible hazards for your home. As compared with your automobile, there is less likelihood of something happening to your home. However, since the potential dollar loss is much higher, you should provide for ample insurance coverage. Because of the lower probability of loss, home insurance premiums are much less than those paid for comparable amounts of auto insurance. Let's first look at the risks; we will then talk about the specifics of home insurance.

## FACTS ABOUT LOSSES

Throughout the ages man has been both blessed and cursed by fire. Properly controlled, it is one of our most helpful servants; uncontrolled it can destroy both life and property. In the 19th century and during the early years of the 20th century, major portions of nine American cities were destroyed by fire. Largest and best known were the great Chicago fire of 1871 and the San Francisco earthquake-fire of 1906. In more recent years, riots and civil disorders caused catastrophic damage—mostly through fire. In 1969, for example, the Insurance Information Institute indicates that these acts caused an estimated $31.3 million insured damage in more than 120 cities and communities across the nation. By comparison, similar losses totaled $80 million in 1968. Beyond the headline-making fires and corresponding statistics are the approximately 2.4 million fires, large and small, reported annually. In 1970 these fires cost Americans more than $2.2 billion. In recent years, residential fires have accounted for about 27 percent of the total fires and approximately 30 percent of the dollar losses.

Apart from fire damage, nature's idiosyncracies inflict a tremendous toll on life and property each year. Though some regions are more severely and regularly affected than others, no state is immune to wind damage. In the last 50 years, 91 hurricanes have reached the continental United States. Hundreds of tornadoes, at their worst in the months of April, May, and June, cause extensive property losses each year. In many parts of the country, property is also frequently damaged from heavy snow and rain storms, flooding, or hazardous freezing conditions.

Crimes can also be costly to the property owner. In recent years, robbers, burglars, embezzlers, and other thieves have been making off with stolen property in excess of $3.5 billion a year—more than $9.5 million, on the average, every day. While about 50 percent of the stolen property is recovered—particularly true of stolen automobiles of which 85 percent are recovered—insured losses run into many millions of dollars annually.

Records of the Federal Bureau of Investigation show that in the last few years crimes against property have been increasing at a greater rate than have crimes of violence such as murder, rape, and aggravated assault. While the FBI's annual Uniform Crime Reports does not include embezzlement losses, other authoritative sources estimate that losses to embezzlers and other persons who misappropriate property of their employers exceed $5 million a day, or more than $1.8 billion a year.

Crimes against property reported by the FBI in 1969 included:

*Robbery* (from the person by force or violence or by putting in fear): 297,580 offenses; property loss $86 million.

*Burglary* (breaking and entering): 1,949,800 offenses; property loss $620 million.

*Larceny* (of goods valued at $50 or more): 1,512,900 offenses; property loss $420 million.

*Automobile theft*: 871,900 offenses; property loss $865 million.

Homeowners, as a general rule, are quite aware of the destructive threat of fire. Mortgage lending institutions normally insist that fire insurance be carried to at least protect their mortgaged interest. Consequently, insurance agents frequently receive invitations to "come to the home and write up a fire insurance policy." Chances are, however, that before leaving his client, the agent will have sold a "homeowner's" policy rather than just a "fire" policy. This is no swindle; for a small additional premium, the insurance coverage is *substantially* broadened. The client has made a wise decision since the home and its contents, as we have seen, face many perils other than fire.

## THE HOMEOWNER'S POLICY

In order to qualify for coverage under a homeowner's policy, the residence must be insured for at least 80 percent of its replacement value. Under such a plan, the entire home, attached or unattached personal structures on the premises such as garages, sheds or storage areas, all personal property owned or used by the family including clothing (excepting pets, autos and aircraft) is protected. At your option, coverage can be increased to include personal property of guests in your home. Permanent landscape features such as trees, shrubs, and bushes are also protected.

Casualty companies—insurance companies that specialize in writing property and liability insurance—currently offer three choices of coverage under the "homeowner's" classification: Standard or Form 1, Broad or Form 2, and Comprehensive or Form 5.

# PROPERTIES COVERED

## YOUR HOME
### (and other structures on your lot)

## PERSONAL PROPERTY

### at HOME

### and AWAY

## ADDITIONAL LIVING EXPENSE
### (If forced to live away from home temporarily)

Least expensive of the three homeowner's policies is the standard form. Though low in cost, it covers an impressive list of *specified* perils, as illustrated by Fig. 15–3. For a small added premium, the broad form can be purchased to include eight more perils in addition to the 11 covered by the standard form. Because of the scope of insurance protection and economy, this form is the most popular homeowner's policy. While the standard and broad forms cover many possible hazards to the homeowner, there are infrequent bizarre accidents or losses which do occur, but are not specified under either policy. The homeowner may, therefore, want to purchase the *comprehensive form*, which lists or specifies *exclusions from coverage* rather than inclusions listing perils covered. Figure 15–3 also compares the perils against which properties are insured for each of the three forms of homeowners' policies.

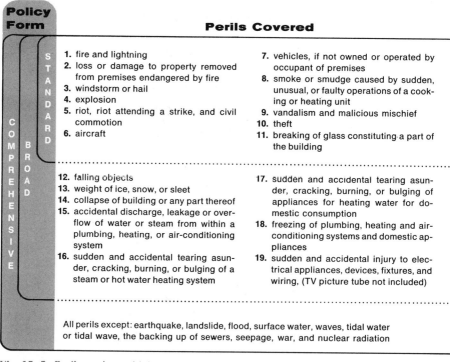

**Policy Form**

**Perils Covered**

STANDARD

1. fire and lightning
2. loss or damage to property removed from premises endangered by fire
3. windstorm or hail
4. explosion
5. riot, riot attending a strike, and civil commotion
6. aircraft

7. vehicles, if not owned or operated by occupant of premises
8. smoke or smudge caused by sudden, unusual, or faulty operations of a cooking or heating unit
9. vandalism and malicious mischief
10. theft
11. breaking of glass constituting a part of the building

BROAD

12. falling objects
13. weight of ice, snow, or sleet
14. collapse of building or any part thereof
15. accidental discharge, leakage or overflow of water or steam from within a plumbing, heating, or air-conditioning system
16. sudden and accidental tearing asunder, cracking, burning, or bulging of a steam or hot water heating system

17. sudden and accidental tearing asunder, cracking, burning, or bulging of appliances for heating water for domestic consumption
18. freezing of plumbing, heating and air-conditioning systems and domestic appliances
19. sudden and accidental injury to electrical appliances, devices, fixtures, and wiring, (TV picture tube not included)

COMPREHENSIVE

All perils except: earthquake, landslide, flood, surface water, waves, tidal water or tidal wave, the backing up of sewers, seepage, war, and nuclear radiation

Fig. 15–3  Perils against which properties are insured under three principal homeowner's policies. Reprinted by permission from *A Family Guide to Property and Liability Insurance.* Insurance Information Institute.

## HOMEOWNER'S LIABILITY COVERAGE

Currently about 115,000 persons are killed accidentally each year. While the motor vehicle is the worst killer, home accidents rank second, causing about 27,000 deaths and untold injuries annually. Many home accidents involve

visitors or other persons who are not members of the family.  The following
example is such a case:

> One morning Mrs. Wallace called her good friend and neighbor on the telephone and
> asked her to drop over for a minute to take a look at a Christmas gift Mrs. Wallace had
> ordered for her husband.  The neighbor arrived in a few moments and made her way
> down the steps to a basement room where Mrs. Wallace was waiting.  The neighbor
> turned the corner of the stairs and tripped on a skateboard that had been left there by
> Mrs. Wallace's three-year old daughter.
>
> The neighbor received severe neck injuries in the fall and was partially paralyzed
> in her right arm.  Naturally, Mrs. Wallace felt terrible about the incident and did every-
> thing she could physically to comfort her friend, but nonetheless the neighbor had
> sustained a serious and permanent injury.  It was not long before the Wallaces were
> contacted by an attorney.  A suit followed which finally proved negligence on the part
> of Mrs. Wallace.  The court awarded the neighbor $14,000 plus $1,700 attorney's fees
> and $1,178 medical expenses.

Fortunately for the Wallaces, their home was covered by a homeowner's
policy in which all of their expenses, including the attorney's fees for defending
the case, were paid.  This policy and all homeowner's policies automatically
include three forms of liability coverage: (1) personal liability; (2) medical
payments; and (3) physical damage to the property of others.

**Personal liability.**  This provision in the homeowner's policy is designed to protect against crippling financial judgments you might receive from a lawsuit.  The
accident that occurred in the Wallaces' home is only an example of the many
unexpected things that could happen.  You may, for instance, be burning leaves
in your back yard.  The fire spreads, a neighbor's property is extensively damaged,
and he sues.  Under a homeowner's policy, the insurance company will pay the
legal costs of defending the policyholder, whether or not he is to blame.  Furthermore, if the insured is declared liable for the damage to the neighbor's property,
his insurance company will pay the damages assessed up to the limits stated in

the policy.  Coverage is not only for accidents occurring elsewhere, if they are caused by the policyholder, a member of his family, or his pets.

# LIABILITY COVERAGES

**BODILY INJURY LIABILITY**

**DAMAGE TO PROPERTY OF OTHERS**

**COST OF LEGAL DEFENSE**

**MEDICAL PAYMENTS**

The minimum coverage for each form of the homeowner's policy is $25,000, and larger amounts can be purchased.  Legal costs which the insurer agrees to pay are those involved in defending the policyholder; they do not include those incurred when the policyholder sues someone else.

If you employ one or more persons in your home or on your premises, you should ask your insurance agent or broker to explain how workmen's compensation insurance laws in your state affect your liability for employees' injuries. In states where workmen's compensation insurance is required by law, the personal liability coverage under your homeowner's policy does not protect you when persons such as your maid or your gardener are injured.

**Medical payments.**  Medical expenses resulting from a *minor accidental injury* suffered by a *visitor* on your property are paid by the insurance company under the medical payments coverage of your homeowner's policy.  Medical payments coverage is similar to the coverage of personal liability in that the coverage applies not only to injuries occurring on the insured's premises, but to those occurring elsewhere if they were caused by him, a member of his family, or his pets.  The two differ, however, in that medical payment coverage is designed for the *small* rather than the *large* claim—the minor rather than the major injury; also, payment is made *without* concern for *legal liability*.  As one would expect, the medical payments provision applies only to bodily injury, whereas the personal liability provision applies to both bodily injury and property damage.  The standard protection is $500 for each person, but larger amounts can be purchased.

An important feature of this coverage is that payment is made regardless of who is at fault.  This makes possible the prompt payment of medical bills since there is no need to go through the time-consuming process of establishing legal liability.

**Physical damage to property of others.**  This coverage applies when the insured or any member of his family accidentally damages someone else's property.  Damage caused by children under 12 years of age is covered, whether accidental or intentional, but the insurance company is not obligated to pay for damage caused intentionally by youngsters 12 years or older.  Payment for damages is made regardless of who is at fault—or, as is sometimes the case, when no one is at fault.  However, the maximum amount that an insurance company will agree to pay for any one accident is $250.  *Physical damage coverage* to the property of others is similar to *medical payments* coverage in that it pertains to *minor* accidents and payment is made by the insurance company no matter who is legally liable for the damage.

### AMOUNT OF COVERAGE NEEDED

Regardless of how vital any insurance may be, it still means a fixed monthly drain on your budget.  Therefore, it is important to know just how much insurance you need.  No one wants to pay for more coverage than he needs, but neither does he want to be under-insured.  In the matter of property insurance, the coverage should be determined solely by the replacement value of the residence or building.  The homeowner's policy requires that the residence be insured for at least 80 percent of its replacement cost.

In determining replacement cost, the values of excavations, underground flues and pipes, underground wiring and drains, and brick, stone or concrete foundations, piers and other supports which are below the surface of the ground are disregarded.  It should be remembered, however, that construction costs for repairing and replacing fire damage are generally 5 to 20 percent more than for new construction.  Replacing fire damage in a home means tearing out burned materials, extensive cleanup, matching new materials to old materials, and so forth.

Even though repair costs run high, the homeowner's policy pays up to the face amount of the policy on any fire damage (usually excluding carpeting and awnings) if the home is insured for 80 percent or more of total value.  Therefore, homes of frame construction or of brick veneer (having internal wood framing) should be insured for full replacement value. A major fire in such a home could inflict such serious damage that the entire residence would have to be rebuilt. A brick or brick and block home might safely be insured for 85 to 90 percent of its replacement value. Even if the home were gutted by fire, the exterior walls would probably stand unhurt, unless the fire were caused by explosion of gas or oil heating units.

A standard 10 percent additional coverage beyond the face value of the homeowner's policy is provided for the garage and other private structures located on the premises. Take this into consideration when you compute the amount of insurance you need. For example, you estimate your home to be worth $26,000 and the attached garage $2,300. If you decided to insure for the full value because the home was of frame construction, you would need purchase only $26,000 worth of insurance since you would automatically be covered for an additional $2,600 (10 percent) on appurtenant private structures.

Regardless of the type of construction, the likelihood of total destruction of a home by fire or explosion is small. Nonetheless, because of the large amount of money involved in the home investment, it is probably wise to insure for almost the full value. Usually one can increase the amount of insurance coverage on the dwelling from the required minimum 80 percent to a full 100 percent without additional premiums by accepting a policy with $50 or $100 deductible provisions on wind and hail damage. This seems to be a sensible approach; by doing this, you get needed additional protection for the "big" potential losses—losses you cannot afford, and at the same time accept liability for smaller damage—losses you can afford.

In determining the coverage necessary, special consideration should be given to the value of household furnishings and contents. Under the homeowner's policy, 40 percent of the policy's face value is automatically provided for personal property. A home insured for $26,000 under a homeowner's policy would have $10,400 worth of coverage of furniture, appliances, clothing, and other personal property. Guessing does not work well in the matter of determining the value of household and personal possessions; careful room-by-room checks ought to be made. If the value of your personal property exceeds 40 percent of the policy, it may be necessary to have the insurance agent write special additional coverage on the household contents. The important point is to know what you have in order to provide adequate insurance protection.

**Adjusting the amount of coverage.** A recent analysis of fire losses on homes in one state revealed that only one homeowner in three carried enough insurance to cover even one-half the replacement value of his home. There are probably two major reasons for this inadequate coverage: (1) the homeowner failed to consider the many home improvements he had made—finished basement space, added rooms, new conveniences; or (2) he had failed to keep track of the actual replacement value of his home due to inflation. Table 15–4 shows how rapidly building costs have risen in the past two decades. A small three-bedroom residence constructed for $13,651 in 1950, for example, would have cost $21,282 in 1970 and more at today's prices.

**Table 15–4** Inflation's effect on home construction costs (1957–59 = 100) annual average

| Year | Index | Year | Index |
|------|-------|------|-------|
| 1950 | 80.3  | 1961 | 104.5 |
| 1951 | 86.6  | 1962 | 106.3 |
| 1952 | 88.8  | 1963 | 108.5 |
| 1953 | 90.4  | 1964 | 111.6 |
| 1954 | 89.7  | 1965 | 115.2 |
| 1955 | 92.4  | 1966 | 120.1 |
| 1956 | 96.5  | 1967 | 127.3 |
| 1957 | 98.3  | 1968 | 136.7 |
| 1958 | 99.2  | 1969 | 148.0 |
| 1959 | 102.5 | 1970 | 155.9 |
| 1960 | 104.2 |      |       |

*Source*: Data shown are from the Boeckh Index of Residential Construction Cost, prepared by E. H. Boeckh and Associates, as appeared in *Savings and Loan Fact Book 1971*, United States Savings and Loan League, p. 27.

The inflationary trend is still with us. Since property insurance is written for three years, building costs may rise 5, 10, 12 percent or more during the policy period. This is another reason for providing near 100 percent coverage each time the policy is rewritten. Chances are that near the end of the policy period, the percent coverage on actual value will have declined due to inflation.

**Cost of homeowners' policies.** There are many factors that influence the actual rate you pay for this type of insurance. For example, a frame or a brick-veneer home requires a higher premium, whereas brick or brick and block homes are insured for minimal premiums. The rates are also influenced by the quality of fire protection available in the community and the statistical loss records for the areas. Urban and suburban rates within the same general metropolitan area often differ.

Let us assume that you own a $20,000 house of frame construction located in a Midwestern town. In order to qualify for the policy, it must be insured for $16,000—or 80 percent of its replacement value. Policies are written for a three-year period. Yearly and monthly prorated figures are shown below:

|                             | Total 3-year premium | Yearly premium | Monthly premium |
|-----------------------------|----------------------|----------------|-----------------|
| Standard—11 perils          | $114.00              | $ 38.00        | $3.17           |
| Broad—19 perils             | $156.00              | $ 52.00        | $4.33           |
| Comprehensive—all risks     | $300.00              | $100.00        | $8.33           |

The premiums quoted are for a policy with a $50.00 deductible provision for wind and hail damage. Keep in mind that these figures are only the cost of insuring one specific home. The best source for actual information on the cost of insuring your home is your local agent or broker.

Under the coverage of a homeowner's policy, the insurance company will pay for such additional living expenses as are required while repair or replacement of the damaged or destroyed property is in progress. For example, payments are provided for rental of temporary living quarters should you and your family have to vacate the home during reconstruction.

**A policy for renters.**  If you live in an apartment or rent the home you occupy, there is a particular policy for you. It is the Residence Contents Broad Form, or Tenants Form, and is also referred to as Form 4. It insures household contents and personal belongings against the same perils as those included in the Broad Form (Form 2). Since the insured does not own the building or appurtenant private structures where he lives, that property is not insured under a Residence Contents Broad Form policy. However, the policy does provide coverage for additional living expense and also includes the three liability coverages discussed previously.

**Special coverage.**  It is usual practice for homeowners' policies to exclude damage from earthquake, landslide, flooding, surface water, tidal waves, seepage, and nuclear radiation. However, many companies will extend the policy to cover earthquake damage. This extension is usually called a "policy assumption endorsement." Rates vary considerably, but as a general rule, the costs for earthquake protection over and above the broad form coverage will amount to an increase in premium of approximately 40 to 50 percent. The cost of extended special coverage differs from one geographical area to another and from one coverage to another.

Recently, a significant milestone was reached when flood insurance became available for the first time with the organization of the National Flood Insurers Association—made up of about 100 insurance companies—in cooperation with the Federal Government. While the Department of Housing and Urban Development initially designated only four areas to qualify for flood insurance, the number of such areas had passed the 150 mark by mid-1970.

Policies will usually specify limits of insurance on money, deeds, securities, manuscripts, jewelry, silver, and furs. If an individual has particularly expensive and valuable items, it is possible to cover this personal property with additional assumption endorsements.

Some homeowners want the greatest possible protection for their dwelling and appurtenant private structures, but do not want to pay for this same extensive coverage on their personal property. Their needs are satisfied by purchasing the Dwelling Special Form (No. 3)—which provides the same coverage for their dwelling and private structures as does the Comprehensive Form (No. 5)—and combining it with the Residence Contents Broad Form (No. 4) which protects their personal property against 19 perils. The Dwelling Special Form (No. 3) cannot be purchased unless it is combined with the Residence Contents Broad Form (No. 4). No matter which form or combination of forms chosen for the protection of property, the policy includes personal liability coverages.

## SELECTING AN INSURANCE COMPANY

Perhaps the most significant consideration in choosing an insurance company is to know something about its reputation for settling claims systematically, speedily, and equitably. Negotiating a settlement with some companies can be extremely difficult and frustrating. For example, in instances where heavy smoke damage has been sustained in a home, the insurance adjustor may refuse claims for anything more than a quick wash of the walls and woodwork. Or if large areas of carpeting have been charred and ruined, the insurance company may quibble over the settlement, since it cannot be proved that the carpeting burst into *open flame*. These companies are not what you want.

**Making sure you can collect.** Even after selecting a reputable insurance company, it is essential for you to take certain precautions to assure collection for serious fire damage. Most insurance companies require, in the event of major loss, that you furnish a complete inventory of the destroyed, damaged and undamaged property, showing in detail quantities, costs, actual cash value, and amount of loss claimed. If your home were destroyed by fire today, could you sit down and itemize every valuable item contained in that house, including clothes, personal belongings, furniture, appliances, carpeting, drapes, etc.? Should you try to do this, you would probably be amazed at how many details you cannot recall.

Insurance companies will supply inventory sheets which should be filled out and kept in a safe deposit box in a bank or other safe depository away from the insured premises. It's also a good idea to supplement these lists from time to time with photographs of every room, closet and storage area of the home. Antiques or other collectors' items of considerable value should be appraised so that their cash worth can be established.

In the event of theft, burglary, or vandalism, it is essential that law enforcement authorities be called immediately. Most companies will refuse payment if this is not done. Also in the event of any loss, one should immediately contact the insurance agent and inquire about the formal procedures required to file a claim.

**Cancellation of policies.** Because of the broad coverage of homeowners' policies, companies usually insist upon including a clause which allows them to cancel the policy at any time upon giving the insured five days' written notice of cancellation. The prorated premium on the unexpired part of the policy is then, of course, refunded. Cancellation usually occurs as a result of the insured filing an excessive number of small claims, such as four or five claims for glass breakage.

Some families seem to be much more accident-prone than others, and certain geographic locations seem to attract more vandalism and malicious mischief. Also, should the company in any way suspect that claims have resulted from careless or negligent action, it is likely that the policy would be immediately cancelled.

### FEEDBACK 15

**A.** Take an inventory of your possessions in your home, whether you are renting or buying. For convenience and accuracy, keep sub-inventories for each room in the house.

- In a sample room, the living room, for example, compute the original cost, the current worth, and the replacement cost for every item in the room (i.e., couch, chairs, television, carpet, drapes, pictures, bookcases, etc.).

- Compare your valuation in the above item with current prices, to be certain that inflation has not eroded your current insurance protection.

   Are any items, from anywhere in the house, of antique value? If so, they deserve special consideration under your policy, and perhaps additional insurance coverage. Similarly, you should also evaluate any art work, considering that your loss will be greater for some of your furnishings if they are rare or prized beyond their simple replacement value.

**B.** Make a hazard survey of your family's traffic and habit patterns to check up on your liability coverage.

- Are all entrances and hallways well lighted?

- Does any family member consistently leave toys, tools, or other "tripping" items lying around?

- Do you have a consistent program for removing snow, ice, and other walking hazards from your walks?

- Is your living area free of hazards generally; like faulty wiring, plumbing, and ventilation?

**C.** Your insurance agent can help you with this inventory, although you are probably informed sufficiently to make an initial appraisal. Recheck your automobile insurance coverage to be sure it is (1) adequate and (2) not more expensive than it need be.

- Have you become 25 years of age since the policy was written?

- Do you commute less frequently, or for less total mileage than your coverage is written to cover?

- If you drive a less or more expensive automobile than before, is your present insurance compatible with this fact?

- If your family status has changed since the policy was written, is there any significance for your insurance coverage or rates?

- Assuming you are a safe, ticket-free driver, is there any advantage you can gain through lower insurance rates?
- Do your insurance rates adequately reflect possible reductions on account of participation in safe-driver classes?

## DISCUSSION QUESTIONS

1. Are insurance companies justified in charging higher auto insurance rates when the economic losses from auto accidents have dropped? Explain.

2. Why has a no-fault system of auto insurance become so popular? Should it be adopted nationwide? Explain.

3. What types of coverage should be mandatory with auto vehicle drivers? Explain.

4. Why are discounts given to farmers on their insurance premiums for their private passenger cars?

5. How can one plan at an early age to be eligible for the lowest auto insurance rates?

6. What are the advantages of a homeowner's policy over just a fire policy?

7. Why are perils such as earthquakes, floods, war, etc. not covered under the comprehensive policy form?

8. How does a person know what amount of insurance he needs to protect his car, home, etc.? Can he have too much insurance? Explain.

9. For what reasons would renters want to buy property insurance? Why would they not want to buy it?

10. Why do most insurance companies insist upon inclusion of a cancellation clause in the policy?

## CASE PROBLEM

The Martins had recently moved into a beautiful new home in an impressive residential area. The home was on a rather steep hill affording an expansive view of the city. The carpeting had just been laid, drapes hung, and furniture put in place. As Mrs. Martin and her neighbor chatted on the sidewalk in front of the new home one morning, they looked up in horror to see a large, rickety old truck wildly swaying back and forth racing down the hill. It was obvious the truck was out of control, and the two women ran screaming around to the rear of the house. In a split second they heard the truck hit the curb and felt the ground rumble as the old truck headed for the house. The garage and front wall of the home were shattered. Fortunately no one was injured or killed, but a great deal of property damage had been done—$8,800 to be exact. The truck driver was out of a job, he was being sued for alimony by his former wife, and he was driving a borrowed truck which had no liability insurance coverage.

a) Who was legally responsible for the damage?

b) Under what conditions would the Martins be reimbursed for the damage?

c) Would it be likely that the truck driver would be permitted to continue driving? Why?


## SUGGESTED READINGS

*A Family Guide to Property & Liability Insurance* (Third Edition). New York: Insurance Information Institute, 1966.

American Management Association. *Facing New Problems in Risk Management.* New York, 1961. 104 pp.

American Mutual Insurance Alliance. *Property and Casualty Insurance Companies: Their Role as Financial Intermediaries.* Englewood Cliffs, N.J.: Prentice-Hall, 1962. 65 pp.

"Automobile Insurance." A Filmstrip on Basic Coverages and Costs, Available for free loan, Insurance Information Institute, 110 Williams Street, New York, New York 10038.

*Careers in Business.* New York: Insurance Information Institute.

*Chances Are . . .* New York: Insurance Information Institute, 1964.

*Do You Know?* New York: Insurance Information Institute.

*Insurance Facts 1966.* New York: Insurance Information Institute, 1966.

Keeton, Robert E., and Jeffrey O'Connell. *After Cars Crash: The Need for Legal and Insurance Reform.* Homewood, Ill.: Dow-Jones and R. D. Irwin, 1967. 145 pp.

Long, John Douglas. *Property and Liability Insurance.* Homewood, Ill.: R. D. Irwin, 1965. 1265 pp.

Magee, John Henry, and Oscar Serbein. *Property and Liability Insurance.* Homewood, Illinois: R. D. Irwin, 1967. 944 pp.

O'Connell, Jeffrey, and Wallace Wilson. *Car Insurance and Consumer Desire.* Urbana: University of Illinois Press, 1969. 115 pp.

"Patterns for Protection." A Filmstrip on Insurance for the Home. Available for free loan, Insurance Information Institute, 110 Williams Street, New York, New York 10038.

Reed, Prentiss B. *Adjustment of Property Losses* (Third Edition). New York: McGraw-Hill, 1953.

Rodda, William H. *Property and Liability Insurance.* Englewood Cliffs, N.J.: Prentice-Hall. 500 pp.

Russell, George Hugh, and Kenneth Black. *Human Behavior and Property and Liability Insurance.* Englewood Cliffs, N.J.: Prentice-Hall, 1963.

Schultz, Robert E., and Edward C. Bardwell. *Property Insurance.* New York: Rinehart, 1959.

APPENDIX TO CHAPTER 15

# GLOSSARY OF PROPERTY INSURANCE TERMS

**Actual Cash Value.**  Theoretically the cost of repairing or replacing the damaged property with other of like kind and quality in the same physical condition; commonly defined as replacement cost less depreciation.

**Agent.**  The *independent* (or local) *agent* is an independent businessman who represents two or more insurance companies under contract in a sales and service capacity and who is paid on a commission basis.  Counterparts are the *exclusive agent*, who represents only one company, usually on a commission basis, and the *direct writer*, who is the salaried employee of a single company.  Agents are licensed in the state or states in which they operate.

**Allied Lines.**  A term that has been adopted to refer to the lines that are allied with property insurance.  These coverages provide protection against perils traditionally written by fire insurance companies, such as sprinkler leakage, water damage, and earthquake.

**Assets.**  All funds, property, goods, securities, rights of action, or resources of any kind owned by an insurance company, less such items as are declared non-admissible by state laws.  Non-admissible items consist mainly of deferred or over-due premiums.

**Automobile Assigned Risk Plan.**  A program operative in each state, under which automobile liability insurance is made available to persons who are unable to obtain such insurance in the voluntary market.  In a growing number of states, these programs are referred to as "Automobile Insurance Plans."

**Automobile Liability Insurance.**  Protection for the insured against loss arising out of his legal liability when his car injures others or damages their property.

**Automobile Physical Damage Insurance.**  Coverage for damages or loss to automobile of policyholder, resulting from collision, fire, theft, and other perils.

**Boiler and Machinery Insurance.**  Coverage for loss arising out of the operation of pressure, mechanical, and electrical equipment.  It may cover loss suffered by the boiler and machinery itself and may include damage done to other property, as well as business interruption losses.

**Broker.**  A marketing specialist who represents buyers of property and liability insurance and who deals with either agents or companies in arranging for the coverage required by the customer.  Some large brokers have offices countrywide and some are active on an international basis.  Like the agent, the broker is licensed in the state or states in which he conducts his business.

**Burglary and Theft Insurance.**  Protection for loss of property due to burglary, robbery, or larceny.

**Business Interruption Insurance.**  Coverage for loss of earnings in case the policyholder's business is shut down by fire, windstorm, explosion, or other insured peril.

**Catastrophe.**  A severe loss, frequently causing widespread damage, resulting from such perils as hurricanes and other violent occurrences.

**Coinsurance.**  A provision in an insurance policy which requires the insured to carry insurance equal to a certain specified percentage of the value of the property.  It provides for the full payment, up to the amount of the policy, of all losses if the insurance carried is at least equal to that amount.  Otherwise, loss payment would be only a percentage of the actual loss.  The insured receives a reduction in his rate when he elects to include this clause in his policy.

**Commercial Multiple Peril Policy.**  A package type of insurance for the commercial establishment, that includes a wide range of essential coverages.

**Comprehensive Personal Liability Insurance.**  A type of insurance that reimburses the policyholder if he becomes liable to pay money for damage or injury he has caused to others.  This form does not include automobile liability, but does include almost every activity of the policyholder except his business operations.

**Credit Insurance.**  A guarantee to manufacturers, wholesalers, and service organizations that they will be paid for goods shipped or services rendered.  It is a guarantee of that part of their working capital represented by accounts receivable.

**Crop-Hail Insurance.**  Protection for monetary loss resulting from hail damage to growing crops.  Although hail is the basic peril named in crop-hail policies, a number of other perils are covered as well, depending on the crop and area.  Crop-hail policies cover fire, lightning, windstorm, aircraft, smoke, and other miscellaneous perils.

**Deductible Insurance.**  A method of coverage under which a policyholder agrees to contribute up to a specified sum per claim or per accident toward the total amount of the insured loss.  Insurance is written on this basis at reduced rates.

**Extended Coverage Insurance.**  Protection for the insured against loss or damage to his property caused by windstorm, hail, smoke, explosion, riot, riot attending a strike, civil commotion, vehicle, and aircraft.  This is provided in conjunction with the fire insurance policy.

**Fidelity Bond.**  A form of protection which reimburses an employer for losses caused by dishonest or fraudulent acts of his employees.

**Fire Insurance.**  Coverage for losses caused by fire and lightning, as well as the resultant damage caused by smoke and water.

**Glass Insurance.**  Protection for loss or damage to glass and its appurtenances by any cause except fire and war.

**Group Insurance.**  Any insurance plan under which a number of employees and their dependents are insured under a single policy, issued to their employer, with individual certificates given to each insured employee.  The most commonly written lines are life and accident and health.

**Homeowner's Policy.**  A package type of insurance for the homowner that includes coverage ranging from fire and extended coverages, theft and personal liability to "all risk" coverages, all in a single policy.

**Hurricane.**  A tropical storm with a wind velocity of 75 or more miles an hour.

**Financial Responsibility Law.**  A law under which a person involved in an automobile accident may be required to furnish security up to certain minimum dollar limits. Each state has some form of such a law.

**Inland Marine Insurance.**   A broad type of insurance, generally covering articles that may be transported from one place to another. The essential condition is that the insured property be movable, though bridges, tunnels, and similar instrumentalities of transportation are also considered inland marine. This form of insurance was developed originally by marine under-writers to cover goods while in transit by other than ocean vessels. It now includes any goods in transit (generally excepting trans-ocean) as well as numerous "floater" policies such as personal effects, personal property, jewelry, furs, fine arts, and others.

**Liability Limits.**   The stipulated sum or sums beyond which an insurance company is not liable to protect the insured.

**Liability other than Automobile.**   A form of coverage that pertains, for the most part, to claims arising out of the insured's liability for injuries or damage caused by ownership of property, manufacturing operations, contracting operations, sale or distribution of products, and the operation of elevators and the like, as well as professional services.

**Medical Payments Insurance.**   A coverage, available in various liability insurance policies, in which the insurer agrees to reimburse the insured and others, without regard for the insured's liability, for medical or funeral expenses incurred as the result of bodily injury or death by accident under the conditions specified in the policy.

**Multiple Line Insurance.**   Policies that combine many perils previously covered by individual policies of fire and liability companies. The homeowner's policy is one example. Other examples are the commercial property policy, the farmowner's policy, and the special multiperil policy for motels and apartments.

**Ocean Marine Insurance.**   Coverage on all types of vessels, including liabilities connected with them, and on their cargoes. The cargo coverage has been expanded to protect the owners from warehouse to warehouse, inclusive of all intermediate transit by rail, truck or otherwise.

**Reinsurance.**   Assumption by one insurance company of all or part of a risk undertaken by another insurance company. Purpose is to reduce or spread liability.

**Surety Bond.**   An agreement providing for monetary compensation should there be a failure to perform certain specified acts within a stated period. The surety company, for example, becomes responsible for fulfillment of a contract if the contractor defaults.

**Tornado.**   A whirling wind, accompanied by a funnel-shaped cloud, very violent and destructive in a narrow path, often for many miles over the land.

**Umbrella Liability.**   A form of insurance protection against losses in excess of amounts covered by other liability insurance policies; also protects the insured in many situations not covered by the usual liability policies.

**Uninsured Motorist Protection.**   A form of insurance which covers the policyholder and members of his family if injured by a hit-and-run motorist or a driver who carries no liability insurance, assuming the other driver is at fault.

**Workman's Compensation Insurance.**   A method of providing for the cost of medical care and weekly payments to injured employees or to dependents of those killed in industry, regardless of blame for the accidents.

# CHAPTER 16

# HOW TO MINIMIZE THE TAX BITE

"Don't complain about the taxes you pay," the author's father once admonished as he heard his son grumbling and growling over a Federal Income Tax Return at 11:30 p.m. one miserable April 15, "That's the price you should gladly pay for the privilege of being an American."

Even though it was difficult to agree with him at *that* particular moment, he was undoubtedly right. After all, what would we do without our interstate highways that speed travel, gigantic dams that supply water and electricity, government agencies that protect our health, the Justice Department which safeguards our personal rights, and the military that watches over our national security?

"I'm going to give you that big raise, Frazier, and let the Government do the rest."

Reprinted with permission of *The Wall Street Journal* (Cartoon Features Syndicate).

Regardless of the wastes inherent in government and regardless of one's political views, few people would give up all the things which the Government provides just to avoid paying Federal taxes. However, no one wants to pay more than his or her fair share. Yet thousands of people do pay more than they should each year because they don't understand the hodgepodge of regulations and the tangle of rules that govern our tax system. For too many Americans, April 15 is preceded by a week or two or three of sleepless nights and crisis-ridden days.

Political shenanigans have muddied tax laws with hundreds of special rules and regulations, exemptions and deductions—helping some people and working to the disadvantage of others. Though there have been many energetic attempts to overhaul and simplify the complicated system, none have succeeded. "By now, even the most dedicated tax reform experts recognize that the day of the sweeping reform is past. As is demonstrated by the piles of stymied tax reform plans (such as Wilbur Mills' 1960 bill), tax reform is no overnight job. It's a tedious, provision-by-provision process, aptly compared by economist Walter Heller, former chairman of President Kennedy's Economic Advisory Council, to the bunker-to-bunker fighting on Iwo Jima during World War II."* New administrations may attempt changes, and some will be made, but nothing drastic seems likely.

Despite the gloomy outlook for reform, there are two very important ways you can reduce the taxes you pay under the present law:

1. By becoming familiar with the provisions of the system, you can claim fully all allowable deductions from your present salary and other income.
2. Through long-range planning, saving, and investing you can gradually supplement salary income with long-term capital gains profits. Receiving special treatment under the law, long-term capital gains are taxed at a much lower rate than are salaries—allowing you to keep much more of what you earn.

This chapter will help make tax time a little easier by first reviewing the general requirements and procedures for filing your return. It then shows you how to cash in on the many deductions which are permissible under the law, concluding with a detailed discussion of how capital gains are taxed. Later chapters will help you select and initiate investment programs which will help you take full advantage of the tax savings on long-term capital gains and depreciation allowance.

## THE BASICS OF FILING YOUR RETURN

Because of the millions of tax returns which the Internal Revenue Service must process, and so it may enforce the tax law equitably, the reporting of income, deductions and exemptions are subject to very rigid requirements and stipulations. By first reviewing these basic filing requirements, it will be easier for you to understand the detailed discussion about tax-saving deductions which follows.

**Who must file a return?** Single persons taxable under 65 years of age who had

---

* Peter Lindberg and George Bush, Editors, "Our Income-Tax Mess," *Better Homes and Gardens*, November, 1968, p. 146.

gross income of $1,700 or more during the taxable year, must file a Federal Return. Single persons 65 years and older on the last day of the tax year are not required to file a return unless they had gross income of $2,300 or more. Married couples must file if their combined income is $2,300 or more; $2,900 if one spouse is 65 or older; $3,500 if both are 65 or older. However, the filing requirement for each spouse is $600 if (1) they file separate returns; or (2) they do not have the same household at the end of the year; or (3) another taxpayer is entitled to an exemption for either spouse. College students and others who receive income from tips may still be required to file a return even though their total income is less than $600—if they had uncollected Social Security tax on those tips.

Although you probably won't have to be prompted to do so, you should file a return and claim your own exemption to obtain the refund of any income tax which was withheld from your salaries and wages, even if you did not have enough income to be *required* to file a return. By the way, you are entitled to this refund even though you are claimed as a dependent by another taxpayer.

A husband and wife may either file separate returns or they may be eligible to combine their income and file a joint return. More will be said about this later in the chapter.

**Include your identifying number.** Your Social Security number, which is also your Taxpayer Identifying Number, must be shown on your individual income tax return form. Don't fail to include this or it may cost you money. A penalty of $5 must be assessed for each failure to include this number on a return, unless a reasonable cause can be shown for not providing it.

College students and others filing their first tax return must first obtain a Social Security number if they do not already have one. Application Form SS-5, available at your nearest Social Security office and at your Internal Revenue office, should be used to obtain such a number. The form is also available in most post offices. If a Social Security number has been issued but the card is lost and you do not have the number, the Social Security Administration will, upon request, locate the account number and send you a new card.

**What income is taxable?** Gross or total income, which is the starting point in determining the amount of tax which Uncle Sam wants from you, includes not

GROSS EARNINGS DEC. 31 + MOST OTHER INCOME = GROSS INCOME

only money but also the fair value of property or services which you receive. All income must be reported except for the special exclusions which are discussed later in this chapter. The following items, sometimes overlooked by taxpayers, are all considered taxable income and *should* be reported:

1. *Kickbacks, push money, side commissions.*

**Example:** An insurance broker kicks back a portion of his insurance commissions to automobile salesmen who refer customers to him. The salesmen must include such kickbacks in their income.

2. *Gambling winnings.* You may deduct your gambling losses incurred during the year, but only to the extent of your winnings, provided you itemize your deductions. Proceeds from lotteries, raffles, etc., are gambling winnings. Bonds, autos, and other non-cash prizes are included as income at their fair market value.

3. *Prizes and awards.* Prizes won in any contest such as a lucky number drawing, television or radio quiz program, door prizes, etc., are all taxable. Awards and bonuses to employees for achievements in their work or for suggestions are taxable.

    However, Pulitzer, Nobel and other prizes received in recognition of past accomplishments in religious, charitable, scientific, educational, artistic, literary, or civic fields are NOT included in income if the recipient is selected without action on his part and is not expected to render any future services for the award.

4. *A canceled debt.* This is generally income to the debtor. But it is not income if the cancellation is intended as a gift or if the cancellation results from bankruptcy proceedings.

5. *Alimony.* This and similar payments are generally considered income to the wife and a deductible expense to the husband.

If you have miscellaneous income receipts during the year besides your regular paycheck, it's a good idea to deposit all the funds in your bank account. Your deposit slips will then assist you in making a full and honest declaration of income at tax time. Copy B of the W-2 Form, a statement of your earnings and the taxes withheld from your salary, must accompany your tax return. If you work for more than one employer during the year, you should have a W-2 form from each job. However, even though you worked for more than one employer, you should file only *one* tax return. Do not file a new return for each W-2 you receive. Your return must be filed on time, however, and if you cannot obtain all your Form W-2's, report all your income on your return and attach a statement explaining how you computed any tax withheld for which you claim credit and for which you have no Form W-2.

**Adjusted gross income.** Some deductions are subtracted from *gross income* (total income) to determine *adjusted gross income*—a figure referred to frequently in the discussions in this chapter. Other deductions, described at length later in this chapter, and your allowable personal exemptions are subtracted from adjusted gross income in arriving at taxable income. To compute your adjusted gross, you total all income receipts and deduct the following items:

1. Businessmen deduct all ordinary and necessary expenses attributable to their trade or business.

2. If you hold property for the production of rents or royalties, you subtract ordinary and necessary expenses and certain other deductions attributable to the property.

3. Outside salesmen deduct all expenses attributable to earning a salary, commission or other compensation.

4. Employees deduct expenses of travel, meals, and lodging while away from home in connection with the performance of their services as employees. They also deduct transportation expenses incurred in connection with the performance of services as employees even though they are not away from home. If you moved your residence because your employer transferred you to a new place of employment or because you went to work for a new employer, you deduct such expenses if they otherwise qualify.

5. Sick pay if included in your gross income is deducted in arriving at Adjusted Gross Income.

6. If you are an income beneficiary of property held in trust or an heir, legatee, or devisee of an estate, you may deduct allowable depreciation and depletion, if not deductible by the estate or trust.

7. Certain losses on sales or exchanges of property are allowable as a deduction in determining your Adjusted Gross.

8. You may also deduct certain capital losses. More information on this will be given later in the chapter.

**Accounting periods and methods.**  The accounting period refers to the time covered by an income tax return, and is usually 12 months.  The calendar year is the most common accounting period.  However, you may also use a fiscal

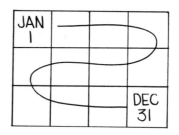

year—any 12-month period.  For example: May 1 to April 30; June 1 to May 31, etc.  The choice is yours; however, once you choose an accounting period, you may not change it without the consent of the Internal Revenue Service.

**Example:**  You went to work for a salary in 1970 and only earned $450.  In 1971 you filed your first income tax return for the calendar year 1970 to obtain a refund of the tax withheld in 1970.  You may not change your accounting period from the calendar year, even if you quit your job and open your own business, without the prior consent of the Internal Revenue Service.

An accounting method refers to the method you use in accounting for your income and deductions. It determines when income is taxable. The *cash* method is most commonly used by individuals. There are other methods, such as the *accrual* method, under which income is reported when *earned* rather than when *received*. If you are interested in using any method other than the cash method, you should obtain Document No. 5175, *Accounting Periods and Methods*, which is available free from your Internal Revenue Office.

As with your accounting period, you may choose your accounting method. Once you use a method, you may not ordinarily change it without the consent of the IRS. You may, however, use a different method for each separate business in which you are engaged.

**Example:** You work for a salary and use the cash method to report that income on your return. You open a restaurant and continue to work for a salary. Even though you use the cash method for your salary, you may use the accrual method of accounting for reporting the income from the restaurant if you wish.

**Accurate records can save tax money.** Every taxpayer is required by law to maintain enough records so that he can prepare a complete and accurate income tax return. However, no particular kinds of records are required. Receipts, cancelled checks, and other evidence may be used to prove the amounts claimed as deductions on your return.

Quite often, taxpayers pay more taxes than they need simply because they don't keep adequate records of deductible items. Small cash contributions of $5 here and $10 there add up to a substantial figure by year's end. Even though you get a receipt for these contributions, it's easy to lose or misplace these little slips of paper. A safer, surer way is to make out a personal check for all tax deductible expenditures. Then at the end of the year, checks can be sorted and deductions tallied. Copies can be made of all the checks claimed as deductions and these can be forwarded to the IRS to verify the return.

Checks as well as other tax records should be retained as long as their contents may be questioned by the Internal Revenue Service. Many persons find it a good idea to keep all cancelled checks permanently since they might come in handy later in establishing the original cost of your home or other property, subsequent improvements, and to verify deductions to a skeptical tax auditor.

From a legal standpoint, records that support an item of income or deduction appearing on an income tax return must be retained until after the expiration of the statute of limitations for such return. Ordinarily this is three years from the date the return was due or filed, or two years from the date the tax was paid, whichever occurs later.

### THE FEDERAL TAX FORMS

Form 1040, *U.S. Individual Income Tax Return*, is the form used by most taxpayers in filing their tax returns. It has been simplified and redesigned a number of times over the years. Currently, it is a basic two-page return with corresponding special schedules which should be used as needed. In most cases the Internal Revenue Service will mail a Form 1040 to you. Use the form you have received in the mail. Peel your address label off the cover of the instructions you received in the mail and place it in the address area of the Form 1040 you use. Also, make any necessary name and address changes right on the label. If you have not received a form in the mail, they are available at your Internal Revenue office, post office, and at many banks.

If all your income is from wages, dividends (not more than $100), and you have no adjustments for sick pay, moving expenses, employee business expenses, or payments to self-employed retirement plans, and you do not itemize your deductions, you need only file Form 1040. (See Fig. 16–1.) No supporting schedules are necessary. However, don't take the quick way out. If you can save money by itemizing deductions, do it.

**Supporting schedules.** If you find it advisable to itemize deductions, use Schedule A.

If your dividends exceed $100 or your interest income exceeds $100, you must list the payers and amounts on Schedule B.

Profit (or loss) from your business or profession must be reported on Schedule C.

Gains and losses on sales or exchanges of property are reported on Schedule D.

Supplemental schedule of income, Schedule E, is used to report income from pensions, annuities, rents, royalties, partnerships, estates, trusts, and small business corporations.

Farm income and expenses are shown on Schedule F.

Income averaging is computed on Schedule G.

If you claim retirement income credit, use Schedule R.

Use Schedule SE to compute your self-employment tax if any.

**Signatures.** One of the frequent oversights of taxpayers is the signature at the bottom of the form. Under law, the form must be signed. A joint return must be signed by both husband and wife even though only one had income.

Also, any person who prepares your return for compensation must sign it

Form **1040** U S Department of the Treasury / Internal Revenue Service
**Individual Income Tax Return** 19

For the year January 1–December 31, 19 , or other taxable year beginning ................., 19 , ending ................., 19

Please print or type

First name and initial (If joint return, use first names and middle initials of both) | Last name | Your social security number

FRANK B. & EVELYN H. | JONES | 516 : 10 : 1776

Present home address (Number and street or rural route) | Spouse's social security number

3700 Mill Way | 575 : 10 : 1492

City, town or post office, State and ZIP code

HOMETOWN, New York 10012

Occu-pation | Yours Electrician
Spouse's Co-Owner of Nursery School

**Filing Status—check only one:**

1 ☐ Single; 2 ☒ Married filing jointly (even if only one had income)
3 ☐ Married filing separately **and** spouse is also filing. If this item checked give spouse's social security number in space above and enter first name here ▶
4 ☐ Unmarried Head of Household
5 ☐ Surviving widow(er) with dependent child
6 ☐ Married filing separately and spouse is not filing

**Exemptions** Regular / 65 or over / Blind Enter number of boxes checked

7 Yourself . . . . . . ☒ ☒ ☐
8 Spouse (applies only if item 2 or 6 is checked) ☒ ☐ ☐ ▶ 3
9 First names of your dependent children who lived with you **marie, james** Enter number ▶ 2
10 Number of other dependents (from line 34) . . . ▶ 2
11 Total exemptions claimed . . . . . . . . . ▶ 7

Income

12 Wages, salaries, tips, etc. (Attach Forms W–2 to back. If unavailable, attach explanation) . | 12 | $7,814. | 65

13a Dividends (see pages 5 and 9 of instr.) $ 462.50 13b Less exclusion $ 180.00 Balance . ▶ | 13c | 282. | 50
(Also list in Part I of Schedule B, if gross dividends and other distributions are over $100)

14 Interest. Enter total here (also list in Part II of Schedule B, if total is over $100) . . . | 14 | 110. | 17

15 Income other than wages, dividends, and interest (from line 40) . . . . . . . . | 15 | 9,817 | 82

16 Total (add lines 12, 13c, 14 and 15) . . . . . . . . . . . . . . . . . | 16 | 18,025 | 14

17 Adjustments to income (such as "sick pay," moving expense, etc. from line 45) . . . | 17 | 60 | 00

18 Adjusted gross income (subtract line 17 from line 16) . . . . . . . . . . . | 18 | 17,965 | 14

- See page 2 of instructions for rules under which the IRS will figure your tax and surcharge.
- If you do not itemize deductions and line 18 is under $10,000, find tax in Tables. Enter tax on line 19.
- If you itemize deductions or line 18 is $10,000 or more, go to line 46 to figure tax.

Tax and Surcharge

19 Tax (Check if from: Tax Tables 1–15 ☐, Tax Rate Schedule X, Y, or Z ☐, Schedule D ☐, or Schedule G ☐) | 19 | 1,598 | 86
20 Tax surcharge. See Tax Surcharge Tables A, B and C in instructions. (If you claim retirement income credit, use Schedule R to figure surcharge.) . . . . . . . . . | 20 | 36 | 00
21 Total (add lines 19 and 20) . . . . . . . . . . . . . . . . . . . . . | 21 | 1,634 | 86

Payments and Credits

22 Total credits (from line 55) . . . . . . . . . . . . . . . . . . . . | 22 | 153 | 60

23 Income tax (subtract line 22 from line 21) . . . . . . . . . . . . . . | 23 | 1,481 | 26

24 Other taxes (from line 61) . . . . . . . . . . . . . . . . . . . . | 24 | 96 | 60

25 Total (add lines 23 and 24) . . . . . . . . . . | 25 | 1,577 | 86
26 Total Federal income tax withheld (attach Forms W–2 to back) . | 26 | 707 | 20 | Make check or money order payable to Internal Revenue Service.
27 1970 Estimated tax payments (include 1969 overpayment allowed as a credit) | 27 | 900 | 00
28 Other payments (from line 65) . . . . . . . . . . | 28 | 32 | 67

29 Total (add lines 26, 27, and 28) . . . . . . . . . . . . . . . . . . | 29 | $1,639 | 87

Bal. Due or Refund

30 If line 25 is larger than line 29, enter BALANCE DUE. Pay in full with return . . . ▶ | 30 |
31 If line 29 is larger than line 25, enter OVERPAYMENT . . . . . . . . . . ▶ | 31 | 62 | 01
32 Line 31 to be: (a) Credited on 1971 estimated tax ▶ $ ; (b) Refunded ▶ $ | | 62 | 01

Under penalties of perjury, I declare that I have examined this return, including accompanying schedules and statements, and to the best of my knowledge and belief it is true, correct, and complete.

Sign here

Your signature *Frank B. Jones* Date
Spouse's signature (if filing jointly, BOTH must sign even if only one had income) *Evelyn H. Jones*

Signature of preparer other than taxpayer, based on all information of which he has any knowledge. Date

Address

16–81168–1

Please attach Copy B of Form W–2 to back
Please attach Check or Money Order here

**Fig. 16–1** Individual income tax return.

Page **2** Form 1040 (1970)                                                              **Attach Copy B of Form W-2 here.** ▶

| Foreign Accounts (check appropriate box) | ▶ Did you, at any time during the taxable year, have any interest in or signature or other authority over a bank, securities, or other financial account in a foreign country (except in a U.S. military banking facility operated by a U.S. financial institution)? . . . . . . . . . . . . ☐ Yes ☐ No. If "Yes," attach Form 4683. (For definitions, see Form 4683.) |
|---|---|

**PART I.—Additional Exemptions (Complete only for other dependents claimed on line 10)**

| 33 (a) NAME | (b) Relationship | (c) Months lived in your home. If born or died during year write "B" or "D" | (d) Did dependent have income of $625 or more? | (e) Amount YOU furnished for dependent's support, if 100% write "ALL" | (f) Amount furnished by OTHERS including dependent. |
|---|---|---|---|---|---|
| Grace Smith | mother | 12 | no | $ 815 | $ 500 |
| Clara Jones | sister | none | no | 350 | 650 |
| (forms 2120 attached) | | | | | |

**34 Total number of dependents listed above.** Enter here and on line 10 . . . . . . . . . . . . . . ▶ 2

**PART II.—Income other than Wages, Dividends, and Interest**

| | | |
|---|---|---|
| 35 Business income (or loss) (attach Schedule C) . | 35 | |
| 36 Sale or exchange of property (attach Schedule D) . . . . . . . . . . . . | 36 | 915 00 |
| 37 Pensions and annuities, rents and royalties, partnerships, estates or trusts, etc. (attach Schedule E) . | 37 | 8,727 82 |
| 38 Farm income (or loss) (attach Schedule F) . . . . . . . . . . . | 38 | |
| 39 Miscellaneous income (state nature and source) *Photography Contest $50.00* *Excess Reimbursement from employer* $25.00 | 39 | 175 00 |
| 40 Total (add lines 35, 36, 37, 38, and 39). Enter here and on line 15 . . . . . . . ▶ | 40 | 9,817 82 |

**PART III.—Adjustments to Income**

| | | |
|---|---|---|
| 41 "Sick pay" if included in line 12 (attach Form 2440 or other required statement) . . . . . . | 41 | 60 00 |
| 42 Moving expense (attach Form 3903) . . . . . . . . . . . . . . . | 42 | |
| 43 Employee business expense (attach Form 2106 or other statement) . . . . . . . . | 43 | |
| 44 Payments as a self-employed person to a retirement plan, etc. (attach Form 2950SE) . . . . | 44 | |
| 45 Total adjustments (add lines 41, 42, 43, and 44). Enter here and on line 17 . . . . . . . ▶ | 45 | 60 00 |

**PART IV.—Tax Computation**

| | | |
|---|---|---|
| 46 Adjusted gross income (from line 18) . . . . . . . . . . . . . . . | 46 | $17,965 14 |
| 47 (a) If you itemize deductions, enter total from Schedule A, line 22<br>(b) If you do not itemize deductions, and line 46 is $10,000 or more, enter $1,000 ($500 if married and filing separately) } . . . . . | 47 | 4,595 30 |
| 48 Subtract line 47 from line 46 . . . . . . . . . . . . . . . . | 48 | 13,369 84 |
| 49 Multiply total number of exemptions claimed on line 11, by $625 . . . . . . . . . | 49 | 4,375 00 |
| 50 Taxable income. Subtract line 49 from line 48. (Figure your tax on this amount by using Tax Rate Schedule X, Y, or Z unless the alternative tax or income averaging is applicable.) Enter tax on line 51 | 50 | 8,994 84 |
| 51 Tax. Enter here and on line 19 . . . . . . . . . . . . . . . . . ▶ | 51 | 1,598 86 |

**PART V.—Credits**

| | | |
|---|---|---|
| 52 Retirement income credit (attach Schedule R) . . . . . . . . . . . | 52 | $ 153 60 |
| 53 Investment credit (attach Form 3468) . . . . . . . . . . . . . | 53 | |
| 54 Foreign tax credit (attach Form 1116) . . . . . . . . . . . . . | 54 | |
| 55 Total credits (add lines 52, 53, and 54). Enter here and on line 22 . . . . . . . . ▶ | 55 | 153 60 |

**PART VI.—Other Taxes**

| | | |
|---|---|---|
| 56 Self-employment tax (attach Schedule SE) . . . . . . . . . . . . | 56 | 96 60 |
| 57 Tax from recomputing prior-year investment credit (attach Form 4255) . . . . . . . | 57 | |
| 58 Minimum tax. See instructions on page 7. Check here ☐, if Form 4625 is attached . . . . | 58 | |
| 59 Social security tax on unreported tip income (attach Form 4137) . . . . . . . . | 59 | |
| 60 Uncollected employee social security tax on tips (from Forms W-2) . . . . . . . . | 60 | |
| 61 Total (add lines 56, 57, 58, 59, and 60). Enter here and on line 24 . . . . . . . . ▶ | 61 | 96 60 |

**PART VII.—Other Payments**

| | | |
|---|---|---|
| 62 Excess F.I.C.A. tax withheld (two or more employers—see instructions on page 7) . . . | 62 | —0— |
| 63 Credit for Federal tax on gasoline, special fuels, and lubricating oil (attach Form 4136) . . . . | 63 | $ 5 12 |
| 64 Regulated Investment Company Credit (attach Form 2439) . . . . . . . . . . | 64 | 27 55 |
| 65 Total (add lines 62, 63, and 64). Enter here and on line 28 . . . . . . . . . . . | 65 | 32 67 |

☆☆☆☆ U.S. GOVERNMENT PRINTING OFFICE:1970—O-970-040                94-1149624        16—81168-1

as the preparer. If it is prepared by a firm or corporation, it should be signed in the company name or, if the firm name is printed or typed, the return must be signed by the person authorized to sign on behalf of the firm. However, the signature is not required if one of your regular full-time employees prepares your return.

**Rounding off dollars.** Money items appearing on your return may be rounded off to whole dollars. This means that amounts under 50 cents are eliminated and amounts from 50 to 99 cents are increased to the next dollar.

### FILING YOUR RETURN

April 15 is usually the final date for filing income tax returns, because most people use the calendar year ending on December 31. However, if the last day for filing a return falls on Saturday, Sunday, or a legal holiday, you may instead procrastinate a bit and file on the next succeeding day (which is not a Saturday, Sunday, or legal holiday).

If you use a fiscal year (a year ending on the last day of any month but December), your return is due on or before the 15th day of the 4th month after the close of your tax year.

If you mail a properly addressed return or tax payment, and it is postmarked no later than the date you were required to file the return or make the payment, you will be considered to have filed your return or paid your tax on time. Sooner or later most of us end up in a freeway jam at 11:45 p.m. on April 15 trying to get to the nearest postal annex.

**Extensions of time for filing.** Under unusual circumstances (illness, accidents, fires, etc.), a person may be granted an extension of time to file a return. If you find an extension desirable, you may make your application for extension by letter or by filing Form 2688 with the Internal Revenue Service where your return will be filed. Your application must include the following information: (1) your reasons for requesting an extension; (2) whether you filed timely income tax returns for the three preceding years; and (3) whether you were required to file an estimated return for the year, and if so whether you filed and paid the estimated tax payments on or before the due dates.

Extensions are not granted as a matter of course, and the reasons for your request must be substantial. If you are unable to sign the request, because of illness or other good cause, another person who stands in close personal or business relationship to you may sign the request on your behalf, stating the reason why you are unable to sign. You should make any request for an extension *early* so that if it is refused, your return may still be filed on time.

**Extensions while abroad.** Lucky citizens of the United States who, on April 15, are not in the United States or Puerto Rico, are allowed an automatic extension of time until June 15 for filing the return for the preceding calendar year. An extension of two months beyond the regular due date for filing is also available to taxpayers abroad who are making returns on a fiscal-year basis.

Military or naval personnel on duty outside the United States and Puerto Rico are also allowed this automatic extension of time for filing their returns. Servicemen in a combat zone (and others supporting combat people—Red Cross workers, Federal civilian employees, accredited correspondents, and others) have an automatic extension of time to file. Their returns will not be due until 180 days after they leave the combat area, or if they were hospitalized outside the United States as a result of combat service, the return is due 180 days after release from the hospital, whichever is later. This extension is available to the spouse of such taxpayers wishing to file a joint return, but not for filing a separate return.

## Addresses of Internal Revenue Offices

| If you are located in: | Use enclosed envelope or this address | If you are located in: | Use this address |
|---|---|---|---|
| Delaware, District of Columbia, Maryland, New Jersey, Pennsylvania, Virginia | Internal Revenue Service Center 11601 Roosevelt Boulevard Philadelphia, Pa. 19155 | Panama Canal Zone, American Samoa, Guam | Director of International Operations Internal Revenue Service Washington, D.C. 20225 |
| Alabama, Florida, Georgia, Mississippi, North Carolina, South Carolina, Tennessee | Internal Revenue Service Center 4800 Buford Highway Chamblee, Georgia 30006 | Puerto Rico (or if excluding income under section 933) | Director of International Operations U.S. Internal Revenue Service Ponce de León Ave. and Bolivia St. Hato Rey, Puerto Rico 00917 |
| Indiana, Kentucky, Michigan, Ohio, West Virginia | Internal Revenue Service Center Cincinnati, Ohio 45298 | Virgin Islands: Permanent residents (For income taxes): | Department of Finance, Tax Division Charlotte Amalie St. Thomas, Virgin Islands 00801 |
| Arkansas, Colorado, Kansas, Louisiana, New Mexico, Oklahoma, Texas, Wyoming | Internal Revenue Service Center 3651 Interregional Highway Austin, Texas 78740 | Permanent residents (For self-employment taxes) and other residents (For income and self-employment taxes) file with Puerto Rico address above. | |
| Alaska, Arizona, California, Hawaii, Idaho, Montana, Nevada, Oregon, Utah, Washington | Internal Revenue Service Center 1160 West 1200 South Street Ogden, Utah 84405 | U.S. citizens with foreign addresses, except A.P.O. and F.P.O., and those excluding income under sec. 911 or 931: file with Director of International Operations, Internal Revenue Service, Washington, D.C. 20225. | |

| Use this address if you are DUE a refund | If you are located in: | Use this address if you are NOT DUE a refund |
|---|---|---|
| Internal Revenue Service Center 310 Lowell Street Andover, Mass. 01812 | CONNECTICUT MAINE MASSACHUSETTS NEW HAMPSHIRE NEW YORK RHODE ISLAND VERMONT | Hartford, Conn. 06115 Augusta, Maine 04330 Boston, Mass. 02203 Portsmouth, N.H. 03801 Albany, N.Y. 12210; 35 Tillary St., Brooklyn, N.Y. 11201; Buffalo, N.Y. 14202; Manhattan District—120 Church St., New York, N.Y. 10007.* Providence, R.I. 02907 Burlington, Vt. 05401 |
| Internal Revenue Service Center 2306 E. Bannister Road Kansas City, Mo. 64170 | ILLINOIS IOWA MINNESOTA MISSOURI NEBRASKA NORTH DAKOTA SOUTH DAKOTA WISCONSIN | Chicago, Ill. 60602; Springfield, Ill. 62704* Des Moines, Iowa 50309 St. Paul, Minn. 55101 St. Louis, Mo. 63101 Omaha, Nebr. 68102 Fargo, N. Dak. 58102 Aberdeen, S. Dak. 57401 Milwaukee, Wis. 53202 |

**Fig. 16–2** Addresses of Internal Revenue Service offices. Since a number of new centralized processing centers have been established in recent years, it is imperative that you send your return to the correct address.

**Where to file.** Address your return to the Internal Revenue Service at the address shown in Fig. 16–2. Note that if you claim a refund, you should send your return to an address different from the one to be used if you owe additional tax. If more than one address is shown for your state and you are not sure which one to use, consult your local post office.

**When payment is due.** If your computations show you owe additional tax, it should be remitted with your return unless you owe less than $1, in which case the IRS shows its generosity, and the extra amount is forgiven.

**Refunds.** If you file Form 1040, and there is an overpayment of tax, you should indicate in the place provided the amount you want refunded and the amount you want credited against your estimated tax. A refund of less than $1 will not be made unless you attach a separate application to your return requesting it.

If you file Form 1040A and the District Director computes your tax, any refund to which you are entitled will be mailed to you.

## IF YOU MAKE AN ERROR

Naturally, before filing your return, you should check carefully to make sure you have reported all of your income and claimed all of the deductions and credits to which you are entitled. But, if after you have filed your return you discover that you failed to report some of your income, erroneously claimed deductions or credits, or are entitled to deductions or credits which you failed to claim, the error can be corrected.

**Error discovered after filing but before due date.** If you filed your return prior to the due date, you may file a corrected return at any time on or before the final due date, and it will be considered to be your original tax return. Print "CORRECTED COPY" at the top of the form.

**Error discovered after filing and after due date.** If you discover after the final filing date that your return contains an error (such as income you failed to report or improper deductions or credits claimed), you should file a new return, clearly marked "AMENDED RETURN," in which your correct tax is shown.

If the error you discovered will result in a refund of tax to you, and the amount is large enough to bother about, you may claim the refund by filing either a Form 1040 marked "AMENDED RETURN," or by filing a claim for refund on Form 843. Either way, the claim for a refund must be filed within three years from the date your original return was filed or within two years from the time the tax was paid, whichever is later. A return filed before the final due date is considered to have been filed on the due date.

The Internal Revenue Service offers you this check list of 10 of the most frequent errors on returns filed last year:

1. Use of the wrong tax table or tax-rate schedule.
2. Calculation from the wrong line of the tax table or tax-rate schedule.
3. Omission of Social Security number, or use of the wrong number.

4. Failure to sign the return or, in the case of a joint return, failure of either the husband or wife to sign.

5. Simple mistakes in mathematics—addition, subtraction, or multiplication.

6. Failure to attach a W-2 form showing earnings and withheld taxes.

7. Lack of explanation for dependents other than children.

8. Entry on the wrong line of refund due or tax owed.

9. Failure to complete the return and, often, failure to compute tax.

10. Lack of explanatory statements for unusual deductions.

## TAX SAVING ELECTIONS AND DEDUCTIONS

To fully explain the entire tax code would take a good many volumes of fine print and to fully understand the code would require very patient reading. For the average taxpayer, however, there are a handful of special deductions which are easy to use and which can save a considerable amount of tax money. This chapter, therefore, limits its discussion to these selected deductions. If you are in business, buy and sell real estate or have other specialized tax problems, you will be able to get detailed information from the Internal Revenue Service. Because tax laws are subject to change from one year to another, it is always a good idea to read thoroughly the instruction booklet included with your annual tax forms.

## INCOME WHICH IS NOT TAXED

Fortunately, not all income is taxable. College students in particular may benefit from nontaxable scholarships and grants. Other excludable income may benefit almost any taxpayer. While some types of income are only partially excludable, other income escapes taxation completely. To avoid paying unnecessary taxes and to save inconvenience and delay as your return is processed, it is important to (1) know your rights—what you can and can't exclude; and (2) clearly identify the source and conditions of excludable income.

**Scholarships and fellowship grants.** If you're lucky enough to receive a scholarship or fellowship grant, you may exclude that amount from your gross income

if you are a candidate for a degree. To qualify for this exclusion, the payment must be for the primary purpose of furthering the recipient's education and training.

A scholarship generally means an amount paid or allowed to, or for the benefit of, a student at an educational institution to aid that person in pursuing his or her studies. A fellowship grant generally means an amount paid or allowed to, or for the benefit of, an individual to aid him in the pursuit of study or research.

Here are other specialized aids that are excludable:

1. *Public Health Service awards.* These awards to students enrolled in advanced courses of training for professional nursing are scholarships.

2. *Work-study programs.* The value of tuition and work payments awarded to students at a college which has no tuition charge and, under its educational philosophy, requires all its students to participate in a work program are scholarships.

3. *Research Fellowship Grant of American Heart Association, Inc.* This grant, to aid individuals to pursue further training subject to the approval of the Association, qualifies as a fellowship.

4. *Student nurse allowances.* The value of room and board furnished by an accredited school of nursing to a student is treated as a scholarship.

5. *Expense payments.* Amounts you receive to cover expenses incident to your scholarship or fellowship grant, such as for travel (including meals and lodging while traveling and an allowance for travel of your family), research, clerical help, or equipment, may be excluded from gross income so long as the amounts are specifically designated as being for expenses under the scholarship or grant. Any amounts not spent to accomplish the purpose of the award and not returned to the grantor must, of course, be included as income.

Amounts received as scholarship prizes in contests where there is no requirement that the prize be used for educational purposes, must be included in the recipient's gross income whether or not the amounts are eventually used for educational purposes.

If you are a candidate for a degree, there is no limitation on the amount of the scholarship or fellowship grant which may be excluded from your income. You may not, however, exclude the portion of the award which is payment for your teaching, research, or other services in the nature of part-time employment required as a condition to receiving a scholarship or fellowship grant, unless such activities are also required of ALL candidates for a particular degree.

If you are not a candidate for a degree, the amount you receive as a scholarship or fellowship, which includes the value of service and accommodations provided to you, may be excluded from gross income only up to the amount of

$300 times the number of months you are under the grant during the tax year. The number of months you may exclude amounts you receive as scholarships or fellowship grants if you are not a candidate for a degree is limited to 36 months during your lifetime. Grants must be from:

1. The Federal Government or an agency thereof, a State, Territory, or a possession of the United States, or any political subdivision thereof, or the District of Columbia; or

2. A nonprofit organization which is exempt from Federal income tax, and operated exclusively for religious, charitable, scientific, testing for public safety, literary, or educational purposes, or the prevention of cruelty to children or animals; or

3. A foreign government; or

4. An international organization, or a binational or multinational educational and cultural foundation or commission created or continued under the Mutual Educational and Cultural Exchange Act of 1961.

**Gifts, inheritances, and insurance.** Whatever you may luckily receive in the way of gifts—a beach home, a new Cadillac, land or money—is not considered taxable income. This applies to money and property which you inherit, and to money received from insurance. If because of the death of the insured you are entitled to receive life insurance in installments, by your election or otherwise, you may exclude a portion of each installment from your income.

To determine the excludable portion, you must prorate the amount held by the insurance company (generally the total lump sum payable at the insured's death) over the period in which the installments are to be paid. Amounts exceeding this excludable portion must be included in income as interest. However, if insurance proceeds are payable to you because of the death of your *spouse*, and you receive them in installments, you may exclude the prorated amount of the lump sum payable at death *plus* up to $1,000 of the interest earned each year on the amount held by the insurer.

**Example:** A widow elects to receive the proceeds of her husband's $75,000 life insurance policy in 10 annual installments of $8,750. The payments are based upon a guaranteed interest return of the insurer. She will include $250 in income and exclude $8,500 each year determined in the following manner:

| | |
|---|---|
| Fixed payment | $8,750 |
| Less prorated amount of insurance principal ($75,000 ÷ 10) | 7,500 |
| Excess over prorated amount | 1,250 |
| Less annual exclusion of interest up to $1,000 | 1,000 |
| Amount included in gross income | $ 250 |

**Social Security and unemployment receipts.** Whether received monthly or in a lump sum, Social Security payments are not taxable. Neither are unemployment benefits paid to you by a state from Social Security funds or payments made under the Railroad Unemployment Insurance Act.

Unemployment benefit payments from a fund to which you voluntarily contribute, whether union established or established as a private non-union fund, are taxable but only to the extent that the amount received exceeds your payments into the fund. Strike and lockout benefits paid by a union from union dues, including both cash and the fair market value of goods received, are includible as income unless the facts clearly show that such benefits were intended as gifts.

Public assistance payments from a general welfare fund in the interest of the general public, such as payments because of blindness, are not included in income.

**Sick pay, disability pay, etc.** You may exclude a limited amount of sick pay from your gross income if the following three conditions are met:

1. You must have been absent from work because of sickness or injury.
2. You must have been paid for the time you were absent under a sick pay plan which was financed by your employer.
3. You must have been absent more than the required waiting period. The length of your waiting period depends on several factors. Therefore, if you received sick pay, it would be a good idea to consult the information service of your Internal Revenue Service to determine your waiting period and how much pay you can exclude.

**Disability pension income.** If you contribute all the cost (premium) of your disability pension, any benefits you may subsequently receive are tax exempt. Similarly, if you contribute part of the premium for disability insurance, when you are absent from work due to an injury or sickness, you may exclude that portion of the benefit attributable to the amount you contributed.

If your employer contributes the cost of your pension, and you pay nothing toward it, amounts you receive as a disability pension when you are absent from work due to an injury or sickness are treated as sick pay until you reach retirement age. When you reach retirement age, the disability receipts are accounted for as an annuity which is explained below.

**Pensions and annuities.** Most pensions require employee contributions. Each payment received from such an annuity then actually consists of two parts: (1) a return of your cost and (2) taxable income. You must first determine what you have invested in the contract—premiums and other considerations which you have paid. This includes the amounts your employer contributed which you were required to include in income at an earlier time, as well as the amounts you contributed.

Next, you must compute the expected return under the contract. If you will receive annuity payments for a fixed number of years, without regard to your life expectancy, the expected return is the total amount you will receive after the annuity starting date. Thus, if you are to receive specific periodic payments which are to be paid for a term, such as a fixed number of years, your expected return is determined by multiplying the fixed number of years or months for which payments are to be made by the amount of the payment specified for each such period.

**Example:**  Edward K. Jones invested a total of $7,500 in an annuity contract which was to pay him $1,000 a year if he remains alive for 10 years starting at age 65. He received his first payment of $1,000. His total expected return on the contract is $10,000 ($1,000 yearly × 10 years). Therefore, he expects to receive a total of $2,500 more than his contract cost. Or another way of stating it, he will receive 25 cents profit on each annuity dollar. The taxable portion of his first year's income ($1,000) would therefore be $250.

If you are to receive annuity payments for the rest of your life, the expected return is found by multiplying the amount of the annual payment by a multiple which is based on your "life expectancy" as of the annuity starting date. These multiples are set out in actuarial tables prescribed by the Internal Revenue Service. Your employer, the administrator of the plan, or the insurance company from which you receive the annuity can generally provide you with the multiple to be used. In any event, it may be obtained from your IRS office.

After you determine your net investment in the contract and your expected return, you obtain the percentage of the annuity to be excluded (the exclusion percentage) by dividing your net investment in the contract by your expected return. This percentage remains the same as long as you draw the annuity as determined on the annuity starting date, even after the payments exceed the expected return. Next, multiply the amount of the annuity income received during the year by this percentage. This gives you the amount of the annuity payments which is a return of your investment and not included in income. Finally, you subtract this amount from the total amount you received during the year. The remainder is the amount which is taxable.

**Example:**  Your annuity, with a net investment of $9,000 pays you $1,000 a year for life. The multiple you use is 15.0 as shown in the IRS actuarial table for your age (male age 65), and your expected return is $15,000 (15 × $1,000). Your net investment of $9,000 divided by your expected return of $15,000 equals 60%, the percentage you will exclude. Each year you will exclude $600 (60% of $1,000) and $400 will be taxable income, as long as payments are received.

If you did not contribute to the cost of your pension, and it was fully paid for by your employer, usually you must pay tax on the full amount you receive each year.

**Reimbursements and allowances.**  If your employer requires you to make an accounting for travel, transportation, gift, and entertainment expenses; and you do not deduct such items from your income tax return, you need not include money you received for reimbursements or allowances in gross income.

**Interest on tax-free securities.**  In an effort to help build better schools, roads, and other public facilities, the Federal Government exempts any interest which one receives from obligations of a state or a political subdivision of a state.  This includes such bodies as port authorities, toll-road commissions, state industrial development boards, utility service authorities, and other similar bodies.

Because of the tax-exempt status of the interest, persons in higher income brackets may find investments in these securities attractive even though interest rates are lower than other investments.  For instance, a person in the 70 percent tax category would prefer a $3\frac{1}{2}$ percent tax-free bond over taxable securities paying $4\frac{1}{2}$ percent.

**Meals and lodging furnished by employer.**  Many students manage apartments or motels to help them get through school or take other jobs which necessitate that they reside where they work.  This kind of work provides a nice tax hedge because the value of the meals or lodging furnished without charge to the student is not considered income.  To qualify for this exclusion, the following tests must be met:

1. The meals or lodging are furnished on the business premises by the employer;
2. The meals or lodging are furnished for the convenience of the employer; and
3. In the case of lodging (but not meals), the employee is required to accept the lodging as a condition of employment.  This means that acceptance of the lodging is required to enable the employee to properly perform the duties of his job, as in a situation where a person is required to be available for duty at all times.

**Military and veterans' benefits.**  Money paid by the Veterans Administration to veterans and their families are exempt from tax.  This includes:

1. Education and training or subsistence allowances
2. Disability compensation and pension payments
3. Grants to seriously disabled veterans
4. Veterans' insurance proceeds
5. Veterans' pensions

Certain military payments are also nontaxable:

1. Payments, equal to six months pay, made by the United States to beneficiaries of Armed Forces personnel who died in active service.
2. Forfeited pay (fines, however, are not excluded).
3. Certain amounts of combat pay.  Servicemen with such income should obtain more information from their APO or other local post office.

**Dividend income.**  The first $100 of ordinary dividends received by you from a domestic corporation may be excluded from your income.  If you are filing a joint return, up to $200 may be deducted. However, neither husband or wife may consider any portion of the dividends received by the other in computing his or her exclusion—excepting most community property states. Thus, if a husband received $120 and his wife received $80 in such dividends, he will exclude $100, and she will exclude $80 or a total of $180 on a joint return. The wife may not use the $20 which her husband was unable to exclude.

## THOSE WELCOME DEDUCTIONS

There are two ways of taking your deductions. You can itemize them on Schedule A of Form 1040 as shown in Fig. 16–3, or if the deductions aren't sizable enough, you may claim a standard deduction. If you own a home and pay interest and property taxes, you will ordinarily find it quite advantageous to itemize deductions. Or if you make generous contributions to qualified charities, have unusually large medical expenses during the year, pay alimony or incur a major uninsured casualty loss, you're probably better off itemizing. Here are some of the general types of things you can deduct:

1. Charitable contributions
2. Interest
3. Taxes (not Federal taxes)
4. Medical and dental expenses (including health insurance premiums)
5. Certain losses and other miscellaneous expenses

For some of these items, only a portion of the total expense can be deducted. More will be said later on in the chapter about each of these items so you can make full use of your legitimate deductions.

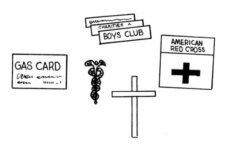

The standard deduction is really an allowance and should be used when it *exceeds* the total of your itemized deductions. Under the Tax Reform Act of 1969, the old 10 percent deduction with a $1,000 ceiling has been replaced with a 15 percent deduction and a $2,000 ceiling. The changes in the standard deduction, like other features of the new law, are to be achieved in stages. For 1971, the standard deduction is 13 percent with a $1,500 ceiling; for 1972, 14 percent with

**Schedules A & B—Itemized Deductions AND Dividend and Interest Income**

(Form 1040)
Department of the Treasury
Internal Revenue Service    ▶ Attach to Form 1040.

**1970**

Name(s) as shown on Form 1040
Frank B. and Evelyn H. Jones

Your Social Security Number
516 04 1492

### Schedule A—Itemized Deductions (Schedule B on back)

Medical and dental expenses (not compensated by insurance or otherwise) for medicine and drugs, doctors, dentists, nurses, hospital care, insurance premiums for medical care, etc.

| | | |
|---|---|---|
| 1 One half (but not more than $150) of insurance premiums for medical care . . | $ 69 | 00 |
| 2 Medicine and drugs · · · · · · · | 250 | 00 |
| 3 Enter 1% of line 18, Form 1040 . . | 179 | 65 |
| 4 Subtract line 3 from line 2. Enter difference (if less than zero, enter zero) . . | 70 | 35 |

5 Itemize other medical and dental expenses. Include hearing aids, dentures, eyeglasses, transportation, balance of insurance premiums for medical care not entered on line 1, etc.

| | | |
|---|---|---|
| One-Half of medical Ins. | 69 | 00 |
| Hometown General Hsptl. | 240 | 35 |
| Dr. Roberts | 185 | 00 |
| Dr. Johnson | 70 | 00 |
| Dr. Smith | 74 | 00 |

| | | |
|---|---|---|
| 6 Total (add lines 4 and 5) . . . . . . | $ 708 | 70 |
| 7 Enter 3% of line 18, Form 1040 . . . | 538 | 95 |
| 8 Subtract line 7 from line 6. Enter difference (if less than zero, enter zero) . . | $ 169 | 75 |
| 9 Total deductible medical and dental expenses (Add lines 1 and 8. Enter here and on line 17, below.) . . . . . . . ▶ | $ 238 | 75 |

| | | |
|---|---|---|
| Taxes.—Real estate . . . . . . . . | 286 | 00 |
| State and local gasoline (see gas tax tables) | 149 | 00 |
| General sales (see sales tax tables) . . . | 320 | 88 |
| State and local income . . . . . . . . | | |
| Personal property . . . . . . . . . | | |

| | | |
|---|---|---|
| 10 Total taxes (Enter here and on line 18, below.) . . . . . . . . . . . ▶ | $ 818 | 88 |

**Contributions.**—Cash—including checks, money orders, etc. (Itemize—see instructions on page 8 for examples)

| | | |
|---|---|---|
| First Church | 260 | 00 |
| Community Fund | 175 | 00 |
| Red Cross | 25 | 00 |
| Boy Scouts | 12 | 00 |
| General Hospital | 20 | 00 |
| Share of Jones Bros. Partnership | 37 | 50 |

| | | |
|---|---|---|
| 11 Total cash contributions . . . . . | 529 | 50 |
| 12 Other than cash (see instructions on page 8 for required statement). Enter total for such items here . . . . . | | |
| 13 Carryover from prior years (see instructions on page 8) . . . . . . | | |
| 14 Total contributions (Add lines 11, 12, and 13. Enter here and on line 19, below. See instructions on page 8 for limitation) . . . . . . . . ▶ | $ 529 | 50 |

| | | |
|---|---|---|
| Interest expense—Home mortgage . . | $ 363 | 77 |
| Installment purchases · · · · · · · | 4 | 90 |
| Other (Itemize) Ace Bldg and Loan Assoc. Mortgage Prepayment Penalty | 60 | 00 |
| 15 Total interest expense (Enter here and on line 20, below.) . . . . . . ▶ | $ 428 | 67 |

**Miscellaneous deductions** for child care, alimony, union dues, casualty losses, etc. (see instructions on page 8).

| | | |
|---|---|---|
| Theft Loss | $ 79 | 50 |
| Alimony—J. Jones N.C.Y, N.Y | 1,900 | 00 |
| Union Dues | 150 | 00 |
| Casualty Loss—Summer cottage (from line 49, Sched.) | 450 | 00 |
| 16 Total miscellaneous deductions (Enter here and on line 21, below.) . . . ▶ | $ 2,579 | 50 |

**A**

### Summary of Itemized Deductions

| | | |
|---|---|---|
| 17 Total deductible medical and dental expenses (from line 9) . . . . . . . . . . . . . . . . . . . | 238 | 75 |
| 18 Total taxes (from line 10) . . . . . . . . . . . . . . . . . . . . . . . . . . . | 818 | 88 |
| 19 Total contributions (from line 14) . . . . . . . . . . . . . . . . . . . . . . . . | 529 | 50 |
| 20 Total interest expense (from line 15) . . . . . . . . . . . . . . . . . . . . . . . | 428 | 67 |
| 21 Total miscellaneous deductions (from line 16) . . . . . . . . . . . . . . . . . . . . | 2,579 | 50 |
| 22 **TOTAL ITEMIZED DEDUCTIONS.** (Add lines 17 through 21. Enter here and on Form 1040, line 47) · · ▶ | $4,595 | 30 |

**Fig. 16–3** Schedule A of individual income tax return.

a $2,000 ceiling; and finally 15 percent with a $2,000 ceiling for 1973 and subsequent tax years. Married persons filing *separate* returns are entitled to one-half of the above figures.

The standard deduction is normally the *larger* of (1) the percentage standard deduction applicable for the particular tax year; or (2) a flat minimum deduction called a low-income allowance. A portion of the tax tables for 1970 returns is shown in Fig. 16–4. The low-income allowance is automatically taken into consideration when you use the Tax Tables.

**Table 2—Returns claiming TWO exemptions (continued) (Do not use this table if you itemize deductions.)**

| If adjusted gross income is— At least | But less than | Single, not head of house-hold | Head of house-hold | Married* filing joint return | Married filing a separate return claiming— Low income allow-ance | %-Stand-ard deduc-tion |
|---|---|---|---|---|---|---|
| $3,900 | $3,950 | $362 | $350 | $334 | $381 | $364 |
| 3,950 | 4,000 | 372 | 359 | 342 | 391 | 372 |
| 4,000 | 4,050 | 381 | 367 | 350 | 400 | 381 |
| 4,050 | 4,100 | 389 | 375 | 357 | 410 | 389 |
| 4,100 | 4,150 | 398 | 383 | 364 | 419 | 398 |
| 4,150 | 4,200 | 406 | 391 | 371 | 429 | 406 |
| 4,200 | 4,250 | 415 | 399 | 378 | 438 | 415 |
| 4,250 | 4,300 | 424 | 408 | 386 | 448 | 424 |
| 4,300 | 4,350 | 432 | 416 | 393 | 457 | 432 |
| 4,350 | 4,400 | 441 | 424 | 400 | 467 | 441 |
| 4,400 | 4,450 | 449 | 432 | 407 | 476 | 449 |
| 4,450 | 4,500 | 458 | 440 | 414 | 486 | 458 |
| 4,500 | 4,550 | 466 | 448 | 422 | 495 | 466 |
| 4,550 | 4,600 | 475 | 456 | 429 | 505 | 475 |
| 4,600 | 4,650 | 483 | 464 | 436 | 514 | 483 |
| 4,650 | 4,700 | 492 | 472 | 443 | 524 | 492 |
| 4,700 | 4,750 | 500 | 480 | 450 | 533 | 500 |
| 4,750 | 4,800 | 509 | 489 | 458 | 543 | 509 |
| 4,800 | 4,850 | 518 | 497 | 466 | 552 | 518 |
| 4,850 | 4,900 | 526 | 505 | 473 | 562 | 526 |
| 4,900 | 4,950 | 535 | 513 | 481 | 571 | 535 |
| 4,950 | 5,000 | 543 | 521 | 489 | 581 | 543 |
| 5,000 | 5,050 | 552 | 529 | 496 | 590 | 552 |
| 5,050 | 5,100 | 560 | 537 | 504 | 600 | 562 |
| 5,100 | 5,150 | 569 | 545 | 512 | 609 | 571 |

| If adjusted gross income is— At least | But less than | Single, not head of house-hold | Head of house-hold | Married* filing joint return | Married filing a separate return claiming— Low income allow-ance | %-Stand-ard deduc-tion |
|---|---|---|---|---|---|---|
| $5,150 | $5,200 | $577 | $553 | $519 | $619 | $581 |
| 5,200 | 5,250 | 586 | 561 | 527 | 628 | 590 |
| 5,250 | 5,300 | 595 | 570 | 535 | 638 | 600 |
| 5,300 | 5,350 | 603 | 578 | 542 | 647 | 609 |
| 5,350 | 5,400 | 612 | 586 | 550 | 657 | 619 |
| 5,400 | 5,450 | 620 | 594 | 558 | 666 | 628 |
| 5,450 | 5,500 | 629 | 602 | 565 | 676 | 638 |
| 5,500 | 5,550 | 637 | 610 | 573 | 685 | 647 |
| 5,550 | 5,600 | 646 | 618 | 580 | 696 | 657 |
| 5,600 | 5,650 | 654 | 626 | 588 | 707 | 666 |
| 5,650 | 5,700 | 663 | 634 | 596 | 718 | 676 |
| 5,700 | 5,750 | 671 | 642 | 603 | 729 | 685 |
| 5,750 | 5,800 | 680 | 651 | 611 | 740 | 696 |
| 5,800 | 5,850 | 689 | 659 | 619 | 751 | 707 |
| 5,850 | 5,900 | 698 | 668 | 627 | 762 | 718 |
| 5,900 | 5,950 | 708 | 677 | 636 | 773 | 729 |
| 5,950 | 6,000 | 718 | 686 | 644 | 784 | 740 |
| 6,000 | 6,050 | 728 | 695 | 653 | 796 | 751 |
| 6,050 | 6,100 | 738 | 704 | 661 | 806 | 762 |
| 6,100 | 6,150 | 748 | 713 | 670 | 817 | 773 |
| 6,150 | 6,200 | 758 | 722 | 678 | 828 | 784 |
| 6,200 | 6,250 | 768 | 731 | 687 | 839 | 795 |
| 6,250 | 6,300 | 777 | 740 | 696 | 850 | 806 |
| 6,300 | 6,350 | 787 | 749 | 704 | 861 | 817 |
| 6,350 | 6,400 | 797 | 758 | 713 | 872 | 828 |

| If adjusted gross income is— At least | But less than | Single, not head of house-hold | Head of house-hold | Married* filing joint return | Married filing a separate return claiming— Low income allow-ance | %-Stand-ard deduc-tion |
|---|---|---|---|---|---|---|
| $6,400 | $6,450 | $807 | $767 | $721 | $883 | $839 |
| 6,450 | 6,500 | 817 | 776 | 730 | 894 | 850 |
| 6,500 | 6,550 | 827 | 785 | 738 | 905 | 861 |
| 6,550 | 6,600 | 837 | 794 | 747 | 916 | 872 |
| 6,600 | 6,650 | 847 | 803 | 755 | 927 | 883 |
| 6,650 | 6,700 | 857 | 812 | 764 | 938 | 894 |
| 6,700 | 6,750 | 867 | 821 | 772 | 949 | 905 |
| 6,750 | 6,800 | 876 | 830 | 781 | 960 | 916 |
| 6,800 | 6,850 | 886 | 839 | 790 | 971 | 927 |
| 6,850 | 6,900 | 896 | 848 | 798 | 982 | 938 |
| 6,900 | 6,950 | 906 | 857 | 807 | 993 | 949 |
| 6,950 | 7,000 | 916 | 866 | 815 | 1,004 | 960 |
| 7,000 | 7,050 | 926 | 875 | 824 | 1,015 | 971 |
| 7,050 | 7,100 | 936 | 884 | 832 | 1,026 | 982 |
| 7,100 | 7,150 | 946 | 893 | 841 | 1,037 | 993 |
| 7,150 | 7,200 | 956 | 902 | 849 | 1,048 | 1,004 |
| 7,200 | 7,250 | 966 | 911 | 858 | 1,059 | 1,015 |
| 7,250 | 7,300 | 975 | 920 | 867 | 1,070 | 1,026 |
| 7,300 | 7,350 | 985 | 929 | 875 | 1,081 | 1,037 |
| 7,350 | 7,400 | 995 | 938 | 884 | 1,092 | 1,048 |
| 7,400 | 7,450 | 1,005 | 947 | 892 | 1,103 | 1,059 |
| 7,450 | 7,500 | 1,015 | 956 | 901 | 1,114 | 1,070 |
| 7,500 | 7,550 | 1,025 | 965 | 909 | 1,125 | 1,081 |
| 7,550 | 7,600 | 1,035 | 974 | 918 | 1,136 | 1,092 |

**Fig. 16–4** Federal income tax tables. The Federal Income Tax Instruction Booklet provides convenient tax tables which show the tax liability for various income levels where expenses are not itemized.

The Tax Tables supplied with your income tax forms provide two columns for married persons filing *separate* returns. You can see in Table 2 of Fig. 16–4 that the one column considers the low-income allowance, the other shows the percentage standard deduction. You cannot use the low-income allowance column if your spouse's tax is computed under the percentage standard deduction column. However, you can use the low-income allowance column if your tax is *higher* than that under the standard deduction column and your spouse's tax is lower under the low-income allowance column than under the standard deduction column. Other rules apply to certain married individuals living apart.

A husband and wife filing separate returns should use the method of claiming deductions most beneficial to them as a unit, even though it may be less advantageous to one of them. They both must use the same method of claiming deductions. If one spouse itemized deductions, the other must itemize. If one spouse claims the standard deduction, the other must also.

Although most persons may choose whether or not to itemize or take the standard deduction, there are those who are *required* to make itemized deductions. This is true even though they might otherwise benefit from taking a standard deduction. They are:

1. Nonresident aliens
2. Estates and trusts
3. United States citizens entitled to special benefits accorded income received from a United States possession
4. Individuals filing a short-year return in case of a change in accounting period
5. One spouse whose spouse itemizes deductions

## DEDUCTIBLE CONTRIBUTIONS

It seems as though every day someone comes by the home or office soliciting a contribution for some worthy cause. If you make donations to these and similar kinds of organizations, be certain to keep track of your contributions so that you can use them to full advantage as a tax deduction when April rolls around:

1. Schools, hospitals, churches, states, political subdivision
2. United Fund, Community Chest, YMCA—YMHA, YWCA—YWHA, Salvation Army
3. Red Cross, Family Service Association, Police Boys Clubs
4. Boys Clubs of America, Boy Scouts, Camp Fire Girls, Girl Scouts, Daughters of the American Revolution, Disabled American Veterans
5. Veterans of Foreign Wars, American Legion, Amvets
6. Multiple Sclerosis Society, CARE, Tuberculosis Society, WAIF, Diabetes Association, Cancer Association, Heart Association, Cerebral Palsy

Other non-profit organizations may also qualify.

In addition to the usual cash contributions, some frequently overlooked items are also deductible. Check these:

1. Dues, membership fees, initiation fees, or assessments which you pay to qualified organizations are deductible as contributions if you are not entitled to benefits and privileges in return. For example, amounts you pay to your church, synagogue, or other religious organization as dues, fees, pew rents, or assessments are considered charitable contributions and are deductible.
2. Payments you make for admission to or other participation in charity balls, banquets, shows, sporting events, etc., are deductible to the extent that they exceed what you would ordinarily have to pay for the admission or other

privileges. If there are no established charges for the event, the amount you would ordinarily have to pay is a reasonable estimate.

3. Out-of-pocket expenses which you pay in rendering services without compensation to a qualified organization are deductible as contributions. This includes amounts you pay for transportation from your home to the place where you serve.

4. You may deduct nonreimbursed out-of-pocket expenses which are directly attributable to service you render to a qualified organization, such as for the operation of your car. If you do not wish to deduct your actual expenses, you may instead use a standard mileage rate of 5¢ per mile as your contribution. However, depreciation and insurance are not deductible.

5. Deductions may also be taken for gifts of property to qualified charitable organizations. Check the yearly instruction guide for special limitations that apply to these gifts.

Contributions to most charities may be deducted up to 50 % of your adjusted gross income. However, contributions to certain private non-operating foundations, veterans organizations, fraternal societies, and cemetery organizations are limited to 20 % of adjusted gross income.

## DEDUCTIBLE INTEREST

Young couples and others with home mortgages should be sure to claim their full interest deduction for the mortgage as well as for any other indebtedness they may have. In the early years of a 20-year, 7 %, $22,000 mortgage, a couple would pay a little more than $1,500 annually for interest. Therefore, it would certainly pay them to itemize deductions, since only $1,000 may be deducted as a maximum standard deduction.

Actually, all interest is deductible which is paid out during the taxable year. Here are some interest items which are sometimes overlooked by taxpayers:

1. Interest on loans from credit union, small-loan company or private individual.

2. Interest may be hidden in other payments such as judgments, tax deficiency payments, etc. All such interest is deductible. However, any amount which you are required to pay for late payments designated as a penalty cannot be deducted.

3. Installment contracts nearly always have interest charges—which should be deducted. If you have difficulty determining how much interest is being paid, ask the creditor to give you a written statement as to how much interest was paid by you for the taxable year.

4. If you purchase personal property, such as clothing, jewelry, a radio, television, etc., on the installment plan in which the carrying charges are separately stated, but the interest cannot be determined (in general these will

be contracts written prior to the effective date for the Truth-in-Lending Law), you may treat a portion of your payments as interest. Similarly if the actual interest charge under a so-called budget charge account cannot be determined, you may treat part of your payment as interest.

You can deduct the lesser of:

a) An amount equal to 6% of the average unpaid balance of your installment contract during the year, or

b) The portion of the total carrying charge allocable to the year.

The average unpaid balance in (a) above is determined by totaling the unpaid balances on the first day of each month in the year and dividing this total by 12. The unpaid balance at the beginning of each month is determined by taking into account the payments in the amount and at the time called for in the contract, even though such payments are not made when due. The amount in (b) is determined by dividing the carrying charge by the total number of monthly payments to obtain a prorated monthly carrying charge. This amount is then multiplied by the number of months in the tax year during which the installment obligation was outstanding.

**Example:** On July 12, Frank Jones purchased a home freezer for $254 plus a carrying charge of $20. He made a down payment of $50 and agreed to make 16 monthly payments of $14 each on the 10th of each month, beginning August 10. He is a cash method, calendar year taxpayer and made no other installment purchases. The portion of the carrying charge which is deductible as interest is computed as follows:

a) Unpaid balance (including carrying charge) outstanding:

| | |
|---|---:|
| August 1 ($254 + $20 − $50) ........................... | $224.00 |
| September 1 ......................................... | 210.00 |
| October 1 ........................................... | 196.00 |
| November 1 ......................................... | 182.00 |
| December 1 ......................................... | 168.00 |
| Total of monthly unpaid balances | $980.00 |
| Average unpaid balance ($980 ÷ 12) ...................... | $ 81.67 |
| 6% of $81.67 ........................................ | $4.90 |

b) Carrying charge ......................................... $ 20.00
Carrying charge per installment ($20 ÷ 16 installments) ........ 1.25
Multiply by number of installments paid ($1.25 × 5) .......... 6.25
Carrying charge allocable to year ..................................... $6.25
Interest deduction—lesser of computation under (a) or (b) ................. $4.90

The amount treated as interest cannot exceed that portion of the total carrying charge which is allocable to the taxable year. Moreover, it cannot exceed the actual amount of the payments you made under the contract in the year.

## DEDUCTIBLE TAXES
Practically every consumer pays a number of different taxes each year. Many

are deductible. If you itemize deductions, you can deduct general state or local retail sales taxes if they are imposed directly upon the consumer, or if they are imposed on the retailer (or wholesaler in case of gasoline taxes) and the amount of the tax is separately stated by the retailer. A convenient way to account for sales tax is to use the Sales Tax Tables provided in your annual tax instruction booklet. A portion of this information is reproduced in Fig. 16–5. This gives the average amount of sales taxes which persons in each state paid according to

## 1970 Optional State Sales Tax Tables

If you itemize your deductions, you may use these tables to determine the general sales tax to be entered on Schedule A. However, if you are able to establish that you paid an amount larger than that shown, you are entitled to deduct the larger amount. The sales tax paid on the purchase of an automobile may be added to the table amount except in Vermont.

If your income was more than $19,999, but less than $100,000, compute your deduction as follows:

Step 1—For the first $19,999, find the amount for your family size in the table for your State.

Step 2—For each $1,000 of income (or fraction thereof) over $19,999, but less than $50,000, add 2 percent of the amount you determined in Step 1, above.

Step 3—For each $1,000 of income (or fraction thereof) over $49,999, but less than $100,000, add 1 percent of the amount you determined in Step 1, above.

If your income was $100,000 or more, simply deduct 210 percent of the amount determined in Step 1, above.

### Colorado [3]

| Income [1] | 1 | 2 | 3 | 4 | 5 | Over 5 |
|---|---|---|---|---|---|---|
| Under $3,000 | $35 | $48 | $49 | $59 | $59 | $60 |
| $3,000-$3,999 | 44 | 58 | 61 | 71 | 73 | 75 |
| $4,000-$4,999 | 51 | 68 | 72 | 82 | 85 | 88 |
| $5,000-$5,999 | 58 | 76 | 82 | 91 | 97 | 100 |
| $6,000-$6,999 | 64 | 84 | 92 | 100 | 107 | 112 |
| $7,000-$7,999 | 72 | 92 | 100 | 109 | 117 | 122 |
| $8,000-$8,999 | 76 | 99 | 108 | 117 | 127 | 133 |
| $9,000-$9,999 | 83 | 106 | 116 | 124 | 136 | 143 |
| $10,000-$10,999 | 86 | 112 | 124 | 131 | 145 | 153 |
| $11,000-$11,999 | 91 | 118 | 132 | 138 | 154 | 163 |
| $12,000-$12,999 | 96 | 124 | 138 | 145 | 162 | 172 |
| $13,000-$13,999 | 101 | 130 | 145 | 151 | 170 | 181 |
| $14,000-$14,999 | 106 | 136 | 153 | 157 | 178 | 190 |
| $15,000-$15,999 | 110 | 141 | 160 | 163 | 186 | 198 |
| $16,000-$16,999 | 114 | 147 | 166 | 173 | 194 | 206 |
| $17,000-$17,999 | 118 | 151 | 173 | 181 | 200 | 214 |
| $18,000-$18,999 | 122 | 156 | 179 | 184 | 208 | 215 |
| $19,000-$19,999 | 126 | 161 | 185 | 186 | 215 | 230 |

Fig. 16–5  A portion of 1968 state sales tax deduction table. The average sales taxes paid in each state may be determined from your total income and size of family.

incomes.  If you purchased an automobile during the year, however, the sales tax paid on its purchase should be added to the amount shown in the table.

If part or all of the cost of your car license plates was based on the value of your automobile, then such amount is deductible as personal property tax.

These are the taxes you CAN deduct:

1. Real estate taxes
2. State and local gasoline taxes
3. General sales taxes
4. State and local income taxes
5. Personal property taxes

Another handy table provided in your instruction booklet which you should use is the State Gasoline Tax Table shown in Fig. 16–6.  It shows at a glance how much you can deduct for gasoline taxes according to the mileage driven during the tax year.  People who do a great deal of driving will find a substantial deduction in this tax.  For example, a college student in California driving 15,000 miles in a year could claim a $75 deduction, providing that he itemizes deductions.

### State Gasoline Tax Table

ou may figure the deduction for State tax on gasoline used in your by using the following table based on information available as August 15, 1970. If all or part of your mileage was driven in a r-cylinder (or less) car, the deduction for that mileage should be e-half of the table amount.

If you can establish that you paid a larger amount, you are entitled to deduct that amount.
Find the rate of gasoline tax for your State in the list below. If the rate of gasoline tax changed in 1970, find the deduction for mileage driven at each rate, and add the two amounts.

| | | | | | |
|---|---|---|---|---|---|
| bama 7¢ | Dist. of Col. 7¢ | Kansas 7¢ | Minnesota 7¢ | New Jersey 7¢ | Oregon 7¢ | Utah 7¢ |
| ska 8¢ | Florida 7¢ | Kentucky 7¢ | Mississippi 8¢ | New Mexico 7¢ | Pennsylvania 7¢ | Vermont 8¢ |
| zona 7¢ | Georgia 6.5¢ | Louisiana 8¢ | Missouri 5¢ | New York 7¢ |   after March 31, 8¢ | Virginia 7¢ |
| ansas 7.5¢ | Hawaii 5¢ | Maine 8¢ | Montana 7¢ | North Carolina 9¢ | Rhode Island 8¢ | Washington 9¢ |
| ifornia 7¢ | Idaho 7¢ | Maryland 7¢ | Nebraska 8.5¢ | North Dakota 7¢ | South Carolina 7¢ | West Virginia 7¢ |
| orado 7¢ | Illinois 7.5¢ | Massachusetts 6.5¢ | Nevada 6¢ | Ohio 7¢ | South Dakota 7¢ |   after June 30, 8.5¢ |
| nnecticut 8¢ | Indiana 8¢ | Michigan 7¢ | New Hampshire 7¢ | Oklahoma 6.58¢ | Tennessee 7¢ | Wisconsin 7¢ |
| aware 7¢ | Iowa 7¢ | | | | Texas 5¢ | Wyoming 7¢ |

| Nonbusiness Mileage Driven | RATE PER GALLON | | | | | | | |
|---|---|---|---|---|---|---|---|---|
| | 5¢ | 6¢ | 6.5¢ & 6.58¢ | 7¢ | 7.5¢ | 8¢ | 8.5¢ | 9¢ |
| der 3,000 | $7 | $9 | $9 | $10 | $11 | $11 | $12 | $13 |
| 00 to 3,499 | 12 | 14 | 15 | 16 | 17 | 19 | 20 | 21 |
| 00 to 3,999 | 13 | 16 | 17 | 19 | 20 | 21 | 23 | 24 |
| 00 to 4,499 | 15 | 18 | 20 | 21 | 23 | 24 | 26 | 27 |
| 00 to 4,999 | 17 | 20 | 22 | 24 | 25 | 27 | 29 | 31 |
| 00 to 5,499 | 19 | 23 | 24 | 26 | 28 | 30 | 32 | 34 |
| 00 to 5,999 | 21 | 25 | 27 | 29 | 31 | 33 | 35 | 37 |
| 00 to 6,499 | 22 | 27 | 29 | 31 | 33 | 36 | 38 | 40 |
| 00 to 6,999 | 24 | 29 | 31 | 34 | 36 | 39 | 41 | 43 |
| 00 to 7,499 | 26 | 31 | 34 | 36 | 39 | 41 | 44 | 47 |
| 00 to 7,999 | 28 | 33 | 3F | 39 | 42 | 44 | 47 | 50 |
| 00 to 8,499 | 29 | 35 | 36 | 41 | 44 | 47 | 50 | 53 |
| 00 to 8,999 | 31 | 38 | 41 | 44 | 47 | 50 | 53 | 56 |
| 00 to 9,499 | 33 | 40 | 43 | 46 | 50 | 53 | 56 | 59 |
| 00 to 9,999 | 35 | 42 | 45 | 49 | 52 | 56 | 59 | 63 |

| Nonbusiness Mileage Driven | RATE PER GALLON | | | | | | | |
|---|---|---|---|---|---|---|---|---|
| | 5¢ | 6¢ | 6.5¢ & 6.58¢ | 7¢ | 7.5¢ | 9¢ | 8.5¢ | 9¢ |
| 10,000 to 10,999 | $38 | $45 | $49 | $53 | $56 | $60 | $64 | $68 |
| 11,000 to 11,999 | 41 | 49 | 53 | 57 | 62 | 66 | 70 | 74 |
| 12,000 to 12,999 | 45 | 54 | 58 | 63 | 67 | 71 | 76 | 80 |
| 13,000 to 13,999 | 48 | 58 | 63 | 67 | 72 | 77 | 82 | 87 |
| 14,000 to 14,999 | 52 | 62 | 67 | 73 | 78 | 83 | 83 | 93 |
| 15,000 to 15,999 | 55 | 66 | 72 | 77 | 83 | 89 | 94 | 100 |
| 16,000 to 16,999 | 59 | 71 | 77 | 83 | 88 | 94 | 100 | 106 |
| 17,000 to 17,999 | 63 | 75 | 81 | 88 | 94 | 100 | 106 | 113 |
| 18,000 to 18,999 | 66 | 79 | 86 | 92 | 99 | 106 | 112 | 119 |
| 19,000 to 19,999 | 70 | 84 | 91 | 98 | 104 | 111 | 118 | 125 |
| 20,000 miles* | 71 | 86 | 93 | 100 | 107 | 114 | 121 | 129 |

*For over 20,000 miles, use table amounts corresponding to total mileage driven. For example, for 25,000 miles, add the deduction for 5,000 to the deduction for 20,000 miles.

g. 16–6   State gasoline tax table.  This important deduction can be found easily by first determin- g the tax rate assessed on gasoline in your state and then looking at the line corresponding with e miles driven during the taxable year.

These are taxes you CANNOT deduct:

1. Any Federal excise taxes on your personal expenditures, such as taxes on transportation, telephone, gasoline, etc.

2. Federal Social Security taxes

3. Hunting licenses, dog licenses, etc.

4. Auto inspection fees, license plates, drivers' licenses

5. Water taxes

6. Taxes you paid for another person

7. Alcoholic beverage, cigarette, and tobacco taxes

8. Selective sales or excise taxes (such as those on admission, room occupancy, etc.) even if they are separately stated or imposed on the purchaser, unless imposed at the same rate as the general sales tax

## DEDUCTIBLE MEDICAL AND DENTAL EXPENSES

Under a new ruling, those who itemize deductions can now deduct one-half the amount paid for medical and hospital insurance without regard to the 3 percent limitation on other such expenses (this limitation is discussed later). This deduction is limited to $150, but any additional amount which you pay for such insurance is deductible, although subject to the regular 3 percent limitation.

Deductions for medical expenses are confined to expenses incurred primarily for the prevention or alleviation of a physical or mental defect or illness. Such deductions include money paid for a wide variety of medical expenses. Fees to physicians, surgeons, dentists and other medical men, expenses for therapy, hospital and nursing services, x-rays, ambulance, and many more items. (A complete list is provided in the instructions to each 1040 Form.)

There is no maximum limitation on the amount of your medical expense deduction. However, such expenses are deductible, only to the extent they exceed 3 percent of your adjusted gross income, except for medical insurance which was discussed earlier.

Medical and dental expenses include the cost of medicine and drugs to the extent such expenses exceed 1 percent of your adjusted gross income. You must deduct such expenses only in the year in which paid, and you must keep very accurate records of payments to substantiate your claims. Your deductions must be for amounts paid for yourself, your spouse, and dependents, and for which you are not reimbursed.

## DEDUCTIBLE EMPLOYEES' TRAVELING, TRANSPORTATION, GIFT AND ENTERTAINMENT EXPENSES

If you are one of the many employees in a full- or part-time job who must do considerable traveling and entertaining in the regular course of your work, you can save a good deal on taxes if you take full advantage of special deductions which the law permits. These include:

**Business travel expenses.** All reasonable and necessary expenses which you may incur for foreign and domestic travel away from home overnight in pursuit of your business or employment are fully deductible. You may include transportation as well as meal and lodging expenses. Use this quick check list to make certain nothing is overlooked:

1. Taxi fares or other costs of transportation from the airport or station to the hotel; from the hotel to the airport or station; from one customer to another; or from one place of business to another
2. Cleaning and laundry expenses
3. Baggage charges and transportation costs for sample and display material
4. Operation and maintenance of house trailers
5. Reasonable tips, to the extent incident to any of the foregoing expenses

The expenses must arise from the fact that your duties require you to travel or to live temporarily at some place other than your principal or regular post of duty.

**Meals and lodging expenses.** These are deductible when you are away from home overnight on business. For travel expense purposes, the IRS considers your home as being your principal place of business, employment, station, or post of duty, regardless of where you maintain your family residence.

**Example:** You live with your family in Chicago, but work in Milwaukee. During the week you stay in a hotel in Milwaukee and eat your meals in a restaurant, but return to your family in Chicago every weekend. You may *not* deduct any of your expenses of traveling, meals, or lodging, as Milwaukee is your tax home and the travel over the weekends is not for a business reason.

**Transportation expenses.** These include the fares charged for traveling by air, rail, bus, taxi, etc., and the cost of operating and maintaining your automobile. It is important to note, too, that your transportation expenses may be deducted even though you were not away from home—if incurred for transportation which was directly attributable to the actual conduct of your employment.

**Automobile expenses.**  If you are required to use your car in your work, and if you use it exclusively for that purpose, you may deduct the entire cost of its operation.  Such expenses include the cost of gasoline, oil, repairs, insurance, and depreciation, and are deductible in addition to garage rent, parking fees, tolls, interest to purchase the car, taxes, etc.

If you use your car for both personal and business purposes, you must apportion your expenses between business travel and personal travel.

**Example:**  You are a salesman and drove your car 20,000 miles during the year.  About 8,000 miles were driven for business travel and 12,000 miles were for personal purposes. Only 8,000/20,000 or 40 percent of the total cost of operating your car may be claimed as a business or employment expense.

A standard mileage rate of 10c a mile for the first 15,000 miles and 7c for each succeeding mile of business may be used, in lieu of actual expenses and depreciation, in determining the deductible costs of operating a passenger auto, including a pickup or panel truck.  You may use the standard mileage rate in one year, change to computing your cost the next, and then change to using the standard mileage rate the next—whichever you find most advantageous.

**Entertainment expenses.**  These may be deducted if paid or incurred by you in the course of your employment.  However, a salaried employee ordinarily may not deduct such expenses unless he can show that his employer required or expected him to incur entertainment expenses in connection with his work. Generally, you may deduct the expense of your own meals incurred while entertaining for business purposes, as long as by doing so you are not claiming deductions for substantial amounts of personal living expenses.

**Gift expenses.**  Business gift costs are deductible.  However, there is one important restriction: Such expenses are deductible only to the extent of $25 for each individual involved.

Records for substantiation of travel, entertainment, and business gift expenditures should be maintained in an account book, diary, statement of expense, or similar record (supported by adequate documentary evidence) which is sufficient to establish the elements for the expenditures you later claim as deductions.  Under IRS rules, your records must be timely—that is, you must record your expenses at or near the time they are incurred.  Figure 16–7 shows a convenient record book specially designed to assist you in keeping good daily tally of deductible items.

## DEDUCTIBLE CASUALTY AND THEFT LOSSES

Should you be one of the unfortunate persons who have property stolen, vandalized, or destroyed, you are entitled to a deduction on your loss.  Damages from a hurricane, tornado, flood, mudslide, storm, fire, or accident are all considered casualties.  Other destruction—partial or complete—of property resulting from an identifiable event of a sudden, unexpected, or unusual nature also qualifies.  A sonic boom damage from jet aircraft is a good example.

**Fig. 16–7** Convenient daily appointment and expense form. Without some easy-to-use form to keep track of daily business expenses one is likely to forget many legitimate deductions. This, and similar guides, permit the businessman to keep an on-going record of tax deductions which can be filed away monthly and summarized at the end of the year. Reprinted by permission from The Bureau of Business Practice.

Not all of one's loss is deductible—only to the extent that the loss exceeds $100 for each casualty or theft. Insurance proceeds or other compensation received must be used to reduce your loss.

**Example:** If you have $100 deductible collision insurance on your automobile used for personal purposes and the automobile is damaged in a collison to the extent of $300, you do not have a deduction for the damage since your recovery of $200 in insurance will reduce the net loss to $100.

Business casualty losses are treated differently, being fully deductible, without consideration of the $100 limitation.

## DEDUCTIBLE EDUCATIONAL EXPENSES OF EMPLOYEES

If you have met the minimum educational requirements for qualification in your employment, and your employer requires you to obtain further education in order to retain your present salary, status, or employment, you may deduct the expenses for the least education which will meet the requirements imposed. Education which extends beyond the minimum requirements may also be deductible if it maintains or improves skills (discussed a little later) required in your employment or other trade or business.

If you are taking courses to meet the increased requirements for retention of your position, you will usually be allowed to claim your expenses even though a new position or a substantial advancement in your position results.

**Example:** Miss Johnson, a qualified high school teacher, is required by her employer to take courses giving six hours academic credit every two years in order to retain her position as a teacher. The nature of the courses is not specified by her employer. During a two-year period, she takes courses providing six hours of credit. Her expenses are deductible, and she need only establish that the education was required by her employer even if, as a result of the education, Miss Johnson eventually receives a master's degree and an increase in salary.

**Example:** Mr. Brown is a machine operator. His employer acquired new machines involving new and advanced operating methods, and he required Mr. Brown to take a special course given by the manufacturer in a distant city. Mr. Brown paid for this course; and, in addition, he incurred expenses for travel, meals, and lodging while away from home. Mr. Brown was given a $10 a week raise after completing the course. Since he took the course to meet the educational requirements of his employer, Mr. Brown may deduct his expenses for the course of study and also for travel, meals, and lodging while away from home.

**Maintaining or improving skills.**  If you voluntarily incur expenses for education to maintain or improve skills needed in your employment or other trade or business, you may deduct such expenses if you can show that the education is related to your duties.  Ordinarily, this would include refresher courses or courses dealing with current developments, in addition to academic or vocational courses.

**Minimum educational requirements.**  You may not, on the other hand, deduct expenses incurred to meet the minimum educational requirements for qualification in your employment or other trade or business. The "minimum" is determined from such factors as the requirements of your employer, the applicable laws and regulations, and the standards of the profession, trade, or business involved. However, the fact that you are already performing services for your employer will not establish that you have met the minimum education required. Note for example:

**Example:** Jack King, a research chemist, was employed as a patent chemist on the condition that he would get a law degree at his own expense. His duties were the filing and prosecution of patent applications. He enrolled in an evening law school program, graduated and was promoted to the position of patent attorney at a substantial increase in salary. His expenses are not deductible, since the education was necessary to meet the minimum requirements for qualification in his trade or business.

## PERSONAL AND DEPENDENT EXEMPTIONS

In addition to a standard deduction or itemized deductions which have been discussed earlier, every taxpayer is entitled to take a personal exemption. The 1969 Tax Reform Act increased these exemptions to $650 for 1971; $700 for 1972; and $750 for 1973 and thereafter. As a student, it's important for you to know that you are entitled to the deduction for yourself—even though you may still be a dependent of another.

Citizens or residents of the United States who are 65 or older by the end of the year, get a *double* personal exemption. You are considered to be 65 on the day before your 65th birthday. Additionally, an added exemption for blindness is allowed, based on the condition on the last day of the year.

**Exemptions for wife or husband.** If you file a joint return, you may also claim a personal exemption for your wife, another exemption if she was 65 by the end of the tax year, and still another if she was blind at that time. If you file a separate return, you may claim the exemptions for your wife, but only if she had no gross income and was not the dependent of another taxpayer. If your wife had income, you may claim her exemptions only if she files a joint return with you.

**Exemptions for dependents.**  You may also claim the personal exemption for children or other relatives who meet all of the following tests:

1. *Income.*  Received less than $625 income. (If the child was under 19 or was a student, this limitation does not apply.)
2. *Support.*  Received more than half of his or her support from you (or from husband or wife if a joint return is filed).
3. *Married Dependents.*  Did not file a joint return with her husband (or his wife).
4. *Nationality.*  Was either a citizen or resident of the United States or a resident of Canada, Mexico, the Republic of Panama or the Canal Zone; or was an alien child adopted by and living abroad with a citizen of the United States.
5. *Relationship.*  Either (a) for your entire taxable year had your home as his principal place of abode and was a member of your household; or (b) was related to you (or to husband or wife if a joint return is filed) in one of the following ways:

| | | |
|---|---|---|
| Child* | Stepbrother | Daughter-in-law |
| Foster child | Stepsister | |
| Stepchild | Stepmother | The following if |
| Mother | Stepfather | related by blood: |
| Father | Mother-in-law | Uncle |
| Grandparent | Father-in-law | Aunt |
| Brother | Brother-in-law | Nephew |
| Sister | Sister-in-law | Niece |
| Grandchild | Son-in-law | |

\* Includes a child who is a member of your household if placed with you by an authorized placement agency for legal adoption.

### HOW TO AVOID TAX WHEN YOU SELL A RESIDENCE
If you sell your home and make a profit, your gain may be taxable. But if you sell your home and sustain a loss, you can't deduct what you lose. Even though this aspect of the law is irksome, actually there is a way to avoid paying tax on profits from a residential sale if you plan ahead.

If within a year before or after the sale, you buy and occupy another residence, the gain is not then taxed if the cost of the new residence equals or exceeds the adjusted sales price of the old residence. The amount realized from the sale after commissions and other selling expenses, minus certain fixing-up expenses is your "adjusted sales price." Any gain not taxed in the year you sell your old residence is subtracted from the cost of the residence acquired to replace it, thus giving you a lower basis to be used in the event of a later taxable sale. Of course, if you sell the new residence in a later year and again replace it as explained before, any tax on the gain you realize will continue to be postponed.

**Example:**  You sold your residence in 1970 and realized a $5,000 gain. Immediately afterward you purchased another residence for $25,000, which is more than the price you received for the old one. The gain is exempt from taxation for the taxable year in which it was realized. However, the $5,000 gain must be subtracted from the $25,000 and the "basis" (your cost for tax purposes) of your new residence is $20,000. If you later sell the new residence for $26,000 and do not acquire and occupy a replacement residence within the required time, you would pay tax on the $6,000 gain in the year the sale is made.

You are allowed additional time if (1) you construct the new residence or (2) you were on active duty in the Armed Forces after you sold the old residence.

Construction of a new residence to replace the residence you sell must have begun either prior to the sale of the old residence or not later than 18 months after the sale. You are entitled to the benefit of the 18-month rule if you build your own residence, or contract to have a residence constructed according to your specifications and on specified land.

In determining the cost of the new home, and the amount of gain on your old residence on which tax is postponed, only the costs of construction of the new home for the 30-month period beginning one year before, and ending 18 months after, the sale of your old residence are included. The running of the one-year period or the 18-month period after the sale of your old residence is suspended during the time you serve on extended active duty in the Armed Forces in any period during which individuals are liable for induction for training and service in the Armed Forces.

You are not considered to have constructed your new residence, and you are not entitled to the benefit of the 18-month rule if you contract to purchase, when completed, a house to be built according to a particular specification on specified land, unless the contract was entered into before construction of that particular house was started.

Persons 65 or older may generally elect to exclude from their gross income part or all of the gain on a residential sale if they owned and used property sold or exchanged as their principal residence for a period (whether continuous or interrupted) of time totaling at least 5 years within the 8-year period ending on the date of such sale or exchange. They can elect to exclude all the gain if the adjusted sale price is $20,000 or less; part of the gain if it is for more than this amount. Such a gain may only be excluded once in a person's lifetime.

## JOINT RETURNS USUALLY SAVE MONEY
Federal Income Tax is based upon progressive rates ranging from 14 to 70 percent. The rate you pay depends upon how much taxable income you have—the higher the income, the higher the tax rate. For example, a person with not more than $500 taxable income would get by with the minimum 14 percent tax. But,

if you're one of the fortunate few whose taxable income is $100,000 or more, you—not so fortunately—are taxed at the maximum 70 percent rate. A glance at Fig. 16–8 shows the 1970 rate structure.

## 1970 Tax Rate Schedules

If you do not use one of the Tax Tables, figure your tax on the amount on line 50, Form 1040, by using the appropriate Tax Rate Schedule on this page. Enter tax on lines 19 and 51, Form 1040. Also see Tax Surcharge Tables below for tax surcharge.

**Schedule X—Single Taxpayers and Married Persons Filing Separate Returns**

If the amount on line 50, Form 1040 is:

Not over $500......14% of the amount on line 50.

| Over— | But not over— | Enter on lines 19 and 51, Form 1040: | of excess over— |
|---|---|---|---|
| $500 | $1,000 | $70+15% | $500 |
| $1,000 | $1,500 | $145+16% | $1,000 |
| $1,500 | $2,000 | $225+17% | $1,500 |
| $2,000 | $4,000 | $310+19% | $2,000 |
| $4,000 | $6,000 | $690+22% | $4,000 |
| $6,000 | $8,000 | $1,130+25% | $6,000 |
| $8,000 | $10,000 | $1,630+28% | $8,000 |
| $10,000 | $12,000 | $2,190+32% | $10,000 |
| $12,000 | $14,000 | $2,830+36% | $12,000 |
| $14,000 | $16,000 | $3,550+39% | $14,000 |
| $16,000 | $18,000 | $4,330+42% | $16,000 |
| $18,000 | $20,000 | $5,170+45% | $18,000 |
| $20,000 | $22,000 | $6,070+48% | $20,000 |
| $22,000 | $26,000 | $7,030+50% | $22,000 |
| $26,000 | $32,000 | $9,030+53% | $26,000 |
| $32,000 | $38,000 | $12,210+55% | $32,000 |
| $38,000 | $44,000 | $15,510+58% | $38,000 |
| $44,000 | $50,000 | $18,990+60% | $44,000 |
| $50,000 | $60,000 | $22,590+62% | $50,000 |
| $60,000 | $70,000 | $28,790+64% | $60,000 |
| $70,000 | $80,000 | $35,190+66% | $70,000 |
| $80,000 | $90,000 | $41,790+68% | $80,000 |
| $90,000 | $100,000 | $48,590+69% | $90,000 |
| $100,000 | ............. | $55,490+70% | $100,000 |

**Schedule Y—Married Taxpayers Filing Joint Returns and Certain Widows and Widowers**

If the amount on line 50, Form 1040 is:

Not over $1,000....14% of the amount on line 50.

| Over— | But not over— | Enter on lines 19 and 51, Form 1040: | of excess over— |
|---|---|---|---|
| $1,000 | $2,000 | $140+15% | $1,000 |
| $2,000 | $3,000 | $290+16% | $2,000 |
| $3,000 | $4,000 | $450+17% | $3,000 |
| $4,000 | $8,000 | $620+19% | $4,000 |
| $8,000 | $12,000 | $1,380+22% | $8,000 |
| $12,000 | $16,000 | $2,260+25% | $12,000 |
| $16,000 | $20,000 | $3,260+28% | $16,000 |
| $20,000 | $24,000 | $4,380+32% | $20,000 |
| $24,000 | $28,000 | $5,660+36% | $24,000 |
| $28,000 | $32,000 | $7,100+39% | $28,000 |
| $32,000 | $36,000 | $8,660+42% | $32,000 |
| $36,000 | $40,000 | $10,340+45% | $36,000 |
| $40,000 | $44,000 | $12,140+48% | $40,000 |
| $44,000 | $52,000 | $14,060+50% | $44,000 |
| $52,000 | $64,000 | $18,060+53% | $52,000 |
| $64,000 | $76,000 | $24,420+55% | $64,000 |
| $76,000 | $88,000 | $31,020+58% | $76,000 |
| $88,000 | $100,000 | $37,980+60% | $88,000 |
| $100,000 | $120,000 | $45,180+62% | $100,000 |
| $120,000 | $140,000 | $57,580+64% | $120,000 |
| $140,000 | $160,000 | $70,380+66% | $140,000 |
| $160,000 | $180,000 | $83,580+68% | $160,000 |
| $180,000 | $200,000 | $97,180+69% | $180,000 |
| $200,000 | ............. | $110,980+70% | $200,000 |

**Schedule Z—Unmarried (or legally separated) Taxpayers Who Qualify as Heads of Household**

If the amount on line 50, Form 1040 is:

Not over $1,000....14% of the amount on line 50.

| Over— | But not over— | Enter on lines 19 and 51, Form 1040: | of excess over— |
|---|---|---|---|
| $1,000 | $2,000 | $140+16% | $1,000 |
| $2,000 | $4,000 | $300+18% | $2,000 |
| $4,000 | $6,000 | $660+20% | $4,000 |
| $6,000 | $8,000 | $1,060+22% | $6,000 |
| $8,000 | $10,000 | $1,500+25% | $8,000 |
| $10,000 | $12,000 | $2,000+27% | $10,000 |
| $12,000 | $14,000 | $2,540+31% | $12,000 |
| $14,000 | $16,000 | $3,160+32% | $14,000 |
| $16,000 | $18,000 | $3,800+35% | $16,000 |
| $18,000 | $20,000 | $4,500+36% | $18,000 |
| $20,000 | $22,000 | $5,220+40% | $20,000 |
| $22,000 | $24,000 | $6,020+41% | $22,000 |
| $24,000 | $26,000 | $6,840+43% | $24,000 |
| $26,000 | $28,000 | $7,700+45% | $26,000 |
| $28,000 | $32,000 | $8,600+46% | $28,000 |
| $32,000 | $36,000 | $10,440+48% | $32,000 |
| $36,000 | $38,000 | $12,360+50% | $36,000 |
| $38,000 | $40,000 | $13,340+52% | $38,000 |
| $40,000 | $44,000 | $14,400+53% | $40,000 |
| $44,000 | $50,000 | $16,520+55% | $44,000 |
| $50,000 | $52,000 | $19,820+56% | $50,000 |
| $52,000 | $64,000 | $20,940+58% | $52,000 |
| $64,000 | $70,000 | $27,900+59% | $64,000 |
| $70,000 | $76,000 | $31,440+61% | $70,000 |
| $76,000 | $80,000 | $35,100+62% | $76,000 |
| $80,000 | $88,000 | $37,580+63% | $80,000 |
| $88,000 | $100,000 | $42,620+64% | $88,000 |
| $100,000 | $120,000 | $50,300+66% | $100,000 |
| $120,000 | $140,000 | $63,500+67% | $120,000 |
| $140,000 | $160,000 | $76,900+68% | $140,000 |
| $160,000 | $180,000 | $90,500+69% | $160,000 |
| $180,000 | ............. | $104,300+70% | $180,000 |

**Fig. 16–8**  Tax rate schedules for 1970. Note how the tax rates become progressively higher as your income advances. Single taxpayers get hit the hardest.

Married persons are given an important tax break by being permitted to file joint income tax returns, in effect splitting the total income earned by both persons. Because of the progressive tax schedule, a joint filing is decidedly advantageous for most couples, especially where the husband (or wife) earns a greater percentage or perhaps all of the total income. By filing jointly, the tax is based upon a lower rate. Here's an illustration of how it works:

**Example:** Tom Yardley has a taxable income of $24,000; his wife Elva does not work. If Tom were to file a separate return, he would pay $8,030 in taxes (plus any surcharge that may be in effect). However, by filing a joint return, the Yardleys' tax bill is lowered to $5,660.

It is important to note that you may file a joint return even if you or your spouse had no income or no deductions. However, if you do file jointly, you must include any and all the income, exemptions, and deductions for both you and your spouse. Marital status is determined as of the last day of the tax year. You are considered married for the entire year, if on the last day of your tax year (December 31 for most taxpayers) you are:

1. Married and living as husband and wife

2. Living together in a common law marriage recognized by the state in which it commenced

3. Married and living apart but not divorced or legally separated

4. Separated under an interlocutory decree of divorce. In such a case, you are not legally separated for purposes of your election to file a joint return.

If you are divorced by a final decree on or before the last day of your tax year, you are considered to have been single for the entire year and may not file a joint return. If your spouse dies during the year, you are considered to have been married for the entire year. If you do not remarry before the close of the tax year, you may file a joint return for you and your deceased spouse.

If you're a foot-loose and fancy-free single college student, you should be heartened to know that the 1969 Tax Reform Act made important changes aimed at relieving, partially at least, the inequities of higher taxes for single as opposed to married persons. At comparable income levels, single persons might pay as much as 40 percent more than a married couple under the old tax law. The new rate structure, effective in 1971 and subsequent taxable years, reduces this differential so that a single person's tax will not be more than 20 percent higher.

**Joint-filing requirements.** Both of you must be either citizens of the United States or resident aliens at all times during the tax year, and you must both use the same accounting period. However, you may use different accounting methods and still file a joint return.

Both husband and wife must sign the return, or it will not be considered a joint return. If the husband or wife is traveling or stationed abroad or otherwise away from home, the return should be prepared, signed by the one who is at home, and mailed or transmitted to the spouse not at home so that he (or she) may also sign it and file it on time.

The Social Security numbers of both you and your spouse should be entered on a joint return, even if one of you had no income. The word "none" should be entered for a spouse who has no Social Security number.

**Separate returns by married persons.** If you and your spouse each have income of your own, you may each file a separate income tax return instead of filing jointly. You may also file a separate return where only you or your husband or wife had income. The choice is yours to make.

For the great majority of couples, the joint return saves taxes. However, if both you and your spouse have income, you should generally figure your tax both ways to make sure you are using the method that will result in the lesser tax.

**Example:** If both husband and wife have income, but one has moderate income and substantial medical expense while the other has little or no medical expense, filing separately may increase the total medical expense deduction because of the 3 percent rule. (See p. 488 for a discussion of medical expenses.) However, if they used their joint checking account to pay the medical expenses, such payment will usually be considered to be made half by each, regardless of who signed the check.

Married persons living in a community property state (Arizona, California, Idaho, Louisiana, Nevada, New Mexico, Texas, or Washington) may, in some circumstances, also be better off filing separate returns. See Document No. 5192, *Community Property*, available free at your IRS office.

If you choose to file separate returns, you should each report only your own income, claim only your own exemptions and take only the deductions to which you are entitled separately. If you and your husband or wife file separate returns and one elects to itemize deductions, the other may not take the standard deduction.

Similarly, if you and your wife or husband take the standard deduction in filing your separate returns, you both must use the same type of standard deduction—the 10 percent standard deduction or the minimum standard deduction.

## TAX ADVANTAGES OF LONG-TERM CAPITAL GAINS

As emphasized at the outset of this chapter, it is of considerable importance to one's financial well-being to get an early start on investments which can potentially yield long-term capital gains. Any supplement to one's income is always welcome and beneficial, whatever the source; however, long-term capital gains are especially desirous since these profits are given very favorable tax concessions.

Land, buildings, corporate stocks and certain other types of property and securities are considered capital assets. Profits made on these investments are classified as long-term capital gains—provided they are held for more than 6 months. Long-term profits of $50,000 or less per return ( $25,000 for married persons filing separately) are currently taxed at a maximum rate of 25 percent, contrasted with a 70 percent maximum rate for other taxable income.

Since the long-term gain is also subject to the benefits of income-splitting in a joint return, the effective tax rate (disregarding any surcharge which may be in effect) may be less than the 25 percent rate. The following schedule for couples filing joint returns with mixed incomes of salaries plus some capital gains shows the approximate effective rate of tax:

| Joint returns up to | Effective tax rate |
|---|---|
| $20,000 | 14 % |
| $24,000 | 16 % |
| $28,000 | 18 % |
| $32,000 | 19.5% |
| $36,000 | 21 % |
| $40,000 | 22.5% |
| $44,000 | 24 % |

The impact which the "source" of funds has upon the average person's finances is even more concretely seen by examining the tax bill of two couples. Each couple has the same combined earnings, but Couple A's income is all from salaries; while Couple B's income comes entirely from long-term capital gains:

| Couple A—income all from salaries | | Couple B—income all from capital gains | |
|---|---|---|---|
| Combined salaries (adjusted gross income) | $28,700 | Combined long-term capital gains | $28,700 |
| | | Less 50% long-term capital gains deduction | 14,350 |
| Less maximum standard deduction | 1,000 | Adjusted Gross Income | $14,350 |
| | $27,700 | Less maximum standard deduction | 1,000 |
| Less personal exemptions for themselves and two children | 2,400 | | $13,350 |
| | | Less personal exemptions for themselves and two children | 2,400 |
| Taxable income | $25,300 | Taxable income | $10,950 |
| Total Federal Taxes: | $ 6,128 | Total Federal Taxes: | $ 3,029 |

Because of the special capital gains treatment, Couple B saves nearly $3,100 in taxes compared with the salaried couple. These extra dollars can be used by Couple B for additional investments or for consumer purposes. Perhaps the old adage, "The rich get rich, and the poor get poorer," should be changed to "Investors get rich on long-term capital gains, and the salaried get poorer because of the taxes they pay."

**Computing tax on capital gains.** As has already been pointed out, if you held a capital asset over 6 months, its sale or exchange results in a long-term capital gain (or loss). If the asset is held less than 6 months, its sale or exchange yields a short-term capital gain or loss. To determine if you held property over 6 months, you begin counting on the day following the day you acquired the property. This same day of each succeeding month is the beginning of a new month regardless of the number of days in the preceding month. In your computation, you include the day you disposed of the property.

After you have classified all of your capital assets which were sold or exchanged during the year as short-term or long-term, your next step is to determine the gain or loss on each transaction. These transactions, and the computation of tax, explained below, are entered on separate Schedule D (Form 1040).

1. Short-term capital gains and losses are merged with each other by adding the gains and the losses separately and subtracting one total from the other to obtain the net short-term capital gain or loss.

2. Long-term capital gains and losses are merged by adding the gains and the losses separately and subtracting one total from the other to obtain the net long-term capital gain or loss.

3. The total net gain or loss is then determined by merging the net short-term capital gain or loss with the net long-term capital gain or loss.

4. If the net long-term capital gain exceeds the net short-term capital loss, you claim a deduction equal to 50% of such excess. If you have no net short-term capital loss, your capital gain deduction is 50% of your net long-term capital gain. The capital gain deduction may be subject to *Minimum Tax on Tax Preferences* which is described later.

5. If you have a net short-term capital gain, it is included in income at 100% unless reduced by a net long-term capital loss.

After net taxable capital gains have been computed (considering the 50% deduction for long-term gains), they are entered on the 1040 Form and treated as ordinary income. However, to cash in on any possible savings, you should be familiar with the long-term capital gains alternative tax.

If your net long-term capital gain does not exceed $50,000 ($25,000 for married persons filing separate returns), your alternative tax is computed in the following manner:

1. Reduce taxable income by the capital gain deduction (see above).

2. Using the regular tax rates, compute a partial tax on the amount determined in (1).

3. Add to this partial tax 50% of the capital gain deduction.

The resultant total represents your alternative tax.

The effect of this computation is to tax your net long-term capital gain at a maximum rate of 25%.

**Example:** You are single and your taxable income (after deducting your itemized deductions and personal exemption) is $28,400. This includes a capital gain deduction of $2,000. The regular tax on $28,400 is $10,302. The alternative tax is computed as follows:

| | |
|---|---:|
| Taxable income | $28,400 |
| Less: Capital gain deduction | 2,000 |
| Balance | $26,400 |
| Tax on $26,400 | 9,242 |

> Add: 50% of amount on line 2 ($2,000)        1,000
> Alternative tax                              $10,242

In this instance, you would use the alternative tax ($10,242) since it is less than the regular tax ($10,302).

If your net long-term capital gain exceeds $50,000 ($25,000 for married persons filing separate returns), and if you did not have gains from October 9, 1969, contracts (discussed later in this chapter), then your alternative tax is increased and is determined in the following manner:

1. Determine the regular tax on ordinary income.

2. Add $12,500 (25% of first $50,000 of net long-term capital gain).

3. Add the lesser of (1) the difference between the regular tax on taxable income (or the amount of capital gain deduction if that amount is greater than the amount of taxable income) and the regular tax on the sum of ordinary income and $25,000 or (2) $29\frac{1}{2}\%$ of the net long-term capital gain in excess of $50,000 ($32\frac{1}{2}\%$ in 1971 and 35% thereafter).

The effect of this computation is to tax the first $50,000 of net long-term capital gain at 25% and the balance of the gain at a higher rate.

**Example:** You are single and your taxable income (after deducting your itemized deductions and personal exemption) is $100,000. This includes $20,000 or ordinary income and $80,000 net capital gain ($160,000 long-term capital gain less $80,000 capital gain deduction). Your alternative tax is computed as follows:

| | | |
|---|---:|---:|
| Tax on $20,000 ordinary income | | $ 6,070 |
| 25% of first $50,000 of long-term capital gain | | 12,500 |
| Regular tax on $100,000 taxable income | $55,490 | |
| Less: Regular tax on $20,000 ordinary income and | | |
| $25,000 ($\frac{1}{2}$ of first $50,000 of capital gain) | 19,590 | |
| Difference | 35,900 | |
| $29\frac{1}{2}\%$ of $110,000 ($160,000 minus $50,000) | 32,450 | |
| Lesser of (3) or (4) | | 32,450 |
| Alternative Tax | | $51,020 |

Enter $51,020 on line 19, Form 1040 and check the box marked "Schedule D" on line 19, Form 1040.

**Gains from October 9, 1969 contracts.**   Capital gains received before January 1, 1975, from sales or other dispositions under binding contracts entered into on or before October 9, 1969, will continue to be subject to the lower 25% rate regardless of their amount, except for timber, coal, domestic iron ore, and patent gains taxed as capital gains. Certain liquidating distributions made by a corporation before October 10, 1970, also qualify for the 25% rate.

## CAPITAL LOSSES

If your capital losses exceed capital gains, you may claim a capital loss deduction. The deduction is limited to the smallest of the following amounts:

1. Your taxable income for the year, computed without regard to either capital gains and losses or deductions for personal exemptions (or adjusted gross income if you use a tax table);

2. $1,000; or

3. Your net capital loss, as described in the following paragraphs.

**Joint and separate returns.** If you and your wife file a joint return, you may deduct up to $1,000 of capital losses between you, as set forth in (2). But if you file separate returns, and both have capital losses, the amount in (2) is limited to $500 for each return.

**Computing your loss.** Prior to January 1, 1970, both short-term and long-term losses were considered at 100% in arriving at your capital loss (subject to limitations (1) and (2), above). Beginning in 1970 this changed. Only 50% of your net long-term capital loss can be used to reduce your income. Therefore, $2,000 of net long-term capital losses are needed to produce a $1,000 deduction, $1,000 to produce $500, and so forth.

**Example:** In 1970 you had wages of $8,000, a net long-term capital loss of $1,600 and you claimed the standard deduction. Your capital loss is $800 ($\frac{1}{2}$ of $1,600).

**Example:** Assume the same facts as in the above example, except that your long-term capital loss was $600. In addition, you had a $500 net short-term capital loss. Your capital loss deduction is $800 computed as follows:

| | |
|---|---|
| Net short-term loss | $500 |
| $\frac{1}{2}$ of net long-term loss ($\frac{1}{2}$ of $600) | 300 |
| Net capital loss | $800 |

*Your net capital loss for the year* is the excess of your net short-term capital loss over your net long-term capital gain plus half the excess of your net long-term capital loss over your net short-term capital gain. If you had capital gains and losses for the year as follows:

**Example:**

| | Short-term | Long-term |
|---|---|---|
| Gains | $1,200 | $ 600 |
| Losses | (1,300) | (2,200) |
| Net gain (or loss) | ( $100) | ($1,600) |

Your net capital loss is $900, computed as follows:

| | | |
|---|---|---|
| Net short-term loss | $ 100 | |
| Less: Net long-term gain | 0 | |
| Excess | | $100 |
| Add: Net long-term loss | $1,600 | |

| Less: Net short-term gain | 0 | |
|---|---|---|
| Excess | $1,600 | |
| Less: Half of excess | 800 | 800 |
| Net capital loss | | $900 |

Your deduction is limited to this $900 or your taxable income as set forth in (a), above, whichever is smaller.

**Capital loss carryover.** If your capital losses are in excess of the limitations listed above, you may carry over the excess to subsequent years until it is completely absorbed. When carried over, the loss will retain its original character as long-term or short-term; thus, a long-term capital loss carried over from a previous year will offset long-term gains of the current year.

When carrying over an unused long-term loss, 100% of the loss is carried to the next year. The reduction for 50% of the long-term loss is made in the year the loss is carried to and deducted.

*In determining the capital loss carryover*, short-term losses are applied first, even if they were incurred after a long-term loss. If, after applying the short-term loss, the limitations under capital losses above have not been reached, apply the long-term losses until the limit has been reached. Since long-term losses are only deducted at 50%, twice the amount needed to reach the limitation represents the long-term loss which may still be deducted.

**Example:** On your 1970 return your capital loss deduction limit is $1,000 and you realized short-term losses of $400 and long-term losses of $2,300. Your carryover to 1971 is computed as follows:

| | |
|---|---|
| Maximum amount of capital loss deduction | $1,000 |
| Less: Short-term capital loss | 400 |
| Remaining available capital loss | 600 |
| Long-term capital loss | $2,300 |
| Amount needed to reach $1,000 limitation at 50% (Line 3 $600 × 2) | 1,200 |
| Long-term capital loss carryover to 1971 | $1,100 |

**Carryovers of pre-1970 losses.** The treatment of carryovers with respect to losses incurred in years beginning before January 1, 1970, remains unchanged. Therefore, long-term capital loss carryovers from these years do not have to be reduced by 50% before being deducted.

**Example:** You are single, had income in 1970 of $6,000, and do not itemize your deductions. You have a long-term capital loss carryover from 1969 of $4,000. On your 1970 return, you may deduct a $1,000 long-term capital loss and you will carry over the remaining $3,000 to 1971 ($4,000–$1,000).

When considering losses carried over from more than one year, always deduct the earliest loss first.

Capital loss carryovers from separate returns must be combined if you file a joint return for the current year. But a capital loss carryover from any joint return can be deducted only on the separate return of the person who actually sustained the loss.

**Installment sales can reduce taxes.** The installment method of reporting income relieves you of the burden of paying tax on income which has not been collected and permits you to include in your gross income only that portion of each collection which constitutes actual profit. For this reason, many persons selling a large piece of property or other capital assets may be much better off making the sale on an installment basis rather than accepting cash for the entire amount. This is true especially if the sale would result in a substantially larger income for the year than you normally earn.

But in order to report on the installment method, you must maintain adequate records. The installment method may be used only for reporting profits on certain sales of real or personal property where the buyer agrees to pay to the seller a part of the sales price in one or more years after the year of sale. It may not be used to report losses. It may be used in the following types of sales:

1. A casual or incidental sale of personal property, such as an automobile, for a price of more than $1,000 where the collections, if any, in the year of the sale do not exceed 30% of the selling price; and

2. The sale of real estate, such as a home, a farm, a piece of land, regardless of the amount of the sale where the collections, if any, in the year of the sale do not exceed 30% of the selling price.

As indicated in the illustrations above, a sale may be treated as an installment sale even though there are no payments made in the year of the sale.

If the property sold by you was a capital asset, and you elect to use the installment method, the income from installment collections must be included each year in your net gain or loss from the sale or exchange of capital assets. Income from installment sales is determined by the use of a gross profit percentage. The gross profit percentage for any sale is the percent that the gross profit to be realized is of the total contract price.

**Example:** If you sell property at a contract price of $2,000, and there is a gross profit of $500, your gross profit percentage is 25% ($500 divided by $2,000). Thus, 25% of each payment collected on the sale (including the down payment) is gain and must be included in gross income for the tax year in which collected. This percentage, once determined, remains the same for all installment payments received on the sale.

Even though you make an installment sale, you could elect to report all the profit in the year in which the sale was made. You might want to do this if you anticipated another large sale of property next year—where the combined profits of the new sale and the installment portion of this year's sale would push you into a much higher tax bracket.

## MINIMUM TAX ON TAX PREFERENCES

Because investors receive favorable tax treatment on many income and expense items, Congress was pressured to tighten some of these provisions in the 1969 Tax Reform Act. The result is that there is now a minimum tax on a number of items that are considered to be of a tax preference nature. The tax is computed by first totaling all the items of tax preference, then reducing this amount by a specific exemption of $30,000 ($15,000 in the case of married persons filing separate returns). The excess is further reduced by your regular tax (including tax surcharge but minus the foreign tax credit and retirement income credit) and then a flat 10% rate is applied against the balance. Some of the items of tax preference are:

1. *Capital gains.* This is one-half of the amount by which your net long-term capital gains exceed your net short-term capital losses for the year.

2. *Accelerated depreciation on real property.* This is the amount of the depreciation deduction during the year on real property that is in excess of the depreciation deduction that would have been allowable had the straight line method of depreciation been used.

3. *Stock options.* Upon the exercise of a qualified or restricted stock option, the amount by which the fair market value of the stock exceeds the option price at the time of exercise is an item of tax preference.

4. *Depletion.* This is the excess of your depletion deduction over the adjusted basis of the property at the end of the year (determined without regard to the depletion deduction for the year).

5. *Excess investment interest.* This is the amount by which your investment interest expense exceeds your net investment income for the year. Excess investment interest will be considered a tax preference item only during years beginning before 1972.

Each member of a partnership must take into account separately his distributive share of items of income and deductions that enter into the computation of items of tax preference.

For beneficiaries of estates and trusts, the total items of tax preference for the tax year are apportioned between the estate or trust and the beneficiaries on the basis of the income of the estate or trust allocable to each.

Tax preference items of corporations electing not to be taxed (Sub-chapter S Corporations) are apportioned pro rata among its shareholders in the same way any corporate losses would be apportioned. Where capital gains are taxed to both the corporation and the shareholder, the capital gains can be an item of tax preference at both the corporate and individual level.

Form 4625 is used to compute your minimum tax. This should be attached to your tax return.

**FEEDBACK 16**

**A.** If you are now using a checking account, prepare a filing system for your cancelled checks which verify payments of tax-deductible amounts. If you do not use a checking account consistently, prepare a filing system to keep accurate records of appropriate receipts. At a minimum, either filing system should include:

- Charitable contributions
- Interest charged by any firm; including mortgage holders, loan companies, charge accounts, bank credit cards, and gasoline credit cards
- Taxes paid during the year, on property, goods, assessments, and any special local taxes
- Medical and dental and prescription expenses, sick pay or disability payments
- Business losses and the special expenses allowable as deductions
- Additionally, you should keep accurate records of all income sources as outlined in Chapter 3.

**B.** From your income tax records, using your income for last year, compute the effective tax rate you were charged. Using the tables of Form 1040, find:

- If that income had been a mix of 50 percent salary and 50 percent capital gains, compute the effective tax rate.
- If all your income had been from capital gains, compute the effective tax rate.

  Note: The effective tax rate is the Tax Charged ÷ Taxable Income.

**C.** Prepare an Action Plan to minimize your tax payments for the next five years. Of course, you will not be able to foresee every development, but you should make provisions for some probable events. What would be your estimate of the effects of the following items on the amount of taxes you will be paying?

- If you get a raise of five percent each year?
- If you buy a home in three years?
- If you marry?
- When you have a child?
- If your investments pay dividends under $100 per year? Over $100 per year?
- If you accept employment in a foreign country for one year? For two years?

**DISCUSSION QUESTIONS**

1. Single individuals pay more Federal tax than do married persons.
   a) What specific provisions in our present tax law favor the marrieds?
   b) Considering the overall effects on our society, should this tax preference for marrieds be continued?

2. In what ways can an individual reduce his tax burden through planning and goal-setting?

3. Define *accounting periods* and *methods.* Can you think of a business which might benefit by choosing other than the calendar year; the cash method?

4. Why isn't it a good idea to wait until year's end to list all your expenses and deductions? What does the law say about the matter?

5. Under what circumstances can you get an extension of time for filing your tax return? How do you go about getting such permission?

6. If you discover you've made a serious error after you have filed your tax return, what can you do about it?

7. What kinds of income, if any, are not taxed by the Federal Government?

8. You are likely to have to sell a home and buy another—perhaps several times in your lifetime as you are transferred or change from one job to another. How is the income received from the sale of a home treated for Federal tax purposes?

9. What are capital gains? Capital losses?

10. How can installment sales of real estate be advantageous to you?

**CASE PROBLEM**

The Federal income tax is a "progressive" tax—the higher the income, the higher the percentage of income tax applicable. There are also many loopholes which benefit some people and work to the disadvantage of others.

a) Discuss the kinds of persons which benefit most from current exclusions and deductions; and the progressive rate structure.

b) What are some of the arguments for and against a taxation scheme based on (a) one flat rate of tax for all income; (b) regressive rates—that is, a lower rate, the higher the income; (c) a negative tax—paying money to persons who earn below a certain poverty level?

c) What changes would you personally like to see made in our tax laws? Why?

**SUGGESTED READINGS**

The following publications and documents may be obtained free of charge from any Internal Revenue Service Office:

Publication No.

| | |
|---|---|
| 5051 | *Business Expenses* |
| 5180 | *Corporations* |
| 14 | *Household Employer's Social Security Tax Guide*—Circular H |
| 5202 | *If Your Return is Examined* |
| 5179 | *Partnerships* |
| 5178 | *Repairs and Improvements* |

| 5181 | *Sale of a Business* |
|---|---|
| 5575 | *Scholarships and Contests* |
| 5569 | *Tax Benefits for Older Americans* |

A Guide to Federal Estate and Gift Taxation, U.S. Treasury Department, Internal Revenue Service. Publication 448. (May be purchased from IRS for 25c.)

Gutkin, Sydney A., and David Back. *Tax Avoidance vs. Tax Evasion.* New York: Ronald Press, 1958. 220 pp.

Hunter, Thomas Willard. *The Tax Climate for Philanthropy.* Washington: American College Public Relations Association, 1968. 207 pp.

Lasser, J. K. *Your Income Tax* (current year's edition). New York: Simon and Schuster.

*Laws and Regulations Relating to Employee Pension, Annuity, Profit-Sharing, Stock Bonus, and Bond Purchase Plans.* U.S. Treasury Department, Internal Revenue Service. Publication 337. (May be purchased from IRS for 60c.)

Lindholm, Richard W. *Property Taxation, USA.* Madison: University of Wisconsin Press, 1967. 315 pp.

Myers, Maxmilian Hardy. *Small Tax Client Practice.* Englewood Cliffs, N.J.: Prentice-Hall, 1963. 137 pp.

Ruskay, Joseph A., and Richard A. Osserman. *Halfway to Tax Reform.* Bloomington: Indiana University Press, 1970. 307 pp.

Seltzer, Lawrence Howard. *The Personal Exemptions in the Income Tax.* New York: National Bureau of Economic Research, Columbia University Press, 1968. 222 pp.

*Tax Guide for Small Business.* U.S. Treasury Department, Internal Revenue Service. (May be purchased from IRS for 50c.)

*Your Federal Income Tax* (current year's edition). U.S. Treasury Department, Internal Revenue Service. Publication No. 17. (May be purchased from IRS for $1.00.)

CHAPTER 17

# INVESTING IN YOUR OWN
# SMALL BUSINESS

Starting or buying a small business is much like getting married! You risk much of your property, money, happiness, and reputation on the outcome. However, with the right amount of preparation and know-how, the chances for success can be enhanced enormously. In this chapter major attention will be devoted to important background data, the mechanics of starting a new business, procedures involved in purchasing an existing small concern, and ways to evaluate franchise opportunities.

## WHAT YOU NEED TO KNOW ABOUT SMALL BUSINESSES

Enterprising men and women with pioneer zeal and spirit often find that their small concerns provide excellent jobs in terms of both money and personal satisfaction. Sometimes, the new company experiences energetic growth and yields millions in profits. This was the case for Dr. Land, inventor of the 10-second camera and organizer of the remarkably successful Polaroid Corporation. But obviously, small business ownership is not for everybody. Before you

"We're expecting a tremendous year, -- might
even break even."

Reprinted with permission of *The Wall Street Journal* (Cartoon Features Syndicate).

can decide whether or not you should get involved in a small business, you must know something about the opportunities as well as the disadvantages, the pressures, the risks.  You must satisfy yourself that you have the right personal qualifications.

### THE ADVANTAGES

Running your own business will give you a sense of independence—an opportunity to use your own ideas.  You will be top man.  You can't be fired.  It will mean a chance for higher income because you can collect a salary plus a profit or return on your investment.  You will experience a pride in ownership—such as you experience if you own your own home or your own automobile.  You can achieve the great satisfaction of building a valuable investment for which there will be a market.

By being top man you can adopt new ideas quickly.  Since your enterprise undoubtedly will be a small business—at least in the beginning—you will have no large, unwieldy organization to retrain each time you wish to try something new.  If the idea doesn't work you can drop it just as quickly.  This opportunity for flexibility will be one of your greatest assets.

These are some of the advantages and pleasures of operating your own business.  But let us take a look at the other side.

### THE DISADVANTAGES AND DIFFICULTIES

If you have employees you must meet a payroll week after week.  You must always have money to pay creditors—the man who sells you goods or materials, the dealer who furnishes you fixtures and equipment, the landlord, if you rent, or the mortgage holder if you are buying your place of business, the publisher running your advertisements, the tax collector, and many others.  You must accept sole responsibility for all final decisions.  Wrong judgment on your part can result in losses not only to yourself but, possibly, to your employees, creditors, and customers as well.  Moreover, you must withstand, alone, adverse situations caused by circumstances beyond your control, such as depressed economic conditions or strong competition.

To overcome these disadvantages and keep your business profitable means long hours of hard work.  Invariably when you become your own boss you will work longer hours than when you were working for someone else.  At least, this will be necessary in the beginning.

Then, after all, you will not be entirely your own boss.  No matter what business you choose—whether a manufacturing, wholesaling, retailing, or service business—you must satisfy your customers.  Your creditors and your competitors will dictate to you.  Health authorities and insurance people will see that you meet certain standards and follow certain regulations.  You will have to abide by wage and hour laws and keep records in accordance with the requirements of the tax system.

Regardless of how successful you may be in raising money for a new business, somehow there is never enough. Physical resources—inventories, buildings, instruments, machinery—all are restricted. With shallow, sometimes non-existent cash reserves, mistakes or set-backs that would be mere annoyances to large corporations may deal a mortal blow to the infant company.

Human resources, too, are affected by finances. Seldom will it be feasible to hire all the specialists that a business needs—management personnel, production engineers, research and development scientists. Consequently, most small firms must get by with few experts. And even where there is money to bring such an array of people together, it takes time to mold and shape them into an effective, harmonious team.

Finally, the new company suffers many hardships because it lacks a public image. This makes wide-scale marketing attempts difficult, costly, and at best, uncertain.

## ARE YOU THE TYPE?

So the first question you should answer after recognizing that there is a dark side as well as a bright side to the prospect of establishing your own business is, "Am I the type?"

Many persons dislike working for someone else; find it difficult to get along with others; get fed up with the pressures, worries, and decisions that clutter their work day. Such individuals seldom make successful employees. And, all too often, incompetent employees, disturbed because they haven't achieved job advancement, take what seems the easy way to the top by hiring themselves as president of their own company. They soon find, however, that running a business *multiplies* rather than *diminishes* their problems. Such a person's chances for success are slim indeed.

Even the dedicated, technically competent person, succeeding as an employee in business, may not have all that it takes to make the grade in the competitive and often rocky world of small business. Here are the special personal qualities that seem to count most. The person should:

1. Have an abundance of perseverance and energy
2. Have a logical, practical mind; be able to conceive systematic, concrete ways to cope with problems and exploit opportunities
3. Have a confident, positive outlook and the ability to recover quickly and press on in the face of disappointments or setbacks
4. Have a competitive attitude—the desire to be not only "better" than the competition, but to better his own records
5. Be adept at handling his personal finances
6. Be willing to make hefty sacrifices to achieve success in his business
7. Be experienced in the particular business line he proposes to enter

The last three points deserve special emphasis.

**Competent at personal finance.**  It is inconceivable that a person inept in handling family money matters could make a go of a small business.  The individual who lets his charge accounts get out of control, who can't find money for insurance, who never has a dollar left for savings, isn't going to manage money much differently in business matters.

Seldom can the new business afford the fanciest offices and plant, the most attractive furniture, and latest equipment.  The new business, quite to the contrary, may have to get by on "second-best" for a very long time.  Repeatedly, however, the author has seen extravagance and undisciplined spending ruin concerns.  One classic example illustrates the point:

> Two brothers, both successful salesmen for a large national manufacturer of kitchen cabinets, decided they would set up a competing firm.  Between them, they had jobbers and other accounts amounting to sales of $400,000 per year.  They felt confident that much of this business could be brought over to the new firm.  The one brother had previous shop experience in making custom cabinetry, and he took over the manufacturing end of the business.  The other brother set up the sales organization.
>
> Within two years, things seemed to be going amazingly well.  They had set up the business on a shoestring.  The sales organization, operating virtually without office space, was bringing in business at the rate of about $600,000 a year.  The plant was producing a beautiful product even though it was operating on a "mini-budget" in an old dingy warehouse with second-hand equipment.
>
> The attitude of the two brothers suddenly took a flip-flop.  Their exuberance over how well things had gone sent them on a wild buying spree.  They signed a five-year lease on a magnificent new building.  It had smart offices and a spacious, well-lighted manufacturing area.  They junked practically all the old equipment which, by the way, was virtually paid for by now, and went heavily in debt to get the latest and best plant equipment.  Their operating capital was soon gobbled up by the increased overhead.  Unpaid bills stacked up for equipment and furniture.  Raw material stocks were soon depleted.  Suppliers began refusing to make shipments without cash advances.  The business was in shambles.  Bankruptcy soon dealt the coup de grâce.

There is little doubt that the business would still be operating successfully had the owners restrained their spending and carefully planned for a long but steady period of modernization and growth.

**Willingness to make personal sacrifices.**  A close personal friend of the author operates a profitable Small Business Investment Company.  Its business is to loan money to small companies—sometimes to start operations, sometimes to finance on-going needs.  It has been his experience that almost every time a new business venture is submitted to his company for financing, the organizers seem willing to make all kinds of commitments, except in the area of personal salaries.  Here is one case in point:

> A bright young patent attorney and the production manager of a large ink manufacturing company came to the loan committee with an elaborately prepared scheme to set up a corporation to manufacture inks for newspapers and magazines.  The attorney had helped a client patent a revolutionary new process to produce inks.  It was less

expensive than customary methods and produced better quality inks. The client had signed over a long-term exclusive license on the patent to the two men, allowing the proposed new company to manufacture the inks. The organizers sought $250,000 to begin the new company. Every detail seemed to be worked out. The loan committee of the Small Business Investment Company was very impressed with the depth of preparation and believed that there was a good chance for success—except for one item. The proposed operating budget showed yearly projected salary draws for each of the two organizers of $24,000 each. Believing these salaries were excessive for the new company, the loan committee offered financing to the venture on the stipulation that annual salaries be limited to $8,500 for each of the officers for the first three years.

The offer was rejected. The organizers were not willing to make such personal sacrifices. To my knowledge, they have not yet been able to find suitable financing. But one thing is crystal clear to the loan company—no new small business could support such high salary withdrawals, at least for the first few years of operation.

Apart from salary, owners of a small business must also be willing to make other personal sacrifices. For example, nearly every small operator must put in a very long day. He works hard, too. Because he lacks money, he often must do disagreeable, nerve-racking tasks that could be delegated to someone else in a larger concern. He frequently faces discouragement, fear, and anxiety in trying to keep his ship afloat.

**Be expert in the business you propose to enter.** Of all the author's clients and friends who own thriving enterprises, virtually all had extensive training and experience in their particular line of business before they started out on their own. Mr. F typifies the successful owner:

> Currently operating three swank men's shops, he started in the men's retail clothing business as a boy of 13 in an uncle's shop. Through high school and college he worked for several other men's stores. After college, he managed the men's shop of a large department store for six years. Then he took to the road for three years working as a customer representative for a famous brand of men's suits. By then he had saved enough money to lease a small shop and go into business for himself. Today his annual sales run well over two million dollars with hefty net profits.

The person inexperienced in the industry has much more stacked against him. He will make many more mistakes. Lacking in experience, he is unable to plan and forecast accurately. Often the "unexpected" occurs, which usually costs money and can quickly wipe out profits. Consider this unhappy case:

A research chemist, a successful realtor, and an up-and-coming young employee of an oil company joined forces to set up a rather large candy factory.  They had been successful in getting a government contract for several million pounds of hard candy to be used for emergency food supplies in civil defense shelters.  None of the people had experience in the candy business, but felt secure that all the details had been worked out.  The chemist had developed the manufacturing process and compiled the basic cost figures for production.  From his estimates total overhead costs and profit margins had been estimated.

However, when the plant finally got into operation, much after the anticipated production date, nothing went as planned.  The chemist had not anticipated any raw-materials waste to speak of—but in the reality of production, thousands of pounds of sugar were ruined each week.  The initial government contract was fulfilled but at a whopping loss to the small firm.  Soon the business was voluntarily terminated at a great disappointment and financial hardship to all concerned.

There are, of course, exceptions.  You may personally know someone who was a complete novice to the type of business he entered who succeeded.  But wherever the inexperienced succeeds, he does so because he has the exceptional ability to quickly search out and master the technical and social skills his operation requires.  Without question, too, he faces greater risks because of his inexperience; and usually his business grows more slowly because of mistakes that might have been avoided by the expert.

## YOUR CHANCES OF SUCCESS

What are your chances of success if you do decide to go into business for yourself?  The number of businesses in this country is growing.  In 1900 there were about $1\frac{2}{3}$ million firms in the United States; today there are more than $11\frac{1}{2}$ million.  This does not mean that the number increases every year.  Year-to-year changes in the number of business firms are determined primarily by year-to-year changes in business conditions.  As a general rule, poor business conditions are followed by a larger than average number of failures or disappearances, causing the total number of business firms to drop.  On the other hand, if business conditions are good, the total number of business firms tends to increase.  Special conditions may alter this pattern.  But over the long run, the number of firms increases along with the population and industrial growth of the country.

This growth is not free of growing pains, however.  For example, a United States Department of Commerce study of the 11 years from 1944 through 1954

(more recent data is not currently available) revealed the following facts: There were 9 million businesses newly acquired during the period—roughly half by transfer and half by establishment. During this same time, 7.8 million concerns were disposed of—about 60 percent were sold, reorganized, or otherwise transferred to new owners, and 40 percent were liquidated.

Some types of firms had a better survival rate than others, according to the study. Wholesale firms had the best survival record. Financial, real estate, construction, and manufacturing businesses did better than average. Service trades were below average, while retail trades had the lowest survival rate of all.

Half of the concerns which were newly established or acquired by transfer were sold or liquidated within two years. Chances were only one out of three that a firm would live to the age of four years, and only one out of five for a ten-year survival.

But the longer a new firm endured, the greater was its life expectancy. Although at birth a firm could be expected to live two years, the study showed that the median firm which passed its two-year-old birthday remained in operation an additional five years. So, your chances of success improve the longer you stay in business.

Besides general business conditions, there are other factors, over which the owners have no control, affecting individual firms. Examples of these are the relocation of highways, sudden changes in style, the replacement of existing products by new products, and local labor situations. While these factors may cause some businesses to fail, they may represent opportunities for others. One local market place may decline in importance, but at the same time new shopping centers are developing. Sudden changes in style or the replacement of existing products may bring troubles to certain businesses but open doors for new ones. Adverse employment situations in some areas may be offset by favorable situations in others. Ingenuity in taking advantage of changing consumer desires and technological improvements will always be rewarded.

The largest single cause of business failures may be attributed to poor management. Lack of managerial experience and aptitude has accounted for some 90 percent of the more than one million failures analyzed by Dun and Bradstreet, Inc., in the space of a century (1857 to 1957).

In the final analysis, it is up to you. Will your management be competent? Will you be able to judge, and then satisfy, your customers' wants? Can you do this so accurately and quickly that risks due to factors beyond your control will be more than compensated for? Such accomplishment requires expert management. However, remember that all statistics, gloomy as they are, reflect summary figures of *everyone* who has attempted running a small business. As a college student, you are far from average. You have better intellect. You are more knowledgeable about how and where to get information and help when you need it. You can avail yourself of excellent training in management, finance, marketing and accounting if you so desire while attending college. So your chances of successfully starting and managing a small business should be much, much better than average.

## STARTING A NEW BUSINESS

Suppose that you have now decided that you are the type who can operate a business of your own. You have given some attention to the overall chances for success. Now you must turn your attention to some of the practical problems of starting the business. You must first find a product or service which fits your background and which has good success prospects. You then need to think about where you will locate the business. You must determine the kind of business organization you will have—individual proprietorship, partnership, or corporation. Finally, you need to determine how much money the new venture will take and how you can obtain the financing.

### PRODUCTS AND SERVICES SUITABLE FOR SMALL CONCERNS

With its inherent limitations, the small firm must have an appropriate product or service. Otherwise, no amount of financial sacrifice, dogged determination or management skill can bring genuine success. The author has been closely associated with hundreds of small firms through management consulting and also through research work sponsored by a Small Business Administration grant. Here are what seem to be the product and service characteristics most suited for the small concern.

**Goods which compete on quality, not quantity or price.**  Many products require massive outlays for complicated machinery and equipment and must be produced in great quantities to achieve competitive selling prices. Autos, household appliances, chemicals, and packaged foods are but a few of many such examples. The small firm cannot hope to compete with the production systems of the billion-dollar giants in these fields. Neither does the small company have the strength to tackle nation-wide marketing and distribution involving consumers of virtually all walks of life.

Instead, the small company is better suited—indeed enviably suited—to low-volume, high-quality, customized production. Items requiring special handling, refinement, processing, control, and exactness make fine candidates. Fortunately for small businesses, there is a major trend in America toward higher personal incomes with corresponding increases in discretionary spending. This trend is certainly expanding small businesses' opportunities to produce unique luxury products—artistic, decorative, recreational, cultural—for the more opulent consumer. The scale of production is smaller, meaning that even with limited finances, adequate machinery and tooling can be used.

Customized and specialized products also have more manageable markets. These goods are aimed at a smaller segment of the population—perhaps a certain income category, educational level, or profession. Consequently, the small business has a better likelihood of making an effective market penetration. Such markets can be made even more manageable by piecemeal regional development.

**Products or services for larger companies.** Many small businesses have prospered by producing items used by large corporations in final assemblies. For example, one small company known by the author grosses about $500,000 yearly by molding plastic parts. These items are used by a major auto manufacturer in the instrument assemblies of its cars. The small concern doesn't have to bear the costs and uncertainties of developing and maintaining a market for its products. Furthermore, the designs and specifications of the items which it makes are supplied by the large manufacturer thus eliminating the usual product research and development costs.

Another small profitable concern does embossing and stamping work on a partially manufactured metal item supplied by a large manufacturer of refrigerators. The small company receives the metal pieces, already roughly machined and shaped. It then runs the parts through a relatively simple embossing and stamping process, finally polishing and painting the part. The items are then returned to the larger company for final assembly in their refrigerators. This company, like the other small firm just described, has no marketing department, no advertising costs, and has one additional advantage—it has no raw-materials inventory.

There is always some danger associated with too much dependence on one or two companies for a small firm's entire production. The contract could be lost to another small producer; or the large company could always decide to make the item itself. The latter is unlikely, however, if the item made by the small company represents but a small cost factor in the overall production of the large firm. (A 10¢ plastic part for a $3,000 auto as opposed to the production of a $50.00 cooling compressor for a $250.00 refrigerator.) Large corporations use thousands of small suppliers, processors, and manufacturers. Generally, the contracts are stable in volume and renewable so long as the small company is well-managed, supplies quality products, and charges reasonable prices.

**Franchised products and services.** The "Business Opportunities" classified column of almost any newspaper typically lists a wide array of available franchises—auto rentals, motels, soft-water service, fried chicken, automatic car washes and many more. Some are pie-in-the-sky ventures. Many others deserve serious study and consideration. Among the more important advantages offered by an established reputable franchise are these:

```
QUICK-BURGER
INTERNATIONAL


                    J. JONES MGR.
```

1. The franchise provides a relatively quick and easy way of getting into a small business.
2. The product is usually well known and nationally advertised.
3. The franchise usually provides the technical data and know-how needed to produce the item or supply the service.
4. Raw materials can be purchased at lower cost through the centralized buying facilities.
5. Standard cost figures are supplied so you know exactly how much it will take to begin operations. It also often provides standard accounting sheets for simplified record keeping.
6. The small business may be allocated a particular geographic area which lessens competition—at least from the same brand of product.

Franchising is discussed in greater detail later in this chapter.

**Product or service resistant to technical change.** Electronics, drugs, data processing, and other industries have experienced dramatic technical changes and exploding markets over the past decade. On the surface, these events would seem to herald considerable promise to a daring small businessman with a new or improved product to market. But such is rarely the case. By the time a

small firm gears up for production, it is quite likely that the product would be superseded by another innovation. At best, marketing time would be of limited duration. Ordinarily, small concerns cannot effectively produce and market products undergoing rapid technical changes. Nor are they well suited for products marketed on a *yearly model basis*. The more unchanging and stable, the more favorable is the item for small business.

**Products and services producing immediate cash flows.**  Few small concerns can afford to engage in long-term development work *prior* to a selling or marketing effort.  Usually small firms are thinly financed.  If they engage in extensive development efforts for 8–12–14 months without sales activity, they usually jeopardize their future.  A more sensible approach is to make sure you have a

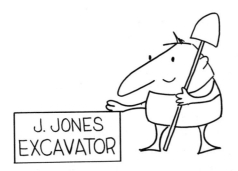

product or service which will start turning a cash flow almost immediately.  Even though sales may not be totally profitable in the beginning, it's better to lose a little each month than to bear the complete burden of development work without sales.  Even if you're fortunate enough to get a public underwriting providing you with substantial amounts of capital from other investors, remember that you've still only got so much time to make the firm self-supporting.  Once a good cash flow is established, you can then begin allocating a portion of the firm's capital to development efforts.

## WHERE TO LOCATE

Once you have decided what type of business you will start, you are ready to select a location.  You may have already picked the community—your home town or some other part of the country in which you would like to live.  While it is important to choose a spot in which you will be happy, you should make sure the community needs the business you plan to open.

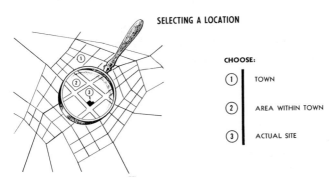

SELECTING A LOCATION

CHOOSE:

①   TOWN

②   AREA WITHIN TOWN

③   ACTUAL SITE

   Picking your location may be considered in three steps: (1) the selection of the town or city; (2) the choice of the area within the town or city; and (3) the selection of a specific site in the chosen area.

**Selecting the town.**    Large companies often spend a great deal of time and study on the problem of selecting a new location, attempting to choose it on a scientific basis.  The small operator may be unable to afford such a detailed scientific study, but he should evaluate the town to the best of his ability.
   If the location of a retail store or service establishment is being considered, assistance may be had from wholesalers or manufacturers who supply merchandise and equipment, Federal, state and local governments, and other sources.
   Consider population.  Is the town growing, or has it already reached the peak of its development?  You should also learn as much as you can about the composition of the population, such as the breakdown by age, occupation, and income.  This will have a bearing on your sales volume if you plan to be a retailer.  If you are starting a manufacturing business, labor supply is important.
   The number of competitive businesses already located in the area should influence your choice of location.  Such data are furnished in the Bureau of Census figures.  For example, it has been found that there is a relationship between the number of inhabitants in a town or city and the number of stores of various types they can support.  Table 17–1 shows how the number of inhabitants per store varies by kinds of retail business.  While one grocery or delicatessen store exists for every 667 inhabitants, one luggage and leather goods store serves an average of nearly 122,500 inhabitants.  These are country-wide averages and may not indicate the ideal number of inhabitants per store in your community.  They are presented here to show how much the number of inhabitants per store may vary in the different lines of business.
   Factors other than the number of stores must be considered.  Even where there are fewer than the average in a location, a store should not be added unless all other advantages and disadvantages have been fully investigated.  Zoning regulations, the enterprise of merchants, the size of the store, and many other special conditions all have an influence.
   In addition to the consideration of present population and competition, you will be interested in the probable future of the city or town.  Is it likely to change from a predominantly agricultural town to an industrial city?  If it is industrial, how old and well established is it?  How aggressive are the civic associations?  What about the town spirit; that is, do the people cooperate well on civic projects?
   Other considerations are the size of the trading area around the city or town, the climate, schools, churches, banks, and amusements.  Are the principal activities seasonal or continuous?  Are most of the residents wealthy, well-to-do, moderately well-off, or poor?

**Table 17–1**  Number of inhabitants per store by selected kinds of business

[National averages]

| Kind of business | Number of inhabitants per store | Kind of business | Number of inhabitants per store |
|---|---|---|---|
| *Food stores* | | *Automotive groups—Continued* | |
| Grocery stores, including delicatessens | 667 | Passenger car dealers (non-franchised) | 6,839 |
| Meat markets | 7,266 | Tire, battery, accessory dealers | 8,284 |
| Fish (seafood markets) | 39,926 | Aircraft, boat, motorcycle dealers | 33,763 |
| Fruit stores, vegetable markets | 13,653 | Household trailer dealers | 56,411 |
| Candy, nut, confectionery stores | 9,847 | | |
| Dairy products stores | 22,711 | *Lumber, building materials, farm equipment dealers* | |
| Bakery products stores | 9,006 | | |
| | | Farm equipment dealers | 9,114 |
| *Eating, drinking places* | | Lumber building materials dealers | 4,969 |
| | | Paint, glass, wallpaper stores | 15,530 |
| Eating places | 754 | Heating, plumbing equipment dealers | 26,392 |
| Drinking places (alcoholic beverages) | 1,507 | Hardware stores | 4,997 |
| | | | |
| *General merchandise* | | *Drug stores, proprietary stores* | |
| | | | |
| Department stores | 54,875 | | |
| Dry goods stores | 19,630 | Drug stores | 3,367 |
| Variety stores | 8,243 | Proprietary stores | 36,212 |
| | | | |
| *Apparel, accessory stores* | | *Other retail stores* | |
| | | | |
| Shoe stores | 7,089 | Fuel, ice dealers | 6,066 |
| Women's clothing, specialty stores | 3,882 | Hay, grain, feed stores | 10,323 |
| | | Farm, garden supply stores | 21,470 |
| | | Jewelry stores | 7,294 |
| *Furniture, home furnishings, appliance dealers* | | Book stores | 60,048 |
| | | Stationery stores | 26,518 |
| | | Sporting goods stores | 17,620 |
| | | Bicycle shops | 100,720 |
| Furniture, home furnishings stores | 3,181 | Florists | 9,034 |
| Household appliances, radio, TV stores | 4,227 | Cigar stores, stands | 32,466 |
| | | News dealers, news stands | 22,979 |
| Music stores, records and musical instruments | 21,725 | Gift, novelty, souvenir stores | 12,386 |
| | | Camera, photographic supply stores | 49,624 |
| *Automotive groups* | | Luggage, leather goods stores | 122,344 |
| | | Optical goods stores | 58,330 |
| Passenger car dealers (franchised) | 4,493 | Antique stores, secondhand stores | 8,189 |

*Source*: Bureau of the Census, U.S. Department of Commerce.  Number of establishments from 1958 Census of Retail Trade.  Number of inhabitants residing in the United States (excluding Armed Forces overseas), as of July 1, 1958.

Rent is a significant expense in the operation of most businesses—particularly in retail businesses. Therefore, the average rental charges in a town should be determined. As a caution, you should not choose a town solely on the basis of low rent, however.

Chambers of commerce, state development agencies, and others may have made, or may be familiar with, local community surveys which would provide the type of information you need. Information from these sources will be helpful in selecting the location for a manufacturing plant as well as mercantile and service outlets.

**Selecting an area within the city.**    Next you must decide in what part of town to locate. If the town is very small and you are establishing a retail or service business, there will probably be little choice. Only one shopping center exists.

In the city, outlying shopping centers appear in addition to the central shopping area, and stores spring up along principal thoroughfares and neighborhood streets. There is a recognized trend toward decentralization of districts.

The kind and variety of merchandise carried helps to determine the type of shopping area which should be chosen. For example, clothing stores, jewelry stores, and department stores are more likely to be successful in the main or outlying central shopping district than elsewhere. On the other hand, grocery stores, drug stores, filling stations, and bakeries do well on principal thoroughfares and neighborhood streets outside the shopping districts. Some kinds of stores customarily pay a low rent per square foot, while others pay a high rent. In the former category are furniture, grocery, and hardware stores, while in the latter are cigar, drug, women's furnishings, and department stores. No hard and fast rule can be laid down, but it is well to observe in what type of area your kind of store appears to flourish most generally.

The size of your store will also help determine the area to be chosen. Your original capital investment may be so small that it would be impossible to obtain sufficient sales volume to pay the high rent of a downtown location. It would then be necessary to select the outlying neighborhood area of a large city—or to locate in a small town.

After determining a likely area best suited to your type of business, be sure to obtain as many facts as you can about it. As pointed out above, you will be interested in the competition. How many businesses of the same kind are located in the area? Can you find out something about their sales volume? If you are establishing a store or service trade, from how many blocks do people come to trade in the area?

If your business is to come primarily from local inhabitants, what is the population of the area? Is the trend of population increasing, stationary, or declining? Are the people native-born, mixed, or chiefly foreign? What do they do for a living? Are they predominantly laborers, clerks, executives, or retired persons? Are they all ages or principally old, middle-aged, or young? To help you gauge their buying power, find out the average rent for homes in the area, the average real estate taxes for homes, the number of telephones, number of automobiles, and, if the figure is available, the per capita income.

The zoning ordinances, parking availability, transportation facilities and natural barriers such as hills and bridges are important in considering the location of any kind of business. How important depends on the business.

Possible sources for this kind of information are chambers of commerce, trade associations, local real estate companies, local newspapers, banks, city officials, and personal observations on your part.

**Selecting a site.** Choosing the actual site within an area may well result in taking what you can get. Not too many buildings or plants will be suitable and at the same time available for use in a given locality. If you do have a choice, be sure to weigh the possibilities carefully.

For a manufacturing plant, consider the condition and suitability of the building, transportation, parking facilities, and the type of lease.

For a store or service establishment, check on the competition, traffic flow, parking facilities, street location, physical aspects of the building, type of lease, history of the site, and the amount, speed, cost, and quality of transportation.

## CHOOSING THE LEGAL STRUCTURE FOR A SMALL FIRM

Shall the small firm be organized as a proprietorship, a partnership, or a corporation? These are the three principal choices. To minimize taxes, provide flexibility for management, and encourage growth, a small firm's legal structure must be right. The life of the firm, its ability to persist after its present owners can no longer function, is also greatly influenced by the legal structure. Let us first take a look at the essential characteristics of each of these firms, then consider in greater depth how they might affect your small firm.

**Proprietorship.** This is the easiest to begin and end (sometimes prematurely), can have the most flexible purpose for its operations, needs no Government approval, other than a city license, has business profits taxed as personal income, and makes the owner personally liable for debts and taxes.

**Partnership.** For two or more people, this is the simplest type of business to start and terminate. It has the same flexibility of objectives as does the proprietorship, has partners taxed separately as personal income, and makes personally liable for debts and taxes all except limited partners.

**Corporation.** The most formal of the structures, it operates under state laws, must comply with regulations of the Securities and Exchange Commission of the Federal Government, has continuous and separate legal life, has its scope of activity and name restricted by a charter. The corporation's profits are taxed separately from earnings of executives and owners, and makes only the company (not the owners nor managers) liable for its debts and taxes—unless such persons sign specific agreements to be responsible for indebtedness.

There are other types of legal structures such as syndicates, joint stock companies, Massachusetts trusts, and pools. However, these are very specialized and rare. For these reasons, they are eliminated from our discussion.

In analyzing your own situation, great care should be taken to make the right decision the first time. In fact, it may well be necessary for you to go to the expense of getting advice and guidance from competent legal counsel. Highlights of major considerations follow and will assist you in making a choice.

**Costs and procedures in starting.** Single proprietorships are the easiest to get started. The costs of formation are low. Basically all you have to do is find out whether you need a city license to carry on your particular business, and whether you have to pay a state tax or license fee.

General partnerships are also started quite simply. You can set one up by having the executives in the business sign what is called a partnership agreement. A written document, however, is not necessarily a prerequisite, since an oral agreement can be equally effective. Moreover, a partnership may even be implied by actions which the managers of an unincorporated business have taken even though no agreement of any kind, oral or written, exists.

Limited partnerships are somewhat more difficult to set up. To form one, you file with the proper state official a written contract drawn according to certain legal requirements. This contract permits you to limit the liability of one or more of the partners to just the amount which they invested. But you must designate at least *one general partner* in addition to the limited partners. And all limited partners must have actually invested in the partnership. According to the Uniform Limited Partnership Act, those investments may be either cash or tangible property, but not services. Lastly, you must conform strictly to the laws of the particular state in which you organize; otherwise your business will be considered as a general partnership.

Corporations are more complicated to form. You can create one only by following strictly the legal procedures of the particular state in which the corporation is being set up. First, responsible people are needed to organize and become officials in the new corporation. Next, they must file with the designated state official a special document called the *articles of incorporation*. Then they must pay an initial tax and certain filing fees. And finally, in order to do the business for which the corporation was formed, various official meetings must be conducted to deal with the specified details of organization and operation. If the incorporators intend to sell stock to other individuals, they must also comply with state and Federal securities laws.

**The size of the risk.**   The degree to which investors in your enterprise risk legal liability for the debts of the business is a *cardinal consideration*. Regardless of legal structure, creditors are always entitled to be paid out of business assets before any equity capital may be withdrawn. In cases where those assets are insufficient, the extent to which owners can be compelled to meet creditors' claims out of their own pockets varies with the type of organization.

A single proprietor is personally liable for all debts of his business—to the extent of his entire property. He cannot restrict his liability in any way. Likewise, each member of a general partnership is, himself, fully responsible for all debts owed by his partnership—irrespective of the amount of his own investment in the business. This can extend to personal indebtedness of the other partner(s), not being restricted just to business debts.

In a limited partnership, however, the limited partners are protected; they risk only the loss of the capital they have invested. But the general partners in a limited partnership are liable jointly and severally for all debts just like any other general partner. And remember, there must be at least one general partner in any limited partnership.

Corporations have a real advantage, as far as risk goes, over other legal structures. Creditors can force payment on their claims only to the limit of the corporation's assets. Thus while a shareholder may lose the money he put into the company, he cannot be forced to contribute additional funds out of his own pocket to meet business debts. This is true even though the corporate assets may be insufficient to meet creditors' claims. Nonetheless, stockholders or managers of corporations could become responsible for satisfaction of corporate debts should they sign special forms specifically agreeing to assume that liability.

**Continuity of the concern.**   In choosing the legal structure for your business, you should also understand clearly how the choice influences the continuity of the business. Although single proprietorships have no time limit on them by law, they are not fundamentally perpetual. Illness of the owner may derange the business, and his death ends it. Partnerships are perishable in the same general sense—they are terminated by the death or withdrawal of any one of the partners.

Corporations have the most permanent legal structure of all. They have a separate, continuous life of their own. The withdrawal, insolvency, injury, illness, or death of a person officially concerned in a corporation does not mean its finish. Moreover, the certificates of stock, which represent investments and ownership in the business, may be transferred from one person to another without hampering the concern's operations.

**Adaptability of administration.**  In the single proprietorship, policy and operations rest, of course, in one individual.  This situation can be both good and bad.  On the one hand, concentration of management avoids the problems of opposing factions and divided responsibilities.  The fact that the chief executive is in full charge, and is in complete control of profits, can be an incentive to careful management.  On the other hand, many a man is not competent to handle all management jobs himself.  To be sure, an owner can, and often does, employ assistants to whom he assigns various details.  But he still reaps the rewards or pays the penalties for what they do.  It is also worth noting that after incorporating a small business, the owner does not necessarily lose control of the enterprise.  In many small, closely held corporations, the former sole owner can and often does retain control by the ownership of a majority of the stock in the newly formed corporation.

In general partnerships, each partner typically has an equal role in administration, with the various operating functions divided among them.  The combined abilities and knowledge of several executives gives the partnership an advantage over the single proprietorship.  But the division of functional responsibility among the several partners may lead to fundamental policy disagreements.  When you compare them with corporations, partnerships have the following administrative features: Decisions may be made and changes adopted simply by oral agreement among the partners.  In limited partnerships, the limited partners may not engage in management functions; if they do, they may be held fully liable as general partners.  Limited partners are, however, entitled to inspect the books and obtain full and complete information regarding the business.

In corporations, the stockholders do not necessarily participate either in operations or in policy formulation, but they may.  Often, however, those functions are centralized in a relatively small group of executives who own only a small percentage of the shares.  Although corporations can get away from the shortcomings of the limited ability or knowledge of one person, they do run some risk of inefficient management where those in control have little or no direct financial interest.  Corporations have an advantage over partnerships in this way: In partnerships each partner can act as general agent for the business; but in corporations, the stockholders cannot bind the firm by their acts just because they have invested capital in it.

**Influences of applicable laws.**  The single proprietorship is the oldest and most widespread legal structure of business.  As a result, little doubt remains as to the influences of laws regulating its legal rights and obligations.  Likewise, the relationships are clear between a sole owner, his agents, his creditors, and others with whom he deals in business.  A private citizen working in Iowa can carry on business in Kansas without paying any greater taxes or incurring any more obligations in Kansas than local Kansas businessmen have.

Broadly speaking, this same situation is also true for a partnership. Of course, a state may require the purchase of a license to carry on a particular kind of business. But the license will be equally available to businessmen of any state so long as they conform to prescribed uniform standards. (This equality of opportunity derives from the United States Constitution which guarantees to citizens of each state *all privileges and immunities* provided to citizens of the other states.) Thus, the legal structures which do not involve any artificial entity (as a corporation does) provide a freedom of action in all states which corporations cannot match.

Corporations owe their legal life solely to the states in which they are organized. No other state is required to recognize them. To be sure, all states do permit out-of-state corporations to function inside their boundaries. Nevertheless, out-of-state corporations must always comply with special in-state obligations such as (1) filing certain legal papers with the proper state officials; (2) appointment of a representative in the state to act as agent in the serving process on the *foreign* corporation; and (3) payment of specified fees and taxes.

Also, corporations are regulated by numerous state laws which vary considerably. Even when the language is similar, these laws can be, and have been, interpreted differently in different places. Therefore, in running a corporation effectively, competent legal counsel is virtually indispensable. The normal course of business, for example, can easily involve statutes and court decisions of a state other than the one where the corporation was founded. Nevertheless, the essential feature of limited liability of stockholders is preserved in every state.

**Attraction of additional capital.** Every business may require additional funds from time to time to carry on operations. If it can't obtain adequate capital, it may well be headed for failure. It is important, therefore, in deciding upon legal structure to take into account the means for attracting new money.

In single proprietorships, the owner may raise additional money by borrowing, by purchasing on credit, and by investing additional amounts himself. Since he is personally liable for all the debts of his business, banks and suppliers will look carefully at his personal wealth. Consequently, the funds he can get will always be limited by his own circumstances. For this reason alone, a business requiring large amounts of capital for successful operation should probably not be organized as a single proprietorship.

Partnerships can often raise funds with greater ease, since the resources of all partners are combined in a single undertaking. Like single proprietors, partners must accept full personal liability for business debts. For this reason, a partnership may be able to borrow on better terms than some corporations. In addition, suppliers and other outsiders may be willing to extend credit because of the security deriving from the individual partners' full liability.

Corporations are usually in the best position of all to attract capital. They may, for example, acquire additional funds by borrowing money by pledging corporate assets.  Also, they may sell securities to the public and attract a wide range of investors.  A shareholder's investment in a corporation will not subject him to any financial risk beyond the amount of his holdings.  And, as a part owner, the stockholder has the prospect of sharing directly, through dividends and rising value of the securities, in any profits the concern makes.  More will be said later in this chapter about using the corporation for raising capital for your small firm.

### GETTING THE MONEY

Once you have established what kind of product or service you will focus on and where you are going to locate, you can start building your financial plans.  This is a critical and vital step in going into business for yourself because you must know as accurately as possible what your money needs are.  These needs include (a) pre-business expenses such as legal fees, license costs, and so forth; (b) set-up expenses—money for advance rentals, equipment purchases or leases, initial inventory, etc.; and (c) additional money which must be put into the business until it can generate sufficient income and profits to be self-supporting.  If you don't know accounting, get a good accountant to check out this phase of your planning.

When you know what it is going to cost to get into business and keep it going for a year or so, you are ready to make a final determination on the legal form of organization and start looking for capital.  If the money needs are relatively small, you may be able to finance the venture through your personal savings or investments.  Then relatives, friends, or other individuals may be found who are willing to venture their savings in your business.  Banks may be willing to help *some*, but usually any loans they make must be personal loans secured by you and not the new company you are organizing.  Trade creditors and equipment manufacturers are other sources of valuable credit for the new business.  The Small Business Administration may be able to offer some help either in making direct loans or in insuring loans made to you by local banks.

When you deal with a banker, sell yourself.  Openly discuss your plans and difficulties with him.  It is his business not to betray confidence.  If you need financial assistance, carefully prepare, in written form, complete information so that anyone approached for aid may gain a thorough understanding of your entire proposition.  Many businessmen or prospective business operators have destroyed their chances of obtaining financial help by the failure to present their proposition properly.

The companies from which you buy equipment or merchandise may also furnish you capital in the form of credit.  Manufacturers of equipment, such as store fixtures, cash registers, and industrial machinery, frequently have financing plans under which you may buy on the installment basis and subsequently pay for the equipment out of income.  Moreover, the wholesalers or suppliers from which you purchase merchandise extend credit.  You are not required to pay for the goods at once. If goods are for resale, no security other than repossession rights of the unsold goods may be involved. However, too extended use of such credit may prove expensive. Usually cash discounts are allowed if a bill is paid within 10, 30, or 60 days. For example, a term of sale quoted as "2–10; net, 30 days" means that a cash discount of 2 percent will be granted if the bill is paid within 10 days. If not paid in that time, the entire amount is due in 30 days. If you do not take advantage of the cash discount, you are paying 2 percent to use money for 20 days, or 36 percent per year. This is high interest.

If your new venture requires large amounts of capital—perhaps $100,000 or $400,000—you will probably want to go to the corporate form or organization and attempt to sell stock to other investors. Since you must comply with very strict state and Federal regulations regarding the sale of securities, it is absolutely essential that you get the advice and services of a qualified securities attorney if you take this route. Some limited local (within the state) stock sales can be made without going through the involved and usually costly Federal Securities and Exchange channels. However, if you want to raise large amounts of capital, it is usually necessary to sell the stock over wide geographic areas. This latter kind of sale does require appropriate SEC clearance.

Two general kinds of public stock offerings may be made: The first is called a "Regulation A Offering" and allows you to sell up to $500,000 in stock. This is the simplest for your attorney to prepare and clear with the SEC and the least expensive initially.

The second type is "An S-1 Registration" and is generally used to sell larger amounts of stock—perhaps $1 or $2 million. It requires more extensive preparation, usually takes longer, and customarily involves sizable attorney's fees.

In either case—Regulation A or S-1—the SEC's procedure is aimed at making you make a full and complete disclosure of what you intend to do with the company and with the money raised in the public sale of stock. The fact that you are able to clear the SEC in no way guarantees that you will be able to sell the stock successfully to investors.

If you need such a stock sale, the best procedure is to first try to find a stock brokerage firm that will attempt to sell the issue for you. This again requires selling yourself as well as your proposed business scheme. You will need lots of documentation and meticulous plans to convince the broker. If you find a broker who believes in you and your business, he will then enter into an underwriting agreement with you. In this document, he will either *guarantee* that he will raise the money for a stipulated commission (underwriting commissions as well as attorney's fees can come out of the proceeds of the stock sale) or he will merely agree to *attempt* to sell the stock on a best efforts basis.

Finding a good underwriter for your business can be the most important day of your life, for it provides a unique method of raising large amounts of capital. Don't get discouraged if you get turned down a few times—or many times. Keep trying.

A good securities attorney may, himself, be able to steer you into an underwriting commitment from some of his business contacts.  He is also essential in assuring that you get the most favorable share of *insider's stock*.  This can mean lots of money in your pocket later if the business succeeds; it can also help assure that you and others associated with you can retain voting control of the corporation.

One of the principal causes of failures among businesses is inadequate financing.  If you do go into business, remember it is your responsibility to provide, or obtain from others, sufficient capital to supply a firm foundation for the enterprise.


## GOVERNMENT HELP FOR SMALL BUSINESSES

The ease with which any citizen can go into business for himself is, undisputably, one of America's truly great qualities.  For the Nation, this *ease of entry* has generated energetic competition among firms in turn contributing to a standard of living unequalled in all the world.  It has also fulfilled the personal dream of millions by providing a society where no one is denied the opportunity of business ownership.

Yet with all the freedom and promise, American business is unquestionably dominated by big corporations.  In numbers, small businesses make up about 95 percent of all concerns.  But in terms of profits, the very big corporations take the lion's share.  Approximately 2 percent of the total number of corporations have assets exceeding $50 million.  However, these relatively few firms generate some 70 percent of *all* corporate profits in an average year.

Concerned with the gloomy plight of the small businessman, Congress in 1958 created the Small Business Administration as a permanent, independent government agency.  In its first decade of work, it has done much to assist and protect small business.  Currently, the S.B.A. has a network of 73 field offices in the principal cities of every state as well as Guam, Puerto Rico, and the Virgin Islands.  It offers financial assistance, management assistance, aid in obtaining government contracts, counseling services, and more than 800 publications covering successful practices in almost every small business field.

**Who is eligible?**  Most small independent businesses—except gambling or speculative firms, newspapers, TV and radio stations, and liquor stores.  For purposes of making loans, S.B.A. defines a small business as one that meets these general size standards:

1. Wholesale—annual sales of not more than $5 million

2. Retail or Service—annual sales or receipts of not more than $1 million

3. Manufacturing—not more than 250 employees

However, size standards for loan assistance vary widely from industry to industry.  Still other standards apply in government contract assistance and in Small

Business Investment Company (S.B.I.C.) assistance. Detailed information on size standards is available at any S.B.A. office.

**Business loans.** Any small businessman with a financial problem may come to the S.B.A. for advice and assistance. Agency specialists will review his problem and suggest possible courses of action. If a businessman needs money and cannot borrow it on reasonable terms, S.B.A. often can help. The Agency will consider either participating in, or guaranteeing up to 90 percent of a bank loan. If the bank cannot provide funds, S.B.A. will consider lending the entire amount as a direct government loan. Two-thirds of S.B.A.'s loans are now made in participation with banks.

S.B.A. looks to past records and future prospects of a small businessman to decide whether he has the ability to repay a loan, and any other debts, out of company profits. Loans may be used for:

1. Business construction, expansion or conversion
2. Purchase of machinery, equipment, facilities, supplies or materials
3. Working capital

The S.B.A. share of a business loan may not exceed $350,000, and may be for up to 10 years; if a substantial part of the loan is for construction, it may be for as long as 15 years. Collateral is required. It may consist of real estate or chattel mortgage; assignment of warehouse receipts for marketable merchandise; assignment of certain types of contracts, guarantees or personal endorsements; and in some instances assignment of current receivables and inventories stored in a bonded or other acceptable warehouse.

**Pool loans.** These are loans made to corporations formed by groups of small businesses. S.B.A. can lend them money to (1) obtain raw materials, equipment, inventory or supplies; (2) obtain the benefits of research and development, or to establish facilities for these purposes. The maximum amount is $250,000 multiplied by the number of pool members—plus whatever amount a participating bank may provide. Such loans can extend for as long as 20 years if construction is involved.

**Economic opportunity loans.** Very small firms, including new businesses in or near needy neighborhoods of larger cities are eligible for these special loans. Many of the persons receiving these loans are members of minority groups. Their business capabilities are evaluated by trained personnel. Volunteer counselors help them until their businesses are operating profitably. They can also take special management training courses. Qualified applicants may borrow up to $15,000 for a maximum of 15 years. S.B.A. also will guarantee the full amount of this type of loan by a private institution.

**Small Business Investment Company loans.** Small Business Investment Companies (S.B.I.C.'s) are privately-owned concerns licensed and sometimes financially assisted by the Small Business Administration. The S.B.I.C.'s, in turn, help the small business community by:

1. Providing long-term loans ranging from 5 to 30 years.
2. Providing "equity" capital (actually investing in the small business) or taking options to purchase stock.

To help S.B.I.C.'s be more effective, the S.B.A. can make operating loans (up to 50 percent of the statutory capital and surplus of an S.B.I.C., but not in excess of $4 million). Capital loans can also be made by the Small Business Administration to match dollar for dollar the private capital raised by an S.B.I.C. up to a maximum of $700,000.

**Disaster loans.** The S.B.A. lends money at 3 percent interest for as long as 30 years to owners of homes, businesses, churches, and privately owned charitable institutions whose property suffered damage from hurricanes, floods, or other natural disasters. The amount of the loan is limited to actual damage suffered, minus insurance. Borrowers must pledge whatever collateral they can provide.

**Special loans.** The S.B.A. lends money at 3 percent interest for as long as 30 years to small firms which have suffered property damage or other economic loss because of natural disasters. They may even make loans to small companies which have suffered substantial economic injury through inability to process or market a food product because of accidental spoilage.

State and local development companies may also receive S.B.A. loans which, in turn, finance specific small firms. The development company is expected to provide at least 20 percent of the cost of the project. Loans may be used to help the company buy land, build a new factory, acquire machinery and equipment, convert an existing plant, or construct shopping center space. Collateral is usually a first mortgage on the project to be financed.

Finally, the S.B.A. is empowered to make loans to small firms that suffer economic injury because of displacement as a result of Federally aided urban renewal, highway, or other construction programs. The loan is based on the cost of re-establishing and reasonably improving the business. Borrowers must pledge whatever collateral they can provide.

**Management assistance.** To strengthen the management of small concerns, the S.B.A. offers a number of interesting and useful services:

1. *Individual counseling.* At regional offices, at key business cities away from S.B.A. offices, and even in remote places, the S.B.A. provides specialists who will give free counseling and information for the small businessman. Through a special management program called SCORE (Service Corps of Retired Executives), more than 3,000 retired businessmen in more than 190 chapters throughout the nation assist businessmen with their problems. The service is free, except for direct expenses.

2. *Conferences, workshops, clinics.* Usually lasting one day, conferences cover such subjects as working capital, business forecasting, and diversification of markets. Workshops generally deal with matters of importance to persons considering starting new businesses. Clinics go into specific problems of small businessmen within a particular industry. A small registration fee is charged to those who enroll.

3. *Association and industry management services.* Through AIMS, the S.B.A. encourages large firms and trade associations to serve as co-sponsors for training programs for their small business customers, suppliers, or members.

## BUYING AN EXISTING SMALL BUSINESS

Purchasing an established, *successful* small business at a reasonable price is less risky than starting one from *scratch.* Not only do you acquire the company's market, but also the productive know-how and many of its operating personnel. To purchase a small concern, you might deal with a *business broker* or directly with the *owners.* Brokers act as *agents* for businesses, much like real estate companies, and earn a commission from the seller. The classified section of your local newspaper, the *New York Times*, and the *Wall Street Journal* list offerings of both owners and brokers of small concerns.

It is probably easier and often safer to deal with a reputable broker than to buy a business direct from its owners. A professional, the broker knows the *in's and out's* of small business. He spends much of his time analyzing companies, representing only those which have good potential for continuing successful operations. Then he helps to negotiate a reasonable sales price, determines the size of down payment, and often assists the buyer in acquiring a loan to finance the balance. The broker may even make a direct loan to the buyer. All the paperwork is handled by the broker, sometimes saving considerable money in attorney's fees.

Nonetheless, if you're interested in small business opportunities, you should explore all the possibilities. Talk to owners of small concerns directly and see what brokers have to offer. As you look at any prospective firm, you will do well to find out why the owner wants to sell his business. It may be any of a larger number of reasons: a personal health problem, a business disagreement, overextension of the company's activities, unfavorable trends in sales, adverse outlook from new competitors, new technology, a desire to retire from business. The possible reasons are many and varied, but very important to you the prospective buyer.

The seller cannot always be relied upon to volunteer his true reasons for wanting to sell. Sometimes the information relating to sales, profits, and other factors are inaccurate or even purposely misstated. The careful buyer, therefore, must ask "What kinds of information do I need?" and "Where can I get this information?"

The needed data can be grouped into three general categories: (1) market information, (2) financial information, and (3) legal information. The kinds of information the buyer should look for and some sources of that information are identified in the following discussions. Not all of the sources listed will apply equally to all kinds of businesses. You will have to determine for yourself the extent to which the specific types of information will help you reach a sound decision.

Some difficulty may arise in the information-gathering stage because of poor records, unavailability of some information, lack of cooperation, and the like. The seller has the advantage as far as internal data are concerned. He has free access to his own records; the buyer does not. You should insist on seeing the company records and be wary of any seller who refuses to give you the information.

Be resigned to the fact that you may have to spend considerable time and effort digging out the information. The sources suggested below, however, should help you gather the basic types of information needed in the decision-making process.

### SOURCES OF MARKET INFORMATION

The first and most logical step in buying a business is to conduct a market analysis. A market analysis is a study of the present position of the business within its market area and of probable future patterns. It should include the growth pattern of the business being sold, the state of the market, the nature and extent of competition—all factors that will show the present market position of the business or that will affect its future.

A market analysis should indicate whether the purchase of the business should be considered further. It will help you decide how much you should pay, and it will also give you a clearer picture of just what you are buying. A market analysis has the added value of making it possible to develop more accurate sales forecasts. It places greater emphasis on fact and less on hunch and guess-work.

The specific nature of the business being bought will determine much of the market information needed. A manufacturing business with problems of marketing and distribution will need information not necessarily pertinent to a retail or service business, with its more localized market. The following areas of market information are designed to suggest sources that may be useful in analyzing the market of the business.

**Sales information.** An investigation should be made of the sales history of the company. At least three years' sales should be examined and preferably ten—or the entire sales history of the company if it is a new one.

The manner in which the records are kept will determine to a large extent the availability of sales information. Many small businesses keep little in the way of sales records—often only what is necessary for tax purposes. Others have bookkeeping systems designed by business-machine manufacturers, trade associations, or professional accounting services. The more standardized the procedure, the more useful the information is likely to be for market analysis.

Most states now have sales taxes, and this may provide a useful source of information. Whether or not a business is required to keep sales-tax records, depends largely on the type of business and the state requirements. Sales-tax laws are not uniform, and what is required in one state may not be required in another.

If most of the business is done on a credit basis, accounts receivable may give useful sales information. If this source is used, the market investigation should be concerned only with the amount of credit sales and not with the effectiveness of the collection of accounts receivable.

Ingenuity and common sense can often turn up sources of sales information. In one case, for example, sales for a self-service laundry were determined by using water capacity per machine, city records of the amount of water consumed by the business, and price per load.

Regardless of where the sales information comes from, the purpose of gathering it is basically the same—to identify the pattern or trend of sales over the past and to use this information to project or estimate sales for the period ahead. Such an investigation is especially useful in determining the value of the business above the value of the assets.

**Cost of goods sold.**    A study of the cost of goods sold is also important in determining the market position of the business. Cost of goods sold is the cost of merchandise purchased by the business for resale, including freight and other charges. The difference between sales and the cost of the goods sold is called *gross margin* or *gross profit*. The higher the cost of goods sold in relation to sales, the lower the gross margin and the net profit.

Many factors, both within the company and in the market of which the business is a part, affect the cost of goods sold. An investigation should be made to determine the following:

1. *Average rate of stock turnover.* This is particularly useful when compared to the normal or typical rate for similar businesses.

2. *Extent to which invoices are being discounted.* Paying invoices in time to earn the cash discount will increase both gross margin and net profit if the discount is recorded as a reduction in the cost of goods sold. A direct increase in net profit will result if the discount is shown as *other income.*

3. *Freight cost.* This is important in determining whether incoming transportation charges are in line.

Among the records to be studied are vendor invoices, records of merchandise payments to vendors, shipper receipts or bills of lading, and records of past physical inventories.

**Sales-effort records.** This information has to do with how much it costs in selling effort to produce a given volume of sales. It involves two types of costs: (1) advertising costs, from invoices and statements for various forms of advertising and promotion; and (2) salaries and wages paid for selling, from payroll or Social Security records. If the business maintains salespeople in the field, as a manufacturer might, information on reimbursable travel expenses should be included.

The purpose of gathering information on selling costs is to determine how well these costs are being utilized and to compare them with average figures for the kind of business being studied.

**Personal observation.** Personal observation of the premises and personnel of the company is another source of information for the buying process. Just what points should be noted will depend on the nature of the business, but the following are offered as examples:

The general appearance of the premises, both internal and external, may be important, particularly if direct customer contact is made at the place of business.

Plant layout and apparent efficiency of operation should be carefully observed if the seller is a manufacturer or otherwise engaged in processing or assembly.

Employee morale and general attitude toward the business should be noted, especially if current employees are to be retained.

Employee records, including wage-payment plans, employee-evaluation and merit-rating programs, training programs, and so on should be studied.

**Market information from outside sources.** Sources of market information outside the business fall into two general classes: (1) competing businesses, and (2) the total market of the business and the factors that enter into it. Analyzing market characteristics involves dealing with constantly changing forces. This is in contrast to the internal analysis, which concerns basically historical records.

**Competition.** Unless the business has a monopoly of some sort, a study of the competition should be included in the market analysis. The competition may be local and well defined, or quite generalized, depending on the nature of the business and of the market.

Trade associations and other-data gathering agencies, both governmental and nongovernmental, are sometimes helpful in this area. A good deal of the information about competition, however, must come from direct investigation business by business.

Such factors as these are of interest: estimated sales, advertising and promotion, services offered, performance of sales personnel, businesses entering and leaving the competition recently, changes in the competitive structure through product mix or services offered, pricing policies, and other factors that form a part of the competitive patterns for specific types of businesses. A very important aspect of competition is the extent to which the total weight of competition has expanded the market for certain types of products or kinds of businesses, and the direction this is taking.

Other relevant factors which we have already discussed concerning site location and population and purchasing power of the area's customers should be analyzed.

**General market conditions.** A much broader yet vital part of the market analysis has to do with what might be called the general state of the market. Most of the discussion of market analysis so far has dealt with factors that have a direct influence on the business being bought or sold: company sale, location, competition, and so on. But these, in turn, are influenced by the overall economic conditions of the country and of the market area. These may be widespread movements such as national cycles of prosperity and depression, or they may be purely local conditions. The two extremes are not necessarily related.

It is to the advantage of the buyer to have a clear understanding of economic factors that affect or are likely to affect the status of the business. The significance of this information becomes clearer when forecasts and estimates are made.

## SOURCES OF FINANCIAL INFORMATION

The buyer can usually find financial information in the following places: (1) financial statements, (2) income-tax returns, (3) other internal records, and (4) other external sources.

The results of the financial transactions of every company *should* be reflected in its periodic financial statements. These statements are extremely important in buying a small business. They were prepared for the seller, of course, and their contents are available to him. But the buyer, too, should be aware during the early stages of a buy-sell transaction of the information contained in financial statements.

**Balance sheet and income statement.** The balance sheet is a statement of the financial position of the business at a given moment in time. The income statement is a summary of the revenue and expenses of the business during a specified period of time. These financial statements show only the past results of the company's transactions. The results of future operations may or may not be similar.

Balance sheets and income statements in themselves contain important information, but they are most useful when a professional accountant makes a detailed analysis of them. A complete analysis includes a review of the manner in which the statements were prepared, and perhaps also a review of the records and control features of the accounting system. This is especially important because the financial statements of smaller companies are not usually as professionally prepared as the statements for larger companies. An accountant should be brought into the picture as early as possible.

**Audited statements.** In many buy-sell transactions, the statements are supplied by the seller, but the buyer reserves the right to conduct an audit of the seller's records.  Or the buyer insists that the seller *warrant* his financial statements.  Warranty of financial statements by the seller should be accepted with caution, however, because there does not seem to be any uniform definition of the term warranty.

If the seller's financial statements are prepared by an independent accountant, the statements should show whether they were (1) prepared after an audit of the seller's accounts, or (2) prepared from the seller's records without verification by audit.  If they were prepared without verification by audit, they may be quite similar or even identical to statements that would have been prepared by the seller's own bookkeeper.  If they were prepared after an audit, they should include a statement of the accountant's opinion.

Financial statements prepared without such an audit may or may not reflect the financial position or results of operation of the company.  Most small companies do not have their records audited annually, but without an audit it is impossible to tell how accurate the statements really are.

**Other considerations.**  The buyer should request balance sheets and income statements for at least three and preferably ten years.  If the seller is a new company, financial statements for the entire life of the company should be requested.

Other financial statements are sometimes available to the buyer.  These include such items as statements of cost of goods manufactured (if the seller is a manufacturer), application of funds, and variances from the budget.

Another point the buyer should consider is the cut-off period for the financial statements.  The statements may have been cut off during the low period of the sales cycle or during the high period.  This has some bearing on the financial position reflected in the statements.

**Income-tax returns.**  If independent accountants did not prepare the financial statements, the seller may or may not have complete sets of statements.  He should have at least an annual income statement—that much is required for income tax purposes.  If the seller is a partnership or corporation, the tax returns should have balance sheets attached.  If the seller is a sole proprietorship, tax returns will not show balance sheet data.

Financial statements prepared for income tax purposes may be very different from statements prepared in conformity with generally accepted accounting principles.  Those prepared for tax returns are designed to present the desired tax position in compliance with the income tax laws.  Financial statements for nontax purposes have different objectives and therefore may reflect different financial information.

The buyer should request copies of tax returns for at least three and preferably ten years or, if the seller is a new company, for the life of the company.  The tax returns are more important in buying the stock of a corporation than in buying the assets of a corporation, partnership, or sole proprietorship.

The corporation is an income tax entity; the partnership and sole proprietorship are not. A partnership is required to file income tax information returns but does not pay income taxes as a company—the taxable income is passed on to the partners, and they pay the tax as individuals. No tax return is filed for a sole proprietorship, but the income statement is included as a part of the sole proprietor's personal income tax return.

The buyer should find out which tax returns have been examined by the Internal Revenue Service and which have not. This is particularly important if the buyer is purchasing the stock of a corporation. If a corporation with an operating loss is being acquired, the loss might have value and the buyer should satisfy himself as to whether this net operating loss can be utilized. In many instances, the only information available to the buyer is that found with the income tax returns.

**Other internal sources.** The financial statements are usually supported by detailed analyses of selected accounts. This might include some of the following items:

1. Sales may have been analyzed by customer, product, division, salesman, time period, and any other classifications necessary.
2. Purchases may be classified according to product, time period, territory, supplier, or other classification.
3. If the seller is a manufacturer, he may have cost-control reports that include analyses of material costs, labor costs, overhead cost, scrap sales, spoiled and defective goods, and other items.
4. There may be a cash-flow statement—perhaps incorporated with the analysis of collections of accounts receivable—and even a projection of cash requirements.
5. The seller may have a regular budgeting program with projections into the near or distant future. It is common practice for the buyer to require the seller to make a projection for at least a year from the date of the proposed transfer. The buyer should insist on this projection.

**Other external sources.** The seller's suppliers are an excellent source of information for the buyer. They can provide records showing the volume of purchases by the seller. This information may be difficult to get in some cases, particularly if the seller informs his suppliers that it is proprietary information.

Another source of data is the seller's banker. A banker can supply information about cash position, line of credit, and other fiscal data. He may, however, be reluctant to release this information.

The seller may have filed payroll-tax reports, sales-tax reports, excise tax reports, ICC reports, or any of many other government reports. Some of this information is available to the buyer.

The buyer may seek information about the seller from credit agencies or credit associations related to trade associations. Usually, the buyer must have a contact with these agencies in order to get the information, but there are many ways to get reports about the seller.

A number of organizations, including trade associations, supply information about industry averages. These averages are very important to the buyer for judging the effectiveness of the seller.

## SOURCES OF LEGAL INFORMATION

The prospective buyer of a business must assume responsibility for checking out possible legal problems that may affect the value of the business and his decision on whether to buy. Legal opinions are the responsibility of the buyer's attorney, of course. But the attorney must often rely on the buyer as his source of internal information about the business—information he will need in making his legal recommendations. It is therefore important that the buyer have some ideas as to what his attorney will expect of him.

As in any sale, the basic legal problem in the purchase of a business involves the transfer of ownership or title to property. How serious the title problem is varies from one business to another, depending on the nature of the assets being purchased.

If the transaction involved only the transfer of a good title to a single piece of real estate, it would be a simple matter. But buying and selling a business typically involves a conglomeration of assets-inventory, fixtures, vehicles, and equipment, all of *which are movable*, and assorted contract rights under leases, sales agreements, patent licenses, and so on, which are *intangible*.

Each asset has its own ownership aspects. It is important to ask this question about each asset: "Is the buyer getting the ownership rights he assumes he is getting?"

An even more careful investigation from a legal point of view is called for when the buyer either assumes liabilities or purchases the stock of a corporation. Even the risk of potential liabilities, those that may occur in the future because of past events, may be reduced by proper investigation.

Both internal and external sources of legal information are usually available to the buyer and his attorney for examination. The buyer should not rely solely on the oral statements of the seller as to important aspects of the business. Any statements of the seller that have to be accepted without support from other sources should be incorporated into the buy-sell contract as warranties.

How much information should a buyer obtain about a business before legally committing himself to purchase? There is no easy answer to this question, but the buyer should realize that the legal risk he assumes is about inversely proportional to the amount of information he has obtained about the business.

**Internal sources of legal information.** Among the internal sources of legal information are copies of contracts, evidences of ownership, and organizational documents. Personally examining the business premises and questioning the seller and his employees may be the only source of information about some assets.

**Contracts.** The buyer is concerned with the rights and obligations created by outstanding contracts with suppliers, customers, creditors, employees, lessors, and the like. The buyer often wants any contractual rights of the seller that are needed in order to maintain the business as a going concern. In legal terminology, the transfer of contractual rights is called an assignment. Generally, a contractual right is assignable, but the original contract may expressly prohibit its assignment.

Such negative provisions are common in printed forms of leases. Loan agreements may prohibit the sale or other change in ownership of substantially all the business assets. Or they may call for speeding up payment of the principal if the assets do change hands. The buyer should get copies of important contracts and review them to determine whether they have nonassignment clauses.

A contract may be nonassignable, however, even without such a provision. This would be true if the contract rights are coupled with obligations of a personal character. For example, the seller's credit arrangements with a supplier are not assignable because they are based on the seller's reputation as a credit risk. A contract for the manufacture of certain goods may not be assignable because the customer, when he signed the contract, knew and was relying on the superior workmanship of the seller. Likewise, a supplier's agreement to supply the seller's manufacturing requirements of certain raw materials may not be assignable because the requirements of the new owner are uncertain.

Both buyer and seller should remember that third parties will, in all probability, have to be reckoned with in carrying out the buy-sell transaction. If the buyer must have a contract that is nonassignable and the seller is not a corporation, the only solution is to renegotiate the contract. In the case of a corporate seller, it may be possible to make the transaction a purchase of stock rather than assets.

Following are some recommendations to the buyer about specific types of contracts and documents:

1. *Copies of real-estate leases* should be obtained from the seller and examined for provisions relating to amount of rent, terms of payment, expiration, renewal, subleasing, repair, improvement, insurance, and so on. The buyer should pay special attention to the duration of the lease. If the term remaining is too short, either the lease should be renegotiated *before the purchase* or an option should be obtained to renew for an additional period. Leases for a specific term are often misleading because of provisions granting to one or both of the parties the right to terminate the lease by giving a stated period of notice.

2. *Copies of patent, trademark, trade-name, and copyright registrations* should be obtained in order to determine the legal status of the right and whether it can be transferred.

3. The main subject of the buy-sell transaction may be a *contract right to be the exclusive agent, dealer, or distributor* of a product or line of products, or the right under license to use a patented process, trade name, or trademark. Copies of such contracts should be obtained to determine the precise nature of the right, its limitations, and the seller's power to transfer. Particular attention should be given to the exclusiveness of the right.

Copies of employment contracts and union agreement should be studied for terms relating to compensation, working conditions, duration of employment, termination, pension and profit-sharing plans, stock option, insurance programs, and so on. The buyer should find out whether key employees will remain with the company if the ownership changes hands. If the employees have not been organized, he should inquire about possible activities of union organizers among them.

4. The buyer should study *outstanding sale and purchase contracts*. Particular attention should be given to trade-credit, discount, installment-payment, and security requirements. The buyer should get from the seller copies of conditional sales contracts, purchase-money chattel mortgages, chattel leases, lease-purchase agreements, consignment contracts, and sale-on-approval and sale-or-return contracts to which the seller is a party.

5. The buyer should also get from the seller copies of *financing agreements* between the seller and commercial banks, finance companies, and other third-party lenders. Attention should be given to the term of the loan, repayment provisions, interest rate, finance charges, insurance requirements, acceleration provisions, security requirements and recourse rights. The buyer will generally have to make his own financing arrangements, but the seller's experience in financing the business will often suggest what the buyer can expect if he purchases the business.

6. A buyer's willingness to purchase *accounts receivable*, apart from his financial ability to do so, should depend on their apparent collectibility. The buyer should require the seller to submit a complete list according to the age of the accounts. Inquiry may disclose factors other than the statute of limitations that would prevent collection.

7. A study of the seller's *insurance policies* may give the buyer some insight into the availability, adequacy, and cost of coverage of such risks as liability arising from manufacture or sale of defective products, liability to customers for injuries sustained on the premises, liability for property damage and bodily injury arising from negligent operation of company vehicles, liability to employees for injury under workmen's compensation laws, and property hazards such as fire, windstorm, and theft. The buyer should be aware, however, that the premiums rated based on the seller's experience may not be available to him.

**Evidences of ownership.** The buyer should get from the seller a certified abstract of title for each parcel of real estate involved in the transaction. The abstract should be examined by the buyer's attorney. In addition to disclosing any defects in the title, examination of the abstract and the abstractor's certificate will usually show whether there are any unreleased mortgages, judgment liens, mechanics' liens, tax liens, or unpaid real estate taxes and special assessments.

The seller should be asked to show evidence of his ownership of principal items of personal property in the form of bills of sales, receipts, assignments, motor vehicle title certificates, and so on. Such evidence will not prove that there are no recorded liens against the property, but lack of it should alert the buyer to the possibility that personal property in the physical possession of the seller is rented, leased, borrowed, or delivered on consignment.

**Organizational documents.** If the seller is a partnership, the buyer should get a copy of the partnership agreement. If there is no written agreement, he should find out who the partners are and whether authority exists to sell the business assets.

If the seller is a corporation, the buyer should get a certified copy of the resolution of the shareholders authorizing the sale of the corporate assets. In a corporation stock transaction, he should get a copy of all organizational documents. These documents include the articles of incorporation and amendments to it, the corporate bylaws, stock-transfer books, and minutes of shareholders' and directors' meetings.

**Observation and inquiry.** Certain types of legal problems can be uncovered only by observation and inquiry. This is true of mechanics' liens. The basis for mechanics' liens against real estate may exist even though no lien is on file. If the buyer learns that there has been repair or construction within the allowable period for filing mechanics' liens, he should check with the contractors and suppliers to find out whether they have been paid.

The real estate should be examined to make sure that it complies with building codes and other ordinances. It is advisable also to have the real estate surveyed to determine whether buildings are located within boundaries in compliance with setback lines, whether adjoining buildings or driveways are encroaching upon the property, and so on.

**External sources of legal information.** Among the more common external sources of legal information are city, county, and state public records, government agencies, and third parties with whom the seller has had dealings.

**Office of record.** A down-to-date abstract of title will ordinarily disclose the existence of liens against a particular parcel of real estate, but liens against personal property of the seller can be discovered only by a search of the office record. Separate filing systems may exist for chattel mortgages, conditional sales contracts, trust receipts, assignment of accounts receivable, and so on. Each of these files must be checked.

A record search will not disclose what items of personal property in possession of the seller have been rented, leased, borrowed, or delivered on consignment. Also, lien notations on motor-vehicle title certificates may take precedence over recording—it depends on state statutes.

**Tax authorities.** Investigation is especially important where the buyer is purchasing the stock of the seller or assuming liability for the payment status of Federal, state, and local income taxes, Social Security and income withholding taxes, Federal excise taxes, state and local taxes, license taxes, and real- and personal-property taxes. Have tax returns been reviewed and approved by the taxing authority?

**Zoning ordinances, planning agencies, building codes.** The buyer should check zoning ordinances and building codes to determine the existence of nonconforming land uses or violations of building codes. Comprehensive zoning plans may provide for steps to be taken toward elimination of nonconforming uses. This can be done by prohibiting alteration or enlarging of buildings or by requiring liquidation of nonconforming use within a prescribed period of time.

City, county, or metropolitan planning agencies and engineering departments should be consulted about the existence of master plans for future re-zoning, redevelopment, and street or highway changes. Highway relocation, limited street or highway access, elimination of on-street parking or changes in the composition of the immediate market area may be enough to destroy the business as a going concern. City annexation policies may be important to businesses located in the suburbs. The cost of planned improvements may affect the buyer's decision.

**Court records.** The buyer should find out from court records whether judgment liens exist against real-estate involved in the buy-sell transaction and whether lawsuits are pending that may retroactively result in the attachment of liens. This is of particular concern to the buyer who either assumes business liabilities or purchases the stock of a corporation. Not only litigation costs and liability must be considered, but also the impact of the publicity on the goodwill of the business.

Even if a court record search is negative, future litigations may arise out of events of the past several years, such as motor-vehicle accidents, manufacture or sale of defective products, accidents on the premises involving customers or employees, breach of contract, violation of wage-and-hour laws, and so on. The best protection is to inquire of the seller and of employees who have been intimately concerned with the business.

## KEEP FINANCIAL COMMITMENTS REALISTIC
Careful attention must be given to the financial commitments required for the purchase. Whether you obtain a loan from a bank, a business broker, or simply agree to make fixed payments to the present owners, you need to know that the

company will generate sufficient profits to meet your commitments. If you are required to make monthly payments, pay special attention to the seasonal or other fluctuations that may be apparent in the company's statements. Even though the business earns enough annually to cover repayments, you must know where each monthly payment is coming from. Otherwise, for your safety a quarterly or semi-annual repayment plan must be negotiated. And before any final arrangements have been made, get the help of a qualified attorney. Never sign any papers until your lawyer has scrutinized every detail.

## WHAT YOU NEED TO KNOW ABOUT FRANCHISING

> "A full time income with only part time effort. Modest investment acquires exclusive franchise territory yielding unlimited earnings potential. No prior experience necessary. We provide you with the intensive training and supervision to guarantee instant success."

Franchising ads are currently appearing in large numbers throughout the country. While most of them offer legitimate business opportunities, some of them do not. Advertisements like the one above which promise *get rich quick* schemes with little effort at no risk, have a deceptive ring about them and frequently lead to disappointment and sometimes to financial disaster.

While franchising has been a part of the legitimate American economy for many years, it has recently experienced a tremendous growth in popularity. The term *franchise boom* has been coined to describe this rapid growth phenomenon which currently accounts for annual sales in the neighborhood of $100 billion.

One of the main reasons for this growth is that franchising has caught the imagination of the small investor by providing him the opportunity to become self-employed with certain distinct advantages. For instance, the risk of failure can be minimized when the franchisee starts in business under the image of a successful corporate name and trademark and when he receives helpful training and management assistance from experienced personnel of the franchisor.

Unfortunately, however, all franchising arrangements do not produce happy results. In other words, franchising does not guarantee success as some promoters would like you to believe. Quite to the contrary, franchising arrangements can produce severe financial loss, and on occasion have caused franchisees to forfeit their total life savings.

Some of these franchisees have experienced disappointment and frustration by falling victim to a deceptive franchising scheme. Perhaps their interest in a franchising venture was initially aroused by an ad similar in nature to the *get rich quick* ad that appears at the beginning of this section. In any event, the rapid growth of franchising has attracted a certain number of unprincipled operators who seek to take advantage of anyone they can. Their methods of operation and techniques are too varied to detail here, but their objectives are the same, i.e., to take your money and give little or nothing in return. For instance, an unscrupulous promoter may, after making wild claims and promises, sell you nothing more than worthless equipment and a catchy business name. Once he receives payment he doesn't care whether you succeed or fail; in fact, contrary to his assurances, you may never see him again.

Other schemes associated with franchising assume more of an air of legitimacy. A letter from a New York woman illustrates an investor's frustration after being bilked by one of these arrangements:

> "My husband and I invested $15,000 of borrowed money in a phony (restaurant) franchise. . . . My husband is working 14 hours a day 7 days a week for $50.00 per week. I work 8 hours a day for no salary. There is not enough money for my salary. I moved from my home in the Bronx to help cut down on salaries so the business could survive. However, this is not enough; the spot just doesn't bring in enough people. He (franchisor) refuses to take the business back and wants 2% royalty which makes it hard for me to sell the business to anyone else. He has you invest between $6,000 to $10,500 as the initial investment which he pockets and obtains loans for you for the building equipment. . . ."

In this instance, in addition to grossly overstating the earning potential of the franchise, the franchisor misrepresented nearly every other aspect of the franchise agreement. The cost of the franchise was much higher than represented and discount supplies were not available as indicated. Moreover, the franchise was not a nationally known chain and the franchisor did not provide planned promotions or helpful training and supervision as he had promised. This is only a sample of the types of franchising deceptions in existence today.

Other franchise arrangements have produced unhappy results either because the franchisee did not have sufficient facts upon which to make a sound

"It's delicious -- how much is the franchise?"

Reprinted with permission of *The Wall Street Journal* (Cartoon Features Syndicate).

evaluation of the franchise prior to entering into the agreement, or because he did not fully understand the terms of the franchise contract with its investment requirements, fees, sometimes oppressive cancellation clauses and various other restrictions.  Too often and too late, franchisees have come to the distressing realization that the franchise agreement can be used by the franchisor as an instrument of repression.

Because the decision to become a franchisee may involve the investment of a lifetime of savings and effort, every prospective franchisee must carefully examine all aspects of a franchise agreement before becoming legally involved. By taking this precaution, the likelihood of financial disaster which may otherwise result from deceptive schemes or ignorance can be greatly reduced.

To help you evaluate a franchise opportunity which may be of interest, it is suggested that you view the proposal in the light of the following points.  If, after this examination, you find areas of uncertainty, it may be well for you to resolve them to your full satisfaction before deciding to embark upon an adventure in franchising.

### WHO IS THE FRANCHISOR?

If the franchisor is well known, has a good reputation, and has an obviously successful franchising operation, you can naturally proceed with greater confidence than if little is known about him.

In either event, however, you should find out everything you can about the operation including the number of years it has been in existence, whether the franchisor has all the successful franchisees he claims to have and whether he has a reputation for honesty and fair dealing with his franchise holders.  It is suggested that personal contact with franchisees is an excellent way to learn about the franchisor.  Obtain the names and addresses, therefore, of a representative number of franchisees, travel to see them, and interview them regarding all aspects of the operation.  In addition to gaining valuable information concerning the franchisor, this will undoubtedly provide you with an opportunity to view samples of the franchise products, equipment, advertising materials, etc., and to obtain profit data and other pertinent information reflective of the operation.  Be wary of a franchisor who does not freely give you the names and addresses of his franchisees.  To assure that you obtain a representative list of franchisees, ask for all franchisees operating in the particular geographical areas in which you plan to make personal contact.

The financial standing and business reputation of the franchisor would also be of utmost interest to you.  In this regard, sources such as Dun and Bradstreet, and the Better Business Bureau should be contacted.

Occasionally, a dishonest promoter will use a franchise name and trade mark deceptively similar to that of a well known franchisor.  Be certain that you are dealing with the particular franchise organization you are in fact interested in and that the individual representing this franchise has authority to act in its behalf.

Be skeptical of franchisors whose major activity is the sale of franchises and whose profit is primarily derived from these sales or from the sale of franchise equipment. This may be the tip-off on an unscrupulous operator. In any event, it appears that such an organization would tend to exhibit far less interest or concern in the continuing success of its franchisees than what would be present in a sound franchise operation.

Remember, the more you learn about the franchisor and his operation before making a decision about the franchise, the less likely you will become involved in a situation that you will regret later.

### WHAT ABOUT THE FRANCHISE COMMODITY?

You should determine the length of time the commodity has been marketed and whether it has been a successful promotion during this time. Is it a proven product or service, and not a gimmick?

Ask yourself whether you are genuinely interested in selling the particular product or service and whether it will have an adequate market in your territory at prices you will have to charge. Will it compare in price and performance with similar products of your potential competitors?

You should also carefully weigh future consumer demand for the commodity. Be skeptical of items which are untested in the market place or which are obviously fads. It may be helpful to you in assessing future market potential to consider whether the commodity is a staple, luxury, or fad item. Generally speaking, the demand for luxury items will tend to be more uncertain than the demand for staples since demand for the former is more apt to be reflective of prevailing economic conditions.

If a product rather than a service is involved, you should be certain that it is safe, that it meets existing quality standards, and that there are no restrictions upon its use. Find out if the product is protected by patent or liability insurance and if the same protection would be afforded you as a franchisee. If the product is to be manufactured by someone other than you, identify the manufacturer and ascertain the manner in which your cost for the item will be established. If a guarantee is involved determine your responsibilities and obligations thereunder as a franchisee.

Finally, would you be compelled under the franchise agreement to sell any new products or services which may be subsequently introduced by the franchisor after you have opened the business? On the other hand, would you be permitted under the agreement to sell products and services other than the franchise commodities, if you would desire to do so at some future date?

### WHAT IS THE COST OF THE FRANCHISE?

In some instances, promoters, in attempting to portray a franchise opportunity in its most favorable light, fail to clearly spell out the total cost of the franchise. The franchise promotion may only refer to the cash outlay that would be needed to purchase the franchise with no mention being made that it is only a down payment or that other charges and assessments may be levied incidentally to the operation of the franchise.

In assessing the total cost of the franchise, therefore, you should determine whether any balance is due over and above the down payment. How is the balance to be financed? (Interest rates would, of course, be a concern to you.) You should also clearly establish what is purchased with the down payment. Is it in whole or in part only a franchise fee? If so, is the franchise fee justified when considering the business reputation you will have purchased with it? Did the down payment purchase any other equity, such as the building, etc?

You will also want to know where to purchase equipment and fixtures necessary for opening the business. If these are purchased through the franchisor, are his prices comparable with competitive prices for these items on the open market?

What about supplies? Frequently, franchisors will attempt to secure income on a continuing basis through the sale of supplies to their franchisees. If this is part of the proposed arrangement, how will the price of these supplies be established? What assurance do you have that the price will be reasonable or competitive? Does the franchise agreement prohibit you from purchasing these supplies from other sources? Could you obtain identical supplies from another source at a lower price?

Another method franchisors use to charge franchisees on a continuing basis is the assessment of royalties based upon a percentage of gross sales. Be careful that these royalties are not out of line with the sales volume and projected net profits for the franchise.

Moreover, you should not overlook the possibility that franchisors also occasionally assess franchisees an additional percentage of gross sales to cover the franchisee's share of advertising costs.

Finally, in evaluating the franchise costs in the light of your financial position, you should also consider the additional miscellaneous funds and operating capital that will be needed to get the business underway and to sustain it during the early weeks and months when profits will undoubtedly be small and expenses unusually high.

### WHAT PROFITS CAN REASONABLY BE EXPECTED?

There is no question that many franchise arrangements provide excellent income producing opportunities. It would be ridiculous to assume, however, that all franchises yield the fantastic profits sometimes promised in franchise promotions or *documented* in human interest stories about franchising. They don't, and in fact many of them produce profits far less than those represented by franchise promoters. Indeed, when purely deceptive promotions are involved, debts rather than fantastic profits are generated.

Since *anticipated profits* are frequently the overriding motivation for entering a franchise business, promoter representations concerning earning potential or projected net profits should not be taken for granted. You should scrutinize these representations carefully, verify them for accuracy, and satisfy yourself that the figures presented are realistic and can in fact be attained by you. Ask to see certified profit figures of franchisees operating on a level of activity you can reasonably expect. You will, of course, in your personal contacts with franchisees, quiz them regarding the financial rewards they have experienced through their respective enterprises. Always remember to evaluate the profit figures and comments of these individuals in the light of the territory and size of operation you have under consideration.

### WHAT TRAINING AND MANAGEMENT ASSISTANCE WILL BE PROVIDED BY THE FRANCHISOR?

Most franchisors purport to train their franchisees. The type and extent of training varies broadly, however, from perhaps one day's indoctrination on the one hand to a more lengthy, meaningful training program on the other. Naturally, when the franchisor provides good training opportunities, the franchisee enjoys brighter prospects for survival and prosperity. Such training will tend to enable him to cope with the specific tasks he must perform in the business.

Frequently, franchise promoters use representations such as "No prior experience necessary." In some instances, however, contrary to the falsely reassuring representations of the promoter, the training provided is inadequate and fails to overcome the inexperience of the franchisee. These circumstances produce unhappy and disappointing results.

It is very important, therefore, that you clearly understand the specific nature of the training that will be provided before making a decision about the franchise. Will the training be more extensive than receiving a manual of instructions or hearing a few lectures? What is the length of training and where must you go to receive it? Who will pay your expenses during the training period? Will the training include an opportunity to observe and perhaps work with a successful franchisee for a meaningful period of time? Do you honestly feel that after taking the training offered you will be capable of operating this franchise successfully?

Continuing management assistance after the business has been established may also be promised by the franchisor. The nature of this assistance is occasionally specified in the franchise agreement, but more often than not only a broad general commitment is included. When being specific, the franchisor may promise to assist with a management or employee training program, an advertising program, merchandising ideas, or in any number of other ways. Here too, it is important to find out precisely the nature of the assistance you can expect to receive and its cost to you. For example, if advertising aid is promised, will it be in the form of handbills, brochures, signs, radio or newspaper advertising etc? If you would be required to participate in a franchisor-sponsored promotion program by contributing a percentage of your profits to an *advertising fund*, what specific advertising benefits can you anticipate and at what dollar cost?

Some franchisors represent that their franchisees will receive management assistance through periodic visits to the business establishment of the franchisee by supervisory personnel of the franchisor. You should find out the specific nature of the assistance offered during these visits and the frequency with which they occur. What assurance do you have that such personnel will be available for consultation in times of crisis or when unusual problems arise?

## WHAT ABOUT THE FRANCHISE TERRITORY?

The franchise territory is a critical factor to consider in evaluating a prospective venture. Following are some questions which may help you to assess this aspect of the franchise.

What specific territory is being offered? Is it clearly defined? What is its potential? Do you have a choice of territories? What competition would you meet in marketing the commodity in the designated territory today? How about five years from now? Has the franchisor represented that a market survey has been made of the proposed territory. If so, who prepared it? Ask him for a copy of it and read it carefully. What assurance do you have that the territory you select is an exclusive territory? In other words, would you be protected from the possibility of the franchisor selling additional franchises within the territory at a later date? On the other hand, are there any limitations upon you in the event you desire to open additional outlets in the territory, or even another territory, at some future time? Has the specific business site within the territory been selected? If not, how will this be decided?

## WHAT PROVISIONS AFFECTING TERMINATION, TRANSFER, AND RENEWAL ARE CONTAINED IN THE FRANCHISE AGREEMENT?

Inasmuch as oppressive termination provisions can cause unexpected and sometimes severe financial loss to a franchisee, careful consideration should be given to this aspect of the agreement.

As an example, some franchise agreements provide that at the end of the contract term, or during the contract term if in the opinion of the franchisor certain conditions have not been met, the franchisor has the absolute right to terminate the agreement. The contract generally provides the franchisor with an option to repurchase the franchise if he desires. If the franchisor should terminate the agreement under these circumstances and if the contract does not provide a means whereby a fair market price for the franchise can be established, it may be possible for the franchisor to repurchase the business at an arbitrarily low and unfair price.

On occasion, franchisors have gone so far as to include a provision in the agreement to the effect that the repurchase price should not exceed the original franchise fee. This means that after a franchisee may have expended considerable effort and funds building the business into a profitable enterprise, he may be faced with the unhappy prospect of having to sell it back to the franchisor at a price no greater than he paid for it years earlier. Under such an obviously unfair provision, the franchisee would not be compensated for the good will or increased equity which he contributed to the business.

Thus, it is important that you, as a prospective franchisee, are aware of the conditions under which the agreement could be terminated and that you clearly understand your rights in the event of termination. You should determine whether the contract extends to the franchisor the right of cancellation for almost any reason or must there be *good cause*? Beware of contracts which, under the threat of cancellation, impose unreasonable obligations such as a minimum monthly purchase of goods or services from the franchisor or unrealistic sales quotas. How would the value of the franchise be determined in the event of termination? Under what circumstances could you terminate the agreement and at what cost to you? Does the contract contain a restrictive covenant which would prohibit you from engaging in a competitive business in the franchise territory in the event termination occurs?

It is equally important that you have a clear understanding of any contract provisions dealing with your ability to transfer or renew the franchise. What restrictions would there be in the event you desired to transfer or sell the franchise? What would happen to the franchise in the event of death? Under what circumstances would you be able to renew the franchise agreement at the end of the contract term?

Remember, a good franchise opportunity should permit you to own and build an equity interest in your franchise which in turn you can sell for whatever value the franchise may have realized under your direction. Some reputable franchisors who have established fair and permanent relationships with their franchisees have made provision for an arbitration clause which allows for a fair evaluation of the franchisee's contribution in the event of termination. In this manner the franchisee will not only recoup his initial investment but will also realize a profit on the sale of whatever goodwill he may have generated in the business.

### IS THE FRANCHISE ATTRACTIVE BECAUSE IT CARRIES THE NAME OF A WELL-KNOWN PERSONALITY?

Some concern has recently been expressed to the effect that franchising may be bursting at the seams with *name* personalities. This is not to suggest that franchises identified with personalities are unworthy of consideration. The important thing to keep in mind is the degree of participation the personality brings to the business. Is he just a figurehead with no actual capital investment of his own in the enterprise? Will he make substantial personal contributions of time and effort to promote the venture to the mutual benefit of all franchisees in the organization? What assurance do you have that he will make personal appearances at your business if such have been promised? Does this personality have a name of lasting value in identifying your franchise to the consuming public? How sound is the basic franchise operation when viewed apart from the prominent name?

## IS THE PROMOTER PRIMARILY INTERESTED IN SELLING DISTRIBUTORSHIPS?

Be wary of promoters who are primarily interested in selling distributorships, probably for some new wonder product. Exaggerated income promises are common in these promotions. Generally, according to the promotional plan, the distributor is to recruit sub-distributors or salesmen who are supposed to sell the product, usually by door-to-door sales. Theoretically, a large portion of the distributor's profits are to be derived from a percentage of his sub-distributors' sales. Unfortunately, however, distributors and those subdistributors he successfully recruits frequently find to their mutual distress after making sizable investments of money, time and effort, that they reap little profit and are "stuck" with a large stock of virtually unsaleable product.

## IS IT A ROUTE SERVICING PROMOTION?

Be alert for deceptive route servicing promotions. Typically, promotions of this kind are characterized by misleading representations (frequently appearing in newspaper want ads) concerning exaggerated profits and the availability of quality routes. If equipment, such as vending machines, is to be purchased in connection with the promotion, it may be poorly made and highly priced. Compare the equipment and prices with those of reputable manufacturers. Carefully check out the validity of all statements made in these promotions, and remember, promoters promises of assistance in locating quality routes after the contract is signed are usually unfulfilled.

## IN SUMMARY, WHAT STEPS CAN YOU TAKE TO PROTECT YOURSELF AS A PROSPECTIVE FRANCHISEE?

Don't be rushed into signing a contract or any other document relating to a franchise promotion. Be wary of pressure for an immediate contract closing for the alleged purpose of precluding others who are supposedly waiting to take the territory if you delay. Don't make any deposits or down payments "to hold a franchise open" or "to demonstrate good faith" or for any other reason, unless you are absolutely certain about your decision to go ahead with the franchise arrangement. Remember, reputable firms don't engage in high-pressure sales tactics.

Find out all you can about the franchise. View the franchise proposal in the light of this discussion and resolve all areas of uncertainty before making a decision. Ask the franchisor for some names and addresses of his franchisees. No reputable franchisor will object to giving you this information. *Personally* contact a representative number of these franchisees and discuss all aspects of the operation. Have they realized all the promises made to them by the franchisor? Has the franchisor met his contractual obligations?

Call your local Better Business Bureau. Ask for a business responsibility report on the franchisor-promoter. The Bureau's report may help you determine if the promoter is legitimate and if complaints have been received from others. If your local Better Business Bureau has no information on the franchisor, contact the National Better Business Bureau, 230 Park Avenue, New York, New York 10017.

Be certain that all terms of the agreement are set forth in a written contract which is not oppressive in its requirements upon you or unfairly weighted in the favor of the franchisor.

Consult a lawyer and have him review all aspects of the agreement before you sign the contract or any papers relating to the franchise. This may turn out to be the soundest investment you could have made.

## FEEDBACK 17

**A.**  Assume that you have an idea for a product or service which you think is worth forming a small business to market.

- Who will buy your product? You can probably eliminate some ideas on this basis alone; for example, making wine racks for people in an area where wine drinking is unheard of is obviously futile and nonprofitable.

- Who is your competition? Is a similar, or even superior product offered where you propose to set up your business?

- Even if you have a unique and superior product, which you can market at a reasonable price, will you have to create the demand your success requires?

**B.**  Does your experience and education match up to the challenge of running your own business? How will you handle the problems which follow:

- A potential financial backer says you lack experience.

- A supplier demands cash on delivery, because you haven't established credit.

- A union organizer wants to represent the workmen you will need in your business.

- Your new firm "takes off" and has a very encouraging sales picture after three months of operation, but your cash reserves are not sufficient to replace your inventory.

**C.**  At the very core of plans for establishing a new business is the problem of raising "start up" money. If your idea needs cash to become reality, how would you approach the problem in your community?

- What are the sources of information about requirements, collateral, and repayment where you hope to start your business?

- How can you arrange for sufficient collateral to put up against a proposed loan?
- If you are not immediately successful in your venture, will your initial or subsequent loan let you ride out the slow period so that you give yourself the best possible chance of success?

**D.** Are you presently training and educating yourself toward success in a small business?

- At your present job, are you constantly studying the way things are done and the decisions which preceded the work itself? How would you manage your business, based on this experience?
- Do you analyze current methods, not just to criticize them, but to improve them? List three proposed improvements and the cost of each. Will the costs be paid for by greater productivity?
- Are you learning about the volume, traffic, employee scheduling, space requirements and hidden costs, for just a few of the important problems you, as a businessman will have, at your present job?
- Have you determined what makes a success in your potential business?
- Have you learned why people have failed in similar businesses?

## DISCUSSION QUESTIONS

1. Everyone knows that starting a small business can be hazardous. Why is this so?
2. Why is it that some people may be quite unsuited to running their own business?
3. *Fortune* magazine publishes a yearly listing of the country's 500 largest corporations. Take a look at the most recent issue. What chance do you think small businessmen have of competing with these giants of industry?
4. What are the unique advantages and satisfactions that come from owning and managing your own enterprise?
5. A person may be very interested in a particular type of business but very inexperienced in that area. How can such a person gain the experience and background needed before he embarks on his own business?
6. Why might your chances for succeeding in a small business be much better than what the averages show?
7. Does the trend toward higher family incomes improve or diminish the opportunities for small concerns? Why?
8. What would you look for in examining a franchise opportunity?
9. An existing small business may be a surer bet than starting a business from scratch. Why?

10. In what ways does the government attempt to assist the small businessman? Why should the government concern itself with this area of commerce?

## CASE PROBLEM

Lynn and Craig have been friends since they were in grade school. They went all through high school together, enrolled in the same college, and were both accepted to do graduate work in business at the university. They will receive their masters this year. Lynn got married when they first entered college and has a small child. Craig is still single.

While doing undergraduate work, Lynn and Craig would often talk about the future and how they would like to open up some kind of business with each other. Now that they will be out of school soon, Lynn is getting very sceptical about starting his own business. Neither of them has had any specific experience in any field of business, and Lynn feels he would be much more secure working for an established firm. Craig, however, is still enthused about opening a business such as a men's clothing store. The two fellows have gone to Mr. Dean, chairman of the department, to talk over the situation.

a) What advantages do you suppose Mr. Dean told them about owning their business? What disadvantages?

b) What do you think Mr. Dean said about the process of starting a business? Capital? Location?

c) Why does Lynn have a different outlook than Craig? What benefits will Lynn get from an established firm?

d) How can Craig convince Lynn to change his mind? Should he change it? Why?

## SUGGESTED READINGS

Allen, Louis L. *Starting and Succeeding In Your Own Small Business*. New York: Grosset & Dunlap, 1968. 157 pp.

American Bankers Association. *Installment Loans to Small Business*. New York: no publisher listed, 1963. 320 pp.

Broom, H. H., and Justin G. Longenecker. *Small Business Management*. Cincinnati: South-Western Publishing Company, 1966.

Burke, William J., and Basil J. Zaloom. *Blueprint for Professional Service Corporations*. New York: Dun & Bradstreet, Business Education Division, in association with Thomas Y. Crowell, 1970. 206 pp.

Carson, Deane. *The Effect of Tight Money on Small Business Financing*. Providence: Brown University, 1963. 137 pp.

Casey, William J. *Forms of Business Agreements with Tax Ideas*. New York: Institute for Business Planning, 1965. 680 pp.

Cossman, Joseph E. *How To Get $50,000 Worth of Services Free, Each Year, From the U.S. Government*. New York: Frederick Fell, 1969. 271 pp.

Crawford, John W. *Advertising: Communications for Management.* Boston: Allyn and Bacon, 1960. 388 pp.

Fisk, McKee, and James C. Snapp. *Applied Business Law.* Cincinnati: South-Western Publishing Company, 1966. 584 pp.

Gross, Harry. *Financing for Small and Medium-Sized Businesses.* Englewood Cliffs, N.J.: Prentice-Hall, 1969. 235 pp.

Hagendorf, Stanley. *Tax Guide for Buying and Selling a Business.* Englewood Cliffs, N.J.: Prentice-Hall, 1967. 225 pp.

Hirshleifer, J. *Investment, Interest, and Capital.* Englewood Cliffs, N.J.: Prentice-Hall, 1970. 319 pp.

Hodgman, Donald R. *Commercial Bank Loan and Investment Policy.* Champaign: Bureau of Economic and Business Research, University of Illinois, 1963.

Kahm, Harold S. *101 Businesses You Can Start and Run with Less Than $1,000.* West Nyack, N.Y.: Parker, 1968. 206 pp.

Kursh, Harry. *The Franchise Boom.* Englewood Cliffs, N.J.: Prentice-Hall, 1968. 477 pp.

Lewellen, Wilbur G. *The Cost of Capital.* Belmont, Calif.: Wadsworth, 1969. 131 pp.

Maw, James Gordan. *Return on Investment: Concept and Application.* New York: American Management Association, Finance Division, 1968. 32 pp.

Robert, William J., and others. *Dillavou and Howard's Principles of Business Law.* Englewood Cliffs, N.J.: Prentice-Hall, 1967. 1074 pp.

Rosenberg, R. Robert, Ed. D., C.P.A., and Floyd L. Crank, Ph.D. *Essentials of Business Law* (Third Edition). New York: Gregg Publishing Division, McGraw-Hill, 1963. 377 pp.

Ruder, William, and Raymond Nathan. *The Businessman's Guide to Washington.* Englewood Cliffs, N.J.: Prentice-Hall, 1964. 252 pp.

Serraino, William J., and others. *Frontiers of Financial Management.* Cincinnati: South-Western Publishing Co., 1971. 462 pp.

Steinmetz, Lawrence L., John B. Kline, and Donald P. Stegall. *Managing the Small Business.* Homewood, Ill.: R. D. Irwin, 1968. 648 pp.

Vatter, William Joseph. *Operating Budgets.* Belmont, Calif.: Wadsworth, 1969. 162 pp.

# CHAPTER 18

# PROFIT OPPORTUNITIES IN REAL ESTATE

Real estate investments are potentially attractive for three compelling reasons. First, the rapid growth in population simply forces more people to compete each year for available homes, apartments, offices and land. According to Census Bureau statisticians, population, currently at about 200 million, is expected to grow to nearly 251 million by 1980; 300 million by 1990; and 361 million by the turn of the century. Second, real property values tend to keep pace with and often outdistance inflationary trends. Land located in pathways of growth has shown particularly rapid price advances. Investment annals are replete with names of those who have made fortunes in land. Thirdly, real estate tends to be a stable investment—not subject to rapid deterioration, technical obsolescence, or violent price changes.

It is little wonder then that we hear about:

a couple who purchased a vacant building lot in an attractive suburb for $8,000 and sold that same lot a year later for $11,000

a college student who spent $5,000 on two acres of raw ground on the outskirts of the city and 18 months later sold the land to a manufacturing corporation for an industrial site at a handy $4,000 gain

a young investment-minded couple who purchased 20 acres of lakeside frontage for $10,000 who five years later subdivided it, making a hefty $80,000 gain

These examples are not included to arouse your speculative appetite foolishly, nor to imply that all real estate investment is profitable. But they are intended to show that there are many interesting real estate speculations to be had by people who know how to recognize a good deal when they see one; and for people who have money set aside so they can back up their judgment with action.

This chapter describes some of the traps and tangles that may ensnare the unwary investor. It also looks at the general characteristics of real estate—land, income property, investment companies, syndicates, and trusts. Finally, there are action plans showing how you can get started in a real estate investment program and suggesting ways in which real estate may be financed.

## THE "WHEELER-DEALERS" AND THEIR DEALS

No matter where you live, you can find a "sure-fire" way to "cash in quick" on some magic real estate investment—at least that is what the land hucksters would have you believe. To be sure, there are all sorts of real estate schemes—enough to fill many books. Here are just a couple of examples:

*Free Lots*: An enterprising real estate man purchased several thousand acres of worthless desert land for $5 an acre. This "sharpie" promoter went from state to state selling one-quarter acre lots which he billed as "ranchettes" with a price tag of $500 each. He would set himself up in a swank downtown hotel, and advertise heavily in the classified columns inviting people to investigate his fine lots—all without cost or obligation, naturally. He didn't really hope to sell the lots for $500, although to his surprise he actually did find a number of willing buyers. Instead, his game was to "give" the lots away—for a small fee, of course. Every time a prospect came in, the promoter went into a canned sales pitch; and, before the prospect left, he was given the opportunity of filling out a "lucky-drawing card" which was placed in a big drum. Investigators were told that the lucky winners would receive a free lot. Actually, about everyone who came in became a "lucky winner." All they had to do to get their lot was to pay a small fee for "bookwork and title transfer costs." The fee was $25. Assuming that the actual recording and deed fees might amount to $5 per lot, that left a nice $75 per acre profit for the promoter—not a bad investment.

*Little Gold Mine in the West*: The scheming owner of a gold mine which had long since ceased profitable operation decided he could still make money on his mine. He subdivided the property into one-foot squares which he sold for $4 each. Needless to say, the only person who could possibly benefit from such an investment is the seller.

There is little doubt that hundreds of thousands of acres of worthless land, gravel, and swamp have been peddled to gullible investors. Fortunately, many states have now passed stiff regulations governing the subdivision and sale of land. But the buyer still must bear the responsibility of finding out for himself. Here are some precautions you should follow before buying any piece of

property—more comprehensive information will be found later in the chapter:

1. Don't ever buy without making a personal examination of the property.

2. Always check out claims and statements made by the seller—proximity to power, telephone, water and sewer facilities, etc.

3. Don't sign a real estate contract without first consulting an attorney. Know what you are signing. Be certain that you will receive a free and clear title to the property.

4. If the seller is to develop roads and other facilities on the property, make certain that part of the property's selling price is put into an escrow account dedicated to development. (An escrow account is usually supervised by a bank or other responsible third party.)

Many land development companies are operating these days building industrial parks, gigantic subdivisions, and even entire cities. While many development companies offer property having good investment potential, it is well to know what you can expect when you sign up for a "free dinner and evening of entertainment" or a "free vacation flight to visit their property." Because of the higher cost of their sales methods, you can be dead certain you will be subjected to intensive, skillful sales attempts for practically every minute these companies have you captive as their "guest." This type of atmosphere is more conducive to impulse buying than to sensibly considered investment purchase. All in all, probably the best real estate investments are those which you turn up yourself, not those offered by professional developers.

## CHARACTERISTICS OF REAL ESTATE INVESTMENTS

There are excellent investment opportunities in real estate. However, there are special characteristics of property investments which may make them suitable for some people and less suitable for others:

1. You usually have to have a fair-sized bank account to get your investment program started.

2. You usually cannot make small fractional additions regularly to your real estate holdings—as you can to a portfolio of common stocks—except when you make installment purchases.

3. Customarily, you must hold your investment for a relatively long time.

4. There may be heavy side costs related to your real estate holdings which must be paid when they arise—property taxes, special assessments for sidewalks, sewer lines, etc.

5. Real estate is not a very liquid type of investment—that is, it is not always easy to convert into cash. In case of financial emergency, you might have considerable difficulty in selling a particular piece of property at any price, let alone at a profit. To play the real estate investment game effectively, you must be able to hold the property until the right buyer comes along.

## OPPORTUNITIES IN LAND INVESTMENTS

Land, over all other types of real property, is an especially interesting speculation in a time of booming population growth, since its quantity is fixed. We can improve upon or change the usefulness of land, but we cannot alter the number of available acres. And even though our country is vast, not all land is available for private investment or commercial ownership—nearly 40 percent is owned by Federal, state, and local governments.

Presently, there seems to be ample land for almost everything. But as our population becomes more dense, there will be more and more people competing for what land there is, unquestionably forcing values to rise. The easiest way to get an idea of what will happen in the next 20 years or so is to look at what has happened in your own city or state in the past two decades. Haven't you often wanted to give yourself a good swift kick for passing up land bargains you could have acquired sometime in the past?

"Land" is a very broad term, actually not meaning very much to the professional real estate investor. He usually refers to a particular type of land, usually categorizing it as (1) raw or unimproved land; or (2) improved land—that which has curb and gutter, sewer lines, power or similar improvements. Let us examine carefully each of these particular kinds of investments.

## RAW, UNIMPROVED LAND—FARMS, GRAZING GROUND, ETC.

One phenomenon of American free enterprise is that the investor who takes the biggest risk stands to gain the most profits. This is certainly the case with the investment in unimproved land. It is undoubtedly the most speculative of land investments, but it also offers the greatest potential reward. Here are the kinds of unimproved property from which you can choose:

1. *Low-cost acreage with recreation potential.* Although it is a commonly held belief that all good investment acreage has already been bought up by big land investors, that is far from correct. Hundreds of thousands of acres still abound often selling from $25 to $200 per acre and some offering good appreciation potential. Particularly worth investigating because of their recreation value and low cost are tracts of land in the mountainous states of the West, parts of the Southern and New England states, and some island and coastal property of the Northwest.

Recreation property near the large population centers will continue to be the most attractive and consequently the most costly. However, improved travel by interstate highways and air makes even distant property which has outstanding recreation features an interesting land speculation. Much of the nation's future recreation ground is now in the hands of farmers and sheep and cattle ranchers. Most of the land they presently hold was acquired in the form of "homestead grants" from the Federal Government for a nominal cost. Consequently, it is not uncommon to find some of the more prosperous stockmen holding several thousand acres of ground—sometimes encompassing beautiful mountainous country with lakes, meadows, and forests. Farming ground, the kind that might have some recreation attraction, is usually found in smaller tracts of 40 to 60 acres.

Land which is currently being used for grazing purposes offers a special attraction to the far-sighted investor. Even though the land is valued by its owners in terms of its marginal agricultural value, the investor should consider that demand for the recreation aspects of the property may materialize. Property taxes are usually small, often negligible, because rural tax assessors usually continue to appraise the land for its agricultural value until it is developed.

2. *Higher-priced acreage near population centers.* Farmland and other acreage near the big cities will continue to boom, especially in California and Florida where there is extraordinary population and industrial growth. Finding investment-quality property in these states, however, is very difficult. Undoubtedly, such property still exists, but literally thousands of land speculators —some legitimate and some not so legitimate—have already acquired much of the acreage. Consequently, property offered for sale usually consists of small pieces of subdivided ground at extremely high prices. Where the land speculators are this intensively at work, it is well to be particularly wary before you invest.

However, being a bit cautious doesn't mean that you should give up the possibilities of finding a good buy. From all projections, the same combination of factors that have already pushed values sky-high in these areas will continue to influence values, perhaps even more intensively in the next two decades. So, if you seem to be paying a lot now, you may get back even more in ten years.

3. *Acreage with oil, gas and other sub-surface potential.* There is a great deal of land which has no obvious use now or in the foreseeable future—as far as its

surface use goes. However, many investors spend all their time looking for just this kind of property to get the oil, gas and mineral rights of the land.

Best qualified for this type of investment purchase are the professional geologists. However, others can and do make such investments, often profitable ones. Geology textbooks, U.S. Geological Services Publications as well as many state documents provide maps showing areas having some potential for sub-surface development. Make no mistake, this type of purchase is "risk" and "speculation" in its purest form. If you don't guess right, and there are no oil leases or other mineral development, you may end up holding the property for a lifetime.

What does make investment sense, however, is for a person attempting to find land with the following combination of attributes:

1. Excellent future recreation potential.
2. Oil, gas, and mineral rights intact.
3. Located in an area with a good potential for mineral exploration.
4. Some immediate income potential—grazing leases, mineral leases, timber sales, etc.

One investor leases much of his land for $2.50 an acre per year to an oil company for exploration purposes; receives $1.25 an acre yearly from a rancher who uses the property for grazing; and sells several thousand dollars worth of timber for his acreage yearly. Having paid only $40 an acre for the ground, the investor in a few years regained his entire investment and still has a slim chance of profiting from the discovery of oil, gas, or other minerals. If he does get lucky, he will be a very wealthy man. If the oil and gas explorations do not pay off, he will probably make a handy profit from subdividing his property into summer home sites. And if and when he sells the home sites, he can still keep the mineral rights—just in case something develops favorably in that direction in the future.

It should be pointed out that not all land—even though you purchase it outright—has underground or mineral rights accompanying it. Often these rights have been sold separately to other investors, or were retained by past owners in a previous transaction. Sometimes the rights are withheld by the Federal or state government, as is the case with some of the late homestead grants. The Bureau of Land Management and U.S. Geological Survey records can usually be searched to find out who holds the mineral rights. An abstract search on the property should also be made.

## IMPROVED URBAN AND SUBURBAN LAND
Somewhat less risky than raw unimproved acreage is property which has already been subdivided and made ready for a particular economic use; i.e., industrial sites, lots for other commercial developments, and residential lots. The discouraging aspect about this kind of property is that the developer has often skimmed off most of the property's profit potential for himself.

If you are interested in this type of investment, try to find property which has a very special personality or a characteristic which makes it distinctive. Hillside lots commanding a fine view, lakeside or oceanside lots, lots near or overlooking golf courses, lots in restricted higher-class subdivisions, wooded or secluded sites are nearly always your best buys, even though you have to pay more for them initially. There is still ample land for ordinary subdivisions, but there are relatively few "quality" sites to be had. In the future, people will pay handsome premiums for these locations.

Usually, you should buy this kind of property as a relatively short-term investment—perhaps being able to see profitable turnover in three to five years. High property taxes may make holding for longer periods unprofitable. Therefore, the price you pay should be closely related to current fair values since you won't have a long holding period to provide as large a markup as you might expect with unimproved land investments.

## HOW TO FIND INVESTMENT ACREAGE

A good start is to get acquainted with a real estate salesman. He will have many urban properties listed which he will be happy to show you. You must remember, of course, that he is a salesman, and that he makes his commission by selling property. Therefore, you have to make sure that you don't get talked into something that is not a suitable investment.

Large tracts of land are advertised in *The Wall Street Journal* as well as your daily newspaper. More often, however, to find something really worthwhile, you have to go out looking for the land yourself. If you have a long summer vacation, plan some year to spend it prospecting for land investments in an area which seems to have a special development potential for:

1. Residential subdivisions.
2. Commercial and industrial developments.
3. Apartments, duplexes, condominiums.
4. Summer or mountain homesites.
5. Sportsmen's clubs, fishing or boating facilities.
6. Golf courses.
7. Dude ranches.
8. Summer camps for children.

Locations that are accessible to main highways, yet which seem secluded and unspoiled from commercial development will become more and more desirable as our population grows, and people find it desirable to "get away from the rest of the world."

## HOW TO UNDERSTAND LEGAL DESCRIPTIONS OF LAND

In order to locate property described in deeds or county records, you should understand how open land or land which has not been subdivided is plotted. To begin with, land in the United States is surveyed into large blocks six miles square called "townships." A township contains 23,040 acres consisting of 36 smaller squares called "sections" which each contain 640 acres. Figure 18–1 shows one such section of ground with a 40-acre tract plotted on it.

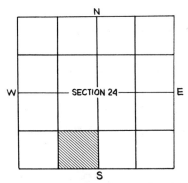

**Fig. 18–1** Section map showing location of 40-acre tract of land.

The 40-acre piece shown might be described on a deed in the following manner:

> The Southeast quarter of the Southwest quarter of Section 24, Range 5 East, Township 18 South, Salt Lake Meridian, containing 40 acres.

The range describes the easterly or westerly location of the tract, while the township notation refers to the northerly or southerly location in relation to a prominent survey point. Further division of the land shown in the foregoing deed notation would be possible—identifying a 10-acre piece within the 40-acre block:

> The Northwest quarter of the Southeast quarter of the Southwest quarter of Section 24, Range 5 East, Township 18 South, Salt Lake Meridian, containing 10 acres.

This 10-acre piece of property is shown in Fig. 18–2.

In order that county records can keep a current account of ownership on land for tax and legal purposes, deeds are (or should be) recorded in County Recorders' Offices. When the recording is made, a book and page number is usually noted on the deed indicating where and when it was recorded.

Irregularities of size and shape are common to surveys, with the result that not all townships are exactly six miles square, nor do they uniformly contain the same number of acres. Portions of the township which are irregular are commonly identified as numbered lots. Developed land, both residential and industrial, is also commonly identified as lots in county records and frequently listed as belonging to a particular subdivision. Here is a typical example of how a tract of land inside a city area would be deeded:

Lot 48 of the Admiral Subdivision, containing 23.92 acres.

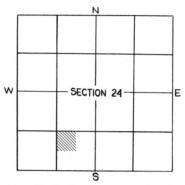

**Fig. 18–2** Section map showing location of 10-acre tract of land.

## SHOULD YOU SUBDIVIDE OR DEVELOP LAND YOURSELF?
Once you have acquired an investment in land, you not only have to decide how long you will hold it, but you must also decide if you should (1) develop or subdivide the property yourself, or (2) sell it in one or two large pieces to someone

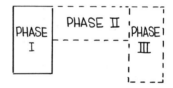

else for development.  Subdividing property can be tricky, but it can also give you the greatest gain.  In a large land development, here are some of the things you will need:

1. Aerial stereo photographic or on-site contour mapping.  (Costs can run from $2 to $300 per acre depending on the size of the project and the terrain. The more acreage you map, the less the cost will be per acre.)

2. Landscape architects' plans and maps.

3. Engineering drawings showing water and sewage drainage.

4. Approval from county and/or city zoning or planning commissions.

5. Approval from state business regulation departments in some states, particularly if you are developing rural land.

Before you decide which way to go, you should weigh carefully the costs, risks, and profit potentials of both the outright sale and the projected development.
    Federal income taxes should also enter into your decision.  If you develop

the property yourself, you will usually be looked upon in the eyes of the Internal Revenue Service as a real estate developer, and you will not be able to take "long-term capital gains treatment provided you have held the property at least six months."

## OPPORTUNITIES IN INCOME PROPERTIES
Although income properties are properly looked upon as real estate investments, they must also be considered businesses. Therefore, income property must not only show good potential for capital appreciation, but it must also have the capability of operating profitably as a business as well.

**Duplexes and apartments.** Generally speaking, duplexes work out to be rather unattractive investments, as do single homes and many condominiums purchased for rental. Property taxes are usually assessed at proportionately higher levels on these types of property than on other rental units. (They shouldn't be, but they are.)

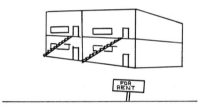

If you have one side of a duplex vacant, 50 percent of your rental income is gone; and if a single home is vacant, all your income ceases. A much better investment therefore is a four- or an eight-plex. Proportionately, each unit in a four- or an eight-plex costs much less to build; the cost drop is especially notice-able for the two-story eight-plex. A young couple might wisely decide to com-bine an investment in living space with an investment in income-producing property. With a good amount of savings, it is often possible for a young couple to make such a purchase. Here are some pros and cons of rental property for you to look at:

| Beneficial aspects of rental properties | Worrisome aspects of rental properties |
|---|---|
| 1. Taxes and interest expenses are fully deductible as business expenses on a yearly basis.* | 1. You may have difficulty renting the property and have to keep up the mortgage payments from other income sources. |
| 2. You are allowed to charge off a | 2. You have constant bother from |

* Except for instances where part of the rental unit is used for personal living quarters.

sizable percentage of the value of the rental property each year for depreciation. This becomes a good tax shelter for your income.

the normal turnover and rental of units.

3. Property may appreciate in value —at least it is a good hedge against inflation.

3. You are tied to the property, not able to come and go as you please. You may have to do much of the maintenance yourself: painting, plumbing, etc.

4. Rentals are not fixed, can be adjusted upward (except in certain rent-controlled areas) if operational costs rise.

4. Rising property taxes may erode profits and make the rental less attractive as an investment property.

5. A good rental unit may not only provide you with a place to live but provide sufficient rental income to pay off the mortgage on the entire investment.

Construction quality, attractiveness of design, and location are prime factors in determining the worth of a rental unit. The size and type of rental is also crucial. For the next decade, there will be a particularly heavy need for small apartments suitable for young marrieds. Because of the baby-boom years following World War II, our population now has an extraordinarily large number of college-aged men and women. As these young people take up housekeeping and move into the rental market, there will be exceptionally good rental opportunities in most areas for investors who have the right kind of units.

**Commercial income property—professional offices, warehouses, retail stores, etc.** Besides housing rentals, there are literally hundreds of different kinds of commercial properties that make excellent income-producing real estate investments. In many cases, the properties can be leased for three to five years to one tenant without the fuss and bother of having to worry about renters coming and going. The lease arrangement also makes it possible to project accurate cash flows—to be discussed later.

A good way to get into the commercial rental business is to search and buy a good lot with appropriate zoning. Later, as your investment funds increase, you can plan and build an appropriate structure for the type of rental you prefer. You might even plan the building for several growth stages—this is quite feasible with professional offices. Here are just a few of the many kinds of commercial income properties you should consider:

1. Medical offices for doctors and dentists.
2. Law offices.

3. Warehouses.

4. Stores, service stations, restaurants.

**How to determine the feasibility of income property.**  Before you purchase any income property, it is essential that you first make an accurate analysis of the net income potential in light of the mortgage or contract payments you must make. Only then can you determine whether or not you can handle the purchase and whether or not it will produce a desirable return on your investment.

For purposes of illustration, assume you are contemplating the purchase of a new four-plex unit. The owner is a builder who is just now putting the finishing touches on the interior of the apartments.  He will sell the property for $44,700 with a downpayment of $11,000.  Furthermore, the builder agrees to take a ten-year contract at 7 percent interest on the balance.  You have the $11,000 in savings, and you think it looks like a good investment.  You plan to live in one unit until the contract is repaid, renting out the other three.  From what you can ascertain from nearby rentals, you ought to be able to rent the units unfurnished for $205 per month.  Table 18–1 shows a simplified income-expense analysis for the property:

**Table 18–1**  Income-expense analysis for prospective four-plex investment

| | |
|---|---|
| Purchase price of four-plex | $44,700.00 |
| Less cash investment | 11,000.00 |
| Balance financed by contract from seller | $33,700.00 |
| (Terms: 10 years, 7% interest; 1/10th of principal to be repaid with interest on July 1 of each year.) | |
| Gross annual income from rental of 3 of 4 units at $205 per month (one unit to be used by purchaser) | $7,380.00 |
| Less estimated revenue loss due to vacancies | 369.00 |
| Anticipated gross annual income from property | $7,011.00 |
| Less estimated operating expenses: | |
| Plumbing repairs, misc. maintenance costs, water, etc.    $ 510.00 | |
| Property taxes    1,030.00 | |
| | 1,540.00 |
| Net anticipated income per year from investment | $5,471.00 |

As you can see, you would receive approximately $5,471.00 annually from the rental of the three units plus the saving you would make from living in one of the units yourself.

Now let us see whether or not the investment is feasible from the standpoint of the income you would receive (just determined) and the outflow required for yearly interest and principal payments. Table 18–2 shows this analysis. Column 1 shows contract year, while columns 2 and 3 detail the interest and principal payments required each year.  Column 4 gives the total contract payment required (interest plus principal). Column 5 gives the yearly deficit or surplus of income after contract payments. The cash-flow analysis for this particular property looks quite good, providing you could keep the apartments rented consistently at the anticipated occupancy rate. You would have to supplement the property's income somewhat for the first two years, but from then on it should pretty well take care of itself. At the end of the 10-year period, you would have the unit free and clear—and it should be worth more than the $44,700 you paid for it.

**Table 18–2** Simple cash-flow analysis for prospective four-plex investment

| Year | Net cash income | Interest on contract | Principal payment on contract | Total contract payment | Deficit or surplus of income after payment |
|------|------|------|------|------|------|
| 1 | $5,471.00 | $2,359.00 | $3,370.00 | $5,729.00 | $−258.00 |
| 2 | 5,471.00 | 2,123.10 | 3,370.00 | 5,493.10 | −22.10 |
| 3 | 5,471.00 | 1,887.20 | 3,370.00 | 5,257.20 | 213.80 |
| 4 | 5,471.00 | 1,651.30 | 3,370.00 | 5,021.30 | 449.70 |
| 5 | 5,471.00 | 1,415.40 | 3,370.00 | 4,785.40 | 685.60 |
| 6 | 5,471.00 | 1,179.50 | 3,370.00 | 4,549.50 | 921.50 |
| 7 | 5,471.00 | 943.60 | 3,370.00 | 4,313.60 | 1,157.40 |
| 8 | 5,471.00 | 707.70 | 3,370.00 | 4,077.70 | 1,393.30 |
| 9 | 5,471.00 | 471.80 | 3,370.00 | 3,841.80 | 1,629.20 |
| 10 | 5,471.00 | 235.90 | 3,370.00 | 3,605.90 | 1,865.10 |

Another bonus feature of rental property, already pointed out in the summary of advantages, is that much of the income generated to pay for the unit escapes taxation. To begin with, all of the interest paid on the contract is deductible. (Actually, 75% is deducted from operating income of the property, with the other 25% deducted as additional interest deduction itemized on Form 1040.) Furthermore, the Internal Revenue Service allows you to estimate a usable life on a piece of property (they consider about 40 years for an apartment house) and subsequently write off for tax purposes a certain amount each year for depreciation.

**DEPRECIATION**
Depreciation is merely a tax deduction. You are not paying it out to anybody. There are several methods of depreciating property. The three most common ones will be discussed later in this chapter. For now, however, let's look at how depreciation helps you avoid taxes. Table 18–3 first shows the taxable income before interest and depreciation deductions. This income is higher than your actual cash income since you may for tax purposes only deduct 75% of the total expenses on the property because you are living in one of the four units. Column

3 shows the total yearly interest on the contract; while Column 4 itemizes 75%
of the total yearly depreciation. The total annual taxable income is given in
Column 5.

**Table 18–3** Summary of taxable income on prospective four-plex investment

| Gross annual income from rentals | $7,380.00 |
|---|---|
| Less 75% of total operating expenses (75% × $1,540 = $1,155) | −1,155.00 |
| Total taxable income before interest and depreciation deductions | $5,856.00 |

| Year | Taxable income before int. and dep. | *Less: Total interest | 75% Depreciation | Annual taxable income |
|---|---|---|---|---|
| 1 | $5,856.00 | $2,359.00 | $1,676.25 | $1,820.75 |
| 2 | 5,856.00 | 2,123.10 | 1,592.44 | 2,140.46 |
| 3 | 5,856.00 | 1,887.20 | 1,512.82 | 2,455.98 |
| 4 | 5,856.00 | 1,651.30 | 1,437.17 | 2,767.53 |
| 5 | 5,856.00 | 1,415.40 | 1,365.32 | 3,075.28 |
| 6 | 5,856.00 | 1,179.50 | 1,297.05 | 3,379.45 |
| 7 | 5,856.00 | 943.60 | 1,232.20 | 3,680.20 |
| 8 | 5,856.00 | 707.70 | 1,170.59 | 3,977.71 |
| 9 | 5,856.00 | 471.80 | 1,112.06 | 4,272.14 |
| 10 | 5,856.00 | 235.90 | 1,056.46 | 4,563.64 |

* *Note*: In order to simplify the illustration, 100% of the contract interest is deducted to arrive at
taxable income. In actually filing a tax return only 75% of interest could be deducted from earnings
statement of income property because one unit is being used for personal use. The other 25%, however, would also be deductible, but would be deducted on page 2 of Form 1040.

Depreciation is computed using the double-declining method based on a 40-year estimated
property life.

Since both interest and allowable depreciation are higher in the earlier years,
the taxable incomes for these corresponding years are reduced. (Remember,
however, that you are receiving a cash income of $5,471 as computed in Table
18–1 each year, regardless of what the taxable income shows.) As the contract
progresses, the taxable income and also your tax burden grow. The income you
receive will be treated as additions to ordinary income on your tax return, and
the amount of tax you will be required to pay each year will depend on your
particular tax bracket.

## HOW DEPRECIATION IS COMPUTED

The first step in determining depreciation is to estimate the usable life of the
property. The easiest way to do this, and at the same time avoid trouble with
the Internal Revenue Service, is to use the tables they have prepared for "Useful
Lives of Depreciable Assets" found in I.R.S. Publication 456, *Depreciation
Guidelines and Rules*.

Then you must decide on one of several methods of figuring depreciation. Three methods are most common—they are described briefly here, showing how each would be used in depreciating the four-plex we have just analyzed.

**Straight-line method.**  Under this procedure, the depreciation for each year is simply determined by dividing the cost of the property (if the property is new and hasn't been depreciated previously), less salvage value, by the remaining useful years of life for the property:

| | |
|---|---:|
| Cost of property | $44,700.00 |
| Estimated salvage value (land and building after 40 years) | 7,000.00 |
| Amount to be depreciated over remaining useful life | $37,700.00 |

$37,700.00 ÷ 40 = $942.50 allowable annual depreciation

**Double-declining balance method.**  This method permits you to take a considerably larger amount of depreciation in the early years of an investment. Since this allows you to keep more income for additional investments early in life, you will usually benefit from using it.  The amount of depreciation you take each year is subtracted from the cost or other basis of the property before computing next year's depreciation, so that the *same depreciation rate* applies to a *smaller* or *declining* balance each year.  Thus, a larger depreciation deduction is taken for the first year, and a gradually smaller deduction is taken in each succeeding year.

Twice the straight-line rate is the maximum rate which may be used to compute depreciation under this method.  Salvage value of the property is not considered.  How this is figured is illustrated here for three years:

Estimated life of apartment

Twice the straight-line rate (1/40th yearly) = 1/20th yearly

1st Year:  Cost of unit $44,700 ÷ 20 = $2,235.00 allowable depreciation

2nd Year:  Cost of unit $44,700.00 — previous depreciation, $2,235.00 = $42,465.00   $42,465 ÷ 20 = $2,123.25 allowable depreciation

3rd Year:  Cost of unit $44,700.00 — previous depreciation, $4,358.25 = $40,341.75   $40,341.75 ÷ 20 = $2,017.09 allowable depreciation

**Sum-of-the-years-digits method.**  Under this method, you apply a different fraction each year to the cost of the property less its salvage value.  The denominator (bottom number) of the fraction is the total of the numbers representing the years of useful life of the property.  Thus, if the useful life is 5 years, the denominator is 15 (1 + 2 + 3 + 4 + 5 = 15).  The numerator (top number of the fraction) is the number of years of life remaining at the beginning of the year for which the computation is made.  Thus, if the useful life is 5 years, the fraction to be applied to figure depreciation for the first year is 5/15.  The fraction for the second year is 4/15 and so on.  Here is how it would work for the four-plex.

Cost of property                                            $44,700.00

$$\frac{\text{Number of years of remaining useful life of property} = 40 \text{ for first year}}{\text{Total of years representing useful life } (1 + 2 + 3 + 4 + 5 \cdots + 40) = 820}$$

Determine depreciation by multiplying cost minus salvage value by the above fraction as follows:

$$\$44{,}700 - \$7{,}000 = \$37{,}700 \times \frac{40}{820} = \$1{,}839.02$$

**Additional first-year depreciation.**  If you acquire personal property for use in your rental or other business, you may be entitled, in the first year, to deduct 20 percent of the cost of such property in addition to your regular depreciation. The additional depreciation is figured *before* you determine the first annual depreciation deduction.

Qualifying property is tangible personal property, such as furniture, having a useful life of at least six years determined from the date you acquire it.  The property may be new or used.  Buildings, land, and intangible property do not qualify.

### SYNDICATES, INVESTMENT COMPANIES AND TRUSTS
Finding a way to pool your money effectively with that of other investors may make sense on certain occasions, especially if your resources are limited.  Here are three ways it can be done:

1. *Through participation in private syndicates.*  Not infrequently, the better real estate bargains are the higher priced ones, simply because there are fewer qualified investors competing for them.  However, one investor may find it impracticable to tackle a large purchase himself.  And even a wealthy investor may prefer to share the risks with others.  One solution for such a purchase is to use a syndicate.

Actually, an investment syndicate is merely a partnership, usually formed for the specific purpose of investing in a particular piece of real estate.  In its simplest form, you and a few friends may decide to join forces to buy a piece of property.  Because of the legal dangers and other disadvantages of partnerships (discussed earlier in Chapter 17, Investing in a Small Business), this type of venture should be undertaken only with people you know and trust.  Ideally, syndicate members should have about the same incomes and net worth:

"The reason you should have syndicate members of roughly the same net worth and annual income is that under most state laws the members of a syndicate are responsible jointly and severally for all the building debts. Say, for example, that you are hit with a major lawsuit because of an accident in the building for which you were not insured. If you lose the case, the court's judgments for damages would be enforced against all the syndicate members together and also against every syndicate member as an individual. If one member is wealthy, compared to the others, he would be the easiest to pick, and might have to bear the major burden."*

2. *Through public syndicates.* Usually public syndicates are formed by a real estate promoter to finance a very large undertaking such as a shopping center or multi-story building. The individual investor buys a "participation share" in the project—which amounts to buying a small part of the equity. The pure syndicate is not a corporation. Therefore, participation in the syndicate may also mean acquiring liability for the syndicate's indebtedness. You could also have trouble in getting your money back. Not only does the value of participations fluctuate but in some instances there is no active market at all.

The record of real estate syndicates is a spotty one—with some excellent performers and some dismal failures. The disadvantages (1) lack of diversification; (2) uncertainty of liability; and (3) questionable marketability make the syndicate too risky especially for the beginning investor.

3. *Through realty investment corporations or trusts.* Any real estate investment could potentially be financed through the sale of corporate securities. For example, promoters desiring to build a multi-million dollar trade center might decide to sell stock for financing the development rather than using mortgage money. In this case, the investor would have very limited diversification—the entire value of the stock being dependent upon what happened to the one project. This kind of company is usually called a real estate investment corporation.

Other real estate corporations may sell stock with the intent to invest the stockholder's money in many different real estate properties—operating in a similar manner to a mutual fund which invests in stocks and giving the investor greater diversification protection. These are also properly referred to as real estate investment corporations, although it is also common for such companies to use the word "trust" in its corporate identification.

The buyer of either such type of corporate stock assumes no liability other than putting his investment at risk. As with any stock, prices fluctuate and marketability may in some cases be uncertain. However, with well-established corporations, there is generally good marketability of shares. There is, however, a very important disadvantage with the realty corporation, and that is that its profits are taxed twice—once by corporate income taxes usually 48 percent and once again when profits are distributed to shareholders.

Some relief to realty corporations was provided in 1960 when Congress passed the Real Estate Investment Trust Act. Upon proper registration, the realty trust can avoid paying corporate income taxes each year it pays 90 percent or more of its income to its stockholders. However, such trusts are limited to a

---

* J. J. Brown, *The Intelligent Investor's Guide to Real Estate.* G. P. Putnam's Sons, New York, 1964, p. 91.

maximum of 30 percent of their gross incomes subject to capital gains treatment; and they may not manage their own investment properties.

This type of investment must be approached with the same caution and selectiveness as any other corporate security. Some real estate investment corporations and trusts have fine records and competent management; while others are outright mediocre. A good REIT, however, is a more conservative, somewhat less risky investment than most public syndicates.

## HOW TO GET STARTED IN REAL ESTATE

Only after you have seriously looked at different real estate properties and compared advantages and disadvantages, their costs, and made one or two purchases and sales, will you acquire a "feel" for what real estate investing actually requires. However, there are a few suggestions which will help make your first attempts at real estate investing profitable:

1. Avoid situations, real or imagined, where you compete pricewise for the property. Determine what you believe to be a property's value in terms of your ultimate use for it; offer that price; then if you don't get it, drop it. You will soon find something else, perhaps something better.

2. Once in a while you may find a real buy when a buyer has an especially urgent need for cash; and, consequently, he must make a sacrifice sale. When you are offered property at a bargain price, don't quibble; pay the price or you may lose your opportunity.

3. Keep your first investment relatively small—not more than $2,500 or $3,000.

4. Pay for this first real estate purchase in cash if possible—or at least put down 70 to 80 percent of its value. And if you have any debt owing on the investment, make sure you have enough other income to cover your payments so you won't be forced into selling the property prematurely—or perhaps run risk of losing the property and your downpayment.

5. Keep your first investment something simple which will not require complicated improvements, subdividing, or other development.

6. If possible, sell your investment on a piecemeal basis—getting some capital returned relatively early so you can get going on another project.

## HOW TO FINANCE REAL ESTATE INVESTMENTS

Contrary to what many persons think, you don't have to be wealthy to invest in real estate. There will be limits as to what the average investor can do in the beginning, but you are not strictly confined to cash purchases. Here are four ways property can be financed:

1. *Conventional mortgage loans.* Banks, insurance companies, private lenders, and credit unions are all sources of mortgage loan funds. Since this type of borrowing was covered thoroughly in Chapter 11 (Renting, Buying,

Building), little needs to be reiterated here. However, you must be certain whenever you take on this type of an obligation that you have the finances to follow through for as long as the investment may require. It is well to note, too, that banks and other lenders may be unwilling to make loans on vacant property because they consider it too speculative.

2. *Sellers' contracts.* You can frequently talk the seller of a piece of property into giving you the property on a long-term installment contract. If he balks, point out that by taking less than 30 percent of the total sales price down and spreading the payments equally over several years, he can report his profits on an installment basis and probably save considerable Federal income tax.

3. *Private syndicates.* This arrangement where several individuals pool resources to enable them to buy a piece of property has been discussed previously in this chapter.

4. *Purchase options.* A purchase option is not strictly a method of financing a purchase, but may be used sometimes in lieu of a purchase just as profitably. Here is how it works: For a small amount of money, the present owner of the property may be willing to give you a "temporary right" to purchase his property. This right, called a purchase option, specifies the purchase terms, and runs for a given length of time. While the option is in force, you have the right to purchase the property; and the owner may not sell to anyone else during this option period. For example: You might spot a piece of property that costs $60,000. You work up plans for the land and find it can be subdivided into 15 residential lots very easily. You don't have the money to buy the property on cash or contract so you talk the owner into giving you a 60-day purchase option for $100. As soon as you have the option, you begin contacting major building contractors in your city. You finally find one that is very interested in the property, and who is willing to pay $74,000 for it. You arrange for the sale to take place at your attorney's office. You actually buy the property for $60,000 and sell it at $74,000 at the same moment making a nice $14,000 gain. Or you could merely sell the "option" you hold to the builder for an agreed upon sum so he could buy the property from the seller himself.

## FEEDBACK 18

**A.** As a potential real estate investor, evaluate your community. Is it a likely location for profitable land acquisition? Commercial buildings? Apartment rentals? Obviously, there are an infinite number of related variables but you should investigate at least the following questions about investing where you live.

● Compared with average growth for your state and the country as a whole, is your community growing in population as rapidly as these?

- Are you aware of specific, not rumored, growth potentialities which may affect the growth of your community's population?
- Can you properly administer your investment until it becomes profitable (say, in 5 to 10 years)? Can you afford the taxes, apart from possible income from the property?
- Can you anticipate the possible improvement costs which you will have to pay if you will hold onto the property?

**B.** Using the real estate want-ads for four-plexes or eight-plexes, and your knowledge of rental characteristics of your community, analyze the income possibilities of two such buildings for sale. Qualify your estimates by assuming (1) you occupy one of the units, (2) you have a 5 percent vacancy loss. (You should also consider greater loss due to vacancy, 10 percent, for example.)

- Compute the Income-Expense potential of the investment, using the price listed for the property. (See page 569 for format.)
- Compute a Simple Cash-Flow for the property. (See page 570 for format.)
- Compute a Summary of Taxable Income for the property. (See page 571 for format.)
- Carefully analyze your ability and willingness to make repairs which may become necessary should you become a landlord.

**C.** Theoretically, each seller makes a profit on real estate when he passes title along to a buyer. When you buy real estate, you do so with the purpose of making a profit through income or capital gains. With this in mind, consider the following questions about property you may be thinking of buying:

- Who will buy the property from you? What purpose will he have in buying? (Will expansion of rental holdings make your property attractive to buyers?)
- Where will the property values be increasing in the next ten years? (Almost everyone wishes he knew the answer to this one, but thinking it through will help you avoid some non-improving property.)
- Is deterioration spreading in your community? Some cities have depreciating property values spreading outward from their centers. You should consider your community for this possibility, and its consequences for your prospective real estate investments. Will rebuilding the central city enhance property value? At what expense? Does potential deterioration make suburban investments more attractive?

**D.** Being objective, and not pessimistic, consider the financing involved in your real estate plans.

- From whom, under what conditions, will you obtain the money to buy the real estate?
- Will you be able to make mortgage payments regardless of vacancies?

### DISCUSSION QUESTIONS

1. Why might raw or undeveloped acreage (such as farming land, grazing ground) be much more attractive as an investment than vacant city lots?

2. Most population authorities predict that our population will continue to grow and continue to concentrate in large urban areas. What effects will this type of growth have on real estate investments? Be specific.

3. More and more state legislatures and county planning authorities are writing stiffer laws and regulations concerning the subdivision of land. What is happening in your county? Your state? What effects are these new regulations having on land development?

4. Real estate investments differ considerably from other investments. What are some of the advantages and disadvantages you see in real estate?

5. How might you profit from oil and gas discoveries without actually owning land?

6. Why is a duplex generally not a good investment?

7. What special tax treatment can you take advantage of when building and renting income property? When selling property for a profit?

8. What is an investment syndicate? What advantages does this kind of investment have over direct purchases of real estate?

9. How might an *option* be used to make you money? Why is the property owner willing to grant an option?

10. Financing real estate investments—even large ones—may be approached in several effective ways. Discuss.

### CASE PROBLEM

Assume that you are married and that you and your spouse are looking for a good rental unit which will provide you with living space and which will also qualify as a good real estate investment. You have found two prospects. One is a duplex; the other is an 8-unit apartment. Originally, you were not interested in duplex properties, but a real estate man found this unit and asked you to take a careful look at it because it has an added advantage—the sale price includes a vacant building lot to the one side of the duplex. The owner of the property will not sell the lot or the duplex separately.

1. Study the information provided here showing your personal income and data on each of the prospective units.

2. Prepare an income-expense statement like the one shown in Table 18–1 for each property; similarly, prepare a cash-flow analysis (Table 18–2) for both the duplex and the apartment.

3. Disregarding the tax shelter from interest and depreciation which each

property would provide, which one would you prefer as an investment? Which, if either, is suitable for your income and financial standing?

*Your income*: Combined gross income of you and your spouse is $15,880 annually. You are presently renting a furnished apartment, paying $167 a month. You pay all utilities additionally. You owe $2,120 balance on your automobile which is repaid monthly at $106; 20 months remain on the contract. You have no other debts. Your savings consist of $4,000 in cash; additionally you have common stock which could be sold now at a long-term capital gain profit yielding $7,450 after estimated income taxes on the gain.

*The duplex*: Each unit has 1,400 square feet of floor space, three bedrooms, and two bathrooms. There is a large, attractive fireplace in the family room; attractive patios privately situated for each unit. You anticipate you could rent the one unit for $245 monthly unfurnished. Property taxes have been assessed at $1,380 yearly on the duplex; plus $176 on the vacant lot. You assume there would be a vacancy rate of about 7%. You estimate the vacant lot which is also zoned for a duplex could be sold on today's market for about $7,600. However, you believe you could make more on the lot by holding it for a few years.

The builder wants a cash deal and will take $37,000. He has arranged with a mortgage loan company for financing—a minimum of $7,000 down is required and the balance is to be repaid monthly on the $7\frac{1}{2}$% 20-year mortgage. Your monthly mortgage payment for interest and principal would be $241.80. You estimate there would be $175 in expenses yearly associated with upkeep and maintainance of the property.

*The apartment*: The apartment has 8 two-bedroom units with floor space of 780 square feet each. A small kitchen with eating space and one bathroom is provided in each unit. You estimate you could rent each unit for $155 unfurnished. Total annual expenses are estimated to be $720 for upkeep and maintenance of the 8 units. A 5% vacancy rate seems likely. Property taxes are assessed at $2,490 yearly.

The builder of the unit must sell outright and will not take a contract. He wants $68,000 for the property. After shopping around for mortgages, you get a commitment from an insurance company for a 20-year $7\frac{1}{2}$% mortgage of the property. You must pay 15% down. After the required downpayment, your monthly principal and interest payment would total $467.87.

## SUGGESTED READINGS

Bennett, Charles. *How Big Ideas Make Big Money Selling Real Estate*. Englewood Cliffs, N.J.: Prentice-Hall, 1961. 274 pp.

Brede, William J. *Creative Thinking in Real Estate*. New York: Harper & Brothers, 1959. 296 pp.

Cadwallader, Clyde T. *How to Buy Real Estate for Profit*. Englewood Cliffs, N.J.: Prentice-Hall, 1960. 308 pp.

Campbell, Don G. *The Handbook of Real Estate Investment.* New York: Bobbs-Merrill, 1968. 366 pp.

Casey, William J. *Real Estate Investments and How to Make Them.* New York: Institute for Business Planning, 1968.

Mair, George. *Guide to Successful Real Estate Investing, Buying, Financing, and Leasing.* Englewood Cliffs, N.J.: Prentice-Hall, 1971. 239 pp.

Martin, Preston. *Real Estate Principles and Practices.* New York: Macmillan, 1959. 434 pp.

Massel, Sherman J. *Financing Real Estate.* New York: McGraw-Hill, 1965. 432 pp.

Peckham, John M. *Master Guide to Income Property Brokerage.* Englewood Cliffs, N.J.: Executive Reports Corporation, 1969.

Ring, Alfred A. *The Valuation of Real Estate.* Englewood Cliffs, N.J.: Prentice-Hall, 1970. 660 pp.

Seldin, Maury and Richard H. Swesnik. *Real Estate Investment Strategy.* New York: Wiley-Interscience, 1970. 248 pp.

Semenow, Robert William. *Questions and Answers on Real Estate.* Englewood Cliffs, N.J.: Prentice-Hall, 1969. 664 pp.

Unger, Maurice Alberto. *Real Estate Principles and Practices.* Cincinnati: South-Western Publishing Company, 1969. 754 pp.

Weimer, Arthur M., and Homer Hoyt. *Principles of Real Estate.* New York: The Ronald Press, 1960. 716 pp.

Wendt, Paul Francis, and Alan R. Cerf. *Real Estate Investment Analysis and Taxation.* New York: McGraw-Hill, 1969. 355 pp.

CHAPTER 19

# INVESTING IN CORPORATE SECURITIES:
# THE BASICS

New York's Wall Street (Fig. 19–1) is a source of curiosity and interest to people, old and young, rich and poor, even those who have never owned a share of stock. The intriguing financial activities taking place there have made the city the world's undisputed financial capital. Because of the widespread public concern and the influence on many facets of the world's economies, the transactions of the New York and American Stock Exchanges are constantly spotlighted by all the news media.

**Fig. 19–1** New York's famous Wall Street. The stock exchanges and concentration of brokers and underwriters make this the financial center of the world. Courtesy of the New York Stock Exchange.

This chapter covers important fundamentals for your study of securities investments. It tells what corporate stocks and bonds are and details the functions and procedures of the unusual markets in which such securities are traded. Importantly, too, it gives you a little of the history behind these markets so that you can better appreciate the temperament and peculiarities of present-day operations.

**CORPORATIONS AND CORPORATE SECURITIES**

In Chapter 17, you studied the three forms of business organizations: the *individual proprietorship*, the *partnership*, and the *corporation*. There, you also learned the essential characteristics of a corporation and a little about the legal requirements for being chartered and registered. Now let us examine more closely some of the important features of corporate securities that affect you as a prospective investor. To begin with, it is important to know about the two basic kinds of stocks sold by corporations—*preferred* and *common*. Although the two stocks have one important similarity, that they both represent fractional corporate ownership, they differ markedly in many other ways.

**Preferred stocks.** As the name implies, this security has certain *preferences* over common stocks. If profit distribution (called dividend payments) are paid by the corporation, preferred stockholders must be paid their share *first*. Although designed to yield a *specified* rate of return, it is important to realize that dividends may be omitted at the discretion of the directors of the corporation. Therefore, the payment of preferred dividends is not comparable to the payment of interest on a bond or a note, which is a *must* to avoid default under the contract. Preferred stock is *junior* or *subordinate* to all debt which the company owes; but it has a claim ahead of the common stock upon the assets of the company in the event the company is dissolved. Preferred stock usually has a call feature which allows the corporation to redeem the shares within a given number of years following issuance if the directors elect to do so. Due to the limited dividends and sometimes indefinite life because of the call feature, preferred stocks do not share fully in the growth and profitability of the firm.

Most preferred stocks are cumulative. This means that dividends, if omitted, build up in arrears and must be paid before dividends can be paid upon common stock. Many preferred stocks do not have voting rights. However, some preferred stock without voting rights becomes voting stock if enough dividends are skipped. *Participating preferred stock* is occasionally sold and allows the stockholder to share dividends in excess of the intial preferred amount with common shareholders. Some preferred stocks are convertible into common stock just as some bonds are.

**Common stocks.** These are by far the most popular type of stock sold and currently traded in the United States. After preferred shareholders have been paid their specified amount of dividend from corporate profits, the common stockholders are eligible to receive any or all of the additional earnings. The amount of the dividends paid to common shareholders, however, is controlled entirely by the corporation's board of directors. It is not necessary to pay any of the corporate earnings to common shareholders unless the board wishes to do so. Common stock usually has voting rights, although certain *classes* of common stock may be designated as non-voting. (See Fig. 19–2.)

**Fig. 19–2** Specimen stock certificate. A certificate is evidence of ownership in a corporation, specifying the exact number of shares which the investor has purchased. The corporation keeps very accurate records of its stockholders so that dividends, when and if they are paid, can be properly distributed.

**Par value.**   When a corporation is first organized, a par value is typically designated and printed on both common and preferred stock certificates. However, common stocks seldom are sold to the public at the par price. Instead an *offering* price (usually higher than par value) is established by the incorporators and cleared by the appropriate state and/or Federal securities agencies. Investors in the original offering must then pay the offering price, not par, if they wish to invest. Once the original stock issue is sold, future transactions (sales) of that stock are normally made with the help of a broker in an auction market. For these reasons, the printed par value is seldom any help in determining the worth of a share of common stock. But much more will be said in a later chapter about judging the value of corporate stock as an investment.

**Corporate bonds.**   In addition to the sale of either preferred or common stocks, both of which represent ownership in the business, corporations have another broad class of investment security which they can issue—corporate bonds. This latter group includes *mortgage bonds* and *debentures*—each of which is an evidence of *indebtedness* as opposed to *ownership*. In another way of speaking, mortgage bonds and debentures represent what a company owes the investor for the use of his money. It is common for both of these debt instruments to be grouped together or referred to simply as *bonds*. Normally, bonds are issued in multiples of $1,000, although $100 and $500 denominations are not uncommon. Since a bondholder is a creditor and not a part owner as is a stockholder, he has no voice in the company, no voting rights.

What distinguishes a mortgage bond from a debenture? Sometimes corporations issue bonds backed by a mortgage on specific company assets—buildings, machinery, patents, land, and so on. Because of the apparent security, the *mortgage bond* may be quite attractive to investors and sell at a very reasonable interest rate. Bonds issued without a specific pledge of assets (a mortgage) are called *debentures*. Even though they lack a specified pledge of assets, debentures are not necessarily less creditworthy than mortgage bonds. Debentures of many large companies are of top credit value. Debentures do, of course, have a general claim on assets in the event the company is liquidated.

In summary, the true nature of a bond is best revealed simply by saying that a bond is a contract to borrow and repay money. This contract binds the issuer of the bond (the corporation or, for that matter, a city or other governmental body) to repay the principal sum plus interest for the use of the borrowed money—the payments to be made as scheduled in the contract.

## NATURE AND OPERATIONS OF SECURITIES MARKETS

Corporate stocks originate or are created either when a company is being formed as a corporate entity or when a business changes from an individual proprietorship or partnership to a corporate form of organization. Usually the stock is sold to the public to get money to run the business. Sometimes, however, stock is issued directly to a family or a small number of people who originate and intend to operate the venture. In these instances the stock may never be offered for public sale. Such businesses would be called *closed* corporations. Or, as happened with the Ford Motor Company, the corporate stock was held in the family for a long time and then finally made available to the investing public—the business being changed from a *closed* to an *open* or *public* corporation.

When stock is *first* issued by a corporation to an investor, most of the money paid for the shares goes directly to the firm; some of it, however, goes as commission to the businesses (called underwriters), brokers, and salesmen, who are involved in selling the new stock to the public.

From that point on, however, the corporation is not directly affected by what the investor does with the stock. The stock need never be redeemed by the company. A stockholder can keep his holdings for a long time if the investment proves good and the company is doing well—either growing rapidly and/or paying reasonable dividends; or the stockholder can sell the shares to someone else.  This latter type of transaction—involving the sale of *previously issued* as opposed to *newly issued* stock from one person to another—accounts for most security transactions.

Although you personally will deal conveniently with a local broker when you buy or sell stock, actual trading of previously issued stocks will take place either (1) in a stock market or (2) in the over-the-counter market.  There is a likelihood that the stock you may wish to buy or sell will be *listed* for trading on one of the stock exchanges that are to be found across the nation.  Many large cities have exchanges—Pacific Coast in San Francisco, Boston, and Detroit Stock Exchanges to mention but a few.  And if the company you are interested in is one of the big and well-known corporations, its shares will probably be listed and traded on either the American or New York Stock Exchange.  These two latter exchanges are the country's largest and handle the lion's share of the business.  Bonds as well as stocks are traded on these exchanges.

However, if the stock or bond you want to buy or sell is not a listed security, your broker would attempt to complete the transaction in the over-the-counter market.*  Also if you are purchasing *newly* issued corporate stocks or bonds (securities from a newly founded corporation, securities just made public from an on-going corporation, or securities issued to expand or finance operations of an existing corporation), these would be purchased in the over-the-counter market.

It is very important that an investor know something about the in's and out's, the basic nature, the types of securities traded, and the temperaments of both the stock exchange and the over-the-counter markets.  For this reason, the following pages trace some of the robust history as well as the current operations of (1) the nation's two largest stock exchanges, the primary trading places of *listed* stocks, and (2) the over-the-counter market which deals in *unlisted* and newly issued stocks.

## THE NEW YORK AND AMERICAN STOCK EXCHANGES
The burgeoning industries of America's economic youth relied heavily upon the sale of corporate stocks and bonds to flourish.  By the final decade of the 1700's there were already many brokers in New York selling new stock issues and trading existing ones between clients.  As the number of corporations and shareholders grew, so were there increasing problems in making stock transactions.  Since communications were slow and cumbersome, brokers began meeting in the streets of lower New York.  They were there from early morning to sundown —in snow, rain, heat, and cold.  It was here in 1792 that 24 brokers banded together to form an unimpressive and informal association that was eventually to become the New York Stock Exchange.

---

* Large blocks of listed securities are also frequently traded on a negotiated basis over-the-counter.

The number of corporations grew by leaps and bounds, especially with the vigorous economic strides that followed the successful conclusion of the American-British War of 1812. By 1817 the associated brokers, pressured from greatly increased business volume, decided that more formal procedures and a stronger association were needed. In that year they drew up the first formal Constitution of the New York Stock and Exchange Board.

The *outdoor* or *street brokers*, however, continued to prosper through the 1800's. Although they were often out to make a *fast buck*, their contributions to the expanding American economy are significant. This was the era when people were heralding the first steam locomotive, the maiden voyage of the steamship, the advent of commercial telegraphy, new territories, mineral discoveries, and industrial expansion.

The American Stock Exchange, as well as the New York Stock Exchange, traces its beginnings to the street brokers who gathered daily in New York's growing financial district. However, as in most famed markets of history, the exact birth date is shaded by time and by the informality of its inception. In 1908 a small group of leading outdoor brokers formed the New York Curb Agency, the first step toward formal organization. Outdoor trading reached its peak on Broad Street between 1900 and 1921. Powerful new industries—steel, munitions, marine, copper—grew during World War I and the years immediately following. New concepts of production helped to launch new types of business endeavors.

**Fig. 19–3** The Old Curb Exchange, about 1920. This remarkable photo shows brokers and investors conducting stock trades amidst a snow storm in New York's streets. Eventually as trading volume grew, the Curb Exchange moved indoors. It is now the nation's second largest exchange, The American Stock Exchange. Courtesy of The American Stock Exchange.

Visitors to New York in those days could witness a scene not likely to be duplicated again in American history. Hundreds of tense, excited brokers, buying and selling stocks and bonds, milled in apparently aimless excitement, waving and shouting to telephone order clerks in rented rooms above the street. Figure 19–3 illustrates with a very rare photograph this unique trading era. In order to be recognized by their clerks, brokers wore bright yellow homburgs, green derbies, or loud-striped jackets.

The growing importance of the market, the increase in the number of stocks, business volume, new brokers, shouting telephone clerks, and tourists created so much noise and confusion that *vocal* communications became a serious problem. Thus was born the hand-signal, a one-handed version of the deaf sign language that still proves an effective way of floor communication for present-day traders on the American Stock Exchange. (See Fig. 19–4.)

**Fig. 19–4** Traders at work on floor of American Stock Exchange. Hand signals, once used in hectic street trading on the outdoor Curb Exchange, are still used today. Courtesy of The American Stock Exchange.

The Curb Market continued to grow; and in 1919, the association decided to move indoors so it could provide improved systems of trading and exercise stronger control over its members and over the securities which it traded. It was not until 1953, however, that the present name, *American Stock Exchange* was adopted.

**Characteristics of trading on the big markets.** The New York and American Stock Exchanges share certain similar characteristics. The exchanges do not buy, sell, or own securities for their own accounts. They are *associations* which are unincorporated. They have a limited number of memberships. Both exchanges are national and international in character and operations, listing and trading numerous foreign as well as domestic securities. The New York Stock Exchange is governed by a 33-man board—29 members and allied members who are elected by the membership; and a president and three governors representing the public viewpoint, who are elected by the board. The American Stock Exchange elect a 32-member Board of Governors which is charged with establishing operating policy. Responsibility for administration of the ASE is centered in the exchange's president.

Both exchanges operate as *auction* markets. Stocks of several different corporations are assigned by exchange officers to a person on the floor of the exchange known as a *stock specialist*. The specialist supervises or conducts all the trades in his assigned securities. Member brokerage houses, across the nation and the world, convey clients' wishes to buy or sell particular securities to floor traders who immediately take the *offers* to the trading posts of the appropriate specialists. Trading action involving the specialists and floor traders on the American and New York Stock Exchanges is shown in Fig. 19.5a and b. The specialist's job is undoubtedly one of the most demanding in Wall Street. He must have quick judgment, split-second timing, a *feel* of the market, money, and a steady nerve. His moment-to-moment responsibility is to help provide *fair* and *orderly markets* in the securities assigned to him. No matter what sharp unexpected turns the market takes, the specialist is expected to buy securities in declining markets for his own account (when the public is selling heavily) and to sell stock in rising (when the public buys). Frequently called *the man in the middle*, his aim is to see that prices move in an orderly way, usually within a narrow range. His job is essentially to act as a stabilizer. He risks his own capital, but also he can make a great deal of money.

Just how does the specialist help the auction markets? Assume that the stock of a particular corporation has last sold at $35. The best public market is $34\frac{1}{2}$ ($34.50) bid, $35\frac{1}{2}$ offered; that is $34\frac{1}{2}$ is the highest any investor is willing to pay, and $35\frac{1}{2}$ is the lowest price at which anyone wishes to sell. With one point ($1) separating buyer and seller, the specialist would normally step in and narrow the quote to, say, $34\frac{3}{4}$ bid, offered at $35\frac{1}{2}$; agreeing to *buy* at the bid or *sell* at the offer for his own account. The investor can now anticipate that the price of the next transaction will be either unchanged from the previous sale at $35, or very close to that price. Narrowing the gap tends to build confidence in the market, and usually results in bringing buyer and seller to bid and offer

**Fig. 19–5** Trading posts and specialists on floor of New York Stock Exchange (19–5a) and American Stock Exchange (19–5b). The actual trading—buying and selling—of stocks takes place under the supervision of a "specialist" in a particular stock who conducts business at an assigned trading post on the Exchange's floor. Courtesy of The New York and American Stock Exchanges.

agreement so that orderly trading will continue. In the extremely active market of recent years, the specialist's role becomes more and more important.

To understand the controlled temperament and agility required of a specialist, consider what may happen when a listed company announces the development of a new space-age project. Investors coast to coast from the storekeeper in Seattle to a major investment company in Boston act on the news. Buy orders for thousands of shares pour onto the exchange trading floor simultaneously, and the sensitive balance between supply and demand is temporarily upset. The last sale before the flood of orders is $30. Because of the increased demand, and the reluctance of public stockholders to sell, the price could jump several dollars immediately unless the specialist helps balance the scales by supplying stock from his own account. The price will no doubt rise as a result of the influx of buy orders, but the rise will remain orderly because the specialist will help establish the supply-demand balance at a price reasonably related to the last sale. The reverse is true in a declining market, with the specialist buying stock to help offset an influx of sell orders.

How, though, can a specialist continually *buck* public trends and still stay financially solvent? Remember that he is buying and selling for his own account to help even things out as well as executing trades between investors. The answer lies in the nature of stock prices. While they are apt to fluctuate widely over a period of time, they almost never move in an absolutely straight line. On the way up they often dip; on the way down, they rise. It is on these fluctuations that the specialist is able to *acquire* or *liquidate* his positions and still play his enormously important stabilizing role.

**Requirements of listing stocks.** There is a wide diversity of corporations. There are thousands of tiny corporations just starting business and selling their stock at 1¢ a share, and many thousands more of the small and large ones just ready to fall into bankruptcy. And on the other side of the fence, there are many hundreds of well-seasoned, stable, consistent profit performers, their shares commonly referred to as the *blue-chip* stocks. Because of the great differences in corporations, both the major stock exchanges have very rigid requirements which must be met before a corporation's securities can be listed and traded.

The American Stock Exchange (Fig. 19–6), the nation's second largest securities marketplace, offers a blend of *blue-chips* and what might be termed *new-chips*. Its listing requirements, although substantial, are less stringent than those of the New York Exchange. For this reason, many younger, less seasoned, yet profitable companies list their stocks on the American Exchange. To qualify for listing on the American Stock Exchange today, a corporation is expected to have the following minimal standards:

1. Demonstrate net earnings after taxes of $150,000 for the latest fiscal year (fiscal year is 12 months of operation not necessarily coinciding with the

beginning and end of the calendar year) and average annual net earnings after taxes of $100,000 for the past three years.

2. Net tangible assets of $1 million.

3. Market value of publicly held shares of $1,250,000 with 750 stockholders, including 500 holders of round lots (round lots are shareholdings of 100 or multiples of 100).

4. For stock issues selling currently below $5 per share, the American Exchange requires 100,000 more publicly distributed shares for each half dollar below $5 per share at which a stock is selling at the time of application for listing.

**Fig. 19–6** The American Stock Exchange building. Visitors are welcome to visit the Exchange and see first hand this interesting market in operation. Courtesy of The American Stock Exchange.

Listing companies are also required to publish quarterly statements of sales and earnings, solicit proxies, and make timely disclosure of important information affecting security values.

Currently, there are nearly 1,100 issues listed for trading on the American

Stock Exchange. These issues total 1.87 billion shares and are valued at about $40 billion. Thirty-two common stock issues traded on the American Stock Exchange have paid annual dividends for 50 to 117 consecutive years.

**Fig. 19–7** The New York Stock Exchange building. The public gallery overlooking the bustling trading floor is a "must" when in New York. In one exciting hour, or less as you wish, you will get a clear picture of how this amazing Exchange operates. Courtesy of the New York Stock Exchange.

To be listed on the New York Stock Exchange (Fig. 19–7), a company must be willing to keep the investing public informed on the progress of its affairs. The company must be a going concern, or be the successor to a going concern. In determining eligibility for listing, particular attention is given to such qualifications as: (1) the degree of national interest in the company; (2) its relative position and stability in the industry; and (3) whether it is engaged in an expanding industry, with prospects of at least maintaining its relative position. While each case is decided on its own merits, the NYSE generally requires the following as a minimum for initial listing:

1. Demonstrated earning power under competitive conditions of $2 million annually before taxes and $1.2 million after all charges and taxes.

2. Net tangible assets of $10 million, but greater emphasis will be placed on the aggregate market value of the common stock, where $12 million or more applicable to publicly-held shares at the time of listing is looked for.

3. One million shares outstanding, of which at least 700,000 common shares are publicly-held among not less than 1,700 round-lot shareholders, and a total of 2,000 shareholders of record.

As a matter of general policy, the NYSE has for many years refused to list non-voting stocks. Therefore, all listed stock on this exchange—common and preferred—must carry voting rights.

Of the 1,400,000 publicly and privately owned corporations filing reports with the United States Treasury, only about 1,300 of these corporations have common stock listed on the New York Stock Exchange. These relatively few companies, however, contribute substantially to the nation's economy. Their assets of $425 billion constitute about 30 percent of the total assets of all corporations, and these same listed corporations employ about 21 percent of all the civilian workers in the United States. For these reasons, a good many of the stocks traded on the NYSE belong to the *blue-chip* category.

Of all the listed stocks on the NYSE, 789 have uninterrupted annual dividend records for at least 20 years, and ten listed companies have paid out some cash dividend to their common stockholders in each and every year for over 100 years.*

Both the American and New York Stock Exchanges have criteria which must be met for continued listing of stocks. Annual reviews are made to determine each stock's eligibility. This pruning or delisting helps insure the quality or nature of stocks traded on each of the exchanges.

**How brokers become exchange members.** You have already learned that the two major stock market exchanges are associations each having a certain number of memberships. Since a brokerage firm must own a membership (or a seat) before it can directly trade in listed stock, memberships are very valuable. Owners of memberships may transfer them, by sale or otherwise, with appropriate approval of the exchange.

The American Stock Exchange has nearly 900 regular and associate members, representing 600 brokerage houses. A membership on the American Stock Exchange is currently worth about $200,000. The New York Stock Exchange now has approximately 1,375 memberships with the value of each seat running about $235,000. About 650 brokerage organizations are represented by these memberships.

---

* *New York Stock Exchange Fact Book 1967.* New York: New York Stock Exchange, 1967, p. 19.

### HOW STOCK EXCHANGE TRADES ARE REPORTED

It is estimated that the number of individuals owning shares in publicly held corporations now exceeds twenty million. These investors are part owners of more than 6,700 companies which have some 18 billion shares of stock outstanding with an estimated total market value of $648 billion.* With such a large number of people owning stock and the significance of the dollar value of their holdings, it is little wonder that there is a great public demand for immediate reporting on stock exchange transactions.

The stock exchanges have for many years operated ticker reporting systems. The ticker is quite similar in operation to a teletypewriter. Data is fed from the exchange in abbreviated form over a wire network to tickers located in brokers' offices. The information is printed by the machine on a narrow paper tape. Because of the growing volume of stock transactions, the older systems of reporting are rapidly being replaced with computerized equipment.

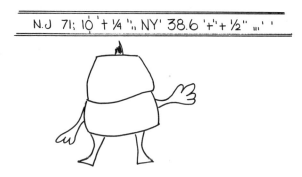

The present ticker operating from the New York Stock Exchange is the fourth such device in the Exchange's history. It is capable of speeds up to 900 characters a minute—close to the limits of readability. Besides the conventional paper-tape ticker, the Exchange also disseminates quotation data through services of several relatively new ticker display and interrogation devices—large electric and electronic boards. As part of the program leading toward automation of the floor operations of the NYSE, optical scanning card reporting has been installed at two of the nineteen trading posts in place of the traditional paper slips. The NYSE system currently feeds 3,962 ticker and display devices in 798 cities in the United States and foreign countries. The total number of devices reporting transaction data—including tickers, displays, interrogation units, panel boards, and television—now numbers more than 16,000 for the New York Stock Exchange.

The American Stock Exchange ticker and information system is similar in many ways to that used by the NYSE. Promptly after transactions are

---

* *New York Stock Exchange Fact Book 1967.* New York: New York Stock Exchange, 1967, p. 35.

# New York Stock Exchange Transactions

| --1971-- High | Low | Stocks Div | Sales in 100s | Open | High | Low | Close | Net Chg. |
|---|---|---|---|---|---|---|---|---|
| 16¼ | 9⅝ | Dymo Ind | 47 | 13½ | 13¾ | 13½ | 13½ | ..... |
| 15½ | 5⅞ | Dynam Am | 136 | 9⅛ | 9¼ | 9 | 9 | ..... |
| 29⅜ | 21 | EaglePic .90 | 9 | 22¾ | 23 | 22¾ | 23 | ..... |
| 24 | 16 | Easco Cp .90 | 32 | 17 | 17¾ | 17 | 17¾ | + ½ |
| 28⅞ | 14⅜ | East Air Lin | 510 | 16⅜ | 16⅞ | 16⅜ | 16⅞ | + ⅝ |
| 51⅜ | 34 | EastGs 1.04t | 128 | 37¾ | 38¾ | 37⅝ | 38¾ | +1¼ |
| 22¾ | 19⅝ | East Util 1.50 | 6 | 21⅜ | 21⅜ | 21⅛ | 21⅛ | .... |
| 86¼ | 72 | EasKodak 1a | 465 | 74⅞ | 77⅛ | 74⅞ | 76¾ | +2⅜ |
| 43½ | 34 | Eaton 1.40 | 46 | 37⅝ | 38¼ | 37⅝ | 38 | + ⅜ |
| 43 | 34⅝ | Eaton pf1.19 | 1 | 37½ | 37½ | 37½ | 37½ | +1⅛ |
| 48⅜ | 30¼ | Echlin Mf .60 | 27 | 44¼ | 45¾ | 44¼ | 45¾ | +1⅞ |
| 27¼ | 23 | EckrdJk .14 | 186 | 24⅝ | 26½ | 24⅝ | 25⅛ | +1 |
| 48½ | 34½ | Eckrd NC .40 | 26 | 41¾ | 43½ | 41¾ | 43½ | +1⅝ |
| 38⅝ | 28½ | EdisonBros 1 | 25 | 29⅞ | 29⅞ | 29½ | 29½ | .... |
| 33 | 14¼ | EG&G .10 | 179 | 27½ | 28 | 26¾ | 26⅞ | − ⅛ |
| 9⅛ | 4¾ | Elect Assoc | 19 | 6¼ | 6¼ | 6¼ | 6¼ | ..... |
| 85¾ | 52 | Electn Data | 134 | 56½ | 58 | 56½ | 58 | +1⅛ |
| 17½ | 8 | El Mem Mag | 233 | 10⅞ | 11⅛ | 10¾ | 11 | + ⅜ |
| 15½ | 10½ | ElMMag pf 1 | 9 | 11¾ | 12 | 11¾ | 12 | + ¼ |
| 7⅝ | 4¾ | Elgin Nat | 27 | 5⅝ | 5⅞ | 5⅝ | 5⅞ | + ⅛ |
| 22⅛ | 17½ | ElPasoNG 1 | 82 | 18⅜ | 18½ | 18⅛ | 18¼ | ..... |
| 29⅜ | 23 | EltraCp 1.20 | 36 | 23⅜ | 24⅛ | 23⅜ | 24⅛ | + ¾ |
| 5⅛ | 3 | EMI Ltd .09g | 93 | 3¼ | 3½ | 3¼ | 3⅜ | + ¼ |
| 78¾ | 65¾ | Emer El 1.16 | 97 | 69⅝ | 70⅝ | 69¼ | 69½ | + ⅜ |
| 53⅛ | 46⅛ | EmEl pf B.90 | 126 | 48⅛ | 48½ | 48 | 48 | ..... |
| 72⅞ | 56½ | EmeryAirF 1 | 19 | 68 | 69⅝ | 68 | 69⅝ | +1⅝ |
| 44⅜ | 29⅛ | Emhart 1.20 | 194 | 29⅜ | 29⅜ | 27 | 27½ | −1⅞ |
| 32⅜ | 27¾ | EmpDist 1.88 | 9 | 28 | 28¼ | 28 | 28 | − ¼ |
| 30 | 17⅝ | Empire Gas | 148 | 19⅜ | 19⅝ | 19¼ | 19½ | − ¼ |
| 36¾ | 26¼ | EnglhMin .40 | 151 | 30⅜ | 30¾ | 30¼ | 30¼ | ..... |
| 13½ | 7¾ | EnnisBF .08p | 34 | 8 | 8 | 7¾ | 7¾ | ..... |
| 33 | 27⅜ | Equimrk .56g | 2 | 27½ | 27¾ | 27½ | 27¾ | ..... |
| 36⅞ | 32½ | Equit Gs 2.32 | 4 | 34¾ | 34¾ | 34⅝ | 34⅝ | − ⅛ |
| 35¼ | 25¾ | EquitLfe .90g | 146 | 27½ | 27⅞ | 27½ | 27¾ | + ⅜ |
| 47 | 23⅞ | EqutyFd .10g | 470 | 38½ | 39⅝ | 38 | 39 | +1 |
| 34⅜ | 21⅛ | ESB Inc 1.20 | 139 | 31¼ | 32½ | 31¼ | 32½ | +1¼ |
| 17¾ | 11 | Esquire .30 | 3 | 11 | 11⅛ | 11 | 11⅛ | + ⅛ |
| 45 | 33⅛ | EssexInt 1.20 | 123 | 40⅜ | 40¾ | 40¼ | 40¼ | + ⅛ |
| 54¾ | 42 | Essex pf2.84 | 2 | 48½ | 48½ | 48½ | 48½ | + ½ |
| 18⅜ | 10 | Esterlin .22g | 20 | 11 | 11⅝ | 11 | 11⅜ | + ¼ |
| 30 | 20½ | Ethyl Cp .84 | 76 | 21 | 21⅝ | 21 | 21⅝ | + ¾ |
| 43⅜ | 34¼ | Ethyl pf2.46 | 26 | 36¾ | 38½ | 36¾ | 38¼ | +2¼ |
| 51⅛ | 40⅛ | EvansP .60b | 1346 | 40⅝ | 40⅝ | 39½ | 40⅜ | − ¼ |
| 24½ | 17½ | ExCellO 1.25 | 35 | 17½ | 18¼ | 17½ | 18¼ | + ¾ |
| 33½ | 18 | Extendcare | 29 | 25⅜ | 25⅞ | 25⅜ | 25⅝ | + ½ |
| 22½ | 12⅞ | Faberge .40 | 173 | 15⅞ | 16⅜ | 15¼ | 15¼ | − ½ |
| 44⅝ | 35¼ | FactorA .60 | 19 | 37⅜ | 37½ | 37⅜ | 37½ | + ⅜ |
| 48⅝ | 21½ | Fairch Cam | 507 | 33¼ | 35½ | 32⅛ | 33⅞ | + ⅝ |
| 13⅜ | 8 | Fair Ind .15g | 13 | 8¼ | 8⅜ | 8¼ | 8¼ | + ⅛ |
| 20¾ | 14⅞ | Fairmont 1 | 19 | 15⅜ | 15⅜ | 15 | 15 | − ⅜ |
| 8⅞ | 5¾ | Falstaff | 20 | 6⅜ | 6½ | 6¼ | 6¼ | ..... |
| 17¼ | 12½ | Family Fi .60 | 7 | 12¾ | 12⅞ | 12⅝ | 12⅝ | .... |
| 16⅛ | 9⅛ | Fansteel Inc | 33 | 9¾ | 10 | 9¾ | 9⅞ | + ¼ |
| 17 | 10⅜ | Far West Fin | 33 | 11⅜ | 11⅜ | 11⅛ | 11¼ | ..... |
| 49¼ | 28 | FarahMfg .44 | 473 | 33⅜ | 35½ | 33⅜ | 33¾ | + ½ |
| 50 | 38 | Fedders .50 | 38 | 43⅝ | 44¼ | 43¼ | 43½ | + ¼ |
| 37¾ | 23½ | Federal 1.20 | 248 | 27⅝ | 28 | 27½ | 27¾ | − ¼ |
| 31⅝ | 25⅞ | FedMog 1.80 | 14 | 27 | 27¼ | 26⅝ | 27 | + ¼ |
| 73 | 55 | Fed NM 1.20 | 351 | 59¼ | 59⅝ | 58¼ | 58¾ | + ⅞ |
| 20⅞ | 14 | FedPacEl | 93 | 20⅞ | 21 | 20⅞ | 20⅞ | ..... |
| 21¾ | 17 | F Pac pf1.26 | 9 | 19¼ | 19¼ | 19 | 19 | − ½ |
| 31⅝ | 18¾ | FedPapBd 1 | 54 | 31 | 31⅜ | 29 | 29 | −1¾ |
| 24 | 16 | FedSigns .60 | 9 | 18½ | 19 | 18½ | 18⅞ | + ⅜ |
| 12½ | 6½ | Federals Inc | 10 | 6⅞ | 7 | 6¾ | 7 | + ⅛ |
| 49 | 38⅛ | FedDeptStr 1 | 272 | 44½ | 45¼ | 44¼ | 44⅝ | + ¼ |
| 12⅛ | 7¾ | Federat Dev | 2 | 9⅛ | 9½ | 9⅛ | 9½ | + ¼ |
| 27⅞ | 20¼ | Ferro Cp .70 | 20 | 23 | 23⅞ | 23 | 23⅞ | +1¼ |
| 35 | 23½ | Fibrebrd .70 | 111 | 24¼ | 24½ | 24⅛ | 24⅛ | ..... |
| 45¾ | 42 | FidUnbn 2.20 | 2 | 42 | 42 | 41⅞ | 41⅞ | − ⅜ |
| 41⅞ | 31¼ | FieldctM 1.40 | 14 | 33⅝ | 33⅞ | 33⅝ | 33⅞ | + ½ |
| 28⅜ | 19¾ | Filtrol 1.40 | 13 | 21 | 21 | 20¾ | 20¾ | − ⅝ |
| 21¼ | 12⅞ | Fin Federatn | 26 | 14¾ | 14⅞ | 14⅝ | 14⅝ | + ⅜ |
| 54⅞ | 47⅜ | Firestne 1.60 | 304 | 52½ | 53¾ | 52½ | 52¾ | + ⅝ |
| 26 | 20 | Fst Chart | 748 | 20½ | 22 | 20½ | 22 | +1⅞ |
| 33⅜ | 23⅞ | Fst Mtg 1.11g | 126 | 27⅜ | 27¾ | 27 | 27¾ | + ⅜ |
| 77½ | 63½ | FstNatBos 3 | 9 | 66 | 66¾ | 66 | 66¾ | + ½ |
| 40½ | 33 | FstNCity 1.32 | 214 | 33¾ | 34½ | 33¾ | 34⅜ | + ½ |
| 40⅛ | 35¼ | FstNStBnc 2 | 2 | 35⅞ | 35⅞ | 35⅞ | 35⅞ | + ⅜ |
| 49½ | 34⅝ | Fst NatStr 1g | 21 | 35 | 35¼ | 35 | 35¼ | + ½ |
| 12 | 9⅞ | FstVaBks .40 | 18 | 10⅜ | 10⅜ | 10⅜ | 10⅜ | .... |
| 40 | 32¾ | Fischbch .80 | x4 | 35¼ | 35⅜ | 35¼ | 35⅜ | + ¾ |
| 18½ | 12⅜ | FishrFd .15g | 53 | 14¾ | 14⅞ | 14⅝ | 14⅞ | + ¼ |
| 19¼ | 10⅝ | Fisher Sci .16 | 102 | 14⅛ | 14⅝ | 14 | 14¼ | + ¼ |
| 50¾ | 29½ | FleetEnt .24 | 84 | 48⅞ | 49⅞ | 48⅞ | 49⅞ | +1⅝ |
| 14¾ | 10¾ | Fleming .50 | 6 | 12½ | 12½ | 12⅛ | 12⅛ | − ⅜ |
| 30½ | 24 | Flintkote 1 | 35 | 26½ | 27⅛ | 26½ | 27⅛ | +1 |
| 41¼ | 33¼ | Flint pfB 2.25 | 1 | 37 | 37 | 37 | 37 | + ½ |

| --1971-- High | Low | Stocks Div | Sales in 100s | Open | High | Low | Close | Net Chg. |
|---|---|---|---|---|---|---|---|---|
| 28¾ | 21½ | Heller Int .76 | 101 | 21⅞ | 22¼ | 21⅞ | 22¼ | + ¼ |
| 17¾ | 14½ | Helm Pd .40b | 21 | 15¼ | 15⅜ | 15⅛ | 15¼ | .... |
| 27⅝ | 21⅛ | HelmrhP .20 | 20 | 25 | 25¼ | 24⅝ | 24⅝ | − ⅜ |
| 5 | 3½ | Hemisph Cap | 3 | 3¾ | 3⅞ | 3¾ | 3⅞ | + ⅛ |
| 8⅛ | 6¾ | HemInc .25g | 23 | 7⅛ | 7¼ | 7⅛ | 7¼ | + ⅛ |
| 50⅞ | 40½ | Hercules .75g | 100 | 45½ | 46⅝ | 45½ | 46⅝ | +1⅜ |
| 31⅜ | 26¼ | HershF 1.10 | 17 | 27⅝ | 28¼ | 27⅝ | 28¼ | + ¼ |
| 50⅛ | 37⅞ | Heublein .85 | 208 | 40¼ | 41⅜ | 40¼ | 41⅛ | + ⅞ |
| 44⅞ | 29½ | Hew Pack .20 | 84 | 39¼ | 40⅛ | 39¼ | 39⅞ | +1⅛ |
| 16¾ | 8⅝ | High Voltge | 191 | 9⅝ | 10⅛ | 9⅝ | 9⅞ | + ¼ |
| 51¾ | 39½ | Hilton Hotl 1 | 86 | 44¾ | 45 | 44¾ | 45 | + ¼ |
| 57¾ | 40½ | Hobart 1.20 | 18 | 51 | 52 | 51 | 52 | +1¼ |
| 30¼ | 23⅛ | HoernWal .90 | 34 | 23¾ | 24¼ | 23¾ | 24¼ | + ¾ |
| 17 | 6⅝ | Hoff Electrn | 38 | 13¼ | 13⅞ | 13¼ | 13⅝ | + ¾ |
| 50⅝ | 34⅝ | HolidyInn .25 | 340 | 43¾ | 44½ | 43⅝ | 44½ | + ⅞ |
| 20⅞ | 13½ | HollySug .30p | 29 | 14¼ | 14¼ | 14. | 14 | − ¼ |
| 31⅞ | 22 | Homestke .40 | 80 | 27¾ | 27⅞ | 27⅛ | 27⅜ | − ⅛ |
| 116½ | 82 | Honywll 1.30 | 196 | 97 | 99 | 96¾ | 99 | +2 |
| 35 | 27¼ | HoovrBl 1.20 | 12 | 31¼ | 31¾ | 31¼ | 31¾ | + ⅜ |
| 44⅞ | 22½ | HospitCp Am | 85 | 36⅝ | 37¾ | 36⅝ | 37⅜ | +1⅜ |
| 39 | 28⅜ | Host Intl .36 | 14 | 33 | 33½ | 33 | 33¼ | + ⅝ |
| 15⅞ | 11⅜ | Houdaille .60 | 33 | 11⅞ | 12 | 11⅝ | 12 | + ⅛ |
| 32 | 27½ | Houdl pf 2.25 | 1 | 28¾ | 28¾ | 28¾ | 28¾ | + ¼ |
| 18⅜ | 13 | Houg Miff .40 | 14 | 14¼ | 14½ | 14¼ | 14¼ | + ¼ |
| 54 | 41¾ | HousehF 1.20 | 325 | 45⅜ | 45⅜ | 44⅞ | 44⅞ | + ⅛ |
| 160½ | 125¾ | HousF pf4.40 | 1 | 134 | 134 | 134 | 134 | +1 |
| 58½ | 48¾ | HousF pf2.50 | 50 | 52¾ | 53¼ | 52¾ | 53⅛ | + ¾ |
| 80½ | 65¾ | HousF pf2.37 | 1 | 69 | 69 | 69 | 69 | +1¾ |
| 49¾ | 41⅝ | HousLP 1.32 | 80 | 44 | 44⅛ | 43½ | 44 | ..... |
| 41¼ | 39¾ | HousNGs .80 | 51 | 41½ | 42¼ | 41½ | 42¼ | +1 |
| 54¾ | 46¼ | HouG pf2.50 | 15 | 46⅝ | 46¾ | 46½ | 46¾ | + ¼ |
| 38 | 20½ | How John .24 | 443 | 35¼ | 35½ | 34¾ | 35¼ | + ⅝ |
| 22¾ | 14 | Howmet .70 | 27 | 14¼ | 14¼ | 14⅛ | 14⅛ | ..... |
| 25½ | 20¼ | Hubbad 1.09g | 24 | 21 | 21⅛ | 20¾ | 21 | + ¼ |
| 24⅝ | 19⅛ | HudBay .30p | 12 | 22¼ | 22¾ | 22¼ | 22¾ | + ½ |
| 14 | 10⅜ | Hugh Hat .40 | 1 | 10⅞ | 10⅞ | 10⅞ | 10⅞ | |
| 21¾ | 16 | Hunt Chm .16 | 42 | 17¼ | 17½ | 17¼ | 17½ | + ½ |
| 50¼ | 31 | Huyck Cp .48 | 20 | 39 | 39⅜ | 38¾ | 39⅜ | + ⅜ |
| 38 | 29¾ | IdahoPw 1.70 | 88 | 30½ | 30¾ | 30⅜ | 30⅜ | − ⅛ |
| 19⅛ | 13¾ | Ideal Bas .60 | 34 | 17⅛ | 17⅜ | 17⅛ | 17¼ | + ⅛ |
| 40⅞ | 29 | Ill Cent 1.14 | 9 | 33¾ | 34 | 33½ | 33½ | − ½ |
| 65 | 50 | Ill Cen pf3.50 | 2 | 55⅜ | 55⅜ | 55 | 55 | ..... |
| 44¾ | 33¾ | Ill Powr 2.20 | 18 | 35¼ | 35¼ | 35 | 35¼ | ..... |
| 33¼ | 29⅜ | Ill Pow pf2.21 | z300 | 29 | 29 | 29 | 29 | − ⅜ |
| 17 | 12¼ | Imprl Cp Am | 889 | 12⅜ | 12⅝ | 12⅜ | 12½ | + ¼ |
| 55⅛ | 34⅞ | INA Cp 1.40 | 460 | 53 | 53⅞ | 53 | 53⅜ | + ⅝ |
| 13 | 9⅞ | Income Capit | 19 | 10⅜ | 10⅝ | 10⅜ | 10⅝ | + ⅜ |
| 11 | 9¾ | IncCCu .68g | 15 | 10⅛ | 10⅛ | 10⅛ | 10⅛ | .... |
| 33⅝ | 25⅞ | Indian Hd .80 | 16 | 29¼ | 29⅜ | 29¼ | 29¼ | + ⅛ |
| 120 | 94½ | Ind Hd pf4.50 | 2 | 105 | 105 | 105 | 105 | + ¾ |
| 30⅝ | 25 | IndnaGs 1.72 | 1 | 26½ | 26½ | 26½ | 26½ | ..... |
| 30 | 23¾ | IndplsPL 1.50 | 55 | 26½ | 26½ | 26 | 26 | − ½ |
| 105 | 93½ | Ind PL pf6.25 | 2 | 93 | 93 | 93 | 93 | −1 |
| 59⅛ | 45 | Inger Rand 2 | 54 | 49⅞ | 50⅜ | 49¾ | 50⅜ | + ¼ |
| 43½ | 37¾ | IngRd pf2.35 | 66 | 38¼ | 38⅜ | 38 | 38⅜ | + ⅛ |
| 32¼ | 26½ | Inland Stl 2 | 82 | 26½ | 26⅝ | 26⅜ | 26½ | − ⅛ |
| 14⅜ | 10⅛ | Inmont Corp | 66 | 12½ | 12⅞ | 12⅜ | 12⅞ | + ⅝ |
| 62 | 51 | Inmont pf4.50 | z40 | 55 | 55 | 55 | 55 | +1¼ |
| 20¾ | 15⅝ | Insilco .70 | 26 | 17⅜ | 17¾ | 17⅜ | 17¾ | + ⅜ |
| 24 | 19⅜ | Insilc pfA1.25 | 16 | 20¾ | 20¾ | 20⅜ | 20⅝ | − ⅛ |
| 51 | 36⅝ | InspirCop 2 | x8 | 39⅞ | 40⅜ | 39⅞ | 40⅜ | +1 |
| 48⅛ | 40¼ | Interco 1.20 | 5 | 44⅞ | 44⅞ | 44½ | 44¾ | ..... |
| 30⅜ | 24¼ | IntrlkInc 1.80 | 21 | 25⅝ | 25¾ | 25⅜ | 25⅝ | − ¼ |
| 365¾ | 283¼ | IBM 5.20 | 429 | 295 | 297½ | 294 | 296¾ | +5½ |
| 29⅞ | 20½ | IntChm Nuc | 414 | 23½ | 23⅞ | 23 | 23⅜ | + ½ |
| 80 | 63 | IntFlaFr .60b | 254 | 72¾ | 73⅝ | 72⅜ | 73⅛ | +1 |
| 33⅞ | 24 | Int Harv 1.40 | 137 | 25 | 25⅝ | 25 | 25⅝ | + ½ |
| 15¾ | 12¾ | IntHoldg .33g | 12 | 13½ | 13⅝ | 13⅜ | 13⅝ | + ⅛ |
| 13⅜ | 5 | Int Indust | 96 | 5½ | 6 | 5½ | 5⅝ | + ⅛ |
| 23⅞ | 9⅛ | IntIndA pf | 14 | 9½ | 9¾ | 9½ | 9½ | + ¼ |
| 20⅝ | 13¾ | Int Mineral | 217 | 16½ | 17 | 16⅜ | 16¾ | + ¾ |
| 15¼ | 9 | Int Mng | 22 | 11 | 11¼ | 10⅞ | 10⅞ | − ⅝ |
| 46¾ | 29½ | Int Nickel 1 | 613 | 31½ | 32 | 31⅜ | 32 | + ⅞ |
| 40⅝ | 31⅝ | Int Pap 1.50 | 309 | 33½ | 33⅞ | 33⅜ | 33½ | + ¼ |
| 66½ | 57 | Int Pap pf 4 | z20 | 57½ | 57½ | 57½ | 57½ | + ½ |
| 9⅝ | 6¼ | Int Rectifier | 15 | 6⅜ | 6½ | 6¼ | 6½ | + ⅛ |
| 67⅜ | 49 | Int T&T 1.15 | 1094 | 56 | 56¾ | 55½ | 56⅝ | +1⅜ |
| 205⅜ | 151 | IntT&T pfE 4 | z10 | 170 | 170 | 170 | 170 | +1¼ |
| 122½ | 94 | IntT&T pfH 4 | 13 | 103 | 104 | 103 | 103⅛ | +2⅛ |
| 118 | 93¾ | IT&T pfI 4.50 | 71 | 99 | 102 | 99 | 102 | +5 |
| 112½ | 90 | IntT&T pfJ 4 | 5 | 96½ | 97 | 96½ | 97 | +1 |
| 112 | 86 | IntT&T pfK4 | 37 | 93½ | 95½ | 93½ | 95½ | +2¾ |
| 84¼ | 62 | IT&TpfN 2.25 | 181 | 70 | 71 | 69⅝ | 70¾ | +2 |
| 110½ | 87½ | IntT&T pfO 5 | 16 | 98 | 98½ | 98 | 98½ | + ½ |
| 44⅞ | 35½ | Int Util 1.40 | 163 | 37⅞ | 39¼ | 37⅞ | 39¼ | +1¾ |
| 50½ | 39¾ | Int Util A | 24 | 42½ | 43¾ | 42¼ | 43¾ | +1¾ |
| 36⅜ | 24¼ | Interpace 1 | 11 | 24⅞ | 25½ | 24⅞ | 25½ | +1 |
| 100 | 77½ | Interpce pf 5 | 3 | 78 | 78 | 77 | 78 | − ½ |

**Fig. 19–8** Stock quotations in daily papers. This illustration shows a portion of the New York Stock Exchange transactions for a typical trading day as reported in *The Wall Street Journal*. Reprinted by permission from Dow Jones & Company, Inc.

completed, they are reported and made public on some 2,000 tickers in nearly 400 cities in the United States and Canada. In addition, about 1,500 Translux screen devices magnify the ticker tape on screens viewed by thousands of brokers and investors. In addition, stock prices are relayed to more than 130 offices of member organizations in foreign cities and even to ships at sea.

The ticker services of both exchanges link the newspapers of the world with the events of these trading centers. The Associated Press and United Press-International send frequent reports into hundreds of newspaper offices during the market day.

Selected quotations or trading information from stocks traded on the New York Stock Exchange are usually summarized in the financial section of local daily papers. In some larger papers, American Stock Exchange quotes may also appear. *The Wall Street Journal* publishes a complete listing of all trading on both the big exchanges, plus other important local or regional exchanges. It also contains excellent up-to-date information on practically every major industry.

It's easy to read the exchange quotations once you understand how the data are presented. Figure 19–8 shows a portion of the New York Stock Exchange transactions as they appeared in one of the daily issues of the *Wall Street Journal*. The first two columns, headed by the current year, show the price range in which the stocks traded during that year.

For example, find the stock of the Firestone Tire and Rubber Corporation. It is abbreviated Firestone in *The Wall Street Journal* listing. Up to that particular date, the stock had traded within a range of $54\frac{7}{8}$ high and $47\frac{3}{8}$ low. These figures reflect *dollars* and fractions of dollars instead of cents with which most people are accustomed to dealing. Therefore, the stock had traded at prices from $54.875 to $47.375. The year's high and low range does not include changes in the latest day's trading. The figure immediately following the name of the stock indicates the annual amount of dividend paid on each share of stock based on the last quarterly or semiannual declaration. Special dividends are designated with a symbol and explained in a footnote. The next column indicates how many 100's of shares of stock were traded. In this instance 30,400 shares of Firestone stock were traded on that particular day. The other columns list the opening or first trading price on the stock for the day; the high, low, and closing prices. The last column indicates the net change from the last transaction of the current trading day as compared with the last transaction from the previous trading day. All these figures are dollar amounts. Thus the high trade of the day was $53.75 while the low was $52.50. Daily newspapers may not have all the data included in *The Wall Street Journal*, but the method of reporting is similar. A check of the column headings will clarify how the information is being presented. Since local papers may have to conserve space, the corporation names are generally abbreviated more than in *The Wall Street Journal*.

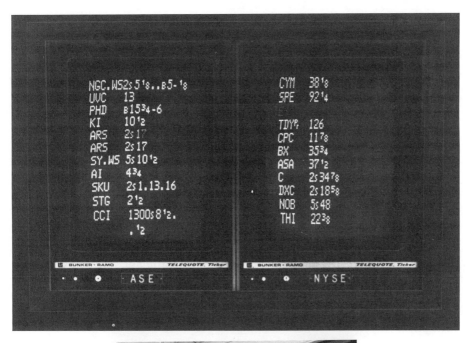

**Fig. 19–9** Modern quotation displays in brokerage offices. Ticker tape quotes are enlarged and projected onto a screen as soon as they are received in office (19–9(a)). Courtesy of Bunker-Ramo Corporation. Figure 19–9(b) shows ASE and NYSE quotations as they appear on new television display devices. Courtesy of Merrill Lynch, Pierce, Fenner & Smith, Inc.

The important thing to remember is that through the ticker and the various quotation services, events of the market place are exposed to public view on a continuing and broad basis helping to provide investors with the daily information they need in order to make their investment decisions. If the daily newspaper or other financial journal is too slow for a particular investor's needs, he can usually get almost instant reporting of market events at his local broker's office. One of the newer electronic boards to be found in the modern broker's office is illustrated in Fig. 19–9. Clients can sit and read tapes showing transactions which occurred only moments earlier on the floor of the NYSE as well as the ASE. Popular stocks are listed by their abbreviated symbols on the electronic board and prices are automatically changed as trades take place on the exchanges.

The exchanges also have interesting voice-quotation systems. Special high-speed access switching equipment links the computer center of either market with telephone lines for direct inquiry by subscribers. By dialing code numbers, member firm subscribers can obtain automatic voice-answer-back data for bid-asked quotations and last sales for any listed stock or for open, high, low, last, and volume information. The New York Stock Exchange system is capable of handling 300 calls simultaneously or up to 400,000 calls each day.

### THE OVER-THE-COUNTER SECURITIES MARKET

All securities trades that occur other than on the floor of one of the stock exchanges are considered over-the-counter transactions. The market is not housed in a single building, nor do the trades occur in any specific geographic place. The over-the-counter market, commonly referred to as the OTC market, consists of thousands of brokerage offices, small and large, scattered from East to West. There are now approximately 5,500 of these broker-dealers registered with the Securities and Exchange Commission, and together they maintain some 4,500 branch offices.*

The OTC market and the stock exchanges complement each other in serving the investing public. It is generally agreed that the greatest volume of trading in securities in the United States takes place over-the-counter, although the exact figures are not really known. The National Security Traders Association, Inc., estimates that 50,000 corporate and governmental issues are traded in this market.**

Sales occur through *negotiation* in the OTC market in contrast to sales by *auction* in the stock exchanges. To illustrate, let us suppose for a moment that a person in Virginia wants to buy 200 shares of stock in a small oil company incorporated and operating in Montana. The investor contacts his broker in

---

* *O.T.C.* New York: National Security Traders Association, Inc., 1961, p. 3.
** *O.T.C.* New York: National Security Traders Association, Inc., 1961, p. 6.

Richmond, Virginia, and inquires about the stock. Not being familiar with the corporation or having previously handled transactions involving this stock, the broker searches for a recent price quote. He finds this quote showing *bid* and *asked* prices on a list collected and published daily by the National Quotation Bureau, Inc. Daily quotes on about 8,000 OTC stocks are available through this company. Detailed lists, called *pink sheets*, are distributed to subscribers. These lists include price information as well as the names of brokers who trade each particular stock. Selected quotes are also reproduced in many newspapers. (See Fig. 19–10.) The prices in such a list do not necessarily reflect actual trades, but instead they are guides showing the approximate prices at which people are willing to buy and sell the stock. The Richmond broker would then probably contact by telephone or telegraph one or more of the brokerage firms shown in the pink sheets. He acts as a negotiator and attempts to bring the buyer and seller to agreement on price.

# Over-the-Counter Markets

*These quotations, supplied by the National Association of Securities Dealers, are bids and offers quoted by over-the-counter dealers to each other as of approximately 3:30 p.m. (Eastern time). The quotations do not include retail markup, markdown or commission, and do not represent actual transactions.*

*Additional quotations are included in a weekly over-the-counter list published each Monday on this page.*

| Stock & Div. | Bid | Asked | Bid Chg. |
|---|---|---|---|
| ComlShear .50 | 14¾ | 15¾ | −1¾ |
| ComwlGs .40b | 12¼ | 13¼ | .... |
| ComwlNGs 1½ | 27 | 27⅜ | +⅛ |
| CmwTlPa 1.10 | 24 | 25 | .... |
| Commun Prop | 8¾ | 9⅛ | .... |
| Com Psych Cn | 14⅝ | 15⅛ | +⅛ |
| Compnt CpAm | 4¼ | 5 | .... |
| Compugraph | 10¾ | 11¼ | −¼ |
| Comp Commu | 7¼ | 7¾ | .... |
| Computer Con | 6½ | 7 | −⅛ |
| Computer Img | 11⅞ | 12⅜ | −⅛ |
| Comput Instal | 4⅜ | 4⅞ | .... |
| Comp Mictech | 2 | 2¼ | .... |
| Computr Tech | 6 | 6¼ | +⅛ |
| Comput Terml | 5⅞ | 6⅛ | −⅛ |
| Computr Usag | 7⅛ | 7⅝ | −⅛ |
| Comress Incor | 2⅛ | 2⅜ | .... |
| ConAgra .50 | 15¾ | 16¼ | −⅛ |
| ConnNtGs 2.40 | 36¼ | 37¼ | +¼ |
| ConsolPaper 1 | 18¾ | 19½ | −¼ |
| ConsRock 1.20 | 26 | 27½ | .... |
| Consyne Corp | 11½ | 12 | −½ |
| ContlCapital k | 6⅝ | 7 | +⅛ |
| ContlCare Cnt | 4⅛ | 4⅜ | −⅛ |
| Contl Invest | 9¼ | 9⅝ | .... |
| Contran Corp | 1⅝ | 1⅞ | .... |
| Context Indust | 6⅛ | 6⅜ | −¼ |
| Convalarium | 3⅛ | 3½ | .... |
| Convenient In | 5⅝ | 6⅛ | .... |
| Conwed Cp .40 | 8 | 8½ | −⅛ |
| Cook Chem .35 | 9¼ | 9¾ | .... |
| CorencoCorp 2 | 30½ | 31½ | −2½ |
| Cornelius Co | 3⅞ | 4⅛ | +⅛ |
| Corporation S | 2⅞ | 3⅛ | .... |
| Cosmet Yours | 7½ | 8½ | .... |
| CousinsPro .14 | 25¼ | 26 | −¼ |
| CradockT .64g | 15⅝ | 16 | .... |
| Crawford .30b | 15 | 15¾ | .... |
| Crawfrd Corp | 4¼ | 4¾ | .... |
| CrossComp .50 | 29¼ | 30 | −½ |
| Crown Crafts | 6⅝ | 7⅛ | +⅛ |
| CRS DesignAs | 12½ | 12⅞ | −⅛ |
| Crutcher Res | 7 | 7¼ | .... |
| Cullum Co .24 | 9⅜ | 9⅝ | +⅛ |
| Curtis Noll .40 | 13¾ | 14½ | .... |
| Cypress Com i | 8¼ | 8⅝ | +⅛ |
| Giffen Indust | 4⅛ | 4½ | −⅛ |
| Gilbert Robin | 6⅝ | 7⅛ | −¼ |
| GilfordInst .12 | 12½ | 13¼ | +¼ |
| Glatfelter 1.40 | 21½ | 23½ | −½ |
| GleasonWk .42 | 24½ | 25 | +¼ |
| GlosserBr .10b | 11 | 11⅜ | −⅛ |
| Godfrey Co .80 | 16¾ | 17½ | .... |
| Gold Medalion | 4¾ | 5¼ | .... |
| Golden Cycle | 16¼ | 16¾ | +¾ |
| Golden Fl .32d | 10 | 10½ | .... |
| Golden Wst Fi | 13 | 13½ | −⅜ |
| Goodwy Copy | 1 | 1⅜ | .... |
| GouldInvs .18e | 8 | 8½ | −⅛ |
| GvEm Cp .40g | 16 | 16½ | −½ |
| GovEmpFl .50 | 29⅞ | 30⅜ | −⅛ |
| Graco Inc .10b | 29 | 29¾ | −½ |
| GrahmMf .15b | 6⅝ | 7⅛ | −⅛ |
| Grand AutoIn | 18¾ | 19¼ | .... |
| Graphic Cont | 9⅝ | 10 | .... |
| Graphic Scien | 22¼ | 22¾ | +⅛ |
| GtAmMt 1.08b | 27¾ | 28¼ | −⅜ |
| GtMarkW Pac | 3⅜ | 3⅞ | +⅛ |
| Gt MidwestCp | 23½ | 25 | .... |
| Great Sowest | 2⅛ | 2⅜ | .... |
| Green MP 1.12 | 14¾ | 15⅛ | .... |
| G R E I T 1.60 | 17⅛ | 17⅝ | .... |
| GreyAdver .50 | 13 | 13¾ | −¼ |
| GRI Computr | 2½ | 2¾ | −⅛ |
| Griggs Equipt | 3¾ | 4¼ | −⅛ |
| Grove Press | 2¼ | 2½ | .... |
| GrwthIntl .15d | 6½ | 7 | .... |
| GRT Corporat | 2½ | 2¾ | +⅛ |
| Grumman Ind | 7½ | 8⅜ | .... |
| Guardian Car | 6⅛ | 6⅝ | .... |
| GulfIntrest .30 | 6¼ | 6¾ | −¼ |
| Gyrodyne .30b | 5⅛ | 5⅝ | −⅛ |
| **H** | | | |
| Hallcraft Hms | 33 | 34 | .... |
| Hamilton Bros | 32¾ | 33¼ | .... |
| HanoverSh .55 | 11½ | 12½ | +¼ |
| HardeesFd .16 | 9½ | 9¾ | −⅛ |
| HardwckCo In | 6 | 6½ | −⅛ |
| Harper Rw .40 | 13⅜ | 13⅞ | −⅝ |
| Harrel Intl 15i | 3 | 3½ | .... |
| Hasbro Indust | (z) | (z) | (z) |
| Hart Carter | 5 | 5½ | −⅛ |
| MadisonGsE 1 | 15 | 15½ | |
| MajorPool Eq | 2⅜ | 2¾ | −¼ |
| Major Realty | 10⅝ | 10⅞ | +1 |
| MallickrdC .80 | 90⅞ | 91⅜ | −⅛ |
| ManorCare In | 6⅛ | 6½ | −⅛ |
| Marcus H .21b | 7 | 7¾ | .... |
| Marion Corpn | 4½ | 5½ | −¼ |
| Maritim Fruit | 13 | 13⅜ | +½ |
| Mark Systems | 3¼ | 3¾ | .... |
| MarshSupr .45 | 7¼ | 7¾ | .... |
| MarthaMan 5i | 4½ | 5 | .... |
| Martha Wh .30 | 8¼ | 8⅝ | .... |
| MartinBw .15b | 26½ | 27¼ | −¼ |
| Mary Kay Inc | 19½ | 20 | −⅛ |
| Maui LndPine | 8⅞ | 9⅜ | −⅛ |
| McCormc .60a | 61½ | 63 | +½ |
| McMoran Exp | 6⅛ | 6⅜ | .... |
| McQuayPx .70 | 18½ | 19¼ | −¼ |
| Median Mtglv | 11½ | 12 | .... |
| Med ElscPhm | 6⅝ | 7 | .... |
| MedicHom En | 5⅝ | 6⅛ | .... |
| Medical Analy | 10¾ | 11¼ | −¼ |
| Medical Invst | 4½ | 5¼ | −½ |
| MedicMt 1.90b | 26⅛ | 26⅝ | −1¼ |
| Medical Servs | 6¼ | 7 | −¼ |
| Medicenters A | 12 | 12½ | .... |
| Medtronic Inc | 39⅝ | 40⅛ | .... |
| Meister Brau | 4⅜ | 4⅝ | .... |
| MercantInd 5k | 9⅞ | 10¼ | .... |
| Merch Inc 1.30 | 24¾ | 25¼ | −¼ |
| MeridianI .65d | 17⅛ | 17⅝ | −¾ |
| Metalfab Inc | 5 | 5½ | −¼ |
| Methode Elect | 3¾ | 4⅛ | .... |
| MeyerFr .60g | 30½ | 31¼ | −⅛ |
| MicrofmDa Sy | 4¼ | 4¾ | .... |
| Midas Intl .40 | 18⅞ | 19⅜ | +¼ |
| MidIndCap .20 | 6⅝ | 7 | −⅛ |
| Midtex Incorp | 1¾ | 2 | .... |
| MidTex Cmun | 15¼ | 15¾ | .... |
| MidwsGasTr 1 | 20½ | 21½ | .... |
| Miller Brother | 9 | 9½ | +⅛ |
| MillerHm .12b | 13½ | 14 | −⅛ |
| Millipore C .42 | 63¾ | 64¾ | +¼ |
| Minn Fabrics | 26 | 26¾ | +¾ |
| Minnpl Gs 2.10 | 34¾ | 35¼ | −¼ |
| MissRvTr 1.08 | 13⅞ | 14¼ | −¼ |
| Porter H K 1 | 20¾ | 21¾ | −¼ |
| Possis Machin | 8¼ | 8¾ | +⅜ |
| Pott Indst .07b | 21¾ | 22¼ | .... |
| Precision Inst | 10½ | 12 | .... |
| PremiMic .15b | 3¾ | 4¼ | .... |
| Pres Fst Lady | 3 | 3⅜ | −⅛ |
| PrewayIn .70g | 12¾ | 13¼ | .... |
| Prochemco In | 5¼ | 5⅝ | .... |
| Professl Golf | 4 | 4¼ | .... |
| Prog Prop Sys | 3¾ | 4 | −⅛ |
| Programg Sys | 2 | 2¼ | .... |
| Provincal Hse | 6 | 6½ | .... |
| Prudent Minrl | 2⅝ | 2⅞ | .... |
| PubSvc N M 1 | 20⅞ | 21¼ | .... |
| Pub Sv NC .80 | 11½ | 11⅞ | .... |
| Publish Co Inc | 5⅜ | 5⅝ | .... |
| Purepac Labs | 14⅝ | 15 | −⅛ |
| Puritan Bennt | 31⅜ | 31⅞ | −⅛ |
| PutnamD Cap | 4⅜ | 4¾ | .... |
| PutnamInc 1a | 15 | 16½ | .... |
| **Q** | | | |
| Qonaar Cp .40 | 10⅛ | 10⅝ | .... |
| Quality Motel | 9¾ | 10⅛ | −⅛ |
| **R** | | | |
| Radi Dyanmic | 9½ | 10 | −¼ |
| Radiant Indus | 4¾ | 5⅛ | .... |
| Ragen Precis | 7⅝ | 8⅛ | .... |
| Rahall Comm | 9½ | 10¼ | −½ |
| Ransburg .50 | 20¼ | 21 | .... |
| Raven Indust | 3¼ | 3¾ | +¼ |
| Raychem Crp | 84¾ | 85¾ | +¾ |
| RayGo Incorp | 5 | 5⅜ | .... |
| Raymond .20g | 13 | 13½ | .... |
| Recogn Equip | 12¾ | 13¼ | .... |
| Red OwlStrs 1 | 29¾ | 30¾ | .... |
| Redcor Corp | 4⅞ | 5¼ | .... |
| Reece Cp .68a | 29¼ | 30¼ | +¼ |
| Regency Eltrn | 19½ | 19⅞ | +¼ |
| Reid ProvLab | 16⅞ | 17⅜ | −⅛ |
| Reliable Inves | 12½ | 13¼ | .... |
| RelianUvl 1.04 | 31½ | 32 | .... |
| RepubFcl 1.20 | 48 | 49 | .... |
| Rep GypsumC | 9 | 9½ | .... |
| Research .20b | 5 | 5¾ | .... |
| Residex Corp | 4¾ | 5⅛ | .... |
| Respon Envir | 4⅛ | 4½ | −¼ |
| Triton Oil Gas | 4⅜ | 4¾ | −⅜ |
| Tuftco Corptn | 10⅜ | 10⅞ | +⅜ |
| Twin Disc 1.10 | 25¾ | 26¾ | .... |
| TysonFds .10h | 10 | 10½ | .... |
| **U** | | | |
| UniCapital Cp | 20¼ | 20¾ | −1⅛ |
| Unitec Indust | 3⅜ | 3¾ | .... |
| Un ArtTh .20g | 9¼ | 10 | −¼ |
| UtdConv Hosp | 2¼ | 2⅝ | .... |
| Utd Illum 2.08 | 29⅛ | 29⅝ | .... |
| UnMcGill .05d | 6½ | 6⅞ | .... |
| Unitd Overton | 3 | 3½ | −¼ |
| Unitek Corpor | 17¼ | 18 | −¼ |
| USBanknot .30 | 6¾ | 7⅛ | .... |
| USEnvelop .60 | 16¼ | 16¾ | −⅛ |
| U S Sugar 2 | 47 | 48½ | .... |
| USTruckLns 1 | 26 | 26¾ | −¼ |
| UniversalFd 1 | x26½ | 27 | +¼ |
| Univ Pub Dist | 3¼ | 4 | +¼ |
| Univ Telephon | 7 | 7½ | .... |
| UpPenPw 1.60 | 20⅞ | 21⅜ | −⅛ |
| Utils&Inds 5k | 24½ | 25½ | .... |
| **V** | | | |
| Vail Associate | 7½ | 7¾ | −⅛ |
| Valley Forge | 7⅜ | 7⅞ | .... |
| Valley Gas .76 | 9⅞ | 10¼ | .... |
| Valmont Indu | 8¼ | 8¾ | +⅛ |
| ValueLDv .11b | 6⅜ | 6⅝ | −⅛ |
| VanceSan 1.20 | 16 | 16½ | .... |
| VanDuAirc .40 | 9¼ | 9⅝ | .... |
| Van Dyk Rsch | 14¼ | 15 | −¼ |
| Varadyne Inc | 3⅞ | 4¼ | −⅜ |
| Velcro Ind .12 | 17⅛ | 17⅝ | −¼ |
| Ventron Cp .40 | 17⅜ | 17⅞ | −⅛ |
| VermAmer .60 | x15½ | 16¼ | +½ |
| Victory Mk .40 | 9⅝ | 10⅛ | .... |
| Villager Indus | 2¾ | 2 15-16 | +1-16 |
| Va Chemcl .56 | 18¼ | 19 | .... |
| Vista Internat | 3¼ | 3¾ | .... |
| Vitramon Incp | 2¼ | 2¾ | .... |
| Vogue Instrm | 7⅛ | 7⅝ | +⅛ |
| Volm Shoe .40 | 54¾ | 55¾ | +1 |
| **W** | | | |
| Wabash Cons | 5½ | 6 | .... |
| Wadswort Pub | 19¼ | 20¼ | +¼ |
| WaittBond Inc | 16½ | 17 | .... |

**Fig. 19–10** Over-the-counter stock quotations. A portion of the OTC transactions of a typical trading day as reported in *The Wall Street Journal*. Reprinted by permission from Dow Jones & Company, Inc., and National Association of Securities Dealers.

Brokers speculate on stock investments just as their clients do. They usually buy and sell stocks for their own account or what is sometimes called the *house account*. Therefore, in many over-the-counter transactions, the broker may actually buy an unlisted security from its own customer; or as the case may be, sell the customer stocks from the house account. In these instances, the broker acts as *principal* of the transaction rather than as an agent. Commissions are charged on over-the-counter transactions which the broker makes as an agent. However, when acting as *principal*, the customer and the broker simply agree on a *fair net amount* for the transaction, and no additional commission is added.

Although most of the over-the-counter transactions involve the securities of small, local corporations, there are some notable exceptions: Anheuser Busch, Avon Products, Ethyl Corporation, Eli Lilly, and others. This market also has the distinction of trading nearly all the bank and insurance company stocks, municipal bonds, and United States Government bonds. Often, the over-the-counter market is referred to as the *unlisted securities market*. This is not an inappropriate reference but many trades of *listed* securities do take place over-the-counter. Particularly is this true where clients have very large holdings of a *listed* corporation which they want to liquidate. Throwing the entire block of stock on the stock market would undoubtedly cause a dent in prices on any auction market. In such instances, therefore, the negotiated over-the-counter market is preferred. Perhaps the broker can find another wealthy client. Or if not, the large block of stock can be broken down into smaller units and sold in an orderly fashion to many investors over a period of time.

Many corporations actually prefer to have their securities traded over-the-counter, even though they could unquestionably satisfy all the requirements of listing by an exchange. One important reason for this is that, in the OTC market, there are many broker-dealers with an active interest in finding buyers and sellers and maintaining a broad, stable market in their securities. The OTC market also serves as the best market for the securities of companies which have a relatively small number of shares outstanding, or those in which trading is primarily of local or regional interest.*

## GOVERNMENT CONTROLS OF SECURITY MARKETS

The Securities Act of 1933 and Securities Exchange Act of 1934 ushered in a new era in American finance. The 1933 Act provides for full and fair disclosure of the character of new issues of securities offered for sale to the public and for the prevention of fraud in the sale of such securities. The 1934 Act provides for the regulation of securities exchanges and of over-the-counter markets to prevent inequitable and unfair practices. Both acts apply only to activities concerned with *interstate* and *foreign commerce*. The Securities and Exchange Commission, with headquarters in Washington and offices in eight other cities, administers the Acts.

Registration with the SEC of all securities listed on the national securities exchanges in mandatory under the 1934 Act, as is disclosure of information

---

* *O.T.C.* New York: National Security Traders Association, Inc., 1961, p. 8.

about a listed security. The Act also bans manipulative operations such as pools, wash or fake sales, false and misleading statements; prohibits "actual or apparent active trading in any security, or raising or depressing the price for the purpose of inducing the purchase or sale of it by others."

In addition, the SEC requires officers, directors and principal stockholders (those owning 10 percent or more of the shares) of companies with securities listed on an exchange to report, within 10 days after the month in which it took place, any transaction by them in the stock of their company. These reports are made public by the SEC and by the exchange with which they are filed. Government controls also regulate the use of *credit* for stock market purchases —buying on margin. This is discussed thoroughly in Chapter 22.

**FEEDBACK 19**
**A.** Select a common stock listed on the New York Stock Exchange and chart it for the past month. Your library or newspaper offices will have old copies of your newspaper for reference. Some smaller newspapers do not carry exchange quotations, so you may have to seek copies of a metropolitan daily for your research.

● Find the highs and lows for the month and the year to date.
● Was there any peak activity in the trading of the stock? Was there any company or industry news which may have affected trading in your stock?
● Compare your stock's dividend payments with others. Can you determine or estimate reasons why yours is paying higher or lower dividends? Is your company a steady blue-chipper or a hot growth company?

**B.** "Organize," with your classmates, an imaginary model company to manufacture motor parts for an automobile manufacturer.

● Determine how much money your company requires to buy heavy machinery and buildings and material handling equipment.
● Assuming that your company directors have sufficient capital to finance the birth of the company, and that they decide to initiate a stock issue to attract that capital; how will they go about it?
● How many shares, at what par value, will be issued? What offering price?
● Will the amount in the third item cover the start-up period, when the company will show little or no profit?
● Does the amount in the third item consider the broker's fee which may be charged for handling your original stock issue?
● What exchange will list your stock?

**C.** Write or visit the appropriate agency for corporation affairs in your state to find out what the laws and regulations of incorporation are.

- How do these laws and regulations affect your proposed (see B above) corporation's plans?
- Report your findings to your nominal "board of directors."

## DISCUSSION QUESTIONS

1. Why are common stocks more popular than preferred stocks?
2. What are the advantages to owning corporate bonds rather than common or preferred stocks? Disadvantages?
3. For what reasons would a corporation want its securities listed on the New York or American Stock Exchanges? For what reasons would it want them handled over-the-counter?
4. Why are the exchanges known as auction markets? Why is the OTC market known as a negotiation market?
5. Why do both of the major stock exchanges have rigid requirements which must be met before a corporation's securities can be listed and traded? Are the requirements justified?
6. Why does the New York Exchange list only those stocks which carry voting rights?
7. Why are memberships on both major exchanges so expensive?
8. How can one identify a blue-chip stock? What would be the advantages to investing in them rather than in a speculative stock? Disadvantages?
9. What are the duties of the Securities and Exchange Commission? Should there be more regulation and control than there is now? Explain.
10. Why does the SEC require officers, directors, and principal stockholders of companies with securities listed on an exchange to report (within 10 days after the month in which it took place), any transaction in the stock of their company?

## CASE PROBLEM

Jessica Alexander is 71 years old and comes from a very prominent and conservative banking family. Her husband died 23 years ago, so her finances have been managed since that time by Mr. Peterson.

Being raised in the banking business and therefore suspicious of speculation, Jessica has insisted that all her money be kept in a bank and has done no investing outside of it. For the last few years, however, Mr. Peterson has been talking to Jessica about buying some corporate bonds from an electronics firm. He feels that just a small portion of her total savings will be needed to invest in some very good bonds.

a) Why does Mr. Peterson feel that Jessica should invest some of her money in corporate securities?

b) Why has he suggested bonds rather than stocks? What objections would Jessica have about stocks?

c) If Jessica were to buy stocks, which would she choose to buy—common or preferred? Why?

d) In what type of bonds would she prefer to invest? Why? Why has Mr. Peterson selected an electronics firm in which to invest?

## SUGGESTED READINGS

Amling, Fredrick. *Investments: An Introduction to Analysis and Management.* Englewood Cliffs, N.J.: Prentice-Hall, 1965.  650 pp.

Badger, Ralph E., Harold W. Torgerson, and Harry G. Guthmann. *Investment Principles and Practices.* Englewood Cliffs, N.J.: Prentice-Hall, 1969.  748 pp.

Bellemore, Douglas H., and John C. Ritchie, Jr. *Investments: Principles, Protection, Analysis.* Cincinnati: South-Western Publishing Company, 1969.  888 pp.

Clendenin, John C., and George A. Christy. *Introduction to Investments.* New York: McGraw-Hill, 1969.  691 pp.

Dice, Charles A., Wilford Eiteman, and David K. Eiteman. *The Stock Market.* New York: McGraw-Hill, 1966.  570 pp.

Eiteman, Wilford J., and Sylvia C. Eiteman. *Nine Leading Stock Exchanges.* Ann Arbor: University of Michigan, 1968.  82 pp.

Kaplan, Gilbert E., and Chris Welles. *The Money Managers.* New York: Random House, 1969.  261 pp.

Loester, John C. *The Over-the-Counter Securities Market.* Los Angeles: National Quotation Bureau, Inc., 1953.

*Nerve Center.* New York: American Stock Exchange.

Robbins, Sidney M. *The Securities Markets: Operations and Issues.* New York: Free Press, 1966.  303 pp.

*Stock Watch.* New York: American Stock Exchange.

*The Language of Investing, A Glossary.* New York: American Stock Exchange.

*The Modern Auction Market.* New York: American Stock Exchange.

*Understanding Preferred Stocks and Bonds.* New York: American Stock Exchange.

*Understanding the Over-the-Counter Securities Market.* New York: Securities Publishing Division of Commodity Research Publications Corporation, 1956.

*Understanding the New York Stock Exchange.* New York: American Stock Exchange.

Wood, James P. *What's the Market? The Story of Stock Exchanges.* New York: Duell, Sloan and Pearce, 1967.  179 pp.

APPENDIX TO CHAPTER 19

# GLOSSARY OF STOCK MARKET TERMS

**Accrued Interest.** Interest accrued on a bond since the last interest payment was made. The buyer of the bond pays the market price plus accrued interest. Exceptions include bonds which are in default and income bonds. (*See also* Flat, Income Bond)

**All-or-None Order.** A market or limited price order which is to be executed in its entirety or not at all, but, unlike a fill or kill order, is not to be treated as cancelled if not executed as soon as it is represented in the Trading Crowd. Bids or offers on behalf of all-or-none orders may not be made in stocks, but may be made in bonds when the number of bonds is fifty or more.

**Alternative Order, Either/Or Order.** An order to do either of two alternatives—such as, either sell (buy) a particular stock at a limit price or sell (buy) on stop. If the order is for one unit of trading when one part of the order is executed on the happenings of one alternative, the order on the other alternative is treated as cancelled. If the order is for an amount larger than one unit of trading, the number of units executed determines the amount of the alternative order to be treated as cancelled.

**Amortization.** A generic term. Includes various specific practices such as depreciation, depletion, write-off of intangibles, prepaid expenses and deferred charges.

**Annual Report.** The formal financial statement issued yearly by a corporation to its share-owners. The annual report shows assets, liabilities, earnings—how the company stood at the close of the business year and how it fared profit-wise during the year.

**Arbitrage.** A technique employed to take advantage of differences in price. If, for example, XYZ stock can be bought in New York for $10 a share and sold in London at $10.50, an arbitrageur may simultaneously purchase XYZ stock here and sell the same amount in London, making a profit of 50 cents a share, less expenses. Arbitrage may also involve the purchase of rights to subscribe to a security, or the purchase of a convertible security— and the sale at or about the same time of the security obtainable through exercise of the rights or of the security obtainable through conversion. (*See also* Convertible, Rights)

**Assets.** Everything a corporation owns or due to it: Cash, investments, money due it, materials and inventories, which are called current assets; buildings and machinery, which are known as fixed assets; and patents and goodwill, called intangible assets. (*See also* Liabilities)

**At the Close Order.** A market order which is to be executed at or as near to the close as practicable.

**At the Opening or At the Opening Only Order.** A market or limited price order which is to be executed at the opening of the stock or not at all, and any such order or portion there-of not so executed is treated as cancelled.

**Averages.** Various ways of measuring the trend of securities prices, the most popular of which is the Dow-Jones average of 30 industrial stocks listed on the New York Stock Exchange. The term average has led to considerable confusion. A simple average for, say, 50 leading stocks would be obtained by totaling the prices of all and dividing by 50. But suppose one of the stocks in the average is split. The price of each share of that stock is then automatically reduced because more shares are outstanding. Thus the average would decline even if all other issues in the average were unchanged. That average thus becomes inaccurate as an indicator of the market's trend.

Various formulas—some very elaborate—have been devised to compensate for stock splits and stock dividends and thus give continuity to the average. Averages and individual stock prices belong in separate compartments.

In the case of the Dow-Jones industrial average, the prices of the 30 stocks are totaled and then divided by a divisor which is intended to compensate for past stock splits and dividends and which is changed from time to time. As a result, point changes in the average have only the vaguest relationship to dollar price changes in stocks included in the average. In August, 1966, the divisor was 2.245, so that a one-point change in the industrial average at that time was actually the equivalent of 7 cents. (*See also* Point, Split, NYSE Common Stock Index)

**Averaging.** (*See* Dollar Cost Averaging)

**Balance Sheet.** A condensed statement showing the nature and amount of a company's assets, liabilities, and capital on a given date. In dollar amounts the balance sheet shows what the company owned, what it owed, and the ownership interest in the company of its stockholders. (*See also* Assets, Earnings Report)

**Bear.** Someone who believes the market will decline. (*See also* Bull)

**Bear Market.** A declining market. (*See also* Bull Market)

**Bearer Bond.** A bond which does not have the owner's name registered on the books of the issuing company and which is payable to the holder. (*See also* Coupon Bond, Registered Bond)

**Bid and Asked.** Often referred to as a quotation or quote. The bid is the highest price anyone has declared that he wants to pay for a security at a given time, the asked is the lowest price anyone will take at the same time. (*See also* Quotation)

**Big Board.** A popular term for the New York Stock Exchange.

**Blue Chip.** Common stock in a company known nationally for the quality and wide acceptance of its products or services, and for its ability to make money and pay dividends. Usually such stocks are relatively high priced and offer relatively low yields.

**Blue Sky Laws.** A popular name for laws various states have enacted to protect the public against security frauds. The term is believed to have originated when a judge ruled that a particular stock had about the same value as a patch of blue sky.

**Board Room.** A room for customers in a broker's office where opening, high, low, and last prices of leading stocks are posted on a board throughout the market day.

**Boiler Room.** High-pressure peddling over the telephone of stocks of dubious value. A typical boiler room is simply a room lined with desks or cubicles, each with a salesman and telephone. The salesmen call what is known in the trade as sucker lists.

**Bond.** Basically an IOU or promissory note of a corporation, usually issued in multiples of $1,000, although $100 and $50 denominations are not uncommon. A bond is evidence of a debt on which the issuing company usually promises to pay the bondholders a specified amount of interest for a specified length of time, and to repay the loan on the expiration date. In every case a bond represents debt—its holder is a creditor of the corporation and not a part owner as is the shareholder. (*See also* Collateral Trust Bond, Convertible, General Mortgage Bond, Income Bond)

**Book.** A notebook the specialist in a stock uses to keep a record of the buy and sell orders at specified prices, in strict sequence of receipt, which are left with him by other brokers. (*See also* Specialist)

**Book Value.** An accounting term. Book value of a stock is determined from a company's records, by adding all assets (generally excluding such intangibles as good will), then deducting all debts and other liabilities, plus the liquidation price of any preferred issues. The sum arrived at is divided by the number of common shares outstanding and the result is book value per common share. Book value of the assets of a company or a security may have little or no significant relationship to market value.

**Broker.** An agent, often a member of a stock exchange firm or an exchange member himself, who handles the public's orders to buy and sell securities or commodities. For this service a commission is charged. (*See also* Commission Broker, Dealer)

**Brokers' Loans.** Money borrowed by brokers from banks for a variety of uses. It may be used by specialists and odd-lot dealers to help finance inventories of stocks they deal in; by brokerage firms to finance the underwriting of new issues of corporate and municipal securities; to help finance a firm's own investments; and to help finance the purchase of securities for customers who prefer to use the broker's credit when they buy securities. (*See also* Call Loan, Margin)

**Bucket Shop.** An illegal operation now almost extinct. The bucket shop operator accepted a client's money without ever actually buying or selling securities as the client ordered. Instead he held the money and gambled that the customer was wrong. When too many customers were right, the bucket shop closed its doors and opened a new office.

**Bull.** One who believes the market will rise. (*See also* Bear)

**Bull Market.** An advancing market. (*See also* Bear Market)

**Call.** (*See* Puts and Calls)

**Call Loan.** A loan which may be terminated or "called" at any time by the lender or borrower. Used to finance purchases of securities. (*See also* Brokers' Loans)

**Callable.** A bond issue, all or part of which may be redeemed by the issuing corporation under definite conditions before maturity. The term also applies to preferred shares which may be redeemed by the issuing corporation.

**Capital Gain or Capital Loss.** Profit or loss from the sale of a capital asset. A capital gain, under current Federal income tax laws, may be either short-term (6 months or less) or long-term (more than 6 months). A short-term capital gain is taxed at the reporting individual's full income tax rate. A long-term capital gain is taxed at a maximum of 25 percent, depending on the reporting individual's tax bracket. Up to $1,000 of net capital loss—that is, when you sell securities at a lower price than you paid for them—is deductible from the individual's taxable income during the year reported. If the capital loss is more than $1,000, as much as $1,000 annually is deductible thereafter until all of the loss has been deducted. The amount of capital loss which may be deducted is reduced by the amount of any capital gain.

**Capital Stock.** All shares representing ownership of a business, including preferred and common. (*See also* Common Stock, Preferred Stock)

**Capitalization.** Total amount of the various securities issued by a corporation. Capitalization may include bonds, debentures, preferred and common stock. Bonds and debentures are usually carried on the books of the issuing company in terms of their par or face value. Preferred and common shares may be carried in terms of par or stated value. Stated value may be an arbitrary figure decided upon by the directors or may represent the amount received by the company from the sale of the securities at the time of issuance. (*See also* Par)

**Cash Flow.** Reported net income of a corporation plus amounts charged off for depreciation, depletion, amortization, extraordinary charges to reserves, which are bookkeeping deductions and not paid out in actual dollars and cents. A yardstick used in recent years because of the larger non-cash deductions appearing to offer a better indication of the ability of a company to pay dividends and finance expansion from self-generated cash than the conventional reported net income figure. (*See also* Amortization, Depletion, Depreciation)

**Cash Sale.** A transaction on the floor of the Stock Exchange which calls for delivery of the securities the same day. In "regular way" trades, the seller is allowed four business days for delivery.

**Certificate.** The actual piece of paper which is evidence of ownership of stock in a corporation. Watermarked paper is finely engraved with delicate etchings to discourage forgery. Loss of a certificate may at the least cause a great deal of inconvenience—at the worst, financial loss.

**Closed-End Investment Trust.** (*See* Investment Trust)

**Collateral.** Securities or other property pledged by a borrower to secure repayment of a loan.

**Collateral Trust Bond.** A bond secured by collateral deposited with a trustee. The collateral is often the stocks or bonds of companies controlled by the issuing company but may be other securities.

**Commission.** The broker's fee for purchasing or selling securities or property for a client. On the New York Stock Exchange the average commission is about 1 percent of the market value of the stocks involved in the transaction.

**Commission Broker.** An agent who executes the public's orders for the purchase or sale of securities or commodities. (*See also* Broker, Dealer)

**Common Stock.** Securities which represent an ownership interest in a corporation. If the company has also issued preferred stock, both common and preferred have ownership rights; but the preferred normally has prior claim on dividends and, in the event of liquidation, assets. Claims of both common and preferred stockholders are junior to claims of bondholders or other creditors of the company. Common stockholders assume the greater risk, but generally exercise the greater control and may gain the greater reward in the form of dividends and capital appreciation. The terms common stock and capital stock are often used interchangeably when the company has no preferred stock. (*See also* Capital Stock, Preferred Stock)

**Consolidated Balance Sheet.** A balance sheet showing the financial condition of a corporation and its subsidiaries. (*See also* Balance Sheet)

**Convertible.** A bond, debenture, or preferred share which may be exchanged by the owner for common stock or another security, usually of the same company, in accordance with the terms of the issue.

**Corner.** Buying of a stock or commodity on a scale large enough to give the buyer, or buying group, control over the price. A person who must buy that stock or commodity, for example, one who is short, is forced to do business at an arbitrarily high price with those who engineered the corner. (*See also* Short Position, Short Sale)

**Correspondent.** A securities firm, bank, or other financial organization which regularly performs services for another in a place or market to which the other does not have direct access. Securities firms may have correspondents in foreign countries or on exchanges of which they are not members. Correspondents are frequently linked by private wires. Member Organizations with offices in New York City also act as correspondents for out-of-town Member Organizations which do not maintain New York City offices.

**Coupon Bond.** Bond with interest coupons attached. The coupons are clipped as they come due and are presented by the holder for payment of interest. (*See also* Bearer Bond, Registered Bond)

**Covering.** Buying a security previously sold short. (*See also* Short Sale, Short Covering)

**Cumulative Preferred.** A stock having a provision that if one or more dividends are omitted, the omitted dividends must be paid before dividends may be paid on the company's common stock.

**Cumulative Voting.** A method of voting for corporate directors which enables the shareholder to multiply the number of his shares by the number of directorships being voted on and cast the total for one director or a selected group of directors. A 10-share holder normally casts 10 votes for each of, say 12 nominees to the board of directors. He thus has 120 votes. Under the cumulative voting principle he may do that or he may cast 120 (10 × 12) votes for only one nominee, 60 for two, 40 for three, or any other distribution he chooses. Cumulative voting is required under the corporate laws of some states, is permitted in most others.

**Curb Exchange.** Former name of the American Stock Exchange, second largest exchange in the country. The term comes from the market's origin on the streets of downtown New York.

**Current Assets.** Those assets of a company which are reasonably expected to be realized in cash, or sold, or consumed during the normal operating cycle of the business. These include cash, United States Government bonds, receivables and money due usually within one year, and inventories.

**Current Liabilities.** Money owed and payable by a company, usually within one year.

**Current Return.** (*See* Yield)

**Day Order.** An order to buy or sell which, if not executed, expires at the end of the trading day on which it was entered.

**Dealer.** An individual or firm in the securities business acting as a principal rather than as an agent. Typically, a dealer buys for his own account and sells to a customer from his own inventory. The dealer's profit or loss is the difference between the price he pays and the price he receives for the same security. The dealer's confirmation must disclose to his customer that he has acted as principal. The same individual or firm may function, at different times, either as broker or dealer. (*See also* NASD, Specialist)

**Debenture.** A promissory note backed by the general credit of a company and usually not secured by a mortgage or lien on any specific property. (*See also* Bond)

**Depletion.** Natural resources, such as metals, oils, gas, and timber, which conceivably can be reduced to zero over the years, present a special problem in capital management. Depletion is an accounting practice consisting of charges against earnings based upon the amount of the asset taken out of the total reserves in the period for which accounting is made. A bookkeeping entry, it does not represent any cash outlay nor are any funds earmarked for the purpose.

**Depreciation.** Normally, charges against earnings to write off the cost, less salvage value, of an asset over its estimated useful life. It is a bookkeeping entry and does not represent any cash outlay, nor are any funds earmarked for the purpose.

**Director.** Person elected by shareholders at the annual meeting to establish company policies. The directors appoint the president, vice presidents, and all other operating officers. Directors decide, among other matters, if and when dividends shall be paid. (*See also* Management, Proxy)

**Discretionary Account.** An account in which the customer gives the broker or someone else discretion, which may be complete or within specific limits, as to the purchase and sales of securities or commodities including selection, timing, and price to be paid or received.

**Discretionary Order.** The customer empowers the broker to act on his behalf with respect to the choice of security to be bought or sold, a total amount of any securities to be bought or sold, and/or whether any such transaction shall be one of purchase or sale.

**Distribution.** Selling of a large block of stock to a large group of investors. (*See also* Exchange Distribution, Liquidation, Primary Distribution, Secondary Distribution, Special Offering)

**Diversification.** Spreading investments among different companies in different fields. Another type of diversification is also offered by the securities of many individual companies because of the wide range of their activities. (*See also* Investment Trust)

**Dividend.** The payment designated by the Board of Directors to be distributed pro rata among the shares outstanding. On preferred shares, it is generally a fixed amount. On common shares, the dividend varies with the fortunes of the company and the amount of cash on hand, and may be omitted if business is poor or the directors determine to withhold earnings to invest in plant and equipment. Sometimes a company will pay a dividend out of past earnings even if it is not currently operating at a profit.

**Dollar Cost Averaging.** A system of buying securities at regular intervals with a fixed dollar amount. Under this sytem the investor buys by the dollars' worth rather than by the number of shares. If each investment is of the same number of dollars, payments buy more when the price is low and fewer when it rises. Thus temporary downswings in price benefit the investor if he continues periodic purchases in both good times and bad and the price at which the shares are sold is more than their average cost. (*See also* Formula Investing)

**Do Not Reduce "DNR" Order.**   A limited order to buy, a stop order to sell, or a stop limit order to sell which is not to be reduced by the amount of an ordinary cash dividend on the ex-dividend date.   A do not reduce order applies only to ordinary cash dividends; it is reduced for other distributions such as a stock dividend or rights.

**Double Taxation.**   Short for Double Taxation of Dividends.   The Federal Government taxes corporate profits once as corporate income; any part of the remaining profits distributed as dividends to stockholders is taxed again as income to the recipient stockholder.

**Dow Theory.**   A theory of market analysis based upon the performance of the Dow Jones industrial and rail stock price averages.   The Theory says that the market is in a basic upward trend if one of these averages advances above a previous important high, accompanied or followed by a similar advance in the other.   When the averages both dip below previous important lows, this is regarded as confirmation of a basic downward trend. The Theory does not attempt to predict how long either trend will continue, although it is widely misinterpreted as a method of forecasting future action.   Whatever the merits of the Theory, it is sometimes a strong factor in the market because many people believe in the Theory—or believe that a great many others do.   (*See also* Technical Position)

**Down Tick.**   (*See* Up Tick)

**Earnings Report.**   A statement—also called an income statement—issued by a company showing its earnings or losses over a given period.   The earnings report lists the income earned, expenses, and the net result.   (*See also* Balance Sheet)

**Equipment Trust Certificate.**   A type of security, generally issued by a railroad, to pay for new equipment.   Title to the equipment, such as a locomotive, is held by a trustee until the notes are paid off.   An equipment trust certificate is usually secured by a first claim on the equipment.

**Equity.**   The ownership interest of common and preferred stockholders in a company. Also refers to excess of value of securities over the debit balance in a margin account.

**Exchange Acquisition.**   A method of filling an order to buy a large block of stock on the floor of the Exchange.   Under certain circumstances, a member-broker can facilitate the purchase of a block by soliciting orders to sell.   All orders to sell the security are lumped together and crossed with the buy order in the regular auction market.   The price to the buyer may be on a net basis or on a commission basis.

**Exchange Distribution.**   A method of disposing of large blocks of stock on the floor of the Exchange.   Under certain circumstances, a member-broker can facilitate the sale of a block of stock by soliciting and getting other member-brokers to solicit orders to buy.   Individual buy orders are lumped together and crossed with the sell order in the regular auction market.   A special commission is usually paid by the seller; ordinarily the buyer pays no commission.

**Ex-Dividend.**   A synonym for "without dividend."   The buyer of a stock selling ex-dividend does not receive the recently declared dividend.   Open buy and sell stop orders, and sell stop limit orders in a stock on the ex-dividend date are ordinarily reduced by the value of that dividend.   In the case of open stop limit orders to sell, both the stop price and the limit price are reduced.   Every dividend is payable on a fixed date to all shareholders recorded on the books of the company as of a previous date of record.

**Ex-Rights.**   Without the rights.   Corporations raising additional money may do so by offering their stockholders the right to subscribe to new or additional stock, usually at a discount from the prevailing market price. The buyer of a stock selling ex-rights is not entitled to the rights. (*See also* Ex-Dividend, Rights)

**Extra.** The short form of "extra dividend." A dividend in the form of stock or cash in addition to the regular or usual dividend the company has been paying.

**Face Value.** The value of a bond that appears on the face of the bond, unless the value is otherwise specified by the issuing company. Face value is ordinarily the amount the issuing company promises to pay at maturity. Face value is not an indication of market value. Sometimes referred to as par value.

**Fill or Kill.** A market or limited price order is to be executed in its entirety as soon as it is represented in the Trading Crowd. If not so executed, the order is treated as cancelled. For purposes of this definition, a "stop" (*See also* Stopped Stock) is considered an execution.

**Fiscal Year.** A corporation's accounting year. Due to the nature of their particular business, some companies do not use the calendar year for their bookkeeping. A typical example is the department store which finds December 31 too early a date to close its books after the Christmas rush. For that reason many stores wind up their accounting year January 31. Their fiscal year, therefore, runs from February 1 of one year through January 31 of the next. The fiscal year of other companies may run from July 1 through the following June 30. Most companies, though, operate on a calendar year basis.

**Fixed Charges.** A company's fixed expenses, such as bond interest, which it has agreed to pay whether or not earned, and which are deducted from income before earnings on equity capital are computed.

**Flat.** This term means that the price at which a bond is traded includes consideration for all unpaid accruals of interest. Bonds which are in default of interest or principal are traded flat. Income bonds, which pay interest only to the extent earned are usually traded flat. All other bonds are usually dealt in "and interest," which means that the buyer pays to the seller the market price plus interest accrued since the last payment date. When applied to a stock loan, flat means without premium or interest. (*See also* Short Sale)

**Floor.** The actual trading area on an exchange where stocks and bonds are bought and sold.

**Floor Broker.** A member of the Stock Exchange who executes orders on the floor of the Exchange to buy or sell any listed securities. (*See also* Commission Broker, Two-Dollar Broker)

**Floor Trader.** (*See* Registered Trader)

**Fluctuation.** (*See* Point)

**Formula Investing.** An investment technique. One formula calls for the shifting of funds from common shares to preferred shares or bonds as the market, on average, rises above a certain predetermined point—and the return of funds to common share investments as the market average declines. (*See also* Dollar Cost Averaging)

**Free and Open Market.** A market in which supply and demand are expressed in terms of price. Contrasts with a controlled market in which supply, demand, and price may all be regulated.

**Funded Debt.** Usually interest-bearing bonds or debentures of a company. Could include long-term bank loans. Does not include short-term loans, preferred or common stock.

**General Mortgage Bond.** A bond which is secured by a blanket mortgage on the company's property, but which is often outranked by one or more other mortgages.

**Gilt-Edged.** High-grade bond issued by a company which has demonstrated its ability to earn a comfortable profit over a period of years and pay its bondholders their interest without interruption.

**Give Up.** A term with two different meanings. For one, a member of the Exchange on the floor may act for a second member by executing an order for him with a third member. The first member tells the third member that he is acting on behalf of the second member and gives the second member's name rather than his own. For another, if you have an account with Doe & Company but you're in a town where Doe has no office, you go to another member firm, tell them you have an account with Doe & Company and would like to buy some stock. After verifying your account with Doe & Company, the firm may execute your order and tell the broker who sells the stock that the firm is acting on behalf of Doe & Company. They give up the name of Doe & Company to the selling broker. Or the firm may simply wire your order to Doe & Company who will execute it for you. In either case you pay only the regular commission.

**Good Delivery.** Certain basic qualifications must be met before a security sold on the Exchange may be delivered. The security must be in proper form to comply with the contract of sale and to transfer title by delivery to the purchaser.

**Good 'Til Cancelled Order (GTC) or Open Order.** An order to buy or sell which remains in effect until it is either executed or cancelled.

**Government Bonds.** Obligations of the United States Government, regarded as the highest grade issues in existence.

**Growth Stock.** Stock of a company with prospects for future growth—a company whose earnings are expected to increase at a relatively rapid rate.

**Guaranteed Bond.** A bond which has interest or principal, or both, guaranteed by a company other than the issuer. Usually found in the railroad industry when large roads, leasing sections of trackage owned by small railroads, may guarantee the bonds of the smaller road.

**Guaranteed Stock.** Usually preferred stock on which dividends are guaranteed by another company, under much the same circumstances as a bond is guaranteed.

**Hedge.** (*See* Arbitrage, Puts & Calls, Selling Against the Box, Short Sale)

**Holding Company.** A corporation which owns the securities of another, in most cases with voting control.

**Hypothecation.** The pledging of securities as collateral for a loan.

**Immediate or Cancel Order.** A market or limited price order which is to be executed in whole or in part as soon as it is represented in the Trading Crowd, and the portion not so executed is to be treated as cancelled. For the purposes of this definition, a "stop" is considered an execution. (*See also* Stopped Stock)

**Inactive Post.** A trading post on the floor of the New York Stock Exchange where inactive securities are traded in units of 10 shares instead of the usual 100-share lots. Better known in the business as Post 30. (*See also* Round Lot)

**Inactive Stock.** An issue traded on an exchange or in the over-the-counter market in which there is a relatively low volume of transactions. Volume may be no more than a few hundred shares a week or even less. On the New York Stock Exchange many inactive stocks are traded in 10-share units rather than the customary 100. (*See also* Round Lot)

**In-and-Out.** Purchase and sale of the same security within a short period—a day, week, even a month. An in-and-out trader is generally more interested in day-to-day price fluctuations than dividends or long-term growth.

**Income Bond.** Generally income bonds promise to repay principal but to pay interest only when earned. In some cases unpaid interest on an income bond may accumulate as a claim against the corporation when the bond becomes due. An income bond may also be issued in lieu of preferred stock.

**Indenture.** A written agreement under which debentures are issued, setting forth maturity date, interest rate, security and other terms.

**Index.** A statistical yardstick expressed in terms of percentages of a base year or years. For instance, the Federal Reserve Board's index of industrial production is based on 1957–1959 as 100. In September, 1965, the index stood at 142.8, which meant that industrial production that month was 42.8 percent higher than in the base period. An index is not an average. (*See also* Averages, NYSE Common Stock Index)

**Interest.** Payments a borrower pays a lender for the use of his money. A corporation pays interest on its bonds to its bondholders. (*See also* Bond, Dividend)

**Investment.** The use of money for the purpose of making more money, to gain income or increase capital, or both. Safety of principal is an important consideration. (*See also* Speculation)

**Investment Banker.** Also known as an underwriter. He is the middleman between the corporation issuing new securities and the public. The usual practice is for one or more investment bankers to buy outright from a corporation a new issue of stocks or bonds. The group forms a syndicate to sell the securities to individuals and institutions. Investment bankers also distribute very large blocks of stock or bonds—perhaps held by an estate. Thereafter the market in the security may be over-the-counter, on a regional stock exchange, the American Exchange or the New York Stock Exchange. (*See also* Over-the-Counter, Primary Distribution, Syndicate)

**Investment Counsel.** One whose principal business consists of acting as investment advisor; a substantial part of his business consists of rendering investment supervisory services.

**Investment Trust.** A company which uses its capital to invest in other companies. There are two principal types: the closed-end and the open-end, or mutual fund. Shares in closed-end investment trusts, some of which are listed on the exchanges, are readily transferable in the open market and are bought and sold like other shares. Capitalization of these companies remains the same unless action is taken to change, which is seldom. Open-end funds sell their own new shares to investors, stand ready to buy back their old shares, and are not listed. Open-end funds are so-called because their capitalization is not fixed; they issue more shares as people want them.

**Investor.** An individual whose principal concerns in the purchase of a security are regular dividend income, safety of the original investment, and, if possible, capital appreciation. (*See also* Speculator)

**Issue.** Any of a company's securities, or the act of distributing such securities.

**Legal List.** A list of investments selected by various states in which certain institutions and fiduciaries, such as insurance companies and banks, may invest. Legal lists are restricted to high quality securities meeting certain specifications. (*See also* Prudent Man Rule)

**Leverage.** The effect on the per share earnings of the common stock of a company when large sums must be paid for bond interest or preferred stock dividends, or both, before the common stock is entitled to share in earnings. Leverage may be advantageous for the common when earnings are good but may work against the common stock when earnings decline. Example: Company A has 1,000,000 shares of common stock outstanding, no other securities. Earnings drop from $1,000,000 to $800,000 or from $1 to 80 cents a share, a decline of 20 percent. Company B also has 1,000,000 shares of common but must pay $500,000 annually in bond interest. If earnings amount to $1,000,000, there is $500,000 available for the common or 50 cents a share. But earnings drop to $800,000 so there is only $300,000 available for the common, or 30 cents a share—a drop of 40 percent. Or suppose earnings of the company with only common stock increased from $1,000,000 to $1,500,000—earnings per share would go from $1 to $1.50, or an increase of 50 percent. But if earnings of the company which had to pay $500,000 in bond interest increased that much, earnings per common share would jump from 50 cents to $1 a share, or 100 percent. When a company has common stock only, no leverage exists because all earnings are available for the common, although relatively large fixed charges payable for lease of substantial plant assets may have an effect similar to that of a bond issue.

**Liabilities.** All the claims against a corporation. Liabilities include accounts and wages and salaries payable, dividends declared payable, accrued taxes payable, fixed or long-term liabilities such as mortgage bonds, debentures, and bank loans. (*See also* Assets, Balance Sheet)

**Lien.** A claim against property which has been pledged or mortgaged to secure the performance of an obligation. A bond is usually secured by a lien against specified property of a company. (*See also* Bond)

**Limit, Limited Order or Limited Price Order.** An order to buy or sell a stated amount of a security at a specified price, or at a better price, if obtainable after the order is represented in the Trading Crowd.

**Liquidation.** The process of converting securities or other property into cash. The dissolution of a company, with cash remaining after sale of its assets and payment of all indebtedness being distributed to the shareholders.

**Liquidity.** The ability of the market in a particular security to absorb a reasonable amount of buying or selling at reasonable price changes. Liquidity is one of the most important characteristics of a good market.

**Listed Stock.** The stock of a company which is traded on a securities exchange, and for which a listing application and a registration statement, giving detailed information about the company and its operations, have been filed with the Securities Exchange Commission, unless otherwise exempted, and the exchange itself.

**Load.** The portion of the offering price of shares of open-end investment companies which covers sales commissions and all other costs of distribution. The load is incurred only on purchase, there being, in most cases, no charge when the shares are sold (redeemed).

**Locked In.** An investor is said to be locked in when he has a profit on a security he owns but does not sell because his profit would immediately become subject to the capital gains tax. (*See also* Capital Gain)

**Long.** Signifies ownership of securities. "I am long 100 U.S. Steel" means the speaker owns 100 shares. (*See also* Short Position, Short Sale)

**Management.** The Board of Directors, elected by the stockholders, and the officers of the corporation, appointed by the Board of Directors.

**Manipulation.** An illegal operation. Buying or selling a security for the purpose of creating false or misleading appearance of active trading or for the purpose of raising or depressing the price to induce purchase or sale by others.

**Margin.** The amount paid by the customer when he uses his broker's credit to buy a security. Under Federal Reserve regulations, the initial margin required in the past 20 years has ranged from 40 percent of the purchase price all the way to 100 percent. (*See also* Brokers' Loans, Equity, Margin Call)

**Margin Call.** A demand upon a customer to put up money or securities with the broker. The call is made when a purchase is made; also if a customer's equity in a margin account declines below a minimum standard set by the Exchange or by the firm. (*See also* Margin)

**Market Order.** An order to buy or sell a stated amount of a security at the most advantageous price obtainable after the order is represented in the Trading Crowd. (*See also* Good 'Til Cancelled Order, Limit Order, Stop Order)

**Market Price.** In the case of a security, market price is usually considered the last reported price at which the stock or bond sold.

**Matched and Lost.** When two bids to buy the same stock are made on the trading floor simultaneously, and each bid is equal to or larger than the amount of stock offered, both bids are considered to be on an equal basis. So the two bidders flip a coin to decide who buys the stock. Also applies to offers to sell.

**Maturity.** The date on which a loan or a bond or debenture comes due and is to be paid off.

**Member Corporation.** A securities brokerage firm, organized as a corporation, with at least one member of an exchange who is a director and a holder of voting stock in the corporation. (*See also* Member Firm)

**Member Firm.** A securities brokerage firm organized as a partnership and having at least one general partner who is a member of an exchange. (*See also* Member Corporation).

**MIP.** Monthly Investment Plan. A pay-as-you-go method of buying New York Stock Exchange listed shares on a regular payment plan for as little as $40 a month, or $40 every three months. Under MIP the investor buys stock by the dollars' worth—if the price advances, he gets fewer shares and if it declines, he gets more shares. He may discontinue purchases at any time without penalty. The commission ranges from 6 percent on small transactions to slightly below $1\frac{1}{2}$ percent on larger transactions. (*See also* Dollar Cost Averaging, Odd-Lot Dealer)

**Mortgage Bond.** A bond secured by a mortgage on a property. The value of the property may or may not equal the value of the so-called mortgage bonds issued against it. (*See also* Bond, Debenture)

**Municipal Bond.** A bond issued by a state or a political subdivision, such as county, city, town, or village. The term also designates bonds issued by state agencies and authorities. In general, interest paid on municipal bonds is exempt from Federal income taxes.

**Mutual Fund.** (*See* Investment Trust)

**NASD.** The National Association of Securities Dealers, Inc. An association of brokers and dealers in the over-the-counter securities business. The Association has the power to expel members who have been determined guilty of unethical practices. NASD is dedicated to—among other objectives—"adopt, administer, and enforce rules of fair practice and rules to prevent fraudulent and manipulative acts and practices, and in general to promote just and equitable principles of trade for the protection of investors."

**Negotiable.** Refers to a security, title to which is transferable by delivery. (*See also* Good Delivery)

**Net Asset Value.** A term usually used in connection with investment trust, meaning net asset value per share. It is common practice for an investment trust to compute its assets daily, or even twice daily, by totaling the market value of all securities owned. All liabilities are deducted, and the balance divided by the number of shares outstanding. The resulting figure is the net asset value per share. (*See also* Assets, Investment Trust)

**Net Change.** The change in the price of a security from the closing price on one day and the closing price on the following day on which the stock is traded. In the case of a stock which is entitled to a dividend one day, but is traded "ex-dividend" the next, the dividend is considered in computing the change. For example, if the closing market price of a stock on Monday—the last day it was entitled to receive a 50-cent dividend—was $45 a share, and $44.50 at the close of the next day, when it was "ex-dividend," the price would be considered unchanged. The same applies to a split-up of shares. A stock selling at $100 the day before a 2-for-1 split and trading the next day at $50 would be considered unchanged. If it sold at $51, it would be considered up $1. The net change is ordinarily the last figure in a stock price list. The mark $+ 1\frac{1}{8}$ means up $1.125 a share from the last sale on the previous day the stock traded. (*See also* Ex-Dividend, Point, Split)

**New Issue.** A stock or bond sold by a corporation for the first time. Proceeds may be issued to retire outstanding securities of the company, for new plant or equipment or for additional working capital.

**Noncumulative.** A preferred stock on which unpaid dividends do not accrue. Omitted dividends are, as a rule, gone forever. (*See also* Cumulative Preferred)

**"Not Held" Order.** A market or limited price order marked "not held," "disregard tape," "take time," or which bears any such qualifying notation. An order marked "or better" is not a "not held" order.

**NYSE Common Stock Index.** A composite index covering price movements of all common stocks listed on the "Big Board." It is based on the close of the market December 31, 1965 as 50.00 and is weighted according to the number of shares listed for each issue. The index is computed continuously by the Exchange's Market Data System and printed on the ticker tape each half hour. Point changes in the index are converted to dollars and cents so as to provide a meaningful measure of changes in the average price of listed stocks. The composite index is supplemented by separate indexes for four industry groups: industrial, transportation, utility, and finance. (*See also* Averages)

**Odd-Lot.** An amount of stock less than the established 100-share unit or 10-share unit of trading: from 1 to 99 shares for the great majority of issues, 1 to 9 for so-called inactive stocks. (*See also* Round Lot, Inactive Stock)

**Odd-Lot Dealer.** A member firm of the Exchange which buys and sells odd lots of stocks —1 to 9 shares in the case of stocks traded in 10-share units and 1 to 99 shares for 100-share units. The odd-lot dealer's customers are commission brokers acting on behalf of their customers. There are one or more odd-lot dealers ready to buy or sell, for their own accounts, odd lots in any stock at any time. Odd-lot prices are geared to the auction market. On an odd-lot market order, the odd-lot dealer's price is based on the first round-lot transaction which occurs on the floor following receipt at the trading post of the odd-lot order. The usual differential between the odd-lot price and the "effective" round-lot price is $12\frac{1}{2}$ cents a share for stock selling below \$55, 25 cents a share for stock at \$55 or more. For example: You decide to buy 20 shares of ABC common at the market. Your order is transmitted by your commission broker to the representative of an odd-lot dealer at the post where ABC is traded. A few minutes later there is a 100-share transaction in ABC at \$10 a share. The odd-lot price at which your order is immediately filled by the odd-lot dealer is \$10.125 a share. If you had sold 20 shares of ABC, you would have received \$9.875 a share. (*See also* Commission Broker, Dealer, Inactive Stock, Round Lot, Transfer Tax)

**Off-Board.** This term may refer to transactions over-the-counter in unlisted securities, or, in a special situation, to a transaction involving listed shares which was not executed on a national securities exchange. (*See also* Over-the-Counter, Secondary Distribution)

**Offer.** The price at which a person is ready to sell. Opposed to bid, the price at which one is ready to buy. (*See also* Bid and Asked)

**Open-End Investment Trust.** (*See* Investment Trust)

**Open Order.** (*See* GTC Order)

**Option.** A right to buy or sell specific securities or properties at a specified price within a specified time. (*See also* Puts and Calls)

**Orders Good Until a Specified Time.** A market or limited price order which is to be represented in the Trading Crowd until a specified time, after which such order or the portion thereof not executed is to be treated as cancelled.

**Overbought.** An opinion as to price levels. May refer to a security which has had a sharp rise or to the market as a whole after a period of vigorous buying, which it may be argued, has left prices "too high." (*See also* Technical Position)

**Oversold.** An opinion—the reverse of overbought. A single security or a market which, it is believed, has declined to an unreasonable level. (*See also* Technical Position)

**Over-the-Counter.** A market for securities made up of securities dealers who may or may not be members of a securities exchange. Over-the-counter is mainly a market made over the telephone. Thousands of companies have insufficient shares outstanding, stockholders, or earnings to warrant application for listing on a stock exchange. Securities of these companies are traded in the over-the-counter market between dealers who act either as principals or as brokers for customers. The over-the-counter market is the principal market for United States Government bonds and municipals. (*See also* NASD, Off-Board)

**Paper Profit.**  An unrealized profit on a security still held.  Paper profits become realized profits only when the security is sold.

**Par.**  In the case of a common share, par means a dollar amount assigned to the share by the company's charter.  Par value may also be used to compute the dollar amount of the common shares on the balance sheet.  Par value has little significance so far as market value of common stock is concerned.  Many companies today issue no-par stock but give a stated per share value on the balance sheet.  Par at one time was supposed to represent the value of the original investment behind each share in cash, goods, or services.  In the case of preferred shares and bonds, however, par is important.  It often signifies the dollar value upon which dividends on preferred stocks, and interest on bonds, are figured.  The issuer of a 3 percent bond promises to pay that percentage of the bond's par value annually. (*See also* Capitalization, Transfer Tax)

**Participating Preferred.**  A preferred stock which is entitled to its stated dividend and, also, to additional dividends on a specified basis upon payment of dividends on the common stock.

**Passed Dividend.**  Omission of a regular or scheduled dividend.

**Penny Stocks.**  Low-priced issues often highly speculative, selling at less than $1 a share.  Frequently used as a term of disparagement, although a few penny stocks have developed into investment-caliber issues.

**Percentage Order.**  A market or limited price order to buy (or sell) a stated amount of a specified stock after a fixed number of shares of such stock have traded.

**Point.**  In the case of shares of stock, a point means $1.  If General Motors shares rise 3 points, each share has risen $3.  In the case of bonds a point means $10, since a bond is quoted as a percentage of $1,000.  A bond which rises 3 points gains 3 percent of $1,000, or $30 in value.  An advance from 87 to 90 would mean an advance in dollar value from $870 to $900 for each $1,000 bond.  In the case of market averages, the word point means merely that and no more.  If, for example, the Dow-Jones industrial average rises from 470.25 to 471.25, it has risen a point.  A point in the averages, however, is not equivalent to $1. (*See also* Averages)

**Portfolio.**  Holdings of securities by an individual or institution.  A portfolio may contain bonds, preferred stocks, and common stocks of various types of enterprises.

**Preferred Stock.**  A class of stock with a claim on the company's earnings before payment may be made on the common stock and usually entitled to priority over common stock if the company liquidates.  Usually entitled to dividends at a specified rate—when declared by the Board of Directors and before payment of a dividend on the common stock— depending upon the terms of the issue. (*See also* Cumulative Preferred, Participating Preferred)

**Premium.**  The amount by which a preferred stock or bond may sell above its par value.  In the case of a new issue of bonds or stocks, premium is the amount the market price rises over the original selling price.  Also refers to a charge sometimes made when a stock is borrowed to make delivery on a short sale.  May refer, also, to redemption price of a bond or preferred stock if it is higher than face value. (*See also* Corner, Short Sale)

**Price-Earnings Ratio.** The current market price of a share of stock dividend by earnings per share for a twelve-month period. For example, a stock selling for $100 a share and earning $5 a share is said to be selling at a price-earnings ratio of 20 to 1.

**Primary Distribution.** Also called primary offering. The original sale of a company's securities. (*See also* Investment Banker, Secondary Distribution)

**Principal.** The person for whom a broker executes an order, or a dealer buying or selling for his own account. The term "principal" may also refer to a person's capital or to the face amount of a bond.

**Prior Preferred.** A preferred stock which usually takes precedence over other preferreds issued by the same company.

**Profit Taking.** Selling to take a profit, the process of converting paper profits into cash.

**Prospectus.** A circular which describes securities being offered for sale to the public. Required by the Securities Act of 1933.

**Proxy.** Written authorization given by a shareholder to someone else to represent him and vote his shares at a shareholders' meeting.

**Proxy Statement.** Information required by SEC to be given stockholders as a prerequisite to solicitation of proxies for a security. Subject to the requirements of the Securities Exchange Act.

**Prudent Man Rule.** An investment standard. In some states, the law requires that a fiduciary, such as a trustee, may invest the fund's money only in a list of securities designated by the state—the so-called legal list. In other states, the trustee may invest in a security if it is one which a prudent man of discretion and intelligence, who is seeking a reasonable income and preservation of capital, would buy.

**Puts and Calls.** Options which give the right to buy or sell a fixed amount of a certain stock at a specified price within a specified time. A put gives the holder the right to sell the stock; a call the right to buy the stock. Puts are purchased by those who think a stock may go down. A put obligates the seller of the contract to take delivery of the stock and pay the specified price to the owner of the option within the time limit of the contract. The price specified in a put or call is usually close to the market price of the stock at the time the contract is made. Calls are purchased by those who think a stock may rise. A call gives the holder the right to buy the stock from the seller of the contract at the specified price within a fixed period of time. Put and call contracts are written for 30, 60 or 90 days, or longer. If the purchaser of a put or call does not wish to exercise the option, the price he paid for the option becomes a loss.

**Quotation.** Often shortened to "quote." The highest bid to buy and the lowest offer to sell a security in a given market at a given time. If you ask your broker for a "quote" on a stock, he may come back with something like "$45\frac{1}{4}$ to $45\frac{1}{2}$." This means that $45.25 is the highest price any buyer wanted to pay at the time the quote was given on the floor of the exchange and that $45.50 was the lowest price which any seller would take at the same time. (*See also* Bid and Asked)

**Rally.** A brisk rise following a decline in the general price level of the market, or in an individual stock.

**Realizing.**  (*See* Profit Taking)

**Record Date.**  The date on which you must be registered on the books of a company as a shareholder in order to receive a declared dividend or, among other things, to vote on company affairs.  (*See also* Ex-Dividend, Transfer)

**Redemption Price.**  The price at which a bond may be redeemed before maturity, at the option of the issuing company.  Redemption value also applies to the price the company must pay to call in certain types of preferred stock.  (*See also* Callable)

**Refinancing.**  Same as refunding.  New securities are sold by a company and the money is used to retire existing securities.  Object may be to save interest costs, extend the maturity of the loan, or both.

**Registered Bond.**  A bond which is registered on the books of the issuing company in the name of the owner.  It can be transferred only when endorsed by the registered owner. (*See also* Bearer Bond, Coupon Bond)

**Registered Trader.**  A member of an exchange who trades in stocks on the floor of an account in which he has an interest.  (*See also* Floor Trader)

**Registrar.**  Usually a trust company or bank charged with the responsibility of preventing the issuance of more stock than authorized by a company.  (*See also* Transfer)

**Registration.**  Before a public offering may be made of new securities by a company, or of outstanding securities by controlling stockholders—through the mails or in interstate commerce—the securities must be registered under the Securities Act of 1933.  Registration statement is filed with the SEC by the issuer.  It must disclose pertinent information relating to the company's operations, securities, management, and purpose of the public offering.  Securities of railroads under jurisdiction of the Interstate Commerce Commission, and certain other types of securities, are exempted.  On security offerings involving less than $300,000 less information is required.

Before a security may be admitted to dealings on a national securities exchange, it must be registered under the Securities Exchange Act of 1934.  The application for registration must be filed with the exchange and the SEC by the company issuing the securities. The application must disclose pertinent information relating to the company's operations, securities, and management.  Registration may become effective 30 days after receipt by the SEC of the certification by the exchange of approval of listing and registration, or sooner by special order of the Commission.

**Regulation T.**  The Federal regulation governing the amount of credit which may be advanced by brokers and dealers to customers for the purchase of securities.  (*See also* Margin)

**Regulation U.**  The Federal regulation governing the amount of credit which may be advanced by a bank to its customers for the purchase of listed stocks.  (*See also* Margin)

**Return.**  (*See* Yield)

**Rights.**  When a company wants to raise more funds by issuing additional securities, it may give its stockholders the opportunity, ahead of others, to buy the new securities in proportion to the number of shares each owns.  The piece of paper evidencing this privilege is called a right. Because the additional stock is usually offered to stockholders below the current market price, rights ordinarily have a market value of their own and are actively traded. In most cases they must be exercised within a relatively short period. Failure to exercise or sell rights may result in actual loss to the holder. (*See also* Warrant)

**Round Lot.** A unit of trading or a multiple thereof. The unit of trading is generally 100 shares in stocks and $1,000 par value in the case of bonds. In some inactive stocks, the unit of trading is 10 shares.

**Scale Order.** An order to buy (or sell) a security which specifies the total amount to be bought (or sold) and the amount to be bought (or sold) at specified price variations.

**Scrip.** A certificate exchangeable for stock or cash before a specified date, after which it may have no value. Usually issued for fractions of shares in connection with a stock dividend or split or in reorganization of a company. For example, a stock dividend might amount to only $\frac{1}{3}$ share so scrip is issued instead of a stock certificate for $\frac{1}{3}$ share. Not traded on New York Stock Exchange. (*See also* Stock Dividend)

**Seat.** A traditional figure-of-speech for a membership on a securities or commodity exchange. Price and admission requirements vary.

**SEC.** The Securities and Exchange Commission, established by Congress to help protect investors. The SEC administers the Securities Act of 1933, the Securities Exchange Act of 1934, the Trust Indenture Act, the Investment Company Act, the Investment Advisers Act, and the Public Utility Holding Company Act.

**Secondary Distribution.** Also known as a secondary offering. The redistribution of a block of stock some time after it has been sold by the issuing company. The sale is handled off an exchange by a securities firm or group of firms and the shares are usually offered at a fixed price which is related to the current market price of the stock. Usually the block is a large one, such as might be involved in the settlement of an estate. The security may be listed or unlisted. (*See also* Exchange Distribution, Investment Banker, Primary Distribution, Special Offering, Syndicate)

**Seller's Option.** A special transaction on the Stock Exchange which gives the seller the right to deliver the stock or bond at any time within a specified period, ranging from not less than five business days to not more than 60 days.

**Selling Against the Box.** A method of protecting paper profit. Let's say you own 100 shares of XYZ which has advanced in price, and you think the price may decline. So you sell 100 shares short, borrowing 100 shares to make delivery. You retain in your security box the 100 shares which you own. If XYZ declines, the profit on your short sale is exactly offset by the loss in the market value of the stock you own. If XYZ advances, the loss on your short sale is exactly offset by the profit in the market value of the stock you have retained. You can close out your short sale by buying 100 shares to return to the person from whom you borrowed, or you can send them the 100 shares which you own. (*See also* Hedge, Short Sale)

**Serial Bond.** An issue which matures in relatively small amounts at periodic stated intervals.

**Short Covering.** Buying stock to return stock previously borrowed to make delivery on a short sale.

**Short Position.** Stocks sold short and not covered as of a particular date. Short position also means the total amount of stock an individual has sold short and has not covered, as of a particular date. Initial margin requirements for a short position are the same as for a long position. (*See also* Margin, Up Tick, Short Sale)

**Short Sale.** A person who believes a stock will decline and sells it, though he does not own any, has made a short sale. For instance: You instruct your broker to sell short 100 shares of ABC. Your broker borrows the stock so he can deliver the 100 shares to the buyer. The money value of the shares borrowed is deposited by your broker with the lender. Sooner or later you must cover your short sale by buying the same amount of stock you borrowed for return to the lender. If you are able to buy ABC at a lower price than you sold it for, your profit is the difference between the two prices—not counting commissions and taxes. But if you have to pay more for the stock than the price you received, that is the amount of your loss. Stock exchange and Federal regulations govern and limit the conditions under which a short sale may be made on a national securities exchange. (*See also* Margin, Premium, Up Tick)

**Sinking Fund.** Money regularly set aside by a company to redeem its bonds, debentures, or preferred stock from time to time as specified in the indenture or charter.

**Special Offering.** Occasionally a large block of stock becomes available for sale which, due to its size and the market in that particular issue, calls for special handling. A notice is printed on the ticker tape announcing that the stock will be offered for sale on the floor of an exchange at a fixed price. Member firms may buy this stock for customers directly from the seller's broker during trading hours. The price is usually based on the last transaction in the regular auction market. If there are more buyers than stock, allotments are made. Only the seller pays a commission on a special offering. (*See also* Secondary Distribution)

**Special Bid.** A method of filling an order to buy a large block of stock on the floor of an exchange. In a special bid, the bidder for the block of stock—a pension fund, for instance, will pay a special commission to the broker who represents him in making the purchase. The seller does not pay a commission. The special bid is made on the floor of an exchange at a fixed price which may not be below the last sale of the security or the current bid in the regular market, whichever is higher. Member firms may sell this stock for customers directly to the buyer's broker during trading hours.

**Specialist.** A member of an exchange who has two functions: First, to maintain an orderly market, insofar as reasonably practicable, in the stocks in which he is registered as a specialist. In order to maintain an orderly market, the exchange expects the specialist to buy or sell for his own account, to a reasonable degree, when there is a temporary disparity between supply and demand. Second, the specialist acts as a broker's broker. When a commission broker on an exchange floor receives a limit order, say, to buy at $50 a stock then selling at $60—he cannot wait at the particular post where the stock is traded until the price reaches the specified level. So he leaves the order with the specialist, who will try to execute it in the market if and when the stock declines to the specified price. At all times the specialist must put his customers' interests above his own. (*See also* Book, Limited Order)

**Specialist Block Purchase.** Purchase by the specialist for his own account of a large block of stock outside the regular market on an exchange. Such purchases may be made only when the sale of the block could not be made in the regular market within a reasonable time and at reasonable prices, and when the purchase by the specialist would aid him in maintaining a fair and orderly market. The specialist need not fill the orders on this book down to the purchase price.

**Specialist Block Sale.** Opposite of the specialist block purchase. Under exceptional circumstances, the specialist may sell a block of stock outside the regular market on an exchange for his own account at a price above the prevailing market. The price is negotiated between the specialist and the broker for the buyer. The specialist need not fill the orders on his book down to the purchase price.

**Speculation.** The employment of funds by a speculator. Safety of principal is a secondary factor. (*See also* Investment)

**Speculator.** One who is willing to assume a relatively large risk in the hope of gain. His principal concern is to increase his capital rather than his dividend income. The speculator may buy and sell the same day or speculate in an enterprise which he does not expect to be profitable for years. (*See also* Investor)

**Split.** The division of the outstanding shares of a corporation into a larger number of shares. A 3-for-1 split by a company with 1 million shares outstanding would result in 3 million shares outstanding. Each holder of 100 shares before the 3-for-1 split would have 300 shares, although his proportionate equity in the company would remain the same, since 100 parts of 1 million are the equivalent of 300 parts of 3 million. Ordinarily splits must be voted by directors and approved by shareholders. (*See also* Stock Dividend)

**Stock Ahead.** Sometimes an investor who has entered an order to buy or sell a stock at a certain price will see transactions at that price reported on the ticker tape while his own order has not been executed. The reason is that other buy and sell orders at the same price came in to the specialist ahead of his and had priority. (*See also* Book, Specialist)

**Stock Clearing Corporation.** A subsidiary of the New York Stock Exchange which acts as a central agency for security deliveries and money payments between member firms of the Exchange.

**Stock Dividend.** A dividend paid in securities rather than cash. The dividend may be additional shares of the issuing company, or in shares of another company (usually a subsidiary) held by the company. (*See also* Ex-Dividend, Split)

**Stockholder of Record.** A stockholder whose name is registered on the books of the issuing corporation. (*See also* Record Date, Ex-Dividend, Ex-Rights)

**Stop Limit Order.** A stop limit order to buy becomes a limit order executable at the limit price, or at a better price, if obtainable, when a transaction in the security occurs at or above the stop price after the order is represented in the Trading Crowd. A stop limit order to sell becomes a limit order executable at the limit price or at a better price, if obtainable, when a transaction in the security occurs at or below the stop price after the order is represented in the Trading Crowd.

**Stop Order.** A stop order to buy becomes a market order when a transaction in the security occurs at or above the stop price after the order is represented in the Trading Crowd.

A stop order to sell becomes a market order when a transaction in the security occurs at or below the stop price after the order is represented in the Trading Crowd. A stop order may be used in an effort to protect a paper profit, or to try to limit a possible loss to a certain amount. Since it becomes a market order when the stop price is reached, there is no certainty that it will be executed at that price. (*See also* Limited Order, Market Order)

**Stopped Stock.** A service performed—in most cases by the specialist—for an order given him by a commission broker. Let's say XYZ just sold at $50 a share; Broker A comes along with an order to buy 100 shares at the market. The lowest offer is $50.50. Broker A believes he can do better for his client than $50.50, perhaps might get the stock at $50.25. But he doesn't want to take a chance that he'll miss the market—that is, the next sale might be $50.50 and the following one even higher. So he asks the specialist if he will stop 100 at $\frac{1}{2}$ ($50.50). The specialist agrees. The specialist guarantees Broker A he will get 100 shares at $50\frac{1}{2}$ if the stock sells at that price. In the meantime, if the specialist or Broker A succeeds in executing the order at $50.25, the stop is called off. (*See also* Specialist)

**Street.** The New York financial community concentrated in the Wall Street area.

**Street Name.** Securities held in the name of a broker instead of his customer's name are said to be carried in a "street name." This occurs when the securities have been bought on margin or when the customer wishes the security to be held by the broker.

**Switch Order—Contingent Order.** An order for the purchase (sale) of one stock and the sale (purchase) of another stock at a stipulated price difference.

**Switching.** Selling one security and buying another.

**Syndicate.** A group of investment bankers who together underwrite and distribute a new issue of securities or a large block of an outstanding issue. (*See also* Investment Banker)

**Tax-Exempt Bonds.** The securities of states, cities and other public authorities specified under Federal law; the interest on which is either wholly or partly exempt from Federal income taxes.

**Technical Position.** A term applied to the various internal factors affecting the market; opposed to external forces such as earnings, dividends, political considerations, and general economic conditions. Some internal factors considered in appraising the market's technical position include the size of the short interest, whether the market has had a sustained advance or decline without interruption, a sharp advance or decline on small volume and the amount of credit in use in the market. (*See also* Overbought, Oversold)

**Thin Market.** A market in which there are comparatively few bids to buy or offers to sell or both. The phrase may apply to a single security or to the entire stock market. In a thin market, price fluctuations between transactions are usually larger than when the market is liquid. A thin market in a particular stock may reflect lack of interest in that issue or a limited supply of or demand for stock in the market. (*See also* Bid and Asked, Liquidity, Offer)

**Ticker.** The instrument which prints prices and volume of security transactions in cities and towns throughout the United States within minutes after each trade on the floor.

**Time Order.** An order which becomes a market or limited price order at a specified time.

**Tips.** Supposedly "inside" information on corporation affairs.

**Trader.** One who buys and sells for his own account for short-term profit. (*See also* Investor, Speculator)

**Trading Floor.** (*See* Floor)

**Trading Post.** One of the 18 horseshoe-shaped trading locations on the floor of the New York Stock Exchange at which stocks assigned to that location are bought and sold. About 75 stocks are traded at each post. (*See also* Inactive Post)

**Transfer.** This term may refer to two different operations. For one, the delivery of a stock certificate from the seller's broker to the buyer's broker and legal change of ownership, normally accomplished within a few days. For another, to record the change of ownership on the books of the corporation by the transfer agent. When the purchaser's name is recorded on the books of the company, dividends, notices of meetings, proxies, financial reports, and all pertinent literature sent by the issuer to its securities holders are mailed direct to the new owner. (*See also* Registrar, Street Name)

**Transfer Agent.** A transfer agent keeps a record of the name of each registered shareowner, his or her address, the number of shares owned, and sees that certificates presented to this office for transfer are properly cancelled and new certificates issued in the name of the transferee. (*See also* Delivery, Registrar, Transfer)

**Transfer Tax.** A tax imposed by New York State when a security is sold or transferred from one person to another. The tax is paid by the seller. The current New York State tax is imposed at rates of from $1\frac{1}{4}$ to 5 cents a share based on the selling price of the stock. The tax is $1\frac{1}{4}$ cents on shares selling for less than $5; $2\frac{1}{2}$ cents on shares selling for $5 to $9.99; $3\frac{3}{4}$ cents on shares selling for $10 to $19.99 and 5 cents for shares selling at $20 or more. The tax also applies to warrants and rights. There is no tax on transfers of bonds.

**Treasury Stock.** Stock issued by a company but later reacquired. It may be held in the company's treasury indefinitely, reissued to the public, or retired. Treasury stock receives no dividends and has no vote while held by the company.

**Turnover.** The volume of business in a security or the entire market. If turnover on the New York Stock Exchange is reported at 5 million shares on a particular day, 5,000,000 shares changed hands. Odd-lot turnover is tabulated separately and ordinarily is not included in reported volume.

**Two-Dollar Broker.** Members on the floor of an exchange who execute orders for other brokers having more business at that time than they can handle themselves, or for firms who do not have their exchange member-partner on the floor. The term derives from the time when these independent brokers received $2 per hundred shares for executing such orders. The fee is paid by the broker and today it varies with the price of the stock. (*See also* Commission Broker)

**Underwriter.** (*See* Investment Banker)

**Unlisted.** A security not listed on a stock exchange. (*See also* Over-the-Counter)

**Unlisted Trading Privileges.** On some exchanges a stock may be traded at the request of a member without any prior application by the company itself. The company has no agreement to conform with standards of the exchange. Companies admitted to unlisted trading privileges prior to enactment of the Securities Exchange Act of 1934 are not subject to the rules and regulations under that Act. Today admission of a stock to unlisted trading privileges requires SEC approval of an application filed by the exchange. The information in the application must be made available by the exchange to the public. No unlisted stocks are traded on an exchange. (*See also* Listed Stock)

**Up Tick.** A term used to designate a transaction made by a price higher than the preceding transaction. Also called a "plus" tick. A stock may be sold short only on an up tick, or on a "zero-plus" tick. A "zero-plus" tick is a term used for a transaction at the same price as the preceding trade but higher than the preceding different price.

Conversely, a down tick, or "minus" tick, is a term used to designate a transaction made by a price lower than the preceding trade. A "zero-minus" tick is a transaction made by the same price as the preceding sale but lower than the preceding different price.

**Voting Right.** The stockholder's right to vote his stock in the affairs of his company. Most common shares have one vote each. Preferred stock usually has the right to vote when preferred dividends are in default for a specified period. The right to vote may be delegated by the stockholder to another person. (*See also* Cumulative Voting, Proxy)

**Warrant.** A certificate giving the holder the right to purchase securities at a stipulated price within a specified time limit or perpetually. Sometimes a warrant is offered with securities as an inducement to buy. (*See also* Rights)

**When Issued.** A short form of "when, as and if issued." The term indicates a conditional transaction in a security authorized for issuance but not as yet actually issued. All "when issued" transactions are on an "if" basis, to be settled if and when the actual security is issued and the Exchange or National Association of Securities Dealers rules the transactions are to be settled.

**Wire House.** A member firm of a stock exchange maintaining a communications network linking either its own branch offices, offices of correspondent firms, or a combination of such offices.

**Working Control.** Theoretically ownership of 51 per cent of a company's voting stock is necessary to exercise control. In practice—and this is particularly true in the case of a large corporation—effective control sometimes can be exerted through ownership, individually or by a group acting in concert, of less than 50 percent.

**Yield.** Also known as return. The dividends or interest paid by a company expressed as a percentage of the current price or, if you own the security, of the price you originally paid. The return on a stock is figured by dividing the total of dividends paid in the preceding 12 months by the current market price—or, if you are the owner, the price you originally paid. A stock with a current market value of $40 a share which has paid $2 in dividends in the preceding 12 months is said to return 5 percent ($2.00 ÷ $40.00). If you paid $20 for the stock five years earlier, the stock would be returning you 10 percent on your original investment. The current return on a bond is figured the same way. A 3 percent $1,000 bond selling at $600 offers a return of 5 percent ($30 ÷ $600). Figuring the yield of a bond to maturity calls for a bond yield table. (*See also* Dividend, Interest)

# CHAPTER 20

# INVESTING IN CORPORATE SECURITIES: THE DANGERS AND THE OPPORTUNITIES

For some, investing in stocks lends an air of sophistication.  Others enjoy being part of the drama, excitement and adventure that often unfolds in swank brokers' offices.  Then there are those who buy stocks to satisfy their urge for dealing with Mother Chance.  While there are legitimate appeals to stock investments, the aforementioned ones are certainly all the *wrong* reasons.  Buying and selling securities is always serious, tricky, tedious, and if done properly, time-consuming.  Any air of sophistication can be quickly shattered, and excitement turned to utter dismay, if an untimely stock investment *sours* and becomes worthless.

**"I should have married Harry Baker -- he bought Polaroid at 37½!"**

Reprinted with permission of *The Wall Street Journal* (Cartoon Features Syndicate).

Millions of Americans, from all walks of life, own shares in large and small corporations.  Some have prospered from their investments; others have experienced various degrees of disappointment.  Like every other type of investment, stocks have certain inherent dangers, plus an added dash of uncertainty.  So before investigating individual issues or as much as committing yourself to the purchase of one single share of stock, you should be thoroughly aware of the many risks as well as opportunities afforded by common stocks.

The objective of this chapter is to provide you with a thorough exploration of the fundamental problems, risks, and advantages of investing in corporate stocks. With this background, you can compare stocks more objectively with other investments. Then, should you decide to buy stocks, not only will you be able to make a more considered choice, but you can also minimize many of the risks of stock ownership due to your awareness of the factors that influence stock values.

## DANGERS OF STOCK INVESTMENTS

There is perhaps nothing more disheartening and tragic than to see people lose hard-earned money on a bad investment. The following short case report tells what actually happened to a young New Jersey couple:

> I got talking to my supervisor, Mr. Larson, at work one day. He told me about this real *hot* investment that his broker had gotten him to buy. Larson said he's put $200 into the stock not more than three months before, and that the stock had gone up until it was worth nearly $1,000. He said he was seriously considering borrowing money from the credit union so he could buy more of the stock, even at its higher price.
>
> The wife and I had been saving faithfully for over five years. We had nearly $4,000 in the bank. I was all excited after hearing what Larson had said. Both the wife and I decided that if Larson thought this was worth doing, we could take the chance too. So we took out all our money from the bank and bought the stock. That was the worst decision of our lives. The stock was nearly $20 a share when we bought it. It continued to go up for a few months—in fact it got up to nearly $28 a share. But then without any warning, it went to hell. In less than six months, it was practically worthless. We kept the stock for nearly three years hoping it might go back up, but finally we sold it so we could write the loss off from our taxes. We only got about $65 back out of our $4,000.

It is almost unbelievable that such sensible people, after years of budgeting, saving, and financial planning, could suddenly let their judgment become so clouded by emotion and greed. Perhaps if they had known more about the dangers, they would have taken greater care in investing their savings.

## MARKETABILITY OF STOCKS

One of the most important questions you try to answer when contemplating the purchase of a new automobile, boat, or home is "How easily and quickly can I resell the item when I desire to do so?" This same question must also be answered for any prospective stock investment. If it is a listed stock on the New York Stock Exchange, you can be reasonably sure that it can be readily sold if the need or desire to sell arises. Orderly trading takes place daily on virtually all the Exchange's listed stocks. Therefore, such listed stocks are said to have a high degree of *liquidity*; that is, they can be readily converted into cash. The majority of the issues listed on the American Stock Exchange also have very good liquidity.

Less certain, however, is the marketability of stocks listed on other smaller exchanges. Some of these stocks have excellent, relatively stable trading records; others have erratic patterns. Similarly, stocks traded on the over-the-counter market show great differences in marketability. Regular trading volumes are common on a great number of OTC favorites, but many other non-listed securities lack any market at all. Therefore, the marketability of stocks traded on small stock exchanges and those traded over-the-counter must be carefully investigated on the basis of each particular issue.

## STABILITY OF STOCK PRICES

Even though listed stocks on the New York and American Stock Exchanges generally can be sold easily, the prospective investor of these securities also wants to know, "How stable is the value of the stocks?" The answer to this question can be found by looking at the basic nature of all auction markets.

Consider what usually happens when several buyers take a special liking to an item being auctioned: They may bid up the price several times over what its reasonable value really is. On the other hand, if only one person shows an interest in an auctioned item, it may go across the auction block for only a small fraction of its worth. Then, too, the auction market may also be influenced by many forces outside the market itself. An especially fine balmy spring day may influence many of the auction's prospective customers to pick up their golf clubs and head for the fairways. An Apollo moon mission may catch their interest and cause them to stay away from the auction. A presidential announcement concerning sweeping economic changes may cause prices to thunder upwards.

Since listed corporate stocks are traded in an auction market, the prices at which they trade are heavily influenced by the number of people bidding for them and the number of shares offered for sale. For example, if *more* investors wish to buy shares of the International Business Machines Corporation than there are *owners willing to sell*, buyers must compete. The successful bidder will be the one willing to pay the highest price. Under such conditions the selling price of IBM shares may soar until the buyers' demands are satisfied, or until other owners of IBM stock are attracted by the higher selling prices and begin to flood the market with additional stock offered for sale. If too many sellers are subsequently attracted to the higher prices, the market may become glutted with sellers. Then shareholders may have to lower their asking price if they are to catch a buyer. In such instances, a downward trend is precipitated.

The vulnerability of corporate stocks to unstable prices is easily verified by looking at the year's high and low prices of NYSE stocks as reported in each issue of *The Wall Street Journal*. A small number of NYSE trades from a random issue of *The Journal* are shown in Fig. 20–1. Notice that IBM's price varied from a high of $365.75 to a low of $283.25. Other stocks in this illustration show similar swings in prices. Some of the stocks were selling at prices near their high for the year; others near their low. Some issues had wide price variations; some traded in a narrower range; but all exhibited the characteristic price swings and churnings of an auction market. Even for a given trading day, prices on a stock may show considerable variation. IBM's high for the trading day shown in Fig. 20–1 was $318, but the stock traded for as low as $314 on that same day.

| ––1971–– | | | Sales in | | | | | Net |
|---|---|---|---|---|---|---|---|---|
| High | Low | Stocks Div | 100s | Open | High | Low | Close | Chg. |
| 65 | 50 | Ill Cen pf3.50 | 13 | 57½ | 59½ | 57½ | 59½ | +2⅛ |
| 44¾ | 33¾ | Ill Powr 2.20 | 62 | 36¼ | 36¼ | 35⅜ | 35½ | − ⅜ |
| 17 | 12¼ | Imprl Cp Am | 584 | 13¾ | 14⅛ | 13⅝ | 14 | + ⅜ |
| 56½ | 34⅞ | INA Cp 1.40 | 576 | 55¾ | 56¼ | 55¼ | 55¾ | − ½ |
| 13 | 9⅞ | Income Capit | 63 | 11¼ | 11¼ | 10¾ | 11 | − ¼ |
| 11 | 9¾ | IncCCu .68g | 28 | 10⅜ | 10⅜ | 10 | 10⅜ | |
| 33⅝ | 25⅞ | Indian Hd .80 | 98 | 31¾ | 32¾ | 31¾ | 32⅝ | +1⅜ |
| 120 | 94½ | Ind Hd pf4.50 | 4 | 116 | 116 | 115 | 115 | +1 |
| 30 | 23¾ | IndplsPL 1.50 | 32 | 26¼ | 26⅝ | 26¼ | 26½ | + ⅛ |
| 21¾ | 18¼ | Indstl Nat .90 | 14 | 19¼ | 19¼ | 19 | 19 | − ⅛ |
| 59⅛ | 45 | Inger Rand 2 | 539 | 56 | 57 | 55¼ | 56⅞ | + ⅞ |
| 43½ | 37¾ | IngRd pf2.35 | 38 | 39½ | 40½ | 39¼ | 40¼ | + ¾ |
| 32¼ | 26¼ | Inland Stl 2 | 409 | 30¼ | 30⅜ | 29¾ | 30¼ | + ¼ |
| 14⅜ | 10⅛ | Inmont Corp | 250 | 14 | 14⅛ | 13½ | 13⅝ | − ⅛ |
| 20¾ | 15⅝ | Insilco .70 | 118 | 18⅝ | 18¾ | 18 | 18¾ | − ⅛ |
| 24 | 19⅜ | Insilc pfA1.25 | 20 | 21¾ | 22 | 21⅜ | 22 | |
| 51 | 36⅝ | InspirCop 2 | 25 | 42½ | 42½ | 41½ | 41½ | −1 |
| 48⅛ | 40¼ | Interco 1.20 | 54 | 47 | 48 | 47 | 48 | +1¾ |
| 30⅜ | 24¼ | IntrlkInc 1.80 | 39 | 28 | 28¼ | 27⅞ | 28⅛ | + ⅛ |
| 365¾ | 283¼ | IBM 5.20 | 841 | 314¾ | 318 | 314 | 315¾ | +1¾ |
| 29⅞ | 20½ | IntChm Nuc | 367 | 24¾ | 25¾ | 24⅜ | 25¼ | +1⅛ |
| 80 | 63 | IntFlaFr .60b | 68 | 77 | 78 | 76¾ | 77⅝ | +3⅝ |
| 33⅞ | 24 | Int Harv 1.40 | 250 | 28⅝ | 29 | 28¼ | 28⅞ | + ½ |
| 15¾ | 12¾ | IntHoldg .33g | 6 | 14⅜ | 14⅝ | 14⅜ | 14⅝ | .... |
| 13⅜ | 5 | Int Indust | 130 | 6⅞ | 6⅞ | 6⅝ | 6⅝ | .... |
| 23⅞ | 9⅛ | IntIndA pf | 25 | 10¼ | 10½ | 10¼ | 10¼ | ..... |
| 20⅝ | 13¾ | IntMiner .05g | 273 | 17½ | 18¼ | 17⅜ | 18¼ | + ¾ |
| 15¼ | 9 | Int Mng | 66 | 10⅝ | 10¾ | 9½ | 9½ | −1⅛ |
| 46¾ | 29½ | Int Nickel 1 | | | | | | |

**Fig. 20–1** Newspaper stock quotations showing year's high and low prices. Notice the wide swings in price shown in the first two columns on the left. Reprinted by permission from Dow Jones & Company, Inc.

In addition to studying price changes of individual stock issues, one can learn much about general trends and price movements by following one or more of the National stock indicators that are published daily. One of the oldest and most widely followed is the Dow Jones Industrial Average. Although more will be said concerning this and other indexes in a later chapter, it will serve our discussion here to merely explain that this average is a composite total of the selling price of common stocks of 30 different large industrial corporations traded on the New York Stock Exchange, adjusted for stock splits and various other relevant factors. Simply stated, these adjustments enable the index *to show trends in stock prices.* While all stocks are not represented in this average, it is, nevertheless, a good basic guide and tells an important story about stock prices. Dow Jones also computes and publishes daily averages of railroad and utility stocks.

Figure 20–2 charts the Dow Jones Averages for a four-month period. The daily trading price range of each index is reflected by individual vertical bars.

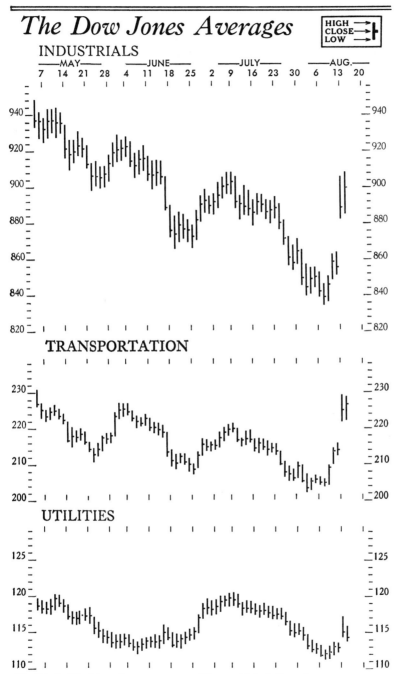

**Fig. 20–2** The Dow Jones averages. These widely followed averages appear daily in *The Wall Street Journal*. Reprinted by permission from Dow Jones & Company, Inc.

The top of the bar gives the high of the day, while the bottom charts the low. The closing average is indicated by a dot on the right side of the bar.

**Fig. 20–3** Comparison of Dow Jones industrial average and National Quotation Bureau industrial average. Reprinted by permission from National Quotation Bureau.

Figure 20–2 is particularly interesting from an historical standpoint. For the most part, it shows stocks riding downward as if on a rollar coaster, reflecting a continuing and severe bear market. The last two trading days shown, however, reflect the unbridled enthusiasm of investors to an economic message of President Nixon effecting wage and price freezes and certain other broad economic changes. The Dow Jones Industrial Average orbited 32.93 points. This particular trading day, Monday, August 16, 1971, chalked up the largest one-day gain in history for the Dow Jones Average. Another record was broken by the New York Stock Exchange on that day with 31,730,000 shares being traded.

Should you examine an issue of *The Wall Street Journal* showing the same averages for a more recent period, you will doubtless find the patterns of stock price variations quite different, but one feature would remain constant—the averages would show the continual fluctuation of stock prices.

Now what about price stability of OTC stocks? We know already that basically the OTC market is conducted by *negotiation* rather than *auction*. Are the prices more stable because of this different method of trading? To help answer this question, Fig. 20–3 plots an indicator compiled by the National Quotation Bureau on 35 OTC stocks along with the Dow Jones Industrial Average. It is easy to see from this comparison that price fluctuations of OTC stocks are quite similar in pattern (although different to some extent in magnitude) to listed stocks. Supply and demand, favorable and unfavorable economic factors, and all the other thousand-and-one things that influence listed stock prices seem to exert similar influences on the OTC issues.

### ECONOMIC AND POLITICAL INFLUENCES

As has already been illustrated, stock prices are extremely sensitive to our nation's economic conditions. And they are also influenced significantly by the business activities of other nations. Nearly all of the industrial giants of the United States have manufacturing facilities or investment abroad. A quick review of our economic history (1920's to 1960's) will help you to understand just how much corporate stock prices can be influenced by the ever-changing political and economic tides.

Although our government had made few if any plans for demobilization and reconstruction following World War I, these events proceeded unbelievably smoothly, perhaps only by accident. There was an acute, but short-lived, depression in 1921. It was followed by four energetic growth years in stock prices. The Dow Jones Industrial Average was 158 at the beginning of 1926. By that year, the automobile manufacturers and road-builders had created millions of new jobs. Similar gains had been made in almost all types of construction. And, a new economic giant, the electrical appliance and machinery industry, was beginning to flex its muscles. It is certainly well documented that the decade of the Twenties was one characterized by optimism and enthusiasm.

Those who were fortunate enough to have bought and sold stocks early in the Twenties made handsome profits. Those investors who didn't sell were bolstered by their unrealized paper profits and made further stock purchases. Prior to this decade, the low- and middle-income person knew little and cared less about stocks and bonds. But now, everybody wanted to get in on what looked like *easy money*. And if you didn't have cash to pay for the stocks, you could buy them on margin (on credit). Bankers seemed to be as optimistic and as greedy as everyone else. They loaned freely to customers who wanted to purchase securities, sometimes at rates of 15 to 20 percent. Nearly everyone seemed to catch stock market fever. You were just out of touch with the times if you didn't jump on the bandwagon. Reading the financial section of the newspaper and making the daily trip to the broker's office became America's new prestige symbols.

Although all the attention seemed to be focused on the *new prosperity*, there were great economic inequities. Many industries were near collapse. Unemployment was high, though almost unnoticed—except by those who were unemployed. Coal miners, leather-goods producers, and railroad equipment manufacturers were nearing bankruptcy. In short, much of the economy was on the verge of economic ruin, yet few people were warned of the impending disaster.

By September of 1929, the feverish speculation had pushed the Dow Jones Industrial Average to 386—a staggering gain of 244 percent in little more than three and a half years. The *impossible* happened—the lovely balloon burst in the surprised and disbelieving faces of hundreds of thousands of investors. The black day was October 29, 1929. In one fell swoop the Dow Jones Average sank to 232, plummeting about 40 percent. At the end of that bleak, frantic day, 16,410,030 shares had traded on the New York Stock Exchange, whereas in 1929 the daily average was only about 3,500,000. In November, stock prices on the Exchange fell to the 200 level. Thus was born this nation's most catastrophic depression.

The break in stock prices was not the cause of the depression, but the crash did dramatize the economic ills which up to that point were either unrecognized or kept neatly swept under political rugs. But now it was all out in the open. Factories were laying off men by the thousands, and soon bread lines would be a daily sight in America's heretofore proud streets. By July of 1932, the Dow Jones Industrial Average had sunk to 41. Stocks that could have been sold for $1,000 at their 1929 peak were now worth only about $89—that is if you could find a buyer for them. The whole tragic picture of what happened to stock prices is pictured in Fig. 20–4. A feeble recovery took place in 1935 and 1936 during Franklin D. Roosevelt's *New Deal*. But it wasn't until November of 1954—some 25 years after the big crash—*that the average once again reached the 1929 level.*

Although stock prices showed an impressive long-term upward trend from the conclusion of World War II to 1966, there have been a good many dips as the Dow Jones Industrial Average traced its upward climb. In most instances, severe declines in stock prices can be traced directly to economic ills and reverses in the nation's economy. Unfortunately, no one can predict with certainty what will happen to stock prices in the future. However, investors can keep track of some of the factors that directly influence stock trading and stock values:

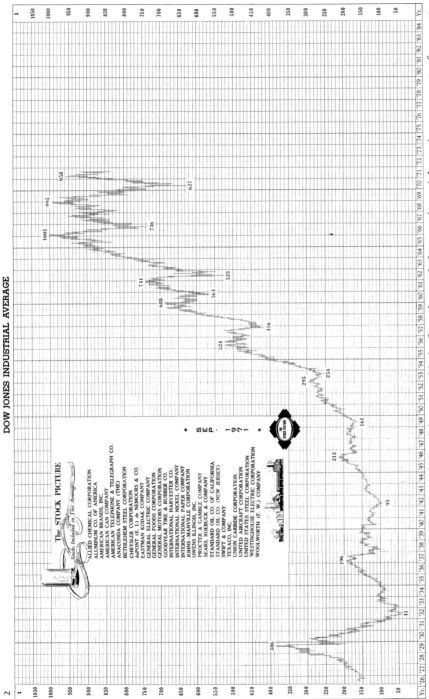

**Fig. 20–4** A historical look at the Dow Jones industrial average. Notice from the graph the sometimes violent price movements of corporate stocks. Reprinted by permission from M. C. Horsey & Company, Publishers.

1. Rising and declining employment figures.
2. Production, sales, and inventory trends.
3. Demands of organized labor on industry, labor unrest, and strikes.
4. Changes in domestic consumer spending and saving rates and patterns.
5. Changes in spending by Federal, state, and local governments.
6. Increases or decreases in imports and exports.
7. International political and economic conditions.
8. Changes in government policies, laws, and taxes.

Although all of these items are important, governmental policies and actions deserve special consideration since they ultimately determine the basic legal and tax framework in which businesses must operate. Here are a few examples: Changes in Federal spending have a pronounced effect on many defense industries and an indirect effect on all business. Small increases or decreases in corporate taxes can substantially reduce or increase the amount of profit which a company is able to keep. Federal controls—such as the recent safety standards which have been imposed on the Nation's automobile manufacturers—certainly have a direct impact upon the producers. Business regulations, changes in interest rates, minimum-wage controls, involvement in limited wars or conflicts, trade relations between this and other countries and many other factors enter the picture. Things both the Democrats and the Republicans do can affect the profitability of the corporation and in turn affect the values of corporate stocks.

Financial publications such as *The Wall Street Journal, Barrons, Business Week, Forbes,* and *Time* provide current information on these and other stock market influences and, more importantly, give meaningful discussion on *how* and *to what extent* the market may react to the changes. Anyone who contemplates making stock investments should certainly take advantage of the invaluable data provided by these reputable journals.

### PSYCHOLOGICAL INFLUENCES

It is easy to understand why stock prices react to general economic conditions that may in a very real way affect future sales and profitability. And there is no difficulty in seeing why the market would react favorably to the good news of inventions or technical discoveries that would enhance a corporation's competitive position. Sometimes, however, the market's reactions are unpredictable and bizarre. It very often over-reacts to changing conditions or anticipated news. A little daring, courage or optimism of a few investors may quickly be copied by thousands of others. When this happens, the price of the particular stock or the entire market may hurtle upward. Unfounded fear and caution has, on a good many occasions, pushed the averages downward in a sweep of unexpected panic selling. When most people want to buy, the market rises. When most people want to sell, the market declines.

Whatever the reasons for the investors' decisions to buy or sell, the law of supply and demand quickly determines the direction prices will go.  News stories of political interest, events of national importance, advice or commentary by public officials may be the trigger.  Frequently, the end result for the market is trading in volumes and at prices far out of proportion to the event which initially provided the trigger.  Consider the following:

> President Eisenhower suffered a mild heart attack on Saturday, September 24, 1955. Everyone was concerned.  Would the President recover?  And if he didn't, what would happen nationally and internationally?  By Monday morning, many investors decided they should get out of the market—sell their stocks—just as a precaution in the event the President should die.  Others took a wait-and-see attitude, but hardly anyone wanted to buy.  As a consequence, the market was overwhelmed with sell orders; prices plummeted.  The New York Stock Exchange traded 2,540,000 shares on the Friday before the President's attack.  The Dow Jones Industrial closing average was 487.45 for that same day.  On Monday, however, it was a far different story.  Heavy trading carried the average down to a low of 446.74 and closed at 455.56, down 31.89 for the day.  When final tallies were made, 7,720,000 shares changed hands during Monday's frantic trading on the NYSE.

## TECHNOLOGY MAKES AND BREAKS COMPANIES AND INDUSTRIES

What would happen to the price of General Motors stock if Westinghouse Corporation were to disclose that it had perfected an entirely new, inexpensive, long-lived power cell capable of furnishing adequate amounts of electrical energy for passenger cars?  Or how would Parke, Davis & Co. stock react to disclosure by the company of a new preventive serum for a broad range of cancers?  With the amount of research and development being conducted today, such discoveries may someday—perhaps very soon—be realities.

Although every new discovery creates investment opportunities, each new advance also inevitably causes problems—both for individual companies and often for entire industries.  Perhaps the most vivid example in recent years is the impact which television has had upon the movie industry.  A comparison of Fig. 20–5a and 20–5b tells the story.  By 1961, the movie industry was beginning to suffer serious declines in revenue as more television sets were purchased.  Instead of going to the movies, people were now being entertained by television at home.

When gains in technology thrust a new competitor on an industry, there are usually serious repercussions.  Some companies respond through dynamic management and make a comeback as have some of the movie companies in more recent years by limiting the number of productions, cutting performer costs and producing pictures specifically for television.  Other companies fail to meet the challenge and their future is seriously jeopardized.

If you are on the winning team as an investor, you will be pleased to see the new technology take over.  However, technological breaks are highly unpredictable.  Even the most careful and astute investor will occasionally be caught holding stocks on the losing side of new developments.

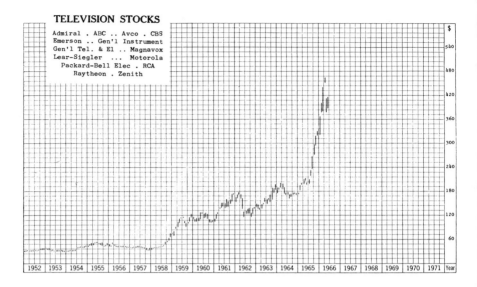

**Fig. 20–5** Comparative performance of television and motion picture company stocks. Technology often gives a boost to one industry and a kick in the pants to another. Reprinted by permission from M. C. Horsey & Company, Publishers.

## INDIVIDUAL WINNERS DIFFICULT TO PICK

Even though all stocks are affected by general economic conditions, political factors, and technology, the actual performance of each stock is always highly individualistic and in the long run greatly dependent on the quality of its management. Expert management may be able to lead even a sick corporation into profitable areas. Or, should unqualified management take over the operations of an otherwise sound corporation, problems of all sorts can arise.

Time seems to be the best guidepost to the quality of a corporation's management. Old, well-established companies with reliable, consistent earnings records are usually referred to as "blue-chip" issues. Even though the values of these stocks fluctuate considerably, the price changes are usually less violent and not quite so unpredictable as for other smaller, newer corporations. Although it is difficult to apply meaningful labels to stocks, you will frequently hear brokers and investors talk about this latter group of unseasoned stocks as *speculative* issues. This is a general term used to indicate that such stocks involve considerable risk. Quite often the market prices of speculative issues fluctuate violently; and, characteristically, over a wider range than blue-chip issues. It is easy to understand why the speculative stock has the lure of much higher profits should things go well, but you must also know that the losses can be staggering if you fail to hit a winner.

## UNCERTAIN GUIDEPOSTS TO DETERMINE VALUES

One of the principal measures used for appraising a stock's worth by experienced investors is the *price-earnings ratio*. It is computed easily by dividing the current market price of the stock by net earnings per share. For example, if a corporation were earning a net profit of $5 on each share of its outstanding stock and the stock were selling at $100 per share on the market, the price-earnings ratio would be 20:1. As a matter of fact, this 20:1 ratio was the average for 425 manufacturing stocks composing the Standard & Poor's Industrials Average in 1971. Interestingly, however, this compares with a ratio of only about 8:1 near the end of 1950.

A glamor issue, such as IBM may at times sell at a ratio of as much as 50:1 as investors anticipate further technological gains and future profits. Other very fine substantial companies typically sell at very low solid ratios of 8:1 or 10:1. Industry groups, too, tend to cluster around a price-earnings ratio peculiar to that industry. For example, bank stocks in 1971 were selling at about a 12:1 ratio compared with the 20:1 manufacturing ratio mentioned earlier. The ratio is a very rough and flexible guide at best. It is easy for investors to get accustomed to buying stocks at very high prices and ratios as they did through the 50's and 60's. As years go by, these same investors may become lulled into a false sense of security. Any small economic misfortune may be just enough to upset the applecart. Prices may race crazily downward as investments are re-evaluated and new price-earnings norms are established. The old statement that "hindsight is always more accurate than foresight" appropriately describes the judgment of any stock market analyst.

Stocks, like people, seem to develop a crowd of friends or a circle of believers. They seem to have very distinctive trading personalities. Many stocks suffer from psychological investor neglect while other glamour issues may be inflated by their popularity. Certainly sentiment has much to do with a stock's market price.

Beyond the current price-earnings status and the investor's sentiment toward a stock, the investors' appraisal of a corporation's future enters prominently into the trading picture. The price which investors are willing to pay *now* is influenced significantly by anticipated technology, and earnings— perhaps looking ahead as much as 2, 3, or 5 years. Personal opinions of investors all over the nation, based on a mixture of fact and fantasy, are then reflected by orders to buy or sell particular stocks at specific prices.

## CORPORATIONS ARE VULNERABLE TO CORRUPT MANAGEMENT

Corporate officers, you will recall, are elected by a vote of the company's stockholders. However, in actual practice, very few investors find it really practical to travel to the city in which the annual corporate meeting is being held. Most stockholders cannot afford the time or the money required to attend corporate annual meetings. Knowing this, the existing corporate officers follow the practice of soliciting proxies from shareholders. The proxy is a legal instrument permitting the person holding it to vote the stock of other shareholders as the holder deems fit. Therefore, if the officers can solicit enough proxies, they can, in effect, vote themselves back into office.

Even though stockholders were unhappy with the way the business was being handled and refuse to sign a proxy, they would find it very difficult to get together enough of a voting block to remove the officers from the corporation. The officers may, in fact, own enough stock among themselves to control the voting without proxies. This is very often the case with a small corporation. And even with a very large corporation, if officers own 5, 10 or perhaps 15 percent of the total outstanding stock and additionally can solicit even a fair number of proxies, they can usually determine the outcome of the voting.

The author does not mean to convey the impression that the practice of soliciting proxies is *bad* or *morally corrupt*. On the contrary, the proxy system usually works to the advantage of the company and the stockholders. If there is qualified management at the helm of the company, voting by proxy can sustain the leadership and give continuity to direction of the firm's activities.

The unfortunate thing is that the management of *any* corporation— whether good or bad—often find it too easy to perpetuate themselves in office. Consider the following case:

> The San Bueno Travel Association, Inc. (pseudo name) was incorporated under the laws of one of the Southwestern states. It was capitalized for 200,000 shares of $1 par value common stock.
>
> The prospectus or information brochure indicated that the corporation's organizers had deeded two acres of vacant property adjacent to a busy highway to the corporation in exchange for 100,000 shares of the corporation's stock. Of the remaining 100,000 shares offered for sale to the public at $2 per share, only 82,000

were sold.  After salesmen's commissions had been paid, the stock sale netted the company $131,200.

Management decided not to go ahead with their plans to build a motel since they felt the motel business had been overbuilt in that particular city.  However, they indicated they were going to look around and find another more suitable location.  At the time this author analyzed the company, eight years had gone by since incorporation.  As far as he could determine, not one transaction had ever been made that would profit the corporation or the stockholders.  Yet the President and Vice President both had drawn good salaries and had been reimbursed for many other expenses:

| | |
|---|---|
| President's salary for 8 years | $80,000 |
| Vice President's part-time salary | $18,640 |
| Travel and miscellaneous expenses | $ 9,456 |

The corporation still owns the two acres of commercial property.  However, cash resources are almost completely gone.  Unless minority stockholders bring suit against the officers and are successful in getting a court judgment, the land will probably be sold and depleted in salaries as have the original proceeds (money) from the stock sale.

Since the President and other organizers of the corporation hold a majority of the stock, there is no chance that the other stockholders can oust management.

## ANTIQUATED MARKET SYSTEMS

During the early years of the seventies, the stock market has been shackled with bad press.  Part of the criticism stemmed from the disheartening bear market which dropped through the 850 level on the Dow Jones Industrial Average.  But another important criticism, one well-founded, has been aimed at the dangers thrust upon the investor by the antiquated, roll-top office procedures of most brokers.  Sometimes the brokers went months before realizing that millions of dollars of their securities had been lost or stolen.  This debacle, one which caused the demise of many large brokerage houses, underscores the need for revamping many of our securities procedures.

Recent comments from the SEC indicate that they will encourage brokerage firms to put more permanent capital into their operations to make them more secure for the investors they serve.  The SEC also is very much concerned that the brokers adopt more modern computerized data handling procedures to provide faster, more accurate service.  It is well recognized that there is a large black market on stocks operated by organized crime.  Studies are currently underway to determine the feasibility of eliminating the physical transfer of stock certificates to help eliminate the black market activities.

## OPPORTUNITIES OF STOCK INVESTMENTS

There is no perfectly safe investment, as was pointed out in the discussion on Savings in Chapter 3.  Money kept in an insured bank or savings and loan association may be safe physically, but the purchasing power or value of the money is subject to the very real risk of inflation.  At current inflationary rates much, if not all, of the interest earned on savings is wiped out by the shrivelling value of the dollar.  To the extent that inflation exceeds interest payments, the net effect is the same as having physically lost part of your savings.  Generally speaking, common stocks have been attractive to investors because they have *variable dollar worth*.  The following pages discuss this important quality as well as many other advantages unique to common stocks.

### COMMON STOCKS MAY BE A GOOD HEDGE AGAINST INFLATION
If the prices of goods and services sold by a corporation advance (along with corresponding increases in expenses), the number of dollars earned on sales will increase even though percentagewise earnings may remain about the same fraction of total sales.  Therefore, the stock would tend to increase proportionately in its dollar worth.  Stated more simply, the value of common stock tends to keep pace with inflation.  Note the following example:

> Let's suppose you were a General Motors shareholder using dividends to purchase the family car.  In 1939, a small Chevrolet cost around $700.  That year, also, GM paid a $3.50 dividend.  So ownership of 200 shares would have allowed you to enjoy a car "on the company."
>
> Since then, General Motors split its stock 2 for 1, in 1950, and 3 for 1 in 1955—your 200 shares would have grown to 1,200.  Total dividends on $5,340 paid on those shares last year will buy a new car today.

And you will note that *common stocks* are specifically mentioned since preferred issues tend to remain more constant in value—yielding as they do only a fixed dollar dividend per share.

Stocks are not a perfect inflationary hedge, however.  Although there are many causes for the prolonged bear market which began in 1966, inflation itself must be partly blamed.  So long as wages and salary increases were outdistanced by increasing worker productivity, corporate profits were secure.  However, in recent years, productivity has ground to a standstill while unions have accelerated their demands for higher salaries and expanded fringe benefits.

So although you may properly look to stock investments as a *good* inflationary hedge; it is well to remember that too much inflation (inflation without corresponding increases in worker productivity) may be *bearish* on the stock market.

### FAVORABLE RATES OF RETURN*
Fisher and Lorie of the University of Chicago recently completed what is

---

* Adapted with permission from Lawrence Fisher and James H. Lorie, "Rates of Return on Investments in Common Stocks (1926–1965)," Chicago: The Center for Research in Security Prices (sponsored by Merrill, Lynch, Pierce, Fenner & Smith, Inc.), Graduate School of Business, University of Chicago, 1969, 13 pp.

undoubtedly the most comprehensive historical study of yields of common stocks listed on the New York Stock Exchange. It shows the rate of return produced by all the common stocks listed on the Big Board beginning in any year from January, 1926, and ending in any other year in December, 1965—a total of 820 possible year-to-year combinations.

One of the key tables of the study is reproduced in Fig. 20–6. It shows how an investor would have made out with reinvestment of dividends but without payment of taxes on dividends or capital gains and without commissions on liquidation; in other words, the data are those that would apply to the portfolio of a tax-exempt investor. Consequently, the rates of return for common stocks shown in this table can be compared most directly to the compound interest rates paid by banks on savings in the various periods and with the published yields on most other investment media, all of which are, of course, pre-tax figures. To arrive at the studies' conclusions, results were computed for every possible combination of month-end purchase and sale dates for every stock throughout the 35-year period. For any one stock, this would have represented 87,900 monthly combinations, and for all Exchange stocks it meant tabulating results on 56,557,538 such possible transactions, a job that would have taken thousands of man-hours without a computer.

Here are the key findings of this study: If an investor (1) had picked a stock at random from the Big Board list; (2) had then picked a purchase date at random between January, 1926 and December, 1960; and (3) had picked at random any later sales date within the same period, he would have made money 78 percent of the time. The median return, assuming reinvestment of all dividends and payment of brokerage commissions on purchase and sale, would have been 9.8 percent per annum compounded annually. At that rate of interest, money doubles in about seven years, and the study showed that the investor would have had a better than 50–50 chance of doing exactly that— doubling his money—with purely random selection. His risk of losing was only one in thirteen whereas his expectation of making as much as 20 percent per annum compounded annually was one in five.

The study demonstrated two other points of vital significance to any investor:

1. If the investor had picked small groups of stocks at random instead of just one, the risk of loss would have been considerably reduced and the probability of a larger profit considerably improved.
2. If the investor had not been forced to sell during a period of economic recession—if he had been able to hold on for a year or two—his chance of making a profit and the amount of profit would have both been significantly increased.

It is important to note here that even though this study reflects bad as well as good stock market times in the past, since 1966 the market has experienced

| To | 1/26 | 12/26 | 12/27 | 12/28 | 12/29 | 12/30 | 12/31 | 12/32 | 12/33 | 12/34 | 12/35 | 12/36 | 12/37 | 12/38 | 12/39 | 12/40 | 12/41 | 12/42 | 12/43 | 12/44 | 12/45 | 12/46 | 12/47 | 12/48 | 12/49 | 12/50 | 12/51 | 12/52 | 12/53 | 12/54 | 12/55 | 12/56 | 12/57 | 12/58 | 12/59 | 12/60 | 12/61 | 12/62 | 12/63 | 12/64 |
|---|---|---|---|---|---|---|---|---|---|---|---|---|---|---|---|---|---|---|---|---|---|---|---|---|---|---|---|---|---|---|---|---|---|---|---|---|---|---|---|---|
| 12/26 | -1.6 | | | | | | | | | | | | | | | | | | | | | | | | | | | | | | | | | | | | | | | |
| 12/27 | 15.3 | 30.0 | | | | | | | | | | | | | | | | | | | | | | | | | | | | | | | | | | | | | | |
| 12/28 | 23.9 | 37.7 | 45.5 | | | | | | | | | | | | | | | | | | | | | | | | | | | | | | | | | | | | | |
| 12/29 | 7.8 | 9.6 | 0.1 | -30.0 | | | | | | | | | | | | | | | | | | | | | | | | | | | | | | | | | | | | |
| 12/30 | -2.3 | -3.5 | -13.0 | -31.7 | -37.2 | | | | | | | | | | | | | | | | | | | | | | | | | | | | | | | | | | | |
| 12/31 | -11.1 | -13.5 | -21.7 | -36.3 | -40.8 | -47.8 | | | | | | | | | | | | | | | | | | | | | | | | | | | | | | | | | | |
| 12/32 | -11.0 | -12.7 | -19.0 | -30.3 | -32.1 | -31.0 | -11.1 | | | | | | | | | | | | | | | | | | | | | | | | | | | | | | | | | |
| 12/33 | -2.7 | -1.6 | -7.7 | -15.6 | -11.8 | -1.3 | 36.9 | 108.4 | | | | | | | | | | | | | | | | | | | | | | | | | | | | | | | | |
| 12/34 | -1.2 | -0.3 | -5.2 | -11.3 | -7.0 | 2.4 | 28.2 | 55.0 | 13.8 | | | | | | | | | | | | | | | | | | | | | | | | | | | | | | | |
| 12/35 | 2.2 | 1.6 | -0.8 | -3.7 | -0.5 | 9.3 | 32.9 | 53.5 | 13.0 | 50.4 | | | | | | | | | | | | | | | | | | | | | | | | | | | | | | |
| 12/36 | 6.6 | 5.5 | 3.1 | -0.4 | 5.3 | 15.3 | 37.5 | 54.5 | 40.9 | 56.8 | 63.9 | | | | | | | | | | | | | | | | | | | | | | | | | | | | | |
| 12/37 | 5.0 | 0.1 | -0.1 | -6.3 | -2.8 | 3.3 | 16.1 | 23.1 | 16.1 | 6.6 | -10.9 | -46.0 | | | | | | | | | | | | | | | | | | | | | | | | | | | | |
| 12/38 | 6.1 | 2.3 | 2.0 | -2.9 | 0.9 | 6.0 | 18.7 | 25.5 | 12.9 | 12.6 | 0.1 | -16.2 | 30.7 | | | | | | | | | | | | | | | | | | | | | | | | | | | |
| 12/39 | 6.3 | 2.3 | 2.0 | -2.6 | 0.9 | 6.0 | 15.7 | 20.5 | 10.1 | 9.4 | 0.4 | -10.0 | 12.9 | -3.3 | | | | | | | | | | | | | | | | | | | | | | | | | | |
| 12/40 | 1.9 | -0.2 | -0.8 | -3.0 | 0.2 | 4.7 | 13.0 | 20.9 | 7.9 | 6.4 | -1.1 | -9.8 | 6.3 | -5.0 | -9.0 | | | | | | | | | | | | | | | | | | | | | | | | | |
| 12/41 | 1.2 | 0.9 | -0.8 | -3.3 | -0.5 | 3.5 | 10.8 | 18.0 | 13.3 | 4.2 | -1.9 | -9.2 | 2.6 | -5.5 | -9.0 | -10.2 | | | | | | | | | | | | | | | | | | | | | | | | |
| 12/42 | 2.0 | 1.9 | 0.4 | -1.9 | 0.9 | 4.8 | 11.6 | 14.6 | 12.4 | 6.0 | 0.9 | -4.9 | 6.1 | 0.6 | 3.5 | 22.2 | 31.1 | | | | | | | | | | | | | | | | | | | | | | | |
| 12/43 | 3.6 | 3.6 | 2.5 | 0.2 | 3.1 | 7.2 | 13.8 | 16.6 | 12.4 | 9.7 | 5.5 | 0.9 | 12.3 | 9.4 | 13.7 | 26.8 | 47.1 | 56.7 | | | | | | | | | | | | | | | | | | | | | | |
| 12/44 | 4.5 | 5.2 | 4.9 | 3.7 | 4.7 | 8.7 | 15.2 | 16.7 | 11.7 | 9.9 | 8.4 | 4.6 | 13.3 | 13.7 | 14.8 | 33.6 | 51.4 | 49.3 | 38.1 | | | | | | | | | | | | | | | | | | | | | |
| 12/45 | 6.3 | 6.5 | 6.0 | 5.9 | 7.0 | 11.3 | 17.6 | 20.4 | 12.9 | 12.5 | 12.4 | 9.3 | 18.3 | 19.4 | 19.1 | 24.2 | 34.8 | 55.4 | 50.1 | 59.8 | | | | | | | | | | | | | | | | | | | | |
| 12/46 | 5.5 | 5.7 | 5.0 | 5.0 | 6.0 | 9.9 | 15.6 | 18.0 | 13.1 | 13.1 | 10.2 | 9.0 | 16.3 | 15.0 | 15.6 | 20.3 | 34.5 | 37.5 | 22.5 | 20.2 | -9.9 | | | | | | | | | | | | | | | | | | | |
| 12/47 | 5.1 | 5.0 | 4.4 | 4.4 | 5.8 | 9.3 | 14.6 | 14.8 | 12.4 | 12.1 | 9.4 | 8.3 | 14.7 | 13.6 | 14.5 | 18.1 | 26.3 | 26.3 | 20.8 | 18.9 | -4.4 | -0.5 | | | | | | | | | | | | | | | | | | |
| 12/48 | 5.7 | 4.5 | 5.0 | 4.9 | 6.3 | 9.1 | 13.9 | 16.6 | 12.4 | 11.1 | 9.1 | 8.3 | 13.5 | 14.2 | 14.8 | 18.2 | 20.8 | 20.8 | 18.0 | 18.0 | -3.5 | -1.0 | -2.9 | | | | | | | | | | | | | | | | | |
| 12/49 | 5.8 | 5.8 | 5.8 | 5.9 | 6.0 | 9.1 | 13.5 | 15.7 | 11.7 | 11.3 | 10.6 | 9.5 | 13.3 | 14.8 | 14.9 | 18.7 | 22.2 | 20.8 | 16.4 | 21.2 | 5.4 | 5.4 | 8.2 | 19.3 | | | | | | | | | | | | | | | | |
| 12/50 | 6.5 | 6.7 | 6.7 | 7.0 | 7.0 | 10.2 | 14.9 | 16.7 | 12.9 | 12.5 | 10.6 | 11.1 | 14.8 | 14.1 | 15.6 | 19.0 | 22.4 | 21.4 | 16.9 | 15.0 | 7.8 | 12.4 | 16.6 | 16.6 | 35.8 | | | | | | | | | | | | | | | |
| 12/51 | 6.9 | 7.1 | 6.4 | 6.4 | 7.6 | 10.6 | 16.7 | 18.0 | 16.7 | 14.4 | 9.0 | 14.5 | 15.6 | 14.5 | 15.6 | 20.8 | 21.6 | 20.2 | 17.7 | 15.2 | 9.4 | 13.3 | 16.4 | 20.0 | 25.2 | 14.9 | | | | | | | | | | | | | | |
| 12/52 | 7.0 | 7.2 | 6.5 | 6.5 | 7.6 | 10.5 | 14.8 | 16.4 | 13.0 | 12.9 | 11.0 | 11.9 | 14.7 | 13.8 | 15.0 | 17.9 | 17.9 | 17.5 | 15.1 | 14.5 | 10.5 | 12.9 | 15.2 | 14.8 | 19.8 | 12.0 | 8.9 | | | | | | | | | | | | | |
| 12/53 | 6.8 | 6.8 | 6.1 | 6.1 | 7.1 | 9.8 | 13.9 | 15.3 | 12.4 | 12.0 | 11.0 | 12.3 | 13.3 | 13.2 | 13.7 | 17.0 | 17.2 | 17.4 | 15.0 | 14.0 | 10.5 | 10.5 | 15.0 | 16.5 | 13.7 | 12.5 | 3.5 | -3.1 | | | | | | | | | | | | |
| 12/54 | 6.1 | 6.1 | 6.1 | 6.4 | 6.4 | 11.4 | 15.5 | 17.4 | 14.5 | 14.5 | 12.7 | 13.1 | 15.9 | 14.8 | 16.2 | 19.0 | 21.0 | 18.8 | 18.6 | 18.6 | 15.5 | 15.5 | 17.7 | 18.5 | 21.7 | 17.9 | 18.5 | 22.8 | 54.8 | | | | | | | | | | | |
| 12/55 | 8.4 | 8.2 | 8.0 | 9.2 | 9.2 | 11.4 | 17.4 | 17.4 | 14.6 | 14.1 | 12.2 | 15.9 | 14.8 | 16.6 | 16.9 | 18.8 | 21.4 | 18.6 | 16.9 | 15.0 | 12.4 | 12.2 | 16.2 | 18.5 | 21.7 | 19.5 | 19.1 | 22.2 | 37.2 | 19.0 | | | | | | | | | | |
| 12/56 | 8.5 | 8.7 | 8.1 | 7.0 | 9.2 | 11.8 | 15.7 | 17.1 | 14.4 | 14.4 | 12.6 | 11.1 | 15.6 | 15.1 | 15.6 | 18.2 | 20.2 | 19.4 | 17.9 | 16.4 | 13.3 | 13.4 | 17.2 | 20.0 | 17.3 | 17.0 | 16.9 | 18.6 | 26.7 | 13.3 | 6.5 | | | | | | | | | |
| 12/57 | 8.8 | 9.0 | 8.4 | 6.3 | 8.3 | 10.7 | 14.3 | 15.3 | 12.9 | 13.0 | 9.7 | 9.7 | 13.2 | 13.9 | 14.2 | 18.3 | 17.5 | 15.1 | 13.6 | 13.6 | 12.3 | 13.2 | 16.7 | 14.8 | 15.3 | 12.0 | 13.0 | 13.0 | 14.5 | 3.4 | -3.7 | -12.9 | | | | | | | | |
| 12/58 | 8.9 | 9.1 | 8.5 | 7.6 | 9.7 | 12.1 | 14.5 | 15.6 | 13.5 | 13.6 | 11.3 | 11.1 | 13.9 | 13.8 | 14.6 | 17.8 | 19.4 | 16.7 | 16.0 | 16.0 | 15.2 | 13.2 | 16.7 | 18.6 | 18.6 | 16.5 | 16.5 | 13.5 | 21.9 | 14.5 | 13.0 | 17.4 | 57.9 | | | | | | | |
| 12/59 | 9.0 | 9.1 | 8.5 | 7.5 | 9.4 | 11.6 | 14.9 | 16.1 | 13.9 | 14.0 | 11.3 | 11.3 | 14.8 | 14.0 | 16.6 | 17.4 | 19.9 | 17.4 | 15.0 | 15.9 | 13.4 | 13.4 | 16.8 | 18.5 | 18.5 | 16.6 | 16.6 | 13.5 | 21.9 | 14.5 | 13.1 | 17.6 | 36.0 | 14.4 | | | | | | |
| 12/60 | 9.4 | 9.5 | 8.7 | 7.5 | 9.1 | 11.6 | 14.9 | 14.8 | 13.5 | 13.7 | 11.6 | 11.5 | 14.8 | 14.2 | 15.1 | 16.0 | 18.7 | 17.9 | 15.9 | 14.4 | 12.2 | 12.2 | 16.8 | 16.5 | 18.5 | 14.9 | 14.8 | 15.3 | 22.8 | 12.4 | 13.1 | 21.9 | 21.9 | 6.4 | -1.9 | | | | | |
| 12/61 | 9.3 | 9.5 | 8.1 | 7.0 | 8.1 | 12.2 | 15.4 | 19.3 | 14.4 | 14.4 | 11.8 | 11.8 | 15.0 | 15.0 | 15.4 | 17.3 | 19.3 | 18.5 | 15.4 | 13.2 | 12.9 | 12.9 | 16.0 | 16.0 | 17.3 | 16.0 | 16.0 | 16.6 | 19.0 | 14.6 | 13.9 | 16.1 | 23.7 | 13.6 | 12.9 | 27.6 | | | | |
| 12/62 | 8.6 | 8.8 | 7.3 | 6.3 | 7.3 | 11.2 | 14.3 | 13.8 | 13.3 | 13.5 | 10.7 | 11.0 | 14.0 | 13.8 | 14.3 | 16.8 | 17.5 | 16.7 | 13.9 | 13.2 | 11.8 | 11.8 | 14.0 | 15.2 | 14.9 | 13.5 | 13.3 | 13.0 | 19.7 | 10.5 | 10.4 | 15.1 | 15.1 | 6.3 | 7.8 | 5.9 | -8.7 | | | |
| 12/63 | 8.0 | 9.1 | 7.6 | 7.6 | 8.5 | 11.6 | 14.5 | 14.6 | 13.5 | 13.6 | 11.3 | 12.3 | 14.3 | 14.0 | 14.7 | 17.4 | 16.7 | 15.0 | 14.9 | 14.2 | 13.4 | 13.2 | 14.2 | 15.3 | 15.0 | 13.7 | 13.5 | 13.5 | 19.3 | 10.4 | 11.2 | 15.7 | 16.2 | 10.4 | 7.4 | 10.4 | 17.7 | 16.3 | | |
| 12/64 | 9.1 | 9.3 | 9.4 | 7.5 | 9.0 | 11.6 | 14.6 | 14.9 | 14.0 | 14.1 | 11.6 | 12.4 | 14.8 | 14.2 | 15.2 | 16.0 | 17.5 | 15.9 | 15.0 | 14.4 | 14.1 | 13.4 | 14.9 | 15.0 | 14.5 | 14.3 | 14.7 | 14.3 | 18.7 | 12.4 | 12.5 | 17.7 | 17.5 | 12.1 | 12.4 | 15.9 | 22.6 | 23.4 | 28.3 | |

**Fig. 20–6** Rates of return on investment in common stocks listed on the New York Stock Exchange. Figures show results with reinvestment of dividends (percent per annum compounded annually) on a cash-to-portfolio, tax-exempt basis. Cash-to-portfolio means the net rate of return which would have been realized after paying commissions on each transaction but continuing to hold the portfolio at the end of each period.

the worst and most prolonged bear conditions since the depression years of the thirties. Hopefully the Fisher and Lorie efforts can be continued and will provide you with new data (from 1966 into the 70's) so that you may evaluate recent trends in yields.

## A WAY TO SHARE IN ECONOMIC GROWTH

By many indicators, America has yet to reach its full economic potential. More new products and industries have evolved in the past decade than in any recorded ten-year span. With the projected growth in population, productivity, and technological development, the closing decades of the twentieth century should chalk up surprising new economic achievements:

1. *Population.* Economists generally agree that population projections form one of the important statistical ingredients necessary for predicting future economic conditions. Figure 20–7 illustrates the way in which our population might grow through the year 2000. Expectations of the Census Bureau are that the United States will grow by more than 100 million persons by the close of the century. This does not mean, however, that it is correct to assume that population growth of itself insures economic growth. If it did, India and China would be far ahead of the rest of the world. It is what is done by the growing population in producing goods and services that determines economic growth.

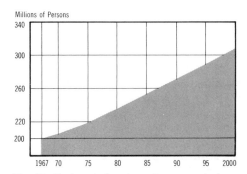

**Fig. 20–7** A growing American population. U.S. Census figures project there will be 100 million more Americans by the year 2000.

A growing population does mean more mouths to feed, more clothing, more roofs over heads. And the production of such items and many others must increase proportionately more than the population grows if the standard of living is to rise. This becomes evident when we consider that, if within a decade the population increases by 20 percent, the total production of the country must increase by 20 percent just to stay even. Over the years, except in periods of depression, the American economy has been able to do *more than just stay even*. It has been able to provide an increasing population with a rising standard of living through an increased production of goods and services by its people.

But what enables the people of a country to produce goods and services faster than it produces new consumers, especially when children, elderly people, members of the armed forces, and other citizens are not part of the civilian labor force? (Even housewives, who are probably the busiest group in the country, are not included in our labor force, for there is no way of recording in precise monetary terms the value of their indispensable services.)

The answer lies not alone in the efficiency of mechanical equipment, but also in the efficiency of the American labor force, and this includes management. It lies in the teamwork of the blue collar and white collar employees. The results so far, as you will see in the following material, have been favorable. Stock investments give you an opportunity to share in this phase of our economic growth.

2. *Output per man-hour*. The efficiency of our labor force, generally called productivity, can be measured in different ways, but the most common measuring rod is called output per man-hour. An illustration will explain its use:

> Let's suppose that the Whitson Appliance Company, a manufacturer of gas ranges in the midwest, employs 100 factory workers, each of whom works an 8-hour day. This gives the company a daily total of 800 man-hours. Now let's suppose that the daily output of gas ranges on the mechanized production line is 160. When we divide this output of 160 ranges by the labor input of 800-man-hours, we learn that the factory has an output per man-hour of .2 gas ranges.
>
> Now let's suppose, that in order to correct a serious limiting factor of production, the company installs a multiple driller and by so doing reduces the time required for drilling flame ports (outlets) in its oven burners. Additionally, it installs new handling equipment on the assembly line which enables the workers to keep up with the faster pace made possible by the installation of the new multiple driller. With this new equipment the 100 men are now able to produce 200 gas ranges each day. When we divide this new output of 200 ranges by the labor input of 800 man-hours, we learn that the factory now has an output per man-hour of .25 gas ranges. Thus, by increasing its output per man-hour from .2 to .25, the company has increased its efficiency or productivity by 25 percent.

So important is this economic measuring rod that both private and government studies have devised criteria by which they measure not only the output per man-hour for manufacturing, for selected industries, and for agriculture, but also for that of the private economy as a whole. The result of their work is generally expressed in terms of index numbers; so let's see what this means. An index-number measuring device calls for the selection of a base period, for example 1957 to 1959, which is considered normal, neither unusually prosperous nor unusually depressed. To this base period is assigned the value of 100. To a period which shows a 10 percent increase over the base period is assigned the index number 110. Conversely, to a period which shows a 10 percent decrease is assigned the index number of 90.

Table 20–1 shows the growing increase in efficiency, in productivity—in terms of output per man-hour—that the United States has demonstrated from 1910 until current years.

**Table 20–1** Productivity efficiency (output per man-hour) in the United States from 1910 to 1969

| Year | Total | Agricultural | Manufacturing |
|------|-------|--------------|---------------|
| 1910 | 35.1 | 33.4 | 40.5 |
| 1920 | 36.5 | 33.7 | 41.9 |
| 1930 | 46.1 | 36.2 | 52.9 |
| 1940 | 58.3 | 43.4 | 66.3 |
| 1950 | 80.3 | 64.4 | 85.0 |
| 1960 | 105.0 | 110.7 | 105.5 |
| 1969 | 139.9 | 182.7 | 142.6 |

*Source*: United States Department of Labor Statistics.

This increase in productivity efficiency—in certain industries it has been sharp—stems principally from the use of more efficient machinery and equipment and the utilization of the skills of a better educated, better trained labor force, a labor force which includes both management and labor. Past trends continued can be positively reflected in securities prices.

3. *Technological development and research.* As we watch one of our manned missiles rise from its pad at Cape Kennedy, how many of us really comprehend its deep significance: the millions of man-hours which have been spent in the teaching and learning of the scientific principles which have made such a missile flight possible?

As each generation of scientists and technicians has built on the knowledge it has inherited and has added to such knowledge the results of its own basic and applied research, technological advance has made amazing rapid strides. It is evidenced not only in our growing ability to explore outer space, but also its fruition is apparent in better machinery, better construction of homes and factories, better modes of communication and of storage of information, better weather detecting apparatus, better modes of transportation, and better methods of mining, manufacturing, and farming. The list goes on and on.

Currently, some $2\frac{1}{2}$ billion dollars are being utilized annually in research and development activities in the United States. (See Fig. 20–8.) This is 5 times as great an effort as existed in 1955; and nearly $2\frac{1}{2}$ times what was expended in 1960. The tremendous expenditures are paying off handsomely. Scientific discoveries are taking place at an amazing pace. The United States Patent Office is currently handling about 100,000 applications a year; some 60 percent being eventually granted. And there is every indication that the significant achievements of recent years and the past several decades have only been the preface to a long era of exciting technological growth. Of all the scientists who ever lived, eight out of ten are alive today.

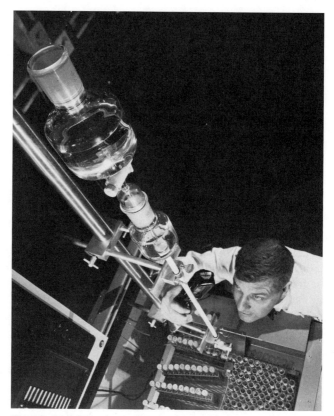

**Fig. 20–8** Advancing technology has many financial rewards. Firms with ample creative talent and research facilities can turn new laboratory discoveries into future profits. Photo shows GM research scientist analyzing the composition of exhaust gases. Courtesy of General Motors.

One of the principal reasons for the high rates of return which common stocks have demonstrated in the past is that the stocks represent a certain share of a business; therefore, they enable the share-owner to participate in the profitability of research and technical development activities and achievements of the company.

## MANY STOCKS PAY GOOD DIVIDENDS

In addition to the growth factors of common stock just discussed, dividend payments should be considered. Many corporations consistently pay moderate to good dividends, thus providing a regular income to the investor. According to records of the New York Stock Exchange, 662 of the common stocks traded there have paid at least one cash dividend every single quarter for the past 20 years.

165 Have paid dividends every quarter for 20 to 25 years.

103 Every quarter for 25 to 30 years.

115 Every quarter for 30 to 35 years.

162 Every quarter for 35 to 50 years.

117 Every quarter for 50 to over 100 years.

If all of these long-term dividend payers—662 as of April 5, 1971—were rolled into a single composite common stock—one share on that date would have cost $33\frac{5}{8}$. Cash dividends on that share based on a median average would have totaled $1.28 in the preceding 12 months—a return of 3.8 percent based on the 1971 price. And cash dividends—every three months—would have traced back to 1934.

Dividend payments have not always been the same from quarter to quarter, or year to year. But stockholders of these companies have received a cash return every three months through good times and bad.

Many corporations do not pay dividends, and therefore may not be suitable for the investment needs of certain individuals. However, many of the more profitable stock investment opportunities occur with corporations that seldom if ever pay dividends. For young persons who are investing small sums each month and who do not need a regular cash return, investments in non-dividend paying companies are fine. However, for the older person nearing retirement or already retired, there may be a very critical need for periodic payments. Although there are many fine companies that do pay consistent dividends, the investment opportunities may be narrowed when periodic return is a requisite of the investment.

**ONLY SMALL AMOUNTS OF MONEY REQUIRED TO INVEST IN STOCKS**
Another reason for the popularity of common stocks is that they may be purchased with relatively small amounts of money. A person with $50 or $60 to invest may be able to buy one or several shares of stock in a real estate, manufacturing, or an oil corporation; while it would be absurd to try to buy an interest in such enterprises in any other way.

**SUMMARY**

In this chapter we have seen that, despite the risks, stocks do offer unique and attractive opportunities for investment. By way of review, here are the unfavorable and favorable aspects of common stock investments:

## THE DANGERS

1. Prices of stock fluctuate constantly, the direction and magnitude of fluctuation depending on how investors interpret the economic, political, and technological changes that comprise the daily news. Most stocks listed on the New York and American Stock Exchanges have good liquidity —that is they can be readily sold. However, the prices at which they can be sold fluctuates widely. Therefore, the price instability of the market would make common stocks particularly unsuitable investments for persons who might be required to convert their investment into cash at any particular time.

2. There are no precise yardsticks by which an investor can easily determine the *worth* of common stocks. Stock prices reflect investors' judgments of both *present* and *anticipated* value. How the corporation is doing *now* profit-wise, the quality of existing management, and current research and development activities help in sizing up the *present*. However, the future is more difficult to predict. Technological developments may or may not favor a particular company. Management efforts may improve or deteriorate. At best, any company's future is apt to be just an educated guess.

3. Once an investor's money is committed to a corporation through the purchase of stock, the only way the investor can recover the money is to sell the stock to someone else. Therefore, stocks of new corporations are particularly risky, since one never knows for certain whether or not there will ever be a ready market for the stock. Unfortunately, too, the corporate form of business makes it all too easy for unscrupulous and unethical management to exploit the unsuspecting investor.

## THE OPPORTUNITIES

1. Common stocks provide a good hedge against inflation. As prices rise, stock values tend to appreciate or grow correspondingly. Today, inflation seems to be one of the more persistent facts of our economic life, and there are good indications that the coming years may see a higher rather than a lower rate of inflation. Consequently, all people need to consider inflation very seriously when making investment decisions.

2. Long-term yields considering both dividends and appreciated value have given common stocks a higher rate of return than many other types of investment over a long span of years.

3. Technological achievements are occuring with ever-increasing frequency in our modern world, and the United States has been particularly fortunate in having such an important part in this world-wide explosion of knowledge. Corporate stocks provide a convenient and easy way for an individual to share in the profits created from technical growth.

4. Many good investments in real estate, service, businesses or manufacturing

concerns involve huge sums of money. For this reason, most persons cannot afford to make such investments. Stocks, on the other hand, usually trade in a price range that permits nearly anybody to purchase at least one share. Even a small investor can, as a consequence, make periodic investments.

The author believes that by careful study, patience, and systematic investment, many persons can substantially profit from common stock investments. But such investments must not be made until a person knows precisely what he is doing. In a free economy, some businesses will do extremely well; while others may make only a fair showing—and some may operate at a loss. Chapter 21 tackles the interesting problems associated with *selecting* stocks.

## FEEDBACK 20

**A.** Study the stock quotation pages found in a recent issue of *The Wall Street Journal* or any newspaper that publishes those quotations. Look down the first two columns and record under the heading WIDE VARIATION five companies that had relatively large differences between their high and low prices for the year (be sure that you are familiar with the companies' types of business). Similarly, record under NARROW VARIATION five companies that had little yearly change in their prices. Compare the two lists of companies.

- Do the companies with wide price variation have any similar business characteristics? What about the companies with little price variation?

- Check each company's current selling price. Indicate which companies are closest to their yearly high selling price. Are there any similar business characteristics between these companies?

- List events which took place last year that may have affected the price of each of your ten listed companies. Would the same events affect all companies the same way? What are some current events that you feel are playing a vital role in affecting the ten companies' prices?

**B.** With the use of your imagination, project yourself ten years into the future. Make a list of any technological changes that you foresee that may have an effect on your life. Keep in mind changes that may occur in industry, transportation, and utilities ten years from now.

- How will those changes be met? Are there any corporations presently in operation that may become antiquated by such changes? Will new corporations have to be formed to meet your ideas of change?

- What types of corporations do you feel will experience exceptional growth if your projected technology comes to reality?

- Write to those corporations that you believe will be able to meet your forecast. Have them send to you their financial publications and information regarding their research and future development. If you believe that they have an optimistic future in this rapidly changing world, consider the possibilities of investing in them.

## DISCUSSION QUESTIONS

1. Why is it that the securities business seems to be a breeding ground for rumors and exaggerations? How can you avoid falling into the rumor trap?

2. If listed stocks have good marketability, why are they potentially dangerous investments?

3. How does the marketability of an OTC stock compare with a listed security? What accounts for the variability; the difference?

4. The OTC market is often referred to as a negotiated market; whereas, the stock exchanges operate on an auction basis. Explain this difference. How might the different procedures affect stock prices? Volume of sales?

5. What recent economic policies of the Federal Government have affected the stock market? What do you anticipate for the next 6 months?

6  What is the present psychology of the market? Is it well founded? Likely to change soon?

7. What technological breakthroughs which have occurred recently are likely to have significant effects on individual companies? Industries?

8. What are the principal attractions of common stocks to investors? Are the attractions of the past likely to be attractions to investors in the future? Why? Why not?

9. From your reading in recent financial publications, what changes do you foresee in (a) the way the securities markets are run; (b) SEC regulations?

10. From the most up-to-date United States Department of Labor figures you can find, what is happening to industrial output per man-hour? What trend seems to be developing? What likely affect will this have on the stock market?

## CASE PROBLEM

Tom Olsen has just inherited $8,000 from his late great-uncle. Not wanting to spend the money immediately, he has decided to invest it in the stock market.

Tom has written to many leading corporations and has asked for sound advice for him as a new investor. To his dismay, all the corporations wrote back explaining to Tom the golden opportunities awaiting him if he would only invest his money in their particular corporation. Realizing that there are also dangers in the market, Tom has come to you for some objective advice.

a) List the advantages or opportunities that Tom may find by investing his money in the stock market. List the disadvantages or dangers.

b) Explain why it is so difficult for Tom to pick a "winning" corporation.

c) Explain why keeping informed on trends in population, productivity, and technology will aid Tom in investing wisely.

## SUGGESTED READINGS

Brealey, Richard A. *An Introduction to Risk and Return from Common Stocks.* Cambridge, Mass.: MIT Press, 1969. 152 pp.

Cobleigh, Ira U. *The $2 Window on Wall Street.* New York: Toucan Press, Doubleday, 1968. 69 pp.

Greiner, Perry, and Hale C. Whitcomb. *The Dow Theory and the Seventy-Year Forecast Record.* Larchmont, N.Y.: Investors Intelligence, Inc., 1969. 190 pp.

*How to Buy Stocks: A Guide to Making More Money in the Market.* Louis Engel (ed.), Third Rev. Ed., Boston: Little, Brown 1962. 272 pp.

Loeb, Gerald M. *The Battle for Investment Survival.* New York: Simon and Schuster, 1965. 320 pp.

Knowlton, Winthrop. *Growth Opportunities in Common Stocks.* New York: Harper and Row, 1965. 176 pp.

Ney, Richard. *The Wall Street Jungle.* New York: Grove Press, 1970. 348 pp.

Ott, David J. *Federal Tax Treatment of State and Local Securities.* Washington: Brookins Institution, 1963. 146 pp.

Sobel, Robert. *Panic on Wall Street; A History of America's Financial Disasters.* New York: Macmillan, 1968. 469 pp.

*What Everybody Ought to Know About This Stock and Bond Business.* New York: Merrill Lynch, Pierce, Fenner and Smith, Inc., 1964.

# CHAPTER 21

# SELECTING YOUR PORTFOLIO OF SECURITIES

After reading about the uncertainties that surround stock investments, you probably now have a healthy skepticism about indiscriminately putting your money into the stock market. However, money is always *at risk* whether it is left in the bank or invested in securities. Any skepticism you have must not overshadow the attractions of common stocks, since such investments do provide a unique opportunity for individuals to share in the country's strong and favorable long-term economic trends. Additionally, such investments offer a sensible way in which one may protect savings against the declining purchasing power which comes from inflation. Even the unpredictable fluctuations in stock prices can be utilized by the astute investor to generate profits.

"Imagine! Come to him for financial advice, and all the time he's trying to sell us some kind of portfolio."

Reprinted with permission of *The Wall Street Journal* (Cartoon Features Syndicate).

If stock investments seem to fit into your overall financial plans, there remain three broad areas for your serious study and consideration: (1) You need to know how to go about choosing stocks. (2) You must know something about investment strategies, timing, and the mechanics of buying and selling. (3) You should become familiar with mutual funds. The purpose of this chapter is to look closely at the first of these problems, the tricky business of choosing stocks. Chapters 22 and 23 deal with the other two stock topics.

"Thanks just the same, Charley, but I can't afford
another tip on the market."

Reprinted with permission of *The Wall Street Journal* (Cartoon Features Syndicate).

Most men and women think nothing about spending several days and sometimes several weeks shopping for a new $75 suit. Yet you may find these same *cautious buyers* deciding in a matter of minutes to purchase $100 or perhaps $500 worth of stock just because someone gave them a hot tip that, "It's a sure bet to triple in price in the next few days." But people who make a serious business of stock investing have learned that you can't make money from following the advice of tipsters. Successful investors know that stock selection deserves a great deal of attention and a certain amount of technical skill.

1. The prospective investor needs to plan out in detail what he expects from his stock investments. For example, does he want long-term growth, does he need periodic income, and so forth?

2. Anyone seriously considering stocks must take the time to become familiar with the many excellent sources of investment and financial data available to him.

3. Since select companies in healthy growth industries are the ones most

likely to succeed (other things being equal), one must know what economists and statisticians project growth-wise for each of the basic industries.

4. The financial soundness of a corporation has much to do with how its stock performs on the market. Therefore, each investor must be able to understand the basic terminology used by accountants in financial statements, and must also be able to analyze and understand the significance of the figures that are given.

5. One must also understand the need for diversification in a stock portfolio and must work toward that end.

6. Finally, the beginning investor must learn why seasoned analysts and financial counselors caution against purchases of stock in new corporations.

Each of these topics make interesting reading and are treated thoroughly in the following pages. Careful study of this chapter should measurably add to your ability to pick and choose high-quality growth securities.

## CLARIFY YOUR INVESTMENT GOALS

Each person or family will have different investment goals, depending on age, type of employment, job outlook, amount of savings and other assets. Since stocks differ considerably in market performance, the prospective investor should strive to pick those stocks that best fit his own particular requirements. Usually stocks are classified according to three basic investment objectives— safety, income, and growth.

**Stocks for safety of principal.** In the previous chapter, we saw how widely the market prices of most stocks fluctuate. However, there are many issues trading both on the big markets and over-the-counter that generally trade in a somewhat narrower price range. These same stocks also seem to be at least partially resistant to many of the adverse factors that trigger short-term price variations on the great majority of common stocks. Generally speaking, this group is made up of stocks of the larger, well-managed gas and electric utility companies. Figure 21–1 charts the trading patterns of four such issues. The less volatile trading patterns coupled with moderate long-term growth possibilities make such stocks particularly appealing to older investors, especially those who may have to sell part of their investment periodically to provide for living expenses. Such stocks not only give some inflation protection to the investor's savings but also favor him in another way: The stocks consistently pay moderately good dividends. For this latter reason, many utility stocks are also frequently classified as *income stocks*.

Why are utility stocks a somewhat safer investment than the average industrial issue? Basically, it is because the earnings and profits of the utility company tend to be more consistent than the earnings and profit patterns of business in general. Regardless of prevailing economic conditions, family

## DETROIT EDISON COMPANY

| Year | 1953 | 1954 | 1955 | 1956 | 1957 | 1958 | 1959 | 1960 | 1961 | 1962 | 1963 | 1964 | 1965 | 1966 | 1967 | 1968 | 1969 | 1970 | 1971 | 1972 |
|---|---|---|---|---|---|---|---|---|---|---|---|---|---|---|---|---|---|---|---|---|
| Earn | .96 | 1.03 | 1.22 | 1.18 | 1.32 | 1.09 | 1.17 | 1.34 | 1.39 | 1.49 | 1.60 | 1.80 | 2.00 | 2.15 | 2.07 | 1.90 | 1.95 | 1.88 | | |
| Div. | .75 | .80 | .80 | .90 | 1.00 | 1.00 | 1.00 | 1.00 | 1.10 | 1.10 | 1.20 | 1.20 | 1.30 | 1.40 | 1.40 | 1.40 | 1.40 | 1.40 | | |

## HOUSTON LIGHTING & POWER CO.

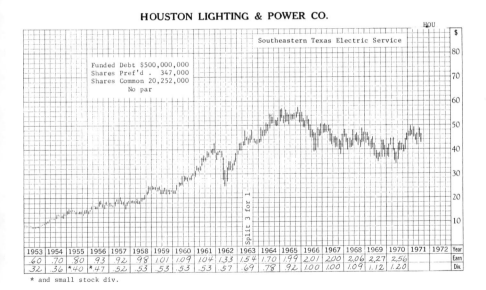

| Year | 1953 | 1954 | 1955 | 1956 | 1957 | 1958 | 1959 | 1960 | 1961 | 1962 | 1963 | 1964 | 1965 | 1966 | 1967 | 1968 | 1969 | 1970 | 1971 | 1972 |
|---|---|---|---|---|---|---|---|---|---|---|---|---|---|---|---|---|---|---|---|---|
| Earn | .60 | .70 | .80 | .93 | .92 | .98 | 1.01 | 1.09 | 1.04 | 1.33 | 1.54 | 1.70 | 1.99 | 2.01 | 2.00 | 2.06 | 2.27 | 2.56 | | |
| Div. | .32 | .36 | *.40 | *.47 | .52 | .53 | .53 | .53 | .53 | .57 | .69 | .78 | .92 | 1.00 | 1.00 | 1.09 | 1.12 | 1.20 | | |

* and small stock div.

**Fig. 21–1** Trading patterns of utility stocks. These and a number of other high-grade utility company stocks seem to be at least partially resistant to the sometimes violent swings in prices which characterize most common stocks. (Continued on next page.) Reprinted by permission from M. C. Horsey & Company, Publishers.

## GENERAL TELEPHONE & ELECTRONICS

| | 1953 | 1954 | 1955 | 1956 | 1957 | 1958 | 1959 | 1960 | 1961 | 1962 | 1963 | 1964 | 1965 | 1966 | 1967 | 1968 | 1969 | 1970 | 1971 | 1972 | Year |
|---|---|---|---|---|---|---|---|---|---|---|---|---|---|---|---|---|---|---|---|---|---|
| | .59 | .95 | .97 | 1.05 | 1.04 | .98 | 1.08 | 1.02 | 1.00 | 1.14 | 1.35 | 1.57 | 1.87 | 2.16 | 2.10 | 2.10 | 2.23 | 2.02 | | | Earn. |
| | .44 | .53 | .44 | .55 | .62 | .67 | .70 | .75 | .76 | .77 | .84 | .69 | 1.03 | 1.16 | 1.31 | 1.42 | 1.49 | 1.52 | | | Div. |

## PHILADELPHIA ELECTRIC CO.

| | 1954 | 1955 | 1956 | 1957 | 1958 | 1959 | 1960 | 1961 | 1962 | 1963 | 1964 | 1965 | 1966 | 1967 | 1968 | 1969 | 1970 | 1971 | 1972 | 1973 | Year |
|---|---|---|---|---|---|---|---|---|---|---|---|---|---|---|---|---|---|---|---|---|---|
| | 1.13 | 1.20 | 1.30 | 1.30 | 1.38 | 1.45 | 1.42 | 1.57 | 1.61 | 1.69 | 1.79 | 1.92 | 2.08 | 2.13 | 1.94 | 1.97 | 1.84 | | | | Earn. |
| | .88 | .90 | .90 | 1.00 | 1.00 | 1.12 | 1.12 | 1.18 | 1.20 | 1.29 | 1.32 | 1.44 | 1.48 | 1.60 | 1.64 | 1.64 | 1.64 | | | | Div. |

**Figure 21–1** (*Continued*).

needs for electricity, heat, and water show little variation. If budget cuts have to be made, discretionary spending will be affected first. A person may quite easily postpone buying a new car, a new suit or dress, or may decide not to take a vacation, but the demand for residential utilities remains amazingly constant. Naturally, however, utility companies that depend heavily on industrial sales could be adversely affected by changing production levels. No stock investment is absolutely safe nor unaffected by changing economic conditions.

## YIELDS OF 5% OR MORE

| | | | | | | |
|---|---|---|---|---|---|---|
| **A** **Acme-Cleveland Corporation** Machines, machine tools | AMT | 1941 | .80 | 1.15 | 15 | 5.3 |
| **Allegheny Power System, Inc.** Holding company—utility | AYP | 1948 | 1.36 | 1.32 | 23⅛ | 5.9 |
| **Amalgamated Sugar Co.** Domestic beet sugar | AGM | 1940 | 1.60 | 1.60 | 29 | 5.5 |
| **American Chain & Cable Co., Inc.** Chains, wire fences, cables | ACN | 1936 | 1.60 | 1.60 | 28¾ | 5.6 |
| **American Crystal Sugar Co.** Domestic beet sugar | ACS | 1946 | 1.40 | 1.40 | 22⅛ | 6.3 |
| **American Distilling Co.** Liquors | ADC | 1946 | 1.00 | 1.00 | 19¾ | 5.1 |
| **American Electric Power Co., Inc.** Holding company—utility | AEP | 1910 | 1.70 | 1.66 | 30 | 5.7 |
| **American Natural Gas Co.** Holding company—utility | ANG | 1904 | 2.20 | 2.08 | 39 | 5.6 |
| **American Smelting & Refining Co.** Metal smelter & refiner | AR | 1936 | 1.90 | 1.90 | 27¼ | 7.0 |
| **Amer. Tel. & Tel. Co.** Bell telephone system | T | 1882 | 2.60 | 2.60 | 49 | 5.3 |
| **Ancorp National Services, Inc.** Vends, distrib. printed matter | ANC | 1864 | 1.00 | 1.00 | 19½ | 5.1 |
| **Atlantic City Electric Co.** Operating public utility | ATE | 1947 | 1.36 | 1.34 | 23⅞ | 5.7 |
| **B** **Baltimore Gas & Electric Co.** Operating public utility | BGE | 1911 | 1.82 | 1.79 | 32⅝ | 5.6 |
| **Basic Incorporated** Refractories | BAI | 1942 | .80 | .80 | 12¾ | 6.3 |
| **Belden Corporation** Electrical wire and cable | BEL | 1939 | 1.60 | 1.60 | 29¼ | 5.5 |
| **Bethlehem Steel Corp.** Steel, shipbuilding | BS | 1939 | 1.20 | 1.80 | 21⅞ | 5.5 |
| **Boston Edison Co.** Operating public utility | BSE | 1892 | 2.36 | 2.20 | 39 | 6.1 |
| **Brooklyn Union Gas Co.** Operating public utility | BU | 1949 | 1.72 | 1.72 | 26½ | 6.5 |
| **C** **Canadian Breweries Ltd.** Holding co.—breweries | CNB | 1945 | .40 | .40 | 7⅜ | 5.4 |
| **Carolina Power & Light Co.** Operating public utility | CPL | 1943 | 1.46 | 1.46 | 27½ | 5.3 |
| **Carpenter Technology Corp.** Specialty steels | CRS | 1908 | 1.60 | 1.60 | 22⅜ | 7.2 |
| **Central Hudson Gas & Elec. Corp.** Operating public utility | CNH | 1903 | 1.48 | 1.48 | 24½ | 6.0 |
| **Central Illinois Light Co.** Operating public utility | CER | 1921 | 1.56 | 1.44 | 26¾ | 5.8 |
| **Central Illinois Pub. Serv. Co.** Operating public utility | CIP | 1947 | 1.20 | 1.16 | 20¾ | 5.8 |
| **Central Maine Power Company** Operating public utility | CTP | 1946 | 1.20 | 1.17 | 21 | 5.7 |

**Fig. 21–2** Common stock dividends. The New York Stock Exchange publishes annually a booklet called "Dividends Over the Years." A portion of one of the pages in a recent issue is illustrated above. For persons interested in stocks for income, this is a good source book of information. Reprinted by permission from the New York Stock Exchange.

**Stocks for dependable income.** If an individual who has retired desires to supplement his private retirement income and Social Security benefits by investing his savings, his prime consideration in selecting appropriate stocks will be the *amount* and *consistency* of dividend payments. The investor who expects that he must periodically sell part of his total investment, should probably stick to those utility company stocks known for both *safety* and *income*. However, many industrial *blue chips* pay good dividends and may turn out to be just as safe in the long run as utility stocks—that is, if the investor can be certain he can weather the ups and downs of the market and choose the most propitious time to sell. And, importantly, industrial stocks may offer greater inflation protection since their earnings and profits are not controlled as are those of the utility firms.

**Stocks for quick profits.** Everyone wants to make a *fast buck*. Unfortunately, though, such opportunities are the exception rather than the rule. Investors who are primarily interested in gambling on the short-term price movements of stocks are generally referred to as *speculators*. Such a person may, for example, buy 100 shares of Syntex anticipating a short-term upward trend in market prices. He watches closely the market activity and quickly sells should the stock make what he considers to be an appropriate price advance.

Beginning investors cannot afford to assume the added uncertainties and risks posed by speculative stocks. Such issues may on occasion yield substantial profits, but more usually lead to staggering losses. You will do well to leave such trading alone until you become a more seasoned, more experienced investor and have a substantial investment portfolio.

**Growth stocks for long-term gains.** The young investor need not be particularly concerned whether or not dividends are paid on stocks which he purchases. His primary concern should be the anticipated growth in market values of the shares. Corporations whose shares have enjoyed the most enviable long-term price advances often pay scanty dividends and sometimes no dividends at all. Instead, these corporations have found that they profit most by plowing the majority of their earnings back into research and development activities which ultimately improve their competitive position through new products and new productive techniques.

It is common for brokerage and investment firms and stock advisory services to classify *growth* stocks according to quality. Although different terms may be used, such headings as these are usual:

Top-Quality Growth Issues—Blue Chips

Medium-Grade Growth Stocks

Patience is very often the key to realizing meaningful stock profits from growth issues. The author strongly believes that the beginning investor should limit his investments to top- and medium-grade investment issues, committing the investment for a long period of time.  Undoubtedly, there will be ups and downs, but if the investment choice is soundly based to begin with, substantial long-term gains are often realizable.

**"Ever since my old man gave me some blue chip
shares the sting has gone out of me."**
Reprinted with permission of *The Wall Street Journal* (Cartoon Features Syndicate).

## BECOME FAMILIAR WITH MAJOR SOURCES
## OF INVESTMENT INFORMATION
In many countries of the world, neither the government nor the people have any major statistical reference tools.  They frequently do not even have a good idea of how many people live in the country, let alone any information concerning such things as production volumes, wage and salary summaries, price

**Table 21-1** Major business and financial periodicals useful to the investor

A. Government Publications

| Publication | Contents | Subscription costs | Where to subscribe |
|---|---|---|---|
| *Business Cycle Developments* U.S. Dept. of Commerce, Bureau of the Census Published monthly | This report brings together many of the economic indicators in convenient form for analysis and interpretation. | $7.00 per year | Supt. of Documents U.S. Government Printing Office Washington, D.C. 20402 or any U.S. Dept. of Commerce Field Office |
| *Economic Indicators* Council of Economic Advisers Published monthly | Latest statistical information (in chart and tabular form) on output, income, spending, employment, wages, prices, money, credit, security prices, and Federal finance. | $2.50 annually $5.40 annually for airmail service | Supt. of Documents U.S. Government Printing Office Washington, D.C.  20402 |
| *Economic   Report   of   the President* | Gives a comprehensive, yet easy-to-read general summary of business and economic conditions and trends for the previous year. This volume also contains the annual report of the Council of Economic Advisers which describes in greater detail patterns in output, money, credit, etc. Prospects and policies for the forthcoming year are also discussed. | $1.25 per copy | Supt. of Documents U.S. Government Printing Office Washington, D.C.  20402 |

**Table 21–1** Major business and financial periodicals useful to the investor

A. Government Publications—*continued*

| Publication | Contents | Subscription costs | Where to subscribe |
|---|---|---|---|
| *Federal Reserve Bulletin*<br>Published monthly | Recent credit and monetary conditions, special economic studies, national summary of business conditions, national and state bank and credit statistics. | $6.00 annually<br>12 issues<br>Make check payable to Board of Governors of The Federal Reserve System Washington, D.C. 20551 | Division of Administration Services<br>Board of Governors of the Federal Reserve System<br>Washington, D.C. 20551 |
| *Survey of Current Business*<br>U.S. Dept. of Commerce, Office of Business Economics<br>Published monthly with weekly statistical supplements | Summarizes current business and monetary statistics. Also includes articles on topics of national economic importance. | $6.00 annually, includes weekly supplements | Supt. of Documents<br>U.S. Government Printing Office<br>Washington, D.C. 20402 or any U.S. Dept. of Commerce Field Office |

B. Newspapers and Chronicles

| Publication | Contents | Subscription cost | Where to subscribe |
|---|---|---|---|
| *Barrons*<br>Published weekly | Weekly summary of financial news and statistics, in-depth articles on noteworthy financial developments, legislation, industry trends. | $15.00 yearly<br>$ 8.50 per 6 months<br>$ 6.00 per 4 months<br>$ 4.75 per 3 months | *Barron's*<br>200 Burnett Road<br>Chicopee, Massachusetts 01021 |

**Table 21-1** Major business and financial periodicals useful to the investor

B. Newspapers and Chronicles — *continued*

| Publication | Contents | Subscription cost | Where to subscribe |
|---|---|---|---|
| *The Commercial & Financial Chronicle* Published twice weekly | Excellent articles and regular features. Includes recent registrations with SEC of new corporate offerings. Also contains a forum in which guest analysts discuss securities favored for current investment. | $90.00 yearly Mon. and Thurs. editions $26.00 yearly Thurs. edition only | William B. Dana Co., Publisher 25 Park Place New York, New York 10007 |
| *The Wall Street Journal* Published daily except Sat., Sun., and general legal holidays | Excellent, comprehensive daily coverage of financial news and interpretation. Includes complete listing of NYSE and ASE transactions, major over-the-counter stocks, mutual funds, bonds, and commodities. A "must" for the serious investor. | $28.00 yearly $15.00 per 6 months $ 8.00 per 3 months | Western Ed: *The Wall Street Journal* 1701 Page Mill Road Palo Alto, California 94304  Eastern Ed: *The Wall Street Journal* 30 Broad Street New York, New York 10004 |

C. Magazines

| Publication | Contents | Subscription cost | Where to subscribe |
|---|---|---|---|
| *Business Week* Published weekly | Summarizes and analyzes the broad trends in business and finance. Feature articles of general interest in domestic and | $8.00 annually | Fulfillment Manager *Business Week* P.O. Box 430 Hightstown, New Jersey 08520 |

**Table 21–1** Major business and financial periodicals useful to the investor

C. Magazines—*continued*

| Magazine | Contents | Subscription costs | Where to subscribe |
|---|---|---|---|
| | foreign business, economics, government, labor, management, marketing, production, research, stock markets, and transportation. | | |
| *Financial World*<br>Published weekly | Interesting weekly features of timely importance to the market, comprehensive industry reviews, depth reports on individual companies, good investment service section. | $24.00 yearly | *Financial World*<br>Guenther Publishing Corp.<br>17 Battery Place<br>New York, New York 10004 |
| *Forbes*<br>Published twice monthly | A magazine denoted to business and financial news and analysis. Regular features include: market comment, stock analysis, technician's perspective, the market outlook, investment pointers, the funds. Two special issues are worth serious study: January issue each year gives a comprehensive review of American Industry; August issue shows comparative performance of all mutual funds. | $7.50 annually | Forbes, Inc.<br>70 Fifth Avenue<br>New York, New York 10011 |

**Table 21–1**  Major business and financial periodicals useful to the investor

C. Magazines—*continued*

| Magazine | Contents | Subscription cost | Where to subscribe |
|---|---|---|---|
| *Fortune*<br>Published monthly, except two issues in June and Sept. | A high-quality business magazine with an elaborate format. Penetrating articles: corporate stories, personal investing, business roundup, technology reports, profiles of interesting businessmen, industry, outlooks. June issue summarizes activities of the nation's 500 largest corporations. | $14.00 yearly | Fortune<br>540 North Michigan Avenue<br>Chicago, Illinois 60611 |
| *Over-the-Counter Securities Review*<br>Published monthly | Business and financial news concerning over-the-counter companies. | $10.00 one year<br>$15.00 two years<br>$20.00 three years | Review Publishing Co.<br>Jenkintown<br>Pennsylvania 19046 |
| *The Magazine of Wall Street*<br>Published twice monthly | Regular departmental features include: The Market, In Washington, In Wall Street, The Business Analyst, The Inquiring Investor, For Profit and Income, and Trends of Events. Additionally each issue contains a number of special reports of interest to stock investors. Accurate, carefully written articles and features. | $25.00 annually | Ticker Publishing Co., Inc.<br>120 Wall Street<br>New York, New York 10005 |

**Table 21-1** Major business and financial periodicals useful to the investor

C. Magazines—*continued*

| Magazine | Contents | Subscription cost | Where to subscribe |
|---|---|---|---|
| *The Exchange* | Published by the New York Stock Exchange, it features general industry reports, new listings to the Exchange, and special articles of interest to investors. | $2.00 yearly<br>$3.50 two years | *The Exchange*<br>11 Wall Street<br>New York, New York 10005 |

levels, etc. Americans are fortunate in having a vast array of economic studies and statistics compiled by government and private sources. The stock investor can significantly benefit from a systematic program of reading and study of business and financial literature. Most of the data can be found at your local library. Some of the publications may be worthy of subscription.

**Business and financial periodicals.** The major publications of interest to the investor are conveniently tabulated in Table 21–1. Here you will find a quick summary of the contents of each publication, subscription costs, and mailing address for subscriptions. The selected government publications listed in this table offer significant data to keep you abreast of general economic developments and trends.

Of the financial newspapers and chronicles, *The Wall Street Journal* is highly recommended. The paper has 18 original news offices located in strategic business and industrial centers across the country. Its pages contain complete daily trading data on the New York and American Stock Exchanges, plus statistics on funds, commodities, bonds, puts, calls, and many more items of interest.

Each of the magazines recommended for reading in Table 21–1 has its own special appeal. Take time to remove them from the library shelf and do some reading. See which one best serves your needs. Since much of the financial analysis reported in these publications is based on expert judgment, compare forecasts and business outlooks of several of the magazines to see if there is some consensus of opinion.

Nearly every library of any size in the United States subscribes to *Moody's Manuals and News Reports*. Quantitatively, these manuals are the most comprehensive source of corporate stock information. Qualitatively, they rank among the most definitive. Over the years, each library subscriber receives more than 23,000 pages. Annually, an entire volume is published on each of the following security groups: Industrials, Banks and Finance, Public Utilities, Transportation, and Municipals and Governments. To keep the data current, twice-weekly news reports are published. Subscribers assemble them in loose-leaf binders.

Another Moody's publication most useful for the investor is *Moody's Handbook of Common Stocks*. A page from this book is shown in Fig. 21–3. For each stock the book gives: (1) A chart portraying its market price history for the past seventeen years (or since first available); (2) A compact package of figures and other information from which can be gained an accurate impression of the stock of an investment; (3) A description of the stock, its quality and general type; and (4) Certain miscellaneous data such as address, names of officers, transfer agent, etc. The *Handbook* is available at most libraries, or it can be purchased by writing to Department HB, Moody's Investors Service, 99 Church Street, New York, New York 10007.

**Brokerage companies.** Most of the very large brokerage firms maintain sizable

# ZENITH RADIO CORPORATION

| LISTED | SYMBOL | INDICATED DIV. | RECENT PRICE | PRICE RANGE (1971) | YIELD |
|---|---|---|---|---|---|
| NYSE | ZE | $1.40 | 49 | 52 - 36 | 2.9% |

THIS INVESTMENT-GRADE STOCK HAS EVIDENCED STRONG PROFIT AND DIVIDEND TRENDS DESPITE ITS DEPENDENCE ON THE CYCLICAL CONSUMER GOODS FIELD.

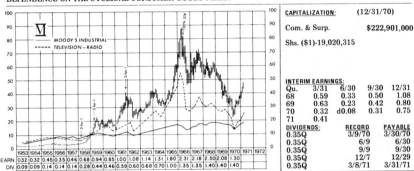

| | 1953 | 1954 | 1955 | 1956 | 1957 | 1958 | 1959 | 1960 | 1961 | 1962 | 1963 | 1964 | 1965 | 1966 | 1967 | 1968 | 1969 | 1970 |
|---|---|---|---|---|---|---|---|---|---|---|---|---|---|---|---|---|---|---|
| EARN. | 0.32 | 0.32 | 0.45 | 0.35 | 0.46 | 0.68 | 0.94 | 0.85 | 1.00 | 1.08 | 1.14 | 1.31 | 1.80 | 2.31 | 2.18 | 2.50 | 2.08 | 1.30 |
| DIV | 0.09 | 0.09 | 0.14 | 0.14 | 0.14 | 0.28 | 0.44 | 0.46 | 0.59 | 0.60 | 0.68 | 0.70 | 1.00 | 1.35 | 1.35 | 1.40 | 1.40 | 1.40 |

**CAPITALIZATION:**    (12/31/70)

Com. & Surp.    $222,901,000

Shs. ($1)-19,020,315

**INTERIM EARNINGS:**

| Qu. | 3/31 | 6/30 | 9/30 | 12/31 |
|---|---|---|---|---|
| 68 | 0.59 | 0.33 | 0.50 | 1.08 |
| 69 | 0.63 | 0.23 | 0.42 | 0.80 |
| 70 | 0.32 | d0.08 | 0.31 | 0.75 |
| 71 | 0.41 | | | |

| DIVIDENDS: | RECORD | PAYABLE |
|---|---|---|
| 0.35Q | 3/9/70 | 3/30/70 |
| 0.35Q | 6/9 | 6/30 |
| 0.35Q | 9/9 | 9/30 |
| 0.35Q | 12/7 | 12/29 |
| 0.35Q | 3/8/71 | 3/31/71 |

## BACKGROUND:

The Company is the number one producer of black and white television sets as well as the number one factor in color TV. The firm is important in radios, particularly the more rapidly growing lines of FM sets. Radio-phonograph combinations and hearing aids are also manufactured. A division manufactures both black and white and color picture tubes. New product developments also include some special electronic products: hearing aids, special electronic components equipment and systems for government and industry. During the past five years, investment in property, plant, and equipment totaled more than $65 million.

## RECENT DEVELOPMENTS:

Sales for the 1970 year were $573.1 mill., a decline of 15% while earnings decreased a greater 38% to $24.7 mill. vs. $39.6 mill. a year ago. Operations during the year had been adversely affected by a decline in unit sales of color and black and white TV sets of 18% and 10%, respectively, by the higher costs of materials, a truckers strike in the second quarter, and the inclusion of labor charges in 90-day color TV warranties. Through Teco, Inc., a Co. affilite, Zenith will begin to market its Phonevision system, a form of subscription television.

## PROSPECTS:

1970 industry sales of color TV's were hurt by the general economic slowdown and by high interest rates, and rising imports of TV sets are cutting into volume. On the expectation of modest economic improvement in 1971 and continued easing of credit, sales and earnings should rise moderately this year. The company's strong position in consumer electronics, its commitment to research and its expansion into other areas, such as subscription television, give the company interesting growth prospects.

## STATISTICS:

| YEAR | GROSS REVS. ($ MILL.) | OPER. PROFIT MARGIN % | NET INCOME ($ 000) | WORK CAP. ($ MILL.) | SENIOR CAPITAL ($ MILL.) | NO. SHS. OUT. (000) | CASH FLOW PER SH. $ | EARN. PER SH. $ | DIV. PER SH. $ | DIV. PAY. % | PRICE RANGE | PRICE X EARN. | AVG. YIELD % |
|---|---|---|---|---|---|---|---|---|---|---|---|---|---|
| 61 | 274.2 | 14.0 | 18,015 | 69.2 | Nil | 18,063 | 1.10 | 1.00 | 0.59 | 59 | $41_7^3 - 16^1$ | 28.9 | 2.0 |
| 62 | 312.2 | 13.1 | 19,637 | 73.2 | Nil | 18,208 | 1.20 | 1.08 | 0.60 | 56 | $37^7 - 22$ | 27.4 | 2.0 |
| 63 | 349.8 | 12.4 | 20,853 | 87.3 | Nil | 18,398 | 1.34 | 1.14 | 0.68 | 59 | $42^1 - 25^4$ | 29.8 | 2.0 |
| 64 | 392.0 | 12.3 | 24,283 | 100.3 | Nil | 18,616 | 1.58 | 1.31 | 0.78 | 59 | $43^5 - 30^4$ | 28.4 | 2.1 |
| 65 | 470.5 | 13.7 | 33,553 | 110.5 | Nil | 18,709 | 2.07 | 1.80 | 1.00 | 56 | $61^1 - 31^3$ | 25.8 | 2.2 |
| 66 | 625.0 | 13.3 | 43,475 | 114.5 | Nil | 18,783 | 2.67 | 2.31 | 1.35 | 58 | $87^6 - 46^1$ | 29.0 | 2.0 |
| 67 | 653.9 | 12.0 | 41,022 | 120.7 | Nil | 18,849 | 2.68 | 2.18 | 1.35 | 62 | $72_2^1 - 47^6$ | 27.5 | 2.3 |
| 68 | 705.4 | 14.1 | 47,315 | 147.0 | Nil | 18,924 | 3.04 | 2.50 | 1.40 | 56 | $65^4 - 50^5$ | 23.2 | 2.4 |
| 69 | 676.6 | 12.6 | 39,621 | 153.4 | Nil | 19,020 | 2.71 | 2.08 | 1.40 | 67 | $58 - 32^7$ | 21.8 | 3.1 |
| 70 | 573.1 | 7.4 | 24,702 | 152.9 | Nil | 19,020 | 1.96 | 1.30 | 1.40 | 93 | $38^4 - 22^2$ | 23.4 | 4.6 |

Note: Adj. for 3-for-1 stk. split, 10/61; also 100% stk. div. 6/66.

| | | | |
|---|---|---|---|
| **INCORPORATED:** July 5, 1923—Illinois | **TRANSFER AGENT:** | First National Bank, Chicago Chemical Bank, N.Y. | **OFFICERS** |
| **PRINCIPAL OFFICE:** 1900 N. Austin Ave. Chicago, Ill. 60639 | | | **CHAIRMAN:** J.S. Wright **PRESIDENT:** |
| **ANNUAL MEETING:** Fourth Tuesday in April | **REGISTRAR:** | Continental Illinois National Bank & Trust, Chicago Chase Manhattan Bank, N.Y. | J.S. Wright **SECRETARY:** E.M. Schroeder |
| **NUMBER OF STOCKHOLDERS:** 50,381 | **INSTIT. HOLDINGS:** | NO.: 98 SHS.: 2,322,935 | **TREASURER:** R.M. Spang |

**Fig. 21-3** Sample page from *Moody's Handbook of Common Stocks.* This comprehensive publication, containing analyses of 1,000 stocks, is designed primarily for individual stock buyers who are looking into the qualifications of individual issues before acting on advice or suggestions. Reprinted by permission from Moody's Investors Service, Inc.

SECURITIES RESEARCH DIVISION

MERRILL LYNCH,
PIERCE, FENNER & SMITH INC

10 stocks for income and appreciation May 1971

In 1966, American Brands, the second-largest domestic manufacturer of cigarettes, sought to lessen its dependence on tobacco products by acquiring producers of food and alcoholic beverages. Additional acquisitions have since given the company such diverse activities as operation of retail optical stores and production of office equipment, toiletries, and locks. About 23% of the $2.67 billion in sales last year was derived from non-tobacco business. We believe that operating income from tobacco products will decline from 86% in 1970 to approximately 77% in 1971.

The company's position in the cigarette industry has been deteriorating in recent years because of its dependence on non-filter cigarettes. Earnings, however, have been aided by acquisitions and by sporadic increases in cigarette prices. During the past five years, per-share earnings, which equaled $4.03 in 1970, have grown at a compound annual rate of 7%. We expect earnings for 1971 to increase to $4.35-to-4.50 a share with the aid of a cigarette price increase, effected in mid-1970, elimination of cigarette advertising from the broadcasting media, improvement in food products, and contributions from acquisitions made last year. First-quarter earnings in 1971 rose to $1.01 a share vs. 83¢ a share a year earlier.

Since 1965 dividends have been increased five times, or by a total of 33%. The current annual rate of $2.20 a share is well covered, and we believe that dividends will continue to rise in line with earnings growth. In our opinion, the good-quality shares of AMB are attractive for intermediate-term appreciation and for income.

**American Brands**

| | PRICE 5/6/71 | P/E RATIO ON 1971 EST. | DIVIDEND | YIELD | 1971 PRICE RANGE |
|---|---|---|---|---|---|
| AMERICAN BRANDS | 48 | 10.8 | $2.20 | 4.6% | 49¾-43½ |
| BORDEN INC. | | | | | |
| CONILL CORPORATION | | | | | |
| DIAMOND SHAMROCK | | | | | |
| FIRST PENNSYLVANIA MORTGAGE TRUST | | | | | |
| NATIONAL STEEL | | | | | |
| ST. LOUIS-SAN FRANCISCO RAILWAY | | | | | |
| STANDARD OIL OF CALIFORNIA | | | | | |
| TIMKEN COMPANY | | | | | |
| WACHOVIA REALTY INVESTMENTS | | | | | |

**Fig. 21–4** Most large investment firms publish investment bulletins such as the one shown here. Reprinted by permission from Merrill Lynch, Pierce, Fenner & Smith, Inc.

research departments, staffed with seasoned financial analysts. Often an analyst or a group of researchers specialize in one particular industry— pharmaceuticals, steel, auto manufacturing, to name but a few examples. Most

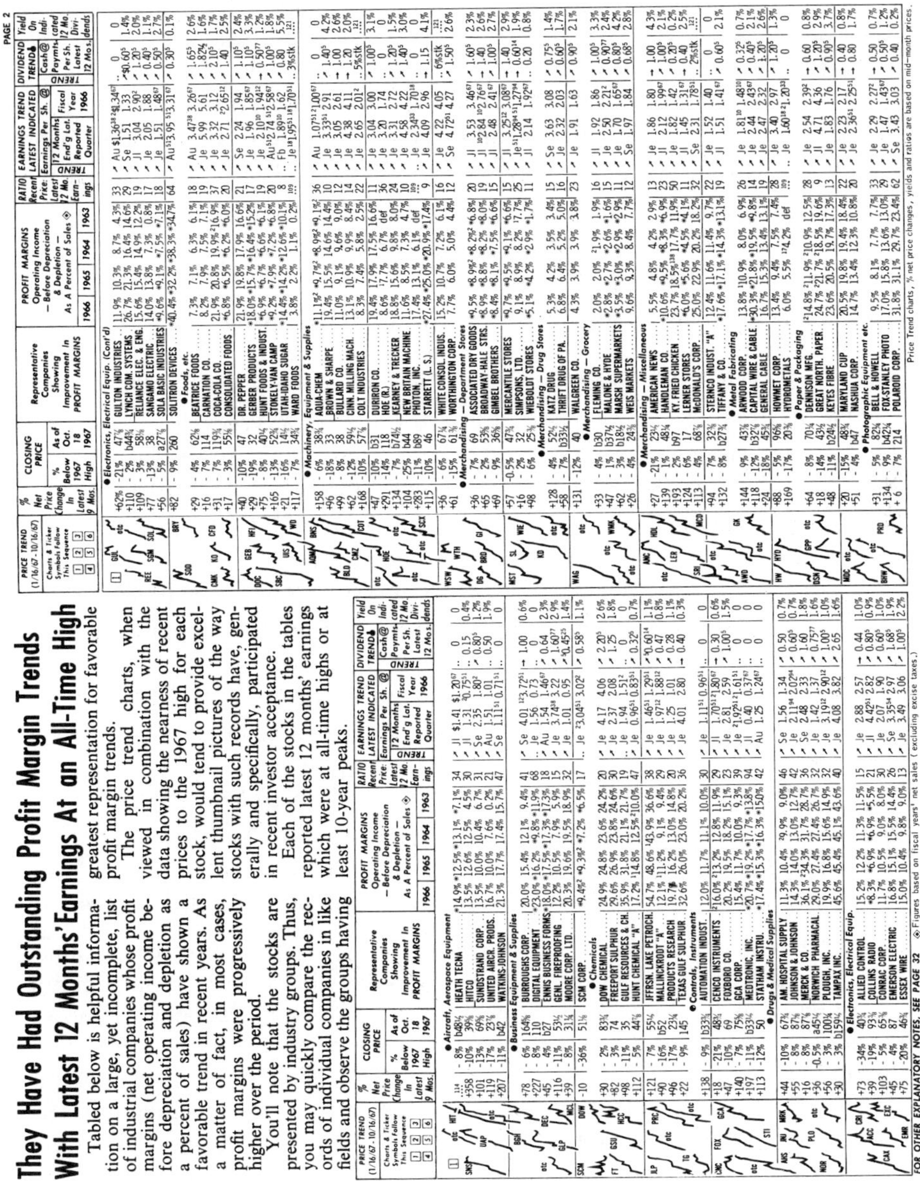

## They Have Had Outstanding Profit Margin Trends With Latest 12 Months' Earnings At an All-Time High

Tabled below is helpful information on a large, yet incomplete, list of industrial companies whose profit margins (net operating income before depreciation and depletion as a percent of sales) have shown a favorable trend in recent years. As a matter of fact, in most cases, profit margins were progressively higher over the period.

You'll note that the stocks are presented by industry groups. Thus, you may quickly compare the records of individual companies in like fields and observe the groups having greatest representation for favorable profit margin trends.

The price trend charts, when viewed in combination with the data showing the nearness of recent prices to the 1967 high for each stock, would tend to provide excellent thumbnail pictures of the way stocks with such records have, generally and specifically, participated in recent investor acceptance.

Each of the stocks in the tables reported latest 12 months' earnings which were at all-time highs or at least 10-year peaks.

**Fig. 21–5** Many investment firms will furnish free copies of the *Monthly Stock Digest* which summarizes data on hundreds of common stocks. Reprinted by permission from Data Digests, Inc.

such firms publish monthly or weekly reports. Special studies are also issued from time to time. Figures 21–4 and 21–5 illustrate two of these publications. On request, the firms will gladly put you on their mailing lists. The reports are free for the asking.  Usually the publications include a discussion of general economic and market factors as well as analyses of companies that look favorable for current investment.  It must be understood, of course, that such recommendations are not infallible, and the quality of reports coming from the different houses differ some in quality.  Names and addresses of some of the nation's largest brokerage firms follow (in random order):

Merrill Lynch, Pierce, Fenner & Smith
70 Pine Street
New York, New York 10005

Paine, Webber, Jackson & Curtis
25 Broad Street
New York, New York 10004

Shearson Hammill & Company
14 Wall Street
New York, New York 10005

Bache & Company
36 Wall Street
New York, New York 10005

Kidder, Peabody & Company
20 Exchange Place
New York, New York 10005

Hornblower & Weeks
One Chase Manhattan Plaza
New York, New York 10005

Walston & Company
75 Wall Street
New York, New York 10005

E. F. Hutton & Company
61 Broadway
New York, New York 10004

Carl M. Loeb, Rhoades, & Company
42 Wall Street
New York, New York 10005

Smith, Barney & Company
20 Broad Street
New York, New York 10004

Francis I. du Pont & Company
One Wall Street
New York, New York 10005

Hirsch & Company
25 Broad Street
New York, New York 10004

Van Alstyne Noel & Company
52 Wall Street
New York, New York 10005

Dean Witter & Company
45 Montgomery Street
San Francisco, California 94104

**Investment counselors.**  Any broker will be happy to discuss your investment problems and goals.  And in most instances, he will make recommendations regarding what he thinks may be a worthwhile stock investment.  However, the decision to buy must be your own.  If yours is a small account, it is unlikely that the broker will be able to offer continued supervision of your stock purchases.  This you must do for yourself.  However, if yours were a very large investment—$25,000 or $100,000—you would be able to turn your account over to an investment counselor who would supervise your program and keep daily track of the general market, as well as the developments affecting the individual stocks making up your portfolio.  The counselor would take a small percentage of the account yearly for its management.  Individuals and firms making investment counselling their specialty differ considerably in the size of investment account which they require.  Also they differ markedly in competence to do the job.

**Investment advisory services.** Many a small investor may want additional assistance and advice beyond what he can get from reading and studying on his own and conferring with his broker. For such a person, one of the investment advisory services may provide the needed information. Usually, such services are offered on a subscription basis. Weekly or monthly publications typically provide:

1. Specific *buy* and *sell* recommendations on favored lists of stocks.
2. Analyses of individual stocks and industries.
3. Easy-to-read summaries of financial and economic news with comments on broad market trends.

Some of the advisory services will also make an individual analysis of the subscriber's present portfolio, recommending changes which are deemed advisable.

In general, the subscription rates for advisory services are high. And, generally speaking, the same type of information can usually be found in one or more of the business and financial magazines. However, if you are interested in finding out more about the advisory services, here are the names and addresses of the leading ones:

Dow Theory Forecasts
7412 Calumet Avenue
Hammond, Indiana 46325

United Business Service
210 Newbury Street
Boston, Massachusetts 02116

Moody's Investors Service, Inc.
99 Church Street
New York, New York 10007

The Value Line Investment Survey
5 East 44th Street
New York, New York 10017

**Annual corporate reports.** At the turn of the century, the New York Stock Exchange influenced the first industrial company to publish an annual report including statements of income and expenditures, along with a balance sheet showing a statement of the company's condition. An age of greater financial disclosure had set in. One after the other, companies brought out annual reports. They were refined during the 1920's and 1930's and in the 1940's too, until today the annual report usually represents a full accounting of a company's earnings, its changes in financial position, its prospects for the future, and even its research, new products, and industrial relations. Now, anyone— whether or not he owns securities—can usually obtain an annual report merely by mailing a written request to the company.

## CONCENTRATE INVESTMENT EFFORTS ON GROWTH INDUSTRIES

The consumer is a whimsical animal! Something just a little new or different often catches the public's fancy and creates a thriving, robust new industry. Waning public opinion may, on the other hand, wreck the best laid marketing plans for an old established item.  One thing is certain—business is never static, but is constantly changing.  One of the basic reasons for change is research. It has already been pointed out that where technology creates a new product or makes an existing one more useful, more attractive, more economical, or more efficient, there is opportunity for corporate expansion and increased profits.

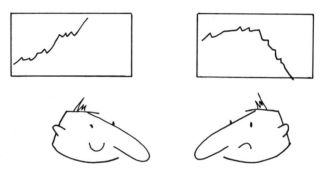

Beginning investors should attempt to limit their stock purchases primarily to select companies in energetic growth industries if they are to get the full benefits of new technology and growing consumer demand.

**KEEP ABREAST OF INDUSTRY TRENDS**

The upswing year, 1971, began a decade of economic growth which started with a gross national product crossing the trillion dollar line and that will end (according to United States Department of Commerce estimates) with its approaching the $2 trillion mark.  With large annual labor force additions of well-educated young adults, advancing technology, and enterprising management, overall growth can readily be predicted.  The relative importance of the components of growth and the evolving *mix* of goods and services are far less certain, however.

Some of these uncertainties are already becoming obvious.  For example, is the current trend toward smaller automobiles a passing fad or does it presage a basic shift toward more economical, safer, and pollution-free cars?  Will there be increasing restrictions on the use of private cars in congested urban areas, thereby favoring expansion of mass rapid transit vehicles and making personal car ownership less desirable?  Will the younger generation, with a different assessment of the relative values of work and leisure, elect to take some of the *fruits of progress* in the form of shorter working hours rather than more material possessions?  How will the undetermined, but potentially enormous, costs of environmental improvement be shared and with what economic reverberations on the stock market?

Answers to these and to myriad other equally significant questions will emerge slowly and partially during the decade and beyond.  But it is reasonably certain that the American economy of 1980 will have a substantially different configuration from that of previous decades.

To assist businessmen as well as investors in assessing intermediate and long-term plans, the United States Commerce Department has recently made projections for activity levels of various industries in 1975 and 1980. These comprehensive reports covering 163 manufacturing industries and 43 non-manufacturing activities can be found in the *United States Industrial Outlook With Projections Through 1980*. This publication is available from the Superintendent of Documents, United States Government Printing Office, Washington, D.C. 20402. This publication coupled with data found in magazines, newspapers, and broker publications should make it possible for you to make intelligent assessments of future trends.

## CHOOSE INDIVIDUAL STOCKS ON A BASIS OF FUNDAMENTAL VALUES

Even though the investor narrows down his choice of stocks to several growth industries, there still are a confusing assortment of stocks from which he must choose. To make an intelligent final selection of *individual issues* for purchase, he must be able to make some basic value determinations. At the very least, he must be able to understand the basis for the recommendations and suggestions which he might receive from brokers and financial reporters. Since stock values are so intimately connected with a firm's financial transactions, one must know something about accounting terminology and the significance of current financial data.

The material that follows will certainly be more easily understood by those who have had a semester or so of basic accounting. But even those without an accounting background will find the data not too difficult to follow. To assist you in understanding accounting terms and analyzing financial data, we will use the balance sheet (Fig. 21–6) and income statement (Fig. 21–7) of a hypothetical corporation, "XYZ Corporation," as might appear in the typical annual corporate report. Since financial data for a single year are not by themselves especially meaningful, figures for the *current* and *previous* years' financial results are compared.* By measuring one year against another, patterns sometimes emerge that can be helpful to the investor.

## THE BALANCE SHEET

Much like a doctor who checks his patient's hospital chart, an investor checks the health of a corporation by carefully studying its balance sheet. This important document shows in convenient summary form (1) what the company "owns"—these are called assets; (2) what the company "owes"—called liabilities; and (3) the amount invested in the corporation by stockholders plus

---

* Most annual reports now include statements for both the current and previous year and in many instances summaries for five- to ten-year periods are provided.

## ASSETS, LIABILITIES AND STOCKHOLDERS' EQUITY

| | Dec. 31 1971 | Dec. 31 1970 |
|---|---|---|
| | *Million* | |
| **Assets** | | |
| *Current Assets* | | |
| Cash | $ 9.0 | $ 6.2 |
| U.S. Government securities | | 2.0 |
| Accounts and notes receivable | 12.4 | 11.4 |
| Inventories | 27.0 | 24.6 |
| Total Current Assets | $ 48.4 | $ 44.2 |
| *Other Assets* | | |
| Surrender value of insurance | 0.2 | 0.2 |
| Investments in subsidiaries | 4.7 | 3.9 |
| Prepaid insurance | 0.6 | 0.5 |
| Total Other Assets | $ 5.5 | $ 4.6 |
| *Fixed Assets* | | |
| Buildings, machinery and equipment at cost | 104.3 | 92.7 |
| Less accumulated Depreciation | 27.6 | 25.0 |
| | $ 76.7 | $ 67.7 |
| Land | 0.9 | 0.7 |
| Total Fixed Assets | $ 77.6 | $ 68.4 |
| Total Assets | $131.5 | $117.2 |
| **Liabilities and Stockholders' Equity** | | |
| *Current Liabilities* | | |
| Accounts payable | $ 6.1 | $ 5.0 |
| Accrued liabilities | 3.6 | 3.3 |
| Current maturity of long term debt | 1.0 | 0.8 |
| Federal income and other taxes | 9.6 | 8.4 |
| Dividends payable | 1.3 | 1.1 |
| Total Current Liabilities | $ 21.6 | $ 18.6 |
| *Reserves* | 3.6 | 2.5 |
| *Long Term Debt* | | |
| 5% Sinking Fund Debentures, due July 31, 1976 | 26.0 | 20.0 |
| *Stockholders' Equity* | | |
| 5% Cum. Preferred Stock ($100 par) | 6.0 | 6.0 |
| Common Stock ($10 par) | 18.3 | 18.3 |
| Capital Surplus | 9.6 | 9.6 |
| Earned Surplus | 46.4 | 42.2 |
| Total Stockholders' Investment | $ 80.3 | $ 76.1 |
| Total Liabilities, and Stockholders' Investment | $131.5 | $117.2 |

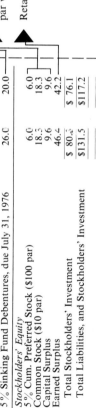

**EXPLANATION**

*The Company Owned*

Cash and U.S. Government securities, the latter generally at either cost or market value, whichever is lower.

Amounts owed the company by its customers and others.

Raw materials, work in process and finished merchandise.

Miscellaneous assets, and advance payments for insurance. Investments in nonconsolidated subsidiary companies.

Land, buildings and equipment and deductions for wear and tear on these properties.

*The Company Owed*

For materials, supplies, wages and salaries to employees, and such things as dividends declared, real estate, social security and income taxes, etc.

May be either a liability of a more or less definite nature, such as provision for possible inventory losses, or a part of earnings not available for dividends and segregated so as not to be included in surplus available for dividends.

For money borrowed (excluding portion due in next 12 months shown as a current liability).

Amount originally invested in the business by the stockholders. Additional capital received from sale of Capital Stock above par value.

Retained earnings reinvested in the business.

**Fig. 21-6**  Balance sheet of a hypothetical corporation.

any profits retained and reinvested in the business. Each of the major balance sheet items and their significance to the potential investor are briefly discussed.

**Assets.** *Current assets.* "XYZ Company's" balance sheet shown on the preceding page had current assets on December 31, 1971, of $48.4 million—*current* because they may be turned into cash more readily than fixed assets.

*Cash.* This item requires no explanation. The bulk will be in the form of bank deposits.

*Receivables.* Usually this figure shows the amounts due from customers for goods sold or services rendered. In different industries, the ordinary terms of payment vary. It is conservative practice to set up a reserve to cover any amounts that may not be collectible.

*Inventories.* This figure represents the total of the raw materials, work in process, supplies used in operations and the finished goods ready for sale. Sometimes these items are shown separately. Since the value of inventories changes with price fluctuations, it is important to know how the inventories are valued. Statements usually indicate the basis, which generally is cost or current market price, whichever is lower. This method avoids overstating earnings and assets as a result of sharp increases in prices on the commodity markets.

A steady drop in the relation of sales to inventories, the so-called *inventory turnover* may be a warning that: (a) inventories are too heavy for the best results, adding to the dangers from falling prices; (b) in the case of merchandising companies, sales policy is not aggressive enough; and (c) buying is not skillful and a large part of the goods on the shelves may depreciate in value because of shifts in public taste or style.

There are a number of methods for valuing inventories. The most widely used is the *first-in-first-out* method (FIFO), in which it is assumed that the oldest items are used or sold before later purchases or productions. Unavoidably, this method leads to the inclusion in income of unrealized appreciation in the value of inventories when commodity prices are rising. This increase is sometimes known as inventory profits or *fool's profits* because if rising prices are followed by a drop in prices, the appreciation may never be realized.

To cushion the impact of rapid price changes, the *last-in-first-out* method (LIFO) of inventory valuation has been adopted by many companies. LIFO is intended principally to match current costs against current revenues. Sales are costed on the basis of inventory acquired most recently, or last-in, while first-in inventory is regarded as unsold. Consequently, in a period of rising prices, LIFO results in the application of a higher unit cost to items sold and a lower unit cost to inventory still unsold. The reverse is true in a period of falling prices.

The rate of inventory turnover varies considerably among different industries. It is much higher in foods and automobiles, for example, than in tobacco or farm machinery.

XYZ Company's current assets increased during the year by $4.2 million mainly because of the $2.4 million increase in inventories and a $1.0 million rise in receivables. Normally these increases would result from a larger dollar sales volume due to the sale of a larger number of units, to higher prices, or to a combination of both.

Studies of industrial companies that failed to show that the proportion of total current assets to fixed assets usually declined persistently. In other words, it may not be wise to expand plant facilities at the sacrifice of current assets.

*Fixed assets (buildings, machinery and equipment less accumulated depreciation and land).* XYZ has plants in Connecticut, Ohio, and North Carolina, but all are lumped together in the balance sheet. This item includes the structures, the machinery and equipment, and such assets as tools and motor vehicles.

Except for land, fixed assets have a limited useful life. Each year a provision is made for depreciation due to wear and tear so the value of the assets will not be overstated.

Usually, gross fixed assets are carried at cost, although such cost usually will be different from the sum for which they could be sold.

An increase in fixed assets is the expected companion of expansion and increased sales. Also, an additional investment in equipment may be made, or new plants built, to cut costs.

If a large gain in fixed assets is not followed by a more or less corresponding gain in sales, management may have over-estimated the ability to sell a larger volume of goods, or the industry may have reached over-capacity. However, if a company's fixed assets show little change for several years during a period of expanding business, the stockholder may have reason to worry about the company's competitive position or about management's keeping up with technological changes and innovations. A company often will state in its annual report that an addition has been made to its plants which will provide so many feet of additional floor space, and that a new warehouse has been acquired, or new equipment is being installed at a plant for the production of a new product.

XYZ's capital expenditures (outlays for new plant and equipment) amounted to $11.6 million, and during the year a provision for depreciation of $2.6 million was made for wear and tear. Gross fixed assets, which include land, show an increase of $11.8 million.

The accumulated depreciation reserve also may be for obsolescence and may include an estimated amount for loss of value due to technological and other changes. Oil and gas and mining companies, as well as other natural resource enterprises, having what is known as "wasting assets," also provide for depletion.

It would be fine if a company could continually produce and sell more merchandise, or mine more ore without adding to its investment. This is practically impossible. Sustained growth almost invariably requires investment in additional facilities—either additional plant structures, machinery and equipment, or in the case of oil and gas companies, additional leases for exploration.

What the investor likes to see is additional production or more efficient production as a result of capital expenditures. Failure to spend to obtain the most efficient equipment in our highly competitive economy can lead to higher costs and thus to the loss of business.

One class of assets, i.e., those known as intangibles because they represent non-physical items, is not contained on the balance sheet of the XYZ Company. Intangibles include good will, trademarks, patents and copyrights, among others. Years ago, it was more common than at present to show items of an intangible nature. In computing the company's net worth or the book value of the stock, the value at which any intangible item is carried in the balance sheet is omitted. It is the tangible net worth or tangible book value that is used for purposes of financial analysis.

**Liabilities.** XYZ's debt is divided into two classes: (1) current debt, money that is payable within a year, and (2) long-term debt, that which need not be paid until after one year.

The XYZ Company's current liabilities as a rule are made up of several classes.

*Accounts payable.* Money owed to suppliers of raw materials, and other costs that have to be met in the usual course of business. Ordinarily, when sales are expanding, there will be some increase in this term.

*Accrued liabilities.* An amount which represents such items as unpaid wages, salaries, and commissions. This item is also likely to vary with the volume of business and many other factors.

*Current maturity of long-term debt.* This merely indicates the amount of such debt due in the next year. Often, a term loan due over a period of many years may provide for serial payments.

*Federal income and other taxes.* Included are all accrued taxes. Sometimes the amount due for Federal income taxes is shown separately. Through payment of local taxes of various kinds, which are not generally set forth in detail in financial statements, corporations make important contributions to the welfare of local communities.

*Dividends payable.* This represents preferred or common dividends, or both, declared by the board of directors but not yet paid. Once a dividend has been declared it becomes an obligation.

The XYZ Company owed $3 million more at the end of 1971 than at the end of the preceding year. Management has to plan carefully to meet current liabilities or obligations. Sometimes rapid growth makes planning all the more difficult. In recent years, a business in a sound financial position has had little or no difficulty in obtaining necessary bank credit.

Important working capital relationships are discussed later in this chapter.

*Reserves.* These reserves, if any, are not to be confused with the accumulated depreciation and depletion, which in the case of XYZ has appeared as a deduction from fixed assets. These reserves earmark appropriations from surplus not to be used for dividend payments. Such reserves may be set up against possible losses from declines in inventory value, or for various other contingencies. Ultimately, contingent reserves may be restored to surplus and become available for dividends.

Sometimes reserve funds are confused with reserves. Reserve funds are assets. For example, a company may set aside a sum in cash for a special construction program.

*Long-term debt.* The amount included in this caption is the face or principal sum due at maturity, less any amount that is payable in less than a year. Sums repaid in the past, of course, have already been eliminated. In the case of XYZ Company, the original issue of debentures was $35 million, which has been reduced to $20 million in 1968. A new period of expansion during 1971 involved the issuance of an additional $7 million of debentures. Debt may consist of several different issues, representing money borrowed at various times and at different rates of interest.

**Stockholders' equity.** This portion of the balance sheet shows what type of stock and how much stock the corporation has sold to its various shareholders. A corporation *must* have common stock—it *may* have other securities.

*Preferred stock.* In this particular instance, the XYZ Company has raised funds through the sale of preferred stock. The rights of the preferred stockholder, like those of a holder of debt securities, are determined by contract. As you have already learned, a preferred stockholder is usually entitled to a fixed dividend before common stockholders may receive dividends, and to priority in the event of dissolution or liquidation. Like bonds and debentures, preferred stocks usually are redeemable at the company's option at fixed prices.

*Common stock.* Common stock may be shown on the books at *par value* or if the stock has no par value, at *stated value*. The thing to remember is that the par value or the stated value of *no-par common stock* is an arbitrary amount, having no relation to the market value of the common stock, or to what would be received in liquidation. Market value is determined by buyers and sellers who take into account earnings, dividends, prospects, the caliber of management, and general business outlook.

*Capital surplus.* Included here are such items as contributed assets or the premium received from the sale of stock over the par value.

*Earned surplus.* This represents past retained earnings, i.e., earnings not paid in dividends.

In other words, surplus is the excess of the total stockholders' equity, or net worth, over the total par value, or stated value, of the capital stock outstanding. *It is not a tangible sum or an amount on deposit in a bank.* Past earnings may have been used in part for the purchase of new machinery. To avoid misunderstanding, more and more companies no longer use the term *surplus* in their financial reports but use *earnings retained and invested in the business* or some similar phrase. Theoretically, at least, the surplus is available for dividends, and the ability of a company to pay dividends depends as much on its financial position as on the amount of surplus in the balance sheet. Sometimes, the creditors place a restriction on the extent to which surplus is available for dividends. Such limitations are usually referred to in a footnote to the balance sheet.

There is no *ideal* capital structure. Even so, the investor should be on guard against too heavy an amount of long-term debt and preferred stock in relation to common stock and surplus. XYZ's capital structure at the end of 1971 was:

|  | Million | Percent of total |
|---|---|---|
| Long-Term Debt | $ 26.0 | 24.4 |
| Preferred Stock | 6.0 | 5.7 |
| Common Stock |  |  |
| Capital Surplus | 74.3 | 69.9 |
| Earned Surplus |  |  |
|  | ——— | ——— |
| TOTAL | $106.3 | 100.0% |

As an ordinary manufacturing enterprise, XYZ has a *sound* or well-balanced capital structure. In other words, the relative amount of different securities gives the senior security holders protection without placing the common stock in a dangerous position.

A one-stock capitalization may be attractive because there are no prior claims ahead of the common stock. But, there may be an advantage in using senior securities provided the funds borrowed can earn more than is needed to pay the interest on debt or dividends on the preferred stock. Long-term debt and preferred stock add what is called *leverage* to a company's capital structure. The degree of leverage is the percentage of the common stock and surplus to the total capitalization. After paying fixed charges and preferred dividends, increased earnings benefit the common stock. Therefore, leverage is an advantage to the common stockholders while earnings are increasing. But a high degree of leverage may be dangerous if a company's earnings are irregular or it is engaged in a cyclical industry. For industrial companies, a rough maximum for bonds and preferred stocks is that they should not exceed 50 percent of the total capitalization.

The smaller the year-to-year fluctuations in earnings, the larger the amount of senior securities outstanding may be without incurring danger. That is why electric and gas utility companies may properly have a 25 to 30 percent common stock equity (ratio of common stock and surplus to total capitalization) whereas this would be considered undesirable for a meat packaging or steel company, or a railroad. A 50 percent common stock equity is generally regarded as a minimum for a manufacturing or retail business.

### THE INCOME STATEMENT

Briefly, the income statement (Fig. 21–7) may be considered to be a blow-by-blow description of the financial transactions of a certain period of time. Statements may be issued quarterly, semi-annually, and in some instances only yearly.

**Sales.** There was a time when quite a few companies did not publish their sales figures, generally because of the mistaken notion that such data would help their competitors. But today no one would think of investing in a company without asking "How much business does the company do?" An income statement begins by providing this information.

In 1971 XYZ had an increase in sales of $5.8 million. The investor likes to see a year-to-year increase in sales. That usually means progress, if the increase also represents increased profits, although it is not always possible to expand sales regularly. In addition, a favorable showing depends on what other companies in the industry have done in the same period. If the whole industry has increased sales by 12 percent and a specific company only 6 percent, the company's results might not be regarded as very satisfactory.

It is always well to determine whether unit sales have expanded or if the larger dollar volume is derived entirely from price increases. More companies now publish unit sales as supplementary information.

*Costs of goods sold.* The expenses of doing business involve outlays for raw materials, wages and salaries, supplies, power and light and other costs.

The XYZ Company was able to keep its expenses down relatively well so that the gain in sales was not entirely eaten up by rising costs. Some companies segregate various parts of the total costs of goods sold. For management purposes costs are broken down further into fixed costs, or those which do not change with volume and variable costs, or those which are flexible.

The lower the cost of goods sold, or the operating cost as it is also called, the larger is the gross profit margin. The investor likes to see a declining operating ratio (percentage of cost of goods sold to sales).

*Selling, general, and administrative expenses.* Costs more directly involved in production, such as wages and raw material purchases are differentiated from selling, general, and administrative expenses. XYZ Company spent a somewhat larger part of last year's receipts for the latter group.

This group of expenses varies considerably with the kind of business. For example, companies selling to consumers usually spend larger sums for advertising than companies selling to other manufacturers or companies that obtain a large part of their orders from government.

*Depreciation and depletion.* These expenses as well as amortization of

STATEMENT OF INCOME—XYZ Company

| | Year Ended December 31 | |
|---|---|---|
| | 1971 | 1970 |
| | Million | |
| **Sales** | $115.8 | $110.0 |
| Less: | | |
| *Costs and Expenses:* | | |
| Cost of goods sold | 74.8 | 73.2 |
| Selling, general and administrative expenses | 14.2 | 13.0 |
| Depreciation and depletion | 4.2 | 3.5 |
| | $ 93.2 | $ 89.7 |
| Operating Profit | $ 22.6 | $ 20.3 |
| Interest Charges | 1.3 | 1.0 |
| Earnings before Income Taxes | $ 21.3 | $ 19.3 |
| Provision for Federal and State Taxes on Income | 11.4 | 9.8 |
| Net Income for the Year | $ 9.9 | $ 9.5 |
| Dividends on Preferred Stock | 0.3 | 0.3 |
| Balance of Net Income Available for Common Stock | $ 9.6 | $ 9.2 |

**STATEMENT OF EARNED SURPLUS**

| | Year Ended December 31 | |
|---|---|---|
| | 1965 | 1964 |
| | Million | |
| Balance at beginning of year | $ 42.2 | $ 37.6 |
| Add—Net Income for the year | 9.9 | 9.5 |
| | 52.1 | 47.1 |
| Less Dividends Paid on | | |
| Preferred Stock | 0.3 | 0.3 |
| Common Stock | 5.4 | 4.6 |
| Balance at End of Year | $ 46.4 | $ 42.2 |

**EXPLANATION**

Amount received or receivable from customers.

Part of income used for wages, salaries, raw materials, fuel and supplies and certain taxes.

Part of income used for salesmen's commissions, advertising, officers' salaries and other general expenses.

Provision from income for the reduction of the service life of machinery and buildings and the use of minerals in mines.

The remainder after deducting the foregoing expenses from sales, but before providing for interest charges and taxes.

Amount required for interest on borrowed funds.

Amount paid or payable for taxes.

This amount was earned for stockholders.

Amount paid to preferred stockholders.

Amount remaining for common stockholders.

Surplus or retained earnings reinvested in the business. Usually not all of the year's earnings can be paid out in dividends, a part being retained in the business for expansion or other purposes.

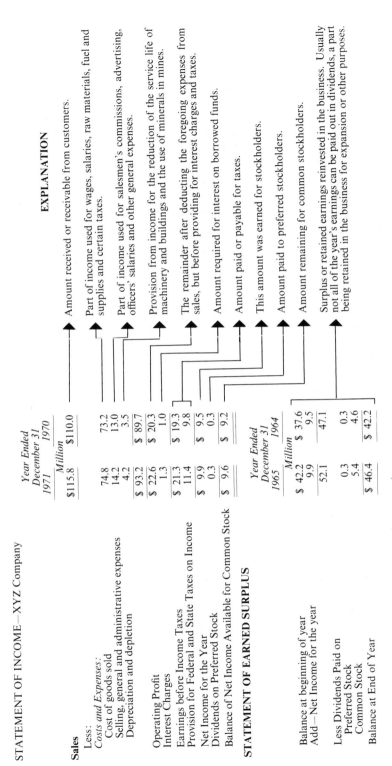

**Fig. 21-7** Income statement of a hypothetical corporation.

various types—differ in a very important respect from the other expenses already considered. While looked upon properly as a cost item, the provision for depreciation does not represent—like other costs—an actual cash outlay. Every piece of machinery and equipment has a limited period of usefulness even when kept in good repair. Thus, XYZ makes a provision for *using up* the service life of each asset, depending on its characteristics. The United States Treasury Department holds that depreciation for tax purposes can be related only to cost. It sets forth maximum depreciation allowances in computing a company's taxable income. If a company did not provide for wear and tear on its production facilities, its profits and net worth would be overstated.

Depletion is somewhat similar to depreciation. It is not a cash outgo and provides for the reduction in the value of natural resources as they are used. Timber, coal, copper, oil, and gas are examples of the types of assets which are subject to depletion.

The higher the amounts provided for depreciation and depletion, the lower is the net reported income. Conversely, large deductions make for a high *cash flow*, which is the total of net income plus the deduction for depreciation and depletion. *Cash flow* is sometimes considered a better guide to future dividend policy than net income. However, working capital and projected capital expenditures should always be considered.

*Operating profit.* This is sometimes referred to as the pre-tax profit. As a percentage of sales, it indicates the pre-tax profit margin. In 1971 and 1970 the pre-tax profit margins were 19.5 and 18.5 percent respectively. For a check on management efficiency, some analysts exclude depreciation and depletion in calculating pre-tax profit margin.

Currently, manufacturing companies have pre-tax profit margins (after depreciation and depletion) of around 6 to 8 percent. Incidentally, small companies do not necessarily have the smallest pre-tax profit margins, nor the big companies the widest.

*Interest charges.* This is the amount required to meet interest payments on debt. Interest being deductible as an expense before taxes, it is often less costly to borrow money than to have funds supplied by stockholders.

The bondholder likes to see at least three dollars of available earnings for each dollar's interest the company must pay. That would mean interest charges were "covered" three times. XYZ's debenture holders can sleep well, for interest charges in 1971 were covered over 17 times before provision for Federal income taxes.

*Earnings before income taxes.* In the case of XYZ, this is simply the operating profit minus interest charges.

*Provision for federal and state taxes on income.* Federal taxes with a 52 percent corporate profits tax rate, have more than a half interest in the earnings of XYZ Company (and others too). Some readers may remember when a 12½ percent rate seemed too high to bear.

The full implications of a 52 percent tax rate have yet to be explored. Some economists and businessmen are sure higher tax rates are passed on to the consumer, but others contend prices are determined in other ways. For obvious reasons, virtually everyone would like to believe that sincere efforts will be made to reduce the tax burden on earnings. If for no other reason than that present tax rates unquestionably hinder small companies more than large businesses, it is often more difficult for a small business to raise needed capital. Thus the rates lessen competition by acting as a barrier against the entry of new firms into business.

*Net income for the year.* This item, also known as earnings or profits is, after all, the acid test of business management. Earnings over the years sum up all the effort, achievement, progress, mistakes, and problems of the business. XYZ's net income in 1971 after all expenses and deductions, including taxes, was about 4.2 percent higher than for the previous year. So far, so good. Since dividends are paid out of profits, a healthy state of affairs requires *good* earnings. But that doesn't necessarily mean earnings must increase each year. Some years will be better than others, although there are valid reasons to believe that the extremes of boom and burst on the scale of 1929 and 1932 can be avoided.

There are two standard tests of how good earnings are. The first is the relation of net income to sales. The XYZ Company in 1971 earned 8.5 percent on each dollar's sales against 8.6 percent in 1970. It will be noted that net income may increase largely because sales have risen, or, on the other hand, mainly because expenses have been reduced in relation to sales.

Average net income to sales varies considerably among different industries and the investor must consider other factors in judging results. For example, chain store grocery companies earn less than 2 cents on each sales dollar, whereas the recent average in manufacturing is about 6 to 8 cents. This does not mean, however, that food distribution is necessarily a poor industry for investment.

The second test concerns net earnings in relation to the amount of the stockholders' investment. Grocery chains earn about 10 percent on the funds the shareholders have in the business. In 1971 XYZ's earnings on the stockholders' investment (net worth) amounted to 12.3 percent.

*Dividends on preferred stock.* The investment quality of a preferred stock is determined largely by the size of net income in relation to annual dividend requirements. The XYZ Company's 1971 net income, in financial language, *covered* the preferred dividends 33 times. That means earnings could shrink drastically without creating any danger signs regarding payment of preferred dividends.

Careful investors also take note of the amount of interest required on a company's indebtedness, for interest comes ahead of the preferred stockholders' dividends. The dividend requirement on the preferred stock is not an obligation in the same way as the interest due a creditor. In a sense, a preferred stockholder is a *limited partner*.

On cumulative preferred stocks, dividends that have not been paid in the past, in addition to current dividends, must be cleared up before dividends may be paid on the common stock.

*Balance of net income available for common stock*. After deducting preferred stock dividends, the remainder represents the balance available for common stocks. This is the most commonly used item to indicate earnings for the common stockholder when reduced to a per share basis. XYZ earned $5.25 per share on the common stock in 1971 compared with $5.03 per share in 1970. Of course, if a company does not have preferred stock, the common stockholders' per share results are found by merely dividing the net income by the number of outstanding shares, or the average number of shares outstanding if there has been a substantial change during the year.

**Earned surplus.** This is also known as income retained in the business. The amount retained from year to year depends on both net income and dividend payments.

Reinvested earnings, it is emphasized, are not as a rule retained in the form of cash. Normally, such reinvested earnings become part of the company's other assets such as inventories and receivables or are used for capital outlays to add to plant and equipment. Or they may be used to repay indebtedness. Over a period of time reinvested earnings should add to a company's earning ability.

### SEVEN KEYS TO VALUE

Over the years, security analysts, brokers, and investors have found that more can be gotten out of financial statements by applying ratios that focus attention on significant relationships in the income account and balance sheet. Those used here are not the only ratios that have been developed, of course, and they are applicable mainly to industrial companies. But even so, the ratios chosen are basic.

The investor should regard his ownership as a proprietary interest. The facts he ought to know are the same as if he were to put his money into running his own business.

1. Pre-tax profit margin.
2. Current (or working capital) ratio.
3. Liquidity ratio.
4. Capitalization ratios.
5. Sales to fixed assets.
6. Sales to inventories.
7. Net income to net worth.

Once the *keys to value* are understood, it is fairly simple to apply them to XYZ's financial statements. The text of annual reports will often clarify the reasons for trends in the ratios. Naturally, interpretation of financial statements cannot provide a magic formula in the appraisal of securities. The economist, accountant, business executive, and financial analyst, in fact, will often differ in their interpretation as to how far financial statements help in determining values.

*1. Pre-tax profit margin.* This is the ratio of profit to sales, before interest and taxes. It is expressed as a percentage of sales and is found by dividing the operating profit by sales. Some analysts compute the pre-tax profit margin without including depreciation and depletion as part of cost because the provision has nothing to do with the efficiency of operations. To illustrate, let's compute the pre-tax profit margin for the XYZ Company: For 1971, it amounted to 19.5 percent; in 1970, the pre-tax profit margin was 18.5 percent. It is usually assumed that a material increase in sales will help widen the profit margin. Certain costs are fixed, i.e., they do not rise or fall in the same proportion as changes in volume. Such costs are interest, rent, and real property taxes. Ordinarily, because of these fixed costs, profits tend to increase and decline more rapidly percentagewise than sales.

*2. Current (or working capital) ratio.* Probably the most generally used for industrial companies, this is the ratio of current assets to current liabilities. A two-for-one ratio is the standard. XYZ's current ratio at the end of 1971 was approximately 2.24 compared to 2.38 in 1970. The change was minor.

A gradual increase in the current ratio usually is a healthy sign of improved financial strength. Ordinarily, a ratio of more than 4 or 5 to 1 is regarded as unnecessary, and may in fact be the result of an insufficient volume of business to produce a desirable level of earnings. To illustrate, in the thirties when railroad equipment orders were extremely small, some railroad equipment companies reported a high current ratio. Earnings, on the other hand, were unsatisfactory. The point again is that the investor should not keep his attention focused solely on the balance sheet or on the income statement. Both are significant in financial analysis.

In 1971, XYZ did not improve its position in this regard because it used substantial funds to increase its plant and equipment. The ratio could have been better if XYZ had spent less for additions to its productive facilities, or had raised more funds for this purpose through the sale of securities, or paid less in dividends. But for one reason or another, none of these alternatives was deemed either necessary or desirable. This particular case illustrates why the entire annual report must be examined and the whole financial statement should be examined.

*3. Liquidity ratio.* This is the ratio of cash and equivalent (marketable securities to total current liabilities. It is also expressed as a percentage figure and results from dividing cash and equivalent by total current liabilities.

This ratio is important as a supplement to the current ratio because the immediate ability of a company to meet current obligations or pay larger dividends may be impaired despite a high current ratio. At the close of 1971, XYZ Company's liquidity ratio was 41.7 percent compared with 44.1 percent in 1970. A decline in the liquidity ratio often takes place during a period of expansion and rising prices because of heavier capital expenditures and larger accounts payable. If the decline persists, it may mean that the company will have to raise additional capital, but unless the decline in the liquidity ratio is drastic, this is something to be watched rather than necessarily a cause for concern.

*4. Capitalization ratios.* These are the percentages of each type of investment in the company to the total investment. As shown previously, the capitalization is made up of Long-Term Debt, Preferred Stock, Common Stock and Surplus.

In financial circles, the word *capitalization* sometimes is loosely used to cover only the outstanding securities, the surplus or retained earnings is an important part of the ownership interest.

The form of capitalization results from the nature of the industry, the company's financial position, and in part from policy. Usually, the higher the ratio of common stock and surplus the more assured is the position of the common stock, as it has less *ahead* of it in the way of debt securities or preferred stock with prior claims. Companies in stable industries, such as electric light and power, may with safety have a higher proportion of debt financing than most industrial companies.

The XYZ Company at the end of 1971, had a common stock equity or ratio of approximately 70 percent. This is the total of common stock, capital surplus, and earned surplus divided by the total of these items plus the outstanding debentures and preferred stock. The common stock ratio was somewhat smaller than in the previous year because of the issuance of additional debentures during the year. Since the surplus was also larger, due to reinvested earnings, the change was slight and the common stock equity remained high.

*5. Sales to fixed assets.* This ratio is computed by dividing the annual sales by the value before depreciation and amortization of plant, equipment, and land at the end of the year. The ratio is important because it helps point up whether or not the funds used to enlarge productive facilities are being spent wisely.

In most cases, of course, a sizable expansion in facilities should lead to larger sales volume. If it doesn't, the added money tied up in the plant, equipment, and land is not producing properly or is not being utilized fully. Or, it may be that sales policies should be altered. After a big increase in capacity, it often takes time for demand to grow up to capacity, and in the meantime, the ratio sales to fixed assets will naturally suffer.

In 1971, XYZ's ratio of sales to fixed assets amounted to approximately

1.1 to 1 compared with 1.2 to 1 in the previous year. But we learn from the annual report that there were delays in getting production under way at the new plant, which isn't uncommon.

In XYZ Company's balance sheet, the fixed assets are shown both as a gross figure, and as a net figure, i.e., before and after accumulated depreciation. Sometimes, the details appear in a footnote to the balance sheet which sets forth the cost of the buildings, machinery, equipment, and land. For our computation we have used the gross figure for all fixed assets, $105.2 million in 1971 and $93.4 million in 1970. The ratio is low, indicating that XYZ probably is in a *heavy* type of industry—possibly steel or paper rather than textiles or drugs, which ordinarily have a larger sales volume in relation to plant investment.

6. *Sales to inventories.* This ratio is computed by dividing the year's sales by the year-end inventories. The so-called *inventory turnover* is important as a guide to whether or not the enterprise is investing too heavily in inventories. In this event a setback in sales or a drop in commodity prices would be particularly unfavorable. A more accurate comparison would result from the use of an average of inventories at the beginning and at the end of the year.

Because inventories are a larger part of the assets of a merchandising enterprise than of most manufacturing companies, this ratio is especially worthy of note in the analysis of a retail business. A high ratio denotes a good quality of merchandise and correct pricing policies. A definite downtrend may be a warning signal of poor merchandising policy, poor location, or *stale* merchandise on the shelves. The nature of the industry has an important part in determining whether a ratio is *high* or *low*.

The XYZ Company's sales-to-inventories ratio in 1971 was approximately 4.3 to 1 compared with 4.5 to 1 in 1970. This decline could have resulted from purchases of raw materials in anticipation of an increase in prices or a falling off in sales toward the end of the year.

7. *Net income to net worth.* This is another ratio given as a percentage and is derived from dividing net income by the total of the preferred stock, common stock, and surplus accounts. This is one of the most significant of all the financial ratios. It supplies the answer to the vital question: "How much is the company earning on the stockholders' investment?" Naturally, a large or increasing ratio is favorable. In a competitive society, of course, an extraordinarily high ratio may invite more intense competition. An increase due to "inventory profits" may be shortlived because of rapid changes of commodity prices.

Broad economic forces may change the general direction of net income to net worth. A higher rate may be due to general prosperity and a decline to a recession or less favorable conditions, or to higher taxes.

The XYZ Company's net income was equivalent to 12.3 percent on net worth in 1971 compared with 12.5 percent in 1970. The change didn't amount to much.  According to general surveys of all manufacturing corporations in the United States a return of over 10 percent appears to be better-than-average. Executives often hesitate to embark on outlays for a new plant and equipment unless they feel that an annual return of at least 10 percent on the new investment may be expected.

It will be observed that XYZ's ratio of return on net worth last year exceeded that of net income to each dollar's sales, which was about 8.6 percent. While the latter ratio is of interest, it is not as significant as the return on the stockholder's investment, as already pointed out.

### INVESTMENT ANALYSIS RATIOS

For investment purposes, a number of ratios in addition to the *seven keys* have been developed to aid in appraising securities.

In the following paragraphs these tests have been applied to the securities of XYZ Company.  A brief description of the terms and their significance has been applied so that the investor will find it easier to apply these tests to other securities.

1. Interest coverage.
2. Earnings per share—preferred stock.
3. Combined or over-all coverage.
4. Earnings per share—common stock.
5. Dividends per share—common stock.
6. Dividend payout.
7. Book value per share—common stock.
8. Price-earnings multiple.
9. Dividend return.

*1. Interest coverage.*  This refers to the number of times interest charges or requirements have been earned.  This ratio is determined by dividing the earnings (or balance) available for such payments—before income taxes—by the annual interest charges.  The practice of showing the interest coverage after income taxes is sometimes followed.  Actually interest is a claim *prior* to income taxes.  Therefore, it is better practice to compute interest coverage before provision for income taxes.

The XYZ Company's interest (or fixed charges) were covered 17.3 times in 1971 and 20 times in 1970, a very high coverage.  In this case, the earnings could decline to only 6 percent of the 1971 results and interest still would be earned. Ordinarily, a manufacturing company's interest coverage is regarded as satisfactory at 5 times; among public utilities, 3 times average coverage is satisfactory.

*2. Earnings per share—preferred stock.*  This ratio is found by merely dividing the net income by the number of shares of preferred stock.  As XYZ had outstanding, 60,000 shares of preferred stock and net income in 1971 amounted to $9.9 million after interest and taxes, the earnings were $165 per share. It could also be said that dividends were earned 33 times. In 1971, earnings per share of preferred stock were approximately $158; and, consequently, preferred dividends were earned 31 times. In both cases earnings were far above *standard* requirements.

3. *Combined or over-all coverage.* A preferred stock of an industrial company with average earnings (before interest on bonds but after taxes) for five years of not less than four times the combined interest and preferred dividend requirements is usually regarded as satisfactory. For a public utility preferred, earnings of around three times the combined requirements make the stock high grade. As a rule of thumb, a preferred stock is considered well protected if dividend payments on the common stock, over a five year period, average upwards of three to four times the preferred dividend requirements.

In 1971, XYZ's combined coverage of interest and preferred dividends after taxes was approximately seven times. To determine this, you divide the adjusted operating profit (profit before interest but after taxes) of $11.2 million, by the total of interest and preferred dividends, which was $1.6 million. This is a more conservative method than merely considering the net income available for the preferred stock.

4. *Earnings per share—common stock.* This is an easy ratio to figure. The balance after preferred dividends is divided by the number of shares of common stock outstanding. In 1971, this balance was $9.6 million and there were outstanding 1,830,000 shares. Accordingly, earnings per share were $5.24 in 1971 and $5.03 in 1970.

If the company sold additional shares during the year it would be customary to show earnings on the average number of shares outstanding during the year, in addition perhaps to the earnings on the outstanding shares at the end of the year. (The company may have had the benefit of the additional funds for only a few months.)

5. *Dividends per share—common stock.* This, too, is a simple computation, and is found by dividing the dividends paid on the common stock by the number of shares. In 1971, XYZ paid $5,490,000 on 1,830,000 common shares —or $3.00 per share. In 1970, it paid $4,575,000—or $2.50 per share.

Dividend policy is a matter for the board of directors. The common shareowner, unlike the bond holder, has no promise from the company that he will be paid a fixed return. The dividends paid to the common stockholder depend on earnings, the availability of funds and the dividend policy.

6. *Dividend payout.* This term refers to the percentage of earnings on the common stock actually paid in dividends. The XYZ Company's dividend payout was approximately 57 percent in 1971 ($3.00 divided by $5.24) and almost 50 percent in 1970.

In practice, the dividend payout will vary, according to many fluctuating factors. Among these are the stability of earnings, the need for new capital, the directors' judgement as to the outlook for earnings and the general views of the management.  Some companies habitually plow back a large part of earnings, in part because of a desire to reduce the amount of funds to be raised from outside sources.

In recent years common stock dividends of industrial companies have averaged about 55 percent of earnings.  In previous decades the payout was somewhat larger.  But electric and gas utility companies have paid an average of over 70 percent of their earnings in recent years because of the greater stability of their income.  On the other hand, growth companies in the chemical and oil industries, have paid substantially less than the average for industrial companies.

7. *Book value per share—common stock.*  Book value is found by adding the stated or par value of the common stock to the surplus accounts and dividing the total by the number of shares.  Accordingly, XYZ's common stock had a book value at the end of 1971 of $40.60 per share.

| | | |
|---|---|---|
| Common stock | $18.3 | million |
| Capital surplus | 9.6 | |
| Earned surplus | 46.4 | |
| | $74.3 | million |

Book value for each of the 1,830,000 shares    $40.60 (Dec. 31, 1971)
(As of Dec. 31, 1970, the figure was $38.31 per share.)

Another method of calculating book value—called the long way—is to deduct from total assets (exclusive of such intangible items as good will and patents) all liabilities and preferred stock, if any.  The remainder is divided by the number of common shares and the result is the book value per share, or net tangible assets per share of common stock.

For industrial companies, book value per share isn't nearly as important as earnings and prospects.  Usually, the largest class of assets is plant and equipment, and the cost is very different from present sales value.  According to an old axiom, assets are worth only what they can earn.

But the book value of the common stock of such money corporations as banks, insurance companies, and investment companies is more significant. The assets of these companies are in securities or other forms that can readily be turned into cash.  The book value of public utility common stocks is also important, since these regulated companies are entitled by law to earn a fair return on their investment, which is made up largely of fixed assets.  Their rates, and hence, earnings are based on the value of their investment in plant and equipment.  Although book value in a single year is almost meaningless in appraising an industrial common stock, the course of book value per share over a period of years may be very significant.

The constant investment of earnings often adds to productive facilities and financial strength.  In other words, the fact that book value per share at the end of last year was $40 per share doesn't tell us much.  However, if the figure was $28 per share four years ago, $12 a share had been added in this period.  Ordinarily, this addition should result in an increase in earning power.

8. *Price-earnings multiple*.  This is a shorthand way of saying that a stock is selling in the market at X times earnings.  If the common stock of XYZ Company is selling at $60 per share, it would be selling at approximately 11.4 times earnings ($60 divided by $5.24).

What is a proper price-earnings multiple?  This is really an agonizing question.  No one knows exactly what it should be.  We do know the average price-earnings multiple has varied widely from time to time.

The price-earnings multiple varies not only with economic conditions but with expectations of the future, or the confidence of buyers that they will be able to sell their stock to other buyers at higher prices.  Interest rates and the level of bond prices are other important factors.

For obvious reasons, investors are willing to pay a higher price for the stocks of companies whose earnings may grow than for stocks of companies in static industries.  Of course, factors applying to individual companies must be considered in each case—management, financial position, capitalization, dividend policy, and the market's appraisal of the stock of other similar companies.

9. *Dividend return* (*dividend yield or income*).  This is determined by dividing the annual dividend per share by the price of the stock.  The indicated return on the common stock of XYZ Company ($3 dividend divided by an assumed price of $60) would be 5 percent.

Returns are generally lower on chemical and oil stocks, for example, than on shoe or textile stocks.  Returns on industrial stocks are usually higher than on bank or public utility stocks, lower than on railroad stocks.  This is, of course, a generality reflecting opinions as to growth of earnings, stability of dividends, and similar factors.  There are wide differences even among stocks of companies in the same industry due to investors' preferences.*

Up to this point in the chapter, we have stressed the importance of clarifying investment goals, limiting investments to growth industries, and selecting stocks on the basis of their fundamental financial soundness.  This is an appropriate place to emphasize another fundamental "selection" pointer: the need for diversification.

## ACHIEVE REASONABLE DIVERSIFICATION

If you are like the average small investor, you will begin by putting a few hundred dollars into the market usually buying stock of only one company.  If your decision to buy that stock is not a wise one, a brief but hectic decline in the price of that issue could virtually wipe out your investment.

---

* Adapted by permission from *Understanding Financial Statements*.  New York: New York Stock Exchange, 1967.

Managers of mutual funds as well as professional and seasoned investors have learned that it is never wise to put all their funds in one or two stocks. No matter how carefully a person tries to select promising stock issues, he simply can't have any guarantee of how that issue will perform. Figure 21–8 shows the wide diversification of a typical mutual fund company as reported in one of its recent quarterly reports. The largest investment in a single stock issue for this particular company amounted to only a small percentage of its total portfolio. The Fund, however, has millions in assets which makes it rather an easy matter to diversify. An individual investor could scarcely expect to ever achieve such diversification.

To illustrate more fully what diversification or a lack of diversification can do, let's assume that you decide to buy a stock of a particular firm—Biotex. The stock looks promising to you from the standpoint of research, recent earnings, and management know-how. A number of large mutual funds are buying the stock; furthermore, it is recommended by several of the investment services to which you subscribe. You purchase 15 shares at $95 per share. You might be very lucky and find in several months after your purchase a headline in *The Wall Street Journal* proclaiming that Biotex had just announced discovery and development of a new anti-viral compound that has proved itself almost 98 percent effective in curing several dozen strains of cold virus as well as cancer. The market reacts to the announcement with a tremendous and wild surge in price. Your stock purchased for $95 per share jumps to over $800;

subsequently it is split twenty for one, after which each share sells for about $72. Your $1,425 investment suddenly is worth a staggering $21,600. Your lack of diversification, your putting all your eggs in one basket, has paid off handsomely.

But perhaps things don't go quite that way. Perhaps *The Wall Street Journal's* headline is something different. Perhaps it reads: "Biotex Sued for $70 Million." You read on and find that apparently one of the corporation's products has not been properly controlled in production and that law suits are being filed from all parts of the country seeking damages. You call your

# Salem Fund INC.

ONE OF THE FIDELITY MANAGEMENT GROUP OF MUTUAL FUNDS

**ANNUAL REPORT**
November 30, 1970

## INVESTMENTS

### NOVEMBER 30, 1970

#### COMMON STOCKS — 90.3%

| Shares | | Market Value |
|---|---|---|
| | **AIRLINES — 1.5%** | |
| 50,000 | Delta Air Lines, Inc. ......... | $ 1,537,500 |
| | **AUTOMOTIVE — 1.4%** | |
| 50,000 | Chrysler Corp. .............. | $ 1,431,250 |
| | **COMMUNICATIONS — 3.0%** | |
| 17,900 | International Telephone & Telegraph Corp. .:......... | $ 816,688 |
| 60,000 | Western Union Corp. ........ | 2,332,500 |
| | | $ 3,149,188 |
| | **CONSUMER PRODUCTS — 14.3%** | |
| 40,000 | Aileen, Inc. ................. | $ 1,400,000 |
| 13,000 | American Home Products Corp. | 874,250 |
| 43,000 | Brunswick Corp. ............. | 757,875 |
| 37,200 | General Foods Corp. ......... | 3,013,200 |
| 13,700 | Jonathan Logan, Inc. .......... | 722,675 |
| 10,000 | Kayser Roth Corp. ............ | 200,000 |
| 30,000 | Norton Simon, Inc. .......... | 1,293,750 |
| 34,000 | PepsiCo, Inc. ................ | 1,717,000 |
| 6,000 | Pfizer, Inc. ................. | 210,000 |
| 30,000 | Procter & Gamble Co. ........ | 1,781,250 |
| 18,000 | Squibb Beech-Nut, Inc. ....... | 1,253,250 |
| 27,000 | Warner-Lambert Pharmaceutical Co. ........ | 1,852,875 |
| | | $ 15,076,125 |
| | **CONSUMER SERVICES — 4.8%** | |
| 22,338 | Disney (Walt) Productions .... | $ 3,350,700 |
| 24,200 | Kinney National Service, Inc. .. | 677,600 |
| 37,400 | Unishops, Inc. .............. | 1,093,950 |
| | | $ 5,122,250 |
| | **DATA PROCESSING — 6.5%** | |
| 12,000 | Control Data Corp. .......... | $ 598,500 |
| 10,000 | International Business Machines Corp. .......... | 3,072,500 |
| 40,000 | Memorex Corp. .............. | 3,210,000 |
| | | $ 6,881,000 |
| | **DIVERSIFIED — 1.0%** | |
| 22,400 | Joy Manufacturing Co. ....... | $ 1,058,400 |
| | **ELECTRICAL and ELECTRONICS — 2.9%** | |
| 35,000 | General Electric Co. .......... | $ 3,093,125 |
| | **FINANCIAL SERVICES — 8.3%** | |
| 40,000 | Continental Mortgage Investors | $ 730,000 |
| 10,000 | Federal National Mortgage Association .............. | 601,250 |

| Shares | | Market Value |
|---|---|---|
| 40,000 | First Charter Financial Corp. ... | $ 1,635,000 |
| 35,000 | Gibralter Financial Corp. of California .............. | 752,500 |
| 101,000 | Great Western Financial Corp. . | 2,222,000 |
| 55,100 | Heller (Walter E.) International Corp. ................... | 1,191,538 |
| 85,000 | Imperial Corp. of America ..... | 1,009,375 |
| 10,900 | MGIC Investment Corp. ...... | 681,250 |
| | | $ 8,822,913 |
| | **HEALTH CARE — 3.9%** | |
| 16,000 | Schering Corp. .............. | $ 930,000 |
| 35,000 | Searle (G.D.) & Co. .......... | 1,763,125 |
| 39,500 | Syntex Corp. ............... | 1,466,438 |
| | | $ 4,159,563 |
| | **MOBILE HOMES — 1.1%** | |
| 35,000 | Skyline Corp. ............... | $ 1,137,500 |
| | **NATURAL RESOURCES — 23.7%** | |
| 26,400 | Coastal States Gas Producing Co. | $ 1,240,800 |
| 113,300 | Eastern Gas & Fuel Associates .. | 4,107,125 |
| 36,000 | Getty Oil Co. ............... | 2,641,500 |
| 70,000 | International Nickel Co. of Canada, Ltd. ............ | 3,211,250 |
| 25,000 | Marathon Oil Co. ........... | 900,000 |
| 25,100 | Mesa Petroleum Co. .......... | 1,063,613 |
| 50,000 | Mobil Oil Corp. ............. | 2,850,000 |
| 35,000 | Occidental Petroleum Corp. .. | 686,875 |
| 50,000 | Pennzoil United, Inc. ......... | 1,668,750 |
| 50,000 | Pittston Co. ................. | 2,006,250 |
| 50,000 | Standard Oil Co. (New Jersey) .. | 3,618,750 |
| 21,000 | Utah Construction & Mining Co. | 1,071,000 |
| | | $ 25,065,913 |
| | **OFFICE EQUIPMENT — 11.5%** | |
| 460,000 | Rank Organisation, Ltd. ADR ord. "A" ............. | $ 7,647,500 |
| 50,000 | Xerox Corp. ................. | 4,468,750 |
| | | $ 12,116,250 |
| | **PHOTOGRAPHIC PRODUCTS — 1.0%** | |
| 14,000 | Polaroid Corp. .............. | $ 1,044,750 |
| | **POLLUTION CONTROL — 1.2%** | |
| 25,000 | Combustion Engineering, Inc. .. | $ 1,303,125 |
| | **MISCELLANEOUS — 4.2%** | |
| 5,000 | American Research & Development Corp. ........ | $ 259,375 |
| 55,000 | City Investing Co. ............ | 845,625 |
| 28,500 | Hercules, Inc. ............... | 1,193,438 |
| 15,500 | Owens Corning Fiberglas Corp. | 573,500 |
| 11,200 | Schlumberger, Ltd. .......... | 970,200 |
| | Other Securities ............. | 640,000 |
| | | $ 4,482,138 |
| | Total Common Stocks .. | $ 95,480,990 |

**Fig. 21–8** Holdings of a mutual fund. This figure shows a portion of an annual report prepared by the Salem Fund Inc. Note the wide variety of industries represented by their holdings and the number of corporations in each industry. Courtesy of Fidelity Management Group.

broker to see what he thinks. He tells you your stock is now trading at $52. But he says, "I think the worst is over. Now would probably be a bad time to sell. It's just gone down too far." You take his advice, but the stock continues to go down and down. Finally when it hits $5.80 a share, you bail out. Your lack of diversification has dealt you a telling loss.

The point is this: If an investor is careful and otherwise uses good sense in investing, he can probably pick more winners than losers. But he can't always pick winners. Even the pros can't always be sure. They don't necessarily spread their investments across great numbers of companies and a score of different industries, but they do seek to distribute their investments selectively among a number of companies representing probably more than one basic growth industry.

At first, you probably can't do much about diversification; but as your investment fund or portfolio grows, look for opportunities to broaden your stock base. If the technology, the products, the discoveries show that a particular industrial segment is going to gain a great deal of market favor in the near future, then attempt to pick two or three of the likely contenders for the consumer race in that industry. Sometimes the late starters are the ones who make the real profits in new technological fields. Perhaps each of your choices will show good market gains. But at least, it is unlikely that all the corporations will be losers.

It is hoped that *all* the selection criteria discussed thus far will be seriously applied to every prospective stock investment. There is, however, one final suggestion regarding common stocks. And like the old saying, "last the best of all the game," the author believes that of all the criteria, this last selection pointer is the most important. Surprisingly, it is also the guideline easiest to follow.

## BE VERY CAUTIOUS OF NEW STOCK ISSUES

At the beginning of the seventies about 9,000 industrial and commercial failures were occurring yearly in the United States. Of those firms which fail, about 3 percent typically do so in their first year of operation; 16 percent in the second year; 17 percent in their third year; and 57 percent within their first five years of operation.

While the exact failure rate of new businesses is not precisely known, it is *high*. Consequently, buying stock of a newly formed corporation is inherently more risky than buying stock of a large, well-established corporation. A 10 or 20 percent price reduction on a blue-chip stock would create a serious loss for the investor; but not nearly so serious as a 100 percent loss of value which so frequently occurs with the failure of a new business. And for those that fail outright, many thousands of other small, new corporations barely survive and fail to make any worthwhile profit for their investors.

It sometimes takes years for the stock of a new corporation to find its place in the over-the-counter market. Only a very few ever make it to one of the big stock exchanges. Even if moderate profits are being made by the corporation, there has to be enough public recognition of the enterprise to send people into the over-the-counter market seeking to buy the corporation's stock.

The investor in a new corporation is immediately put at another disadvantage. There are a great many costs associated with advertising, promoting, and selling new corporate stock. It is not uncommon for a new small corporation to receive only 70 or 75 percent of the total money paid in by investors for the new stock. Therefore, on a strictly balance sheet basis, your initial investment might depreciate by 25 or 30 percent as soon as the purchase is made. The organizers or promoters of the new corporation are also frequently issued a considerable number of shares of stock for their efforts in getting the corporation going. These shares further water down your equity per share and compete on the over-the-counter market (tending to lower its price) when you later want to sell.

All in all, the results of a new corporation have to be really outstanding and truly unusual before the initial investor can expect to make any profit. In most cases, the investor is very lucky to get back just a portion of his money. There are, of course, many success stories written by new companies. If you happen to be in on the ground floor with such a company, the profit potential can be handsome. But remember that the odds are certainly in the other direction. If you are interested in small speculative companies, hold off investing in them until they have at least some operating experience. Chances are you will be able to invest at or below the initial offering price. Even if you have to pay more, you will have the added advantage of being able to judge better the caliber of management and consumer acceptance of the corporation's products before investing.

However, if you want to invest in a new corporation, be sure to read the prospectus or offering circular carefully. (See Fig. 21–9.) Know what stock position the insiders have; learn something about the business, the competition, and the industry trends.

Another reason new corporations have difficulty making profits is the fierce competition which they face from the giant corporation. In concluding years of the previous decade, the corporations with assets totaling $50 million or more generated about 45 percent of all corporate revenues reported in the United States. These same corporations, however, equalled only 2.49 percent of the total number of corporations making tax returns. The uncomfortable facts of life for new firms are that they have to compete with product quality, efficiency, and dependability of goods produced by the billion-dollar giants. It is an understatement to say that is no easy job.

## DON'T OVERLOOK INVESTMENT OPPORTUNITIES IN CORPORATE AND MUNICIPAL BONDS

Often when prospects are dim for common stock investments, you can find a good investment in a corporate or municipal bond. Once considered the exclusive investing province of the sophisticated financier, corporate and

PROSPECTUS

# Abe Schrader Corporation

## 250,000 Shares of Common Stock

### (Par Value, $.10 per share)

The shares offered hereby are being sold for the account of certain stockholders of the Company (see "Principal and Selling Stockholders"). The Company will not receive any of the proceeds from the sale of these shares. Prior to this offering, there has been no market for the Company's shares and the public offering price has been determined by negotiation between the Selling Stockholders and the Underwriters.

THESE SECURITIES HAVE NOT BEEN APPROVED OR DISAPPROVED BY THE SECURITIES AND EXCHANGE COMMISSION NOR HAS THE COMMISSION PASSED UPON THE ACCURACY OR ADEQUACY OF THIS PROSPECTUS. ANY REPRESENTATION TO THE CONTRARY IS A CRIMINAL OFFENSE.

|  | Price to Public | Underwriting Discounts and Commissions | Proceeds to the Selling Stockholders(1) |
|---|---|---|---|
| Per Share | $11.00 | $.88 | $10.12 |
| Total | $2,750,000 | $220,000 | $2,530,000 |

(1) Before deducting expenses payable by the Selling Stockholders, estimated at approximately $78,000.

The Underwriters have agreed, at the request of the Selling Stockholders, to reserve 47,000 of the shares offered hereby for sale at the public offering price to certain employees, officers, directors, suppliers, customers and friends of the Company. The number of shares available for offering to the general public will be reduced to the extent that such persons purchase the shares so reserved.

The above shares of Common Stock are offered when, as and if received by the Underwriters, subject to prior sale and to withdrawal of such offer without notice, and subject to approval of counsel and certain other conditions. The Underwriters reserve the right to cancel or modify this offer and to reject orders in whole or in part. It is expected that delivery of the certificates for the shares of Common Stock will be made on or about January 16, 1969, at the office of Bear, Stearns & Co., One Wall Street, New York, N. Y. 10005, against payment therefor in New York funds.

# Bear, Stearns & Co.

The date of this Prospectus is January 9, 1969.

**Fig. 21–9** Prospectus of a public stock offering. This document is intended to make as full disclosure as possible of pertinent facts about the corporation. Don't buy securities in a public offering by word of mouth. Ask the salesman for a prospectus so you can research the facts yourself.

municipal bonds are now commonly used by men and women from all walks of life to bolster their investment programs.

As with Treasury bills and notes (Chapter 3), the buyer of corporate bonds cannot be assured a specific return unless he holds the bond until maturity. Because of the longer maturities—sometimes 20, 30 years and longer—there is certainly a greater chance that the bonds will have to be sold before they mature. In this eventuality, you may gain or lose depending on the whims of the bond market at the time of the sale.

Another element of risk is also involved—that is the ability of the issuer to repay the obligation plus interest. There are two commonly used ratings for bonds which can help you judge the risk factor. They are:

| Moody Investment Service: | Aaa; Aa; A |
| | Baa; Ba; B |
| | Caa; Ca; C |
| Standard and Poor: | AAA; AA; A |
| | BBB; BB; B |
| | CCC; CC; C |
| | DDD; DD; D |

Although the "A" rated bonds usually offer excellent safety, the rating is no guarantee since ratings are necessarily based on *past* financial statements and performance of the issuers.

As a young person just starting your investing career, it is probably not wise to tie your funds up in municipal or corporate bonds with long maturities. However, if you can find particular issues of these bonds which will mature in two or three years and which will yield a higher rate than Treasury bills and notes or expected appreciation on common stocks, they would be worthy of your consideration.

**Corporate bonds.** Issued by large business corporations to help supply their money needs for new plants, equipment, and operating capital, corporate bonds are generally in denominations of $1,000. However, they are quoted in financial journals in terms of $100 units. Thus a quotation of $86 would indicate that you could buy the bond for $860. Additionally, a small commission of $5 or $10 is tacked onto your purchase. Banks will usually buy corporate bonds for you from a bond dealer; or you can buy directly from a securities broker.

**Tax-exempt municipal bonds.** These bonds are issued by state and local governments and are quoted and traded as are corporate bonds. There is one very important difference, however, for the investor: interest on municipals is exempted from Federal income tax and frequently from State income tax in the state where the bonds are issued. Because of this advantage, the effective interest of such bonds will compare with significantly higher interest returns on taxable bonds. For instance, a married taxpayer filing a joint return on $10,000 of taxable income would find a 6.5 percent municipal bond the equivalent of about an 8.5 percent yield on taxable bonds. For persons with higher incomes, the advantage of municipal bonds is even greater.

## FEEDBACK 21

**A.** To become a successful investor, you must keep constantly informed about any trends that may affect your investments. Review Table 21–1 concerning the publications that are available to you and the sort of information that may be found in them.

- Go to your school library or your nearest public library and check which of the publications can be found there. Take time to read through as many of them as possible. Make a list of those you feel give the best information needed.

- Consider the possibility of subscribing to one or more business publications. Check with any business course instructor about student rates on subscriptions.

- Write to one or more brokerage firms in order to have your name placed on their mailing list. Carefully analyze the information that is sent to you. Compare it with other firms' information or with findings from other business publications. Major differences of opinion should be studied further to answer any questions that you may have.

**B.** Set up an imaginary charge account of $25,000 to be divided among five different corporations—investing $5,000 in each. From a current issue of *The Wall Street Journal*, choose five corporations in which to invest your $5,000 at their common stock's closing price for that day. Try to analyze which corporations will give the best return for your investment—do not choose randomly (just as you would not if you were using real money).

- Make a chart to watch your financial standing during a two month period. List in a column the five corporations, why you invested in them, the number of shares that were bought, and the price at which you bought them.

- Check daily with the price quotations to see if the price is changing. Every two weeks, take your stocks' closing price for each corporation and multiply it by the number of shares you originally bought in that corporation. Sum the five investments to get a total investment figure and compare it with the previous totals. At the end of two months, compare the final total investment figure with the original $25,000 investment that you made. Did you gain money or did you lose it? Analyze what may have happened in the market to cause any change.

- Study the price changes that took place in each of your individual corporations. Did certain stock prices go up, while others went down? Which corporation's stock gave you the best return for your $25,000 investment? Which gave you the poorest return? In your opinion, why did some stock prices gain more than others?

## DISCUSSION QUESTIONS

1. Specific clear-cut personal financial goals have a direct bearing on the stocks one chooses for investment. Discuss the foregoing statement, illustrating its meaning.

2. What types of stocks typically show the most consistent prices? What types of stocks might be expected to react most wildly to changing economic conditions?

3. If a person needed periodic income from his stock investments, what kinds of stocks might he choose. Consult *Moody's Handbook of Common Stocks* and give several examples of stocks that have paid consistent dividends.

4. What is an investment advisory service? Would you follow their recommendations to the letter—providing you had the money to invest?

5. Some investment analysts believe that you're better off investing in a company that may be the second or third entry into a new field, rather than investing in the company that pioneered the new technology. Why might this be true?

6. How might a balance sheet (found in an annual report of a corporation) help you to make an investment decision? How does it differ from the income statement?

7. New corporations pose a special problem or dilemma for the investor. Why?

## CASE PROBLEM

Joseph Hall is a retired building contractor. He was self-employed for 30 years and was able to earn a substantial income from his business. Through the years, Joe was very conservative and has put all his earnings into a savings bank. He was well known for "holding tightly" onto his money; and although he made a good living, money was not spent freely in Joe's home. His children are now all married and have homes of their own, so Joe and his wife Marjorie are left with more than enough money on which to retire.

One evening, Joe read in the newspaper that the current inflation was eating away at everyone's savings—that the interests rates earned in a bank were presently not giving the best rate of return. Being the money manager that he is, Joe began to consider putting some of his "surplus" cash into the stock market. However, he wanted to be perfectly certain that none of his money would be lost. Since Joe went for two years studying business in college and had kept his own financial books while in business, he has taken it upon himself to analyze the market to find the best stocks in which to invest.

a) Where should Joe begin his search in analyzing the market? What sort of publications would best meet his needs?

b) Would you suggest that Joe subscribe to one of the investment advisor services? Explain.

c) What sort of information from the balance sheet would be valuable to Joe as a prospective investor? What sort of information from the income statement?

d) What are the advantages of relying on ratios in statement analyses? Disadvantages?

e) Should Joe remain conservative and spread his total investment over many corporations, or should he place it all in one corporation that he finds to be steadily growing? Explain.

## SUGGESTED READINGS

Bellemore, Douglas H. *The Strategic Investor; Individual Portfolio Management.* New York: Simmons-Boardman, 1963. 394 pp.

Bowyer, John W. *Investment Analysis and Management.* Homewood, Ill.: R. D. Irwin, 1969. 498 pp.

Clarkson, Geoffrey P. *Portfolio Selection: A Simulation of Trust Investment.* Englewood, N. J.: Prentice-Hall, 1962. 143 pp.

Cobleigh, Ira U. *Happiness Is a Stock That Doubles in a Year.* New York: Geis Associates, Grove Press, 1968. 243 pp.

Coe, James C. *Common Stocks for Investors and Traders.* New York: Vantage Press, 1961. 284 pp.

D'Ambrosio, Charles A. *A Guide to Successful Investing.* Englewood Cliffs, N.J.: Prentice-Hall, 1970. 332 pp.

Golde, Roger A. *Can You Be Sure of Your Experts? A Complete Manual on How to Choose and Use Doctors, Lawyers, Brokers, and All the Other Experts in Your Life.* New York: Macmillan, 1969. 245 pp.

*How to Get Help When You Invest.* New York: American Stock Exchange.

*How to Invest in Stocks and Bonds.* New York: Merrill Lynch, Pierce, Fenner and Smith, 1967. 30 pp.

*Investment Facts.* New York: American Stock Exchange.

Latane, Henry A. *Security Analysis and Portfolio Management.* New York: Ronald Press, 1970. 752 pp.

McDonald, Patrick J. (ed.). *Moody's Handbook of Common Stocks* (Second 1971 Edition). New York: Moody's Investors Service, Inc., 1971. 1056 pp.

Sharpe, William. *Portfolio Theory and Capital Markets.* New York: McGraw-Hill, 1970. 316 pp.

*Stocks Grouped by Industry.* New York: American Stock Exchange, 1965.

*Understanding Financial Statements.* New York: American Stock Exchange.

United States Department of Commerce. *U.S. Industrial Outlook 1971.* Washington, D.C.: U.S. Government Printing Office, 1971. 495 pp.

CHAPTER 22

# WHEN AND HOW
# TO BUY AND SELL STOCKS

Once you decide to invest in stocks and do enough reading and investigating to choose with confidence one or more securities, there remain the problems of *when* to make the transactions and *how* to go about your dealings with a broker. These topics, from the point of view of the novice investor, are thoroughly covered in this chapter.

## FORMULA INVESTMENT PLANS

To someone just beginning a stock investment program, price fluctuations can prove unsettling. It is characteristic, for example, for small investors to be overly optimistic when the business horizon seems bright, overly timid during declines in stock prices, and often wrong to boot. To sophisticated investors, however, the *ups and downs* of stock prices provide ways to add to their resources through special investing strategies. Two such plans, *dollar-cost averaging* and *automatic trend following*, which many investors have followed with success are illustrated in the following pages for you.

**Dollar-cost averaging.** Simply explained, dollar-cost averaging is a formula of spacing investments over a long-term investment period, and in the process, acquiring shares at an *average cost* that is below the *average price*, as will be explained in the example below. By investing a fixed sum regularly in stocks at a variety of price levels—some high, some low, some in-between—the investor frees himself from the very tricky business of trying to outguess market turns.

This is basically a good, yet very simple technique for the beginning investor. It is extremely easy to follow and has helped many people accumulate sizable portfolios. Here is how it works: Assume you budget $30 each month for stock investments. You decide to purchase a particular corporate stock that is selling for $15 a share. The first year's investment record is shown in Table 22–1. This illustration shows what may have happened during a downward or *bear* market and the months preceding and following it. The investor had to go against all the negative psychological pressures (fear, panic) which typically build up as prices plunge downward. When everything looked the worst, our investor continued putting the regulated budgeted amount in the stock. But at this lowest ebb—psychologically and price-wise—the $30 purchased five times as many shares as the same amount did when the first investment was made. As a consequence, the $360 invested over the year had purchased 45 total shares. Although the market price of the shares in December was no higher than when the investment program was begun, our investor's shares were worth $675.

**Table 22–1**  First year's stock investment record

| Month | Stock's current market price | Number of shares $30 will purchase | Number of shares owned by investor | Average cost of the shares owned by investor |
|---|---|---|---|---|
| January | $15.00 | 2 | 2 | $15.00 |
| February | 10.00 | 3 | 5 | 12.00 |
| March | 10.00 | 3 | 8 | 11.25 |
| April | 5.00 | 6 | 14 | 8.57 |
| May | 10.00 | 3 | 17 | 8.83 |
| June | 10.00 | 3 | 20 | 9.00 |
| July | 5.00 | 6 | 26 | 8.07 |
| August | 3.00 | 10 | 36 | 6.66 |
| September | 10.00 | 3 | 39 | 6.92 |
| October | 15.00 | 2 | 41 | 7.31 |
| November | 15.00 | 2 | 43 | 7.67 |
| December | 15.00 | 2 | 45 | 8.00 |

You can put a similar investment plan to work for you by following these four steps:

1. Choose a well-managed, well-seasoned corporation in a likely growth industry.

2. Decide on a fixed sum of money which will be set aside from each paycheck for stock investment.

3. Decide on a definite time interval for investment of funds. If the amount you are setting aside for investment will purchase one or more shares of stock monthly, this is desirable. If the budgeted investment amount will not pay for a share monthly, then plan your purchases for each two or three months.

4. Follow through with your investment commitments. You should be looking forward to continued investment for at least 25 to 30 years. (This does not, of course, mean that you can't spend some of it along the way for a little fun.) Do not get discouraged when prices drop—the dips in prices are what makes the plan work.

**Table 22–2** Actual case example of dollar-cost averaging over a six-year period ($30 contributed monthly to investment fund)

| | | Total dollars available for investment at end of each quarter | Number of shares purchased | Cost of each share purchased (excluding commissions) | Number of shares owned | Cost of all shares owned | Total market value of shares owned |
|---|---|---|---|---|---|---|---|
| First year | 1 | $90.00 | 1 | $75.00 | 1 | $75.00 | $75.00 |
| | 2 | $105.00 | 1 | $90.00 | 2 | $165.00 | $180.00 |
| | 3 | $105.00 | 1 | $72.00 | 3 | $237.00 | $216.00 |
| | 4 | $123.00 | 1 | $75.00 | 4 | $312.00 | $300.00 |
| Second year | 1 | $138.00 | 1 | $72.00 | 5 | $384.00 | $360.00 |
| | 2 | $156.00 | 2 | $66.00 | 7 | $516.00 | $462.00 |
| | 3 | $114.00 | 2 | $45.00 | 9 | $606.00 | $405.00 |
| | 4 | $114.00 | 2 | $46.00 | 11 | $698.00 | $506.00 |
| Third year | 1 | $112.00 | 3 | $36.00 | 14 | $806.00 | $504.00 |
| | 2 | $94.00 | 3 | $24.00 | 17 | $878.00 | $408.00 |
| | 3 | $112.00 | 4 | $28.00 | 21 | $990.00 | $588.00 |
| | 4 | $90.00 | 3 | $24.00 | 24 | $1062.00 | $576.00 |
| Fourth year | 1 | $108.00 | 4 | $24.00 | 28 | $1158.00 | $672.00 |
| | 2 | $101.00 | 3 | $33.00 | 31 | $1257.00 | $777.00 |
| | 3 | $93.00 | 2 | $34.00 | 33 | $1325.00 | $1122.00 |
| | 4 | $115.00 | 3 | $35.00 | 36 | $1430.00 | $1260.00 |
| Fifth year | 1 | $100.00 | 2 | $36.00 | 38 | $1502.00 | $1368.00 |
| | 2 | $118.00 | 3 | $36.00 | 41 | $1610.00 | $1476.00 |
| | 3 | $100.00 | 2 | $39.00 | 43 | $1688.00 | $1677.00 |
| | 4 | $112.00 | 2 | $45.00 | 45 | $1778.00 | $2025.00 |
| Sixth year | 1 | $112.00 | 2 | $50.00 | 47 | $1878.00 | $2350.00 |
| | 2 | $102.00 | 2 | $51.00 | 49 | $1980.00 | $2499.00 |
| | 3 | $90.00 | 1 | $69.00 | 50 | $2049.00 | $3450.00 |
| | 4 | $111.00 | 1 | $90.00 | 51 | $2139.00 | $4590.00 |

Table 22–2 shows what dollar-cost averaging did for one small investor whom we shall call Bill. He began his investment program when he was a Junior in college. He decided to set aside $30 per month and maintained this investment rate for six years.

Since the investor was dealing with a stock which initially had a market value higher than the monthly dollar amount set aside for investment, Bill decided to make the stock purchases quarterly for as many shares as the fund would buy.  Any amount left over from the quarterly purchase was kept in the fund to assist in subsequent purchases.  As the trading price of his stock declined, the same fixed dollar investment bought proportionately more shares of stock each time a purchase was made.  On the average then, *more shares were purchased at lower prices than were purchased at higher prices.*

Dollar-cost averaging gives no absolute assurance of stock profits.  But if a person has the financial ability and the emotional stability to continue such a program over a long period of time through all price levels, chances for success are reasonably good.

**Automatic trend following.**  It would be easy to beat the results of dollar-cost averaging if an investor could accurately predict the upswings (bull markets) and downturns (bear markets).  He could always buy at a stock's lowest price and sell at the top figure.  Unfortunately, investors do not have access to a genie or a magic lamp that would permit them to have such insights into market activity; and no one has ever been able to interpret with complete precision all of the complex factors that influence market prices.  Forecasts are, at best, rough indicators—helpful but not completely reliable, and sometimes dead wrong.

Automatic trend following is an investment strategy that attempts to take greater advantage of the market's ups and downs than does dollar-cost averaging. It is a technique that *forces* the individual to react to the *bearish* and *bullish* trends.  This is how it works:

1. The investor bases his sales or purchases decisions upon the trend in prices on the stock market as shown by one of the published market indicators. The Dow-Jones Industrial Index is commonly used.

2. A *sell* indication occurs when the Dow-Jones average (or other average which one is following) declines by a fixed percentage, say 10 percent, from the average's previous high.  (The investor decides what percentage factor he is going to use—usually it varies from 7 to 11 percent.)

3. A *buy* signal occurs when the average increases by the agreed-upon percentage from the average's previous low.

Those who follow such a plan liquidate all or a high percentage of their stock holdings when the *sell* signal develops and subsequently put their money into bonds or short-term government notes.  Stocks are not purchased again until the *buy* signal develops, indicating the market has turned around and is starting on its upward swing.  Then all or a large portion of the money is taken out of bonds or notes and stocks are once again purchased.

Such a plan means that you never benefit for selling at the very *highest* point in the market, nor from buying at the *lowest*.  But it does help you react in such a way that you get the major benefit from the market movements. It helps one to resist the temptation to hang on too long in hopes of making more money; and encourages you to buy while panic and fear still dominate market psychology.

Regardless of the investment strategy you decide to use, do not cling too stubbornly to stocks that turn out to be losers. Now and then investors make mistakes, and sometimes they can be quite costly. Your author is no exception. He had been following with considerable interest a certain electronics corporation which had seemingly phenomenal market success and envious profits. A number of mutual funds were holding the stock; several of the market services and numerous brokers were recommending it highly. At about $19 per share, the author decided to make a substantial purchase. The price of the shares continued upward for a short time, but suddenly declined as that particular stock was hit by a tremendous surge of selling. Soon the word was out that the company's profit picture had drastically changed. Foreign competition on transistors and other electronic devices had severely cut prices, and profits were out of the window. Several law suits were filed against the company claiming that there had been inadequate disclosure of competitive factors at the time the corporation went public (offered its shares for sale to the public). Prior to that time the corporation had been privately held.

To shorten an otherwise long and unhappy story, the price of the stock continued to tumble. The author stubbornly held on, believing all the while that things just could not get much worse. But they did; and, finally, he sold at a whopping loss when the stock reached about $7 a share.

By the time the stock had plummeted to $11 or $12, most of the facts were known, and the author should have reacted by promptly selling his interests in the company. Disbelief and stubbornness lead to nothing but greater loss. When a mistake has been made, even though it is a whopper, one should face up to it and get out. You'll usually lose money by doing so, but probably much less than by holding on and refusing to face facts.

Sudden, jarring bolts of selling on an issue with marked price declines usually have some special significance, especially when the over-all market is not generally moving in that direction. Sporadic waves of heavy selling are often the first signs that serious trouble is ahead for the company. Perhaps insiders with heavy holdings in the corporation have information that makes them decide to dump their shares before others find out. Certainly such heavy selling should be followed closely. Further dips or jolts to the stock usually warrant immediate sale to minimize losses.

### HOW TO BUY AND SELL SECURITIES

Now that you have some notion about how to select quality stocks and apply market strategy, it is appropriate to turn our attention to the details of actual brokerage transactions. Within the complex machinery and system of regulations created by more than 175 years of organized stock trading, how does one actually go about buying and selling securities?

**Opening a brokerage account.** A person wishing to buy or sell corporate stocks first visits a reputable stock broker's office and opens up an account in his or her name. This is really a very simple, routine operation requiring but a few minutes. It is much the same as opening a credit account at any department or furniture store. Figure 22–1 illustrates the type of application which the person is asked to fill out. It calls for name, address, telephone number, social security number, age, and citizenship. Also the applicant must supply information regarding occupation and employer, name of bank, and one or two credit references. Once an account has been established, most of the future dealings can conveniently take place by telephone.

**M**
✚ *TO OPEN AN ACCOUNT FOR THE PURCHASE AND SALE OF SECURITIES WITH*

**MERRILL LYNCH, PIERCE, FENNER & SMITH INC**

Name (Please print) _____

Full mailing address _____
City _____ State _____ Zip Code _____
Business phone_____Residence phone_____
Are you over 21 ?_____Citizen of what country ?_____
Have you ever been a customer ?_____What office ?_____
Name of your bank _____

TO COMPLY WITH NEW YORK STOCK EXCHANGE REGULATIONS, PLEASE SUPPLY THE FOLLOWING
INFORMATION ABOUT YOURSELF — OR IF YOU ARE A HOUSEWIFE, ABOUT YOUR HUSBAND.

Name of employer _____

Kind of business _____ Position _____

Signature _____

SOCIAL SECURITY NO.

CODE 32 R 1/65 Printed in U.S.A. D&N

**Fig. 22–1** Application for a brokerage account. This typical application shows the standard information items which the applicant supplies. Opening a brokerage account is much like opening a charge account at a department store.

Customer transactions with a brokerage house are carried out with the cooperation of an *account executive—a broker salesman.*  The competence of account executives differs considerably; therefore, it is a good idea to pick the person by reputation and recommendation much the same as one would choose a physician, a lawyer, an architect, or an engineer.  However, if the new customer has no preference, the manager of the firm will assign the account to the broker salesman he believes can best serve the new client.

**Fig. 22–2** Customer and account executive discussing investment program.  Brokers are quite willing to discuss overall investment plans as well as give information and advice on buying or selling individual stock issues.  The customer however, must learn enough about stock to make the final decision.  Courtesy of Merrill Lynch, Pierce, Fenner & Smith Inc.

Brokers, like their customers, are people.  The brokerage industry is a personal service industry in which the human factor forms the basis for any continuing relationship (see Fig. 22–2).  Customers range all the way from millionaires to people with one or two modest investments.

People sometimes feel embarrassed about the amount of money they have to invest. If they have only a few hundred dollars, they feel a broker may not want to be bothered with such a small sum. Nothing could be further from the truth. Many brokerage firms, as well as the stock exchanges, are spending millions of dollars in advertising every year to tell the small investor that they definitely are interested in him.

You have every right to decide what kind of investment program you want and to ask for your broker's cooperation in helping you carry it out. Devices such as the one shown in Fig. 22–3 provide brokers and their customers up-to-date information. You can ask your broker to give you information which he has concerning securities that interest you. But do not expect your broker to make your decisions for you. He will want you to do the deciding.

When you have made up your mind, your broker will, of course, see that your order is executed. Later, if you wish, and if your broker has the facilities to do so, you can have him keep your securities for you and send you a check whenever dividends are paid.

**Fig. 22–3** Telequote desk unit. This compact device gives brokers and their customers instantaneous data directly from the exchanges. The data are continually processed, verified, and stored by high-speed computers. Courtesy of Bunker-Ramo Corporation.

**Mechanics of buying and selling.**   Once an account is opened, buying and selling stocks are matters of routine.  (It is knowing what and when to buy and sell in order to make a profit that are the real problems.)  Let's follow a typical *sell* order to illustrate how trades are made:  After holding 100 shares of XX securities for some time, our fictitious investor friend, Mr. McGavern, decides that it is time for him to sell his stock.  He picks up the telephone, calls his broker's office and asks to speak to his account executive, Mr. Pinney:

Investor: This is McGavern speaking.  Would you please give me a quote on XX this morning?

Broker: Yes, certainly.  Just a moment.  Last trade was $77\frac{1}{2}$ ($77.50).

Investor: I'm getting concerned about XX's competitive position.  The stock has been weak for some time, and it doesn't look as though things are going to get better.  Would you recommend I sell my 100 shares?

Broker: From what information I've seen, I'd agree that it might be wise to sell.

Investor: O.K., go ahead and sell 100 shares.

Broker: Do you wish to sell at the going market price?

Investor: Yes, sell at market (the current price at which trading is taking place).

If we assume that XX stock is a *listed* security and traded on the New York Stock Exchange, this is what will happen to McGavern's order:  As soon as the order is given to the account executive, it is quickly written up and handed to a teletype or telephone operator.  The information will be sent immediately to the floor broker at the NYSE.  This person is in the employ of the member brokerage house with which the order was placed.  The floor broker has a communication booth on the outer edge of the stock exchange floor.  As soon as he receives the order, he walks to the XX trading post.

As the broker nears the post where XX is traded, he may encounter a number of other brokers also desirous of buying or selling XX stock.  He loudly calls out, "How's XX?"  The stock specialist, who is delegated the responsibility by the stock exchange to conduct the actual buying and selling of that particular stock, continuously keeps track of the number of shares of stock and the prices at which brokers are willing to sell XX stock.  Our friend, Broker A., gets a quick response.  "Five hundred shares offered at $76\frac{1}{4}$."  At this point our broker has given no indication whether he wishes to buy or sell XX stock.  Another person, Broker B., interjects, "Take it."  The five hundred shares that were offered have now been sold to the Broker B.

Our broker then offers the 100 shares McGavern wishes to sell.  Broker C. rushes up and asks, "How's XX?"  The specialist says, "One hundred shares offered at $76\frac{1}{4}$."  Broker C. says, "Take it," and McGavern's shares have been sold.  The sell order is then processed by the exchange.  In a few minutes the details of the sale are wired back to the local brokerage office where the sell order originated.  The account executive then picks up the telephone and calls McGavern to report that his stock was sold.  The entire trading process for listed securities is vividly illustrated by the interesting sequence of photos in Figs. 22–4a–g.

**(a)**  An account executive receives a round-lot market order from an investor by telephone.

**(b)**  The order goes to the wire room of the local office, where it is sent by teletype to New York headquarters.

**Fig. 22–4(a–g)**  Photo story showing how listed stocks are bought and sold.  Courtesy of Merrill Lynch, Pierce, Fenner & Smith Inc.

**(c)** From there a clerk telephones it to the floor of the New York Stock Exchange.

**(d)** The order is given to the firm's floor broker, who executes it, bargaining for the best possible price, at the appropriate trading post.

(e)  Confirmation is telephoned back to the firm's headquarters.

(f)  From there the information is teletyped to the local office.

**(g)** At the local office the confirmation is received.

**Round and odd-lots.** This is a good place to point out that most stocks trade on the stock exchanges in terms of 100 shares or multiples of 100 called *round lots*. Had McGavern wanted to sell fewer than 100 shares of XX stock, or should he have wished to purchase fewer than 100 shares of any listed stock, his broker would have entered the order as an *odd-lot order*. The broker's floor clerk would have then sent the order to an odd-lot dealer at the post where XX is traded. The odd-lot dealer would have bought XX stocks at a price based on the next round-lot transaction in XX after he received the order. Assuming the round-lot trade was $76\frac{1}{4}$, the odd-lot dealer would have bought XX at $76\frac{1}{4}$ minus $\frac{1}{4}$ or 76; or had it been a purchase order, the odd-lot dealer would have sold XX at $76\frac{1}{4}$ plus $\frac{1}{4}$ or $76\frac{1}{2}$. The additional $\pm$ one-quarter point or 25 cents per share, included in the odd-lot price is known as odd-lot differential. On stocks selling at less than $55, it is $12\frac{1}{2}$ cents a share above the round-lot price on purchases and $12\frac{1}{2}$ cents below on sales.

**Special buy and sell orders.** McGavern's order used in the previous illustrations involved a *market order*—an instruction to the broker to sell at the *going* market price. Here are other kinds of useful orders which brokers will accept:

*1. A limit order.* This is an order which specifies a price. If a round-lot order is entered to buy a stock at $35, for example, it cannot be executed at a price higher than $35. If an order is entered to sell at $35, it cannot be executed below that price. In all cases, though, the broker will do his best to get the best price available to him on the floor.

*2. Stop order.* This order may be used in an effort to protect a paper profit or to try to limit a possible loss to a certain amount. To illustrate: If you bought stock at $35 a share, you could enter an order to *sell at 30 stop*. In the event the stock declines to $30 or below, your order automatically becomes a market order and is executed at the best possible price—which would be at $30, or below or above $30, depending upon the market in the stock at that time.

Or, if stock bought at $35 a share should rise to $55, the customer could enter a *stop order to sell* at $50. Should the stock decline to $50 or below, the stop order would automatically become a market order and the stock would be sold at the best price then available to him on the floor. Stop orders may also be used when *buying* stock.

When he gives his broker a limit order or stop order, the customer can specify that it is to be good for only one day—this is known as a *day order*. Or he can give a week order or a month order. If the order is not executed during the period designated, it automatically expires.

*3. GTC order.* If the customer wants his order to hold good indefinitely, he gives his broker a *good-'til-cancelled* order. This type of order is carried as an open order until the broker is able to execute it, or until the customer cancels it.

**Costs of buying and selling stock.** Although brokerage houses have a variety of ways in which they make profits, their principal source of revenue is the purchase and sale of corporate securities. For his efforts, your account executive receives a portion of the total commission paid the broker. The exact rate of commission varies according to the price and number of shares of stock which are bought or sold. As we have seen, orders are classified as *round-* or *odd-lot* transactions. Round lots are traded at the following commission rates: 2 percent plus $3, if the round-lot transactions totals $100 to $399; 1 percent plus $7, on transactions of $400 to $2,399; $\frac{1}{2}$ percent plus $19 on orders of $2,400 to $4,999; $\frac{1}{10}$ percent, plus $39 on all transactions of $5,000 or more.

On odd lots, the commission is $2 lower per transaction, with a minimum of $6 for transactions involving $100 or less. However, in effect, the stock bought on an odd-lot basis costs more because of the odd-lot differential which is added to purchases or subtracted from sales. In any instance, commissions are not to exceed $1.50 per share nor more than $75 for any one transaction. On top of the commission is added a *service charge* which is 50 percent of the commission, but not to exceed $15.00. New rates were being negotiated when this book went to press and may differ from those presented here.

New York State levies a transfer tax of from $1\frac{1}{4}$ to 5 cents a share, based on selling price of the stock. This tax is paid by the seller.

**Settling your brokerage account.** As soon as a transaction is completed by your broker, the office will prepare and mail you a written *confirmation* such as that shown in Fig. 22–5. This will give all the pertinent data such as date, number of shares traded, name of stock, purchase or sale price, commission charged, and total proceeds of sale or cost of purchase. You then have four days in which to remit a check for payment of the securities purchased or in which to supply the stock certificates of the securities sold. The proceeds of a sale will normally be credited to your brokerage account, or you may have your broker mail you a check. When you purchase securities, the actual stock certificates should be mailed to you within a week or so after payment has been made.

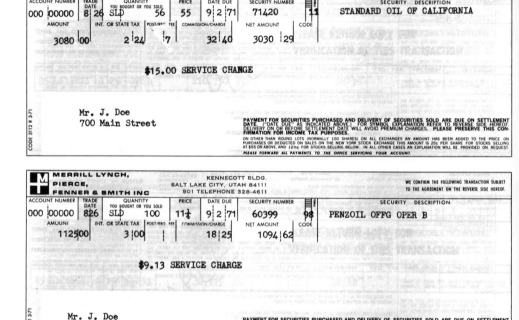

**Fig. 22–5** Specimen brokerage confirmations of buy and sell orders. Purchase or sale price, taxes, commissions, number of shares traded, and settlement date are all clearly shown on the broker's confirmation which is mailed to the customer. This record is important for tax purposes and should be retained permanently.

Since the information contained in the *confirmation* is essential for completing your income tax returns, it should be kept permanently in a safe place with other important documents.

**Monthly investment plan.** Realizing that most investors are unable to contribute large amounts initially toward stock investment, the New York Stock

Exchange in cooperation with all those firms which hold membership or seats on the exchange inaugurated in 1954 a plan known as the *monthly investment program*. Since that time it has become very popular. Approximately 11 million shares of stock have now been purchased under the provisions of this plan. It is possible for a person to contribute as little as $40 monthly or quarterly. The person may select the corporation stock which he desires, and contributions are credited in full or fractional shares to the investor's account as each contribution is made. The commission on such monthly investment plan transactions ranges between 6 to 3 percent, depending on the amount of the contribution. It is a very flexible plan and although one signs up (Fig. 22–6) for a definite contribution program, should personal involvements necessitate changes, the contributions can be revised upward or downward. For that matter, the person can withdraw completely from the program at any time.

If you already have an account with a broker, he will be happy to arrange for contributions to this monthly investment plan. All major investment brokerage houses having membership in the New York Stock Exchange will gladly provide you with further information and counsel concerning the advisability of your participating in such a purchase arrangement.

**Margin stock purchases.*** When you buy stock on margin, you pay only a portion of the total cost and borrow the balance from your brokerage firm paying him interest on the amount you borrow. From then on, the price of your stock may go up or down, but the amount you owe your broker will remain the same. In general, only listed stocks may be bought on margin.

Suppose you want to buy $10,000 worth of an acceptable stock, but you do not want to use $10,000 at the moment. If the margin requirement at that time is 50 percent, you need put up only $5,000 and your brokerage house will lend you the other 50 percent or $5,000. If the requirement is 80 percent, you put up $8,000, and your brokerage house puts up the other $2,000. Just how much of the total cost you have to put up when you buy stocks on margin is determined by the Board of Governors of the Federal Reserve System and is binding on all brokers. Federal regulation of credit extended for the purpose of securities dates from 1934. From that time until the present, the initial margin requirements have ranged from 40 percent to 100 percent. Once the original margin requirement has been met, a subsequent change in the initial margin requirement will not affect purchases already made, since initial margin requirements are not retroactive. In other words, if you put up $5,000 to buy $10,000 worth of stock at a time when the margin requirement was 50 percent, you do not have to put up more money just because the Board raises the initial margin requirement to 70 percent.

---

* Adapted by permission from *What Is Margin?* New York: Merrill Lynch, Pierce, Fenner & Smith, Inc., 1969.

# MONTHLY INVESTMENT PLAN
of
### Members New York Stock Exchange

## PURCHASE ORDER

................19.....

............................
(Name of Member Firm to be filled in)

Gentlemen:

IT IS MY PRESENT INTENTION TO INVEST WITH $.................. monthly / quarterly

PAYMENTS IN ................................................. LISTED ON THE
(fill in name of stock)

NEW YORK STOCK EXCHANGE, COMMENCING WITH AN INITIAL PAYMENT OF $.................., FOR WHICH MY CHECK OR MONEY ORDER IS ATTACHED.

Each remittance for my account ($40 minimum), less your commission, will be applied by you, as my broker, to the purchase of full shares of the stock named above and/or fractional interest in such a share. Purchases will be made at the first odd-lot price established after the day the payment is credited to my account. See Terms and Conditions #2, #3 and #4.

Cash dividends, and proceeds from the sale of rights or special distributions are to be automatically reinvested in my account, unless you are otherwise notified by me in writing with respect to future cash dividends and proceeds.

I reserve the right to cancel this order at any time, without penalty or charge, by written notice to you. You also may cancel this order at any time by written notice to me. Purchases made before the receipt of a cancellation notice will not be affected by such notice.

THE TERMS AND CONDITIONS SET FORTH ON THE
REVERSE SIDE ARE PART OF THIS PURCHASE ORDER.

Mr.
Mrs.
Miss...................

(Print Full Legal Name)            (Legal Signature)

(Street Address)            (Business or Occupation)

(City, State and Zip)        (Citizenship        Social Security No.)

FOR OFFICE USE ONLY

(Member Firm Identifying        (Name of Member Firm)        (Authorized Initials for
Number – Not Over 4 Digits)                              Opening a New Account)

**Fig. 22–6** Purchase order for monthly investment plan. Investor selects the stock he wishes to purchase. Under the plan he may invest as little as $40.00 per month. If the stock is a high-priced one, fractional shares may be purchased.

There is another initial margin requirement that you must meet, and that one is set by the New York Stock Exchange. It is that no person may open a margin account with a member firm without depositing at least $2,000 or its equivalent in securities. The Exchange also sets requirements for the maintenance of margins, as distinguished from the initial margin requirements of the Federal Reserve Board. Generally speaking, a customer's equity may at no time be less than 25 percent of the market value of securities carried. Member brokers frequently also have rules which are higher than 25 percent.

Such rules exist for the protection of the broker, who must be sure that the loans he makes for margin buying are not endangered in a falling market. In practice, this is how the rule works. If the stock you bought on margin has a current market value of $7,500, your equity must be at least $2,000, even though 25 percent of $7,500 is only $1,875. However, most brokers require more. So let us assume that the broker's minimum is 30 percent or $2 per share, "whichever is greater." Thus, if you bought on margin 200 shares of a stock currently selling at $50 and costing $10,000, you would have to maintain an equity of the greater of these two amounts: $3,000 (30 percent) or $400 ($2 a share)—obviously $3,000. In practice, the $2 rule would affect only stocks selling below $7 a share.

If the price of your stock goes down and your equity thereby falls below the minimum; that is, 30 percent of the market value or $2 a share, you become subject to a margin call, which must be met as promptly as possible. That means that you received a notice from your broker asking you to deposit more cash or acceptable securities.

**Uses and advantages of margin buying.**\* Why do people buy stocks on margin? For a variety of reasons, but primarily to increase their buying power.

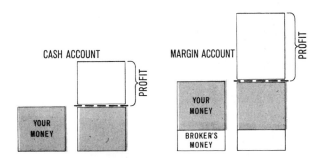

By borrowing from your broker, you increase the size of the profit you may realize beyond what would be possible if you used only your own funds— if the price of the stock goes up. Obviously, since you can buy more stock with the additional money you borrow from your broker, you can increase the amount of capital appreciation that you may realize and obtain more in dividends than you could with a smaller cash purchase.

Capital appreciation is the chief objective of the margin buyer. If you choose a stock that you think will increase in price fairly rapidly, it stands to

---

\* Adapted by permission from *What Is Margin?* New York: Merrill Lynch, Pierce, Fenner & Smith, Inc., 1969.

reason that you will make more profit by buying a greater number of shares on margin than by buying a smaller number for cash—if the stock actually does go up in price.  For example:

| | |
|---|---:|
| If you buy 75 shares of ABC at $50 in cash account, and you pay | $3,750 |
| and if ABC goes up $60, your stock is then worth | 4,500 |
| and you have a profit of | $  750 |
| If you take that $3,750 and buy ABC stock at 75 percent margin, you pay | $3,750 |
| and your broker puts up an additional | 1,250 |
| and you would have 100 shares of stock worth | 5,000 |
| And if ABC goes to $60, your 100 shares are then worth | 6,000 |
| and your profit is | $1,000 |

The amount of your dividends will be larger, too.  However, few people are likely to buy stocks on margin for the sake of dividends unless those dividends are substantially greater than the interest to be paid on the amount borrowed.*

**Dangers and disadvantages of margin buying.***  Margin is a useful device for the speculator or trader in securities, but it can be dangerous and is not appropriate for the small- or long-term or conservative investor, because the risk of loss is multiplied just as much as the possibility of gain when you buy on margin.  No one should buy stock on margin unless he has both the temperament to speculate —the temperament to accept price fluctuations with equanimity—and the financial resources to meet margin calls and to absorb losses because of a drop in the price of the stock.

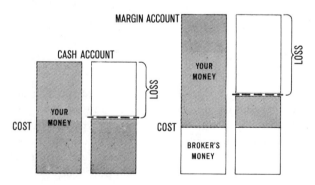

Nor is there likely to be any real advantage in using margin with relatively small amounts of money.  Higher commission charges on odd-lots and interest

* Adapted by permission from *What is Margin?* New York: Merrill Lynch, Pierce, Fenner & Smith, Inc., 1969.

payments on the amount borrowed eat up much of the profit that may be made on such small transactions.

Remember, too, that when you buy stock on margin, the decision on when to sell will be, in effect, out of your hands in the event of your inability to meet a margin call, since the decision will be dictated by market performance rather than by your convictions about the desirability of selling. You may, in fact, be forced to sell at an unfavorable price and thus incur a loss.*

**Short selling.*** This type of sale is in a sense the reverse of a normal transaction. You sell first and buy back later instead of buying first and selling later. When you sell short, you borrow stock from or through your broker and place an order to sell it, usually because you expect the stock to decline in price.

This is how short selling works. You borrow stock from or through your broker (hence you are "short" the stock) and you sell it. If the price of the stock declines, as you expect, you can buy it back later at a lower price and replace the stock you borrowed. Your gross profit will be the difference between the price at which you sold the original borrowed stock and the price at which you were able to buy the stock back.

Of course, the price of the stock may go up, and you may ultimately have to buy it at a higher price in order to replace what you borrowed. In that case, you suffer a loss.

Here are two examples. If you sell a stock short at $50 a share and buy it back for replacement at $40 a share, you make a profit of $10 a share. If you sell it short at $50 and have to buy it back at $60, you lose $10 a share.

Short selling can be done only in a margin account and only with your broker's knowledge. It may be necessary for your broker to decline orders for short sales of listed securities if the stock cannot be borrowed.

When you sell a stock short, the proceeds of the sale are retained by your broker, and the Federal Reserve Board requires that you deposit margin based on the net proceeds of the sale. That margin is the same as the percentage of the total amount you would have to put up for a regular margin purchase— 50 percent or 70 percent or 90 percent, for example. To illustrate:

You sell short 100 shares of JKL at $100 and your broker retains  $10,000
If the initial margin requirement is 50 percent, you must deposit        5,000
If the initial margin requirement is 70 percent, you must deposit        7,000

The rules of the New York Stock Exchange call for the short seller to deposit the prevailing Federal Reserve Board requirement (50 percent or 70 percent or 90 percent or whatever the initial margin requirement is currently) and maintain $5 a share or 30 percent of the market value of any stock sold short. In practice, this means that if you are short $10,000 worth of stock, you must maintain an equity of $3,000, and if the securities you are short happen to sell under $17 a share, your equity must be at least $5 a share.*

* Adapted by permission from *What is Margin?* New York: Merrill Lynch, Pierce, Fenner & Smith, Inc., 1969.

**FEEDBACK 22**

**A.**  Make a visit to the nearest brokerage firm.  Take time to look around and study the acitivity that takes place there.  Pick up any printed information that they may have explaining the operation of the firm.  Also ask for an application blank for a brokerage account.  Answer the following questions after leaving.

- What was your first impression about the brokerage firm?  Was the atmosphere quieter or more confused than you expected?  Did there appear to be a normal routine to the employees' duties?

- What information is asked for on the account application?  Why do they need that sort of information?  Do you believe that you meet their requirements for credit?

- If you do not live near a brokerage firm, write to a reputable one in order to obtain their printed information and application.

**B.**  List on a piece of paper the process of buying 100 shares of common stock listed on the New York Stock Exchange.  Specify numerically each step of the process from the original order to the final affirmation of sale.

- What would have happened if you placed a limited order for $50, and the current price of the stock was $60?  What would a stop order have done?

- Do the same for the selling process.

**DISCUSSION QUESTIONS**

1. Explain why and how dollar-cost averaging works.  Why may some individuals be unable to make such a plan succeed?

2. Would a dollar-cost averaging investment plan—say for 2 or 3 years duration—be appropriate for an older retired couple?  Why?  Why not?

3. Generally speaking, novice investors are afraid of the ups and downs in prices of stocks, while many professionals welcome such swings.  Can you explain why this is so?

4. What advantages or disadvantages do you see to the automatic trend following plan?

5. Explain what happens from the time you pick up your phone to call in a sell order to your broker until that sale is confirmed to you.

6. How do round- and odd-lot sales differ?

7. Why might the monthly investment plan of the NYSE be attractive to new stock investors?

8. What is a margin purchase?  Why might an investor wish to use this procedure?

9. If you sold a stock short, what expectations should you have about that stock?  How would you go about making a short sale?

**CASE PROBLEM**

John Freeman is a student at a small business college located in a large city. He is living at home, and his parents are paying his tuition at the school. John has worked part-time most of his life since he was a newspaper boy at age 10. He has saved his earnings until he now has a $2,500 savings account.

John became interested in the stock market while studying about it in a finance class that he was taking at school. He has decided to invest his $2,500 in a corporation that he is certain is strong and will earn for him a good rate of return. He has studied the corporation's statements and is sure that the stock is a good buy; therefore, he wishes to invest at least $3,500—at a large brokerage firm in his city.

a) If the margin requirement is 70 percent, explain the advantages of buying the stock on margin.

b) Explain the disadvantages of buying stock on margin.

c) What would you advise John if the stock is known to give exceptionally high returns yet is classified as "risky"?

**SUGGESTED READINGS**

*American Stock Exchange Index System.* New York: American Stock Exchange.

Bowen, Bruce B. *An Analysis of the Hypothesis "Buy High, Sell Higher," and Its Profitability.* Salt Lake City: University of Utah, 1965. 63 pp.

Engel Louis. *How to Buy Stocks.* New York: Bantam Books, 1967. 259 pp.

Farrel, Maurice L. (ed.). *The Dow-Jones Investor's Handbook.* New Jersey: Dow-Jones Company, Inc., 1966.

*Fortune. Fortune's Guide to Personal Investing.* New York: McGraw-Hill, 1963. 216 pp.

Graham, Benjamin. *The Intelligent Investor; A Book of Practical Counsel.* New York: Harper and Row, 1965. 332 pp.

Granville, Joseph E. *A Strategy of Daily Stock Market Timing for Maximum Profit.* Englewood Cliffs, N.J.: Prentice-Hall, 1960. 289 pp.

*How to Invest on a Budget.* New York: American Stock Exchange.

*Investment Clubs ... What Are They ... How Are They Started?* New York: American Stock Exchange.

Lishan, John M., and David T. Crary. *The Investment Process.* Scranton, Pa.: International Textbook, 1970. 497 pp.

Rosen, Lawrence R. *Go Where the Money Is; A Guide to Understanding and Entering the Securities Business.* Homewood, Ill.: Dow-Jones-Irwin, 1969. 270 pp.

*The Specialist*: A look at one of the world's most exacting occupations. Reprinted from *American Investor.* New York: American Stock Exchange.

Williamson, Ellen. *Wall Street Made Easy: An Unconventional Guide to Profitable Investing.* Garden City, N.Y.: Doubleday, 1965. 211 pp.

Williamson, J. Peter. *Investments, New Analytic Techniques.* New York: Praeger, 1971. 325 pp.

# CHAPTER 23

# MANAGEMENT INVESTMENT COMPANIES: "MUTUAL FUNDS"

Some readers will want to continue their study of stock investments and will eventually choose to manage their own portfolios. Others may wish to benefit from stock investments but have no desire to get involved with selecting stocks, watching the market, and handling the mechanics of buying and selling. It is to this latter group of people that this chapter is directed.

"Get me some crumbs of whatever the mutual funds are gobbling up."

Reprinted with permission of *The Wall Street Journal* (Cartoon Features Syndicate).

To take full advantage of compound interest growth on dividends and profits, young persons should begin making stock investments as soon as possible. This means that your beginning investment fund will probably be small, perhaps only $500. It's obvious that you couldn't afford the services of an experienced team of investment analysts. However, if you and 100,000 other small investors pooled your money, each putting $500 into an investment account, there would be a hefty $50 million. And if each of the investors paid a management fee of just $5, there would be ample money—$500,000—to hire your team of experts.

Fortunately, you don't have to go out and find 100,000 other individuals to get an investment company started. The work has already been done for you by the sponsors of existing investment companies. These companies are generally corporations. The money which the company collects from the sale of its stock is usually invested in common stocks, sometimes in bonds.

High quality professional investment management is undoubtedly the most important advantage provided by the investment company. The proper selection and continuous supervision of investments require extensive research, substantial experience, and that rare quality *investment judgment*. To assure these essential services, most investment companies retain a large staff of research and investment personnel. These advisors have extensive educational backgrounds in economics, finance, and business.

In addition to brainpower, investment companies provide an additional important safeguard for your investment money—*diversification*. Because of the large amount of money in the fund, the managers can buy stocks in a hundred or more different corporations. This enables you as a shareholder in the investment company to benefit from the conservative principle of spreading risk. Then, should something unexpected happen to push down the stock price of one particular company or even an entire industry, one's total investment would not be jeopardized.

Each shareholder of an investment company owns a fractional interest in the investment corporation's stock investments (usually called its *portfolio*). Hopefully, the stocks which the company buys will rise in value and profits will ultimately result. In turn, most of this profit, called capital gains, is distributed to the investment company's shareholders. This kind of distribution receives favorable income-tax treatment just as if you had purchased and sold stock individually. Substantially all of the dividends received by the company are also returned to the shareholders. Just as the investor of the fund shares in gains, so also he assumes his share of any losses.

Although there are a great number of funds from which to choose, there are really only two types of management investment companies: (1) *closed-end* companies and (2) *open-end* companies, which are commonly referred to as mutual funds. Since there are significant differences in structure and performance of these two types of companies, it is important for you to understand thoroughly the basic features of each.

## CLOSED-END INVESTMENT COMPANIES

The most distinguishing characteristic of the *closed-end* investment corporation is that it has a relatively fixed number of capital shares. Although subject to certain special Securities and Exchange Commission regulations, the closed-end company is very similar to any regular corporation, except, of course, that it is organized for the purpose of reinvesting its stockholders' money. Once the initial subscription or offering of shares is sold, the money collected from the stock sale constitutes the basic investment fund. *The closed-end company does not redeem its shares.* In order for an investor to recover his money, it is necessary to offer the stock for sale to another investor either over-the-counter or in one of the organized stock exchanges.

Because of the way they are organized and operated, closed-end investment corporations have a definite, known amount of money which they invest. This, of course, has advantages as well as drawbacks. For example, in times of rising markets, more money cannot be attracted for investment. But the closed-end fund is never plagued by the possibility of large numbers of stockholders wanting to redeem their shares. Since the managers of closed-end corporations are not always competing for new investment money after the initial stock is sold, they may tend to be not as aggressive and productive in their investments as they should be. On the other hand, managers of closed-end funds are not pushed by public sentiment to include stocks of questionable value in their portfolios just because they happen to be in the public's favor. As far as management considerations are concerned, *there seems to be no obvious superiority to either type of investment company.*

Common sense would tell us that the price of closed-end corporate shares should be determined by the actual worth of such a corporation's investments. For example, let us assume that a corporation had outstanding one million shares of stock which it sold for $1 per share. Subsequently, the corporation invested the $1 million in shares of 40 different corporations. Then, assume that a month later the market value of those 40 securities which the corporation owns totals $1,500,000. Therefore, each share of the closed-end company should be worth $1.50 ($1,500,000 the value of its investment divided by 1,000,000 total shares of stock). Actually, however, this is not the way it works. The shares of closed-end funds could sell at a *premium*—a price higher than the book value of its shares or, such shares could be selling at a *discount*—a price less than the pro-rata value of its investment.

At the end of 1970 there was an average discount of 3 percent on 10 *diversified* closed-end companies. Seven were selling at discounts ranging from 18 percent to 2 percent, three were selling at premiums ranging from 5 percent to 16 percent. Comparable figures existed among some of the *specialized* closed-end companies.* A historical summary of average discounts or premiums for closed-end companies as a group is given in Fig. 23–1.

There appear to be two reasons for most closed-end funds selling at discounts. First and foremost, brokers generally fail to recommend such stocks to their clients. The broker's sales commission is much smaller for closed-end

---

* Wiesenberger, Arthur. *Investment Companies, Mutual Funds and Other Types.* New York: Arthur Wiesenberger & Company, 1971, p. 20.

stocks than for open-end or mutual fund shares. As an illustration, assume that you go to a broker with $1,000 to invest. If you buy into a closed-end fund which is traded on the New York Stock Exchange, the broker will get about $5.10 for making the sale. This is identical to the commission he would receive on any listed security. But if you purchase a mutual fund, the broker will earn a commission of approximately $30.00, nearly six times as much.

The second reason for the lack of investor interest in the closed-end corporation is that such corporations do little by comparison with open-end funds in advertising and promotion. Since open-end funds depend on new money for growth or for money to pay people who wish to redeem stock, they typically have a very effective sales organization with huge advertising and promotion budgets.

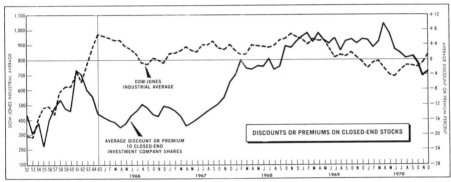

**Fig. 23–1** Discounts or premiums on closed-end stocks. Historically, closed-end firms have rather mysteriously sold at discounts. The fickle nature of the investor could write quite a different future for the closed-end company, however. Reprinted by permission from Wiesenberger Financial Services.

## OPEN-END COMPANIES—MUTUAL FUNDS

Managers of closed-end investment companies soon realized that having a fixed-number of shares severely limited economic efficiency and profit potential of their operations. Actually, it costs little more to manage $20 million in investments than it does to manage $1 million. The same painstaking research and daily follow-through must be done regardless of the number of dollars invested. Therefore, a new type of investment company called the *mutual fund* was conceived. It was given legal sanction under the Investment Company Act of 1940.

Mutual-fund shares are not traded like other securities. The corporation agrees to *repurchase* or *redeem* its own stock. This it will do at a price equivalent to the pro-rated value of its investments at any time. Therefore, if an open-end fund had 20 million shares of stock outstanding and its portfolio had a market value of $200 million, the fund would at the request of any of its shareholders redeem its shares for $10 each.

Likewise, mutual funds agree to *sell* their shares to any and all comers for the same pro-rated amount plus a sales commission of approximately 8 percent. The current prices of popular mutual funds are usually listed in the daily newspaper and other financial journals. Figure 23–2 shows how fund prices are usually reported. The *bid* price is the redemption price, or the pro-rated market value of the funds.* The *asked price* is market value plus the purchase commission. The large majority of funds appraise the market value of their portfolios twice daily, at 1:00 p.m. and 3:30 p.m. New York time, and establish bid and offered prices effective one hour later.

Mutual fund companies have found that they can usually provide sufficient cash from new sales to replace the money lost through shareholder redemption. Until 1971 most mutual funds grew rapidly, continually selling more stock than they redeemed. In 1971, however, some funds began to see redemptions out-distance sales. Naturally funds like to keep sales ahead of redemption so that they can keep their funds fully invested—and not be forced to liquidate a portion of their holdings to keep money on hand to meet redemption requirements.

Mutual funds have become by far the most popular form of investment company. For every $1 invested in closed-end companies, $17.50 goes into mutual funds. Because of their importance, the balance of this chapter is devoted primarily to further discussion of the mutual funds.

**The structure of mutual fund management and distributing functions.** Most mutual fund companies obtain investment advice and office services from the investment adviser companies who created the funds. Such services are provided according to terms of contracts between the mutual fund companies and the advisory companies. Compensation for the services, known as the management or advisory fee, is based on a percentage of net assets. These may not exceed 5 percent. Initially, contracts must be approved by shareholders. Thereafter, contract renewals are confirmed annually either by the stockholders or by the directors of the mutual funds.

**Basic reasons for growth of the mutual fund industry.** In a little over a quarter of a century, the number of mutual fund accounts has risen from fewer than 300,000 to over 11 million. Data from Wiesenberger Financial Services provided in Fig. 23–3 shows that the net assets of the mutual funds and closed-end investment companies have increased from about $450 million at the end of 1940 to over $50 billion at present. The growth in assets and number of shareholders provides clear evidence that mutual funds are meeting an important public need.

Two factors have contributed most significantly to the growth of mutual funds: First, investors have increasingly recognized that fixed income programs for their savings should be supplemented by stock investments to

---

* There are a few funds that charge a small redemption fee.

# Mutual Funds

Price ranges for investment companies, as quoted by the National Association of Securities Dealers:

| | Bid | Ask | Bid Chg. |
|---|---|---|---|
| Aberdeen | 2.24 | 2.45+ | .02 |
| **Admiralty Funds:** | | | |
| Growth | 6.99 | 7.66+ | .04 |
| Income | 4.47 | 4.90+ | .03 |
| Insuran | 10.45 | 11.45+ | .03 |
| Adviser Fd | 5.51 | 6.02+ | .06 |
| Aetna Fnd | 10.56 | 11.54+ | .05 |
| Affilated | 7.42 | 8.03+ | .10 |
| Afutur (v) | 10.99 | 10.99+ | .03 |
| AGE Fund | 5.23 | 5.36+ | .03 |
| Allstate | 11.58 | 12.45+ | .04 |
| Alpha Fnd | 13.08 | 14.30+ | .11 |
| Amcap Fd | 6.50 | 7.10+ | .04 |
| Am Bus Sh | 3.29 | 3.56+ | .02 |
| AmDiv Inv | 10.98 | 12.00+ | .11 |
| Am Equity | 5.49 | 6.02+ | .05 |
| **American Express Funds:** | | | |
| Capital | 9.05 | 9.89+ | .12 |
| Income | 9.30 | 10.16+ | .05 |
| Invest | 8.96 | 9.76+ | .04 |
| Spec Fnd | 9.01 | + | .07 |
| Stock Fd | 9.14 | 9.99+ | .07 |
| Am Grwth | 6.84 | 7.48+ | .10 |
| AmInv (v) | 5.73 | 5.73+ | .07 |
| Am Mutual | 9.51 | 10.39+ | .06 |
| AmNat Gw | 3.56 | 3.89+ | .02 |
| **Anchor Group:** | | | |
| Cap Fnd | 8.70 | 9.53+ | .08 |
| Fund Inv | 9.46 | 10.37+ | .07 |
| Growth | 11.89 | 13.03+ | .11 |
| Income | 8.10 | 8.88+ | .05 |
| Venture | 45.48 | 49.84+ | .31 |
| Astron Fnd | 4.73 | 5.17+ | .02 |
| **Axe-Houghton:** | | | |
| Fund A | 5.85 | 6.36+ | .04 |
| Fund B | 8.12 | 8.83+ | .04 |
| Stock Fd | 6.16 | 6.73 | |
| Axe Scie | 4.85 | 5.27+ | .02 |
| Babson (v) | 9.53 | 9.53+ | .09 |
| Bayrock | 8.66 | 9.46+ | .08 |
| Bayrok gth | 5.77 | 6.31+ | .06 |
| BeacHI (v) | 10.82 | 10.82+ | .07 |
| Beacnl (v) | 14.14 | 14.14+ | .16 |
| Berger (v) | (z) | (z) | (z) |
| Berksh Gw | 6.34 | 6.93+ | .04 |
| Bondstk cp | 6.60 | 7.21+ | .04 |
| Bost cm st | 8.78 | 9.60+ | .09 |
| Bos Found | 11.40 | 12.46+ | .08 |
| Bostn Fd | 8.23 | 8.99+ | .04 |
| Brown Fnd | 3.95 | 4.32 | |
| **Bullock Calvin Funds:** | | | |
| Bullock | 15.38 | 16.85+ | .16 |
| Canadn | 19.41 | 21.30+ | .12 |
| Div Shrs | 3.79 | 4.16+ | .03 |
| Ntwide | 10.66 | 11.67+ | .07 |
| NY Vent | 11.69 | 12.80+ | .09 |
| Burnham | 12.27 | 12.27+ | .17 |
| Busmn Fd | 7.57 | 8.30+ | .04 |
| C G Fund | 10.25 | 11.08+ | .09 |
| Capamer | 8.11 | 8.89+ | .08 |
| Capital Inv | 3.64 | 3.99+ | .07 |
| Capitl Shrs | 6.72 | 7.36+ | .06 |
| Cap Trnity | 13.57 | 14.83+ | .11 |
| Century Sh | 14.40 | 15.74+ | .10 |
| **Channing Funds:** | | | |
| Balanc | 11.99 | 13.10+ | .06 |
| Com Stk | 1.78 | 1.95+ | .01 |
| Growth | 6.02 | 6.58+ | .10 |
| Income | 7.75 | 8.47+ | .03 |
| Special | (z) | (z) | (z) |
| **Chase Group of Boston:** | | | |
| Capital | 7.91 | 8.64+ | .04 |
| Fnd Bost | 10.48 | 11.45+ | .04 |
| Frontir | 91.45 | + | .84 |
| ShTr Bos | 12.16 | 13.29+ | .07 |
| Special | 10.35 | 11.31+ | .05 |
| Chem Fnd | 18.89 | 20.75+ | .06 |

| | Bid | Ask | Bid Chg. |
|---|---|---|---|
| Istel Fund | 22.49 | 23.19+ | .10 |
| IvyFnd (v) | 8.46 | 8.46+ | .06 |
| JHanc Gth | 8.07 | 8.77+ | .10 |
| Johnst (v) | 24.10 | 24.10+ | .18 |
| **Keystone Custodian Funds:** | | | |
| Cust B 1 | 18.98 | 19.85+ | .04 |
| Cust B 2 | 19.75 | 21.65+ | .01 |
| Disct B 4 | 8.61 | 9.43+ | .01 |
| Cust K 1 | 7.96 | 8.72+ | .04 |
| Cust K 2 | 5.71 | 6.26+ | .04 |
| Cust S 1 | 20.26 | 22.20+ | .17 |
| Cust S 2 | 10.96 | 12.01+ | .06 |
| Cust S 3 | 8.62 | 9.44+ | .10 |
| Cust S 4 | 5.20 | 5.70+ | .05 |
| Apollo | 11.07 | 12.13+ | .07 |
| Polaris | 4.21 | 4.60+ | .03 |
| Knickr Fd | 7.54 | 8.27+ | .07 |
| Knickr Gth | 9.94 | 10.89+ | .15 |
| Lenox Fnd | 6.63 | 7.25 | |
| Lex Grwth | 10.52 | 11.50+ | .08 |
| Lex Resch | 17.08 | 18.67+ | .13 |
| Liberty Fd | 6.74 | 7.37+ | .04 |
| Lifelns Inv | 8.50 | 9.29+ | .05 |
| Life & Grw | 6.20 | 6.77+ | .04 |
| Lincln Cap | 11.54 | 12.61+ | .16 |
| Ling Fund | 4.92 | — | .01 |
| **Loomis Sayles Funds (v):** | | | |
| Canadn | 29.84 | 29.84+ | .38 |
| Cap Dev | 11.95 | 11.95+ | .10 |
| Mutual | 15.08 | 15.08+ | .12 |
| Lord Ab bd | 10.77 | + | .05 |
| Lutheran | 12.24 | 13.38+ | .08 |
| Magna Inc | 8.79 | 9.61+ | .01 |
| Manhattn | 5.37 | 5.87+ | .06 |
| Mrktgr (v) | 6.13 | 6.13— | .02 |
| **Mass Company:** | | | |
| Freedm | 8.44 | 9.25+ | .08 |
| Indep Fd | 6.93 | 7.59+ | .03 |
| Mass Fd | 11.57 | 12.68+ | .07 |
| **Mass Financial Svcs:** | | | |
| MIT | 14.50 | 15.85+ | .13 |
| MIG | 13.18 | 14.40+ | .12 |
| MID | 15.48 | 16.92+ | .08 |
| Mates (v) | 3.97 | 3.97+ | .03 |
| Mather (v) | 13.84 | 13.84+ | .02 |
| Mid Amer | 5.71 | 6.24 | |
| Moody Cap | 12.81 | 12.81+ | .10 |
| Moodys Fd | 12.73 | 12.73+ | .09 |
| M FdGvt S | 10.41 | 10.57— | .01 |
| M I F Fd | 8.92 | 9.65+ | .08 |
| M I F Gro | 5.80 | 6.27+ | .05 |
| MOmah gh | 6.09 | 6.62+ | .08 |
| MOmah In | 10.92 | 11.87+ | .07 |
| MutShs (v) | (z) | (z) | (z) |
| MutlTr (v) | 2.00 | 2.00 | |
| NatInd (v) | 11.38 | 11.38+ | .14 |
| **National Securities Series:** | | | |
| Balanc | 11.02 | 12.04+ | .07 |
| Bond Srl | 5.01 | 5.48 | |
| Dividnd | 4.36 | 4.77+ | .02 |
| Preferd | 7.28 | 7.96+ | .03 |
| Income | 5.41 | 5.91 | |
| Stock Sr | 8.13 | 8.89+ | .07 |
| Grwth | 9.60 | 10.49+ | .08 |
| NEL GrFd | 9.98 | 10.85+ | .10 |
| N E A Mut | 10.83 | 11.05+ | .16 |
| Neuw Cent | 6.53 | 7.14+ | .01 |
| Neuwirth | 11.59 | 12.67+ | .10 |
| Newton Fd | 15.47 | 16.90+ | .20 |
| New World | 13.22 | 14.45+ | .10 |
| Nic Str (v) | 17.51 | 17.51+ | .03 |
| Noeast (v) | 15.25 | 15.25+ | .01 |
| Oceang (v) | 7.83 | 7.83+ | .01 |
| Omega Fd | 6.85 | 6.97+ | .01 |
| O Neil (v) | (z) | (z) | (z) |
| 100 Fund | 14.58 | 15.93+ | .10 |
| 101 Fund | 9.24 | 10.10+ | .01 |
| 1 Will (v) | 16.36 | 16.36+ | .15 |

**Fig. 23–2** Many mutual funds are quoted in *The Wall Street Journal*. The redemption price is shown here as the *bid price*. If purchasing the fund, you would pay the *asked price*—this figure includes commission. Reprinted by permission from Dow Jones & Company, Inc.

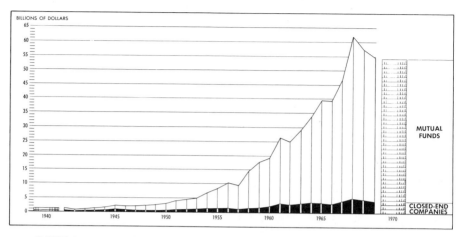

† Including funded debt and bank loans.
Sources: Open-End—Wiesenberger Financial Services 1960-1970. Investment Company Institute 1940-1958. Data include ICI member companies only.
Closed-End—Wiesenberger Financial Services 1948-1970. Investment Company Institute 1940-1946.

| TABLE 1 | Growth of Investment Company Assets Since 1940 | | |
|---|---|---|---|
| Year | Mutual Funds | Closed-End Companies† | Total |
| 1970 | $50,654,900,000 | $4,024,200,000 | $54,679,100,000 |
| 1969 | 52,621,400,000 | 4,743,700,000 | 57,365,100,000 |
| 1968 | 56,953,600,000 | 5,170,800,000 | 62,124,400,000 |
| 1966 | 36,294,600,000 | 3,162,900,000 | 39,457,500,000 |
| 1964 | 30,370,300,000 | 3,523,413,000 | 33,893,713,000 |
| 1962 | 22,408,900,000 | 2,783,219,000 | 25,192,119,000 |
| 1960 | 17,383,300,000 | 2,083,898,000 | 19,467,198,000 |
| 1958 | 13,242,388,000 | 1,931,402,000 | 15,173,790,000 |
| 1956 | 9,046,431,000 | 1,525,748,000 | 10,572,179,000 |
| 1954 | 6,109,390,000 | 1,246,351,000 | 7,355,741,000 |
| 1952 | 3,931,407,000 | 1,011,089,000 | 4,942,496,000 |
| 1950 | 2,530,563,000 | 871,962,000 | 3,402,525,000 |
| 1948 | 1,505,762,000 | 767,028,000 | 2,272,790,000 |
| 1946 | 1,311,108,000 | 851,409,000 | 2,162,517,000 |
| 1944 | 882,191,000 | 739,021,000 | 1,621,212,000 |
| 1942 | 486,850,000 | 557,264,000 | 1,044,114,000 |
| 1940 | 447,959,000 | 613,589,000 | 1,061,548,000 |

**Fig. 23–3**  Growth of investment company assets since 1940. The popularity of investment companies has pushed assets of these companies to nearly $55 billion. Most of the money has gone into open-ended companies or mutual funds. Reprinted by permission from Wiesenberger Financial Services.

offset the long-term effects of inflation. Accordingly, they have taken advantage of the fact that mutual funds, through their diversified investments in securities of leading corporations, provide an opportunity to participate at relatively low-risk in the growth of the American economy; and second, mutual funds have grown because they have performed well for their shareholders.

**Sales charges for mutual funds.**  The prevailing pattern of sales charges for mutual funds ranges from 7.5 to 8.75 percent. While there are some investment funds, called *no-load funds*, which do not charge a sales commission, about four out of five funds add the sales fee. The latter group are called *loaded funds* —meaning that the investment you make has been loaded with the added burden of a selling commission.

Many people feel that the sales charges for mutual fund shares are far too high. Although this question was debated at great length before passage of the 1970 Investment Company Amendments Act, the existing fee schedules were left intact with the modification that "sales charges may not be unconscionable or grossly excessive."

The mutual fund people and the security dealers say that the existing sales charges are justified. They point to the results of a recent study made by the National Association of Securities Dealers which indicates that in his mutual fund activities the typical salesman makes about 18 sales contacts per week. Each sales contact consumes about two hours. The salesman average 1.7 sales per week, which means that he works approximately 19 hours for each completed sale. They argue that because so much more time is required to make a proper sale of mutual funds, the higher rate is needed to provide adequate compensation for the salesman.

Normally the salesman's portion of the sales charge is about 3 percent out of an $8\frac{1}{2}$ percent maximum sales charge. Another portion of the sales charge, generally 3 percent, is retained by the salesman's employer, the securities dealer firm, to offset its overhead—including the cost of recruiting, training, and supervising salesmen and the maintenance of long-term customer services. The final portion of the sales charge (about $2\frac{1}{2}$ percent of the maximum charge) is retained by the mutual fund underwriter to pay various costs including the expense of printing prospectuses, preparing sales literature, maintaining regional offices and sales representatives, and advertising and promoting the sale of fund shares. This role, essential to the widespread distribution of mutual fund shares, simply does not exist in the day-to-day trading of individual stocks.

In fairness to the mutual fund industry, it is improper to compare the cost of purchasing a mutual fund with that of purchasing a single ordinary common stock. Actually, a mutual fund share is not a single stock, but represents a share in a diversified, managed portfolio of securities, with a variety of special services. Any such comparison would have to take into consideration the costs to an investor of obtaining a minimum amount of diversification by buying a number of stocks instead of just one.

The investor would pay far more in commissions if he were to buy and sell stocks of just 20 of the 50 to 100 or more companies held in a mutual fund's portfolio. To illustrate: The median mutual fund purchase by regular account holders is $1,240. An 8 percent mutual fund sales charge covers both the *purchase* and *sale* of a $1,240 mutual fund transactions. The stock exchange commissions and charges payable on the *purchase* and *sale* of $1,240 worth of 20 listed stocks would approximate 12 percent.

No-load funds are able to exist because they are operated as sideline businesses to investment advisory organizations with other clients, or by brokerage firms, part of whose profit is derived from handling the funds' portfolio transactions. In most instances, purchase of no-load funds is made directly from the sponsoring company. Naturally, if you can find a no-load fund with management policies equal to those of a loaded fund, your investment results will be improved. By saving the usual 8 percent commission, you can put that much more money to work for you in actual investments. Management performance is the key to buying funds, *load* or *no-load*. Before you buy any fund, you need to check first to make sure that you get the quality of management which you need. No-load companies are currently receiving favorable attention from investors, and there are a number of well-managed diversified companies to select from.

Special long-term contractual plans are now being actively pushed by many security salesmen. Undoubtedly, their popularity can be attributed to the lucrative broker commissions. These plans usually set specified time and money targets. The money target is not a guarantee of what the investment will be worth ultimately, but rather a commitment of how much the investor is willing to put into the fund during the life of the contract. The time target is most commonly ten years, although plans are available for longer or shorter periods. Even though they may provide more psychological inducement for a person to invest reguarly, they have one serious disadvantage. Usually the funds are *front-loaded*. This means that up to 50 percent of all the money which the investor pays into the program during the first year can go to the broker as his commission. For example, if you signed up for a ten-year $12,000 contractual plan, contributing $100 monthly, the total broker's commission could be as much as $1,080. Of the $1,200 which you would pay into the program during the first year, the broker could take as much as $600 as pay toward his total fee. This means that only one-half of your payments would be working for you in actual investments. And if something forced you to discontinue the program and sell out at the end of the first year, you could recover only the current value of the stock which the $600 had purchased.

It is important to note that even though these plans are referred to as contracts, the investors are not bound legally to fulfill the agreements. Payments may be stopped at any time. Under the 1970 Act, buyers of front-loaded funds may rescind the transaction within 45 days. Also a buyer may over the first 18 months ask for a refund of all his payments except for a 15 percent commission. Let him know that you know something about how such plans operate, and he will soon find a better solution for you.

**Variety of mutual funds.** In order to accommodate a wide variety of investor needs, mutual funds have been created with many different investment policies and objectives. Some funds seek safety of principal. Others want to maximize current dividend income. Still others attempt to secure long-term growth of capital along with moderate income. Many funds combine two or more of these investment objectives.

A number of funds limit their investments principally to the blue chip stocks of leading corporations, while others will purchase the more venturesome securities of companies that offer prospects of above average growth. There are bond funds, common stock funds, income funds, and balanced funds. The last provide balanced investment programs consisting of bonds, preferred stocks, and common stocks. There are funds that invest in particular industries where scientific and technical knowledge are of great importance, such as the aerospace or chemical industries.

The investment objective is described in a booklet (called a *prospectus*) published by each fund. The fundamental investment policy of a fund set forth in the prospectus cannot be changed without approval of the shareholders. Thus, an investor has a wide choice, and may select the mutual fund whose investment objective and investment record most closely matches his particular needs. However, mutual funds are intended to be long-term investments. Because of the 8 percent purchase fee, short-term trading of mutual funds shares is usually unprofitable. With a mutual fund you will need time to achieve your investment goal. Most shareholders retain and add to their mutual fund investments for periods often exceeding 15 years.

**Choosing a mutual fund.** If you do decide that a mutual fund or other type of investment company would be the best way for you to make securities investments, how do you go about picking which fund to buy? Here are a few suggestions:

1. Pick a fund which has investment objectives dovetailing your own needs.
2. Look at the long-term performance of the candidate funds. Don't be too concerned with what happened this year or in any single year.
3. Consider and compare all types of funds—no-load, loaded, closed-end. Remember, the sales fee may be justified if the long-term performance of the fund promises to be superior.

While there are many good sources of comparative information on investment companies, two which are particularly recommended are described below:

*Investment Companies—Mutual Funds and Other Types*
Latest Yearly Edition
By Arthur Wiesenberger
Published by Arthur Wiesenberger & Company
60 Broadway
New York, New York 10006

This comprehensive publication gives a very fine, in depth coverage of the investment company business. Additionally, it gives valuable comparative statistical data on all major investment companies. It can be found in most libraries or can be ordered directly from the publisher.

*Forbes Magazine*
Latest Yearly Edition
Published by Forbes, Inc.
60 Fifth Avenue
New York, New York 10011

This publication gives ratings on all the mutual funds. This appears in the August 15 issue. The data are reliable and in very easy-to-use form. Figure 23–4 shows one page of the 1971 ratings.

**Reinvestment of dividends and capital distributions.**  Unless you have a definite need for supplementary income from your mutual fund investment, it is wise to have the fund automatically reinvest all dividends and income payments. If your mutual fund investment is small to begin with, the periodic payments of dividends and capital distributions will be very small.  However, in the long run, continuous reinvestment will substantially add to your investment objective.  This service is provided by all mutual funds and by a few of the closed-end investment companies.

The investor should realize, too, that the capital gains distributions are his share of the money received by the company when it decides to sell a particular issue or issues of stock.  The company is forced to distribute most of the proceeds to avoid taxation.  The important point to remember about this income is that it is really *part of your original capital investment* plus any profit made on the sale.  Therefore, if you take these distributions in cash, you are in effect spending part of your capital.

All the funds will provide automatic reinvestment service for you.  They also supply periodically a comprehensive summary useful for your personal information and for tax purposes.  This shows the number of shares owned and the dividends and capital distributions for the period.

**Taxes on dividends and profit distribution.**  As far as the individual investor is concerned, for tax purposes he treats the *dividends* received from an investment company as ordinary income.  However, each person is allowed to exclude from taxable income the first $100 of dividends received.  Profits from stock sales are designated as *long-term capital gains*.  Such amounts are not eligible for the $100 dividend exclusion, but are taxable at the lower Federal rate for long-term gains.

**Special programs for people who need regular income payments.**  Stocks have not been particularly attractive to older persons, widows, and others who need to make regular withdrawls from their investments.  If such persons do buy stocks, they usually have the worry and bother of selling a few shares each month in order to supplement their other finances.  To remedy this inconvenience, many reliable mutual funds now offer special automatic withdrawal plans. The mutual fund shares are purchased in the usual way, but the person must

## Forbes Fund Ratings 1971

| PERFORMANCE RATINGS | | | DOLLAR RESULTS | | | | | |
|---|---|---|---|---|---|---|---|---|
| In UP Markets | In DOWN Markets | | 1962-71 | Latest 12 Months | Dividend Return | Assets in Millions | Maximum Sales Charge | Annual Expenses (Cents per $100) |
| | | | **$100 ENDED AS ...** | | | | | |
| — | — | Standard & Poor's 500 Stock Average | $139.34 | $137.10 | 3.1% | | | |
| C | C | FORBES Stock Fund Average | $153.34 | $138.25 | 2.5% | | | |
| | | **STOCK FUNDS (LOAD)** | | | | | | |
| •D | •B | Diversified Fund of State Bond & Mortgage Co. (started 6/64) | — | $131.80 | 3.5% | $ 2.5 | 8.50% | $1.00 |
| D | B | Dividend Shares | $141.32 | 131.11 | 3.1 | 376.2 | 8.67 | 0.52 |
| C | C | Dreyfus Fund | 180.26 | 135.81 | 3.0 | 2,489.1 | 8.75 | 0.56 |
| D | C | Eaton & Howard Stock Fund | 131.11 | 137.22 | 2.8 | 237.2 | 8.50 | 0.62 |
| •C | •C | Egret Growth Fund (started 9/64) | — | 133.80 | 2.4 | 37.4 | 8.00 | 0.67 |
| A | F | Enterprise Fund | 351.65 | 134.60 | 6.2 | 510.7 | 8.50 | 0.93 |
| C | F | Equity Fund | 143.43 | 135.54 | 3.3 | 44.6 | 8.50 | 0.64 |
| A | F | Equity Progress Fund (formerly Republic Technology Fund) | 96.08 | 145.34 | none | 24.3 | 8.75 | 1.02 |
| D | F | F-D Capital | 74.86 | 121.28 | none | 1.4 | 8.00 | 4.30 |
| A | F | Fairfield Fund | 160.88 | 143.84 | 1.5 | 54.9 | 8.50 | 0.76 |
| C | C | Fidelity Capital Fund | 202.68 | 134.66 | 3.1 | 658.4 | 8.50 | 0.54 |
| D | B | Fidelity Fund | 169.48 | 130.09 | 3.5 | 871.8 | 8.50 | 0.47 |
| B | D | Fidelity Trend Fund | 230.62 | 137.57 | 2.4 | 1,113.0 | 8.50 | 0.52 |
| D | D | Financial Industrial Fund | 123.75 | 125.00 | 3.6 | 317.7 | 8.50 | 0.68 |
| D | B | First Investors Fund | 131.41 | 139.18 | 2.3 | 34.1 | 8.75 | 0.70 |
| C | •D | First National Fund | — | 132.12 | 2.4 | 9.2 | 8.50 | 0.95 |
| B | B | First Sierra Fund | 226.44 | 161.33 | 2.0 | 36.9 | 8.80 | 0.95 |
| A | •F | Founders Growth Fund (formerly Gryphon Fund) (started 4/63) | — | 137.20 | 3.0 | 67.4 | 8.50 | 0.78 |
| C | C | Founders Mutual Fund | 135.39 | 135.46 | 3.0 | 203.4 | 8.50 | 0.44 |
| B | •F | Foursquare Fund | — | 141.41 | 2.7 | 11.9 | 8.50 | 1.00 |
| B | C | Franklin Custodian Funds Growth Series (formerly Common Stock Series Shares) | 163.02 | 141.23 | 0.6 | 14.5 | 8.75 | 0.87 |
| D | B | Utilities Series | 91.75 | 124.59 | 3.6 | 20.3 | 8.75 | 0.88 |
| C | F | Fund of America | 122.34 | 131.81 | 3.3 | 83.1 | 8.75 | 0.64 |
| C | D | Fundamental Investors | 132.62 | 134.44 | 2.7 | 1,134.5 | 8.75 | 0.54 |
| | | Group Securities | | | | | | |
| A | F | Apex Fund | 142.89 | 151.04 | 1.1 | 23.7 | 8.50 | 0.80 |
| D | B | Common Stock Fund | 128.23 | 126.27 | 3.8 | 328.3 | 8.50 | 0.76 |
| C | F | Hamilton Funds Series H-DA | 113.95 | 140.12 | 3.8 | 680.2 | 8.50 | 0.76 |
| D | C | Harbor Fund | 160.70 | 124.56 | 5.7 | 159.6 | 8.50 | 0.91 |
| B | C | Hedberg & Gordon Fund | 223.51 | 142.50 | 1.8 | 15.7 | 8.50 | 1.07 |
| — | — | The Heritage Fund° | — | 148.48 | none | 2.0 | 8.75 | 6.10 |
| D | C | ICM Financial Fund | 116.80 | 129.40 | 1.6 | 2.5 | 8.75 | 1.00 |
| C | C | Imperial Capital Fund | 151.68 | 137.34 | 2.6 | 38.8 | 8.50 | 0.84 |
| •A | •C | Imperial Growth Fund (started 4/63) | — | 144.43 | 1.7 | 20.1 | 8.50 | 0.93 |
| •A | •D | Independence Fund (started 1/66) | — | 145.96 | 0.9 | 28.0 | 8.75 | 0.98 |
| •B | •C | Industries Trend Fund (started 2/65) | — | 136.49 | 2.2 | 104.3 | 8.50 | 0.63 |
| B | D | Integon Growth Fund | 123.09 | 144.08 | 2.1 | 10.1 | 7.50 | 0.70 |
| B | C | The Investment Co. of America | 191.57 | 136.90 | 2.8 | 1,327.8 | 8.50 | 0.55 |
| D | C | Investment Trust of Boston | 137.07 | 133.19 | 2.7 | 84.2 | 8.50 | 1.59 |
| B | C | Investors Research Fund | 215.53 | 128.39 | 1.7 | 5.5 | 8.50 | 1.18 |
| D | C | Investors Stock Fund | 117.28 | 138.84 | 2.5 | 2,459.4 | 8.00 | 0.33 |
| B | F | Investors Variable Payment Fund | 134.80 | 143.49 | 1.9 | 1,008.0 | 8.00 | 0.39 |

• Fund rated for two periods only; maximum allowable rating A.
° Changed investment policy in 1967; not ranked.

**EXPLANATION OF COLUMN HEADINGS**

Annual expenses include management fees and operating expenses as a percentage of average net assets.

Only funds in existence for at least six of the measured periods are given a FORBES performance rating. All capital gains distributions have been reinvested, but income dividends have not. All ratings are based on investments at net asset value and do not allow for sales charges. In Dollar Results section, the 1962-71 period covers the period from January 1, 1962 to June 30, 1971; the latest 12 months covers the period from June 30, 1970 to June 30, 1971. Dividend Return is based on June 30, 1971 net asset value and the income payout for the preceding 12-month period.

**Fig. 23-4** Forbes Fund Ratings 1971. (Continued on next page.) Reprinted by permission from Forbes, Inc.

# Forbes
## Fund Ratings
## 1971

PERFORMANCE
RATINGS

DOLLAR RESULTS

| In UP Markets | In DOWN Markets | | 1962-71 | Latest 12 Months | Dividend Return | Assets in Millions | Maximum Sales Charge | Annual Expenses (Cents per $100) |
|---|---|---|---|---|---|---|---|---|
| | | | **$100 ENDED AS...** | | | | | |
| C | C | Standard & Poor's 500 Stock Average | $139.34 | $137.10 | 3.1% | | | |
| | | FORBES Stock Fund Average | $153.34 | $138.25 | 2.5% | | | |
| | | **STOCK FUNDS (LOAD)** | | | | | | |
| C | D | Aberdeen Fund | $132.88 | $135.63 | 2.4% | $ 40.7 | 8.75% | $0.77 |
| | | Admiralty Funds | | | | | | |
| A+ | F | Growth Series | 138.13 | 154.99 | 0.3 | 38.8 | 8.75 | 0.99 |
| D | A | Income Series | 140.96 | 129.08 | 5.3 | 9.3 | 8.75 | 0.99 |
| C | C | Insurance Series | 150.38 | 179.90 | 0.3 | 5.3 | 8.75 | 0.99 |
| C | F | Advisers Fund | 114.47 | 139.80 | 2.3 | 3.3 | 8.50 | 1.00 |
| D | B | Affiliated Fund | 136.38 | 131.38 | 4.0 | 1,713.9 | 7.50 | 0.36 |
| •C | •F | All American Fund (started 2/64) | — | 154.90 | 1.3 | 2.7 | 8.50 | 0.99 |
| •D | •B | American Diversified Investors Fund (started 12/64) | — | 130.99 | 2.8 | 2.8 | 8.50 | 1.12 |
| B | F | American Express Capital Fund | 184.26 | 143.74 | 2.3 | 222.7 | 8.50 | 0.77 |
| C | D | American Express Stock Fund | 142.35 | 138.70 | 2.9 | 84.4 | 8.50 | 0.71 |
| B | D | American Growth Fund | 165.45 | 143.59 | 2.5 | 16.8 | 8.50 | 1.00 |
| C | B | American Mutual Fund | 153.59 | 136.88 | 3.8 | 405.0 | 8.50 | 0.66 |
| A+ | F | American National Growth Fund | 210.21 | 164.79 | 1.7 | 10.6 | 8.50 | 1.00 |
| B | F | Anchor Growth Fund | 152.20 | 143.78 | 1.7 | 558.0 | 8.75 | 0.63 |
| A | D | Axe-Houghton Stock Fund | 277.97 | 128.67 | 4.3 | 86.1 | 8.50 | 1.00 |
| A | F | Axe Science Corp. | 195.67 | 132.95 | 3.5 | 52.6 | 8.00 | 0.90 |
| C | F | Bayrock Growth Fund (formerly Florida Growth Fund) | 144.17 | 129.82 | none | 9.1 | 8.50 | 1.00 |
| C | C | Bondstock Corp. | 145.29 | 137.93 | 3.7 | 33.6 | 8.50 | 0.69 |
| D | B | Broad Street Investing Corp. | 152.07 | 141.40 | 2.8 | 412.2 | 8.50 | 0.29 |
| D | B | The Brown Fund of Hawaii | 129.23 | 118.62 | 2.7 | 5.8 | 8.50 | 1.00 |
| C | B | Bullock Fund | 157.97 | 145.36 | 2.6 | 180.0 | 8.67 | 0.43 |
| B | F | Businessman's Fund | 103.35 | 128.79 | 2.7 | 18.0 | 8.75 | 1.01 |
| •D | •A | Capamerica Fund (started 2/65) | — | 124.50 | 4.5 | 2.3 | 8.75 | 1.00 |
| B | F | Capital Investors Growth Fund | 125.84 | 135.39 | 1.4 | 3.0 | 8.75 | 1.00 |
| D | F | Capital Shares | 77.96 | 129.96 | 1.6 | 51.5 | 8.75 | 1.00 |
| D | C | Century Shares Trust | 117.01 | 154.40 | 2.1 | 112.3 | 8.50 | 0.54 |
| | | Channing Funds | | | | | | |
| C | B | Common Stock Fund | 142.42 | 133.59 | 2.9 | 34.0 | 8.50 | 0.82 |
| A+ | F | Growth Fund | 147.89 | 146.99 | 1.5 | 289.6 | 8.50 | 0.75 |
| A | F | Special Fund | 137.17 | 142.86 | 0.5 | 118.2 | 8.50 | 0.80 |
| A+ | F | The Chase Fund of Boston | 182.37 | 161.63 | 1.1 | 115.4 | 8.50 | 0.85 |
| B | B | Chemical Fund | 213.61 | 137.40 | 1.8 | 620.4 | 8.50 | 0.54 |
| D | B | The Colonial Fund | 133.01 | 127.04 | 4.1 | 231.0 | 8.50 | 0.60 |
| A | F | Colonial Growth Shares | 181.62 | 148.76 | 1.7 | 76.5 | 8.50 | 0.71 |
| B | D | Commerce Fund | 147.89 | 146.99 | 2.1 | 95.4 | 8.50 | 0.67 |
| C | •B | Common Stock Fund of State Bond & Mortgage Co. | — | 137.53 | 1.9 | 32.9 | 8.50 | 0.93 |
| D | D | Commonwealth Fund Indenture of Trust Plans A & B | 118.39 | 127.78 | 3.7 | 34.1 | 7.65 | 0.71 |
| D | C | Commonwealth Fund Indenture of Trust Plan C | 122.12 | 129.77 | 4.2 | 56.2 | 7.50 | 0.74 |
| C | B | Composite Fund | 181.13 | 136.84 | 3.4 | 49.3 | 8.00 | 0.77 |
| D | B | Corporate Leaders Tr Fund Certificates, Series "B" | 101.91 | 131.66 | 3.6 | 65.7 | 7.64 | 0.20 |
| | | Crown Western Investments | | | | | | |
| C | F | Dallas Fund | 127.58 | 139.36 | 0.7 | 9.5 | 8.50 | 1.00 |
| C | D | Diversified Fund | 133.57 | 134.96 | 3.8 | 20.4 | 8.50 | 1.00 |
| D | B | Decatur Income Fund | 176.92 | 128.62 | 5.2 | 154.1 | 8.50 | 0.78 |
| B | D | Delaware Fund | 193.14 | 139.48 | 3.7 | 518.9 | 8.50 | 0.69 |

• Fund rated for two periods only; maximum allowable rating A.

WHAT THE
RATINGS MEAN

FORBES rates mutual funds on the basis of their performance in three rising markets and three falling markets. We rate funds against each other rather than on an absolute scale. In up markets the top 12.5% get an A+; the next 12.5% get an A, the next 25% get B; the next 25% get C; the lowest 25% get D. Funds that failed to perform as well as their overall average in the recent up market were penalized one rank. In down markets, reflecting the poor performance in the last crash, we also give F ratings. As a result, a fund gets a B rating in down markets only if its average performance over the three down markets was better than the S&P 500. Funds that did an outstanding job got an A or A+. Those that didn't beat the averages at all got a C, D, or F depending on how poorly they fared. Funds that failed to perform as well as their overall average in the last crash were penalized one rank.

**Figure 23–4** (*Continued*).

invest $7,500 or more initially in the plan. Usually under such plans, capital distributions and dividends are automatically reinvested. Additional shares can be purchased later if desired. The person merely indicates on the purchase contract *when* the payments are to be made to him and in *what* amount. No charges are made for this additional service.

If the annual total of the monthly withdrawals is in excess of the income for any year, the balance is paid out from principal. One popular withdrawal plan provides that all income dividends and capital gain distributions are invested in additional shares at net asset value and sufficient shares are sold from the shareholder's account at the time of each withdrawal payment to provide for such payment. Continued withdrawals in excess of current income eventually exhausts the principal particularly in a period of declining market prices.

## FEEDBACK 23

**A.** Compare the growth performance of five "load" mutual funds against five "no-load" mutual funds.

● Determine if the sales commission is recovered and surpassed by the load funds.

● Compare the *net* worth of portfolios in each type of fund; which exhibits the greatest return for your investment dollars?

● Can you choose between the two types, basing your judgment only on performances of the last ten years?

● Based on holdings, which of the funds exhibits the most aggressive investment policies? Which might suffer directly from rapid technological changes?

**B.** Using one year or ten year stock quotation comparisons, assemble a portfolio of ten stocks. Use your best judgment and diversify your imaginary holdings.

● At the end of your charted investment period, what is your portfolio worth?

● Can you find mutual funds (of any type) which equal or exceed your portfolio in investment/worth ratio for a similar period?

● If the answer to the second item is yes, what do you suppose are some of the reasons? Consider diversification, management, information, and capital.

**C.** Determine your investment objectives in terms of income, growth, and security. In the most current *Forbes Magazine* annual mutual fund ratings, find one or more funds whose objectives most nearly match your own.

● Compare performances. Chart an investment (say $500) for five years for each of these funds.

- Which is the best growth fund for your purposes? (Remember to compute the sales charges too.)

## DISCUSSION QUESTIONS

1. Some legislators and other concerned citizens are afraid of the effects of mutual funds on the stock market. Why might such concerns arise? How well founded are these fears?

2. Describe the difference between a closed-end and open-end investment company.

3. Should an investor even bother to find out whether a prospective investment fund is a closed-end or an open-end type?

4. What do these terms mean: loaded fund; no-load fund; front-loaded fund?

5. Why might a relatively small new fund be able to show better performance for the investor than one of the nation's largest funds? What uncertainties would there be with the new-comer?

6. Why is an investment fund a safer way to invest in stocks for most people?

7. What is a capital distribution?

## CASE PROBLEM

Mrs. Smith's husband died one year ago and his insurance policy left her a large sum of money on which to live. She feels that she does not need all of that cash right away and would like to put about $2,000 to work for her in some investments. She is very skeptical of the stock market, however, since Mr. Smith lost $10,000 four years ago on a speculative stock that failed. Still, she does want to get the best return on her money and knows that a good stock investment can do it. So she goes to her son-in-law, Al, about the situation. Al studied finance in school, and suggests that she put her money into some kind of mutual fund investment.

a) What do you suppose were some of the reasons Al gave to support his suggestion?

b) Mutual funds have many different investment policies and objectives; in what type of fund should Mrs. Smith invest? Explain.

c) If Mrs. Smith decides to invest, would you advise her to have her dividends automatically reinvested? Explain.

## SUGGESTED READINGS

Bradley, Bryce. *The Effect of the Investment Company Act of 1940 and the Subsequent Regulations Upon Management Investment Companies.* Salt Lake City: Unpublished Master's Thesis, University of Utah, 1965. 57 pp.

Dacey, Norman. *Dacey on Mutual Funds.* New York: Crown Publishers, 1970. 272 pp.

Etherington, Edwin D. "The American Stock Exchange and Mutual Funds: Patterns of Growth and Responsibility." Address before Investment Company Institute. New York, April 29, 1965.

Friend, Irwin. *Mutual Funds and Other Institutional Investors: A New Perspective.* New York: McGraw-Hill, 1970.

Investment Company Institute. *Management Investment Companies.* Englewood Cliffs, N.J.: Prentice-Hall, 1962. 111 pp.

Markstein, David L. *How to Make Money with Mutual Funds.* New York: McGraw-Hill, 1969. 258 pp.

Ohlman, Maxwell. *Ohlman's Manual on Mutual Fund Management Companies.* New York: Laird, Bissell & Meeds, 1962. 128 pp.

# INDEX

ABCDEFGH798765432